CHRONIN

VOLUME 1: THE KNIFE AT YOUR BACK

CHRONIN

VOLUME 1: THE KNIFE AT YOUR BACK

Alison Wilgus

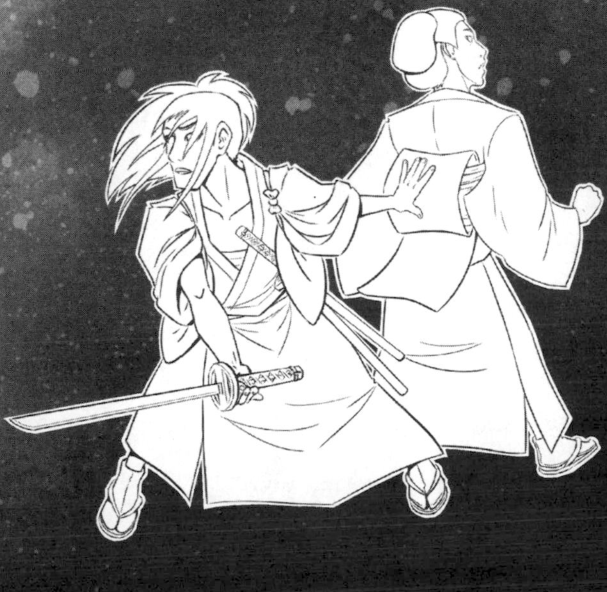

TOR

A TOM DOHERTY ASSOCIATES BOOK • NEW YORK

CHRONIN VOLUME I: THE KNIFE AT YOUR BACK

Interior artwork was created digitally in Adobe Photoshop on a Cintiq 12WX.

A Tor Book
Published by Tom Doherty Associates
175 Fifth Avenue
New York, NY 10010

www.tor-forge.com

Tor® is a registered trademark of Macmillan Publishing Group, LLC.

The Library of Congress Cataloging-in-Publication Data
is available upon request

ISBN 978-0-7653-9163-6 (trade paperback)
ISBN 978-0-7653-9287-9 (ebook)

Our books may be purchased in bulk for promotional, educational, or business use. Please contact your local bookseller or the Macmillan Corporate and Premium Sales Department at 1-800-221-7945, extension 5442, or by email at MacmillanSpecialMarkets@macmillan.com

First Edition: February 2019

Printed in the United States of America

0 9 8 7 6 5 4 3 2 1

For my mom and my sister,
who have been with me through everything.

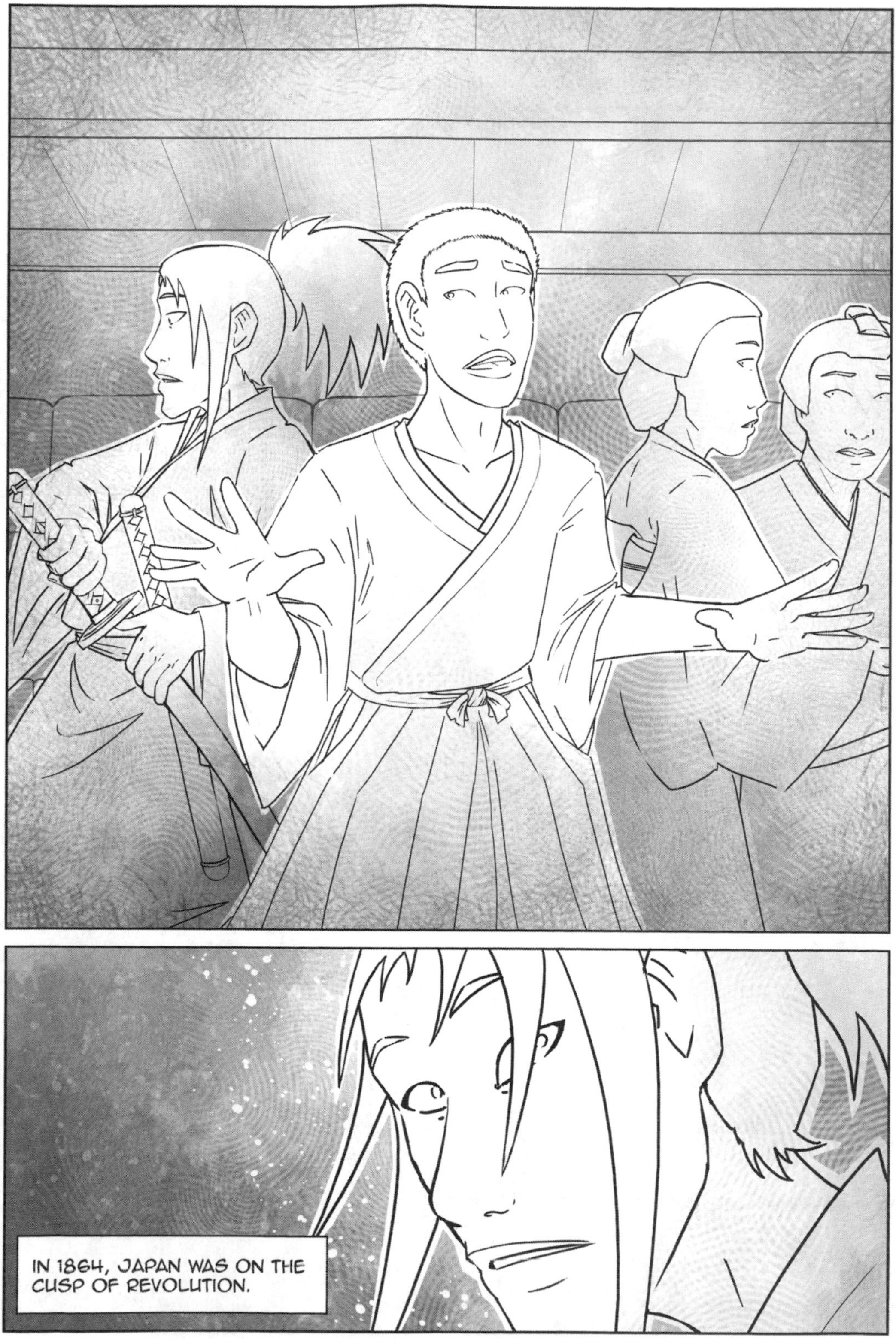
IN 1864, JAPAN WAS ON THE CUSP OF REVOLUTION.

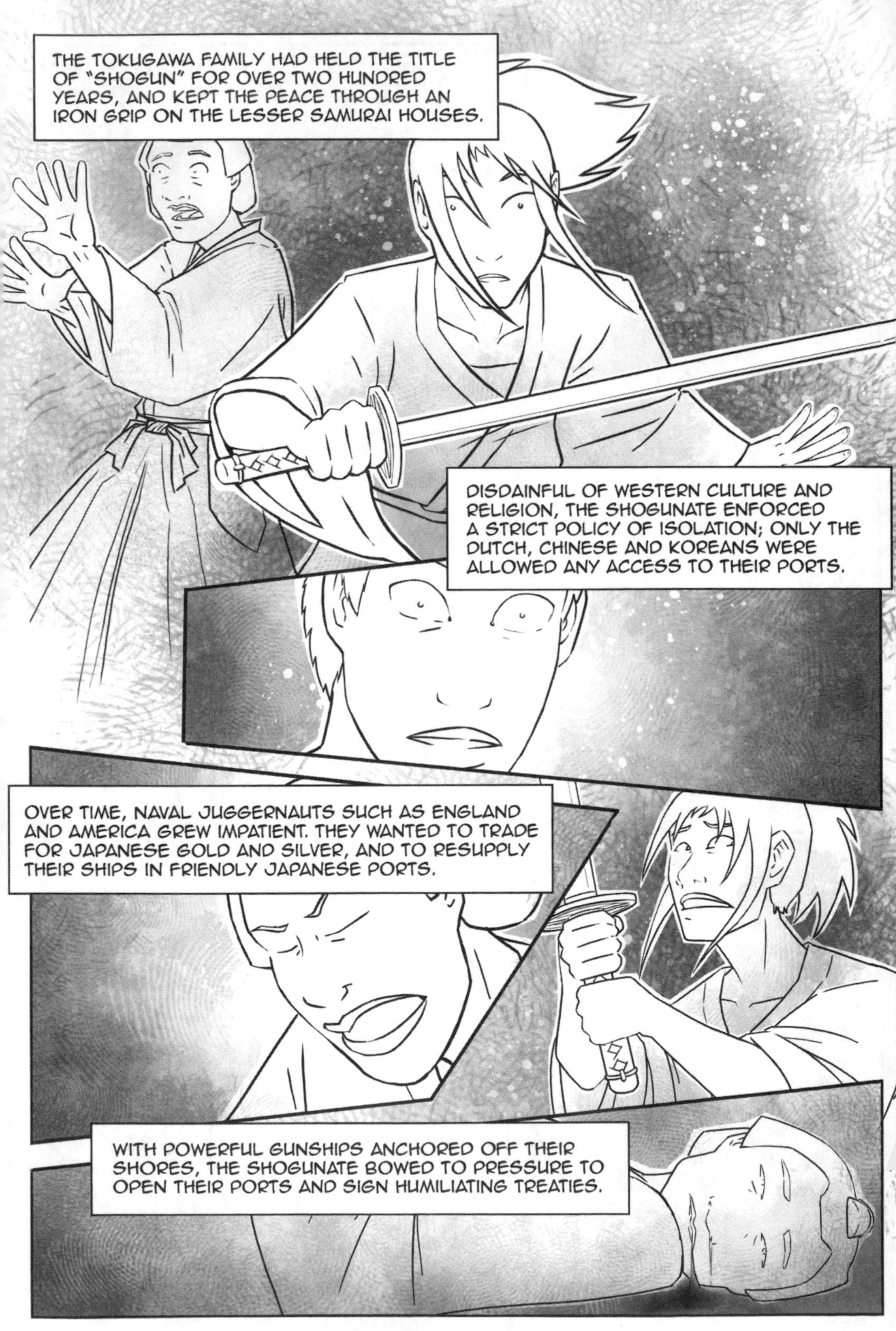
THE TOKUGAWA FAMILY HAD HELD THE TITLE OF "SHOGUN" FOR OVER TWO HUNDRED YEARS, AND KEPT THE PEACE THROUGH AN IRON GRIP ON THE LESSER SAMURAI HOUSES.
DISDAINFUL OF WESTERN CULTURE AND RELIGION, THE SHOGUNATE ENFORCED A STRICT POLICY OF ISOLATION; ONLY THE DUTCH, CHINESE AND KOREANS WERE ALLOWED ANY ACCESS TO THEIR PORTS.
OVER TIME, NAVAL JUGGERNAUTS SUCH AS ENGLAND AND AMERICA GREW IMPATIENT. THEY WANTED TO TRADE FOR JAPANESE GOLD AND SILVER, AND TO RESUPPLY THEIR SHIPS IN FRIENDLY JAPANESE PORTS.
WITH POWERFUL GUNSHIPS ANCHORED OFF THEIR SHORES, THE SHOGUNATE BOWED TO PRESSURE TO OPEN THEIR PORTS AND SIGN HUMILIATING TREATIES.

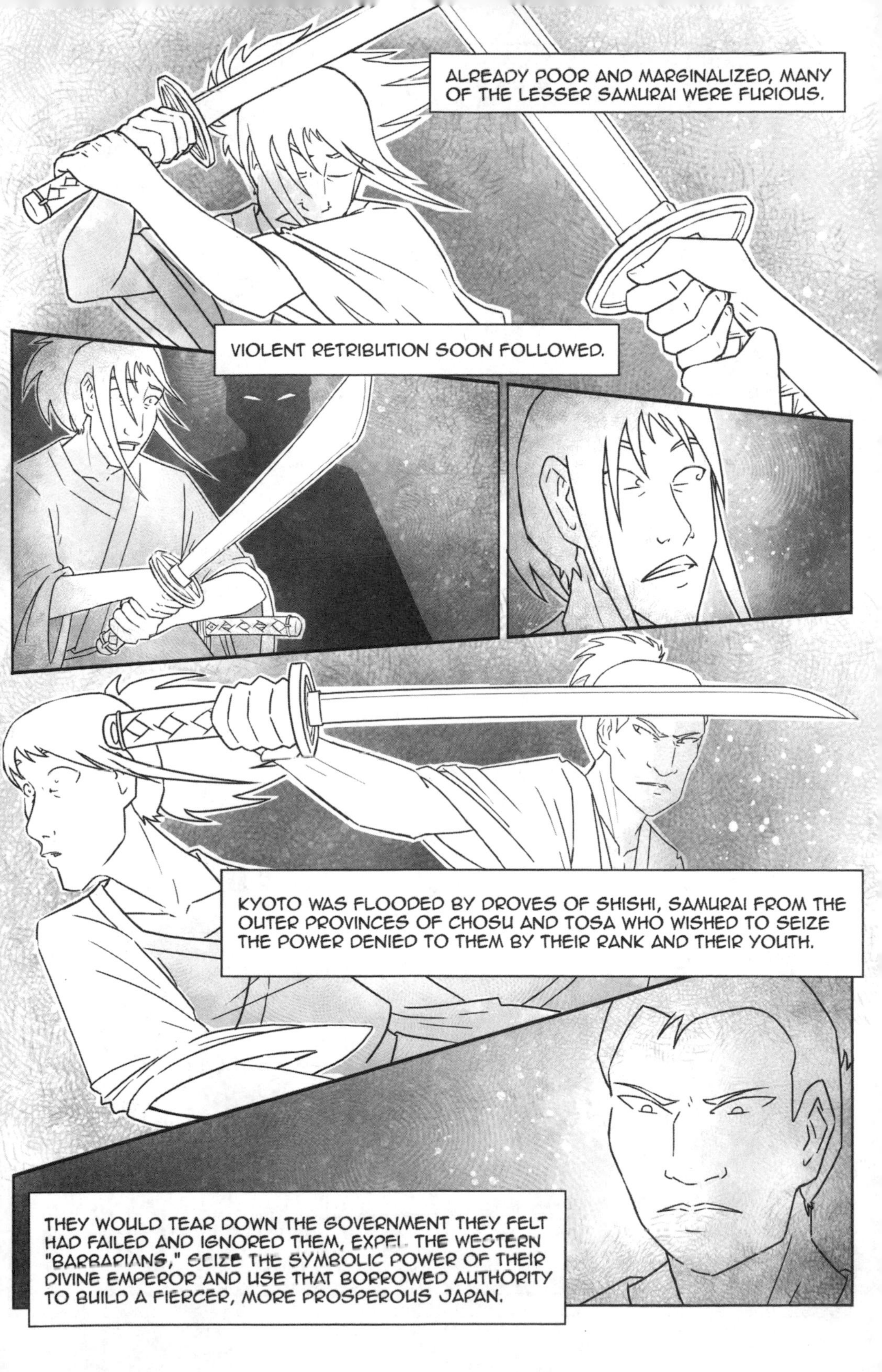
ALREADY POOR AND MARGINALIZED, MANY OF THE LESSER SAMURAI WERE FURIOUS.
VIOLENT RETRIBUTION SOON FOLLOWED.
KYOTO WAS FLOODED BY DROVES OF SHISHI, SAMURAI FROM THE OUTER PROVINCES OF CHOSU AND TOSA WHO WISHED TO SEIZE THE POWER DENIED TO THEM BY THEIR RANK AND THEIR YOUTH.
THEY WOULD TEAR DOWN THE GOVERNMENT THEY FELT HAD FAILED AND IGNORED THEM, EXPEL THE WESTERN "BARBARIANS," SEIZE THE SYMBOLIC POWER OF THEIR DIVINE EMPEROR AND USE THAT BORROWED AUTHORITY TO BUILD A FIERCER, MORE PROSPEROUS JAPAN.

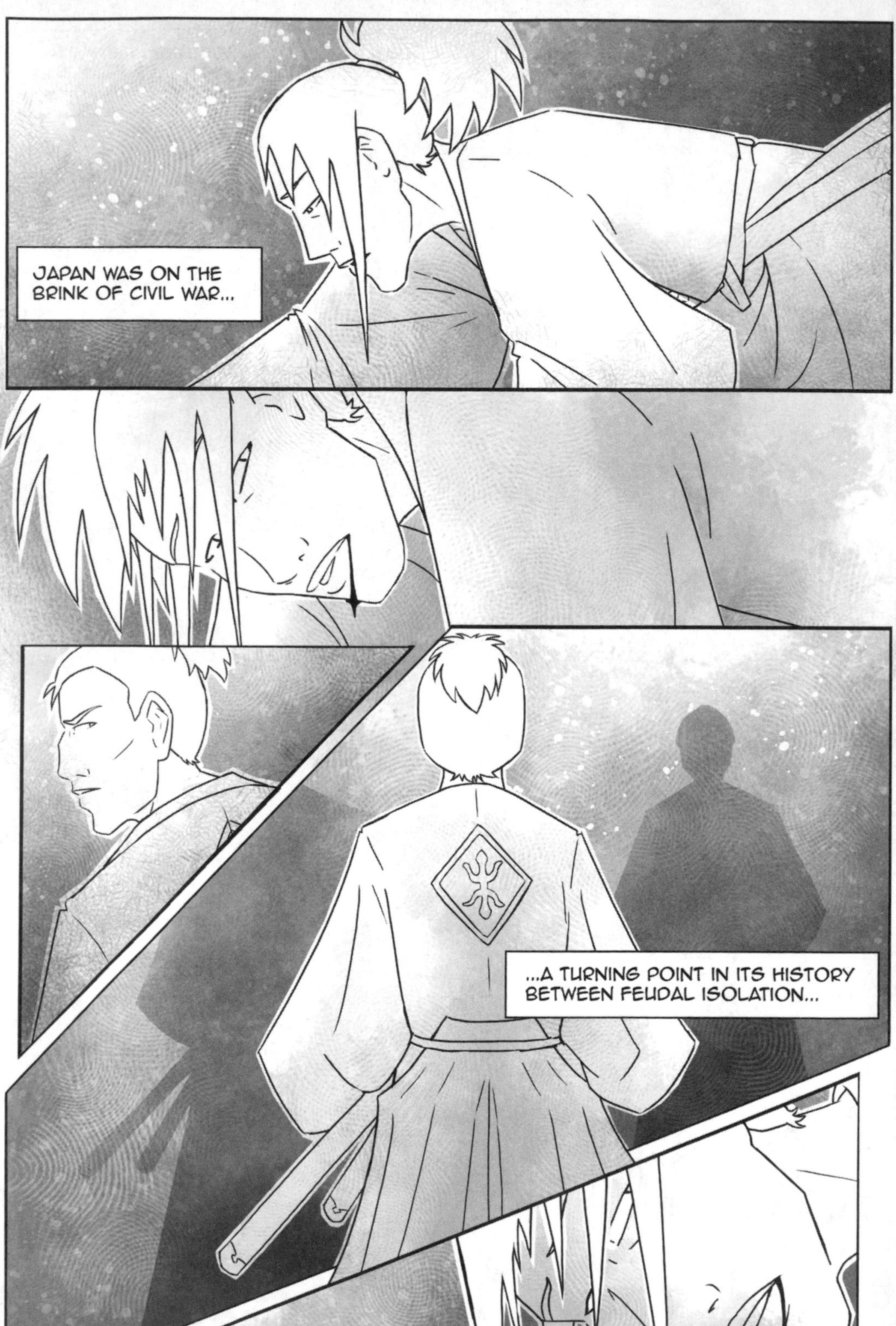
JAPAN WAS ON THE BRINK OF CIVIL WAR...
...A TURNING POINT IN ITS HISTORY BETWEEN FEUDAL ISOLATION...

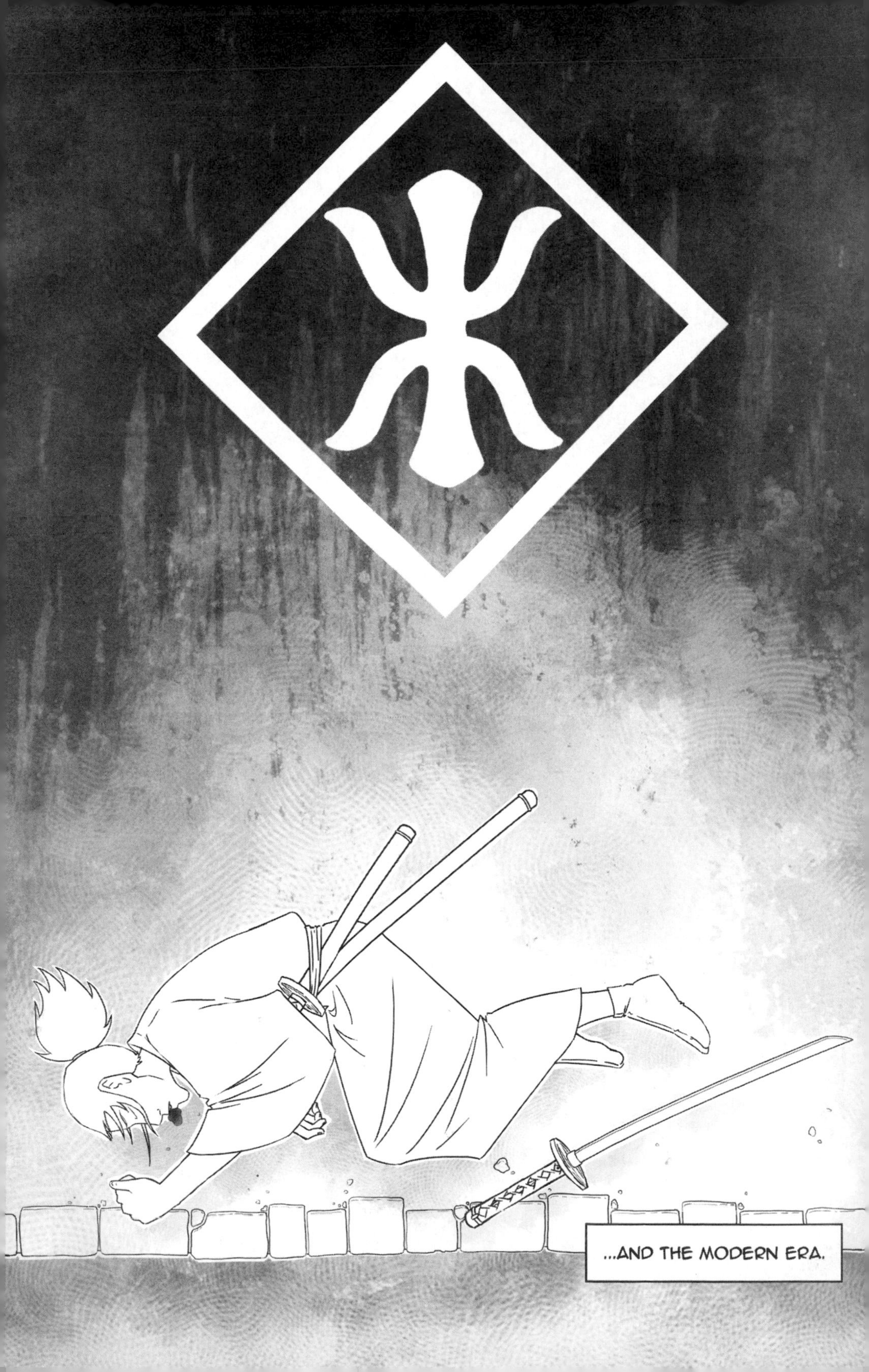
...AND THE MODERN ERA.

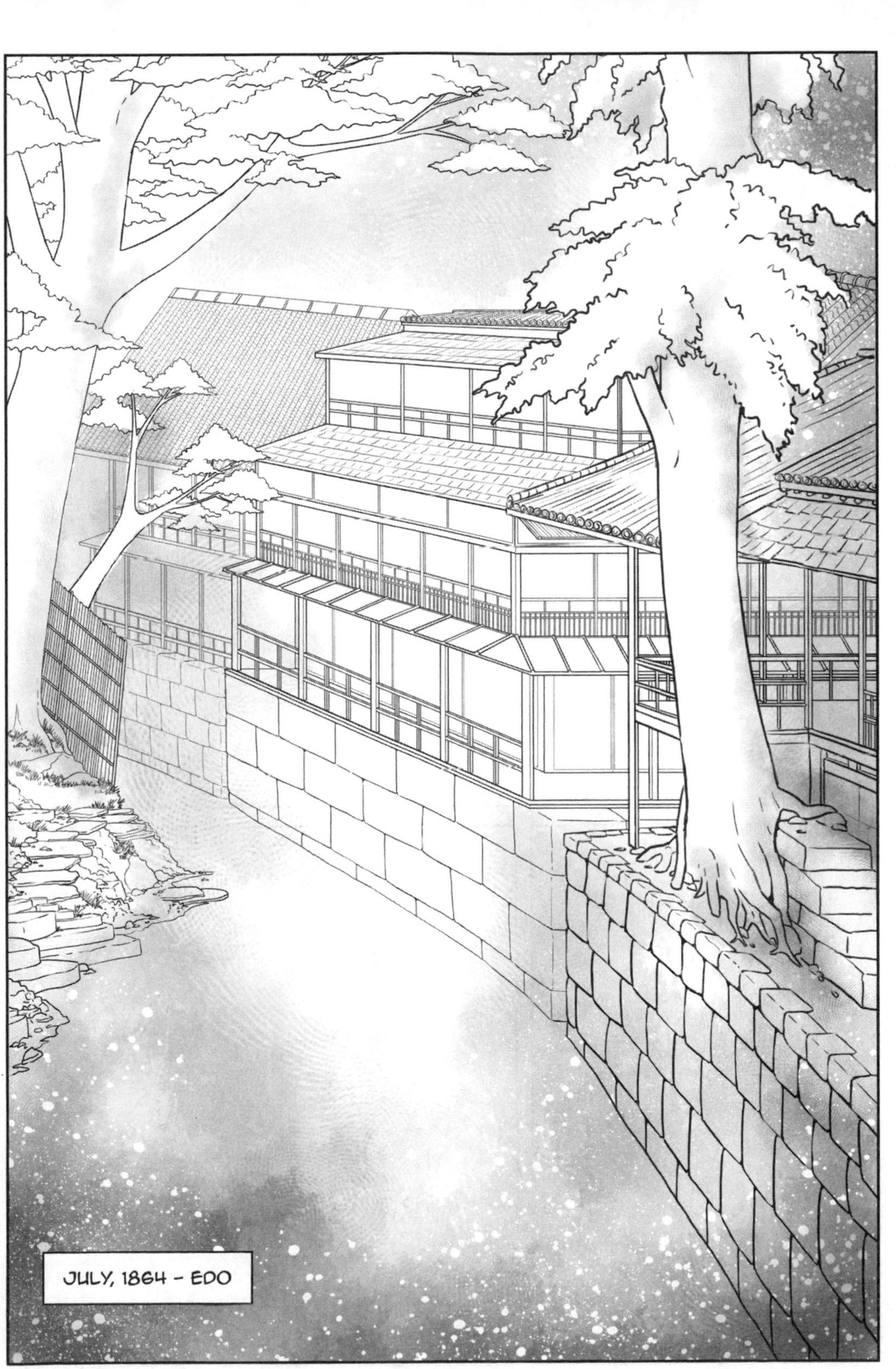
JULY, 1864 - EDO

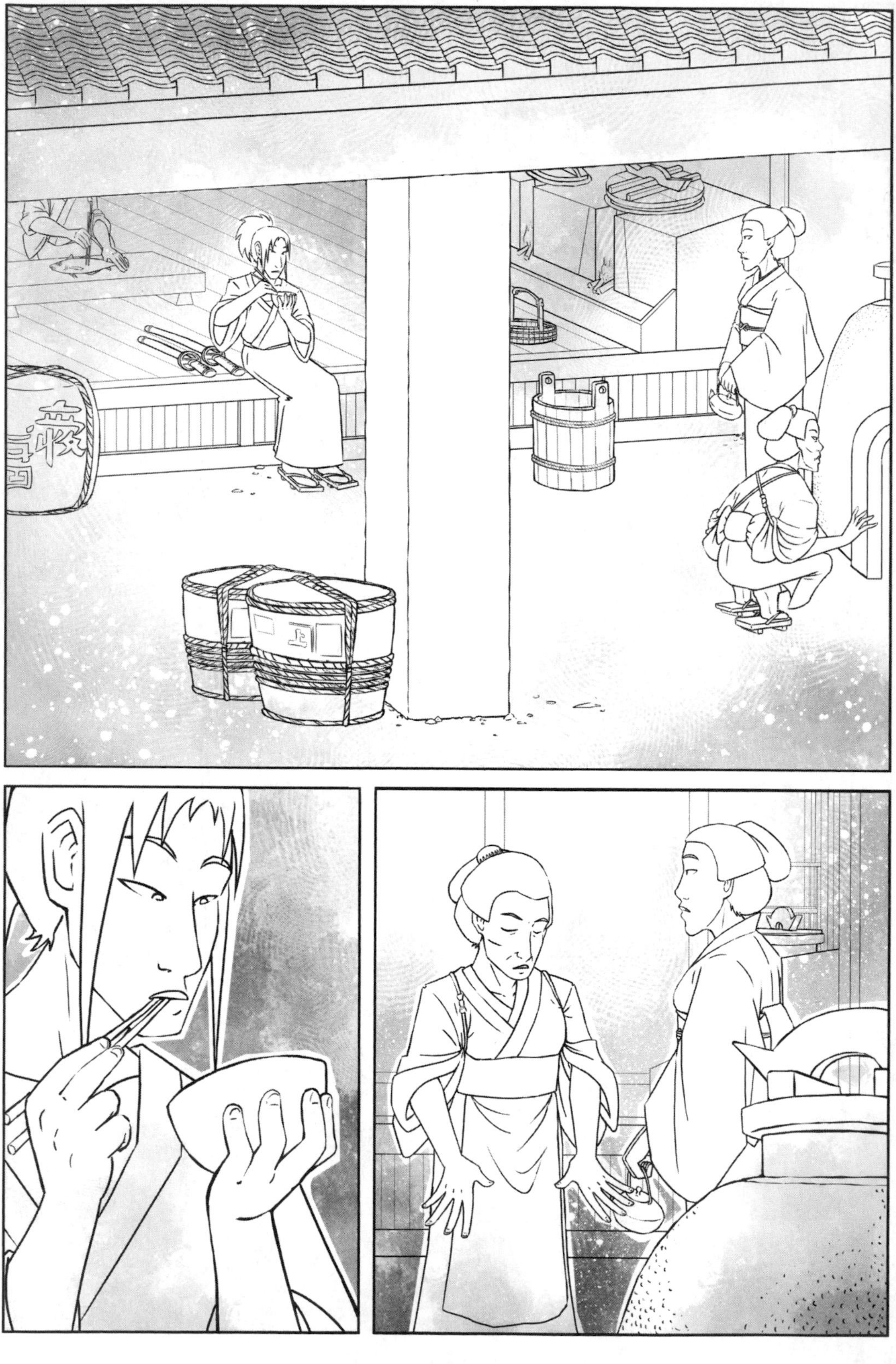
上

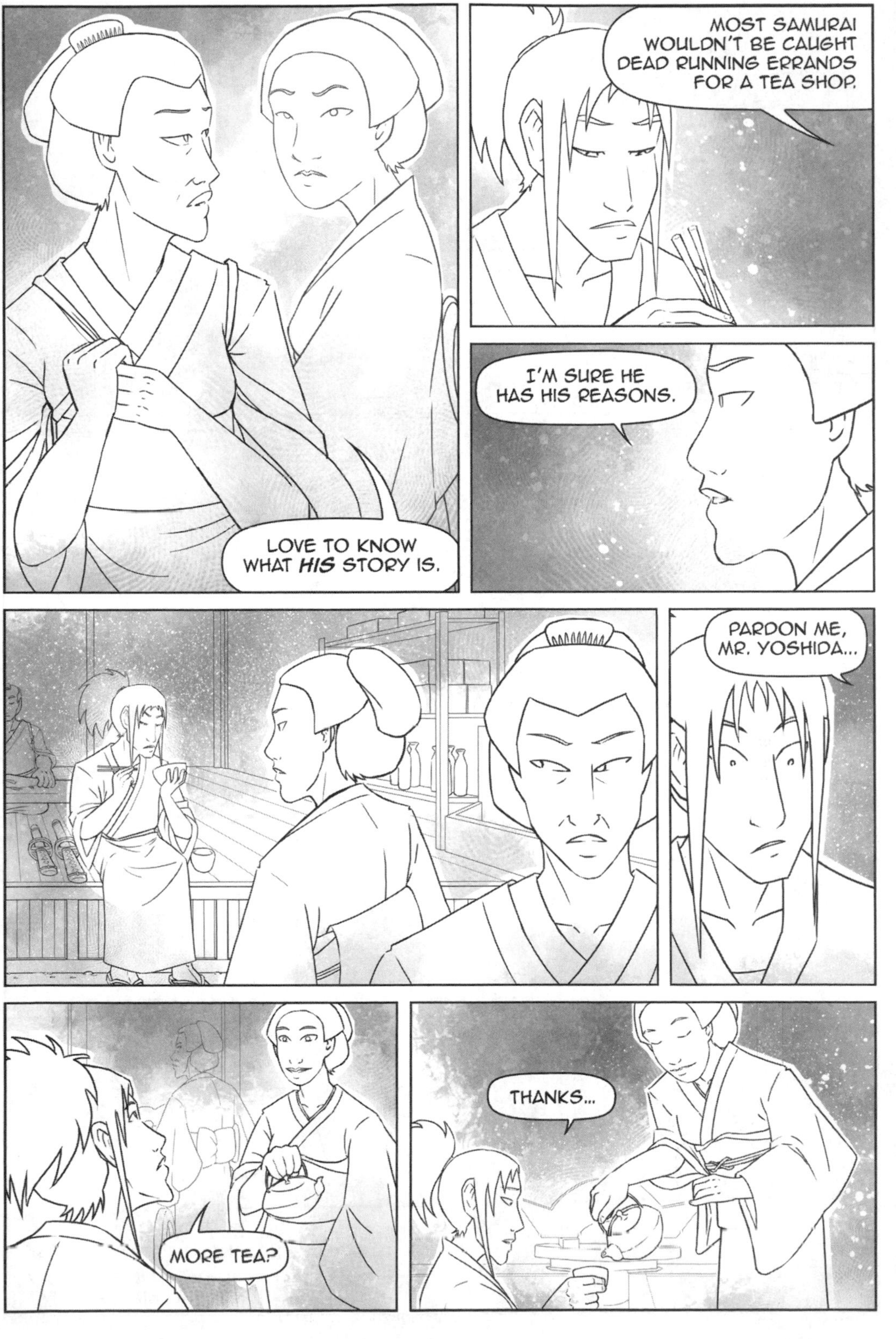
LOVE TO KNOW WHAT ***HIS*** STORY IS.
MOST SAMURAI WOULDN'T BE CAUGHT DEAD RUNNING ERRANDS FOR A TEA SHOP.
I'M SURE HE HAS HIS REASONS.
PARDON ME, MR. YOSHIDA...
MORE TEA?
THANKS...

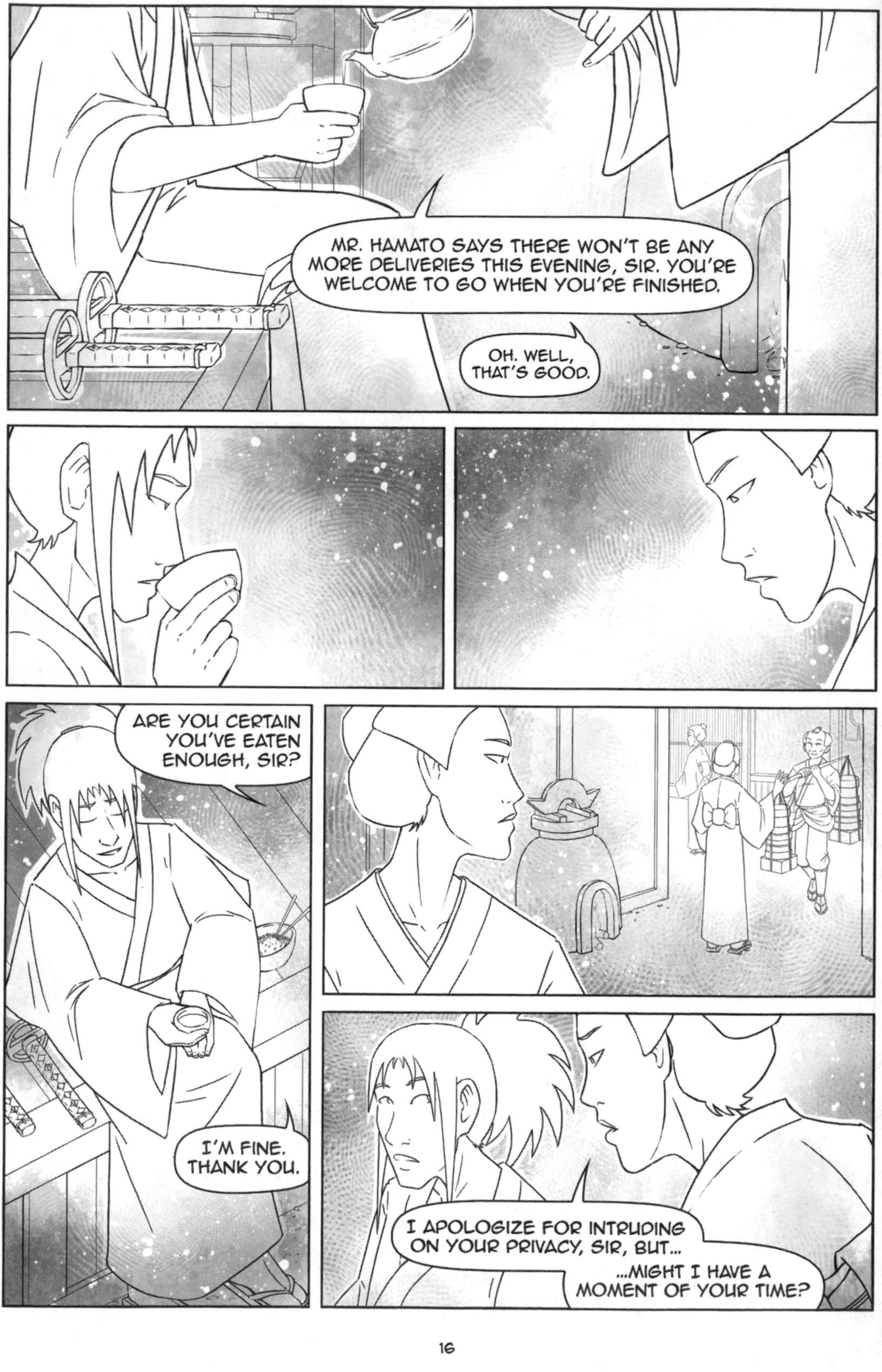
MR. HAMATO SAYS THERE WON'T BE ANY MORE DELIVERIES THIS EVENING, SIR. YOU'RE WELCOME TO GO WHEN YOU'RE FINISHED.
OH. WELL, THAT'S GOOD.
ARE YOU CERTAIN YOU'VE EATEN ENOUGH, SIR?
I'M FINE. THANK YOU.
I APOLOGIZE FOR INTRUDING ON YOUR PRIVACY, SIR, BUT...
...MIGHT I HAVE A MOMENT OF YOUR TIME?

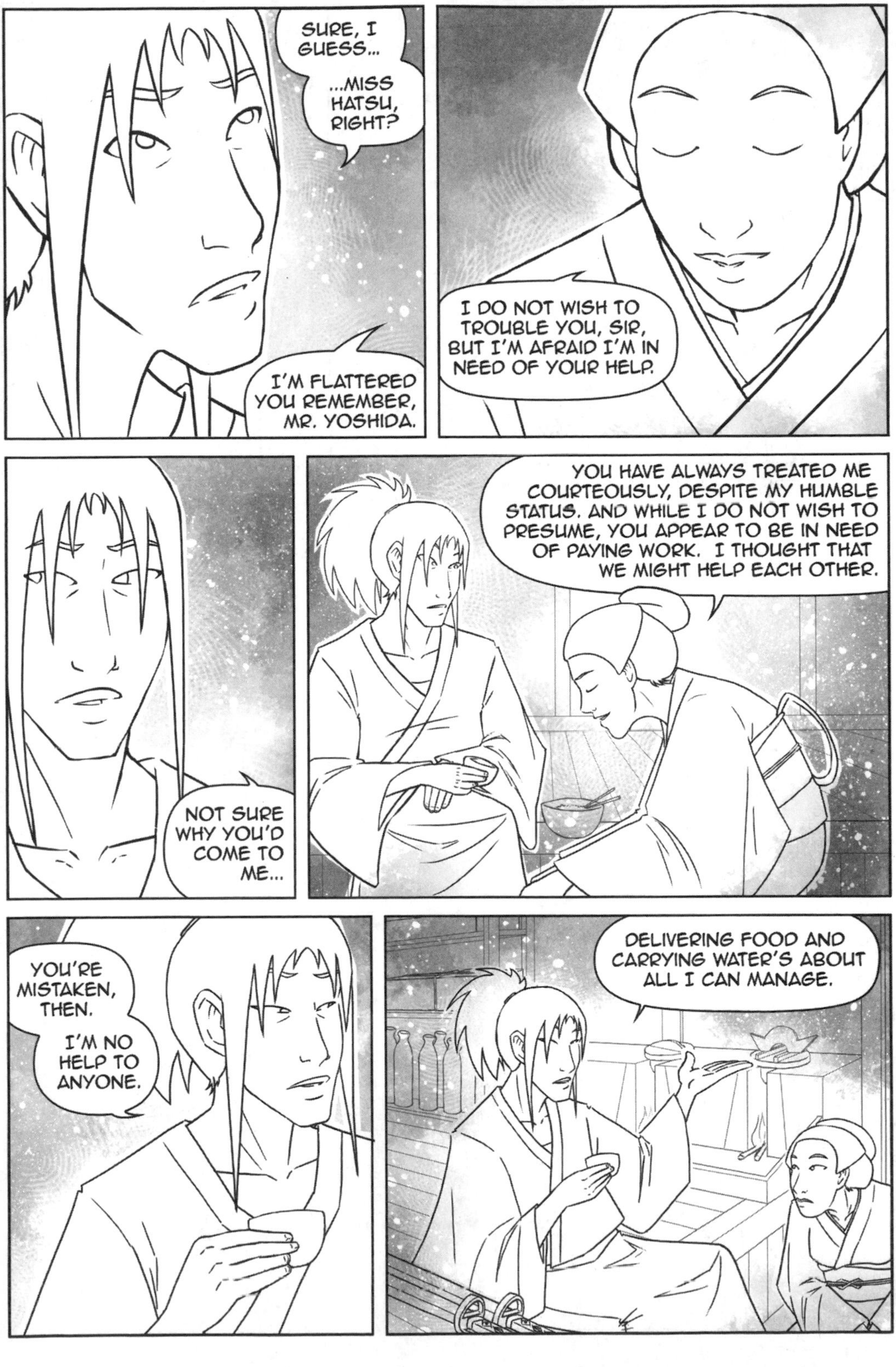
SURE, I GUESS...
...MISS HATSU, RIGHT?
I'M FLATTERED YOU REMEMBER, MR. YOSHIDA.
I DO NOT WISH TO TROUBLE YOU, SIR, BUT I'M AFRAID I'M IN NEED OF YOUR HELP.
NOT SURE WHY YOU'D COME TO ME...
YOU HAVE ALWAYS TREATED ME COURTEOUSLY, DESPITE MY HUMBLE STATUS. AND WHILE I DO NOT WISH TO PRESUME, YOU APPEAR TO BE IN NEED OF PAYING WORK. I THOUGHT THAT WE MIGHT HELP EACH OTHER.
YOU'RE MISTAKEN, THEN.
I'M NO HELP TO ANYONE.
DELIVERING FOOD AND CARRYING WATER'S ABOUT ALL I CAN MANAGE.

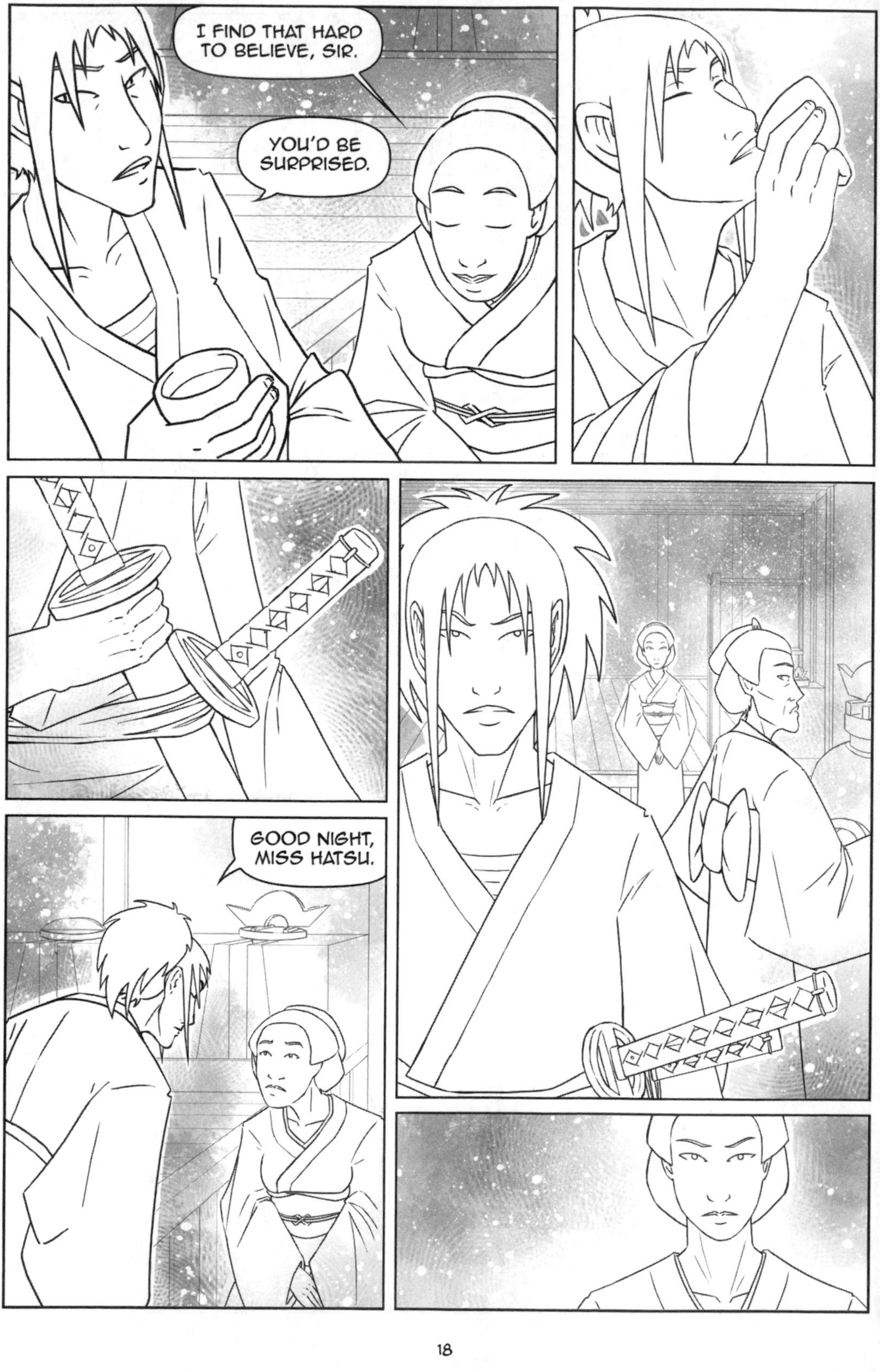
I FIND THAT HARD TO BELIEVE, SIR.
YOU'D BE SURPRISED.
GOOD NIGHT, MISS HATSU.

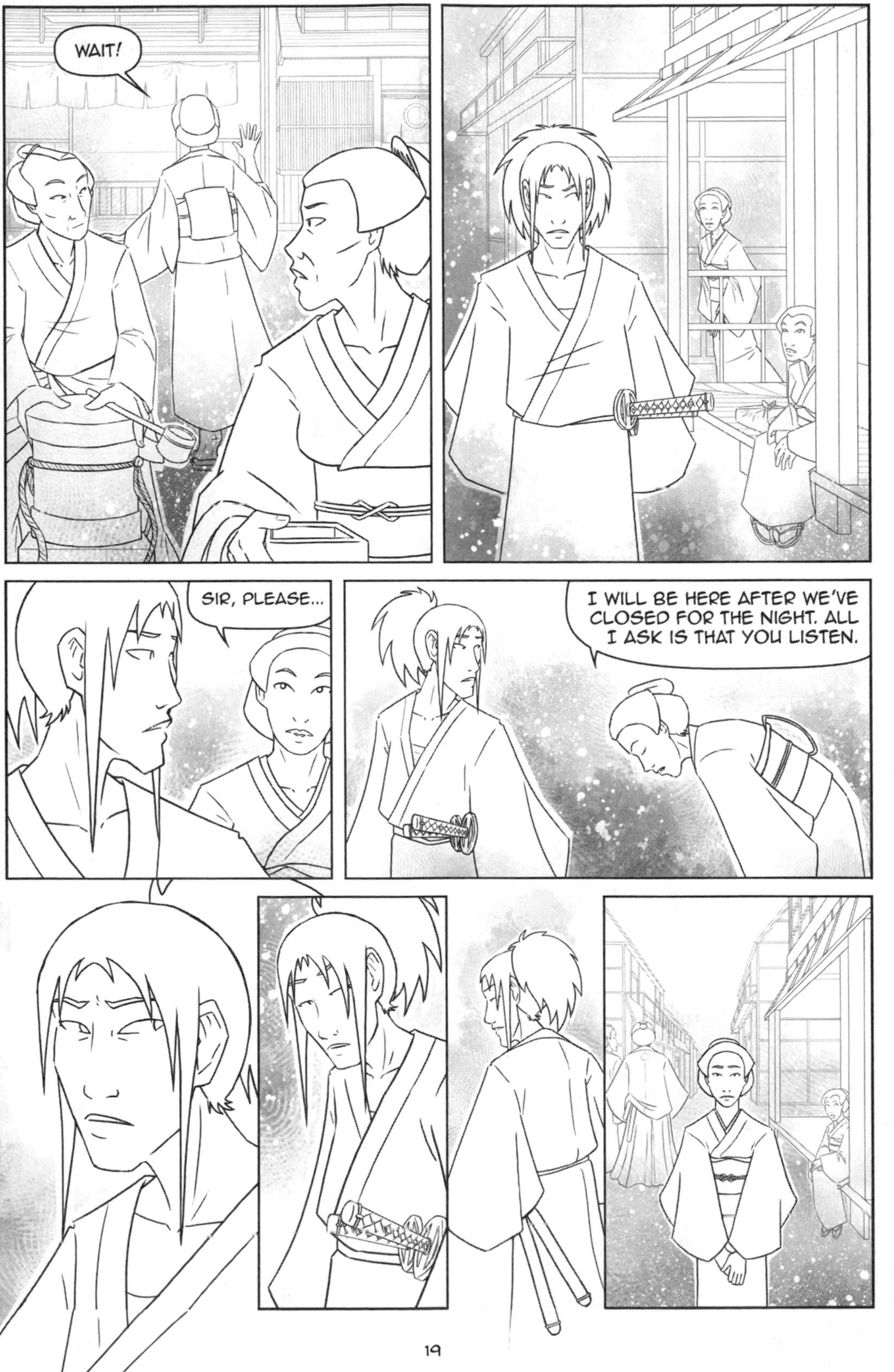
WAIT!
SIR, PLEASE...
I WILL BE HERE AFTER WE'VE CLOSED FOR THE NIGHT. ALL I ASK IS THAT YOU LISTEN.

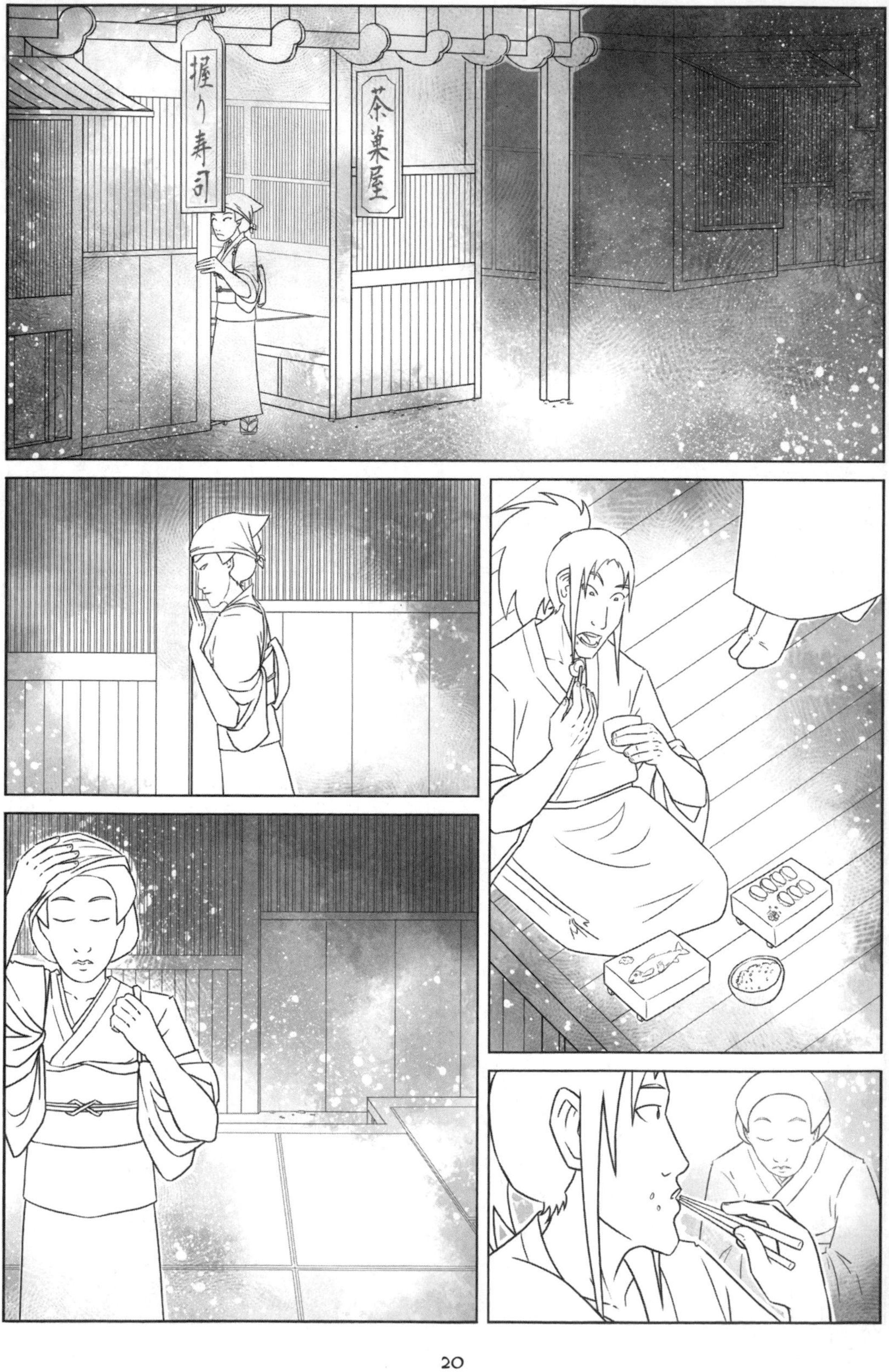
握り寿司
茶菓屋

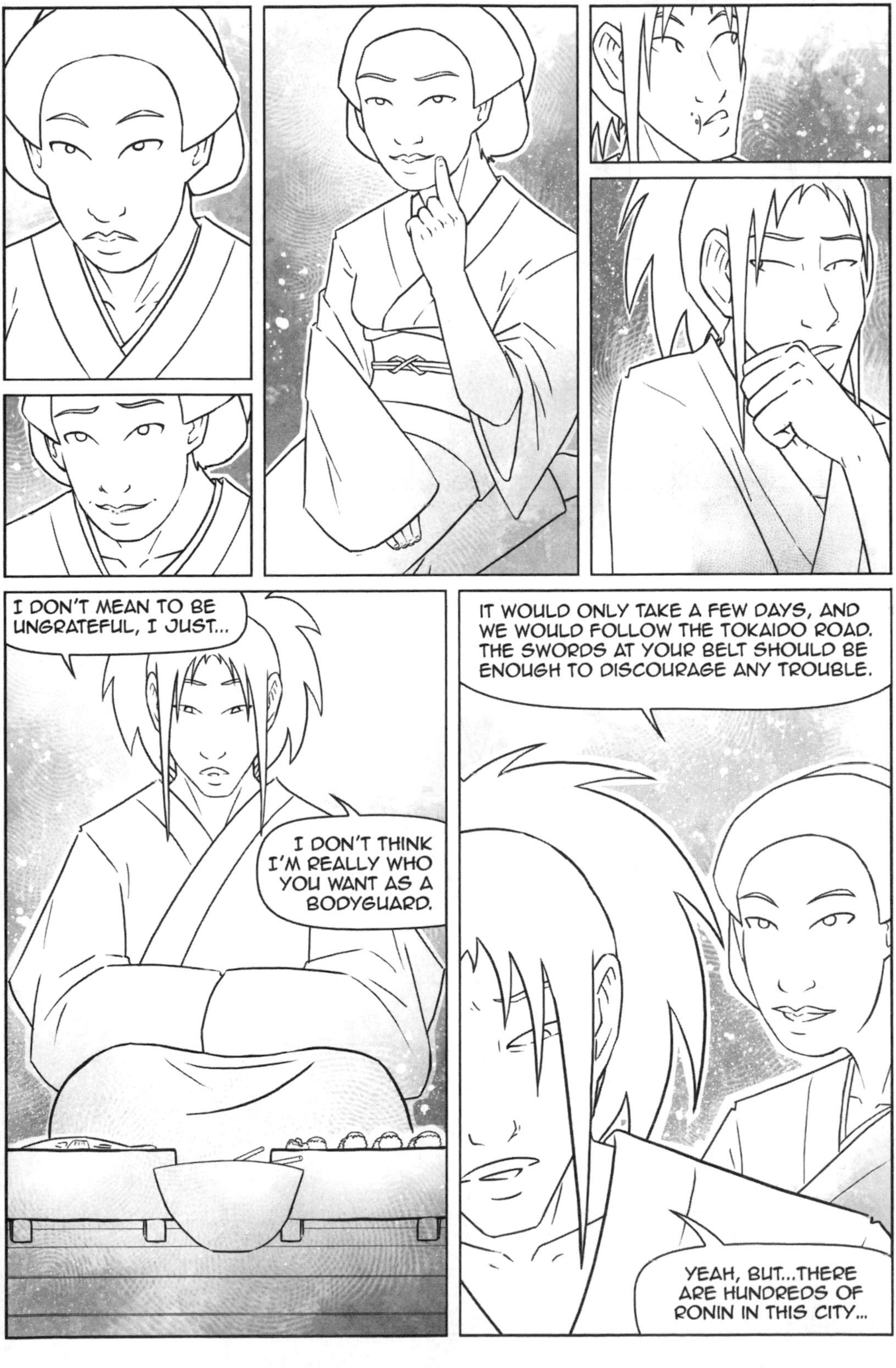
I DON'T MEAN TO BE UNGRATEFUL, I JUST...
I DON'T THINK I'M REALLY WHO YOU WANT AS A BODYGUARD.
IT WOULD ONLY TAKE A FEW DAYS, AND WE WOULD FOLLOW THE TOKAIDO ROAD. THE SWORDS AT YOUR BELT SHOULD BE ENOUGH TO DISCOURAGE ANY TROUBLE.
YEAH, BUT...THERE ARE HUNDREDS OF RONIN IN THIS CITY...

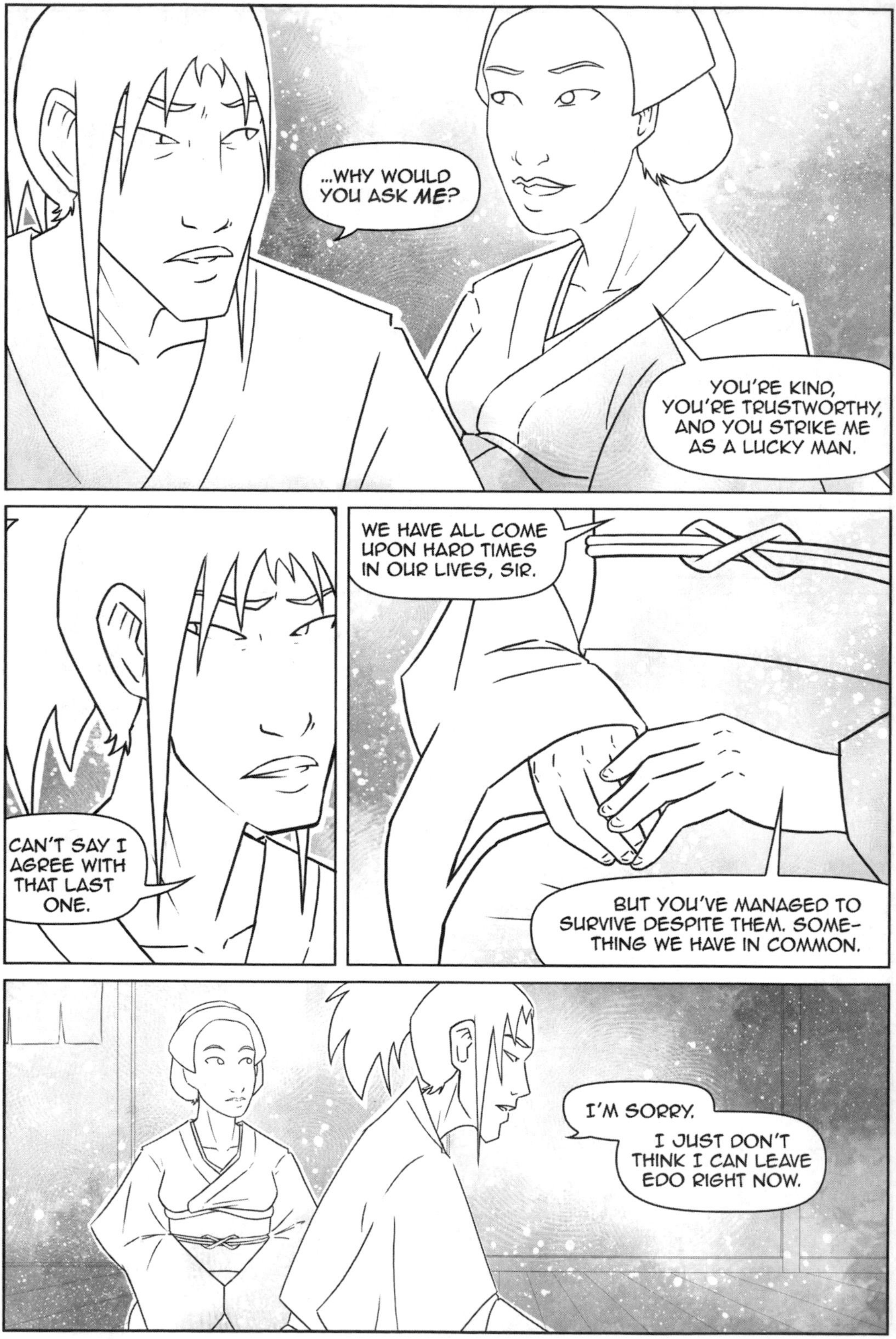
...WHY WOULD YOU ASK *ME*?
YOU'RE KIND, YOU'RE TRUSTWORTHY, AND YOU STRIKE ME AS A LUCKY MAN.
CAN'T SAY I AGREE WITH THAT LAST ONE.
WE HAVE ALL COME UPON HARD TIMES IN OUR LIVES, SIR.
BUT YOU'VE MANAGED TO SURVIVE DESPITE THEM. SOME-THING WE HAVE IN COMMON.
I'M SORRY.
I JUST DON'T THINK I CAN LEAVE EDO RIGHT NOW.

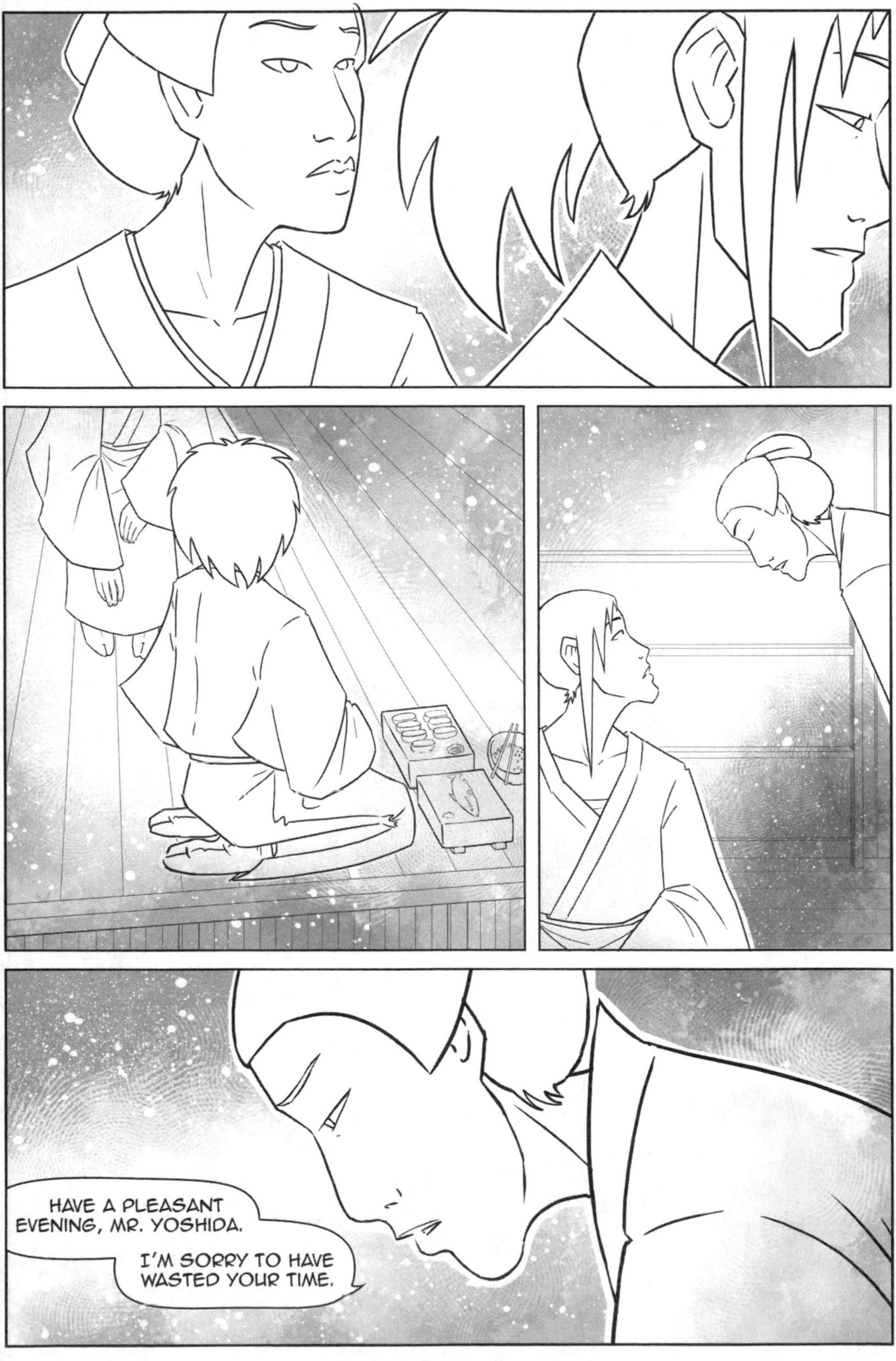
HAVE A PLEASANT EVENING, MR. YOSHIDA.
I'M SORRY TO HAVE WASTED YOUR TIME.

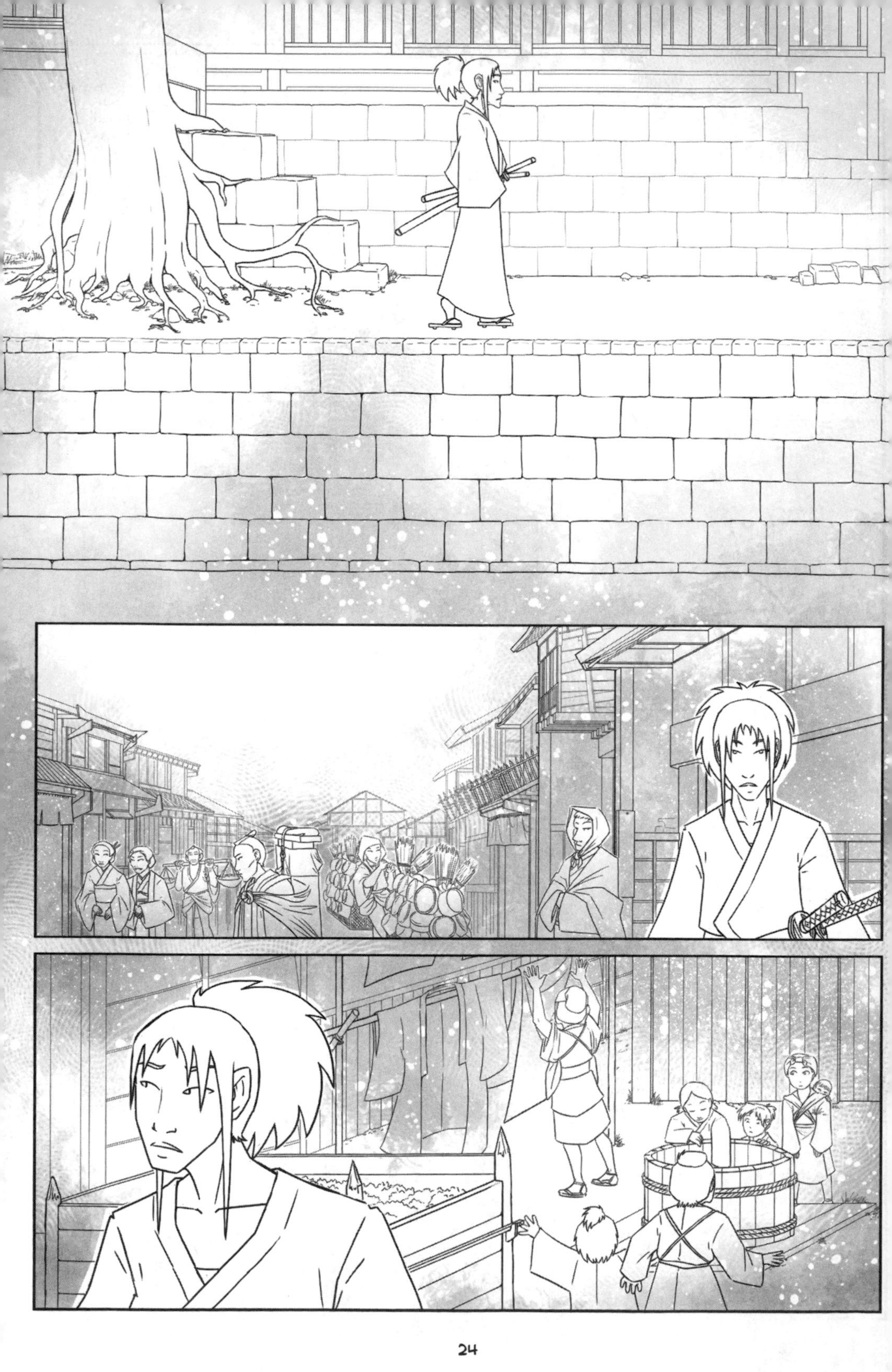

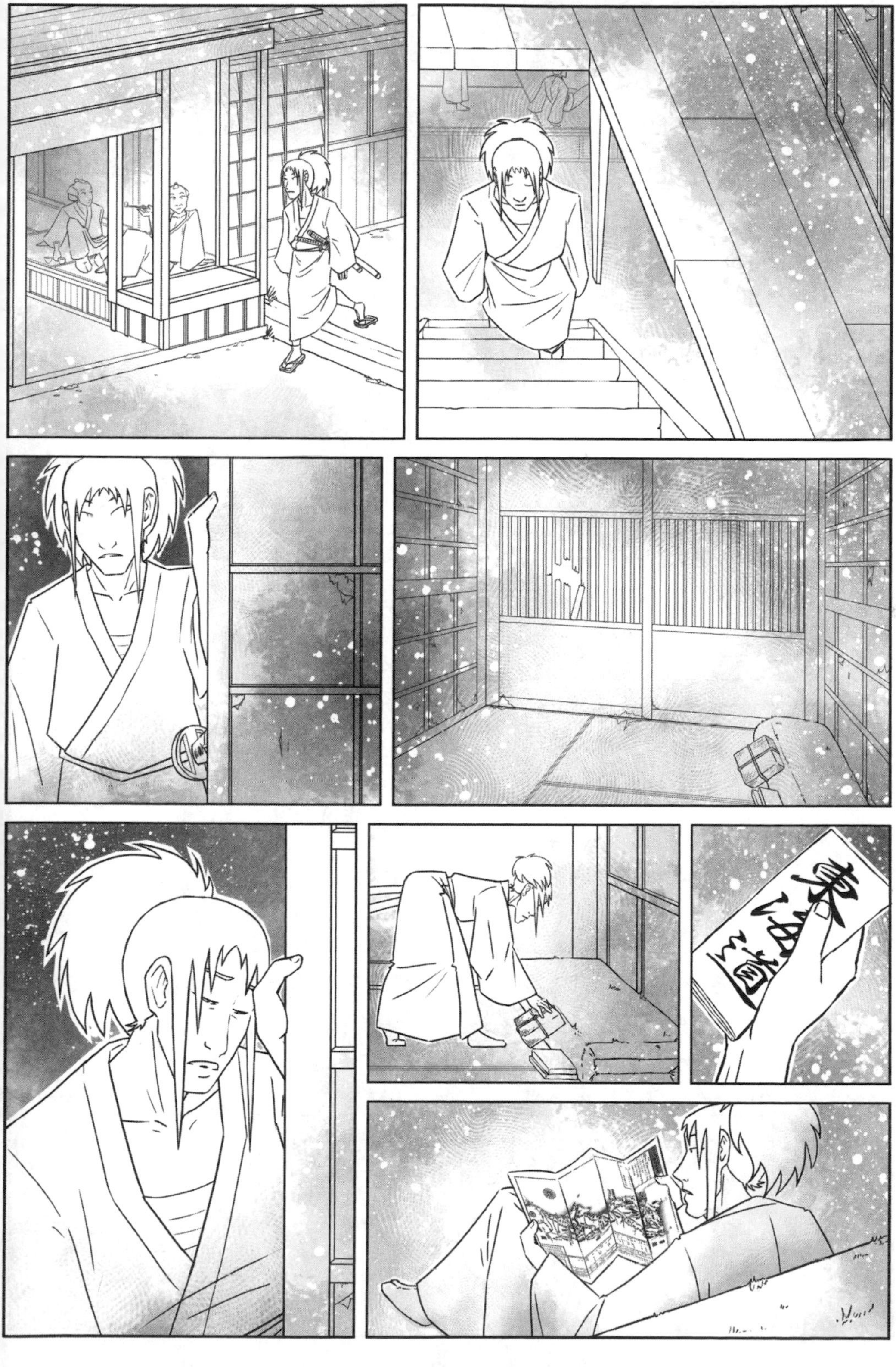
東海道

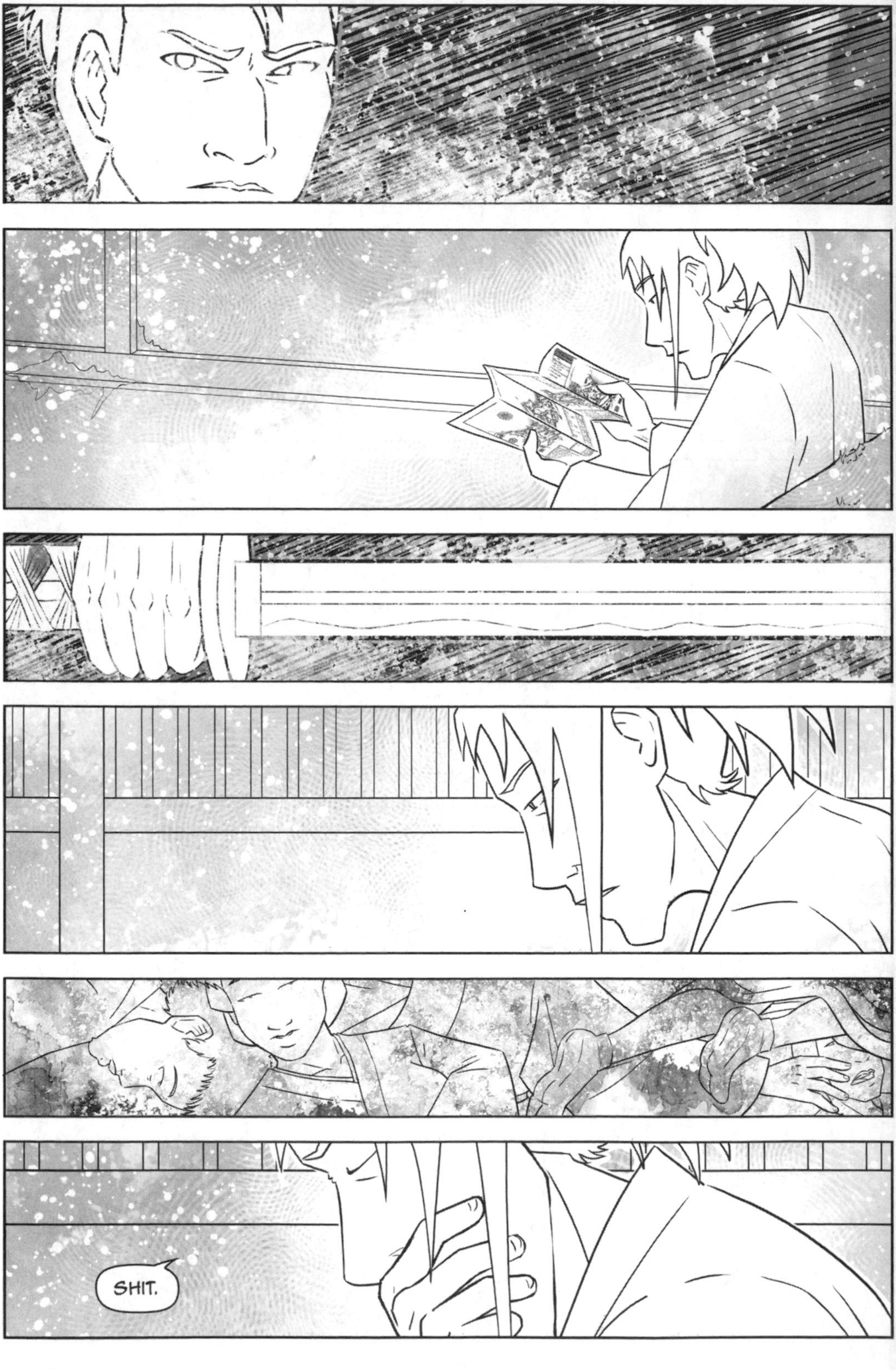
SHIT.

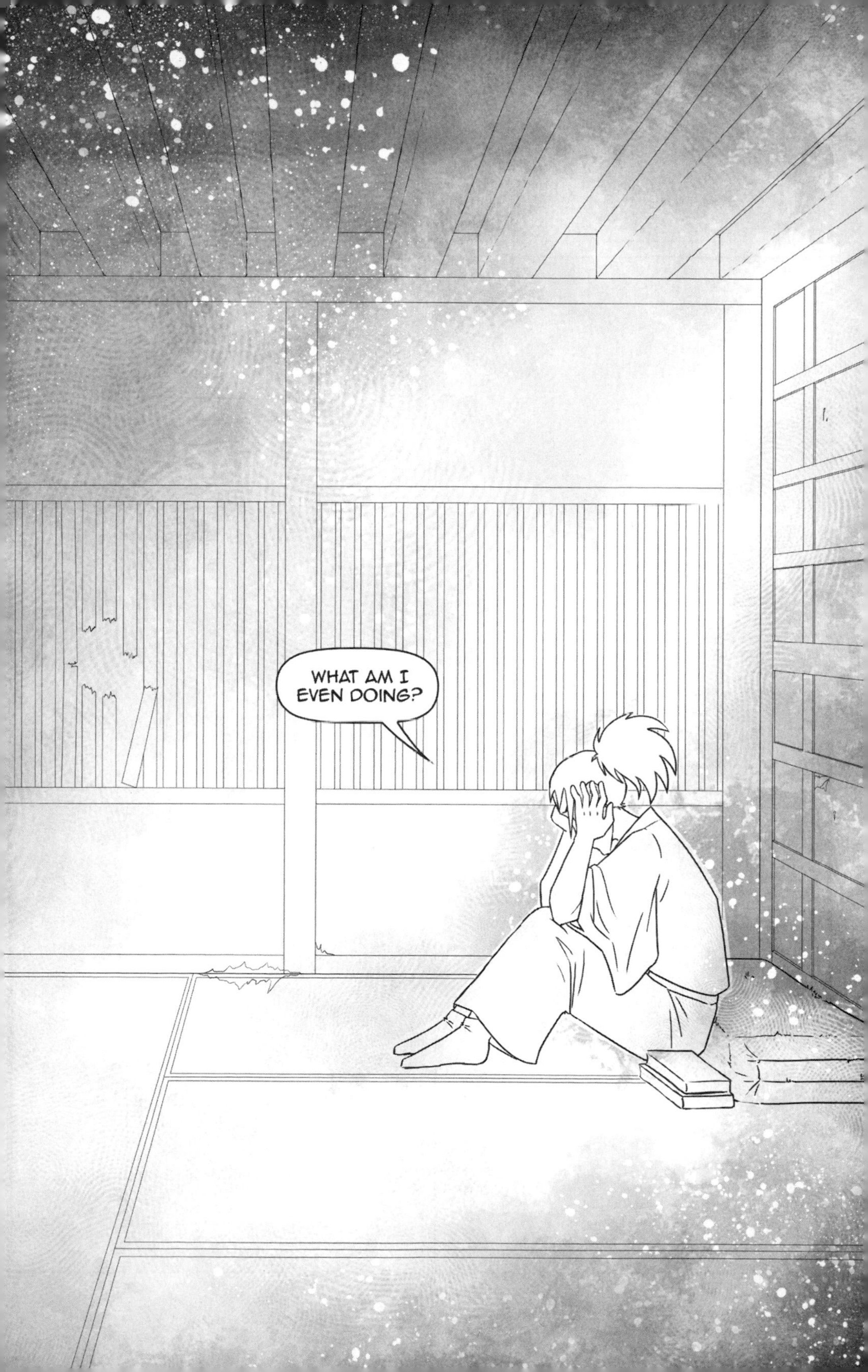
WHAT AM I
EVEN DOING?

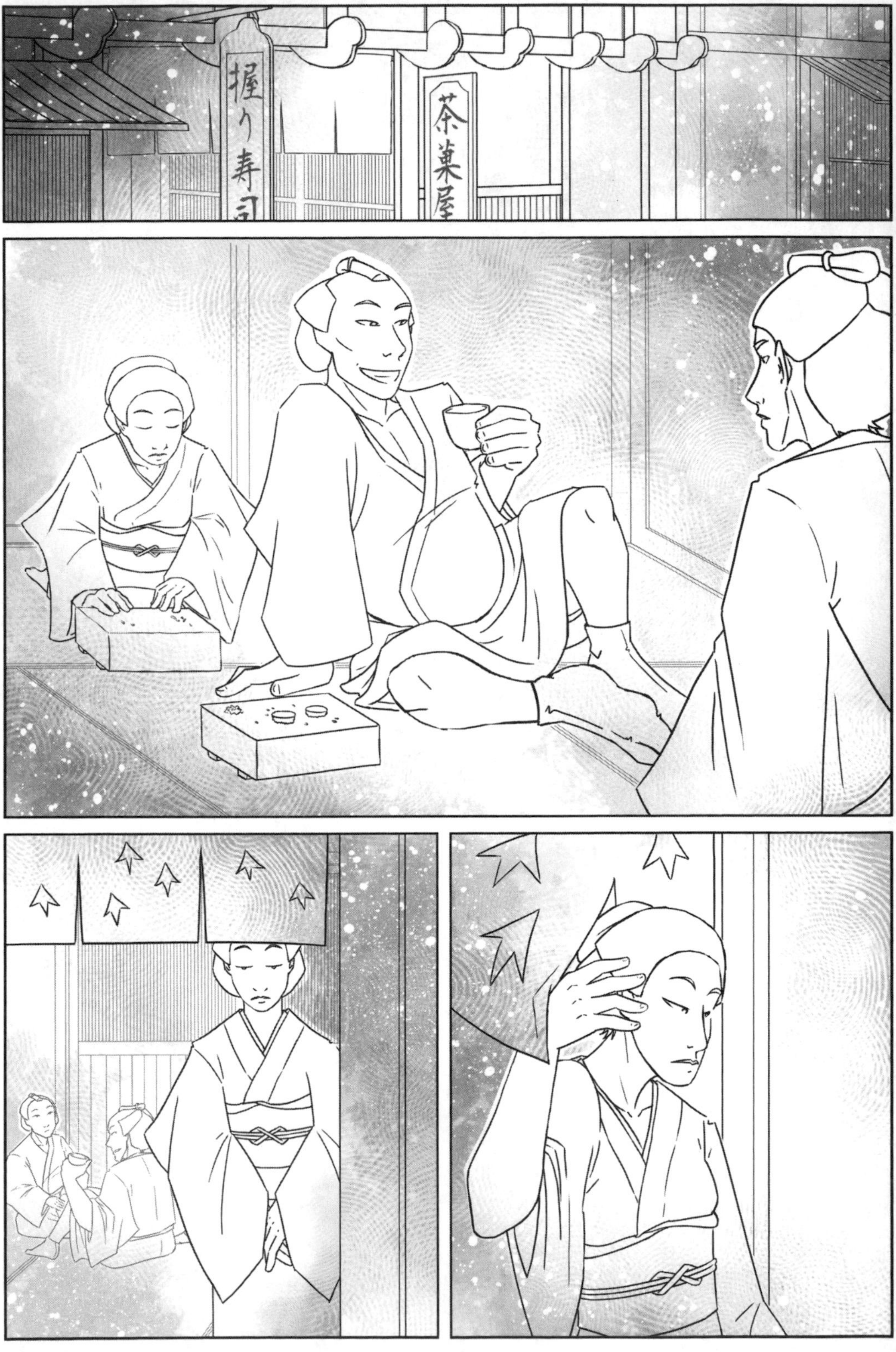
握り寿司
茶菓屋

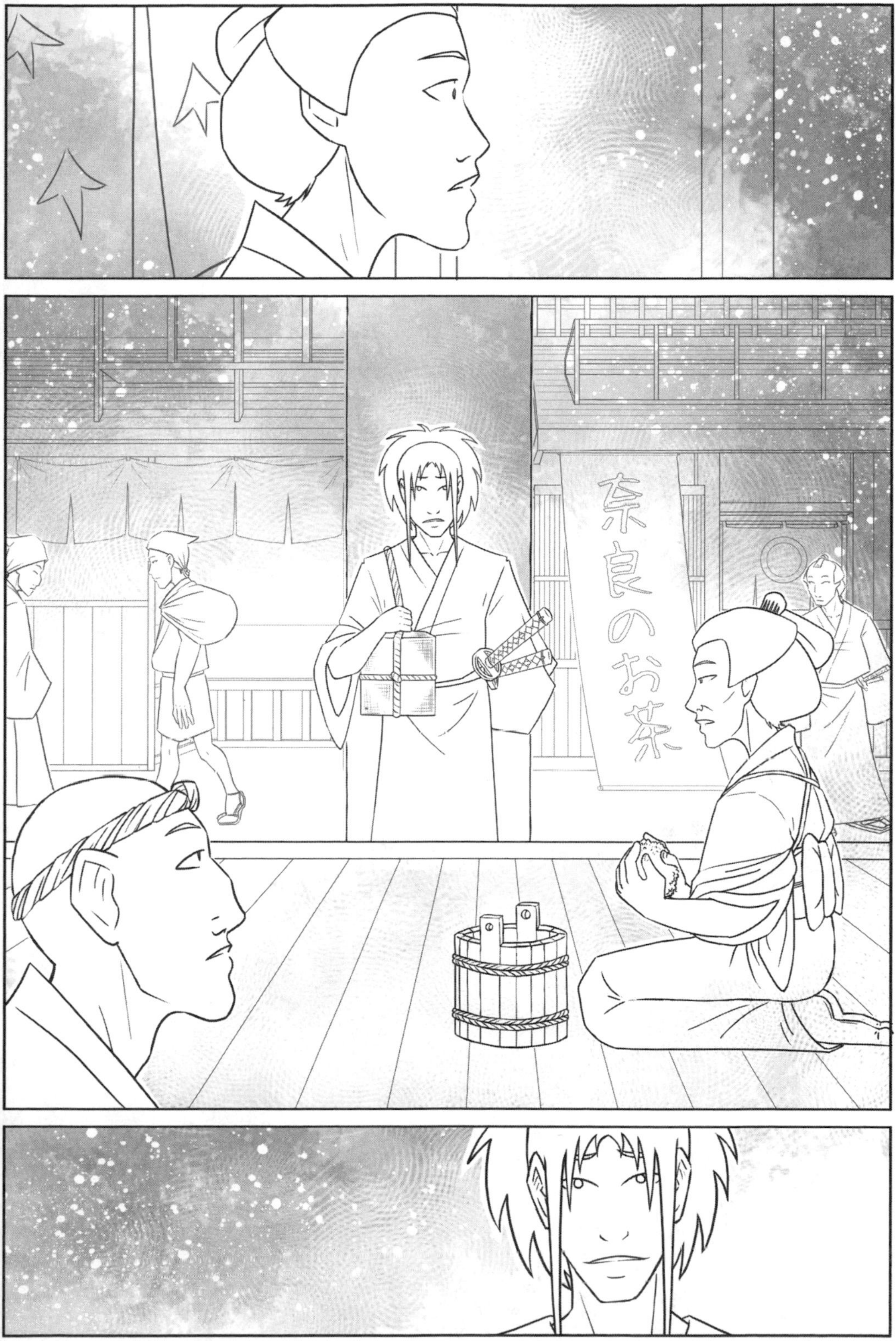
奈良のお茶

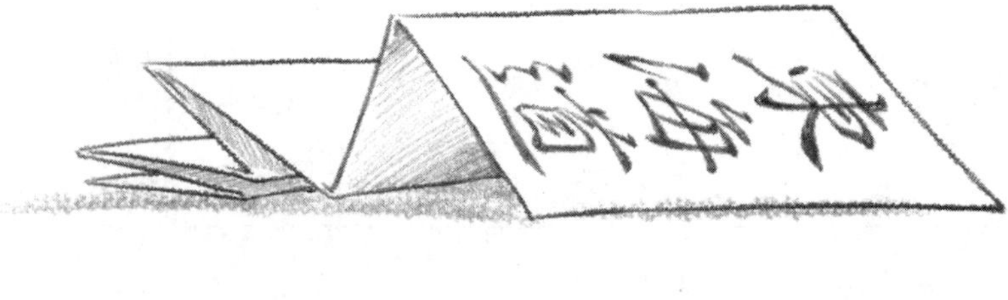
東海道

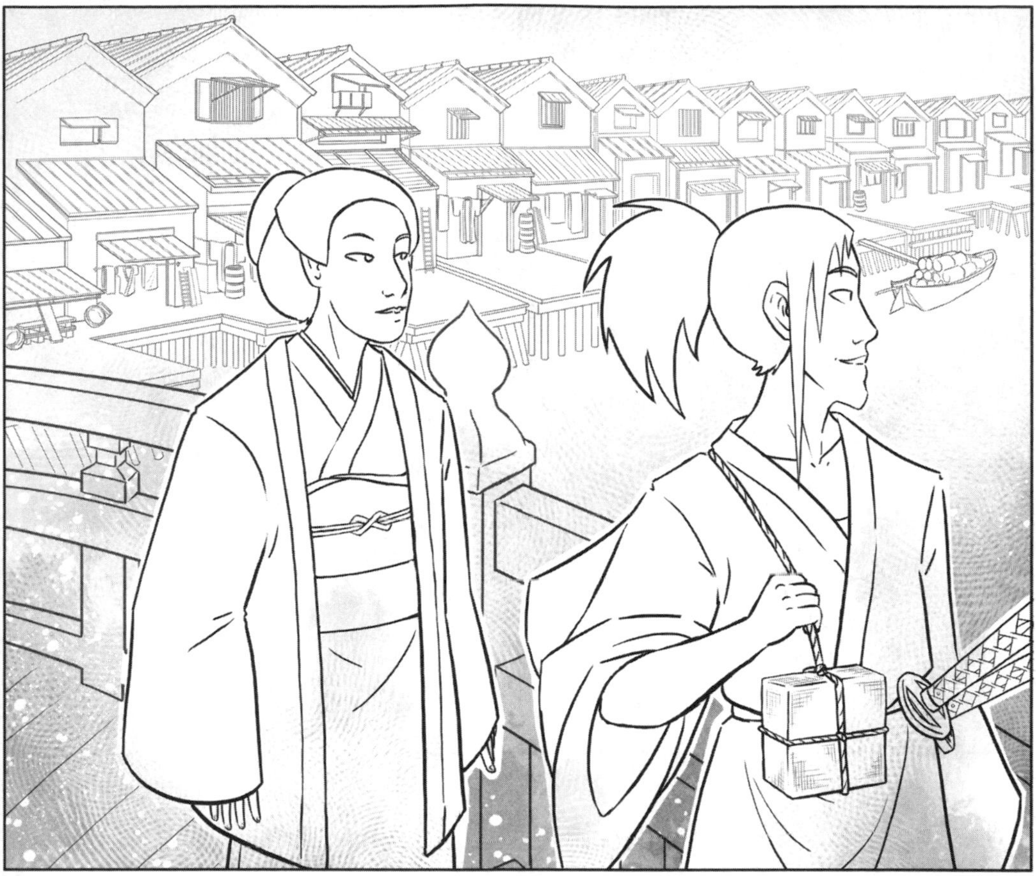

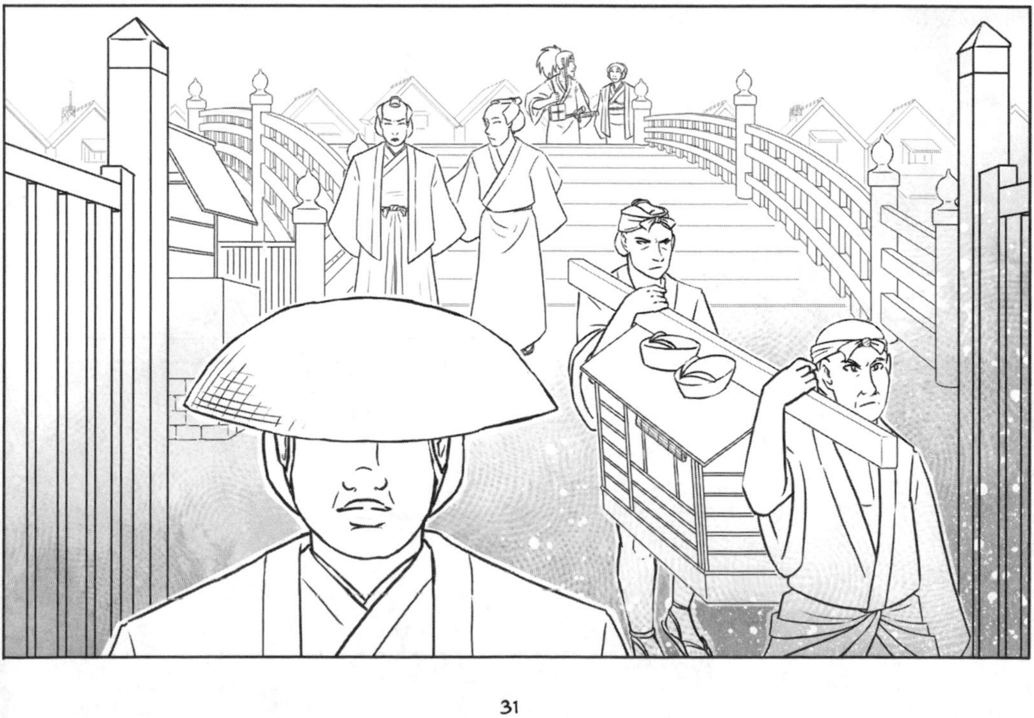

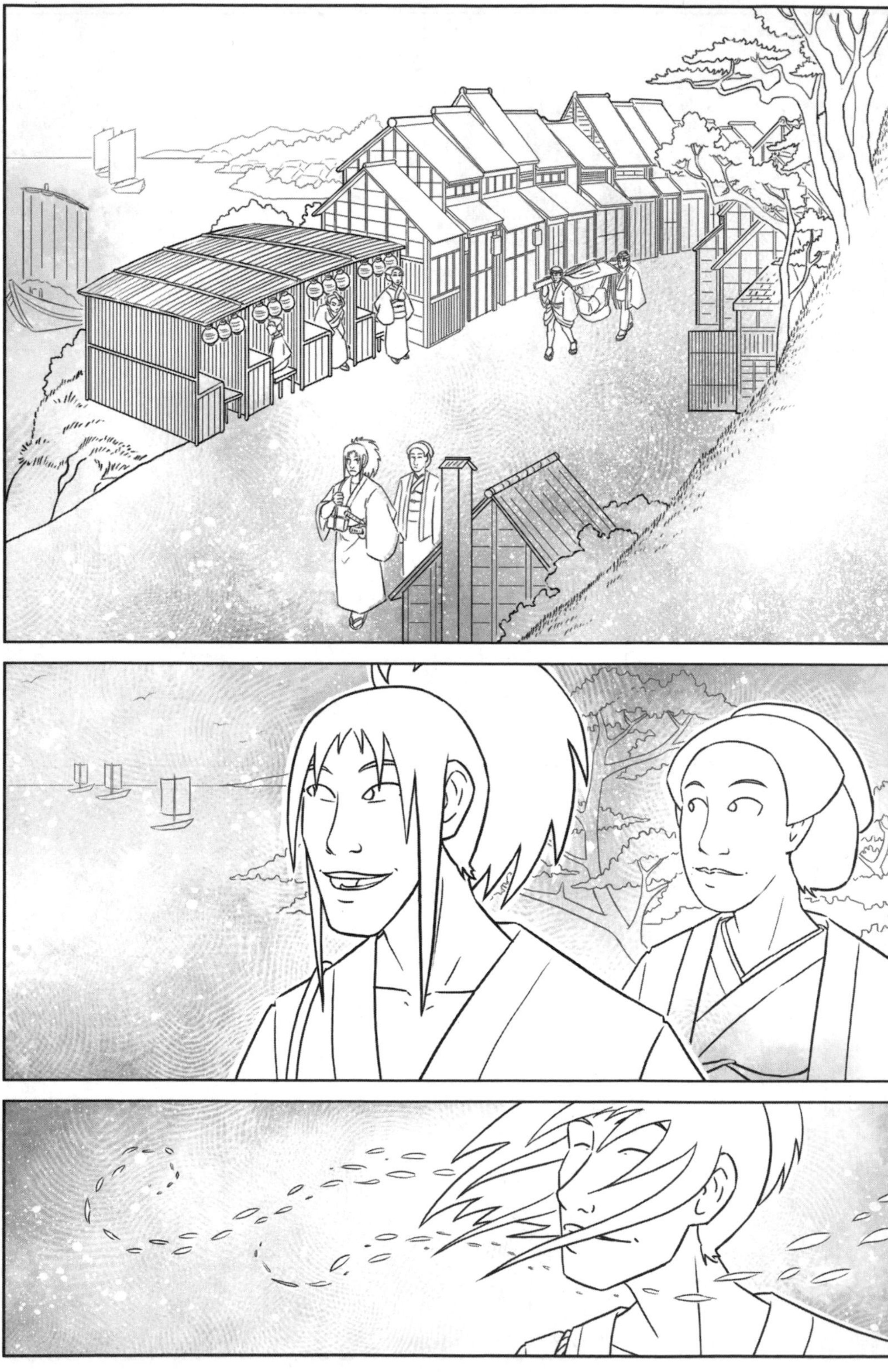

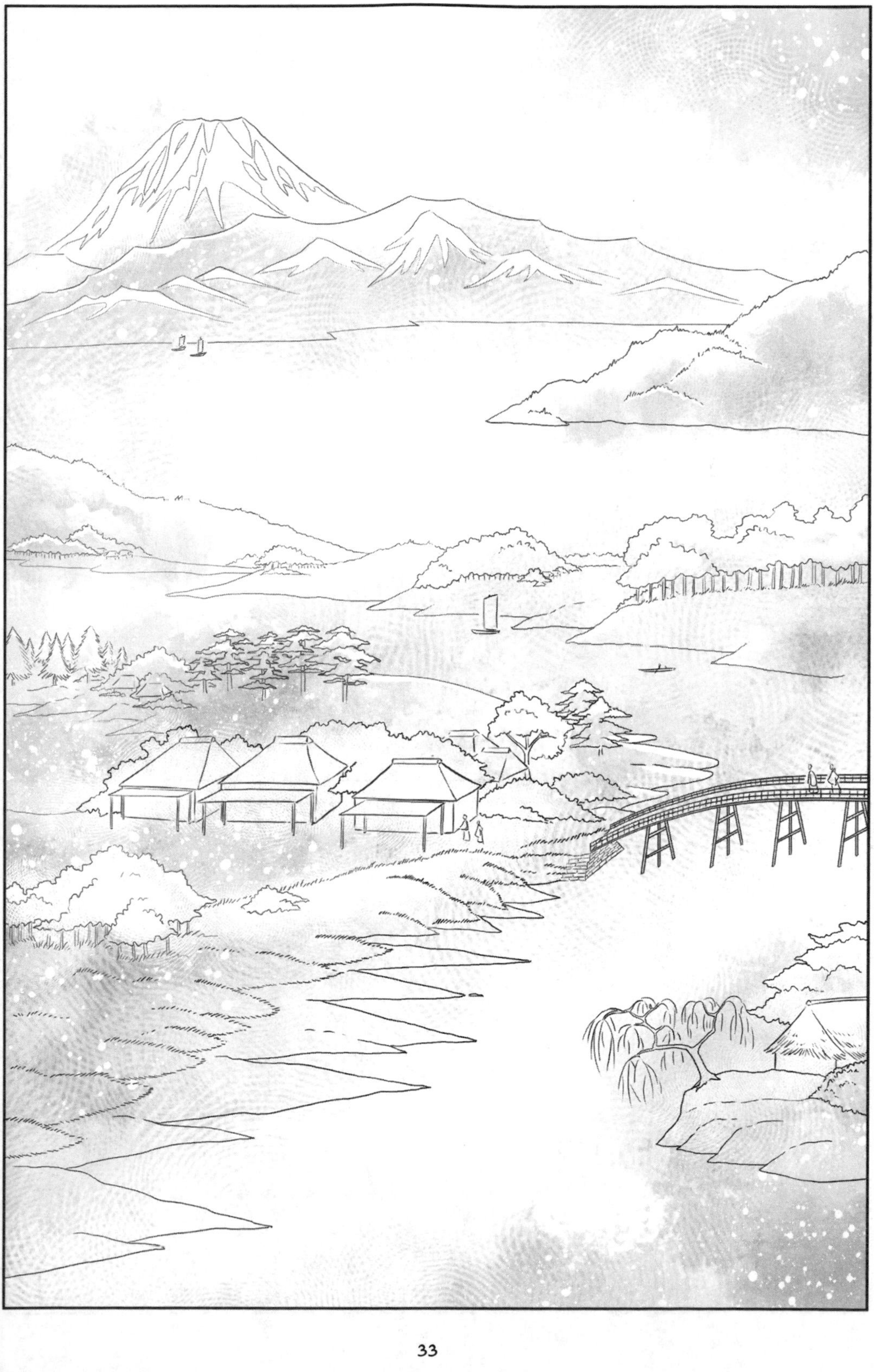

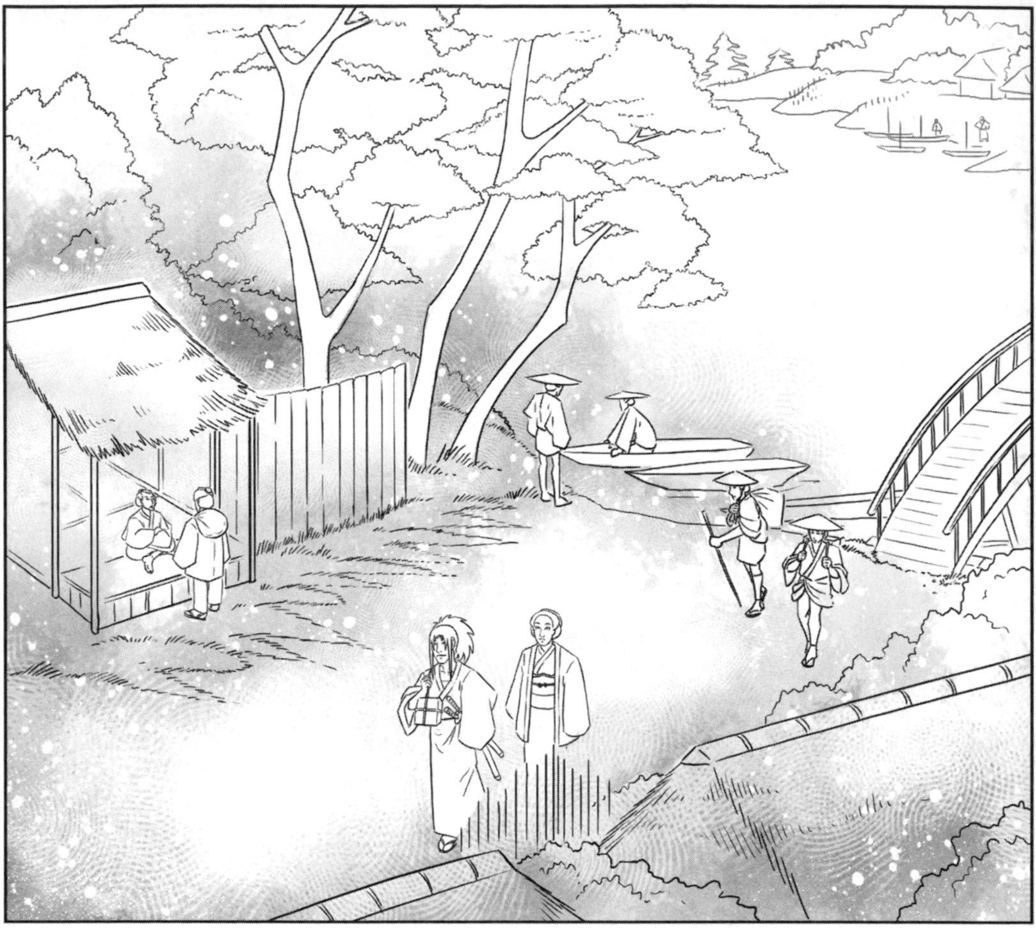

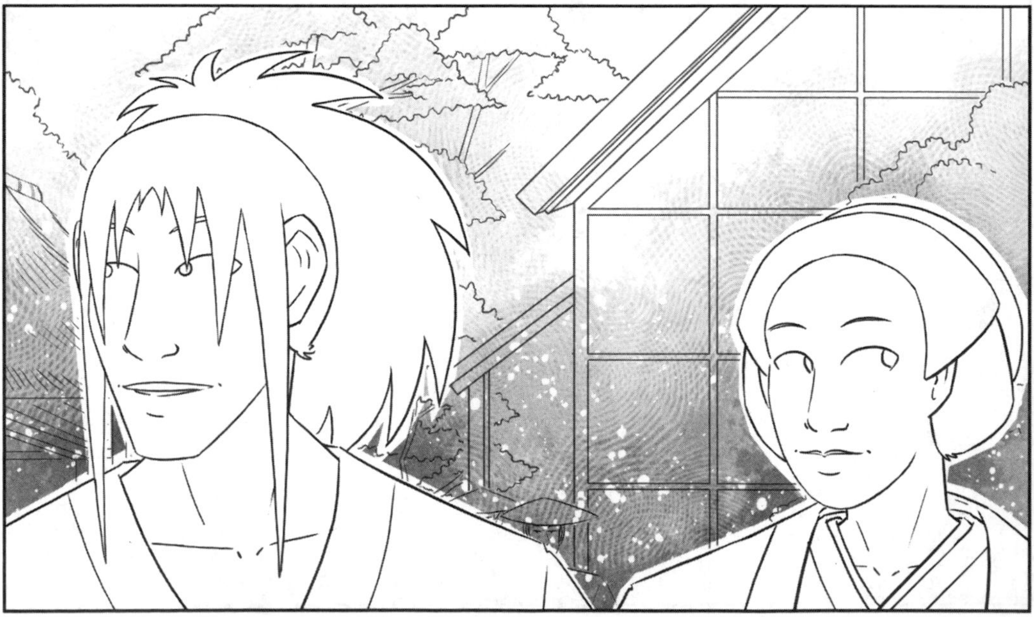

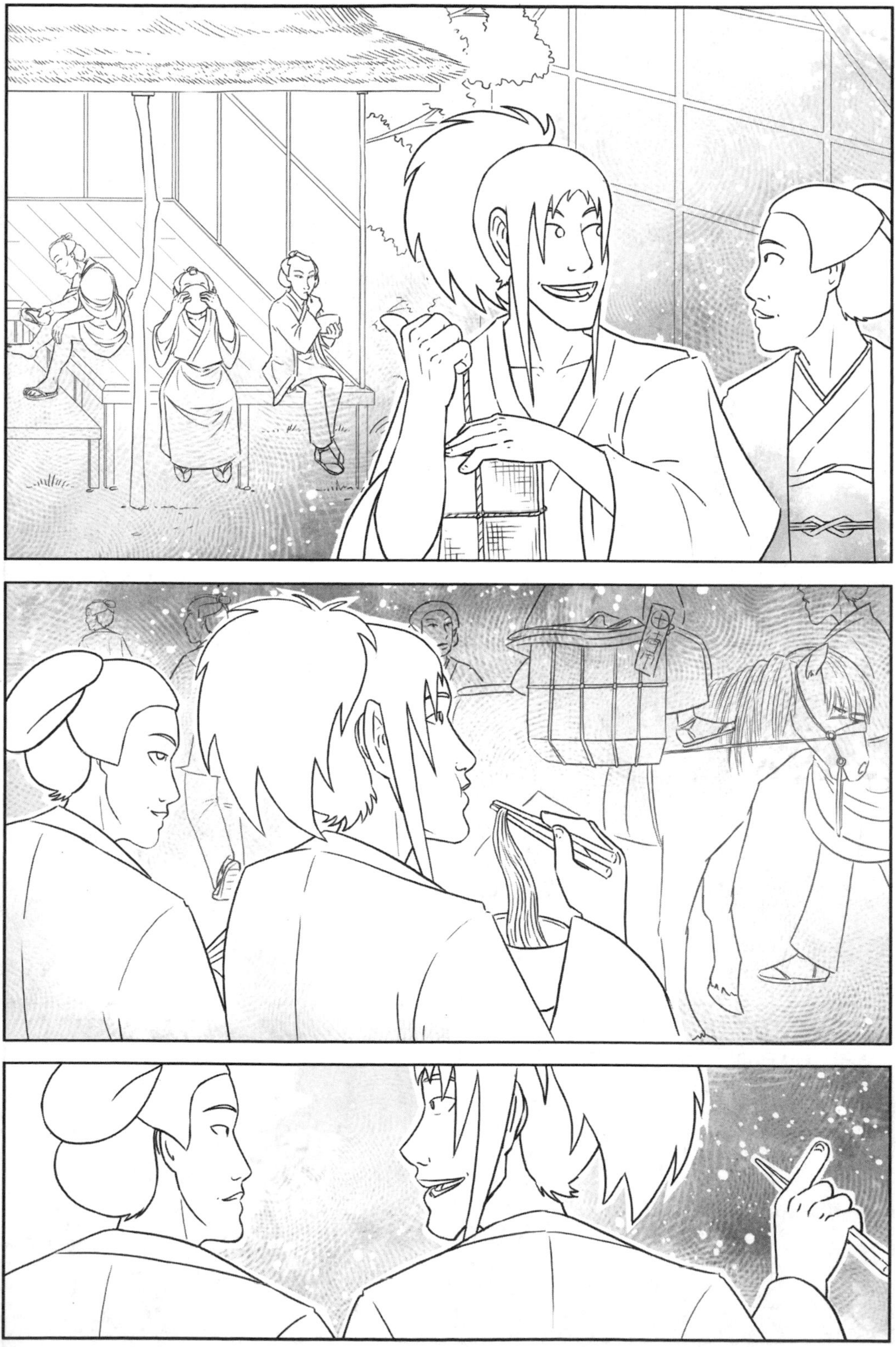

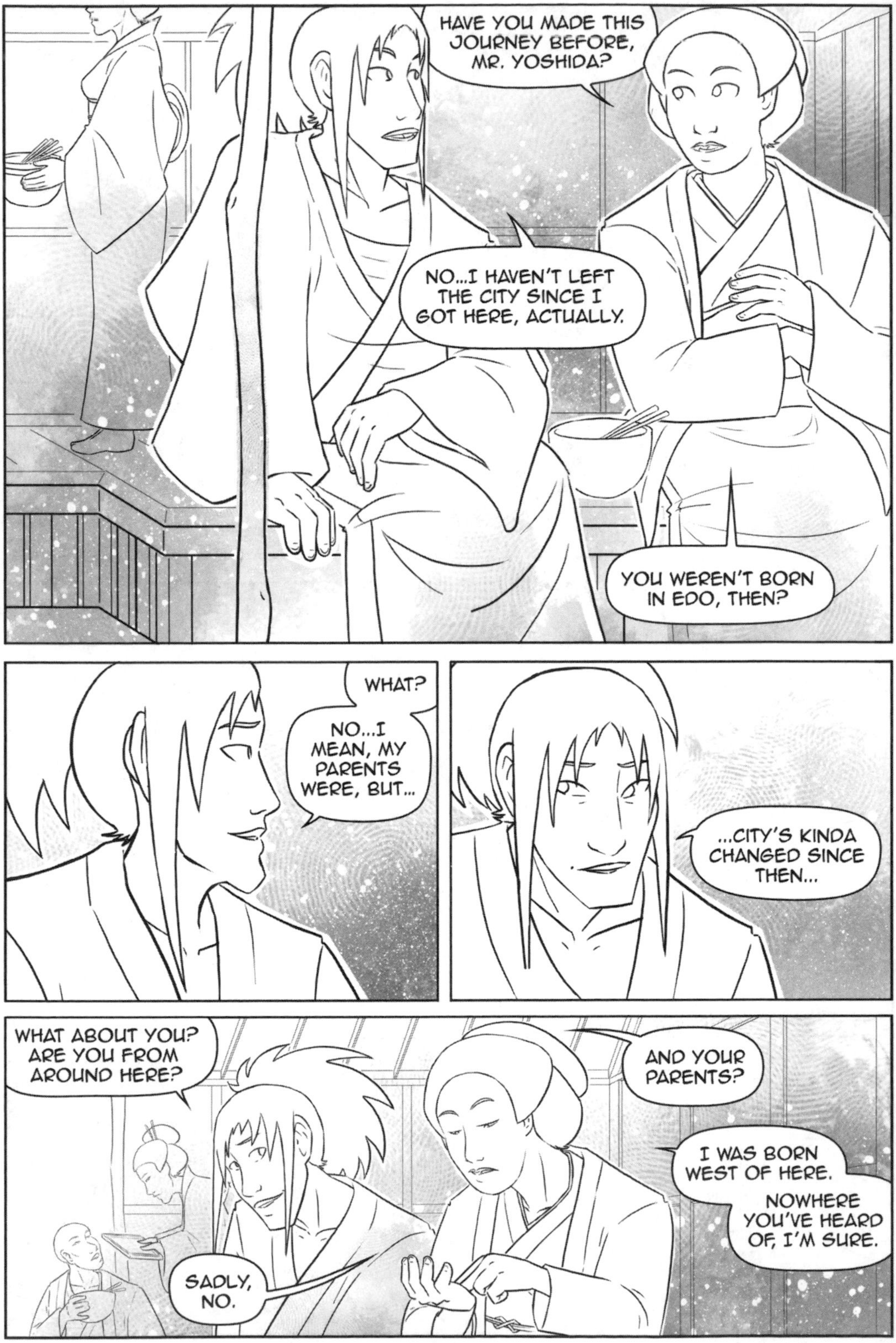
HAVE YOU MADE THIS JOURNEY BEFORE, MR. YOSHIDA?
NO...I HAVEN'T LEFT THE CITY SINCE I GOT HERE, ACTUALLY.
YOU WEREN'T BORN IN EDO, THEN?
WHAT?
NO...I MEAN, MY PARENTS WERE, BUT...
...CITY'S KINDA CHANGED SINCE THEN...
WHAT ABOUT YOU? ARE YOU FROM AROUND HERE?
AND YOUR PARENTS?
I WAS BORN WEST OF HERE.
NOWHERE YOU'VE HEARD OF, I'M SURE.
SADLY, NO.

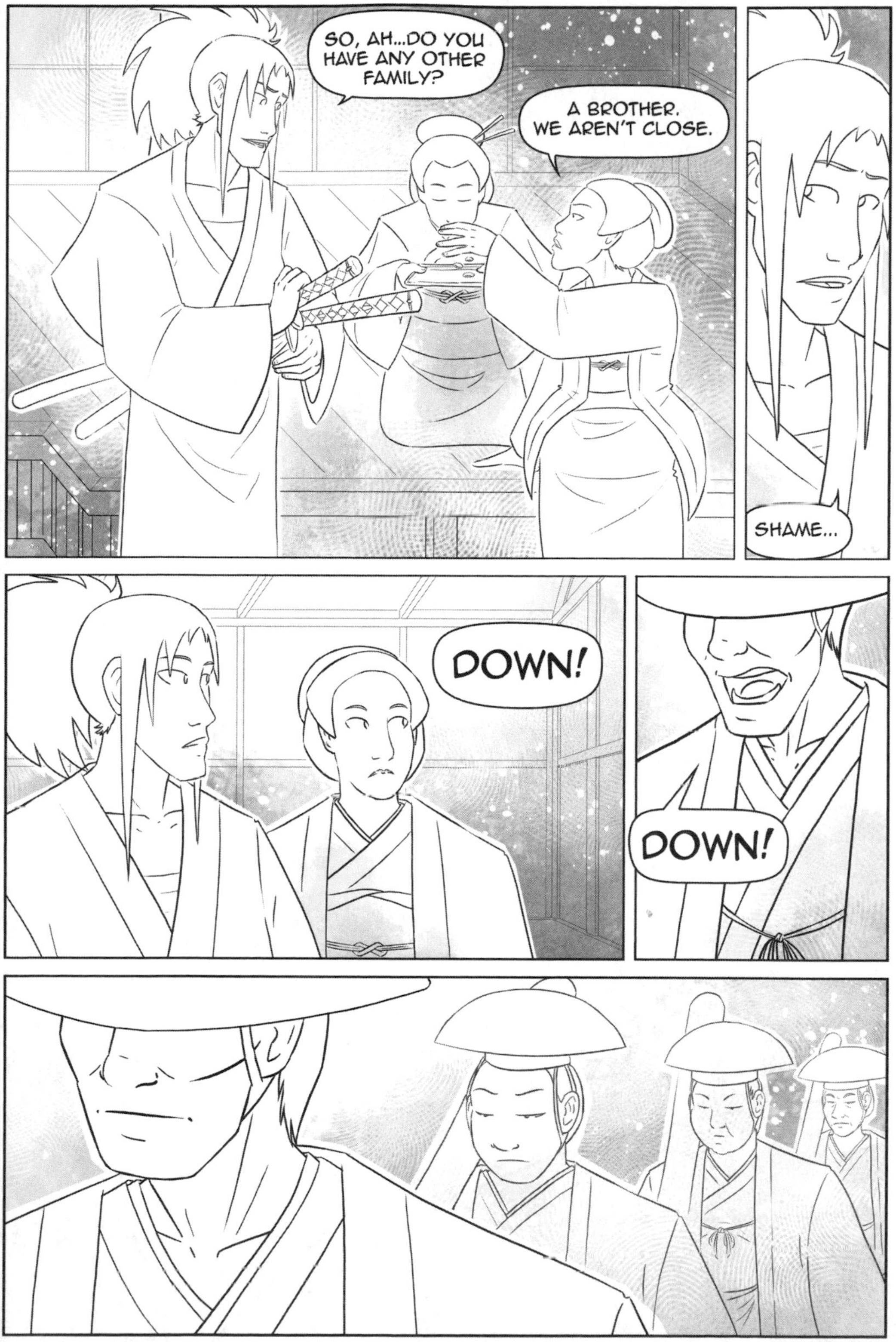
SO, AH...DO YOU HAVE ANY OTHER FAMILY?
A BROTHER. WE AREN'T CLOSE.
SHAME...
DOWN!
DOWN!

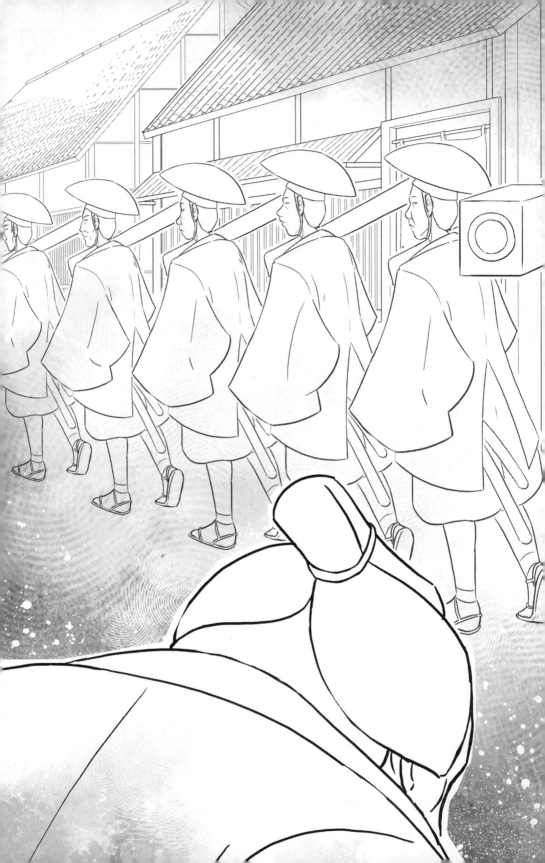

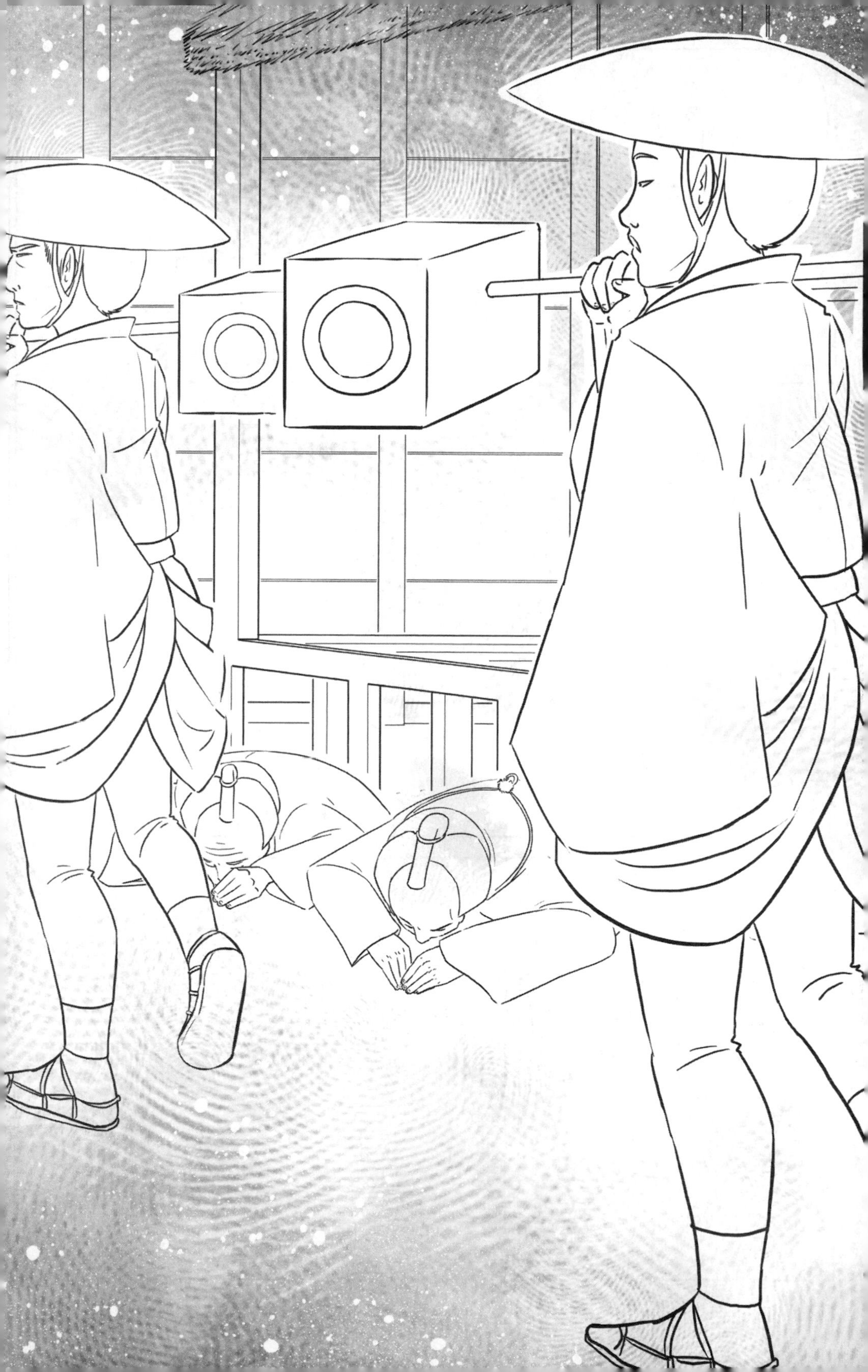

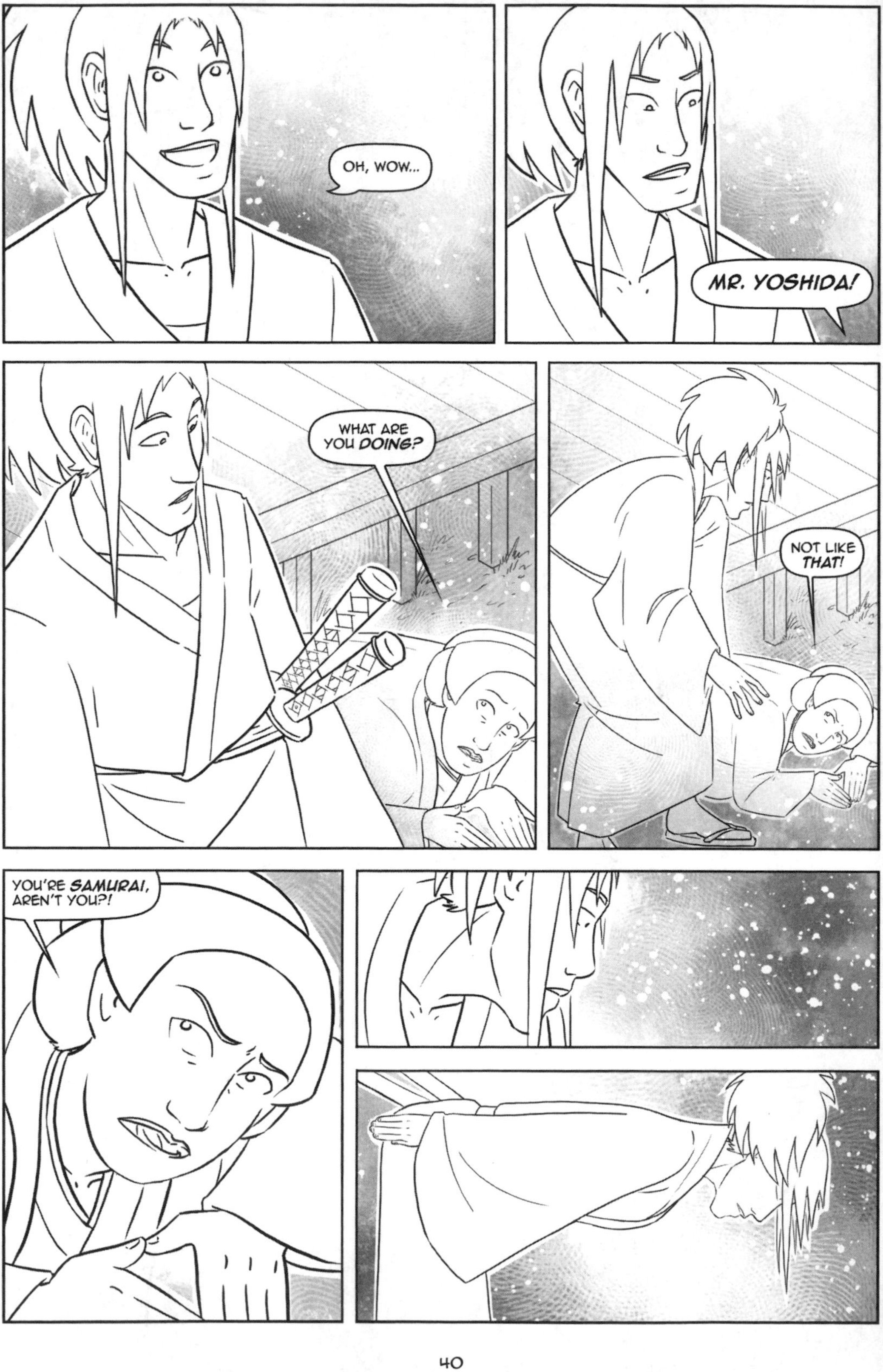
OH, WOW...
MR. YOSHIDA!
WHAT ARE YOU DOING?
NOT LIKE THAT!
YOU'RE SAMURAI, AREN'T YOU?!

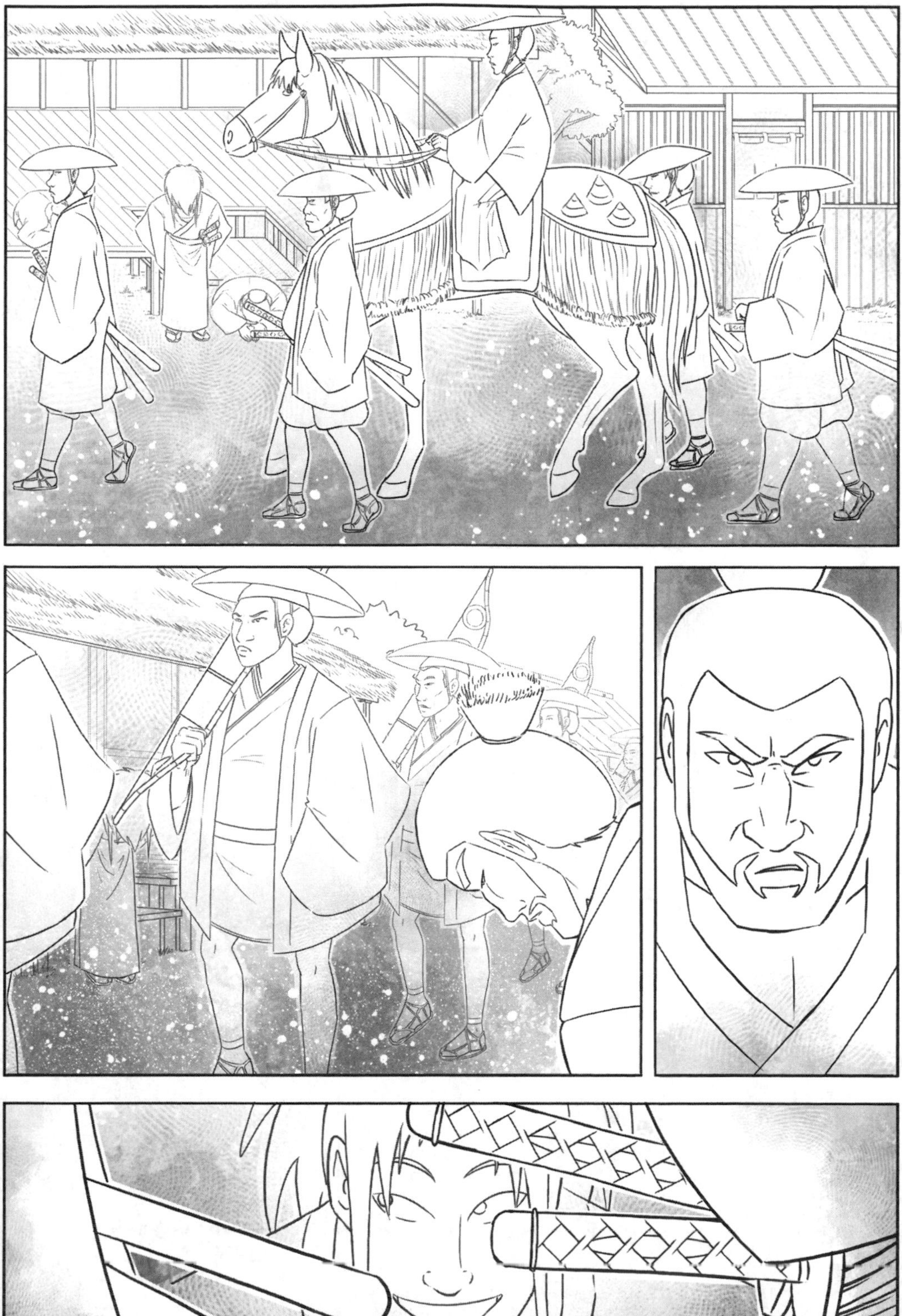

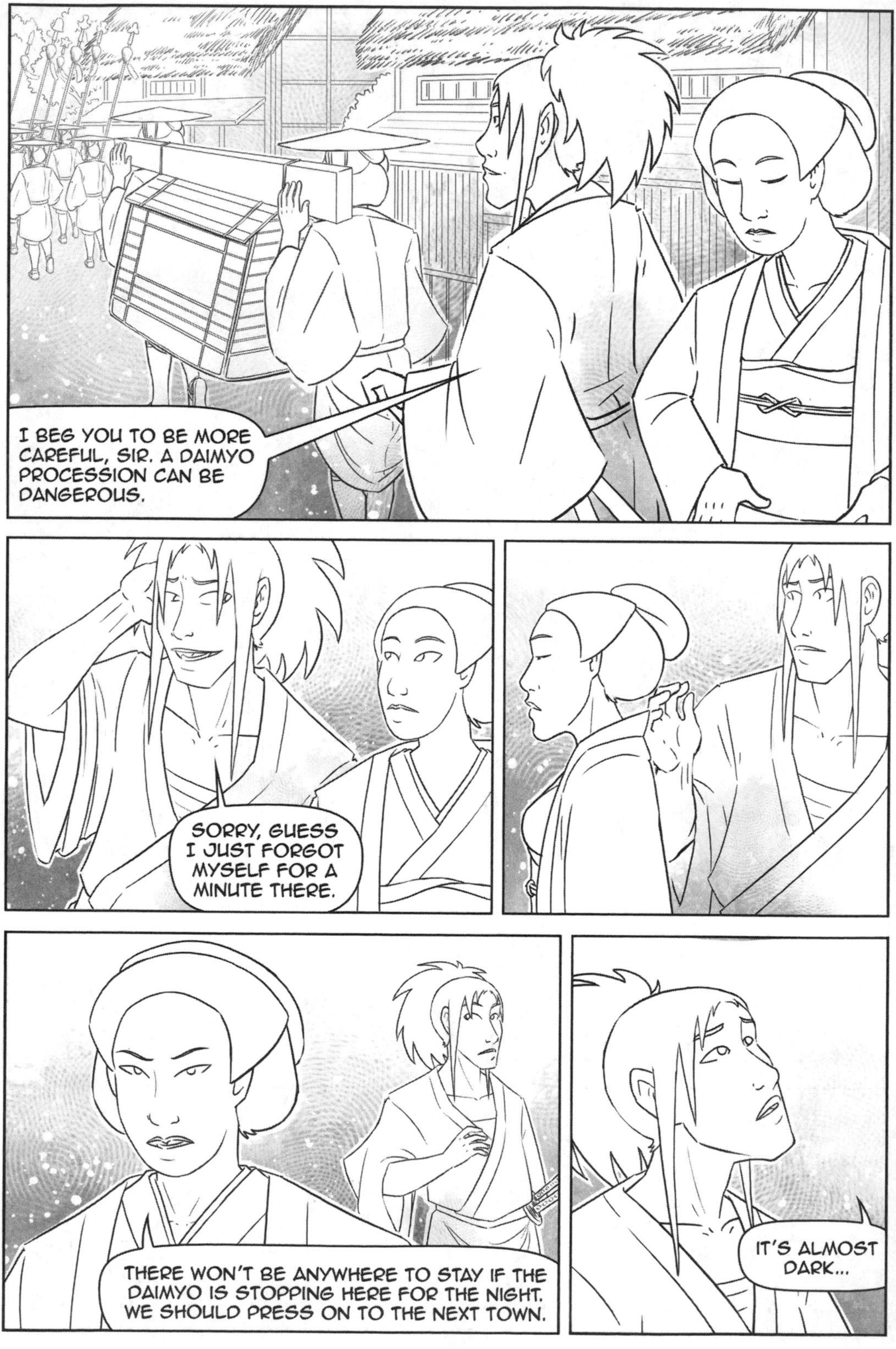
I BEG YOU TO BE MORE CAREFUL, SIR. A DAIMYO PROCESSION CAN BE DANGEROUS.
SORRY, GUESS I JUST FORGOT MYSELF FOR A MINUTE THERE.
THERE WON'T BE ANYWHERE TO STAY IF THE DAIMYO IS STOPPING HERE FOR THE NIGHT. WE SHOULD PRESS ON TO THE NEXT TOWN.
IT'S ALMOST DARK...

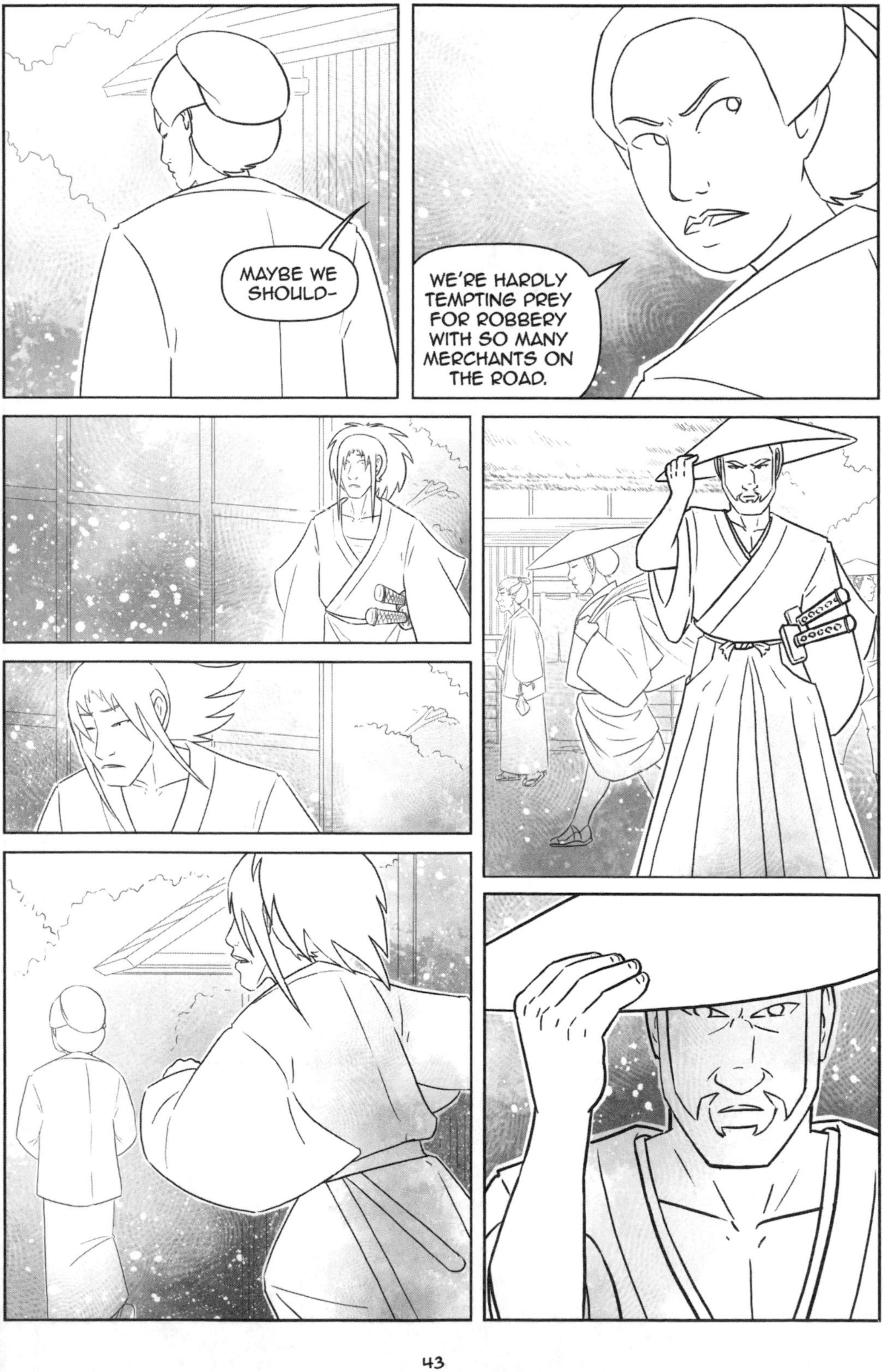

MAYBE WE SHOULD-
WE'RE HARDLY TEMPTING PREY FOR ROBBERY WITH SO MANY MERCHANTS ON THE ROAD.

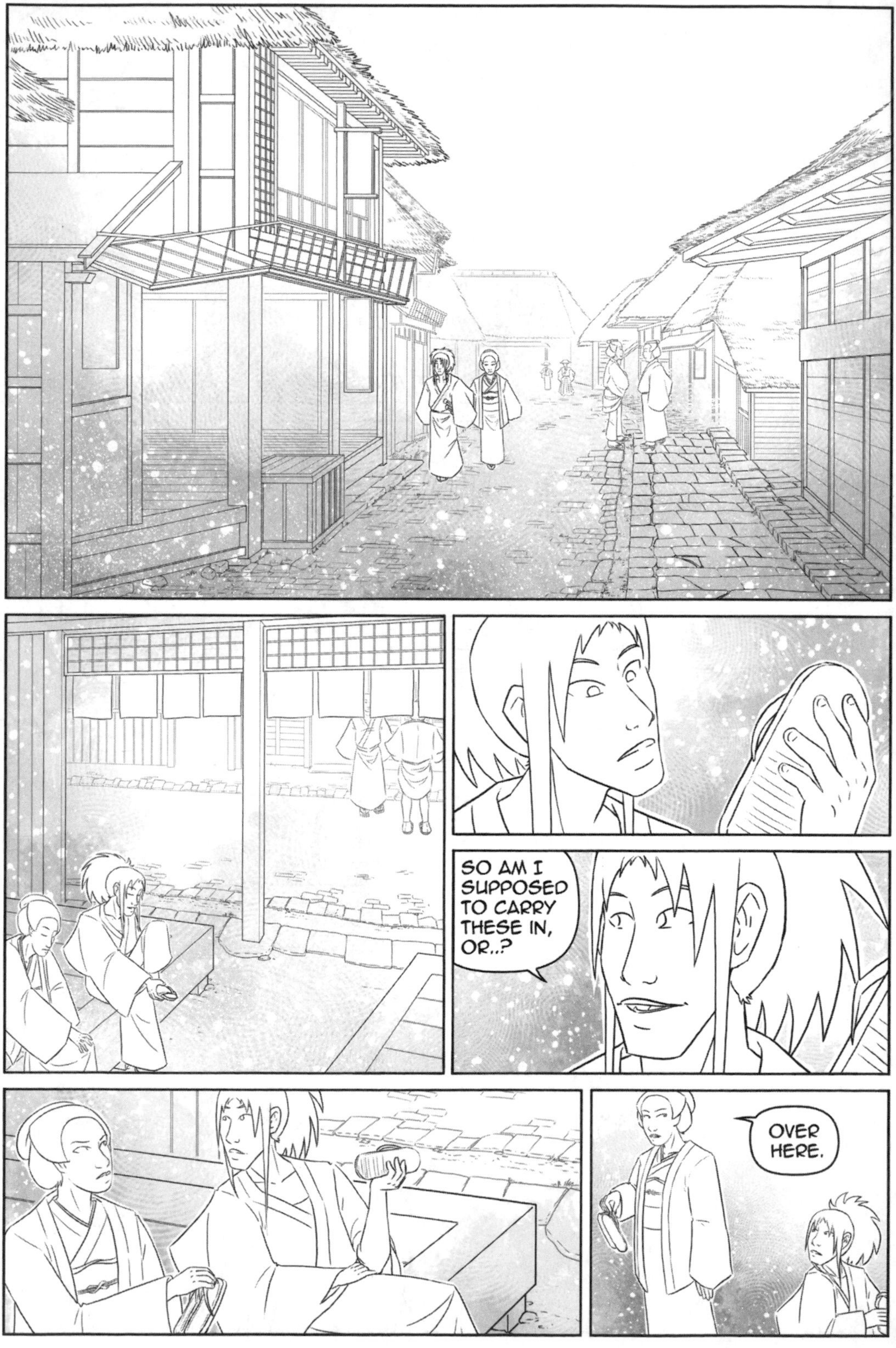
SO AM I SUPPOSED TO CARRY THESE IN, OR..?
OVER HERE.

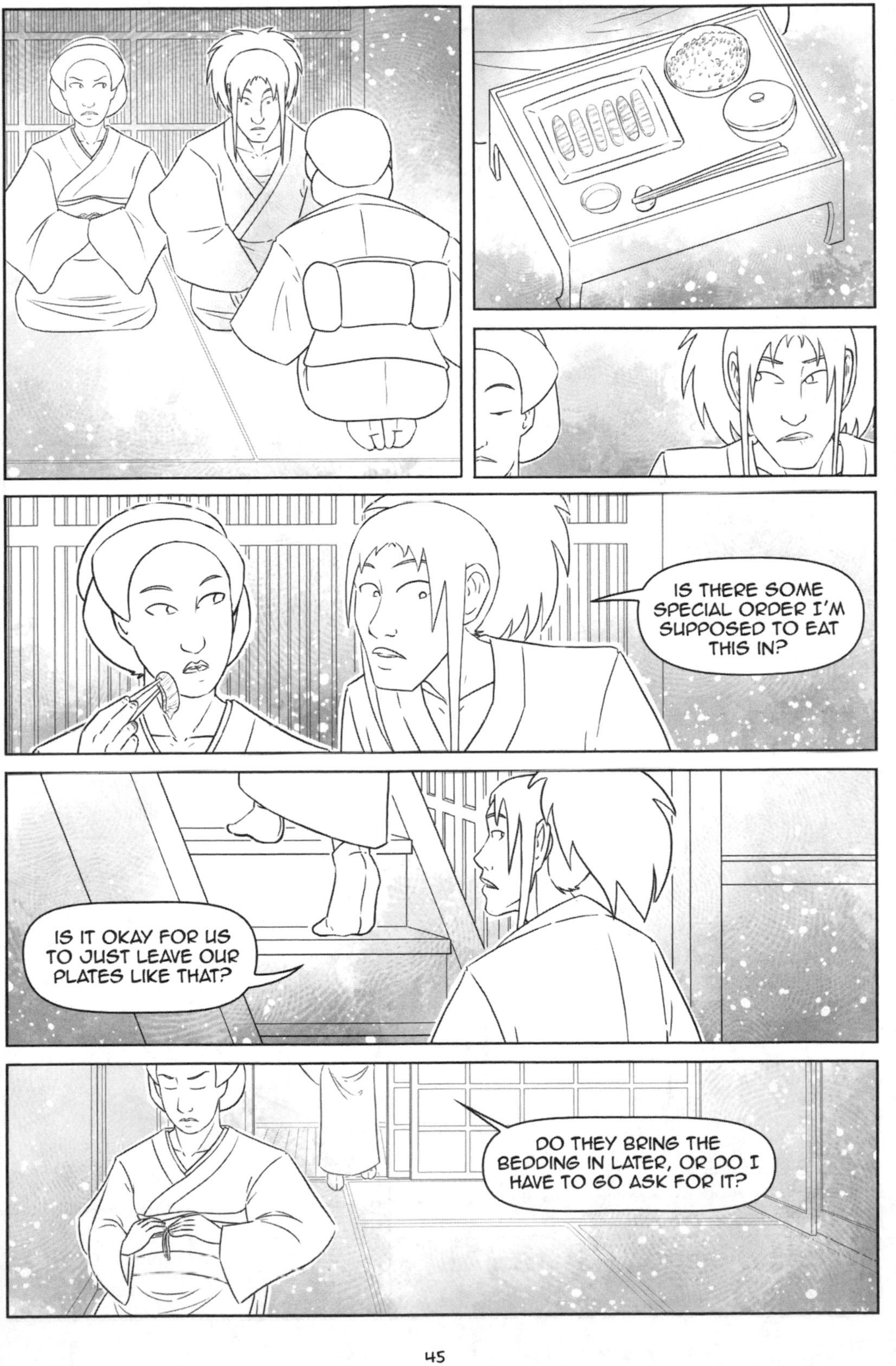
IS THERE SOME SPECIAL ORDER I'M SUPPOSED TO EAT THIS IN?
IS IT OKAY FOR US TO JUST LEAVE OUR PLATES LIKE THAT?
DO THEY BRING THE BEDDING IN LATER, OR DO I HAVE TO GO ASK FOR IT?

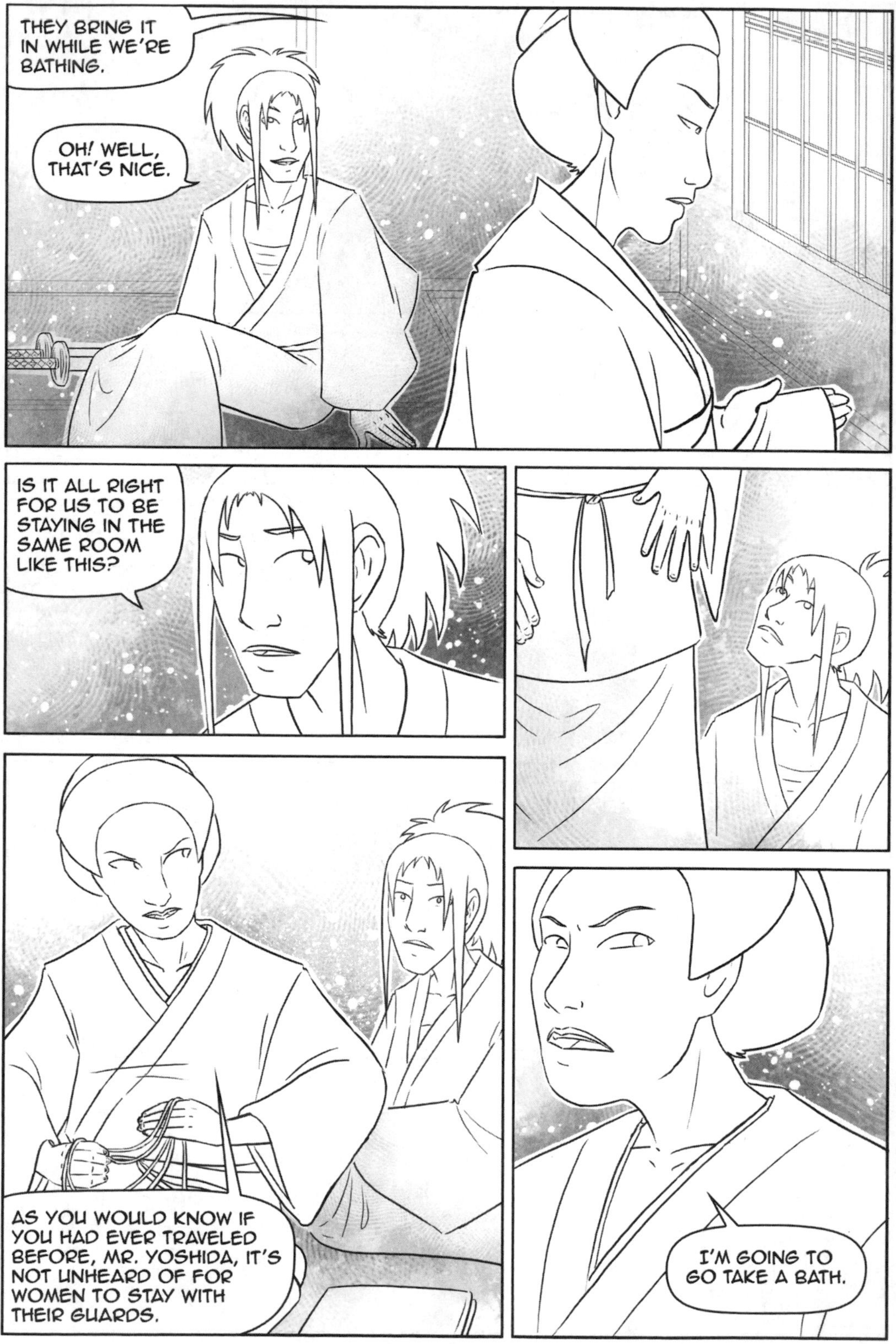
THEY BRING IT IN WHILE WE'RE BATHING.
OH! WELL, THAT'S NICE.
IS IT ALL RIGHT FOR US TO BE STAYING IN THE SAME ROOM LIKE THIS?
AS YOU WOULD KNOW IF YOU HAD EVER TRAVELED BEFORE, MR. YOSHIDA, IT'S NOT UNHEARD OF FOR WOMEN TO STAY WITH THEIR GUARDS.
I'M GOING TO GO TAKE A BATH.

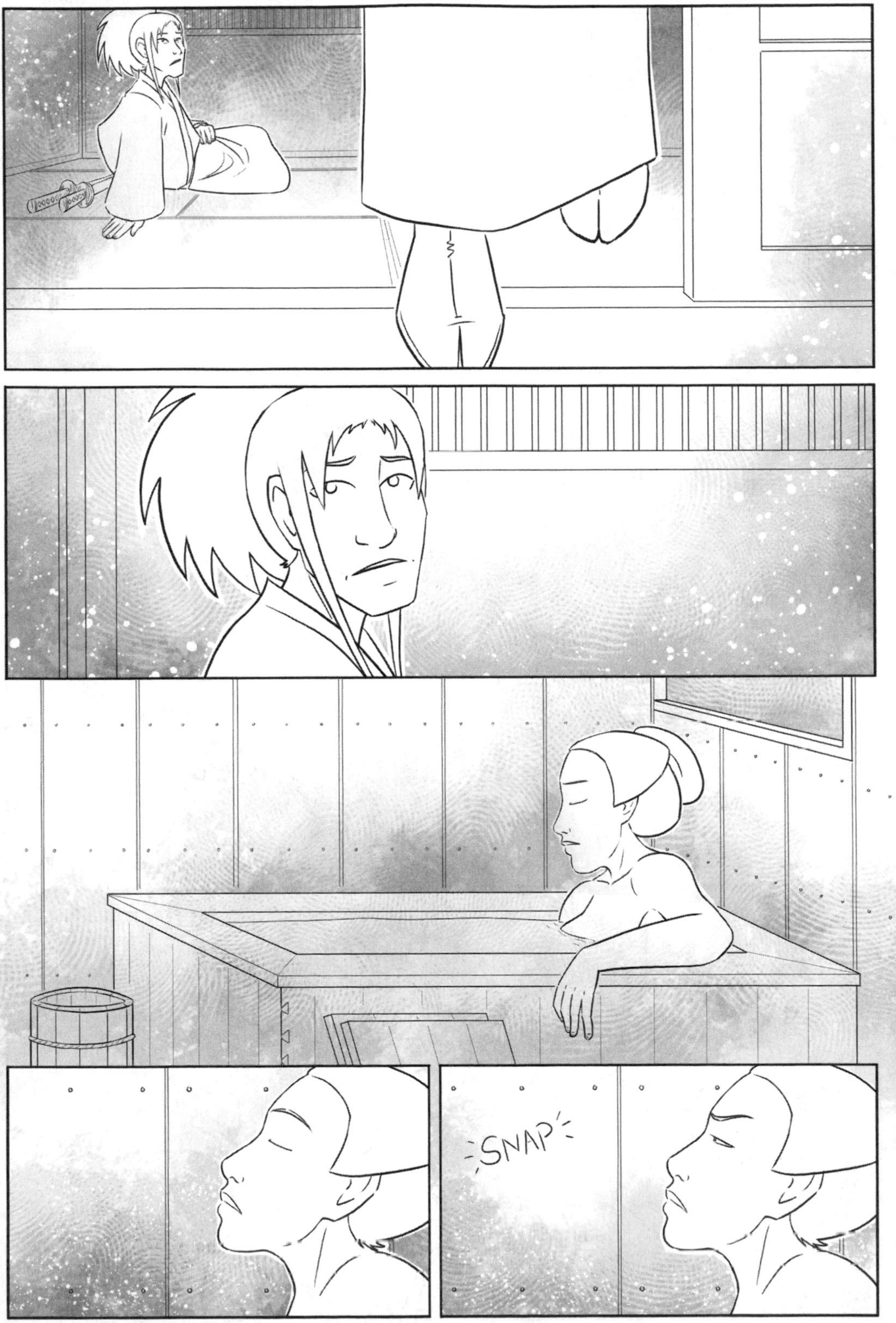
SNAP

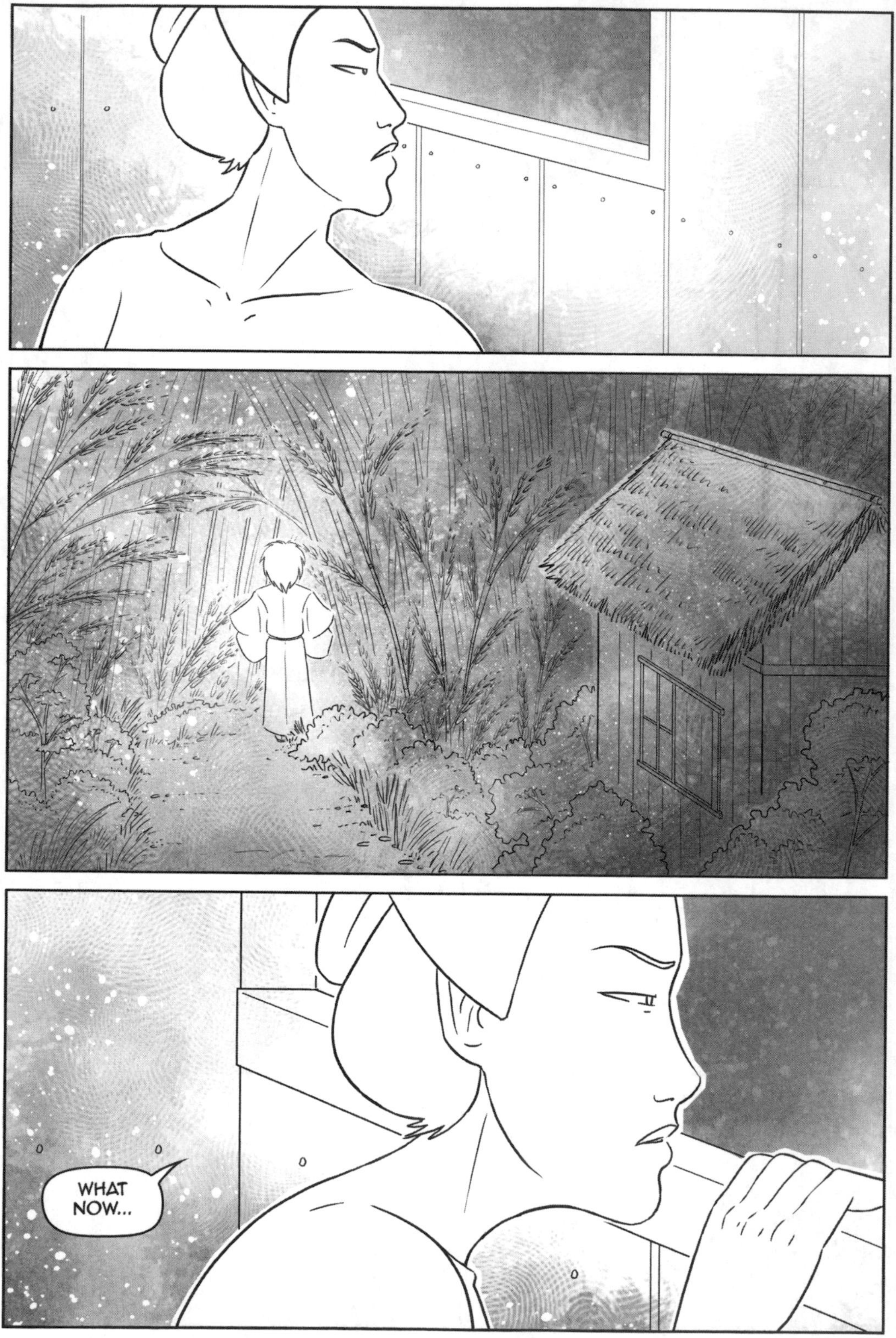
WHAT NOW...

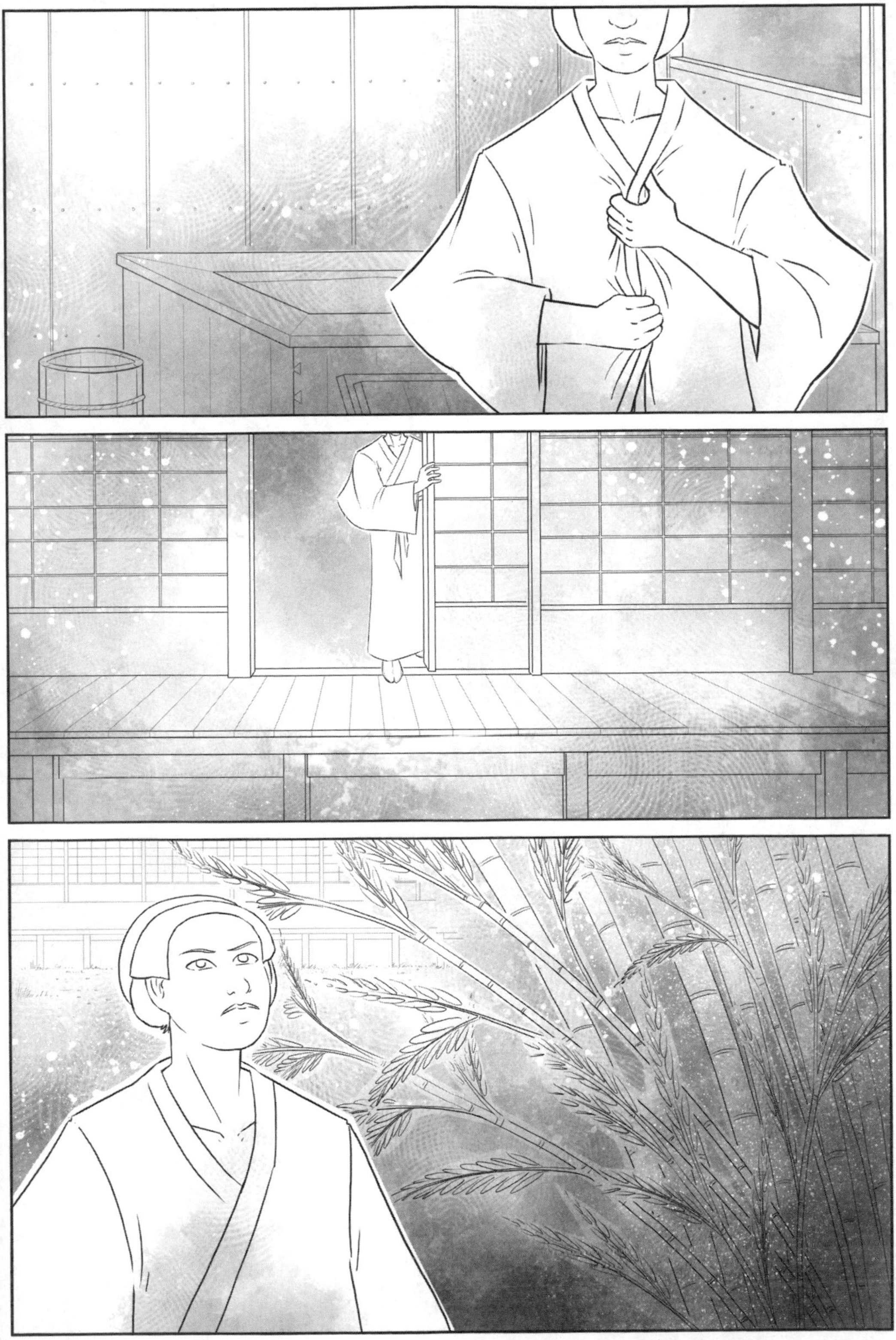

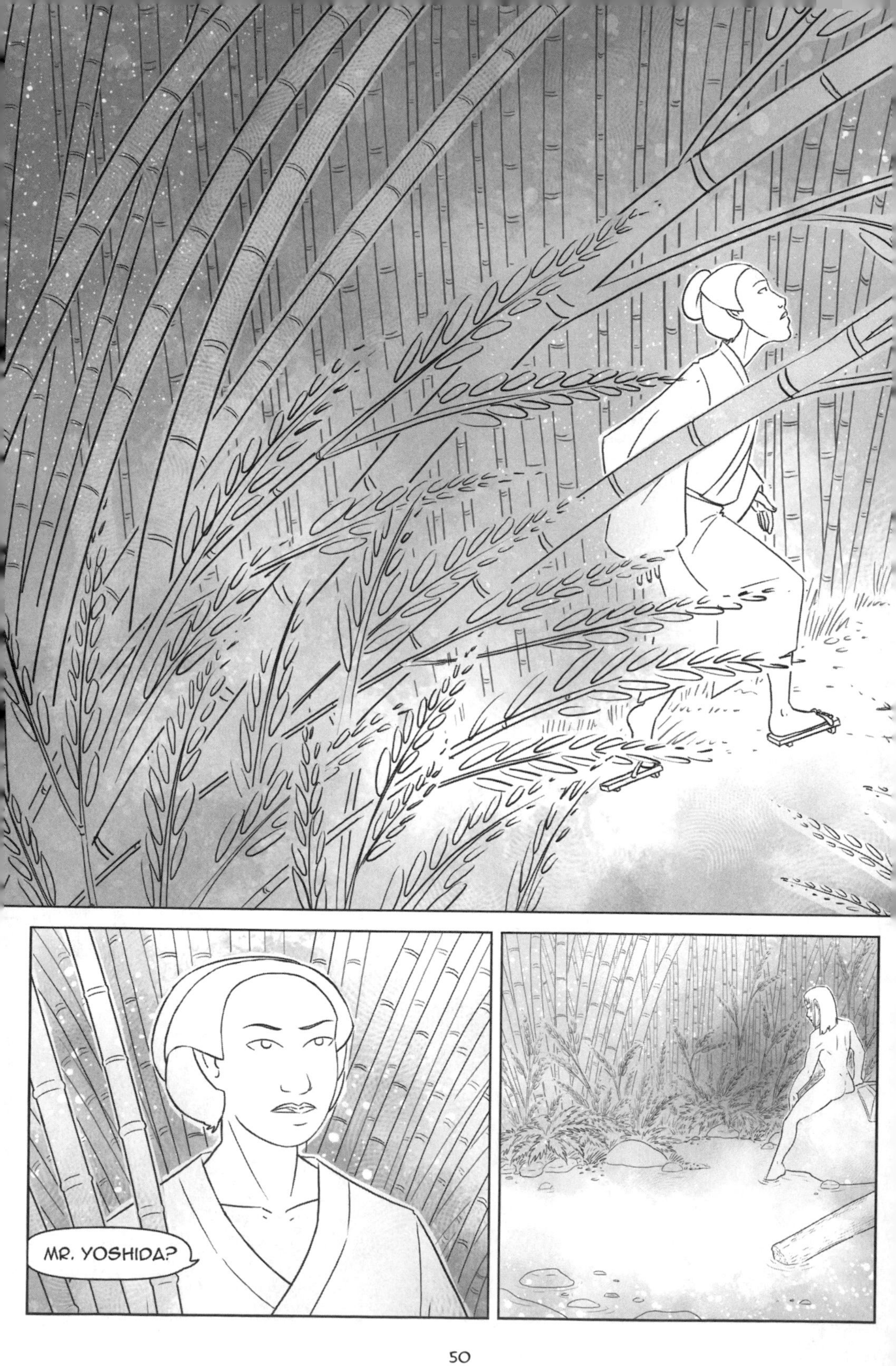
MR. YOSHIDA?

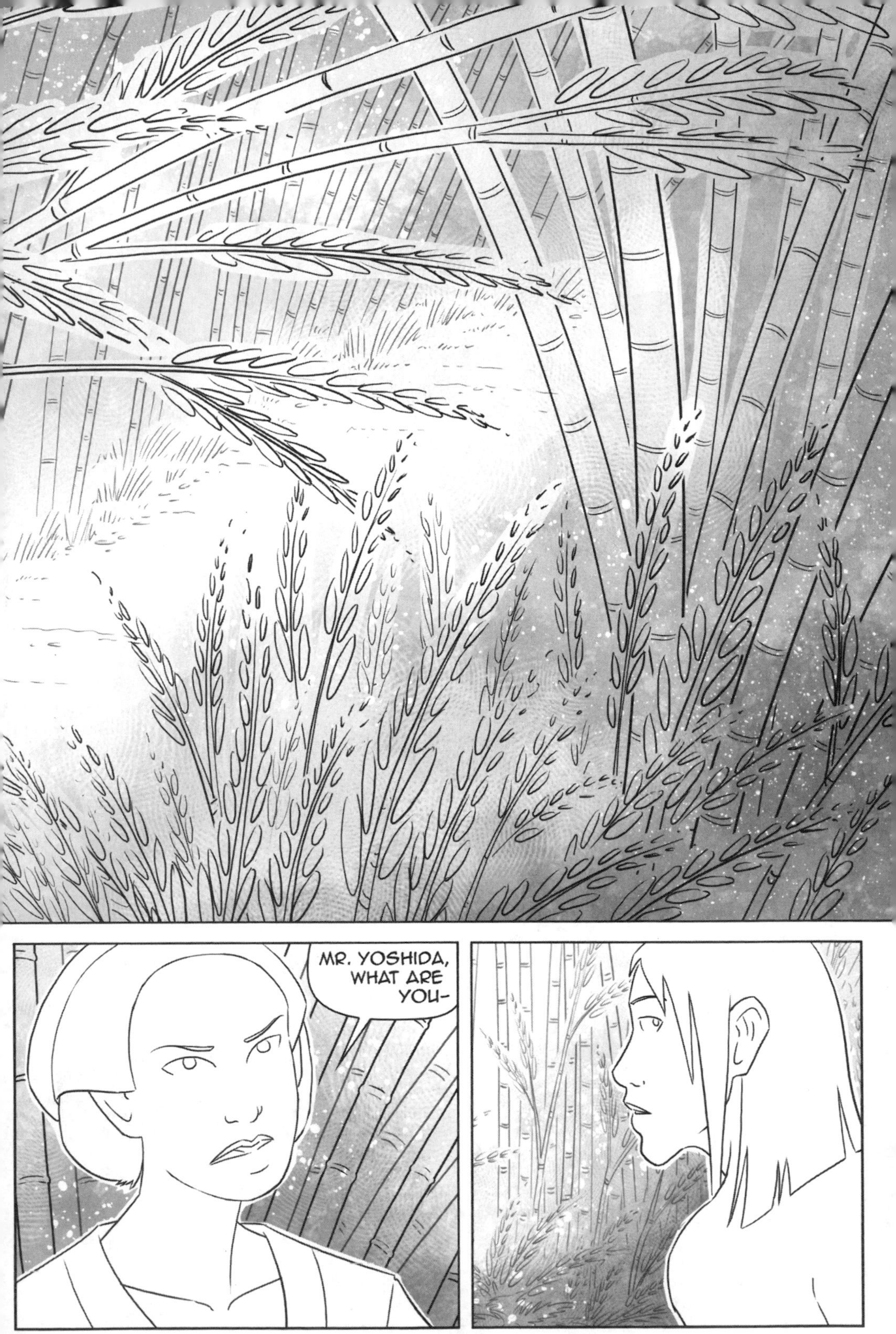
MR. YOSHIDA, WHAT ARE YOU-

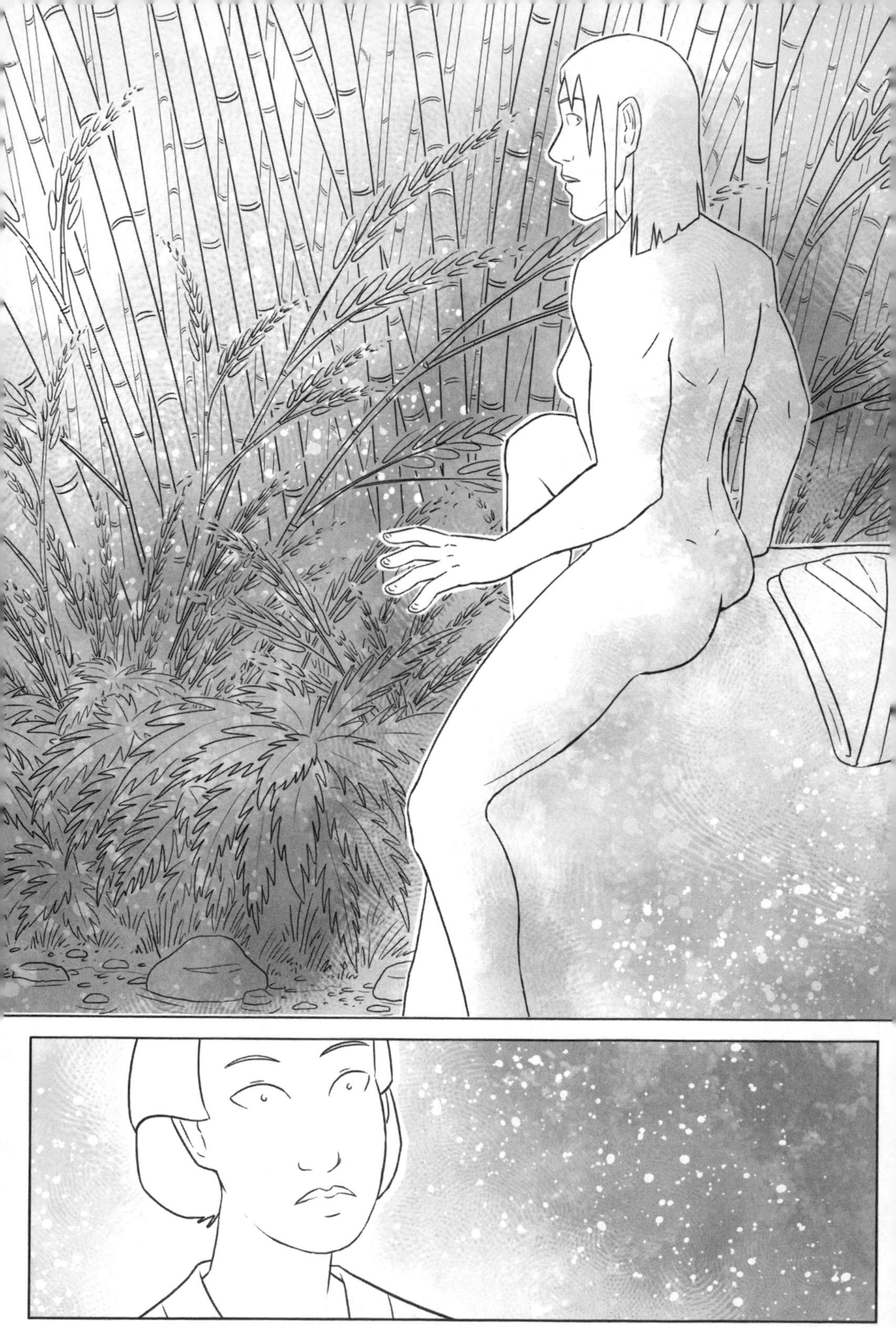

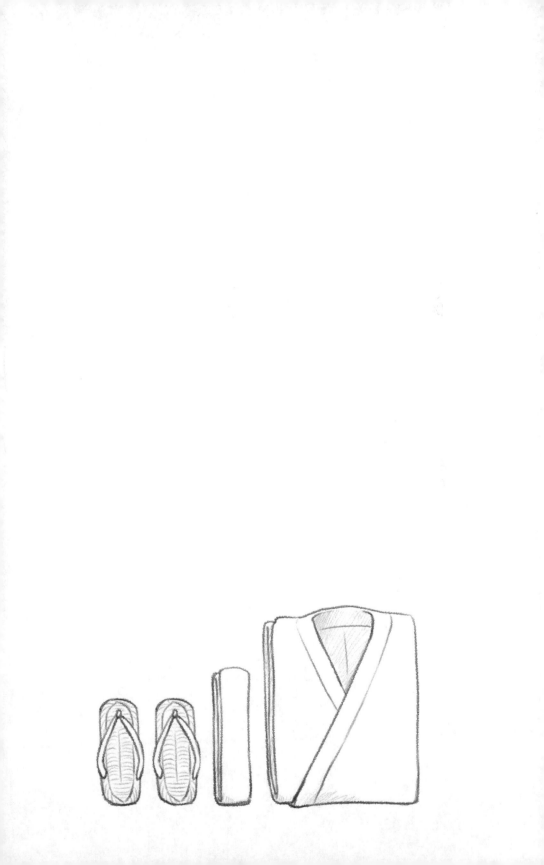

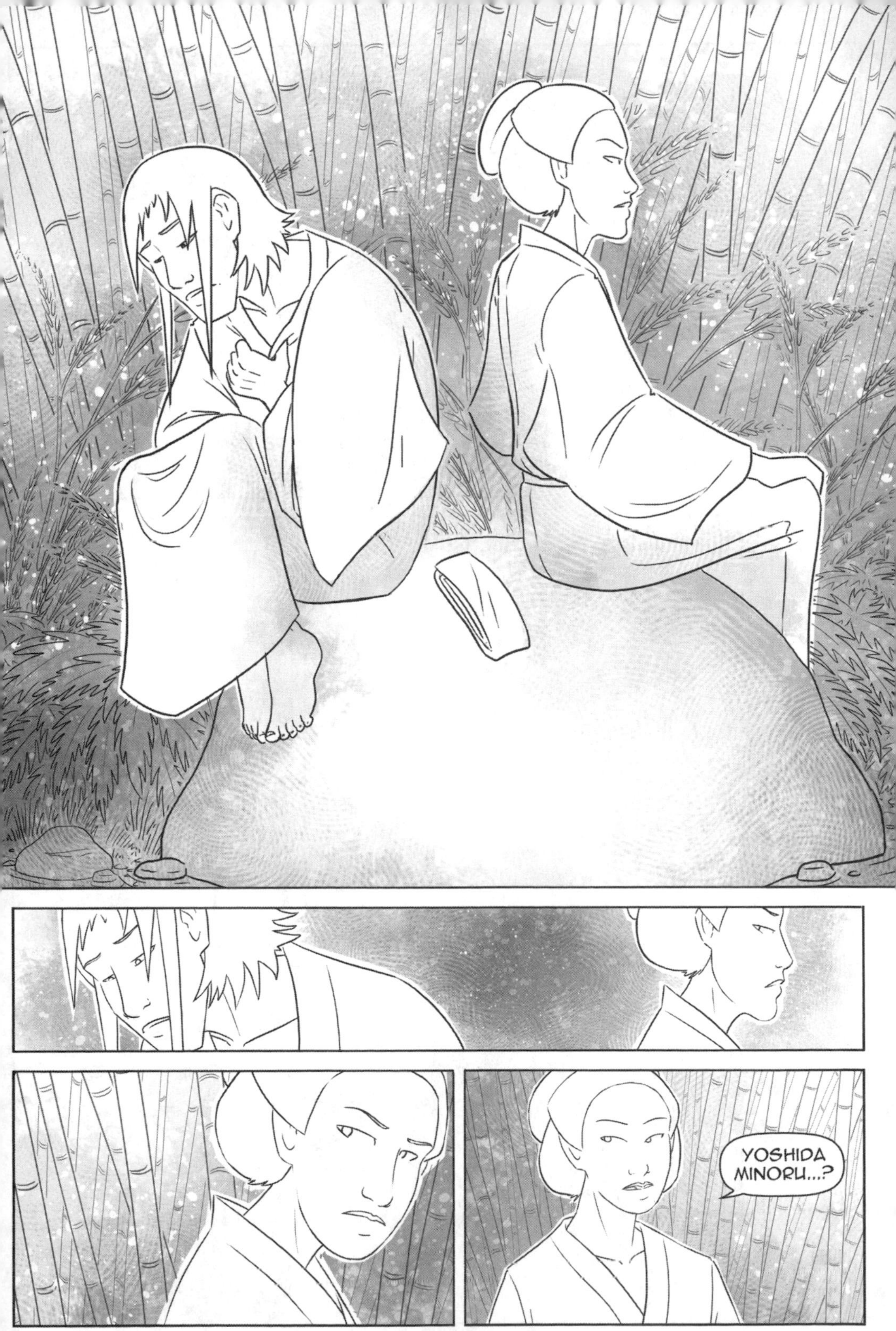
YOSHIDA MINORU...?

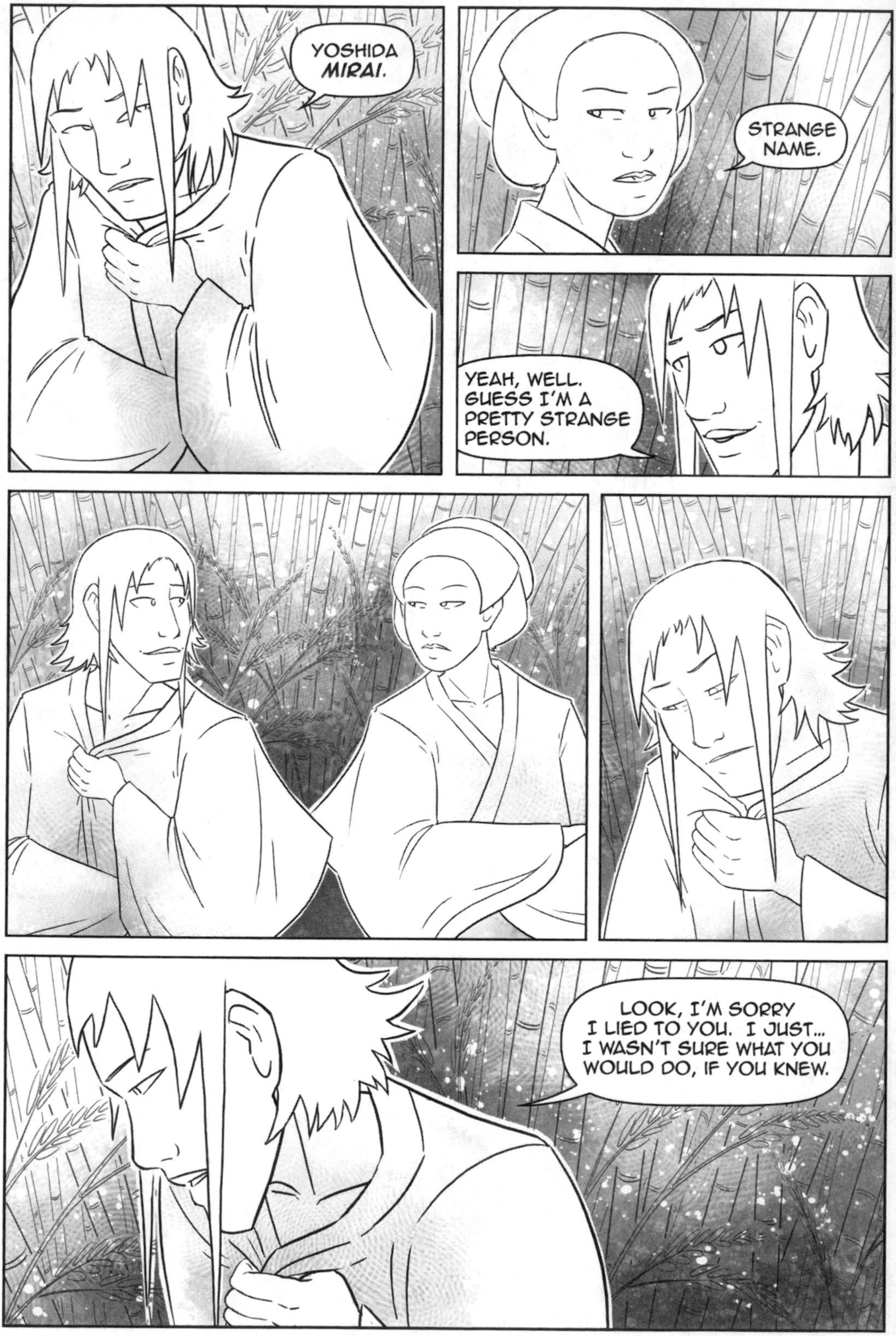
YOSHIDA MIRAI.
STRANGE NAME.
YEAH, WELL. GUESS I'M A PRETTY STRANGE PERSON.
LOOK, I'M SORRY I LIED TO YOU. I JUST... I WASN'T SURE WHAT YOU WOULD DO, IF YOU KNEW.

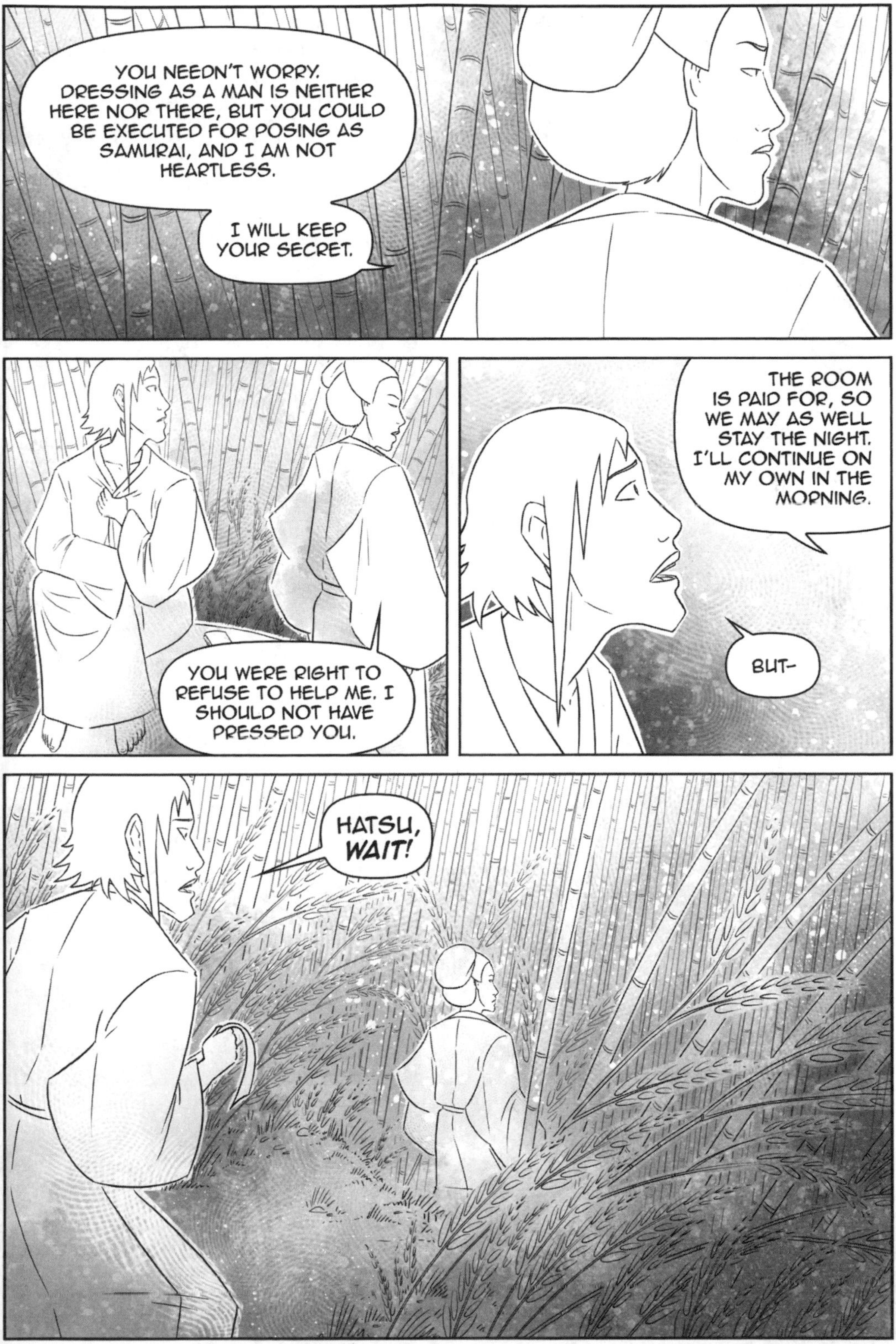
YOU NEEDN'T WORRY. DRESSING AS A MAN IS NEITHER HERE NOR THERE, BUT YOU COULD BE EXECUTED FOR POSING AS SAMURAI, AND I AM NOT HEARTLESS.
I WILL KEEP YOUR SECRET.
YOU WERE RIGHT TO REFUSE TO HELP ME. I SHOULD NOT HAVE PRESSED YOU.
THE ROOM IS PAID FOR, SO WE MAY AS WELL STAY THE NIGHT. I'LL CONTINUE ON MY OWN IN THE MORNING.
BUT-
HATSU, *WAIT!*

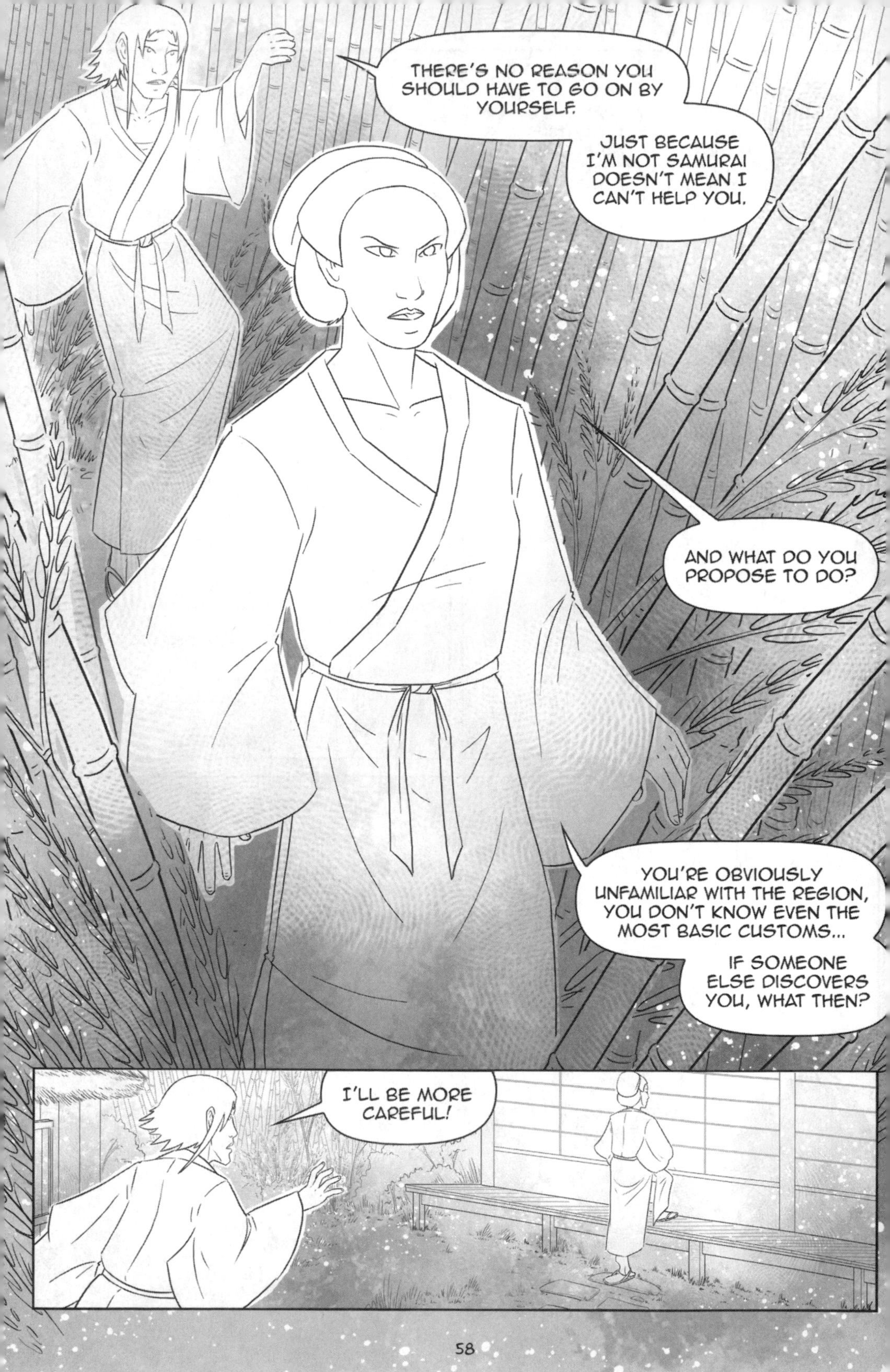
THERE'S NO REASON YOU SHOULD HAVE TO GO ON BY YOURSELF.
JUST BECAUSE I'M NOT SAMURAI DOESN'T MEAN I CAN'T HELP YOU.
AND WHAT DO YOU PROPOSE TO DO?
YOU'RE OBVIOUSLY UNFAMILIAR WITH THE REGION, YOU DON'T KNOW EVEN THE MOST BASIC CUSTOMS...
IF SOMEONE ELSE DISCOVERS YOU, WHAT THEN?
I'LL BE MORE CAREFUL!

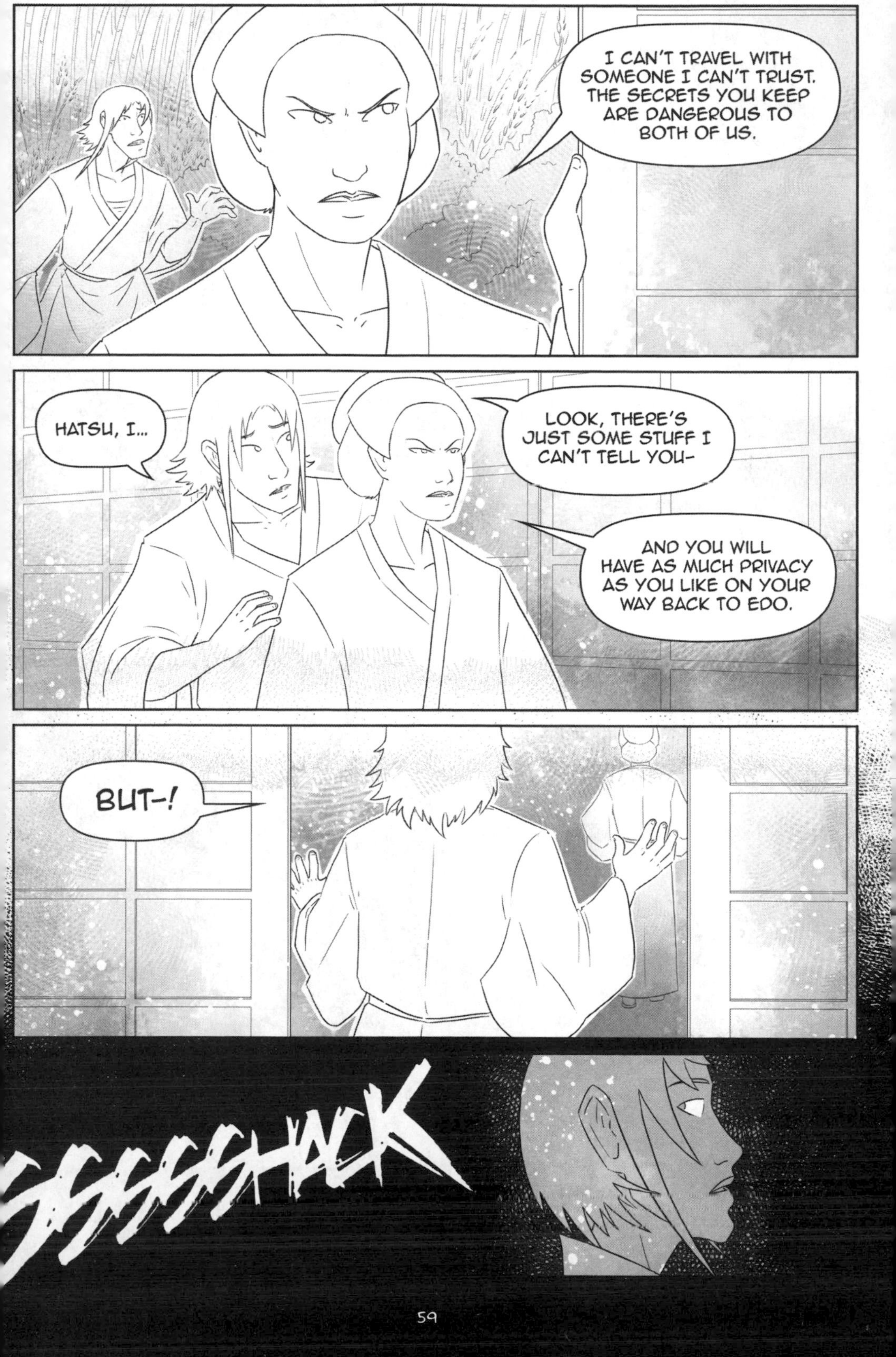
I CAN'T TRAVEL WITH SOMEONE I CAN'T TRUST. THE SECRETS YOU KEEP ARE DANGEROUS TO BOTH OF US.
HATSU, I...
LOOK, THERE'S JUST SOME STUFF I CAN'T TELL YOU-
AND YOU WILL HAVE AS MUCH PRIVACY AS YOU LIKE ON YOUR WAY BACK TO EDO.
BUT-!
SSSSSHACK

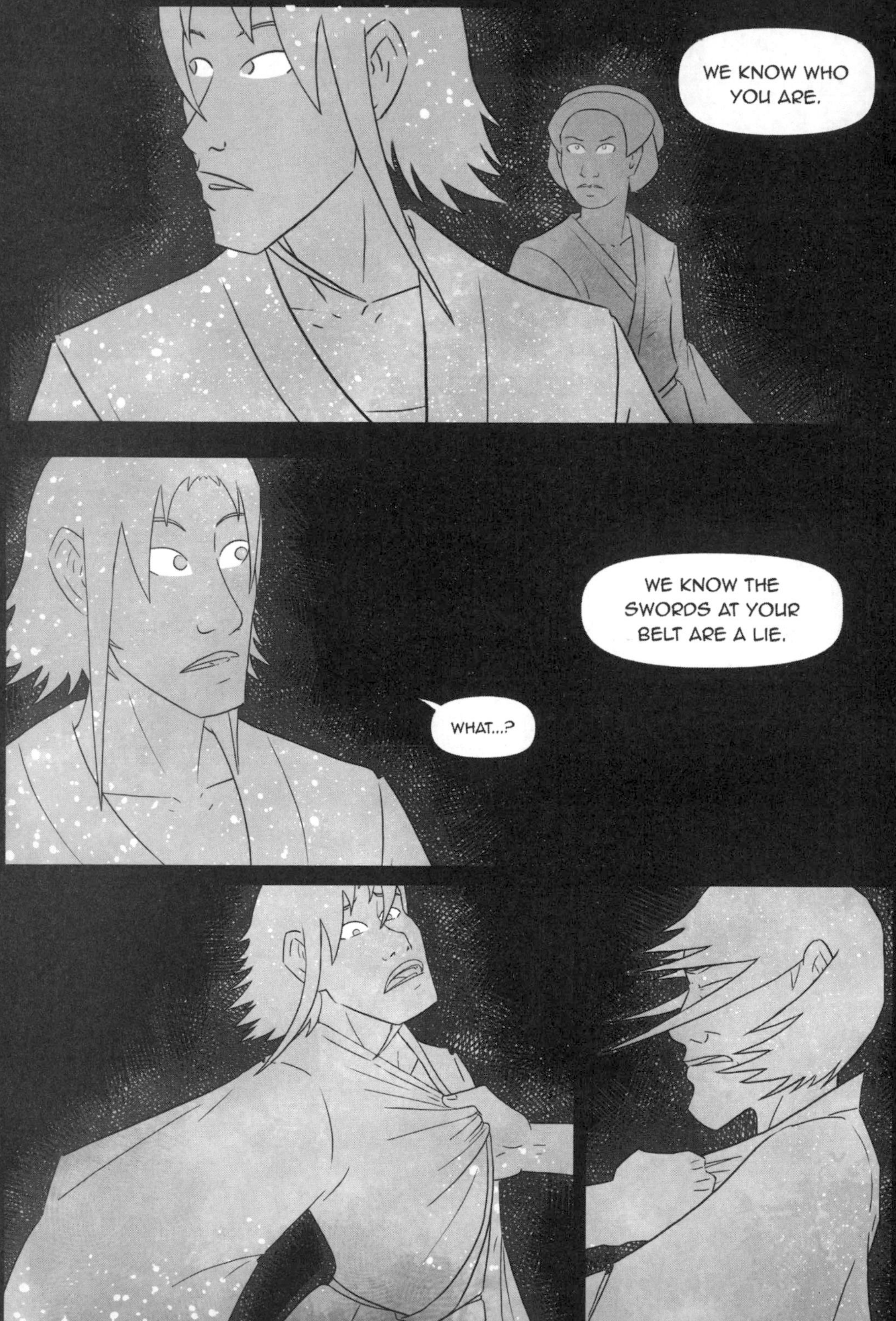
WE KNOW WHO YOU ARE.
WE KNOW THE SWORDS AT YOUR BELT ARE A LIE.
WHAT...?

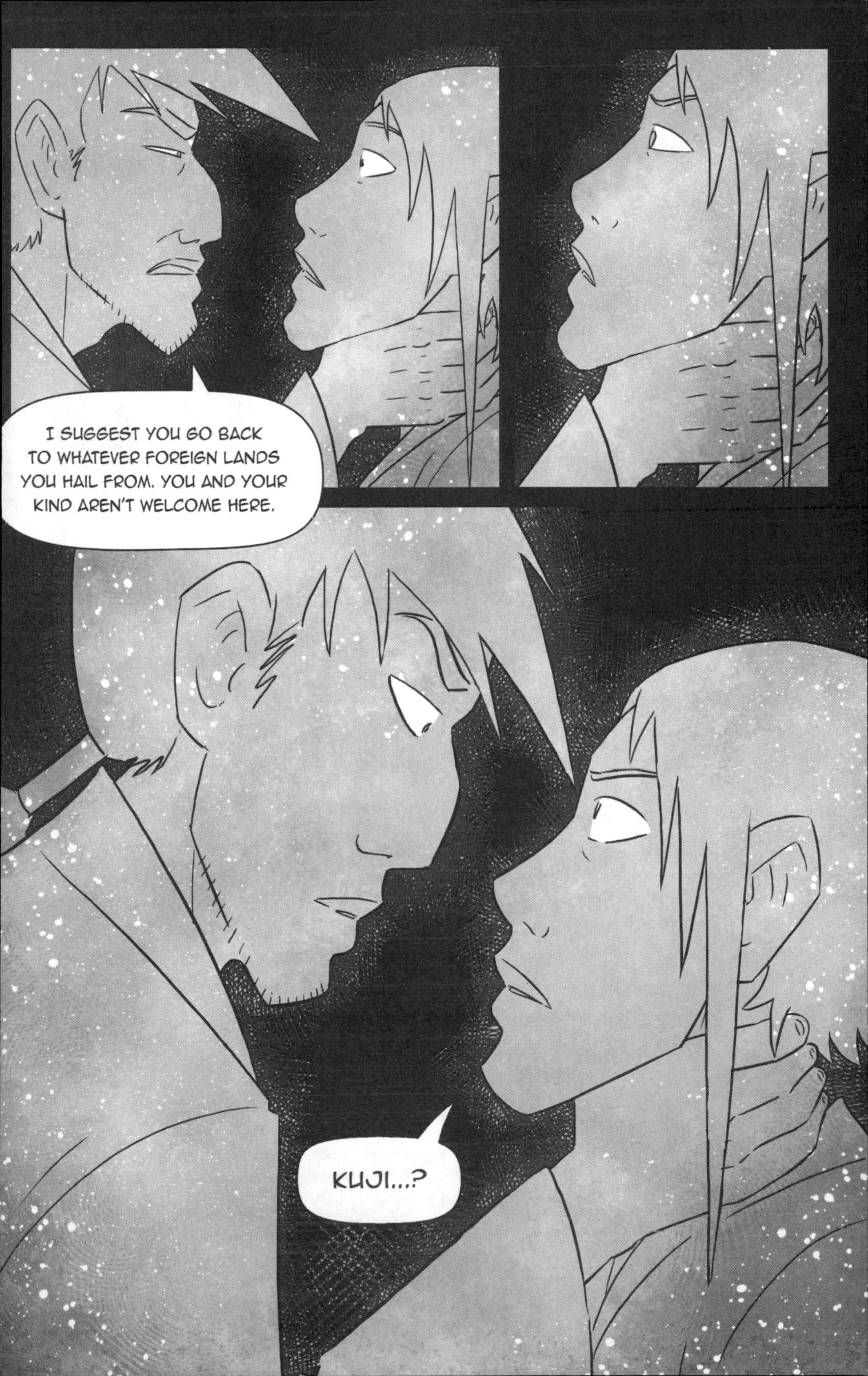
I SUGGEST YOU GO BACK TO WHATEVER FOREIGN LANDS YOU HAIL FROM. YOU AND YOUR KIND AREN'T WELCOME HERE.
KUJI...?

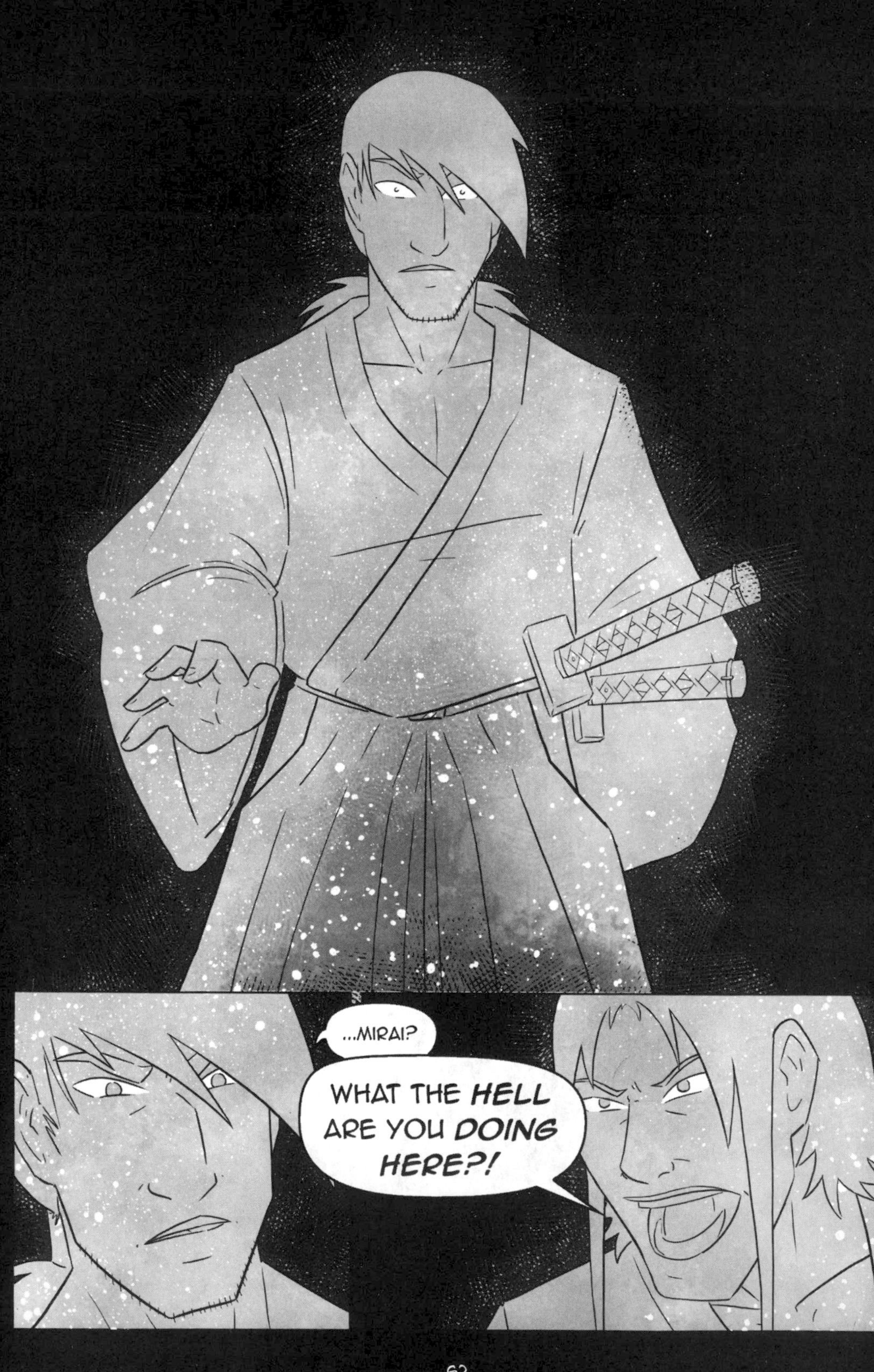
...MIRAI?
WHAT THE **HELL** ARE YOU **DOING HERE?!**

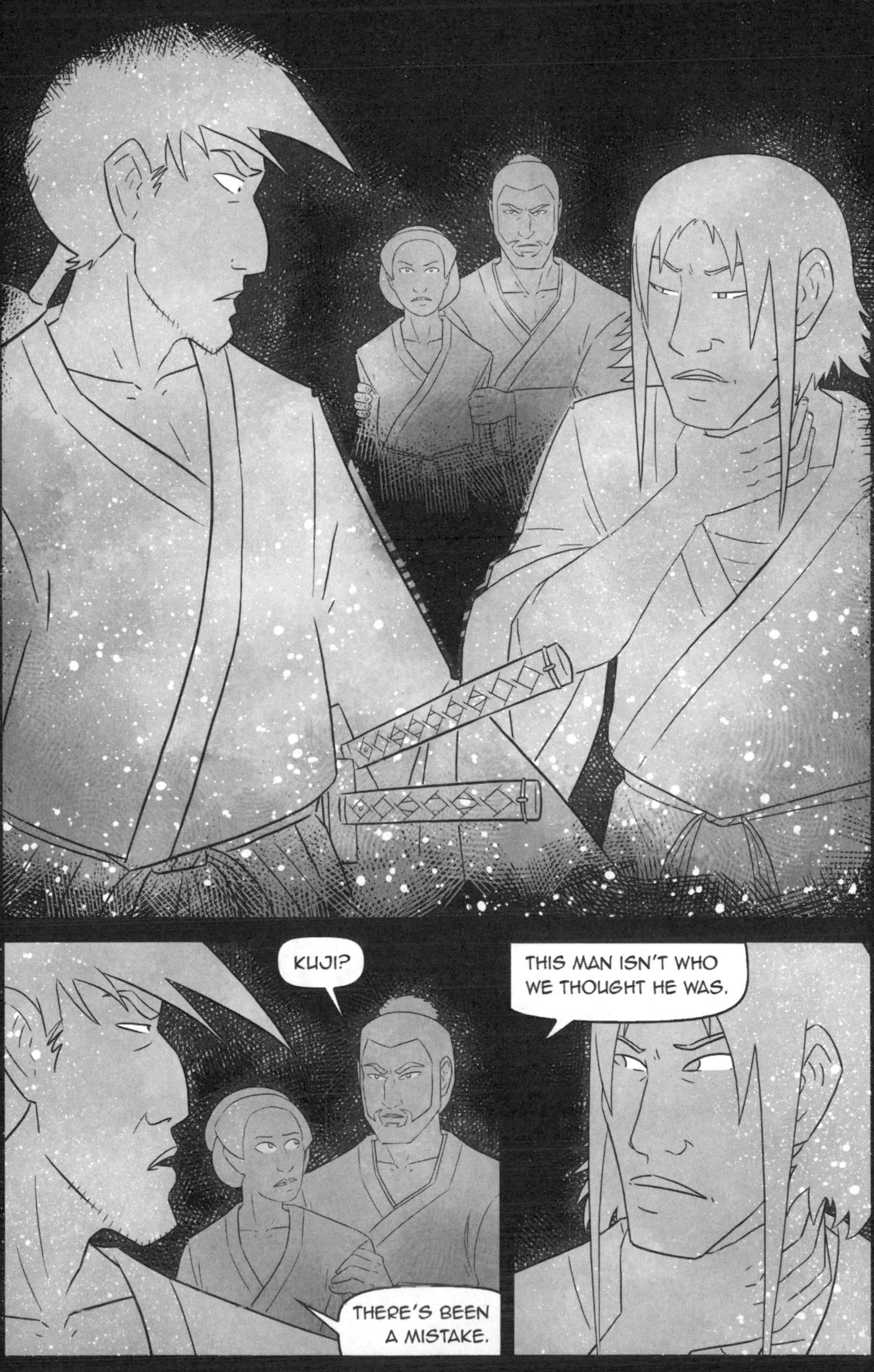
KUJI?
THERE'S BEEN A MISTAKE.
THIS MAN ISN'T WHO WE THOUGHT HE WAS.

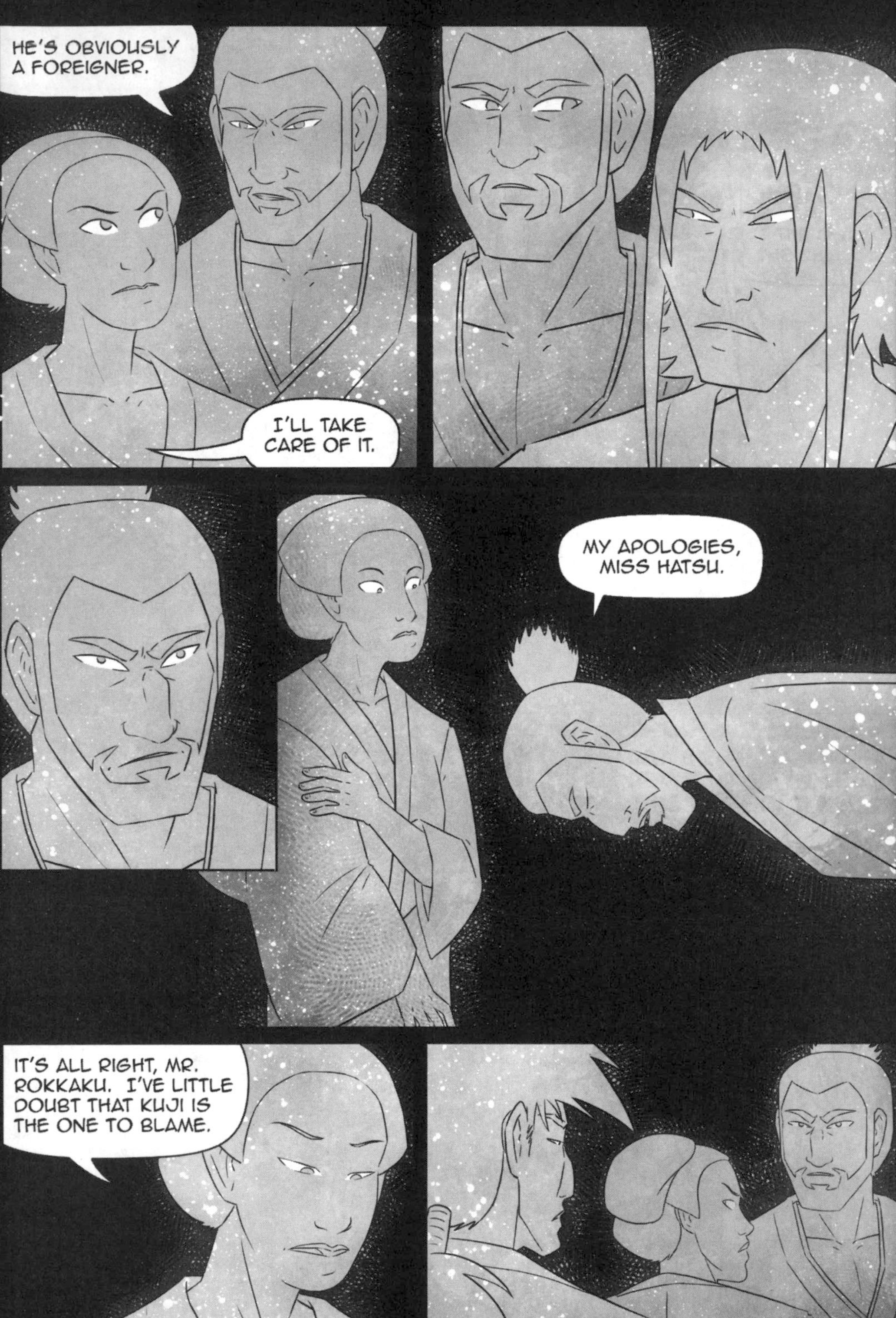
HE'S OBVIOUSLY A FOREIGNER.
I'LL TAKE CARE OF IT.
MY APOLOGIES, MISS HATSU.
IT'S ALL RIGHT, MR. ROKKAKU. I'VE LITTLE DOUBT THAT KUJI IS THE ONE TO BLAME.

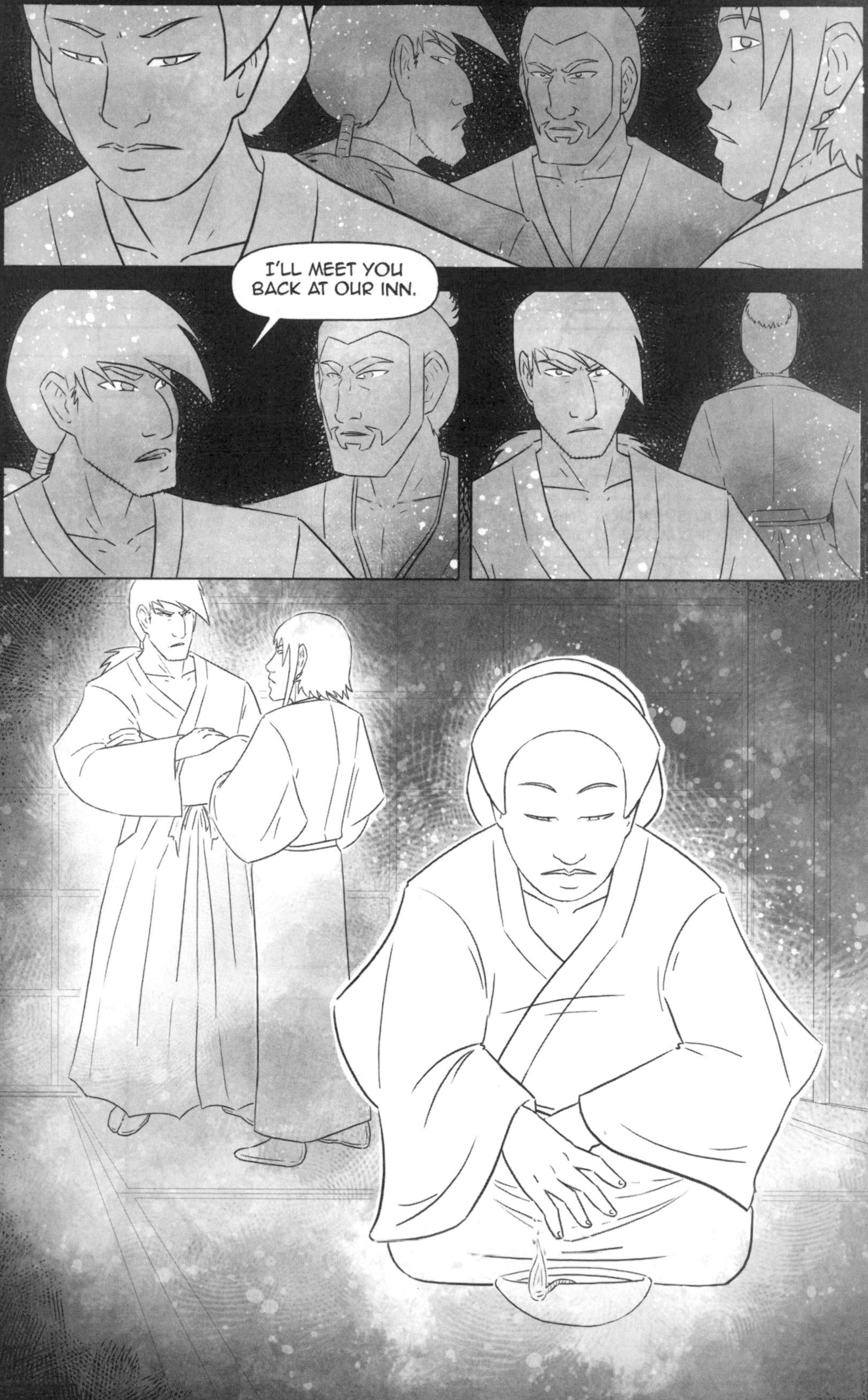
I'LL MEET YOU BACK AT OUR INN.

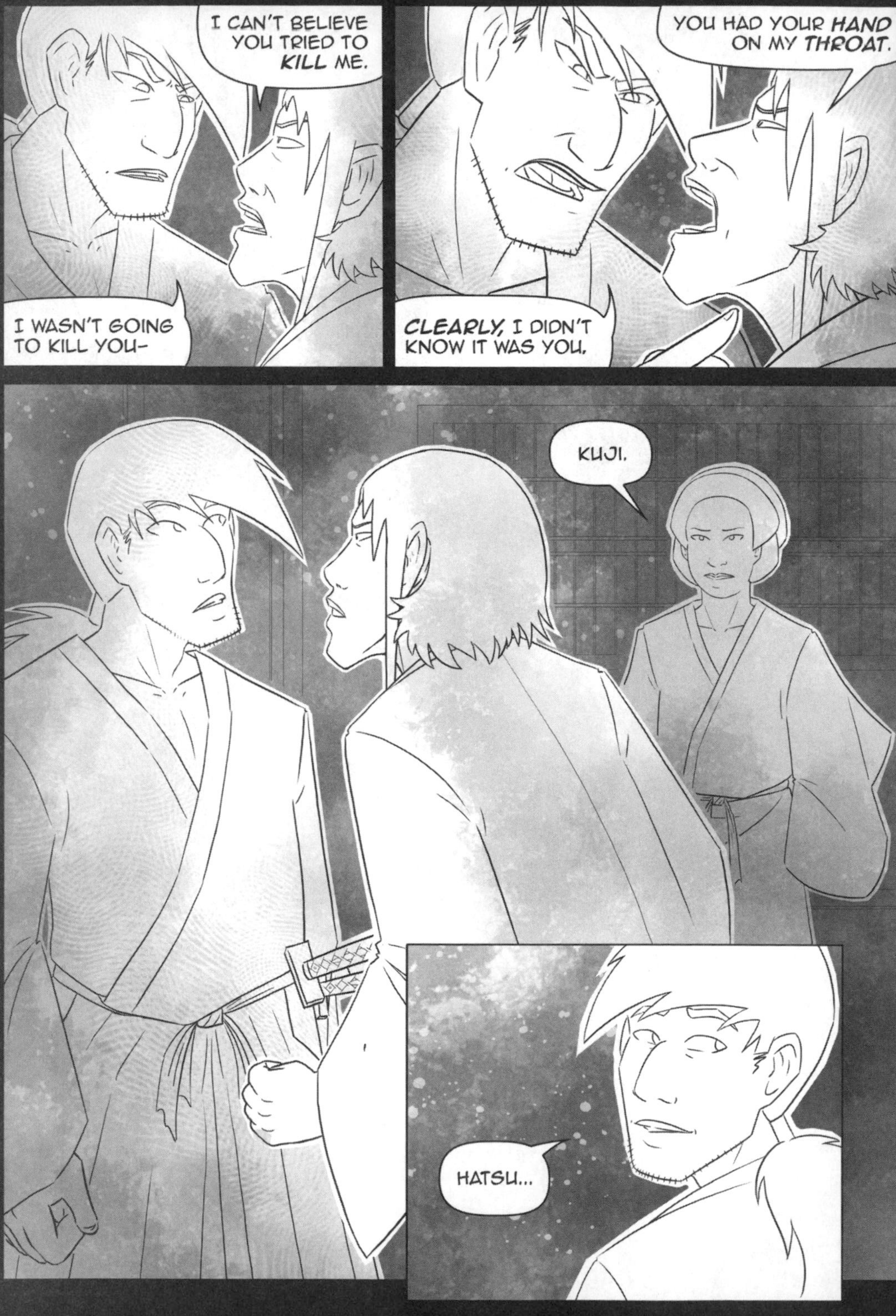
I CAN'T BELIEVE YOU TRIED TO KILL ME.
I WASN'T GOING TO KILL YOU-
YOU HAD YOUR HAND ON MY THROAT.
CLEARLY, I DIDN'T KNOW IT WAS YOU.
KUJI.
HATSU...

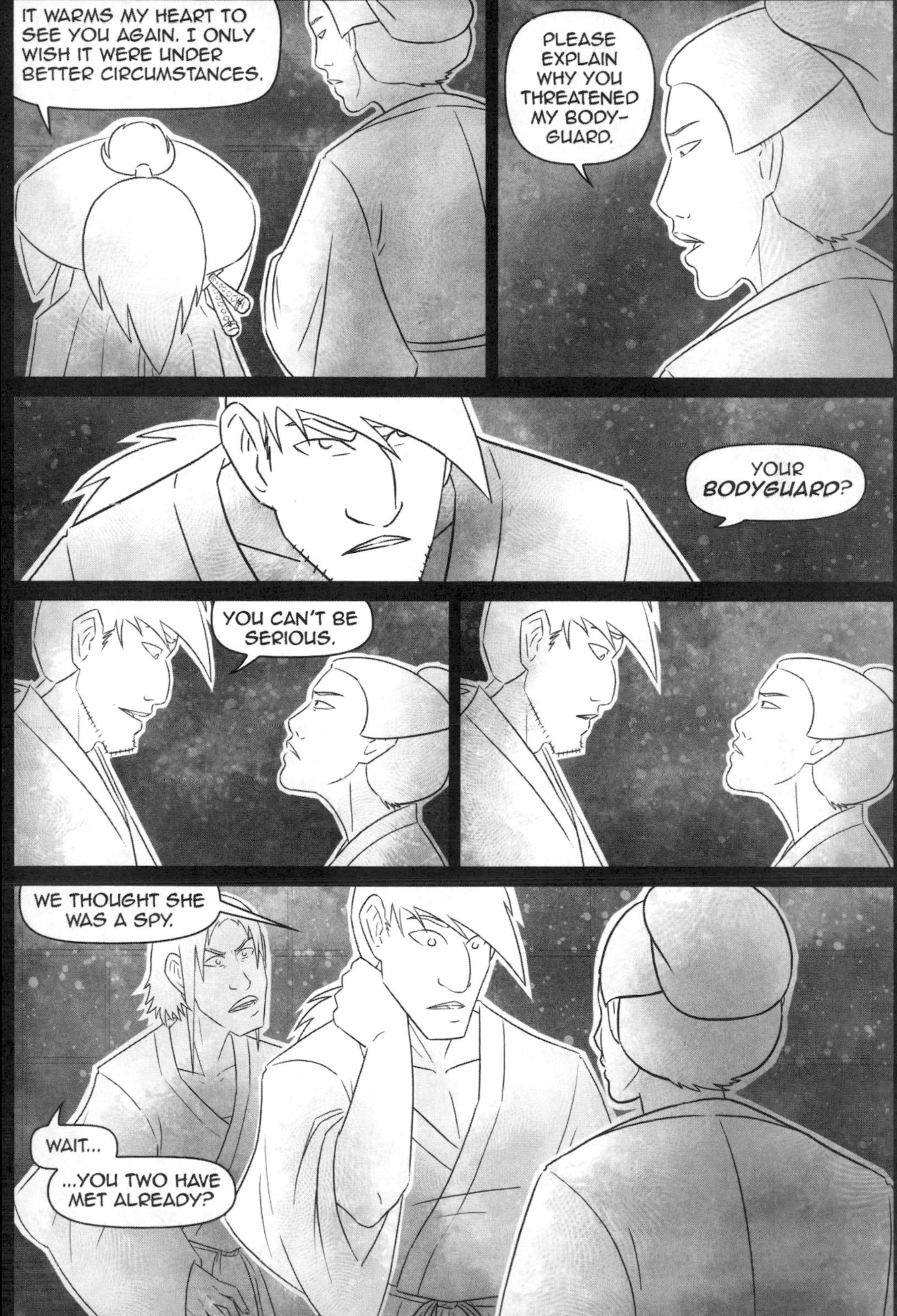
IT WARMS MY HEART TO SEE YOU AGAIN. I ONLY WISH IT WERE UNDER BETTER CIRCUMSTANCES.
PLEASE EXPLAIN WHY YOU THREATENED MY BODY-GUARD.
YOUR BODYGUARD?
YOU CAN'T BE SERIOUS.
WE THOUGHT SHE WAS A SPY.
WAIT...
...YOU TWO HAVE MET ALREADY?

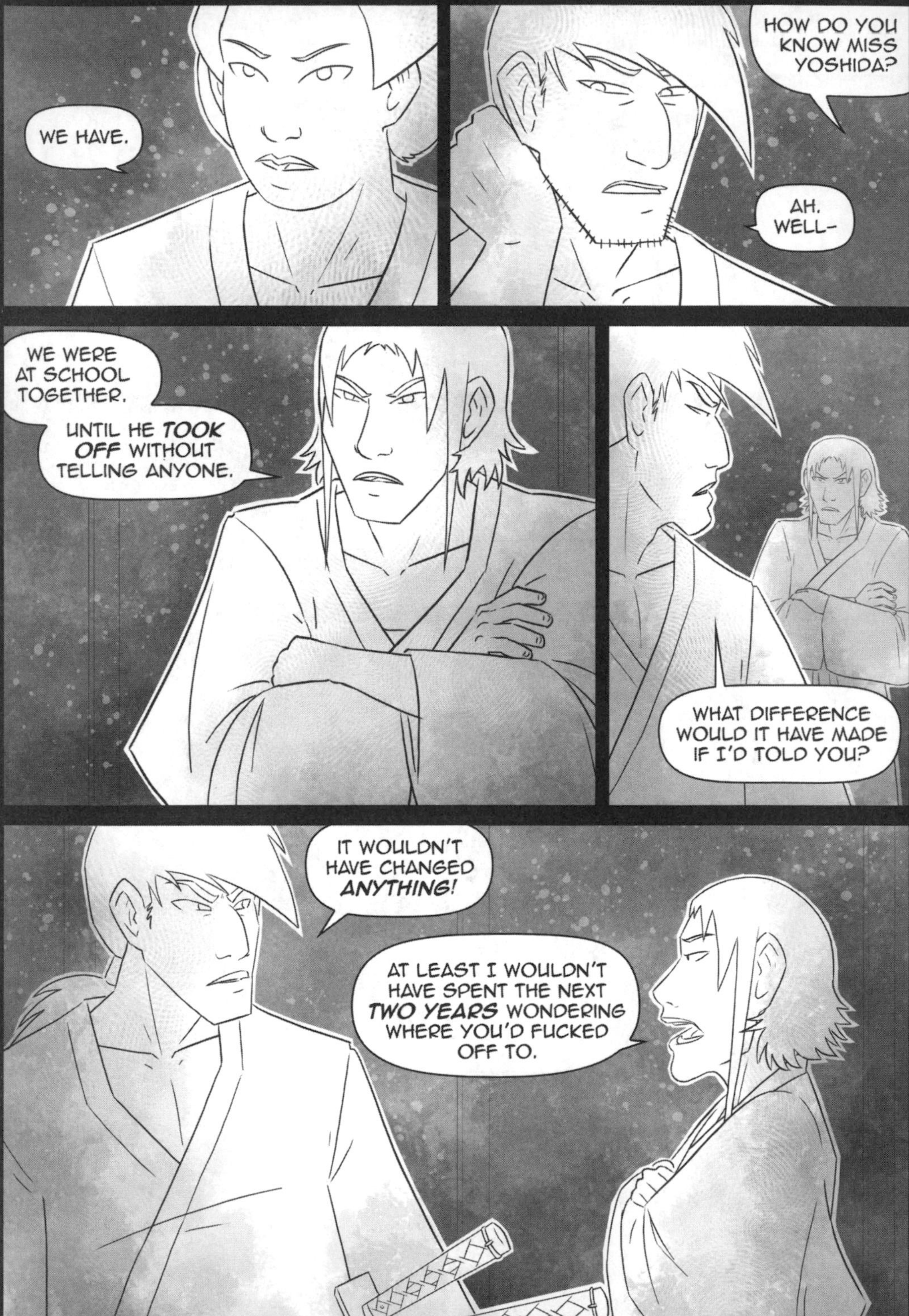
WE HAVE.
HOW DO YOU KNOW MISS YOSHIDA?
AH. WELL-
WE WERE AT SCHOOL TOGETHER.
UNTIL HE TOOK OFF WITHOUT TELLING ANYONE.
WHAT DIFFERENCE WOULD IT HAVE MADE IF I'D TOLD YOU?
IT WOULDN'T HAVE CHANGED ANYTHING!
AT LEAST I WOULDN'T HAVE SPENT THE NEXT TWO YEARS WONDERING WHERE YOU'D FUCKED OFF TO.

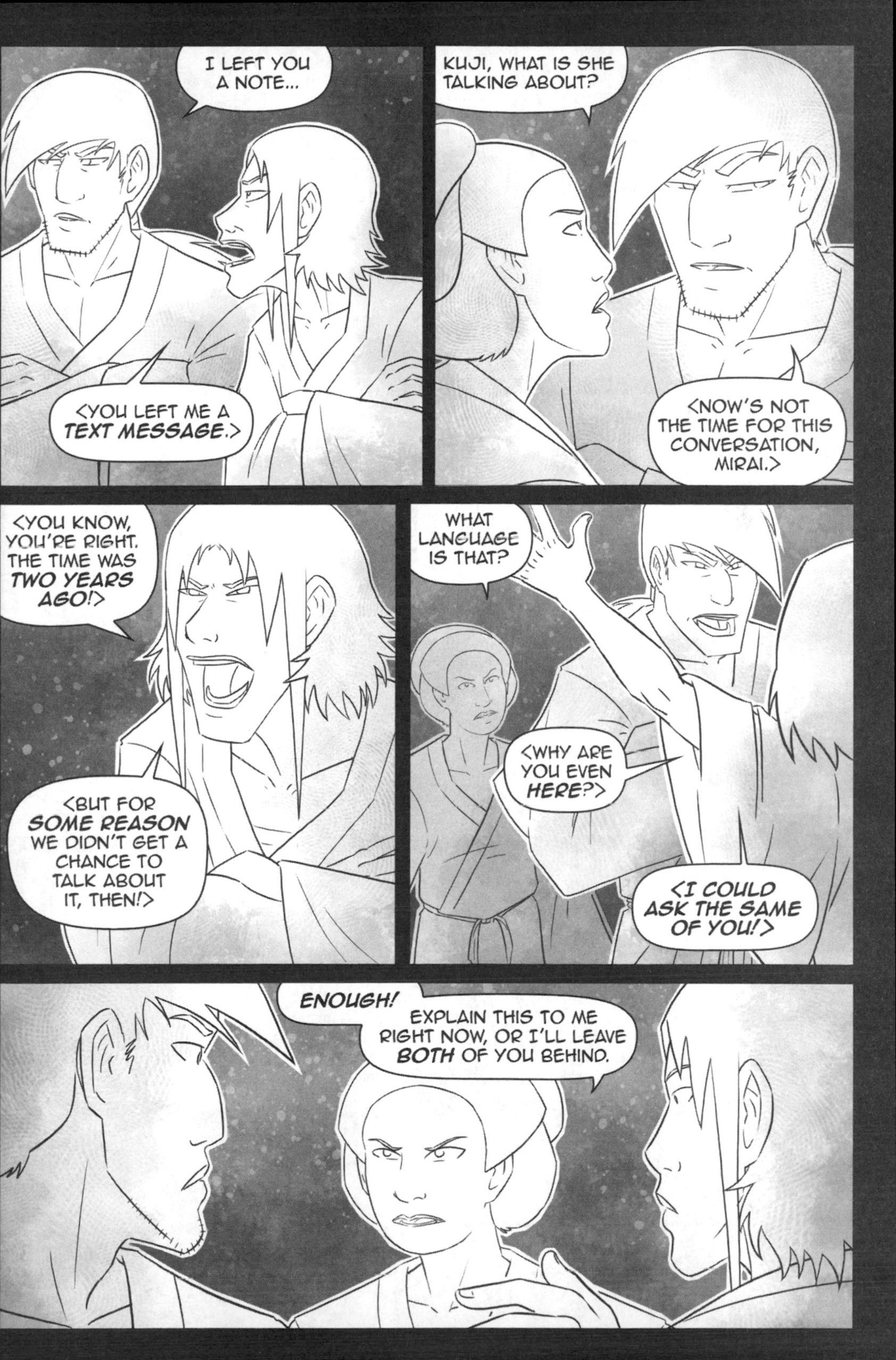
I LEFT YOU A NOTE...
<YOU LEFT ME A *TEXT MESSAGE*.>
KUJI, WHAT IS SHE TALKING ABOUT?
<NOW'S NOT THE TIME FOR THIS CONVERSATION, MIRAI.>
<YOU KNOW, YOU'RE RIGHT. THE TIME WAS *TWO YEARS AGO!*>
<BUT FOR *SOME REASON* WE DIDN'T GET A CHANCE TO TALK ABOUT IT, THEN!>
WHAT LANGUAGE IS THAT?
<WHY ARE YOU EVEN *HERE*?>
<*I COULD ASK THE SAME OF YOU!*>
ENOUGH! EXPLAIN THIS TO ME RIGHT NOW, OR I'LL LEAVE *BOTH* OF YOU BEHIND.

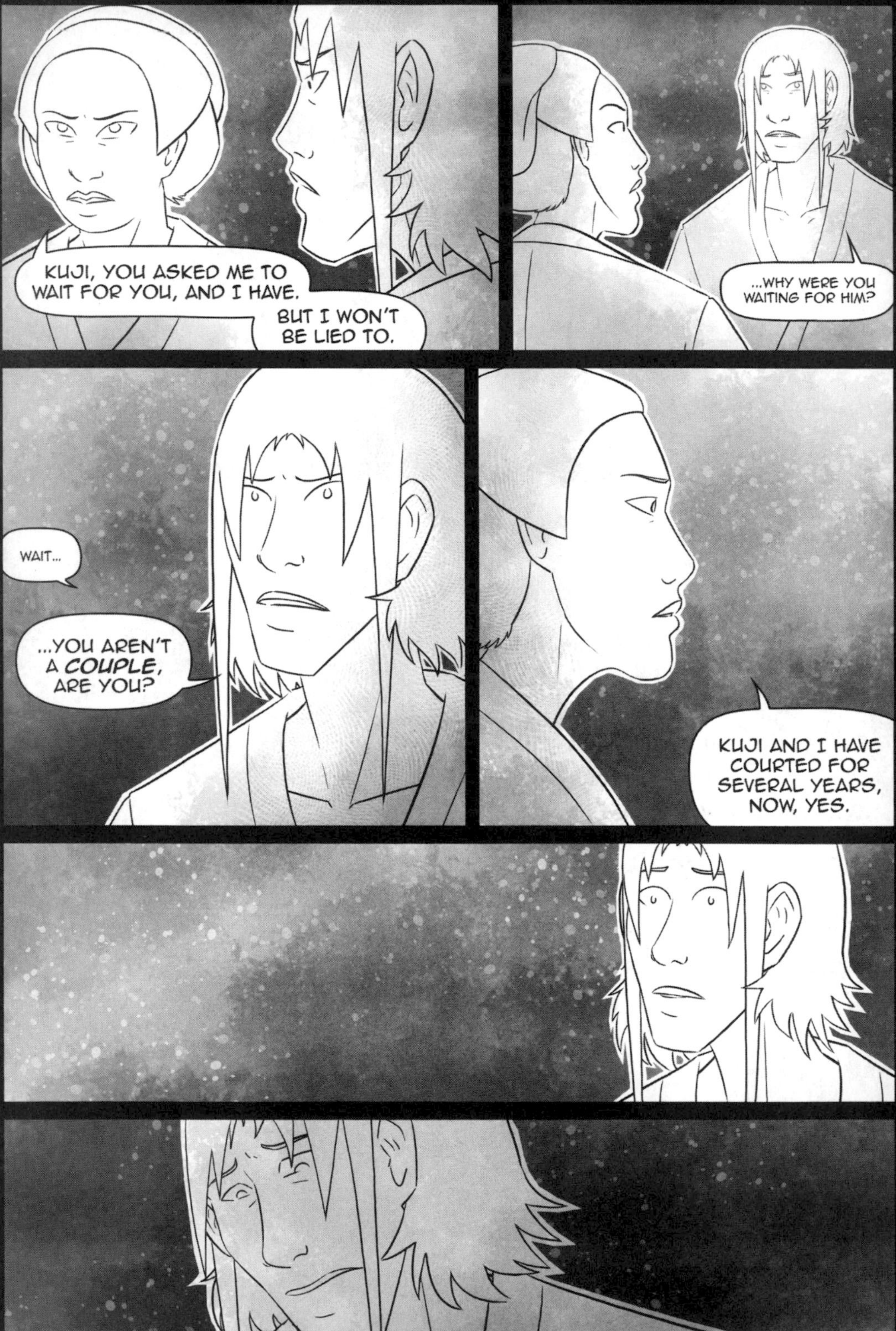
KUJI, YOU ASKED ME TO WAIT FOR YOU, AND I HAVE.
BUT I WON'T BE LIED TO.
...WHY WERE YOU WAITING FOR HIM?
WAIT...
...YOU AREN'T A *COUPLE*, ARE YOU?
KUJI AND I HAVE COURTED FOR SEVERAL YEARS, NOW, YES.

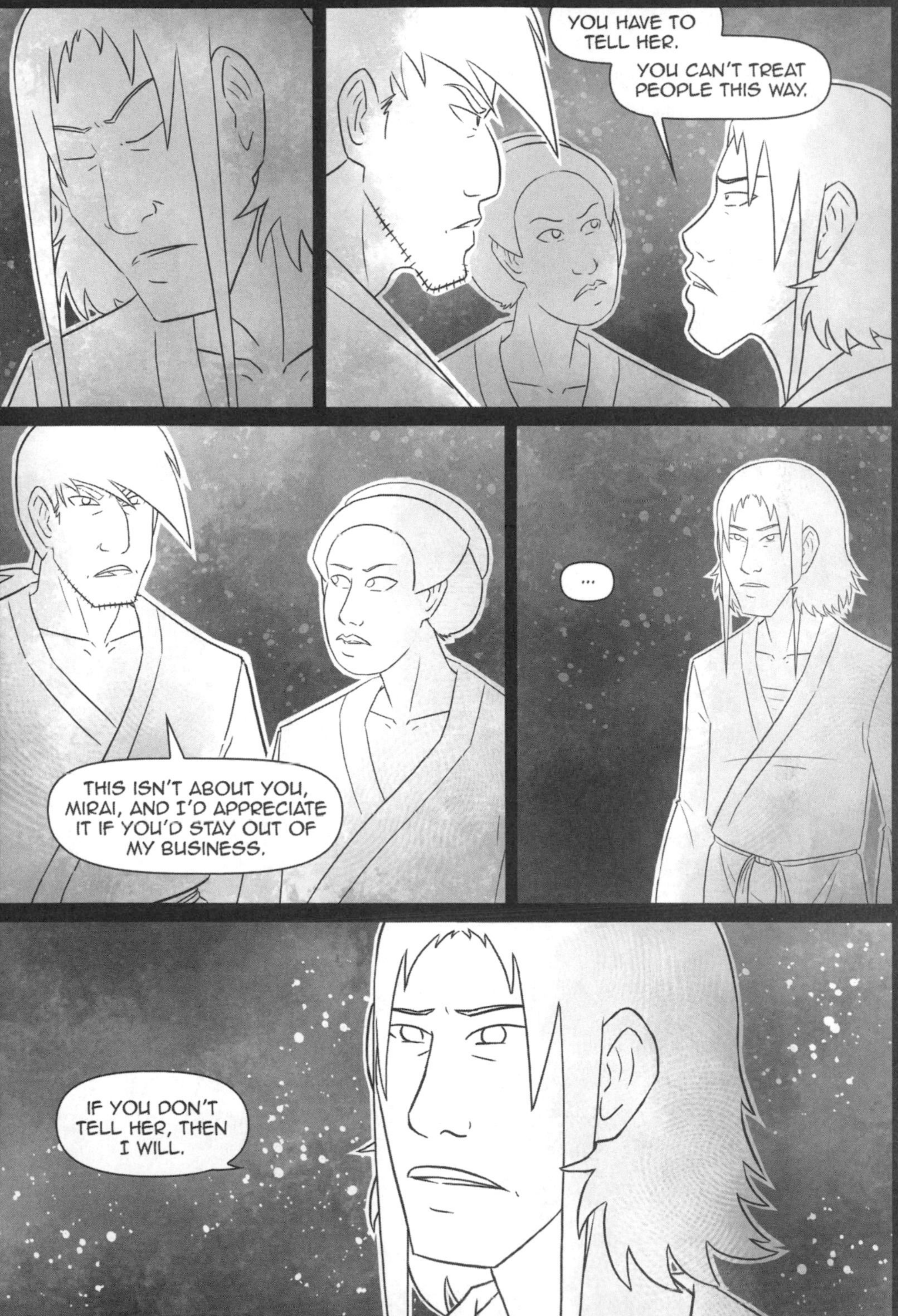
YOU HAVE TO TELL HER.
YOU CAN'T TREAT PEOPLE THIS WAY.
THIS ISN'T ABOUT YOU, MIRAI, AND I'D APPRECIATE IT IF YOU'D STAY OUT OF MY BUSINESS.
...
IF YOU DON'T TELL HER, THEN I WILL.

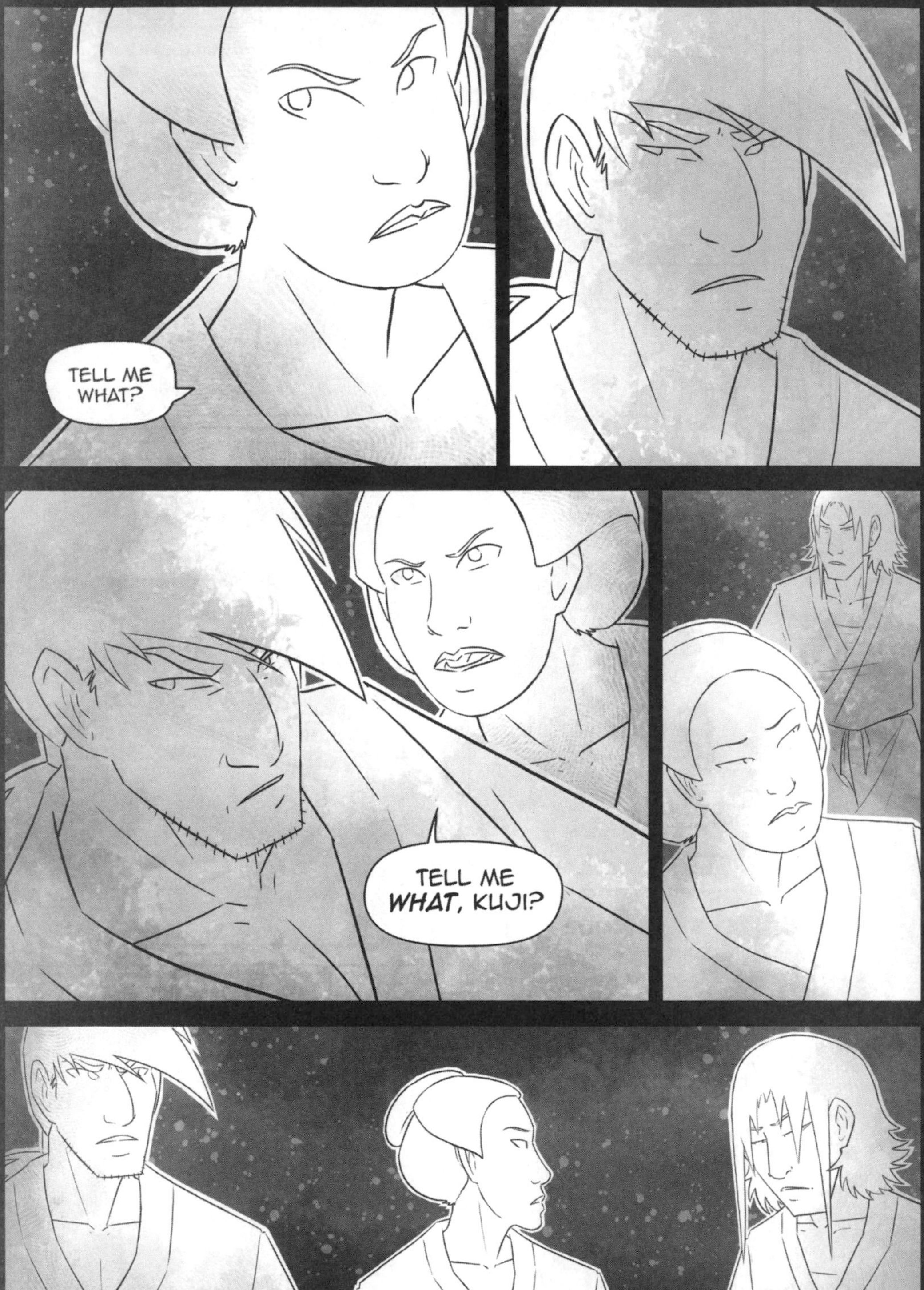
TELL ME WHAT?
TELL ME *WHAT*, KUJI?

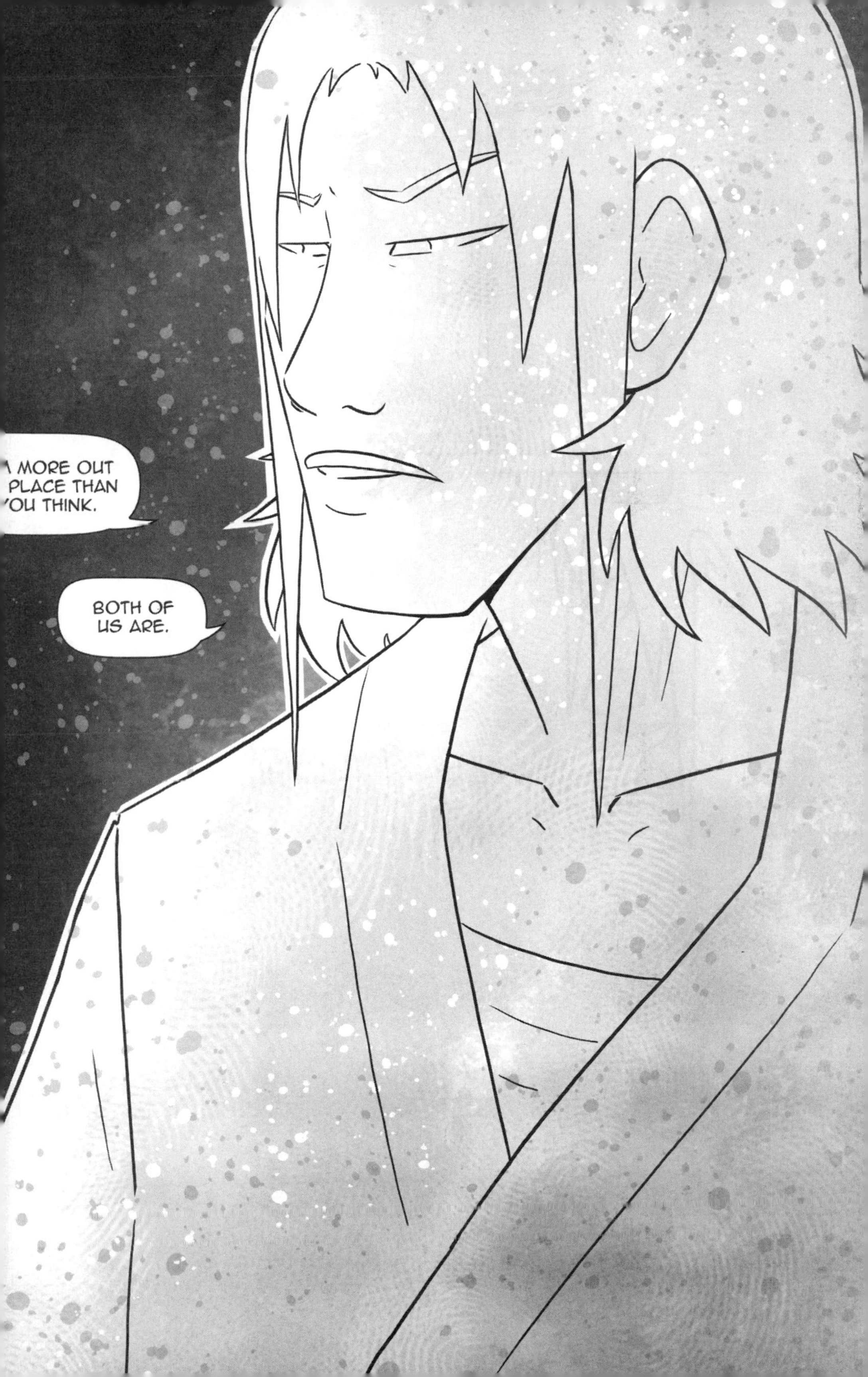
MORE OUT PLACE THAN OU THINK.
BOTH OF US ARE.

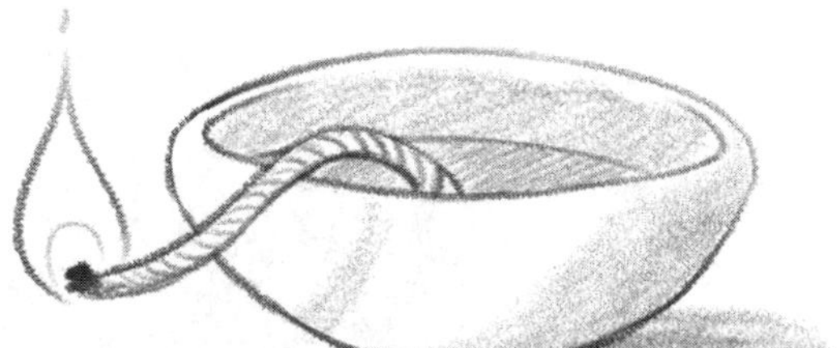

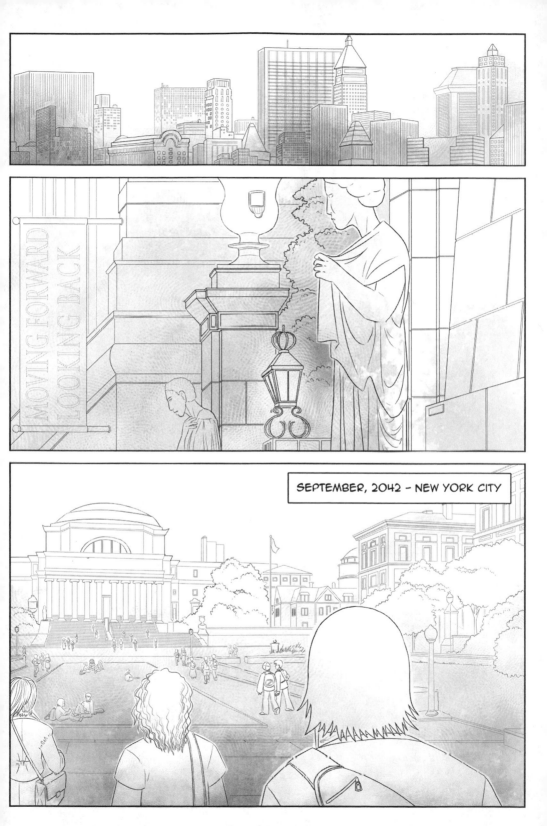

MOVING FORWARD LOOKING BACK

SEPTEMBER, 2042 – NEW YORK CITY

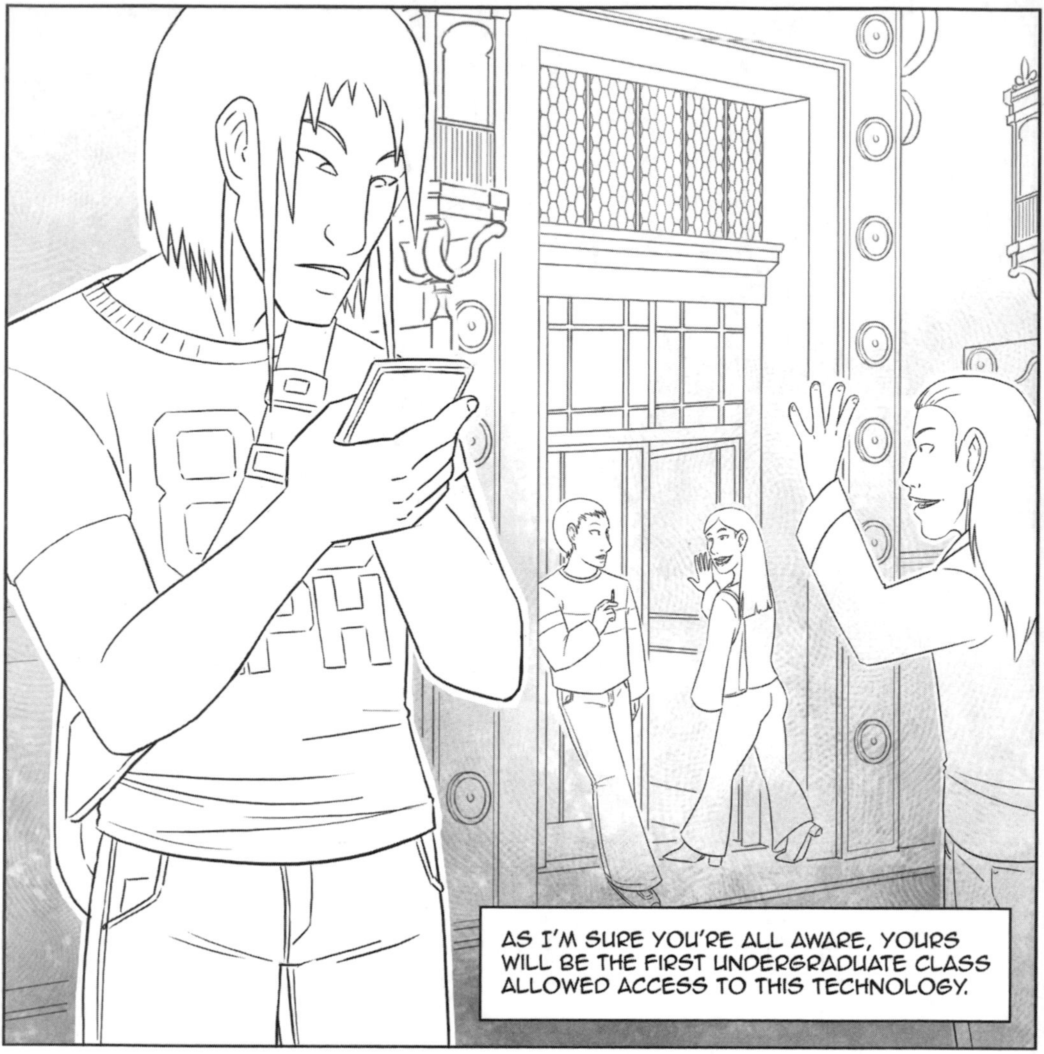
AS I'M SURE YOU'RE ALL AWARE, YOURS WILL BE THE FIRST UNDERGRADUATE CLASS ALLOWED ACCESS TO THIS TECHNOLOGY.

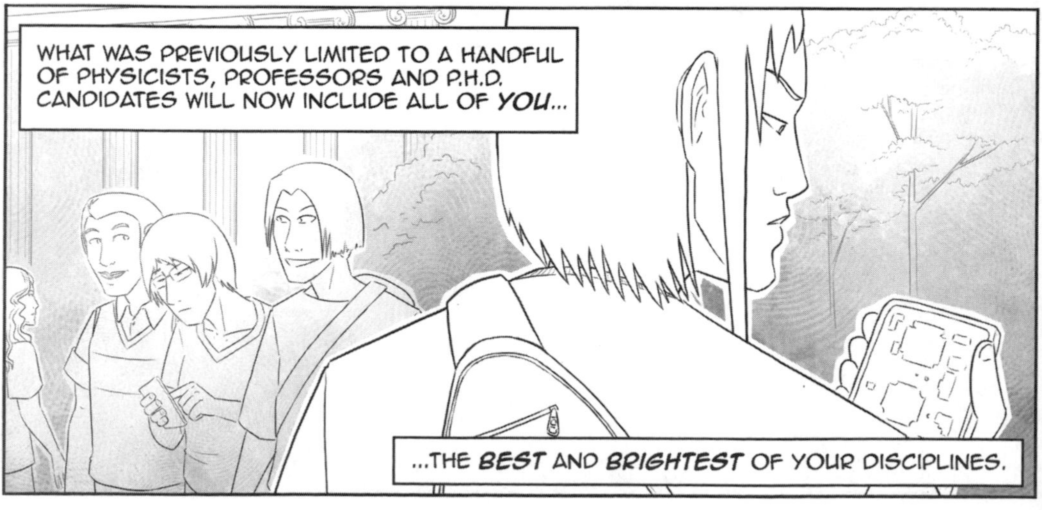
WHAT WAS PREVIOUSLY LIMITED TO A HANDFUL OF PHYSICISTS, PROFESSORS AND P.H.D. CANDIDATES WILL NOW INCLUDE ALL OF *YOU*...
...THE ***BEST*** AND ***BRIGHTEST*** OF YOUR DISCIPLINES.

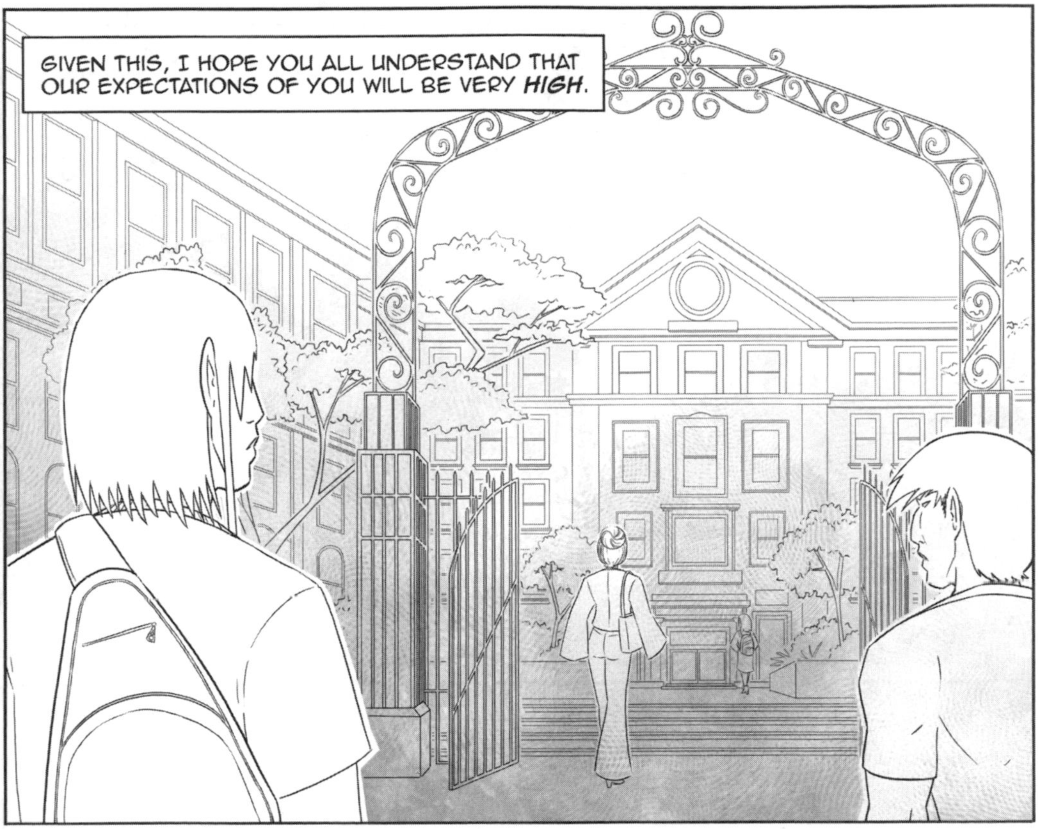
GIVEN THIS, I HOPE YOU ALL UNDERSTAND THAT OUR EXPECTATIONS OF YOU WILL BE VERY *HIGH*.

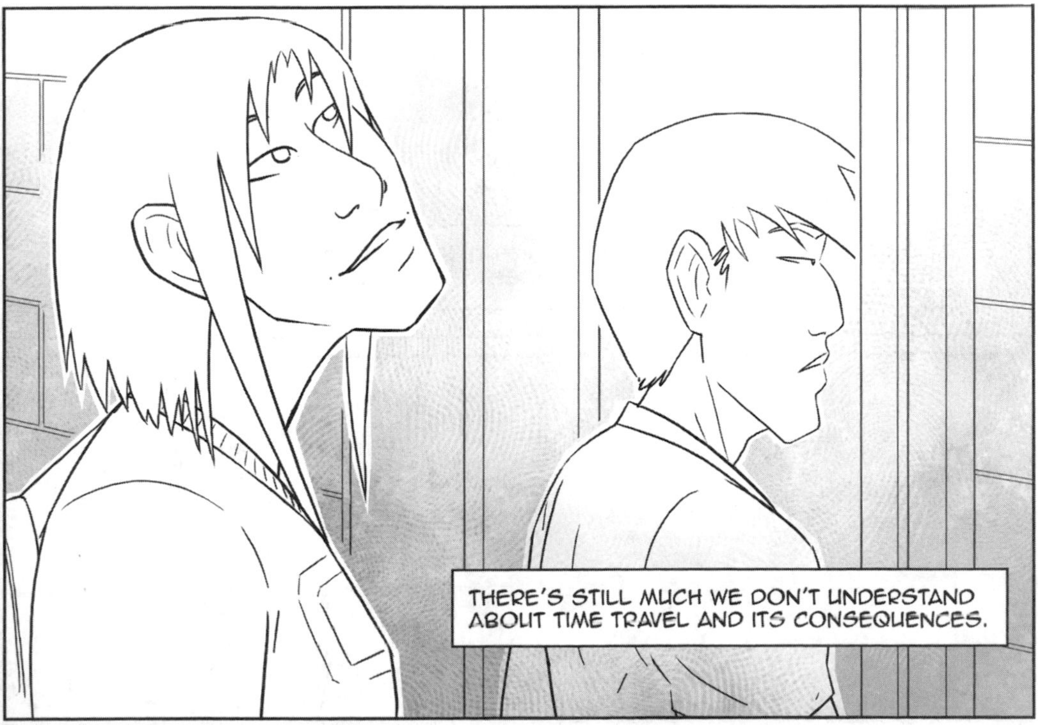
THERE'S STILL MUCH WE DON'T UNDERSTAND ABOUT TIME TRAVEL AND ITS CONSEQUENCES.

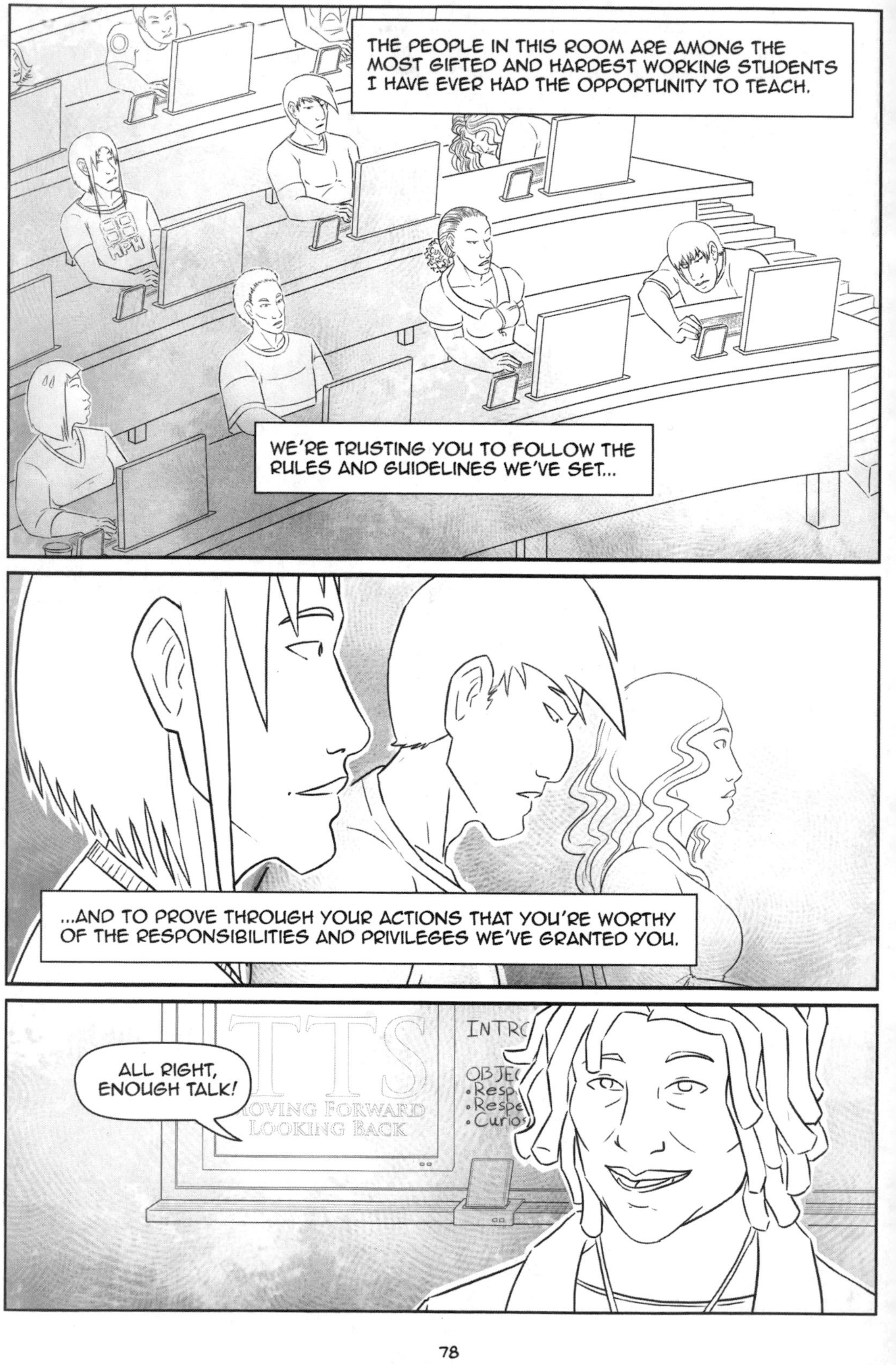
THE PEOPLE IN THIS ROOM ARE AMONG THE MOST GIFTED AND HARDEST WORKING STUDENTS I HAVE EVER HAD THE OPPORTUNITY TO TEACH.
WE'RE TRUSTING YOU TO FOLLOW THE RULES AND GUIDELINES WE'VE SET...
...AND TO PROVE THROUGH YOUR ACTIONS THAT YOU'RE WORTHY OF THE RESPONSIBILITIES AND PRIVILEGES WE'VE GRANTED YOU.
TTS
LOOKING BACK
ALL RIGHT, ENOUGH TALK!

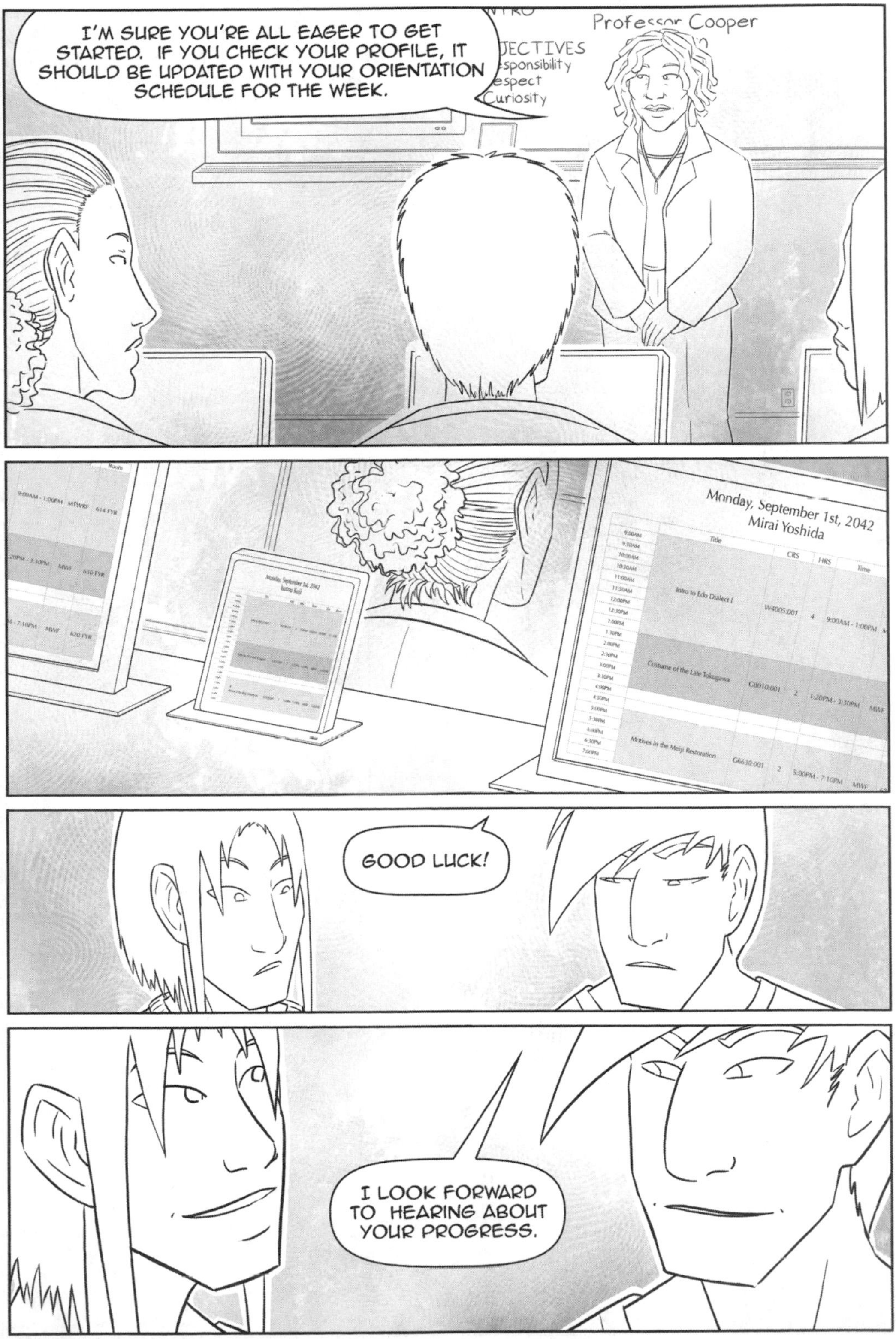
I'M SURE YOU'RE ALL EAGER TO GET STARTED. IF YOU CHECK YOUR PROFILE, IT SHOULD BE UPDATED WITH YOUR ORIENTATION SCHEDULE FOR THE WEEK.
Professor Cooper
JECTIVES
esponsibility
espect
Curiosity
Monday, September 1st, 2042
Mirai Yoshida
Title
CRS
HRS
Time
Intro to Edo Dialect I
W4005:001
4
9:00AM - 1:00PM
Costume of the Late Tokugawa
G8010:001
2
1:20PM - 3:30PM
MWF
Motives in the Meiji Restoration
G6630:001
2
5:00PM - 7:10PM
MWF
GOOD LUCK!
I LOOK FORWARD TO HEARING ABOUT YOUR PROGRESS.

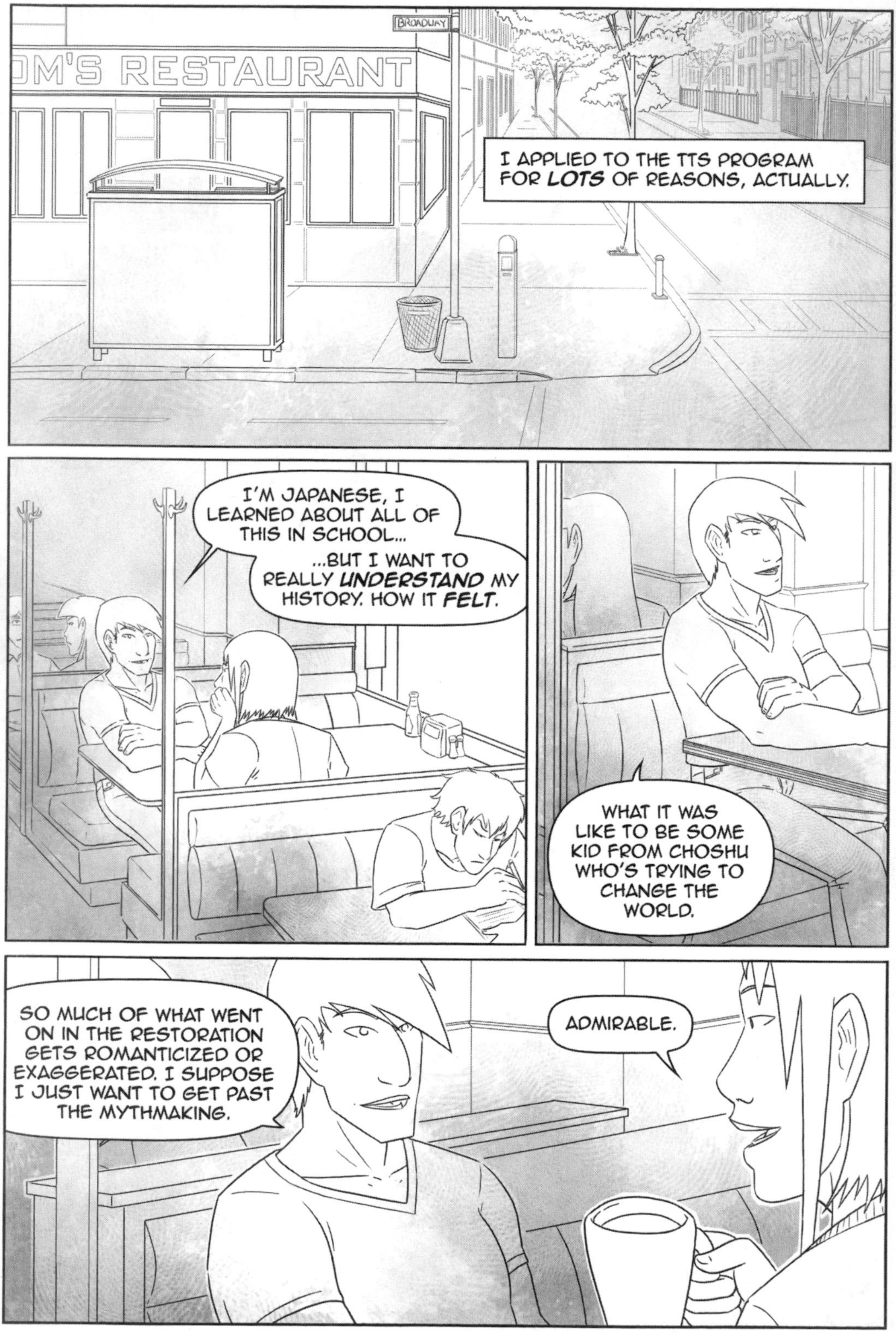
BROADWAY
OM'S RESTAURANT
I APPLIED TO THE TTS PROGRAM FOR **LOTS** OF REASONS, ACTUALLY.
I'M JAPANESE, I LEARNED ABOUT ALL OF THIS IN SCHOOL...
...BUT I WANT TO REALLY **UNDERSTAND** MY HISTORY. HOW IT **FELT**.
WHAT IT WAS LIKE TO BE SOME KID FROM CHOSHU WHO'S TRYING TO CHANGE THE WORLD.
SO MUCH OF WHAT WENT ON IN THE RESTORATION GETS ROMANTICIZED OR EXAGGERATED. I SUPPOSE I JUST WANT TO GET PAST THE MYTHMAKING.
ADMIRABLE.

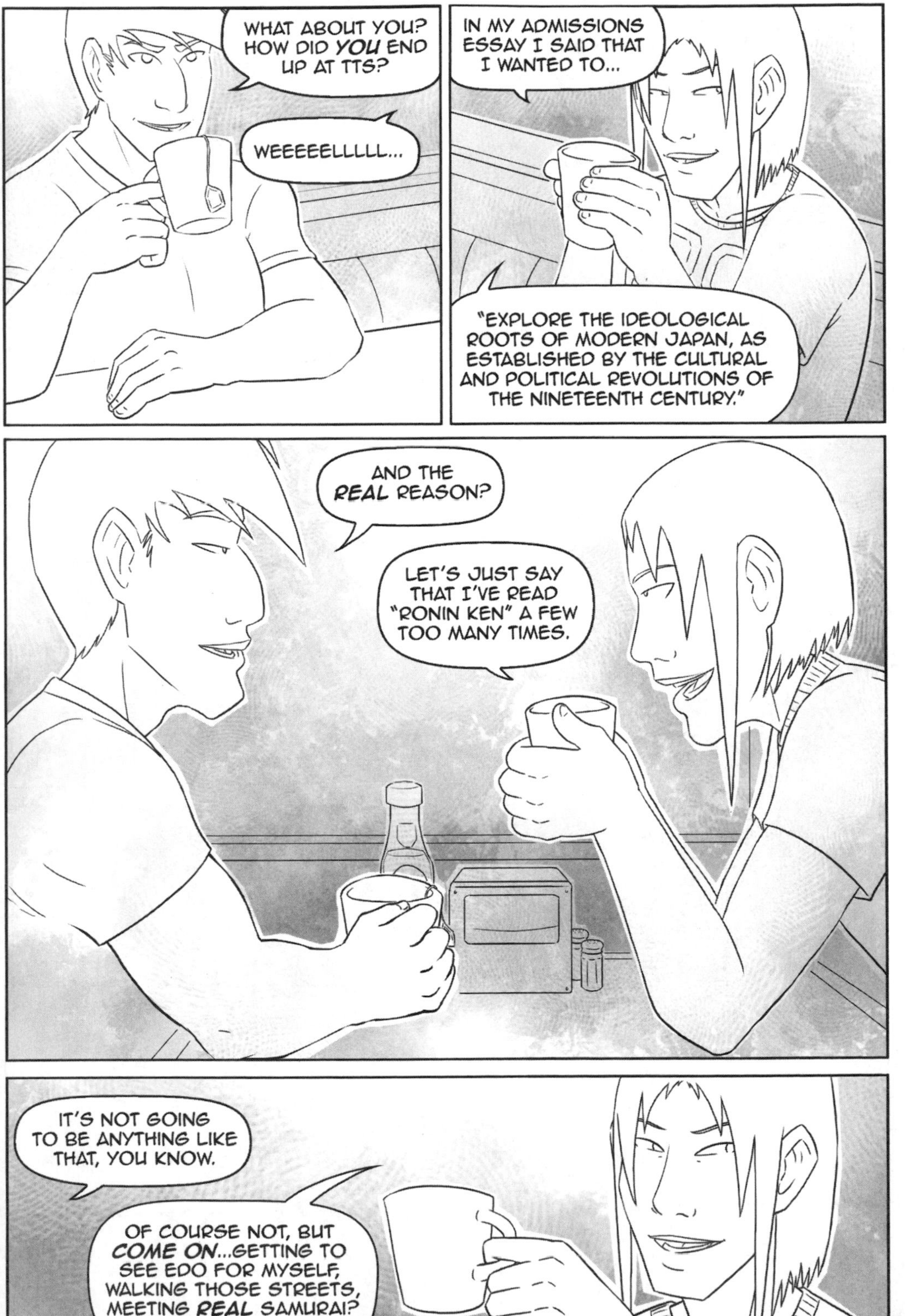
WHAT ABOUT YOU? HOW DID YOU END UP AT TTS?
WEEEEELLLLL...
IN MY ADMISSIONS ESSAY I SAID THAT I WANTED TO...
"EXPLORE THE IDEOLOGICAL ROOTS OF MODERN JAPAN, AS ESTABLISHED BY THE CULTURAL AND POLITICAL REVOLUTIONS OF THE NINETEENTH CENTURY."
AND THE REAL REASON?
LET'S JUST SAY THAT I'VE READ "RONIN KEN" A FEW TOO MANY TIMES.
IT'S NOT GOING TO BE ANYTHING LIKE THAT, YOU KNOW.
OF COURSE NOT, BUT COME ON...GETTING TO SEE EDO FOR MYSELF, WALKING THOSE STREETS, MEETING REAL SAMURAI?

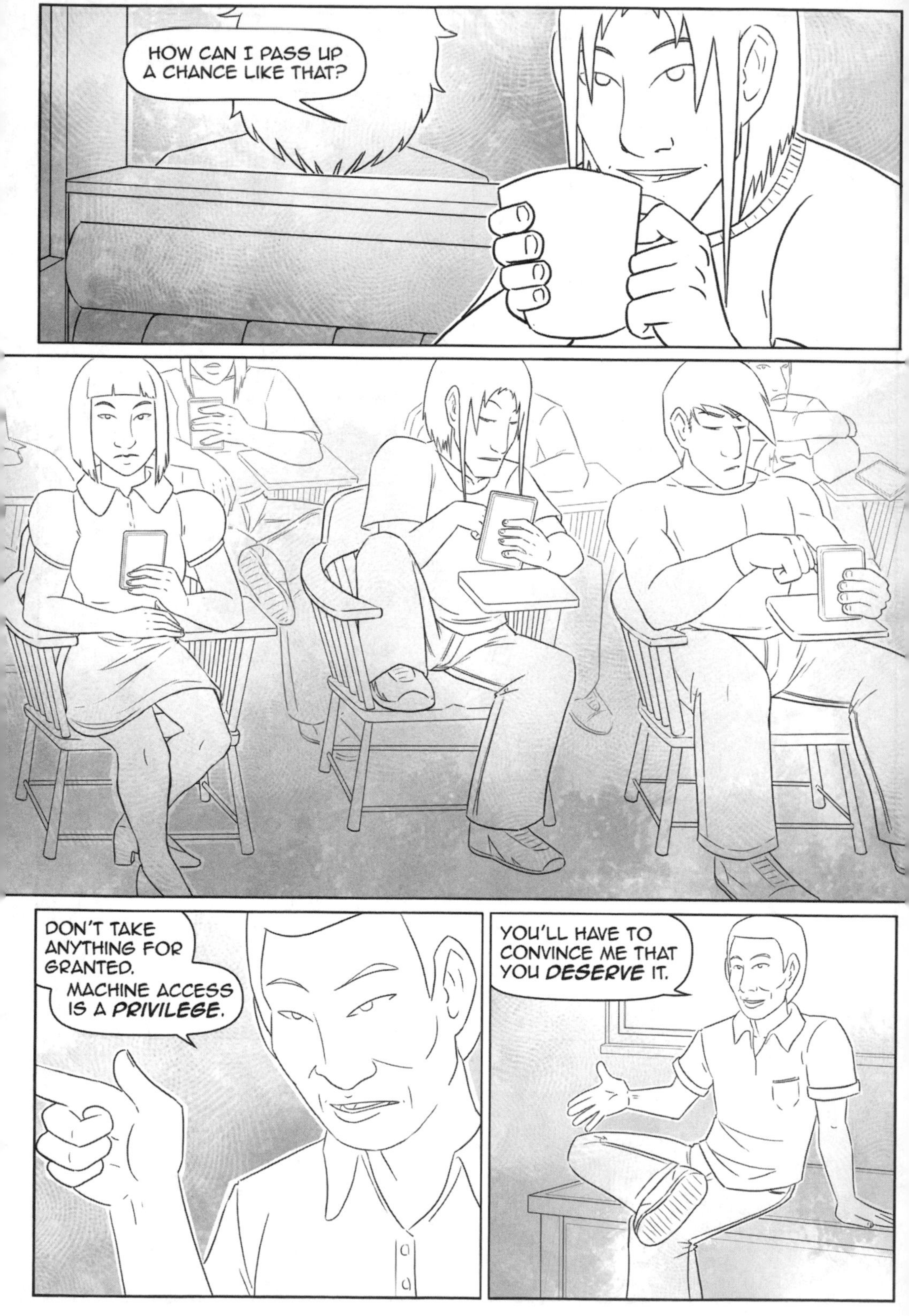
HOW CAN I PASS UP A CHANCE LIKE THAT?
DON'T TAKE ANYTHING FOR GRANTED.
MACHINE ACCESS IS A *PRIVILEGE*.
YOU'LL HAVE TO CONVINCE ME THAT YOU *DESERVE* IT.

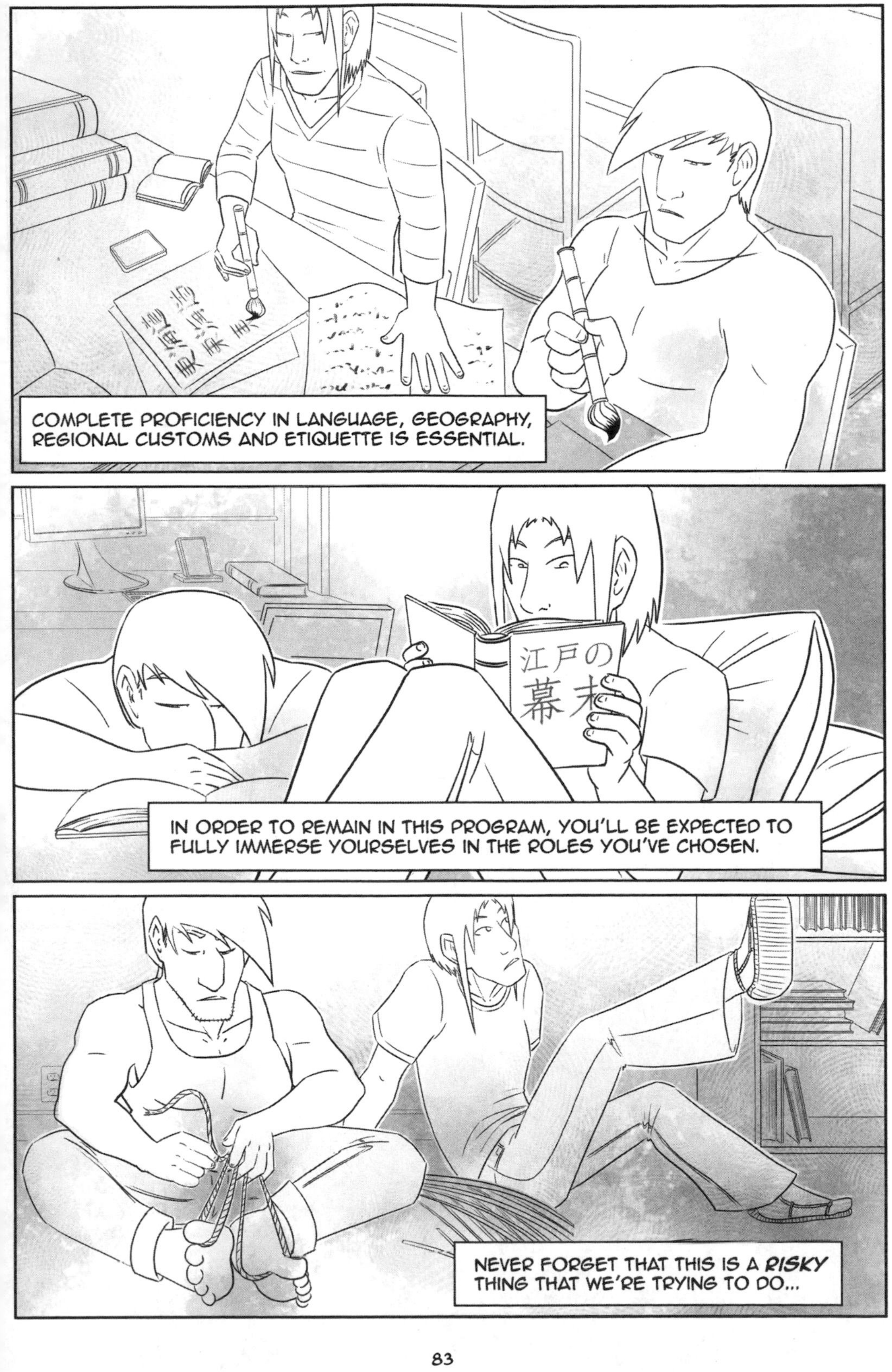
COMPLETE PROFICIENCY IN LANGUAGE, GEOGRAPHY, REGIONAL CUSTOMS AND ETIQUETTE IS ESSENTIAL.
江戸の
幕末
IN ORDER TO REMAIN IN THIS PROGRAM, YOU'LL BE EXPECTED TO FULLY IMMERSE YOURSELVES IN THE ROLES YOU'VE CHOSEN.
NEVER FORGET THAT THIS IS A *RISKY* THING THAT WE'RE TRYING TO DO...

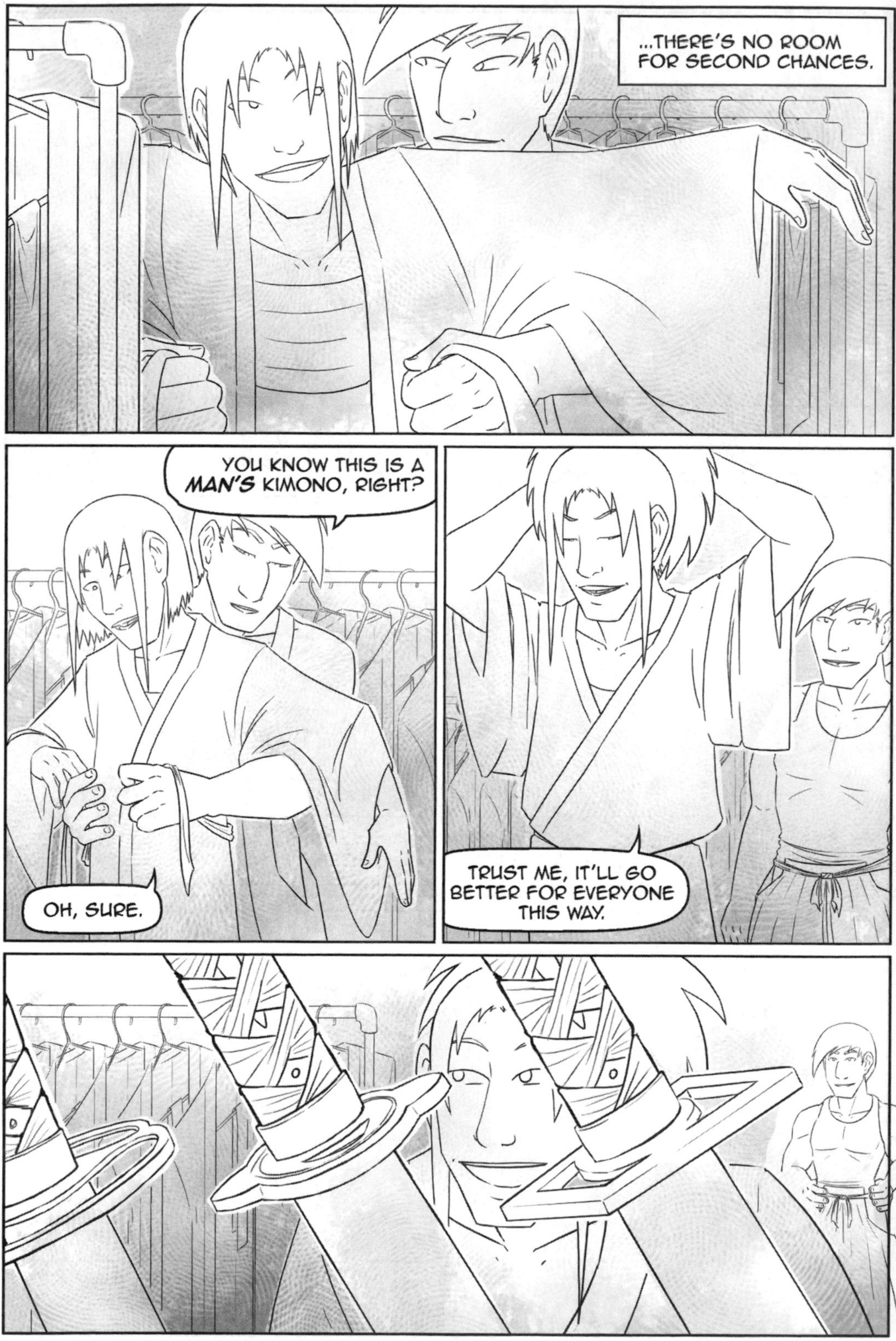
...THERE'S NO ROOM FOR SECOND CHANCES.
YOU KNOW THIS IS A MAN'S KIMONO, RIGHT?
OH, SURE.
TRUST ME, IT'LL GO BETTER FOR EVERYONE THIS WAY.

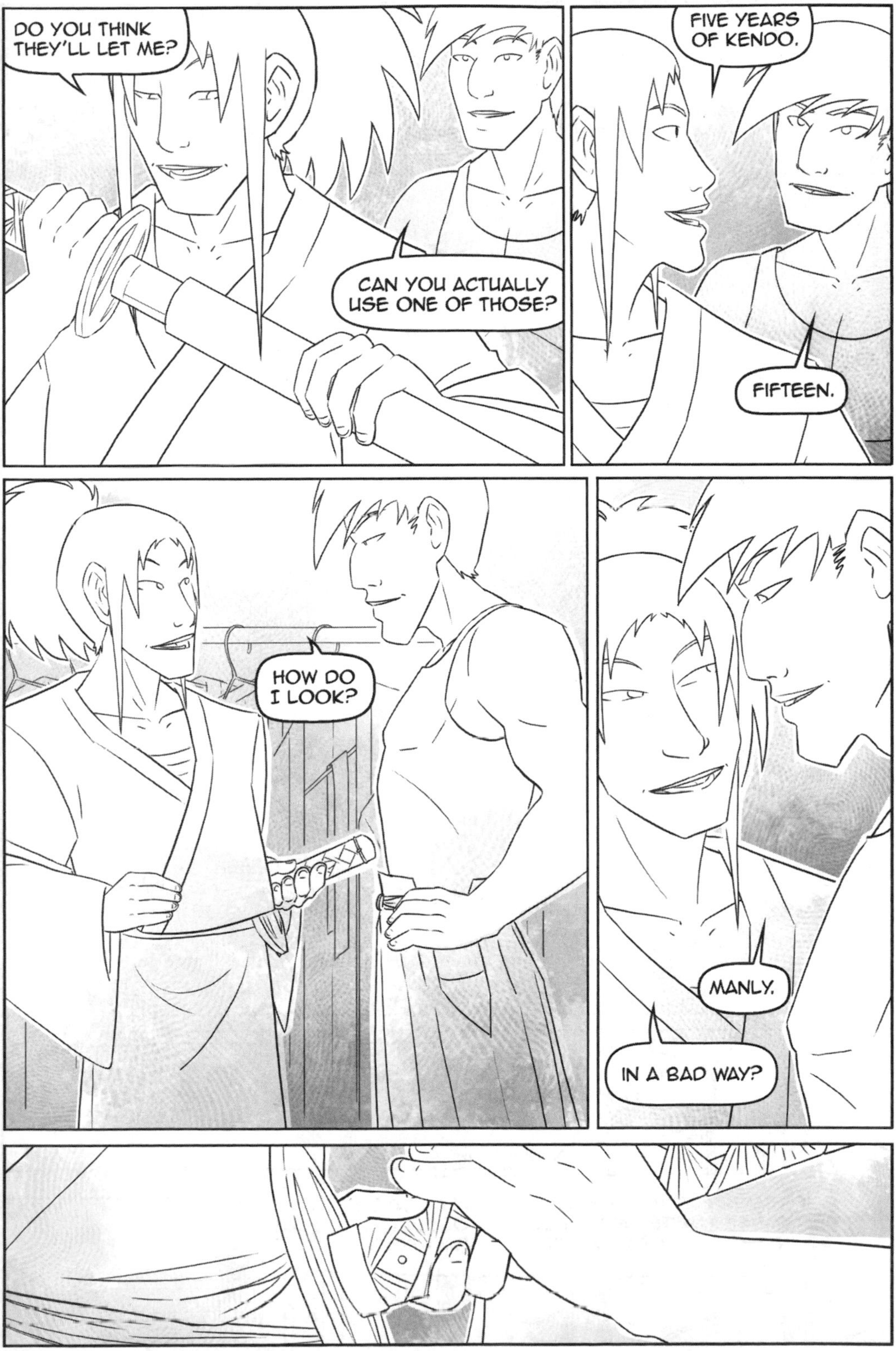
DO YOU THINK THEY'LL LET ME?
CAN YOU ACTUALLY USE ONE OF THOSE?
FIVE YEARS OF KENDO.
FIFTEEN.
HOW DO I LOOK?
MANLY.
IN A BAD WAY?

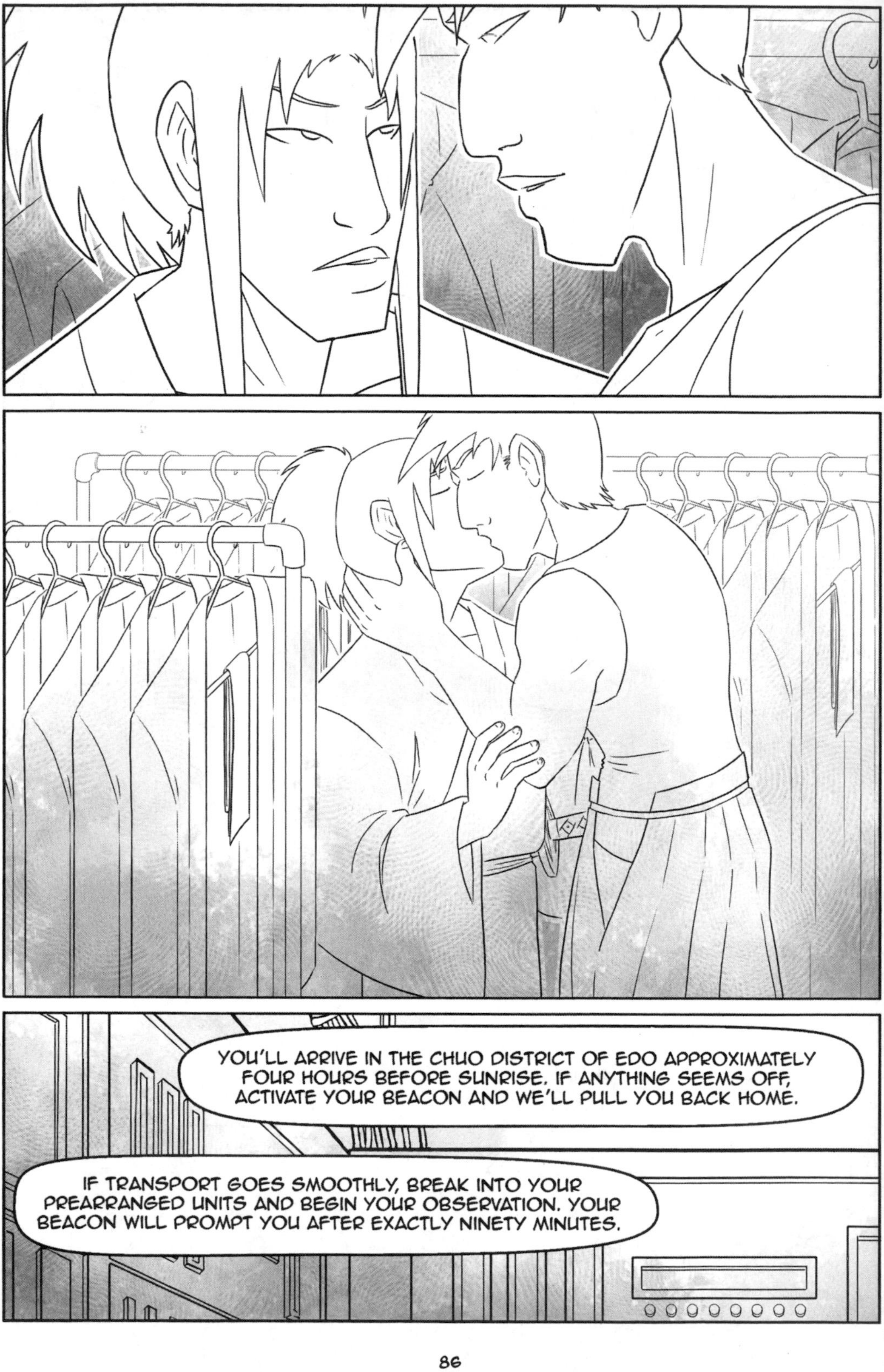
YOU'LL ARRIVE IN THE CHUO DISTRICT OF EDO APPROXIMATELY FOUR HOURS BEFORE SUNRISE. IF ANYTHING SEEMS OFF, ACTIVATE YOUR BEACON AND WE'LL PULL YOU BACK HOME.
IF TRANSPORT GOES SMOOTHLY, BREAK INTO YOUR PREARRANGED UNITS AND BEGIN YOUR OBSERVATION. YOUR BEACON WILL PROMPT YOU AFTER EXACTLY NINETY MINUTES.

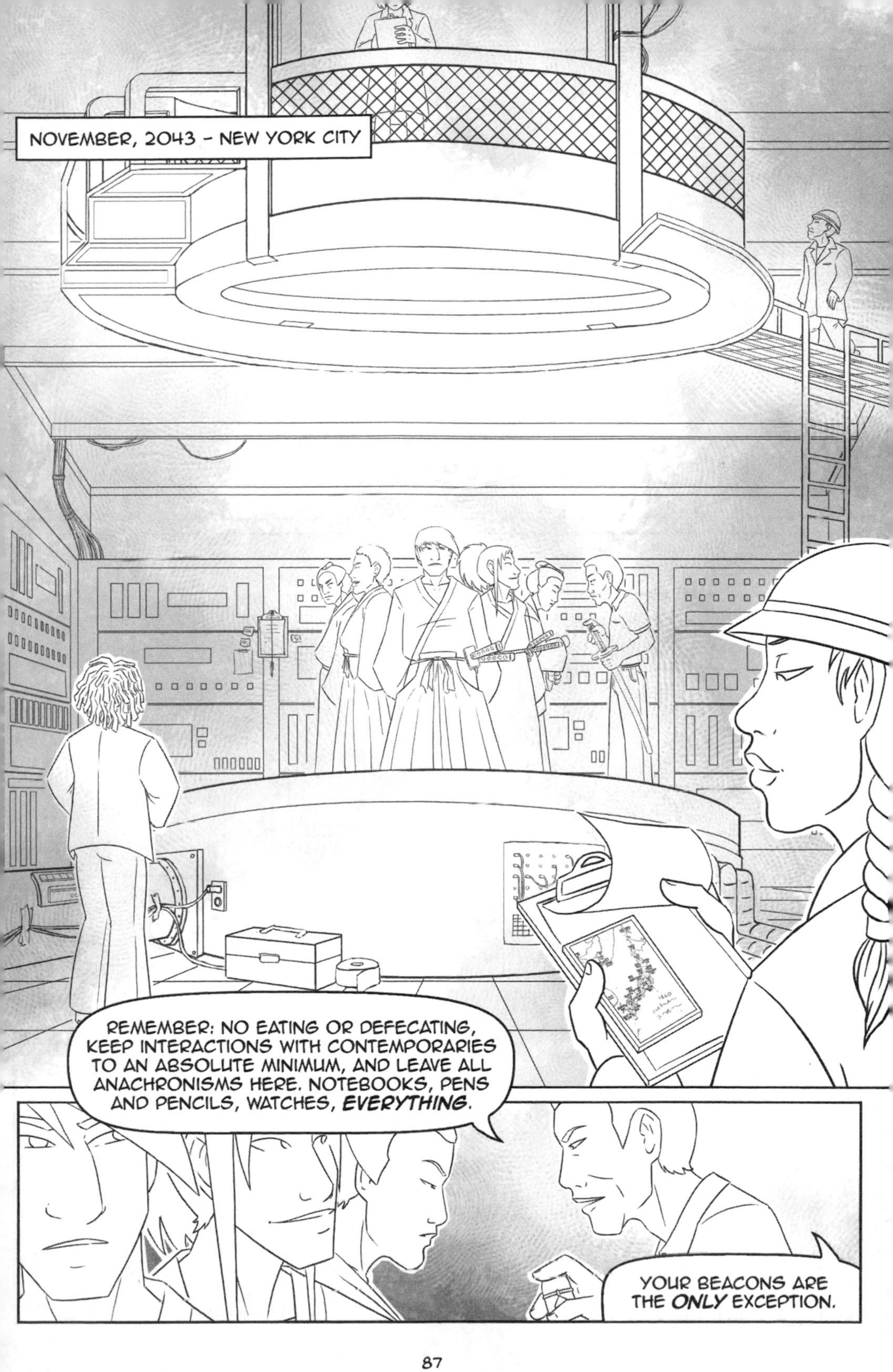
NOVEMBER, 2043 - NEW YORK CITY
REMEMBER: NO EATING OR DEFECATING, KEEP INTERACTIONS WITH CONTEMPORARIES TO AN ABSOLUTE MINIMUM, AND LEAVE ALL ANACHRONISMS HERE. NOTEBOOKS, PENS AND PENCILS, WATCHES, *EVERYTHING*.
YOUR BEACONS ARE THE *ONLY* EXCEPTION.

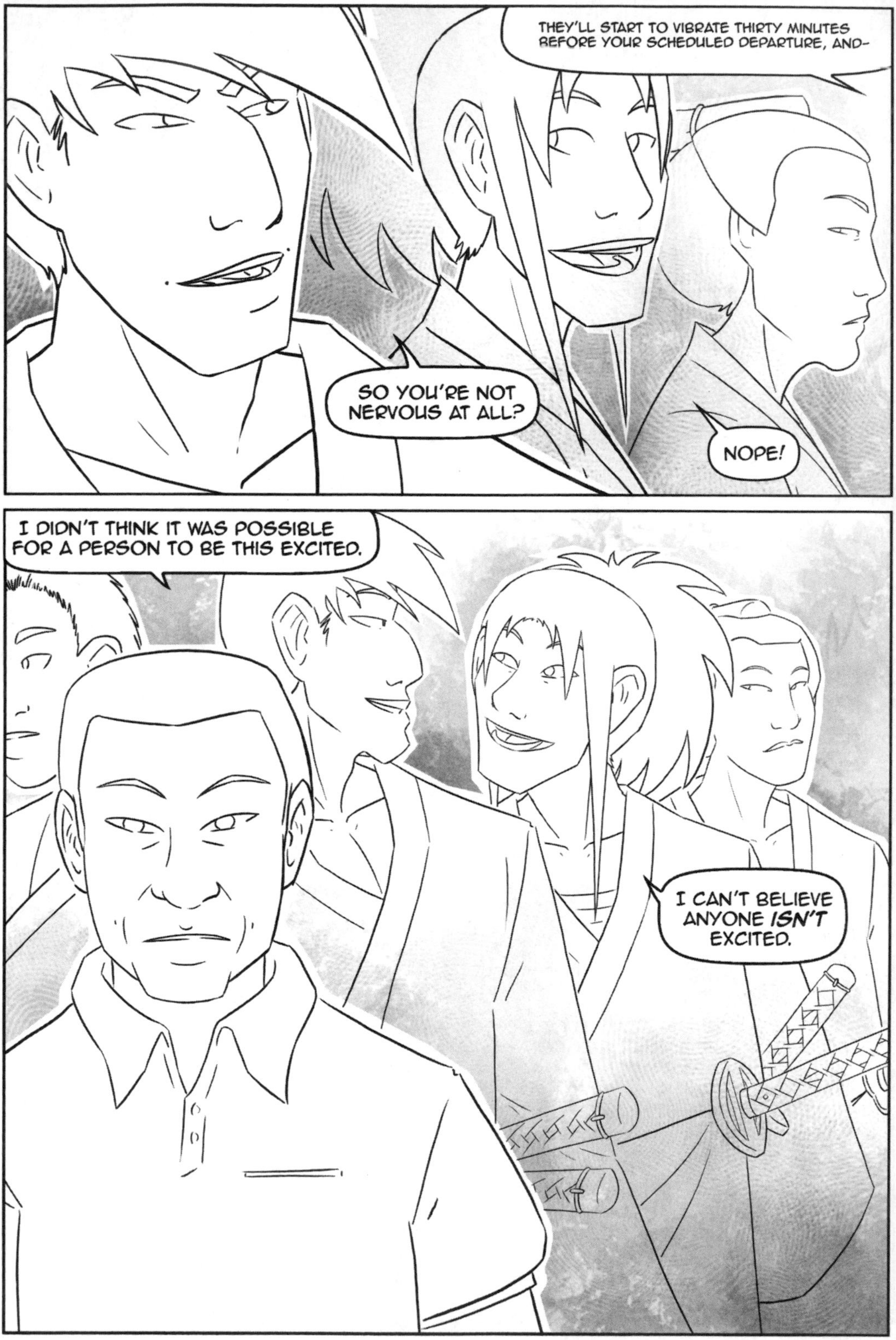
THEY'LL START TO VIBRATE THIRTY MINUTES BEFORE YOUR SCHEDULED DEPARTURE, AND-
SO YOU'RE NOT NERVOUS AT ALL?
NOPE!
I DIDN'T THINK IT WAS POSSIBLE FOR A PERSON TO BE THIS EXCITED.
I CAN'T BELIEVE ANYONE *ISN'T* EXCITED.

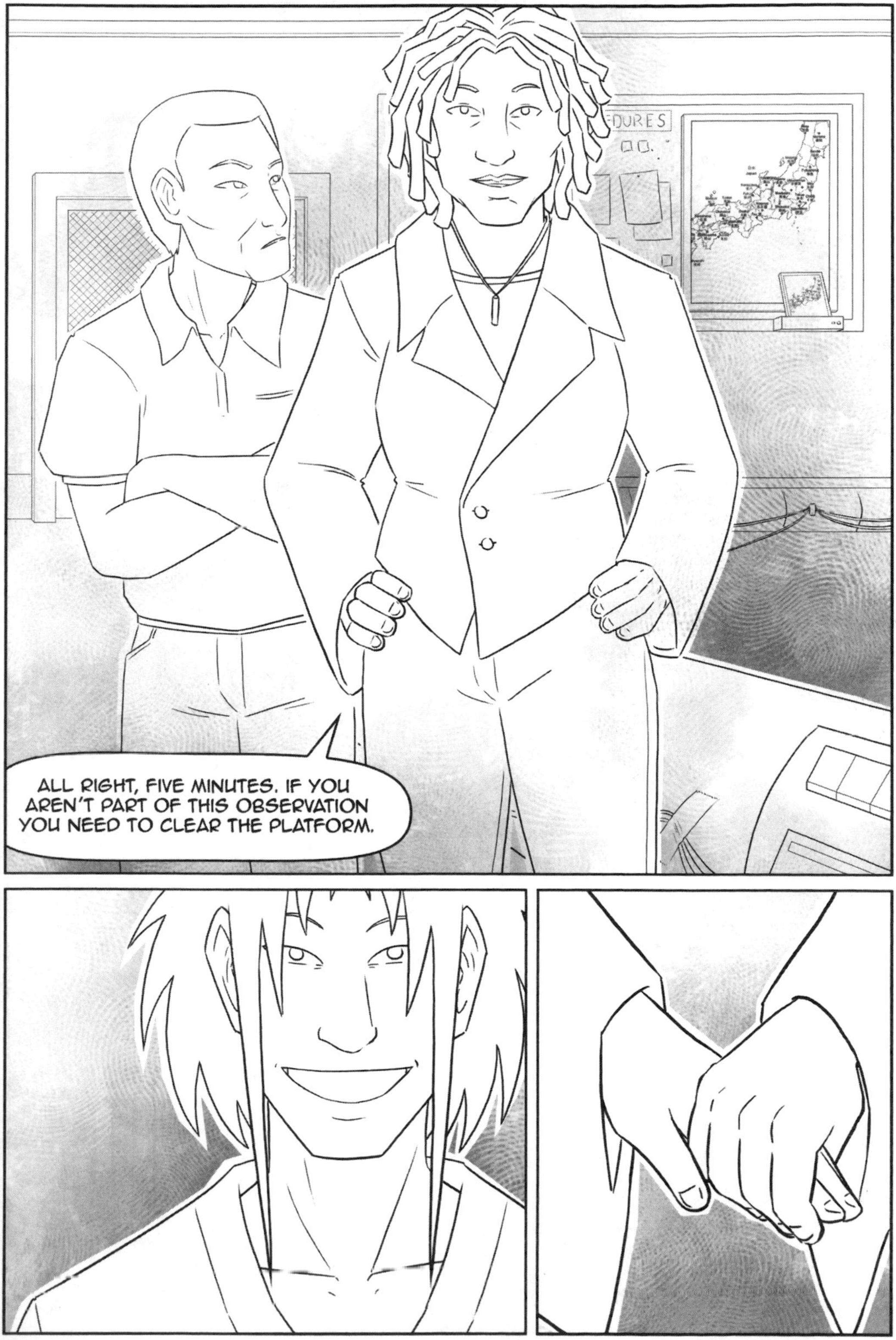
ALL RIGHT, FIVE MINUTES. IF YOU AREN'T PART OF THIS OBSERVATION YOU NEED TO CLEAR THE PLATFORM.

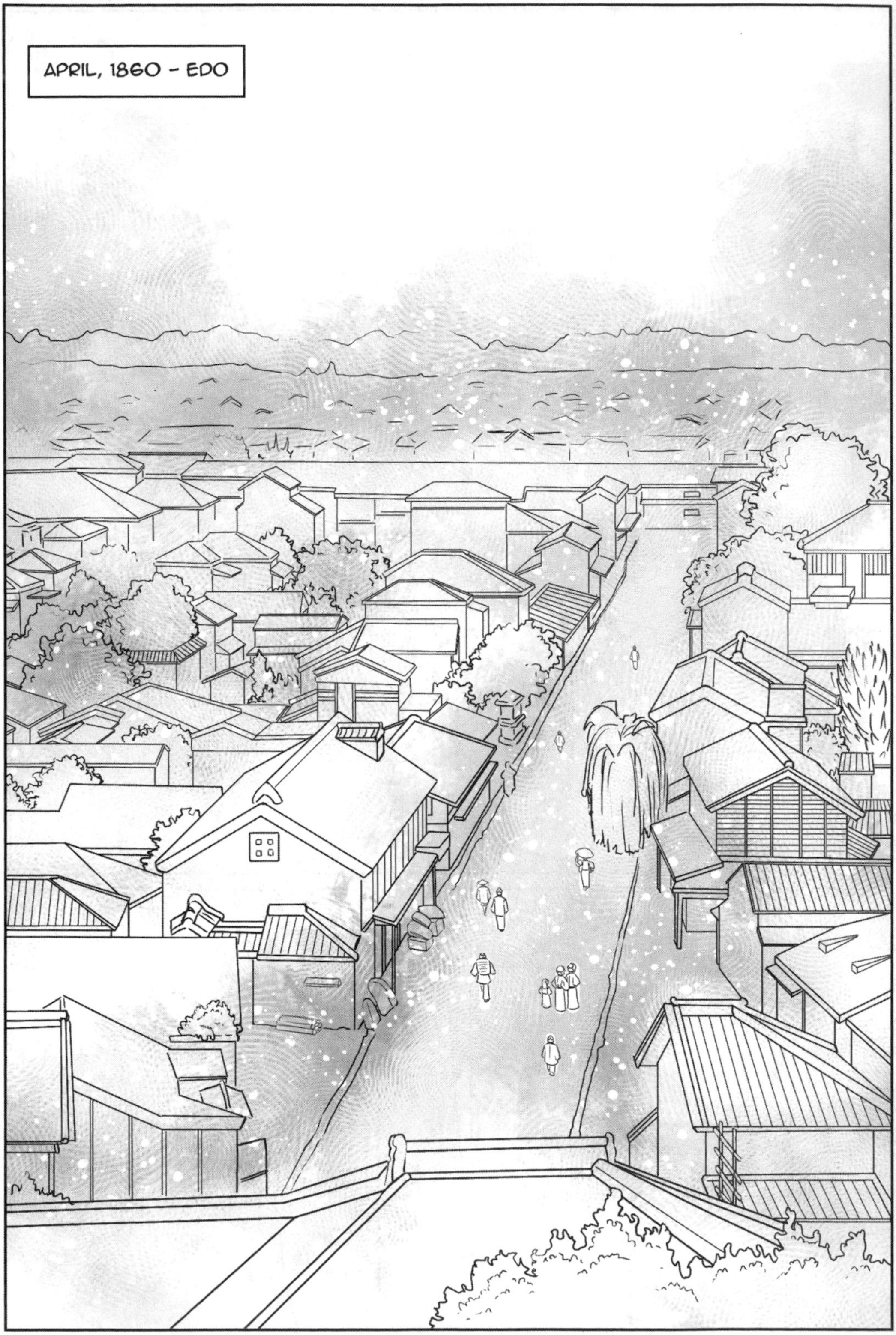
APRIL, 1860 - EDO

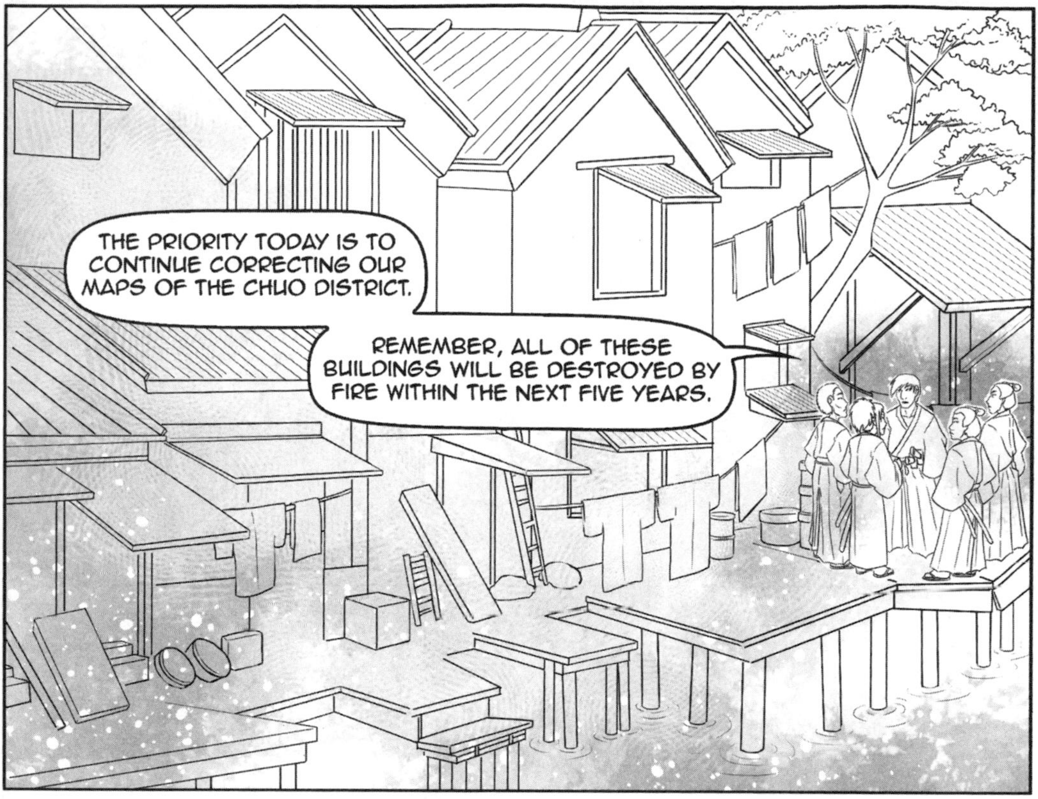
THE PRIORITY TODAY IS TO CONTINUE CORRECTING OUR MAPS OF THE CHUO DISTRICT.
REMEMBER, ALL OF THESE BUILDINGS WILL BE DESTROYED BY FIRE WITHIN THE NEXT FIVE YEARS.

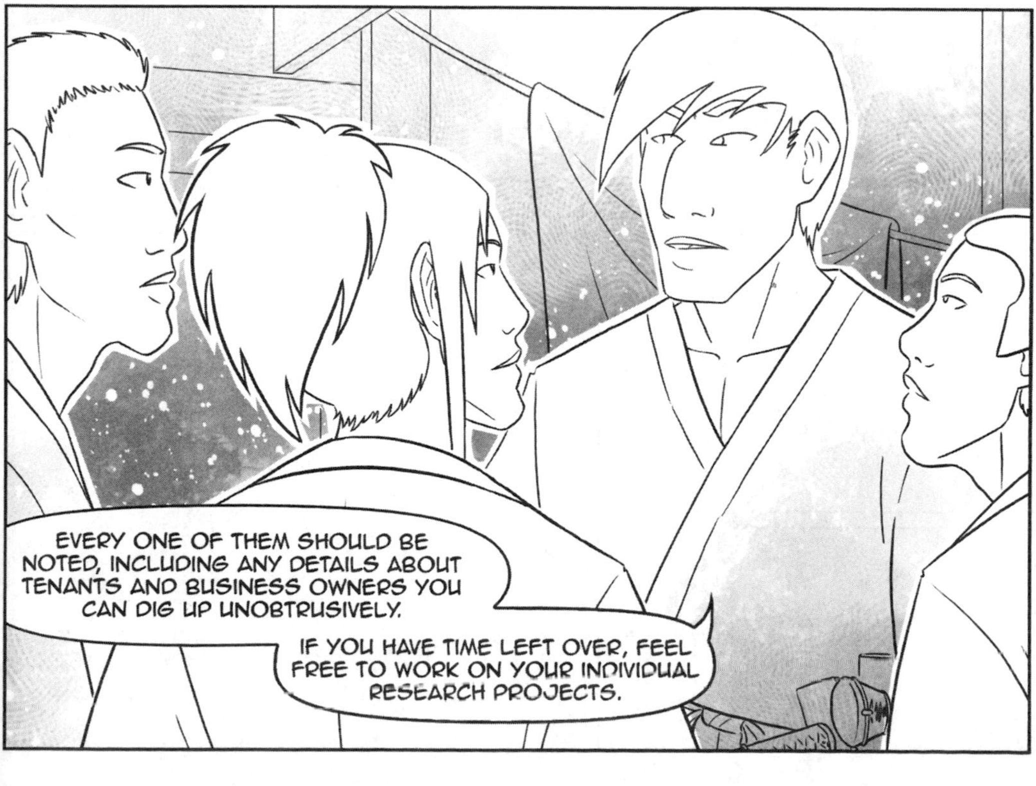
EVERY ONE OF THEM SHOULD BE NOTED, INCLUDING ANY DETAILS ABOUT TENANTS AND BUSINESS OWNERS YOU CAN DIG UP UNOBTRUSIVELY.
IF YOU HAVE TIME LEFT OVER, FEEL FREE TO WORK ON YOUR INDIVIDUAL RESEARCH PROJECTS.

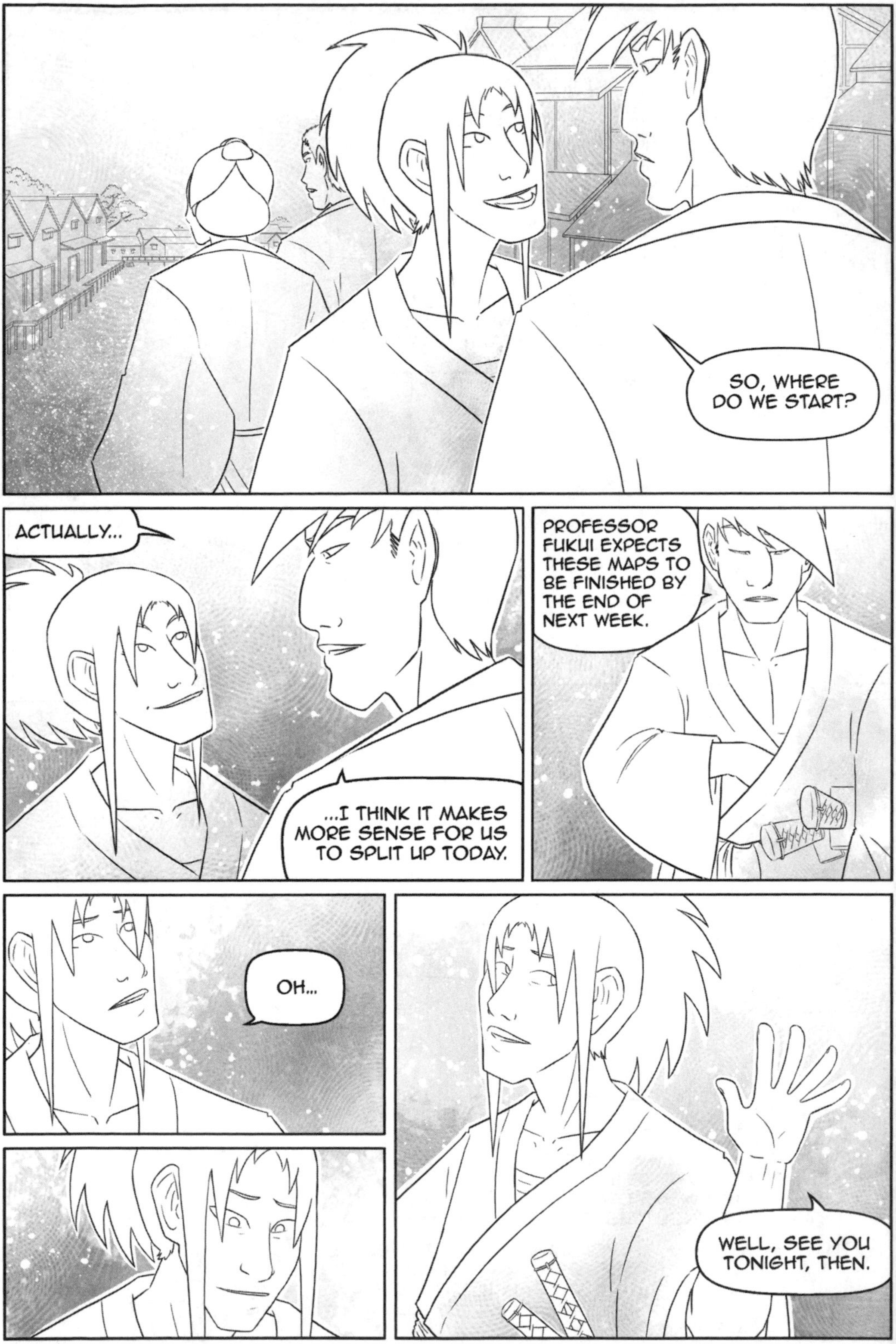
SO, WHERE DO WE START?
ACTUALLY...
...I THINK IT MAKES MORE SENSE FOR US TO SPLIT UP TODAY.
PROFESSOR FUKUI EXPECTS THESE MAPS TO BE FINISHED BY THE END OF NEXT WEEK.
OH...
WELL, SEE YOU TONIGHT, THEN.

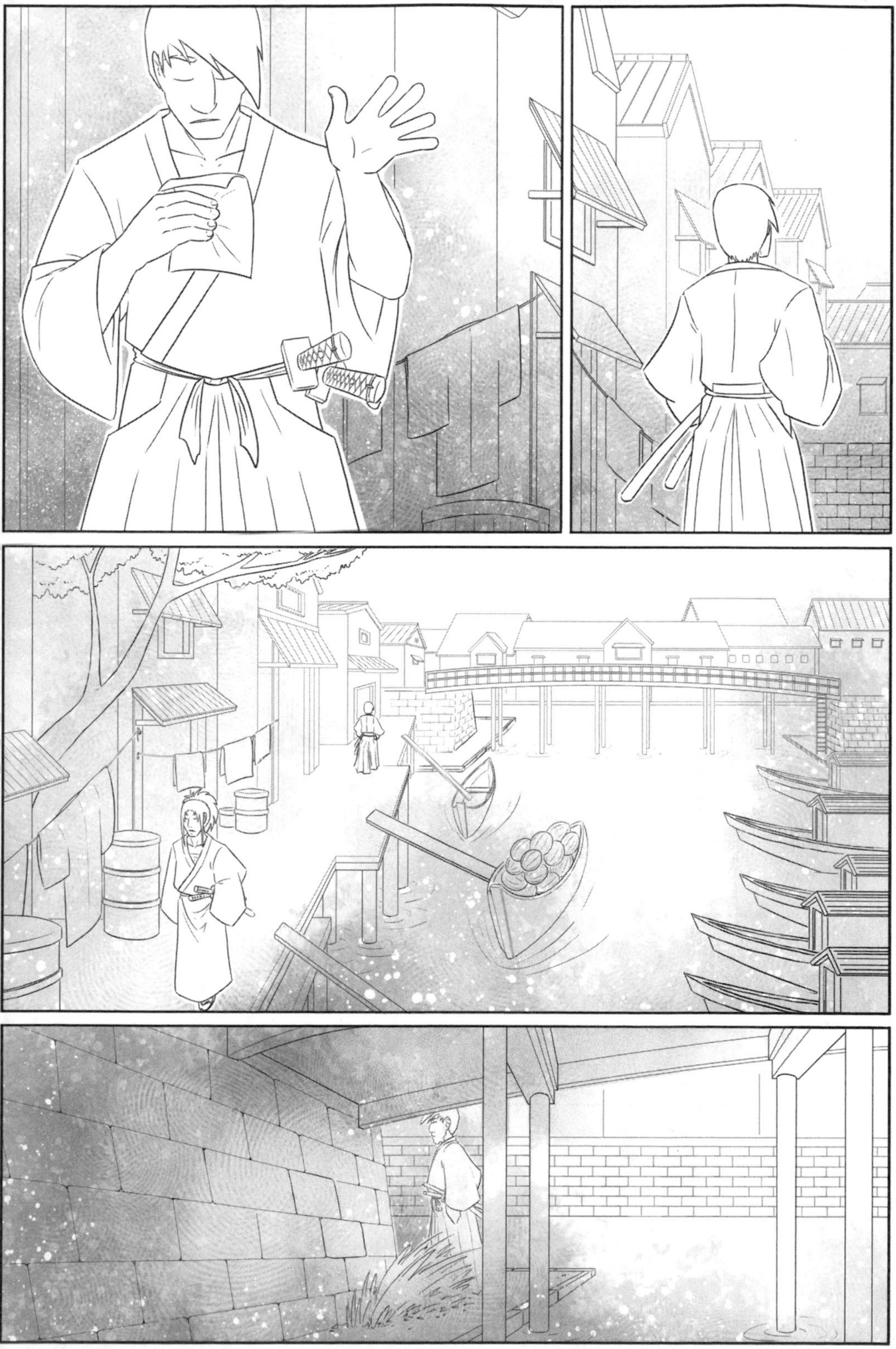

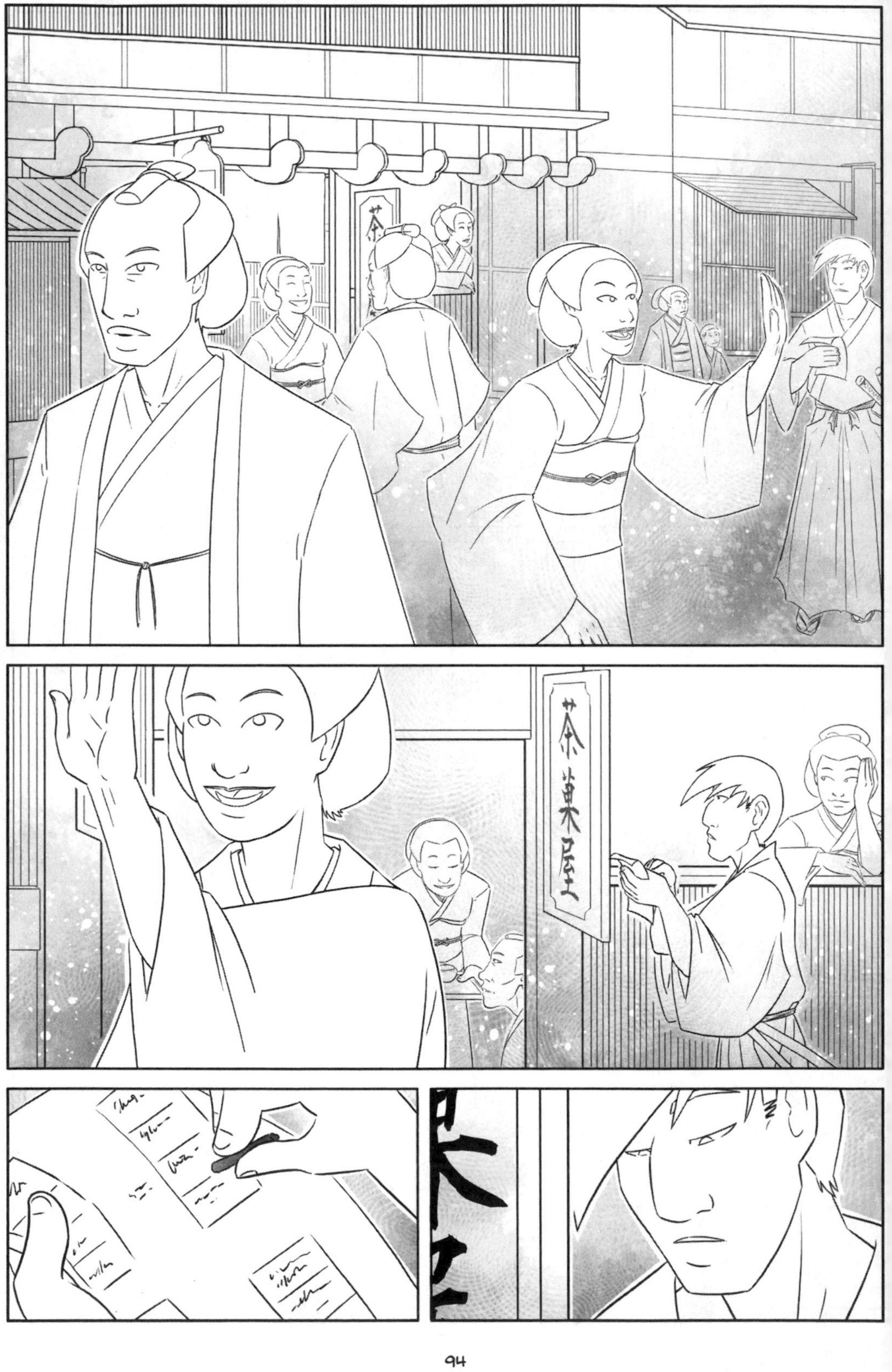
茶菓屋

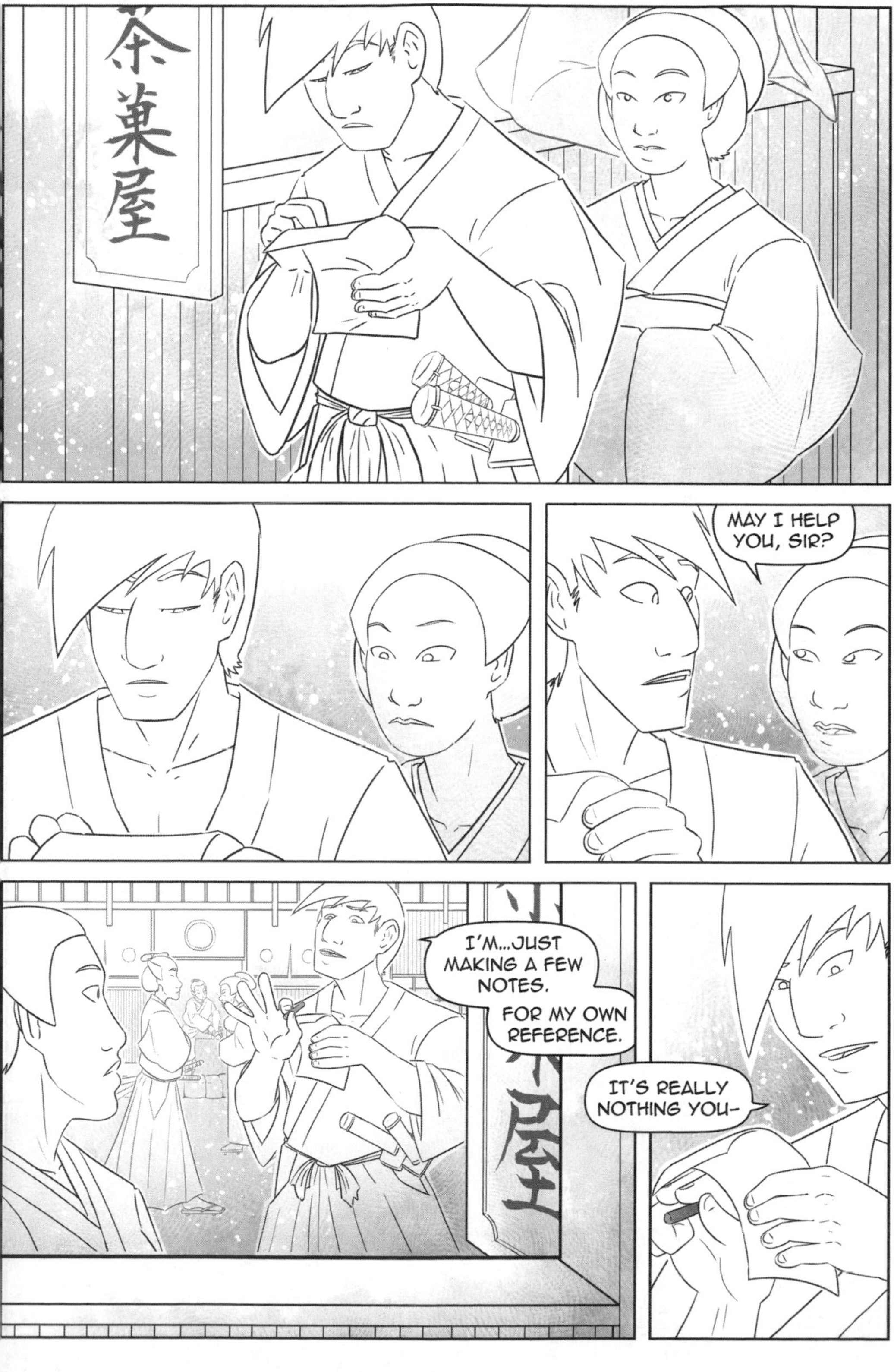

茶菓屋
MAY I HELP YOU, SIR?
I'M...JUST MAKING A FEW NOTES.
FOR MY OWN REFERENCE.
IT'S REALLY NOTHING YOU-

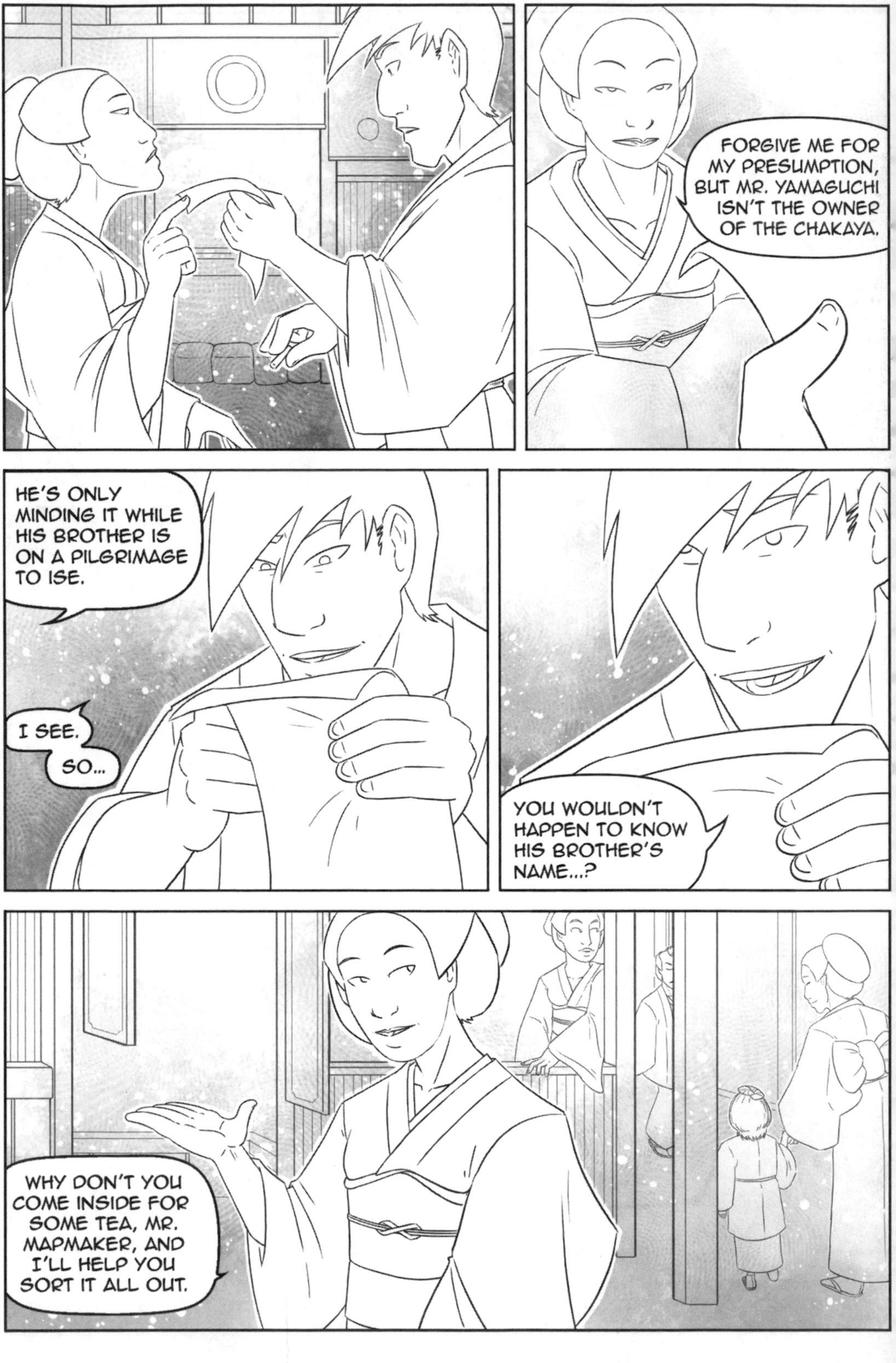
FORGIVE ME FOR MY PRESUMPTION, BUT MR. YAMAGUCHI ISN'T THE OWNER OF THE CHAKAYA.
HE'S ONLY MINDING IT WHILE HIS BROTHER IS ON A PILGRIMAGE TO ISE.
I SEE.
SO...
YOU WOULDN'T HAPPEN TO KNOW HIS BROTHER'S NAME...?
WHY DON'T YOU COME INSIDE FOR SOME TEA, MR. MAPMAKER, AND I'LL HELP YOU SORT IT ALL OUT.

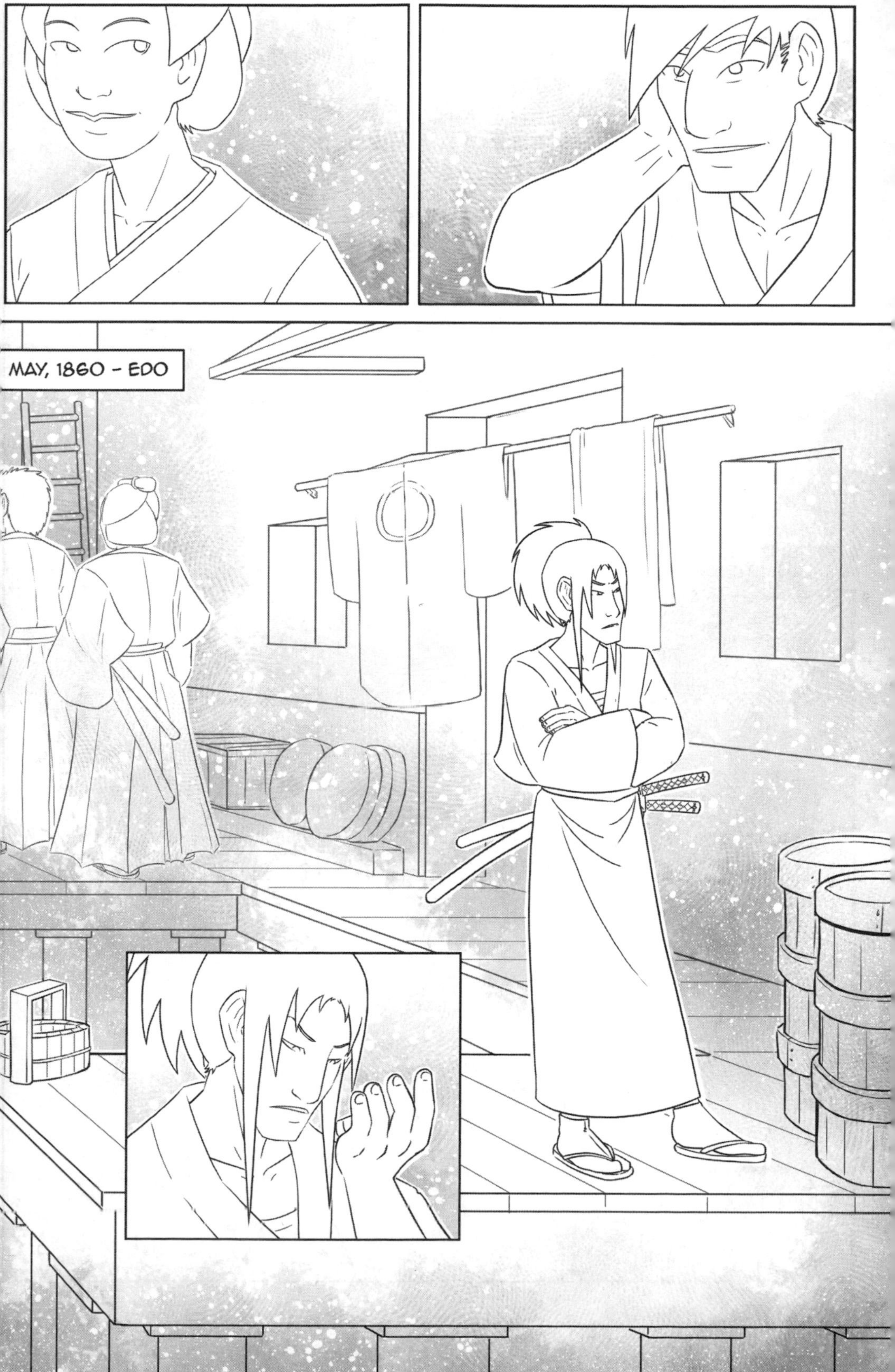
MAY, 1860 - EDO

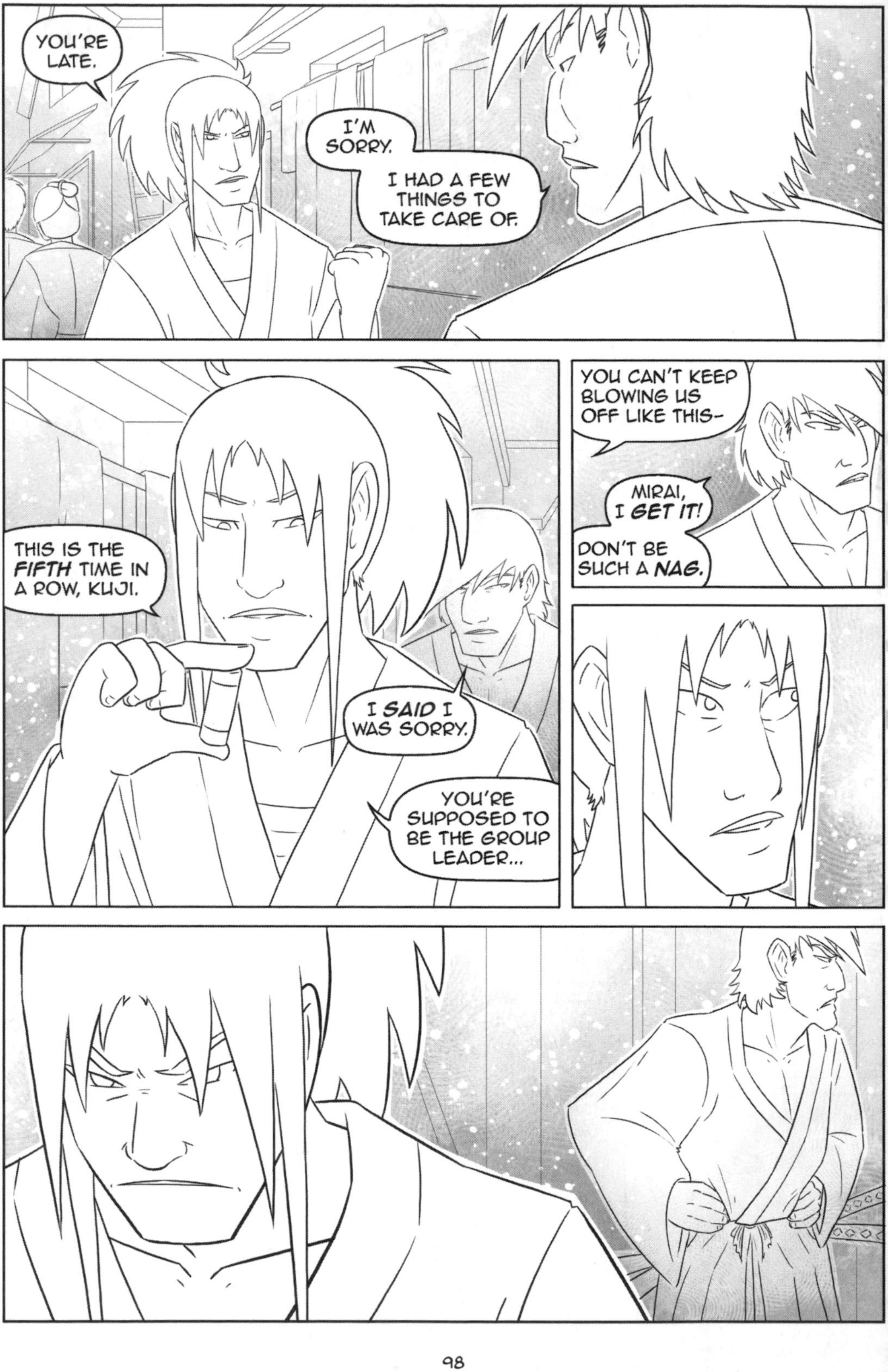
YOU'RE LATE.
I'M SORRY.
I HAD A FEW THINGS TO TAKE CARE OF.
THIS IS THE FIFTH TIME IN A ROW, KUJI.
I SAID I WAS SORRY.
YOU'RE SUPPOSED TO BE THE GROUP LEADER...
YOU CAN'T KEEP BLOWING US OFF LIKE THIS-
MIRAI, I GET IT!
DON'T BE SUCH A NAG.

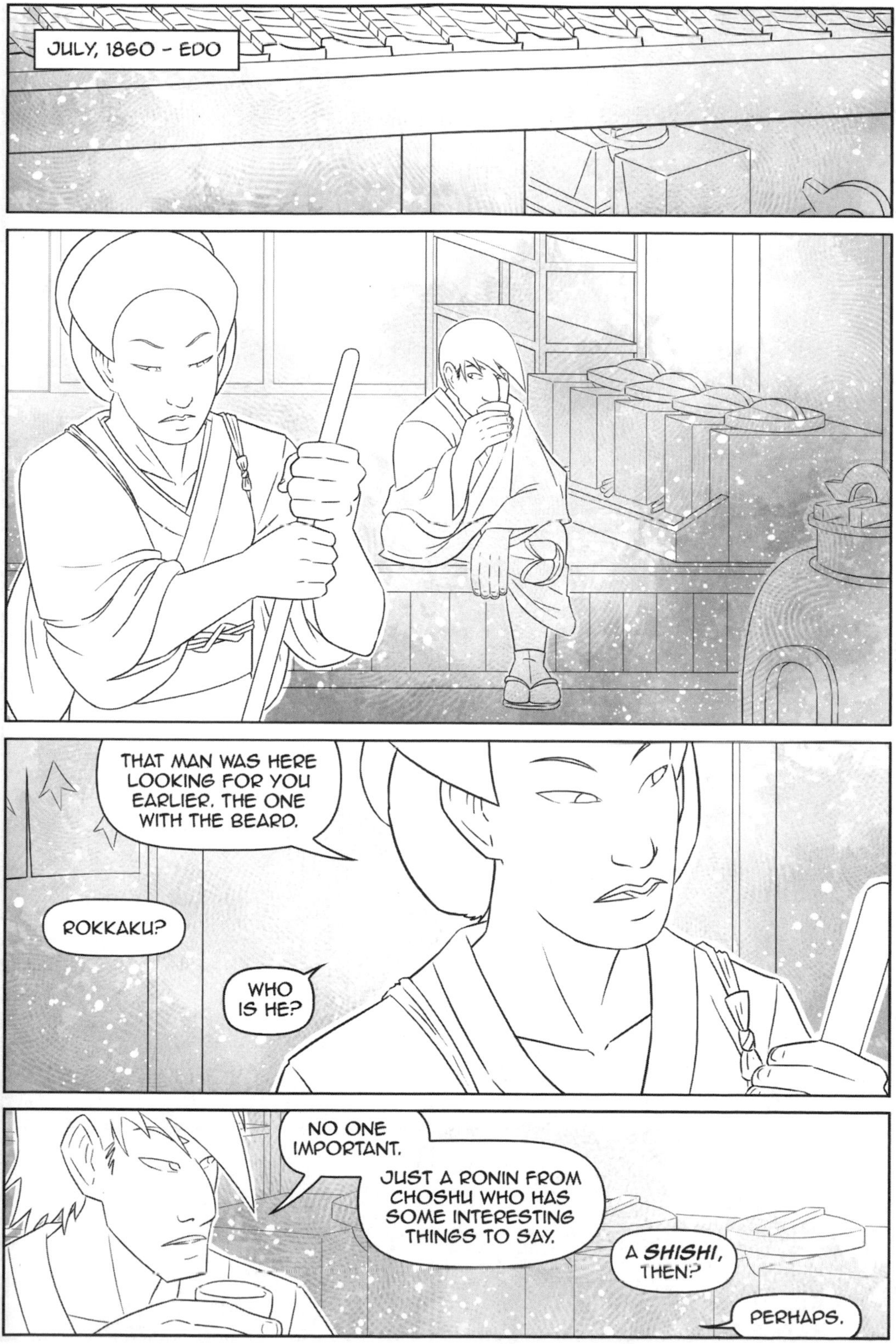
JULY, 1860 - EDO
THAT MAN WAS HERE LOOKING FOR YOU EARLIER. THE ONE WITH THE BEARD.
ROKKAKU?
WHO IS HE?
NO ONE IMPORTANT.
JUST A RONIN FROM CHOSHU WHO HAS SOME INTERESTING THINGS TO SAY.
A *SHISHI*, THEN?
PERHAPS.

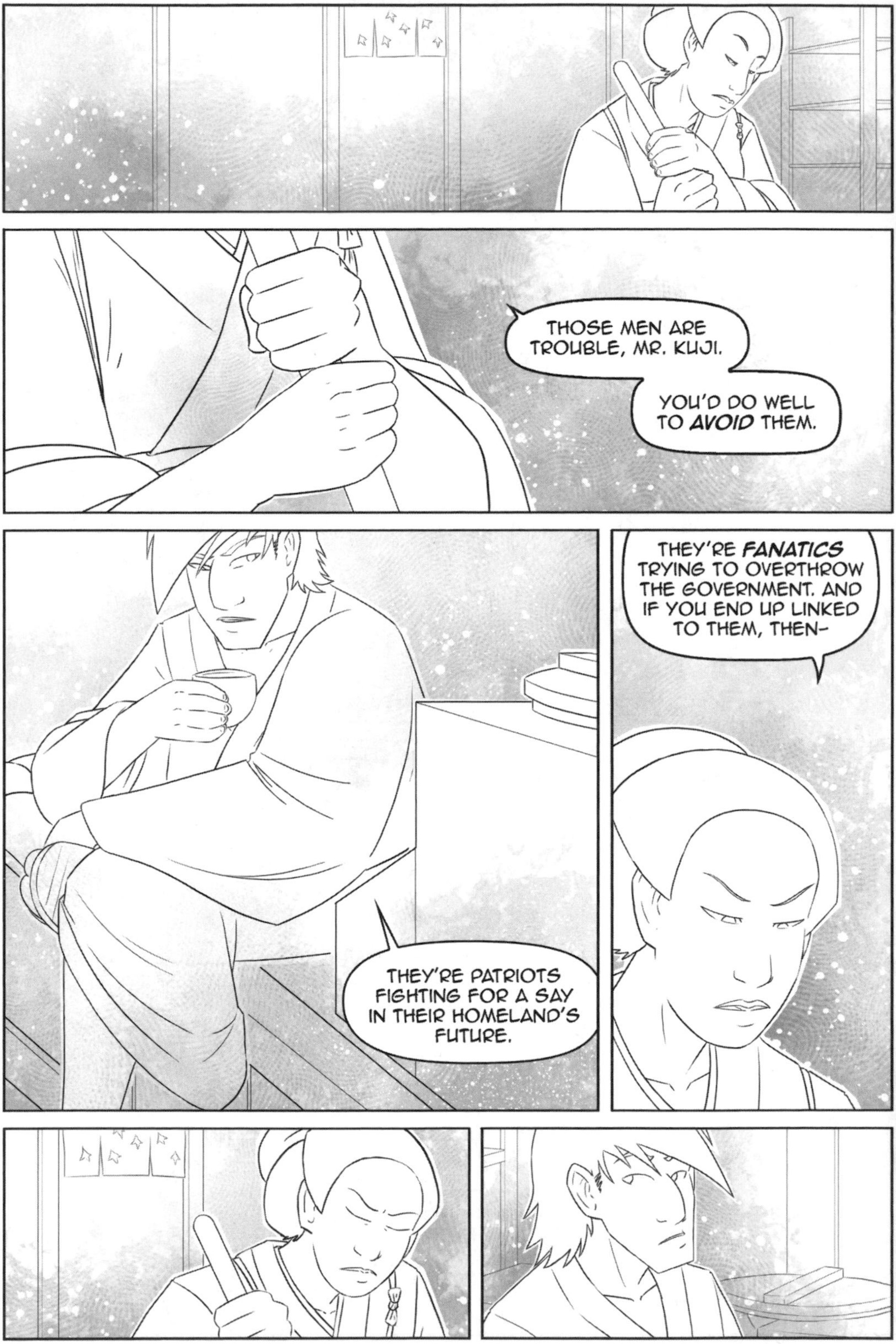
THOSE MEN ARE TROUBLE, MR. KUJI.
YOU'D DO WELL TO ***AVOID*** THEM.
THEY'RE PATRIOTS FIGHTING FOR A SAY IN THEIR HOMELAND'S FUTURE.
THEY'RE ***FANATICS*** TRYING TO OVERTHROW THE GOVERNMENT. AND IF YOU END UP LINKED TO THEM, THEN-

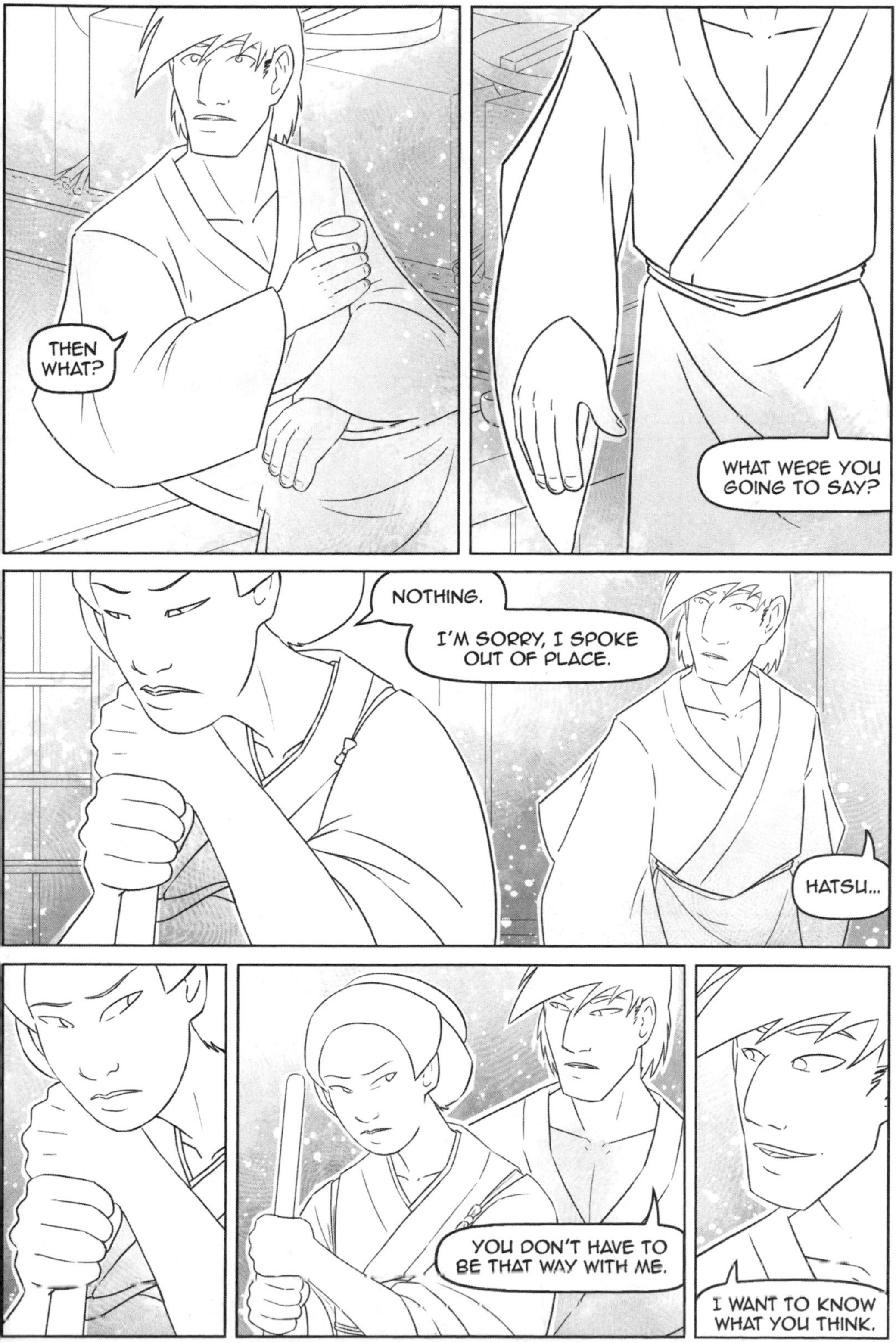
THEN WHAT?
WHAT WERE YOU GOING TO SAY?
NOTHING.
I'M SORRY, I SPOKE OUT OF PLACE.
HATSU...
YOU DON'T HAVE TO BE THAT WAY WITH ME.
I WANT TO KNOW WHAT YOU THINK.

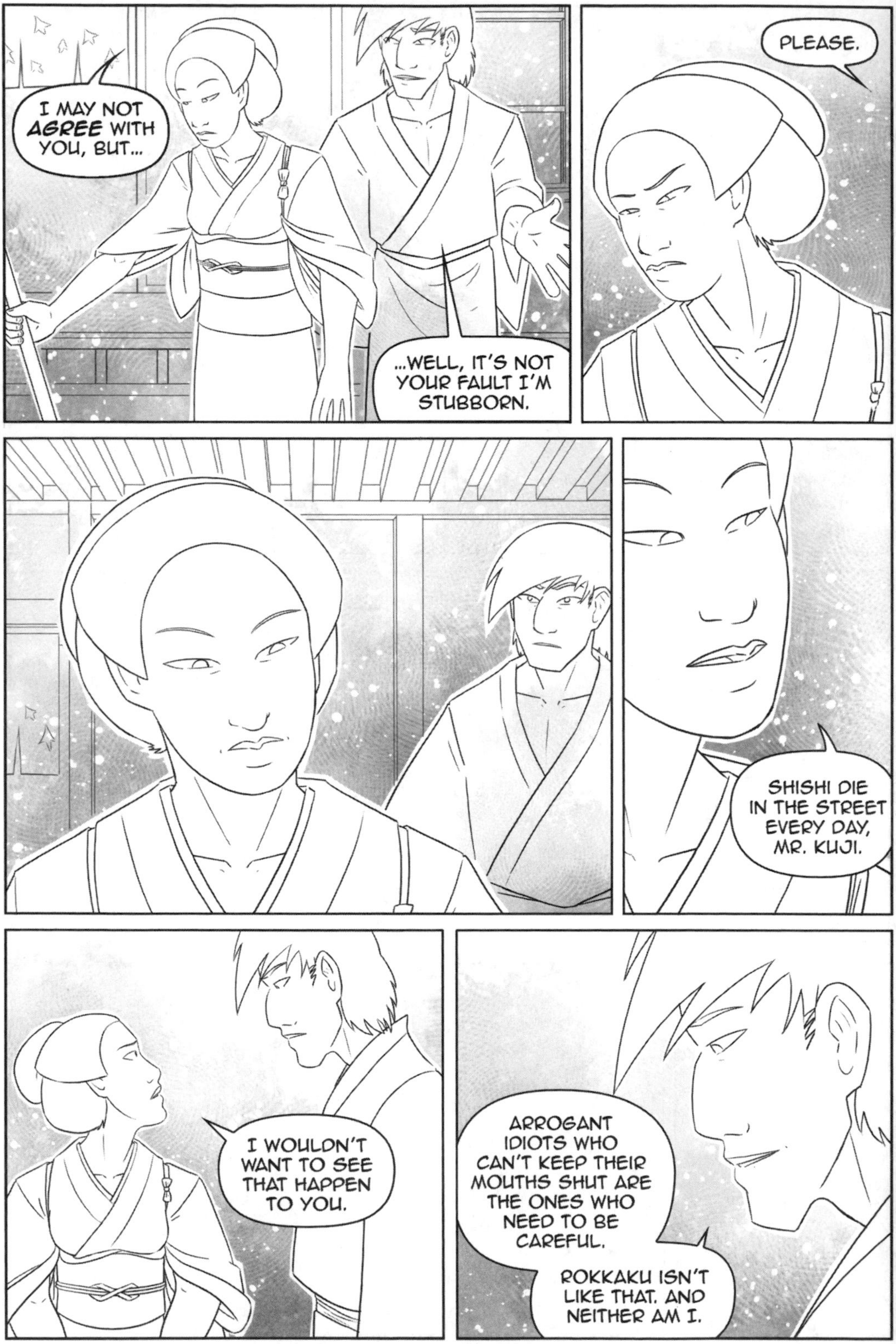
I MAY NOT AGREE WITH YOU, BUT...
...WELL, IT'S NOT YOUR FAULT I'M STUBBORN.
PLEASE.
SHISHI DIE IN THE STREET EVERY DAY, MR. KUJI.
I WOULDN'T WANT TO SEE THAT HAPPEN TO YOU.
ARROGANT IDIOTS WHO CAN'T KEEP THEIR MOUTHS SHUT ARE THE ONES WHO NEED TO BE CAREFUL.
ROKKAKU ISN'T LIKE THAT. AND NEITHER AM I.

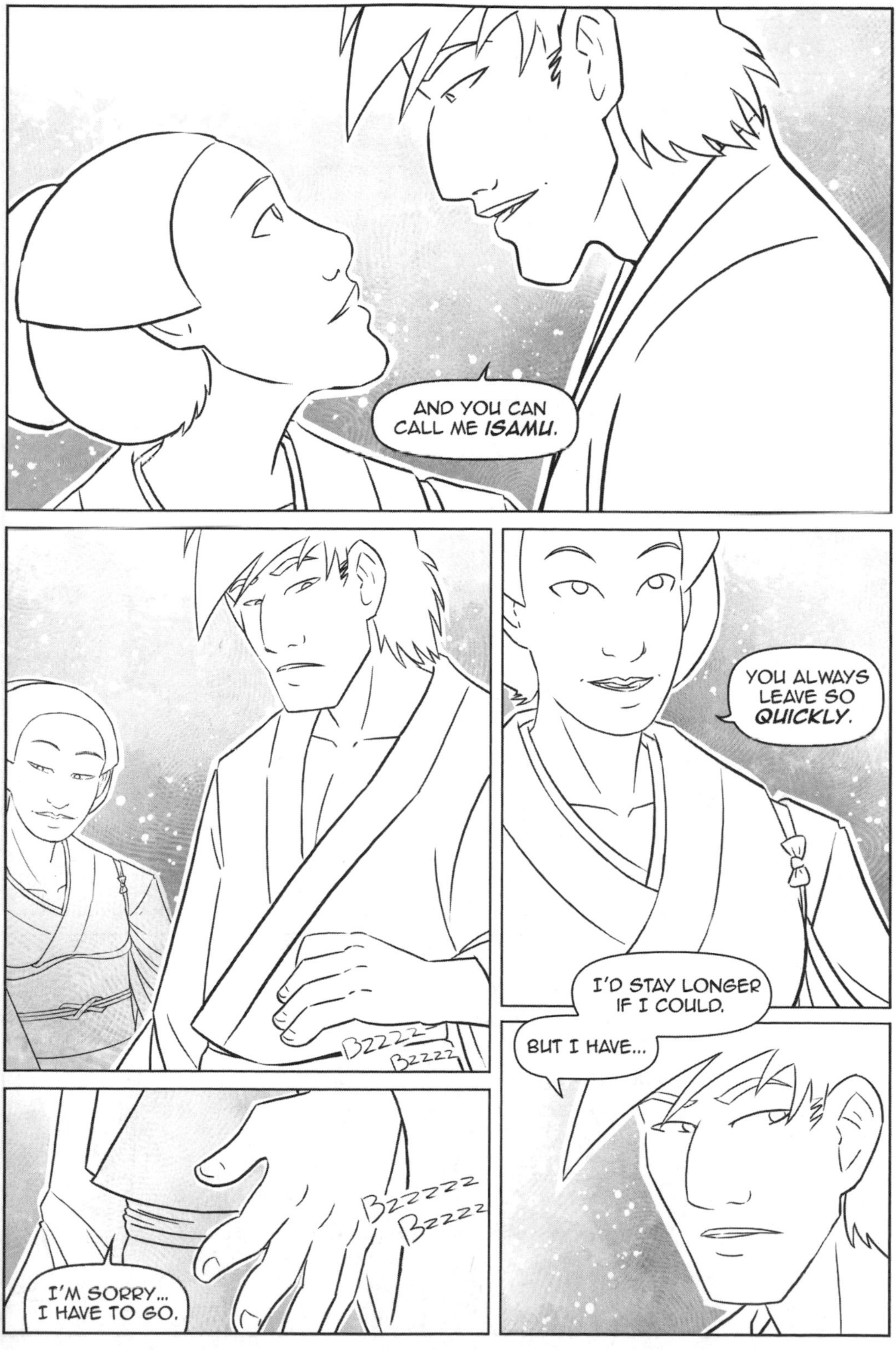
AND YOU CAN CALL ME ISAMU.
BZZZZ BZZZZ
YOU ALWAYS LEAVE SO QUICKLY.
I'D STAY LONGER IF I COULD.
BUT I HAVE...
BZZZZZ BZZZZ
I'M SORRY... I HAVE TO GO.

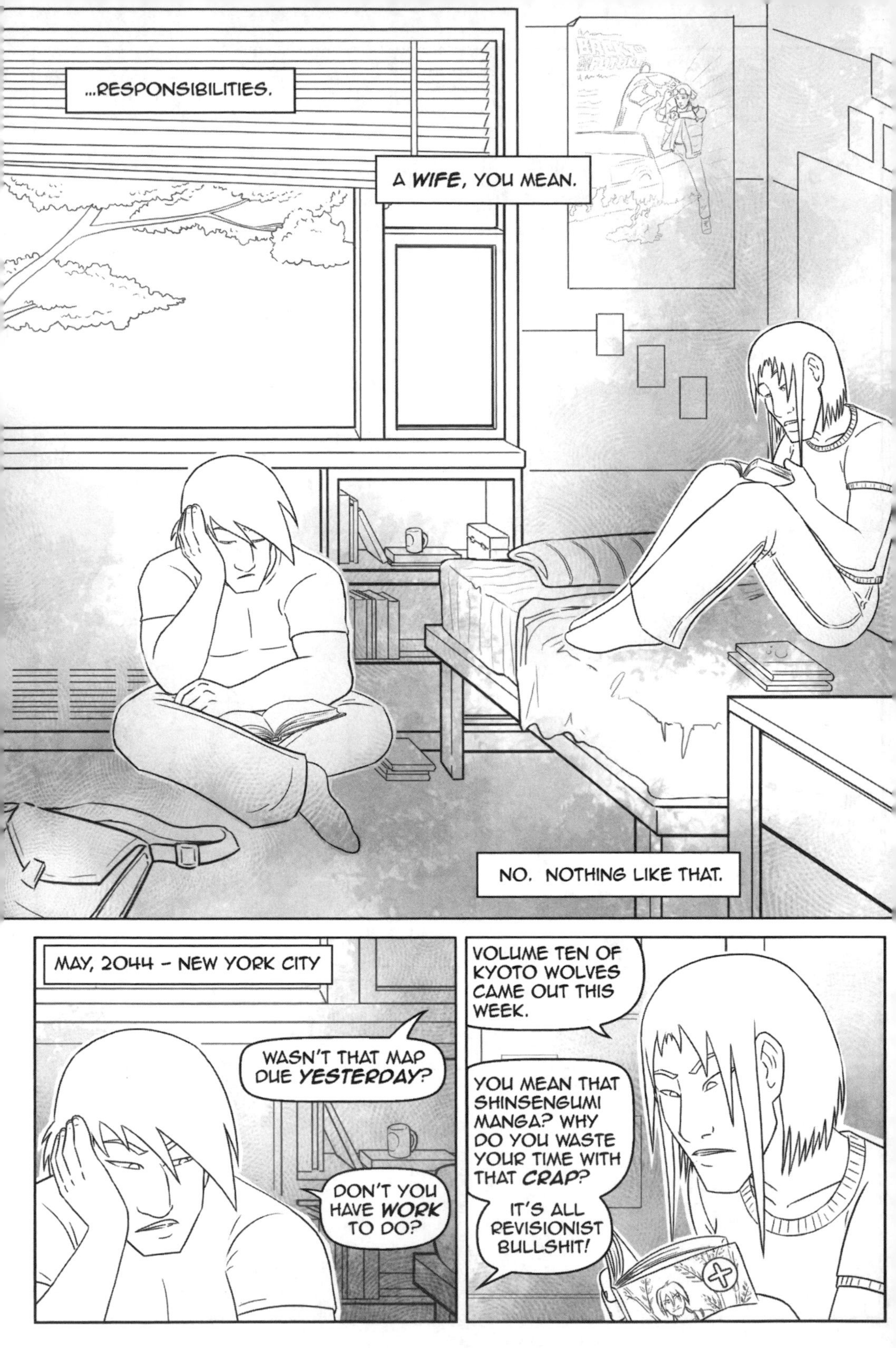
...RESPONSIBILITIES.
A WIFE, YOU MEAN.
NO. NOTHING LIKE THAT.
MAY, 2044 - NEW YORK CITY
WASN'T THAT MAP DUE YESTERDAY?
DON'T YOU HAVE WORK TO DO?
VOLUME TEN OF KYOTO WOLVES CAME OUT THIS WEEK.
YOU MEAN THAT SHINSENGUMI MANGA? WHY DO YOU WASTE YOUR TIME WITH THAT CRAP?
IT'S ALL REVISIONIST BULLSHIT!

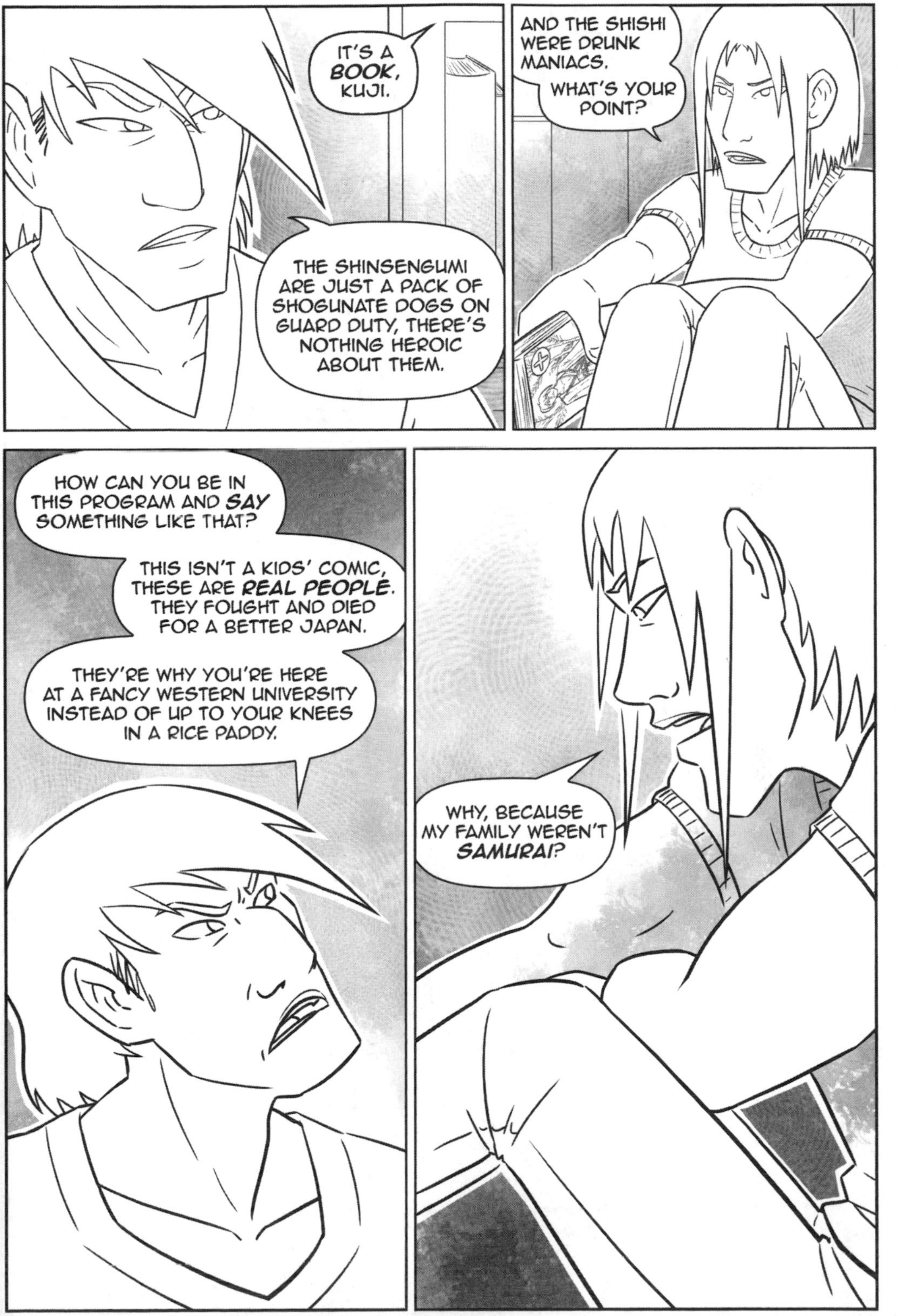
IT'S A **BOOK**, KUJI.
THE SHINSENGUMI ARE JUST A PACK OF SHOGUNATE DOGS ON GUARD DUTY, THERE'S NOTHING HEROIC ABOUT THEM.
AND THE SHISHI WERE DRUNK MANIACS.
WHAT'S YOUR POINT?
HOW CAN YOU BE IN THIS PROGRAM AND ***SAY*** SOMETHING LIKE THAT?
THIS ISN'T A KIDS' COMIC, THESE ARE ***REAL PEOPLE***. THEY FOUGHT AND DIED FOR A BETTER JAPAN.
THEY'RE WHY YOU'RE HERE AT A FANCY WESTERN UNIVERSITY INSTEAD OF UP TO YOUR KNEES IN A RICE PADDY.
WHY, BECAUSE MY FAMILY WEREN'T ***SAMURAI***?

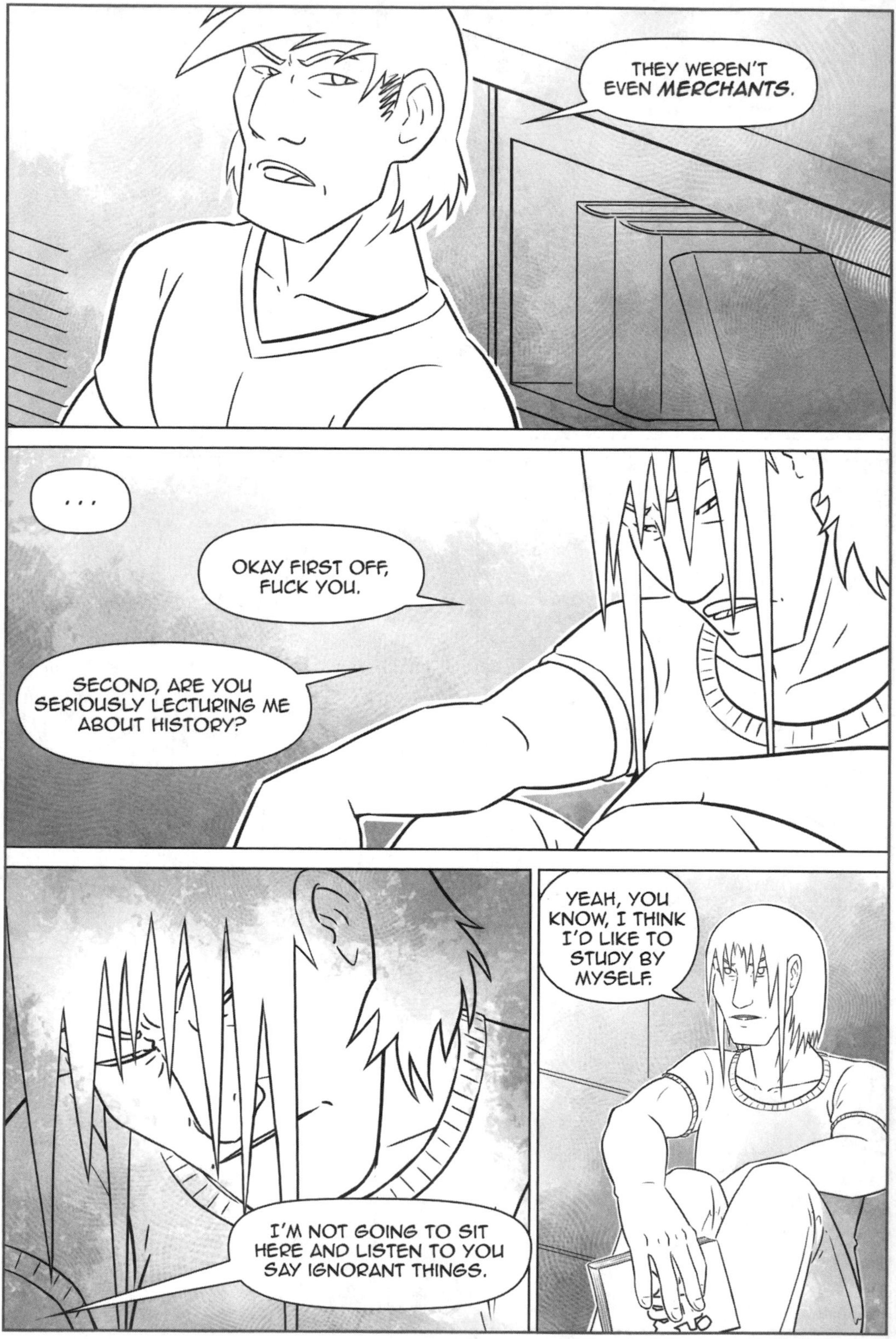
THEY WEREN'T EVEN MERCHANTS.
. . .
OKAY FIRST OFF, FUCK YOU.
SECOND, ARE YOU SERIOUSLY LECTURING ME ABOUT HISTORY?
I'M NOT GOING TO SIT HERE AND LISTEN TO YOU SAY IGNORANT THINGS.
YEAH, YOU KNOW, I THINK I'D LIKE TO STUDY BY MYSELF.

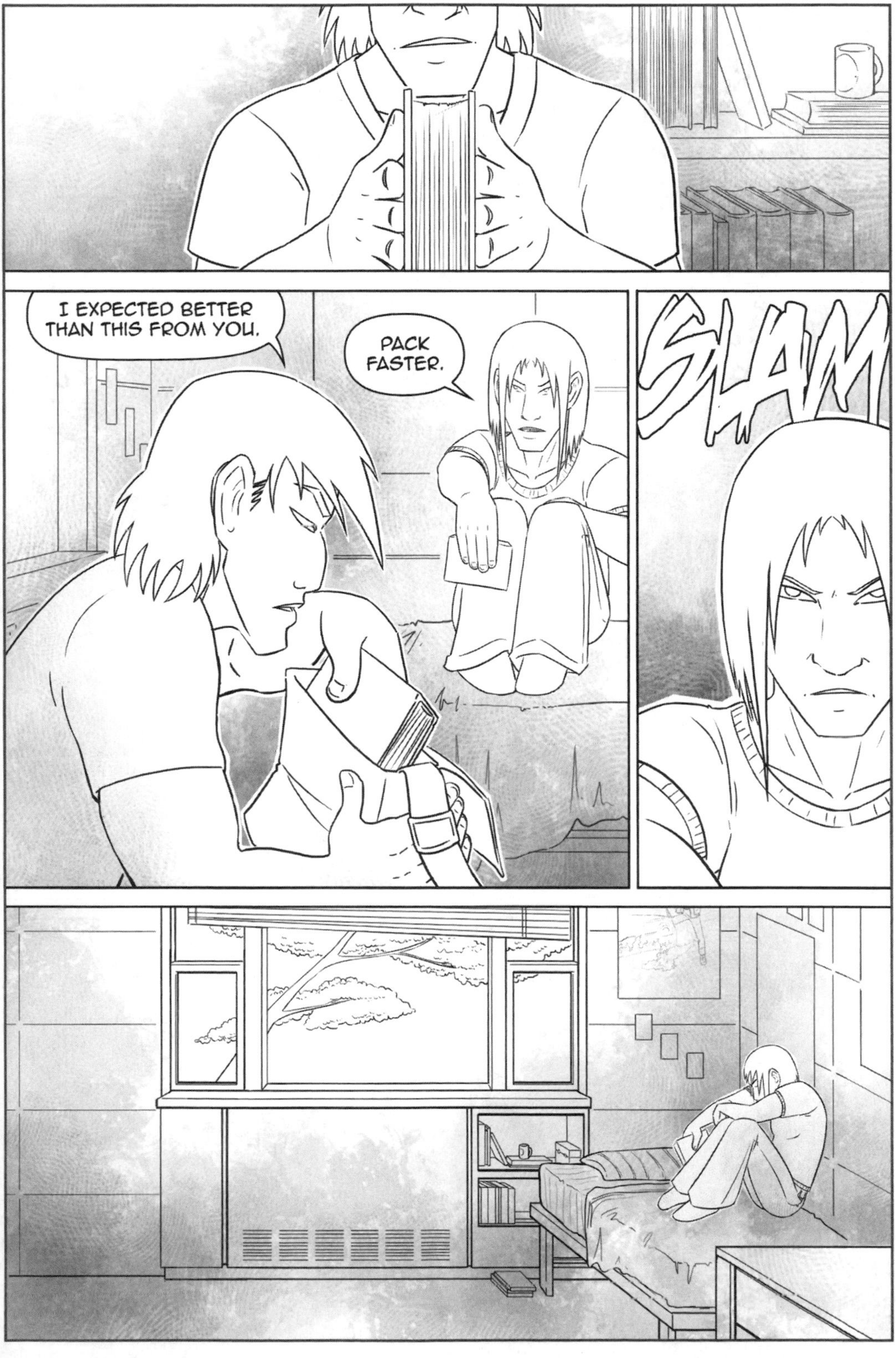
I EXPECTED BETTER THAN THIS FROM YOU.
PACK FASTER.
SLAM

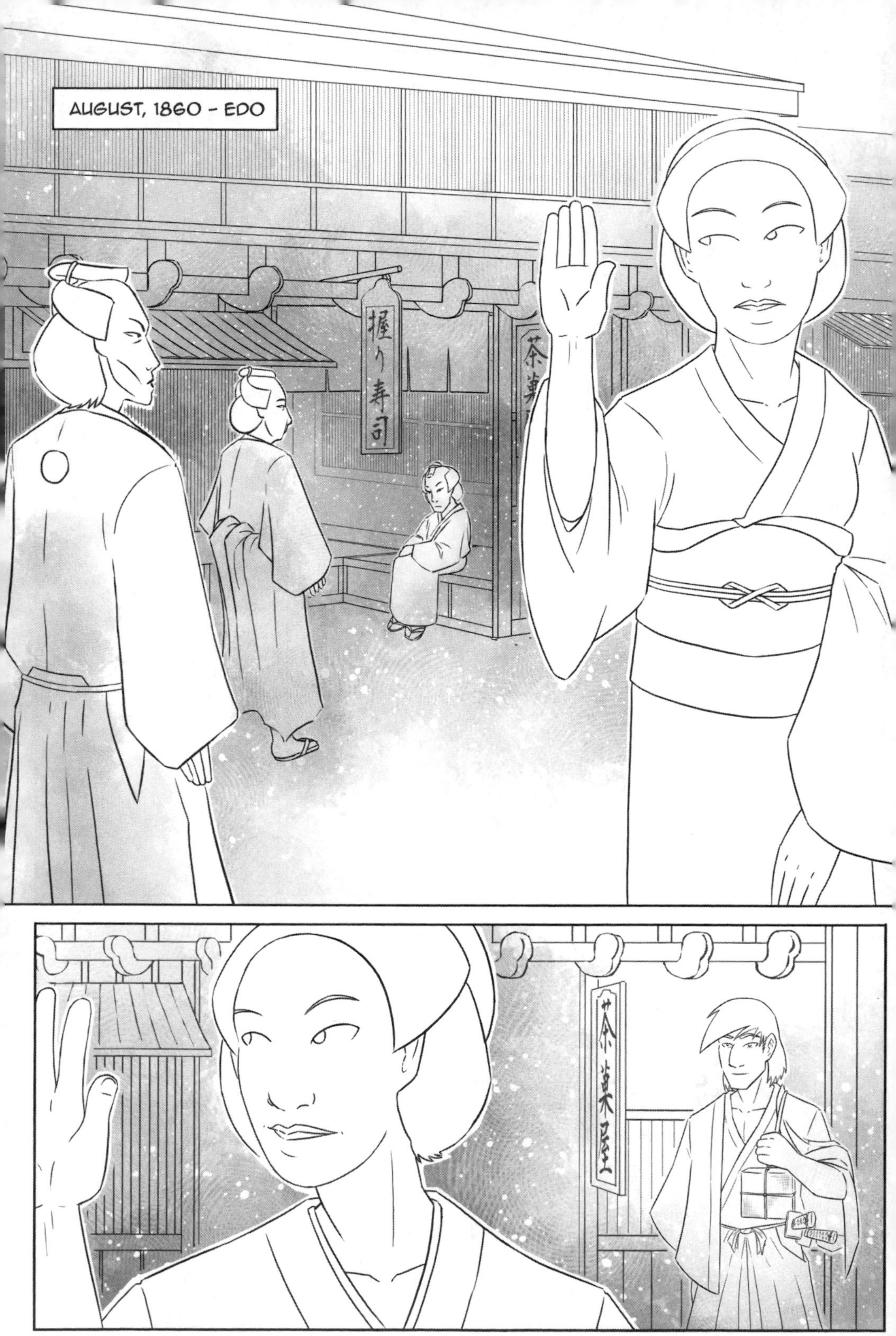
AUGUST, 1860 - EDO
握り寿司
茶菓屋

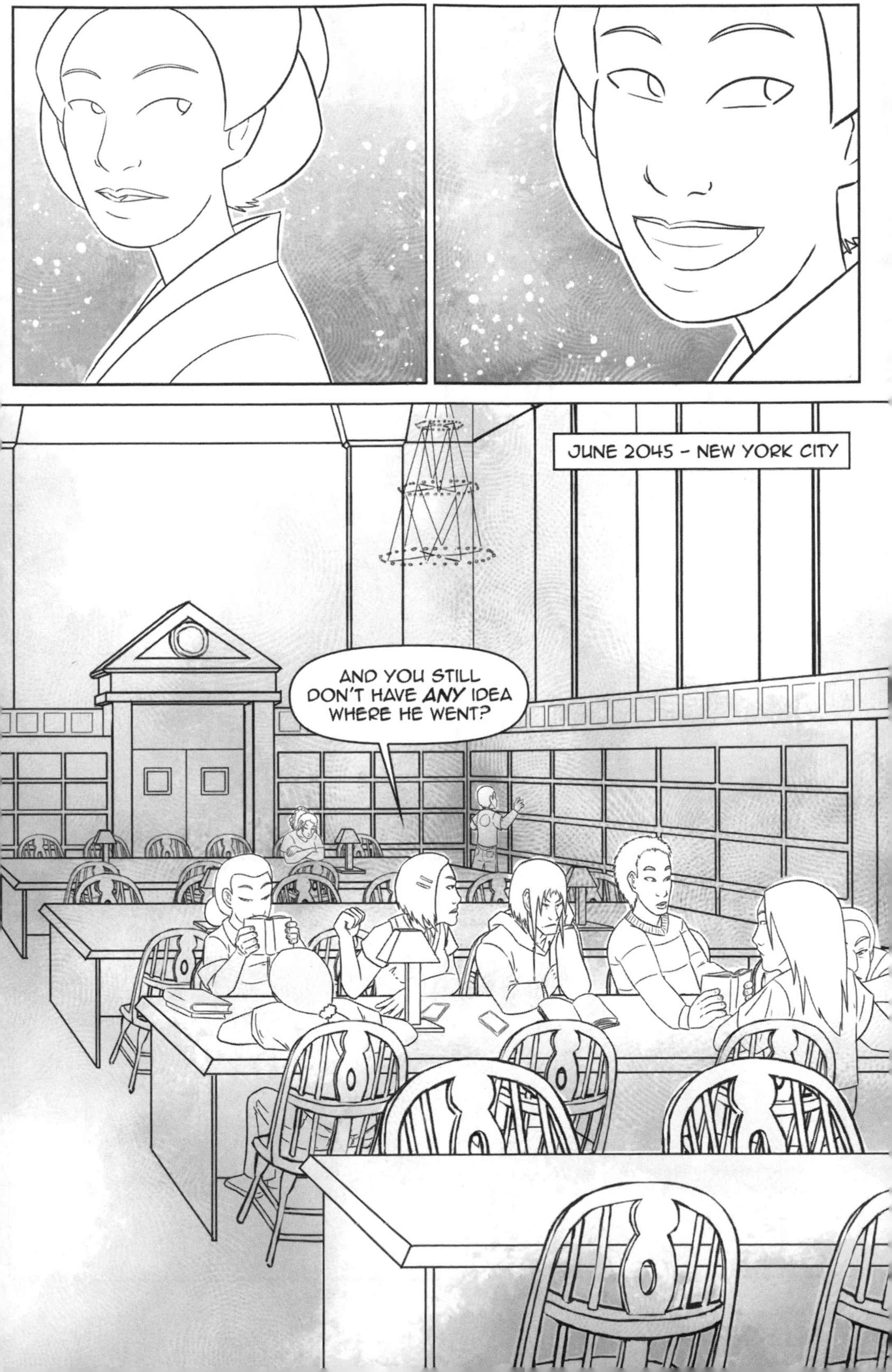
JUNE 2045 - NEW YORK CITY
AND YOU STILL DON'T HAVE *ANY* IDEA WHERE HE WENT?

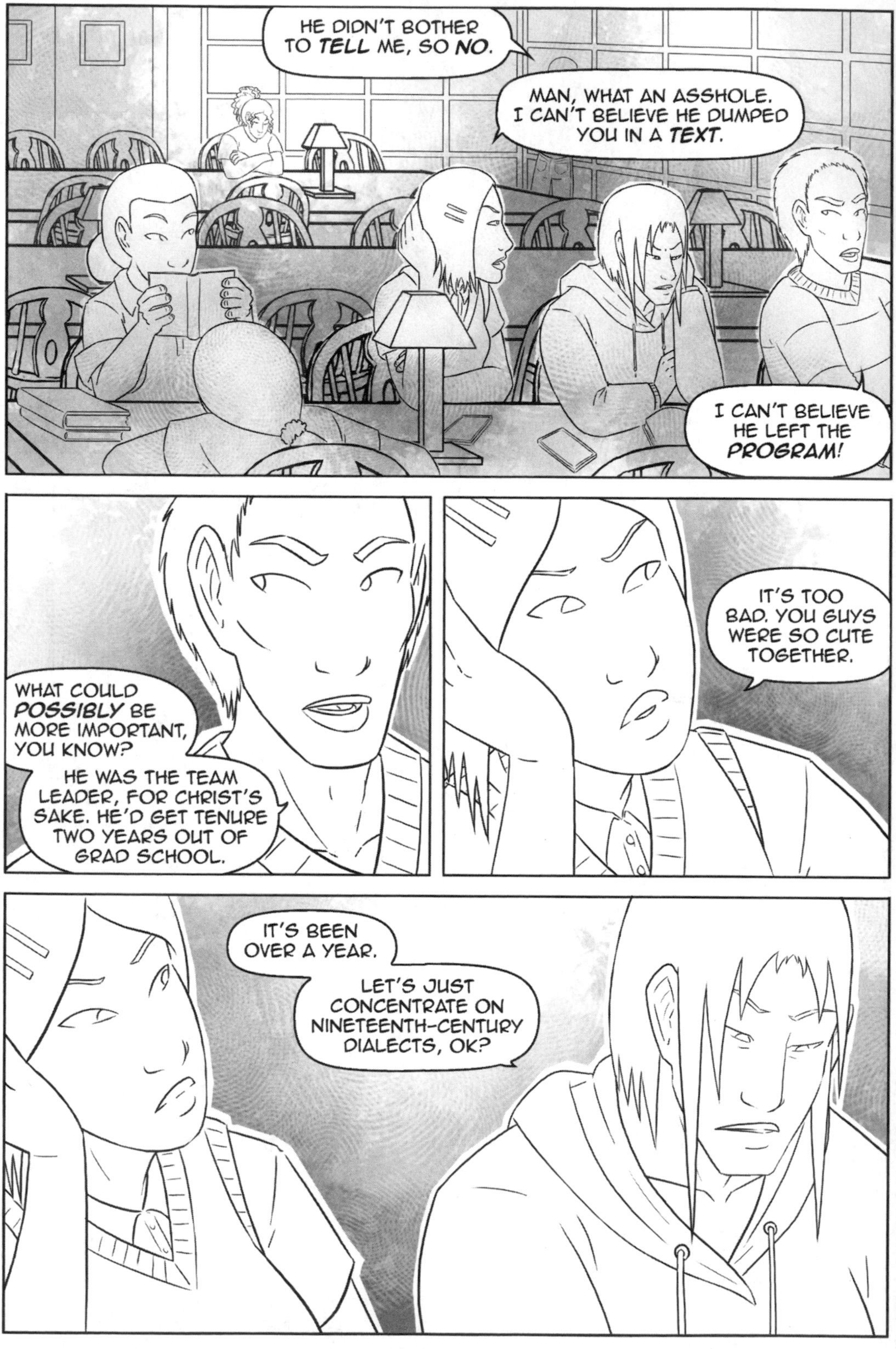
HE DIDN'T BOTHER TO TELL ME, SO NO.
MAN, WHAT AN ASSHOLE. I CAN'T BELIEVE HE DUMPED YOU IN A TEXT.
I CAN'T BELIEVE HE LEFT THE PROGRAM!
WHAT COULD POSSIBLY BE MORE IMPORTANT, YOU KNOW?
HE WAS THE TEAM LEADER, FOR CHRIST'S SAKE. HE'D GET TENURE TWO YEARS OUT OF GRAD SCHOOL.
IT'S TOO BAD. YOU GUYS WERE SO CUTE TOGETHER.
IT'S BEEN OVER A YEAR.
LET'S JUST CONCENTRATE ON NINETEENTH-CENTURY DIALECTS, OK?

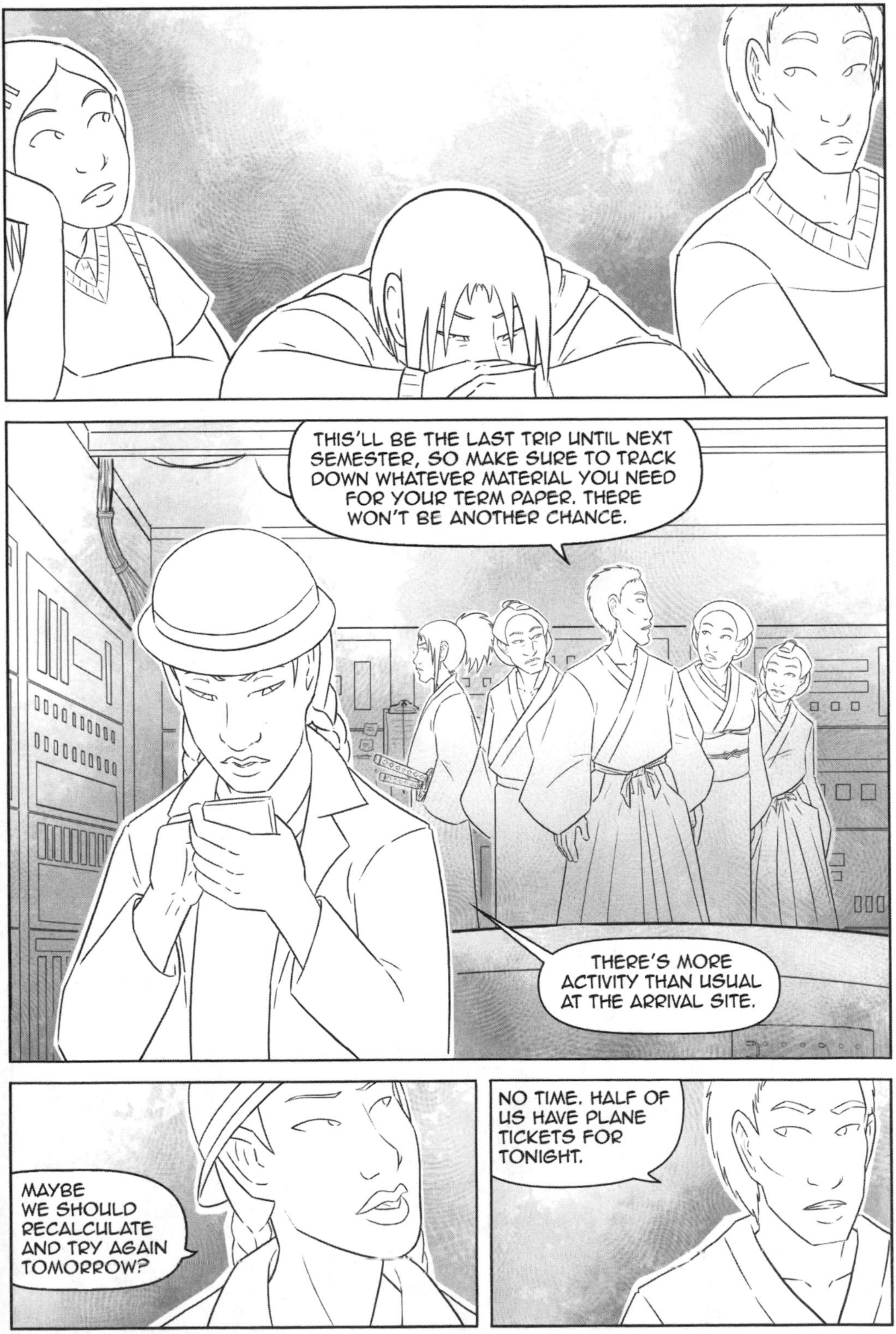
THIS'LL BE THE LAST TRIP UNTIL NEXT SEMESTER, SO MAKE SURE TO TRACK DOWN WHATEVER MATERIAL YOU NEED FOR YOUR TERM PAPER. THERE WON'T BE ANOTHER CHANCE.
THERE'S MORE ACTIVITY THAN USUAL AT THE ARRIVAL SITE.
MAYBE WE SHOULD RECALCULATE AND TRY AGAIN TOMORROW?
NO TIME. HALF OF US HAVE PLANE TICKETS FOR TONIGHT.

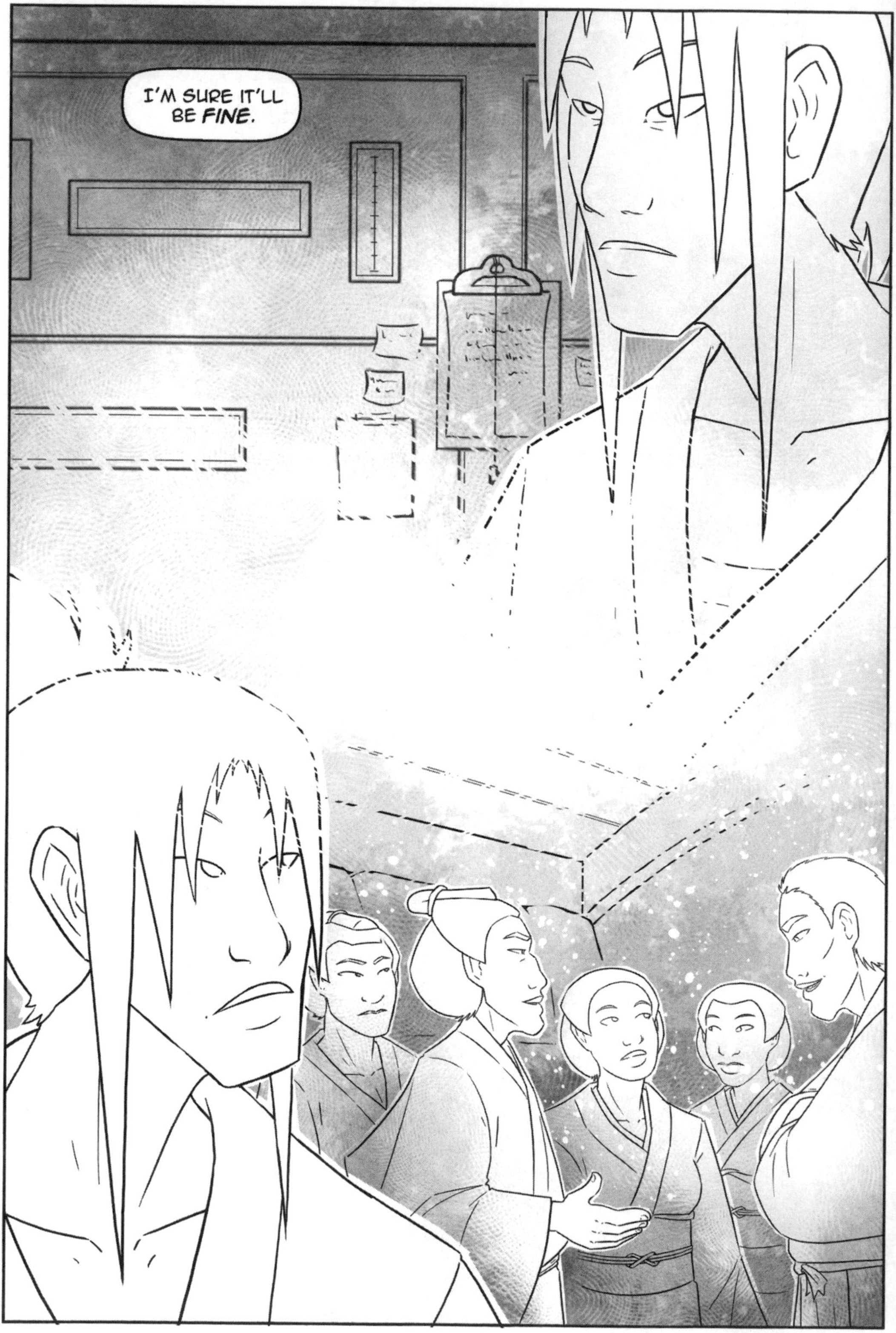
I'M SURE IT'LL BE FINE.

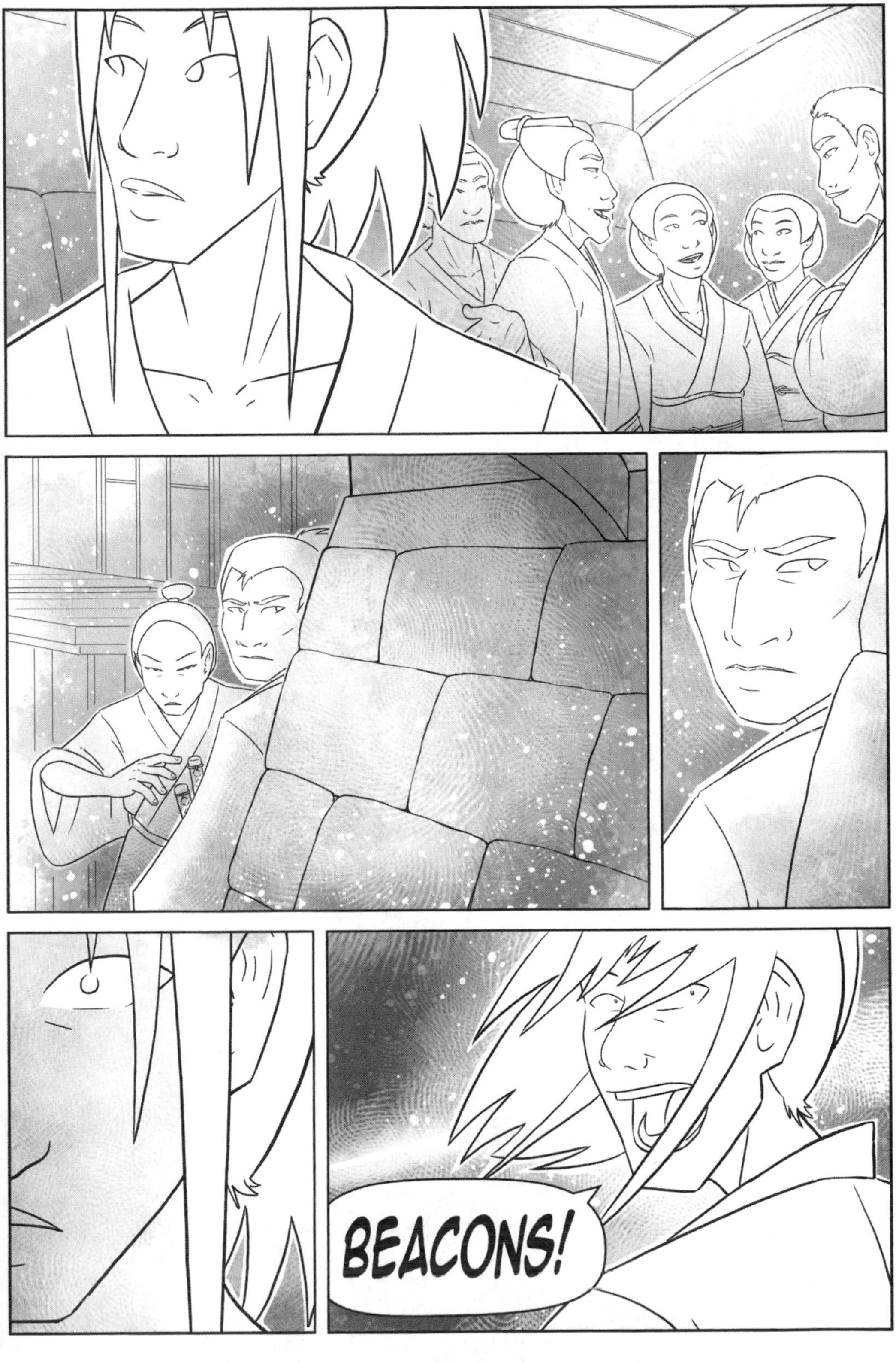
BEACONS!

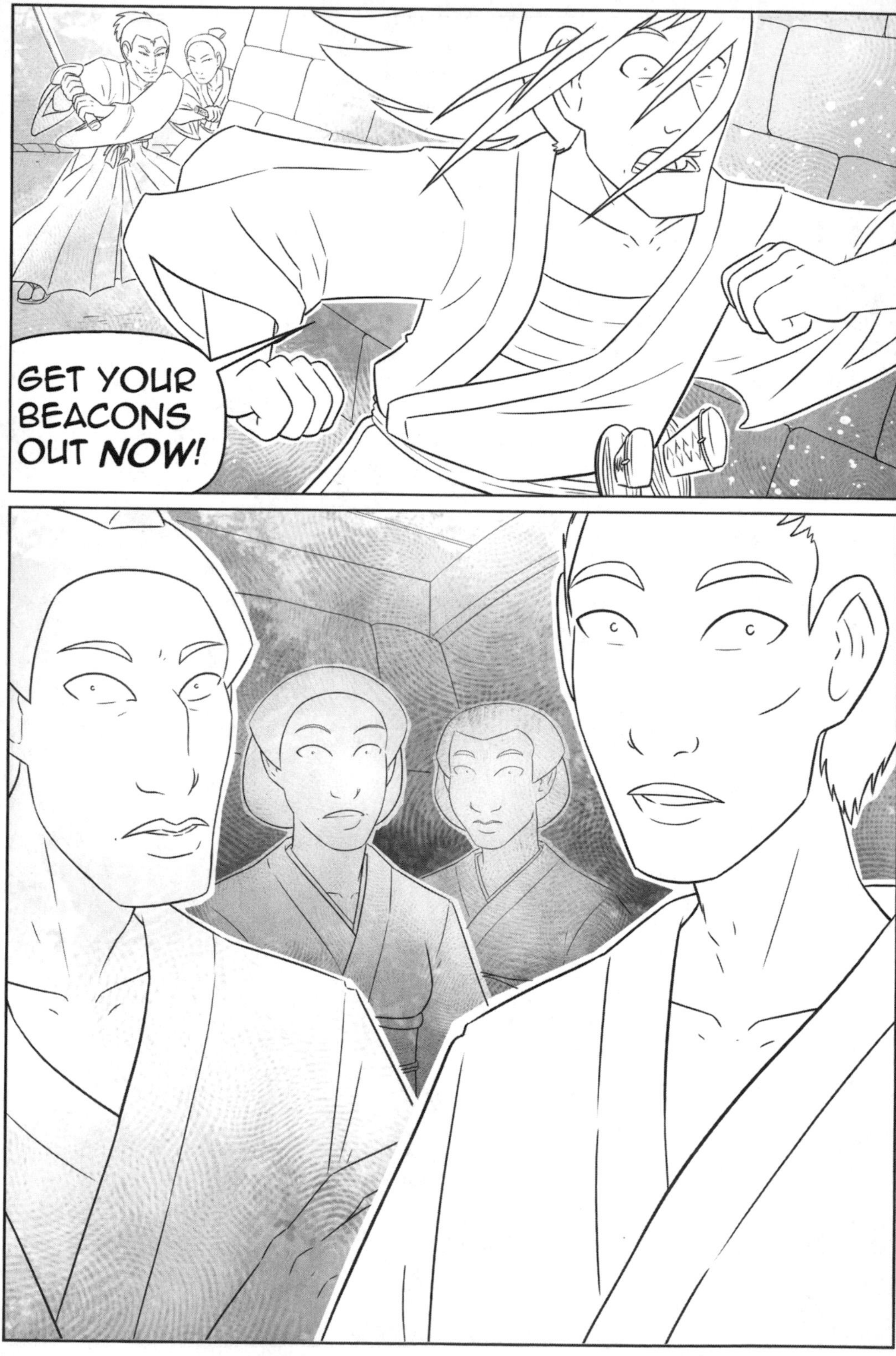
GET YOUR BEACONS OUT NOW!

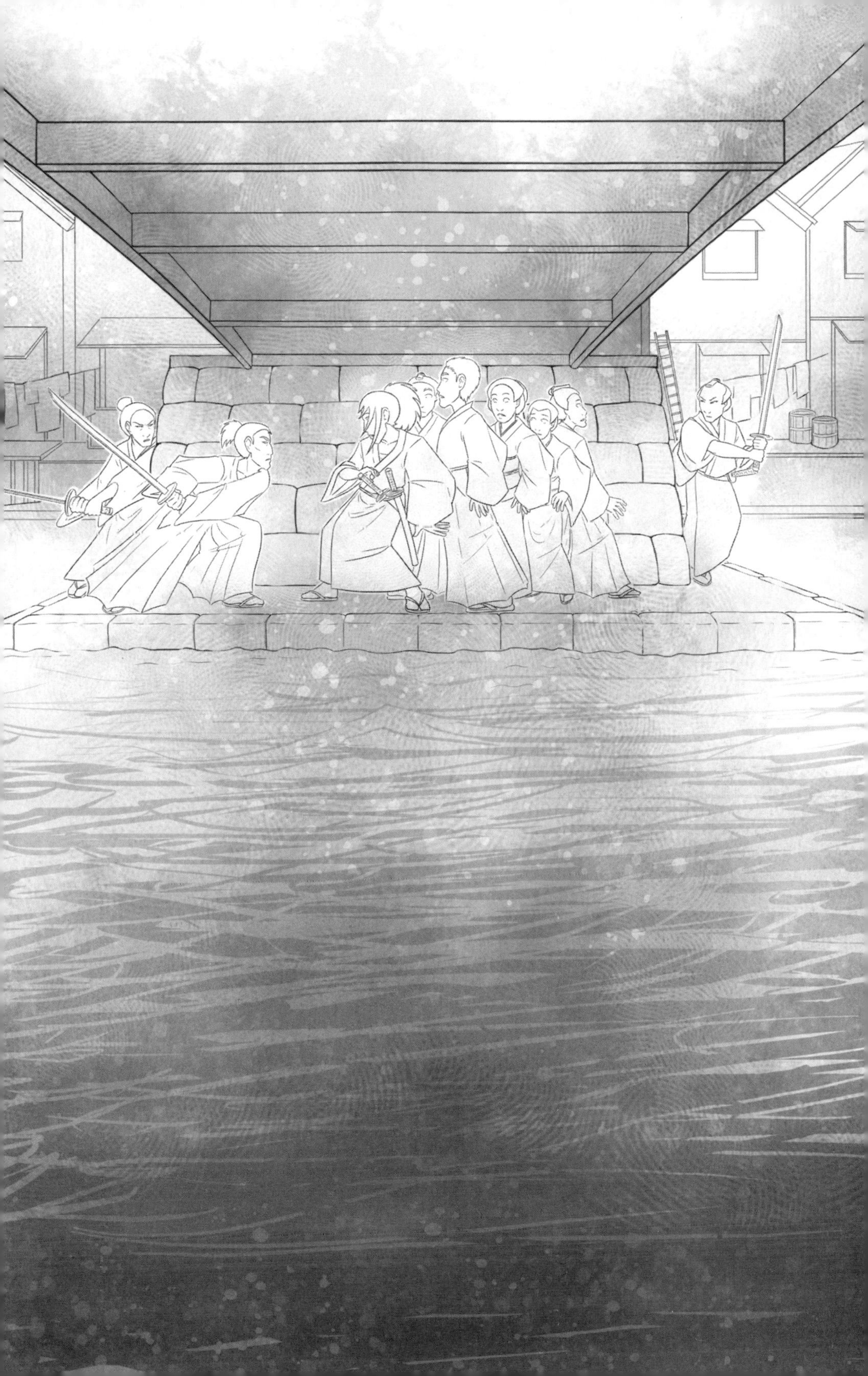

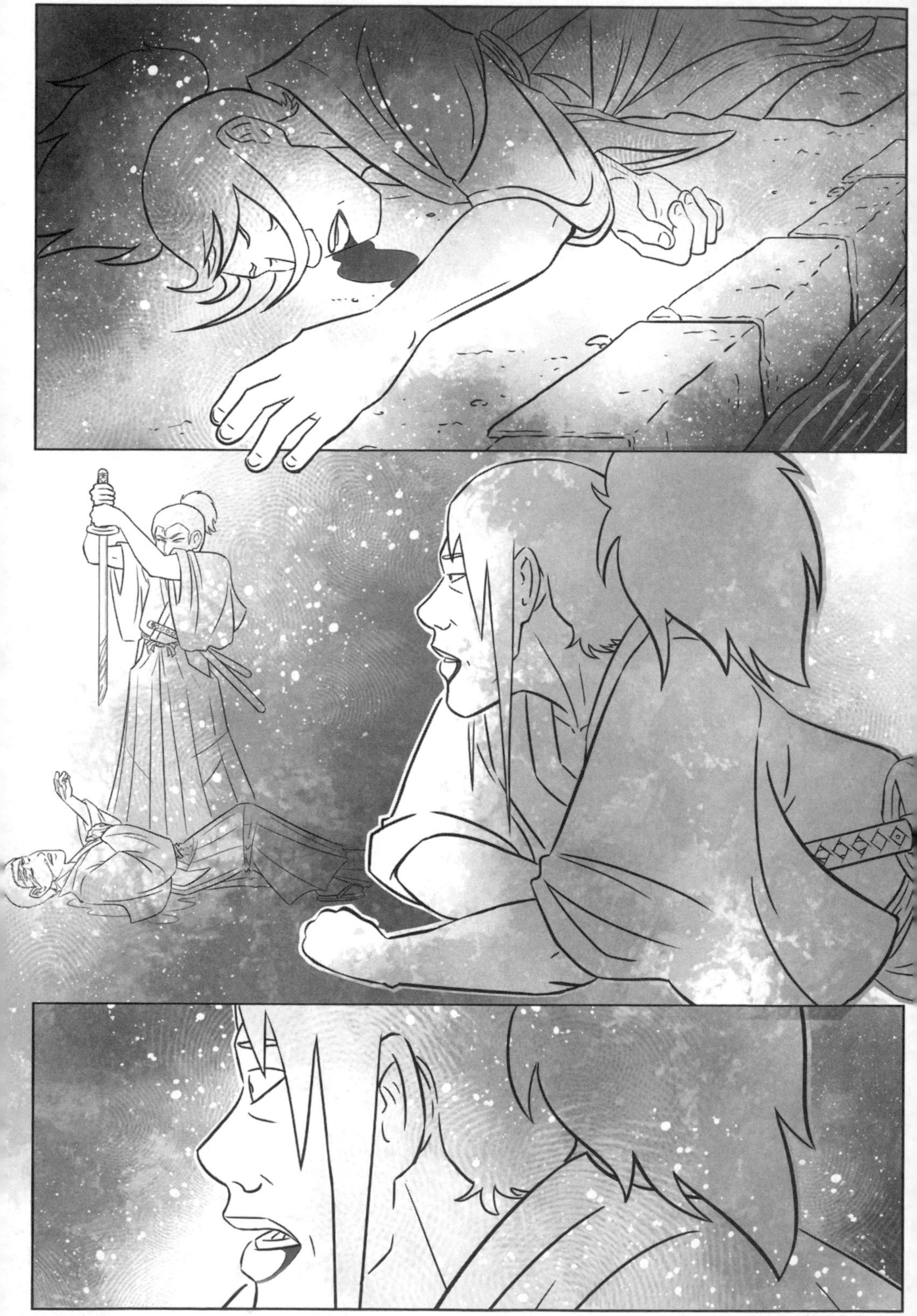

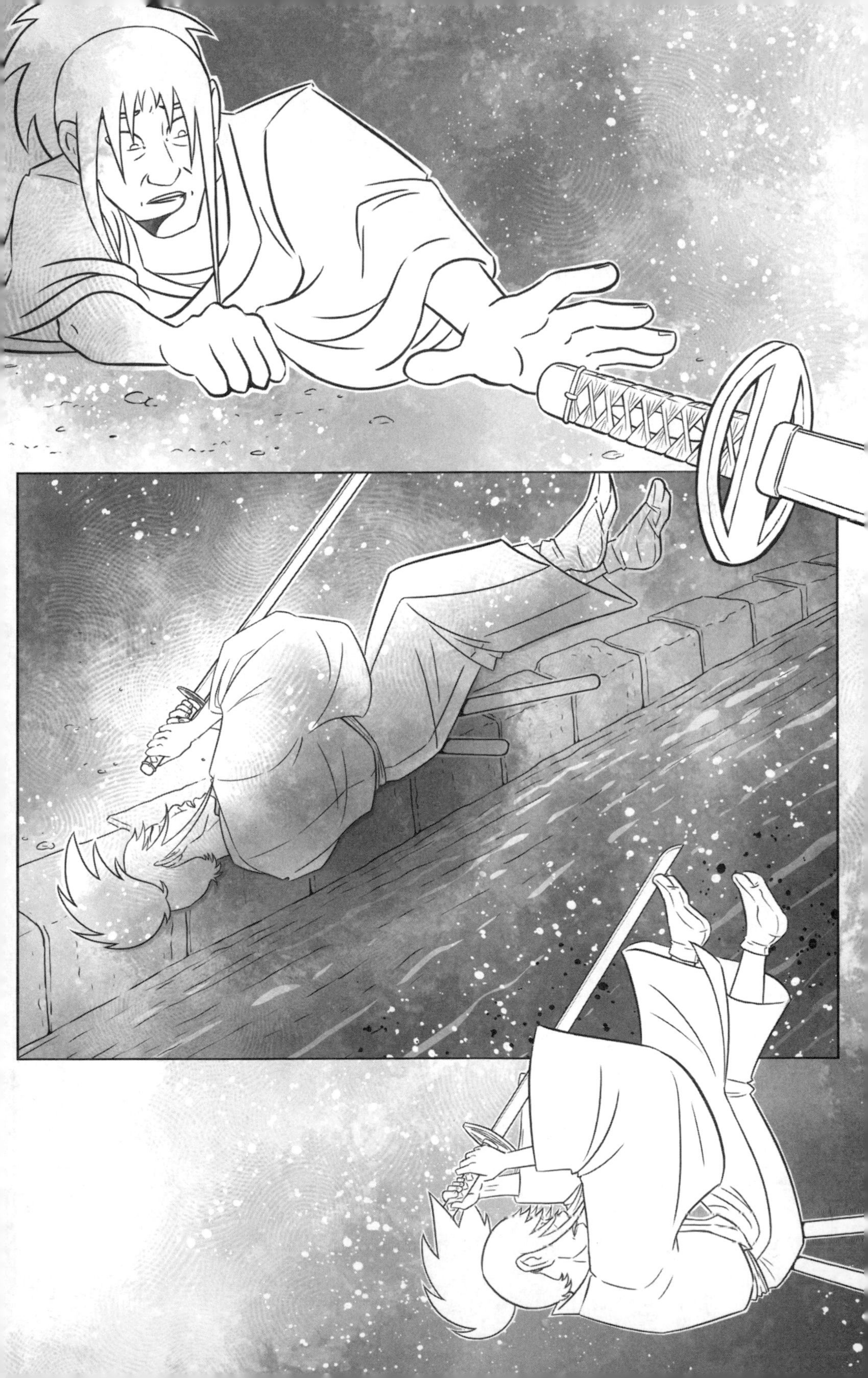

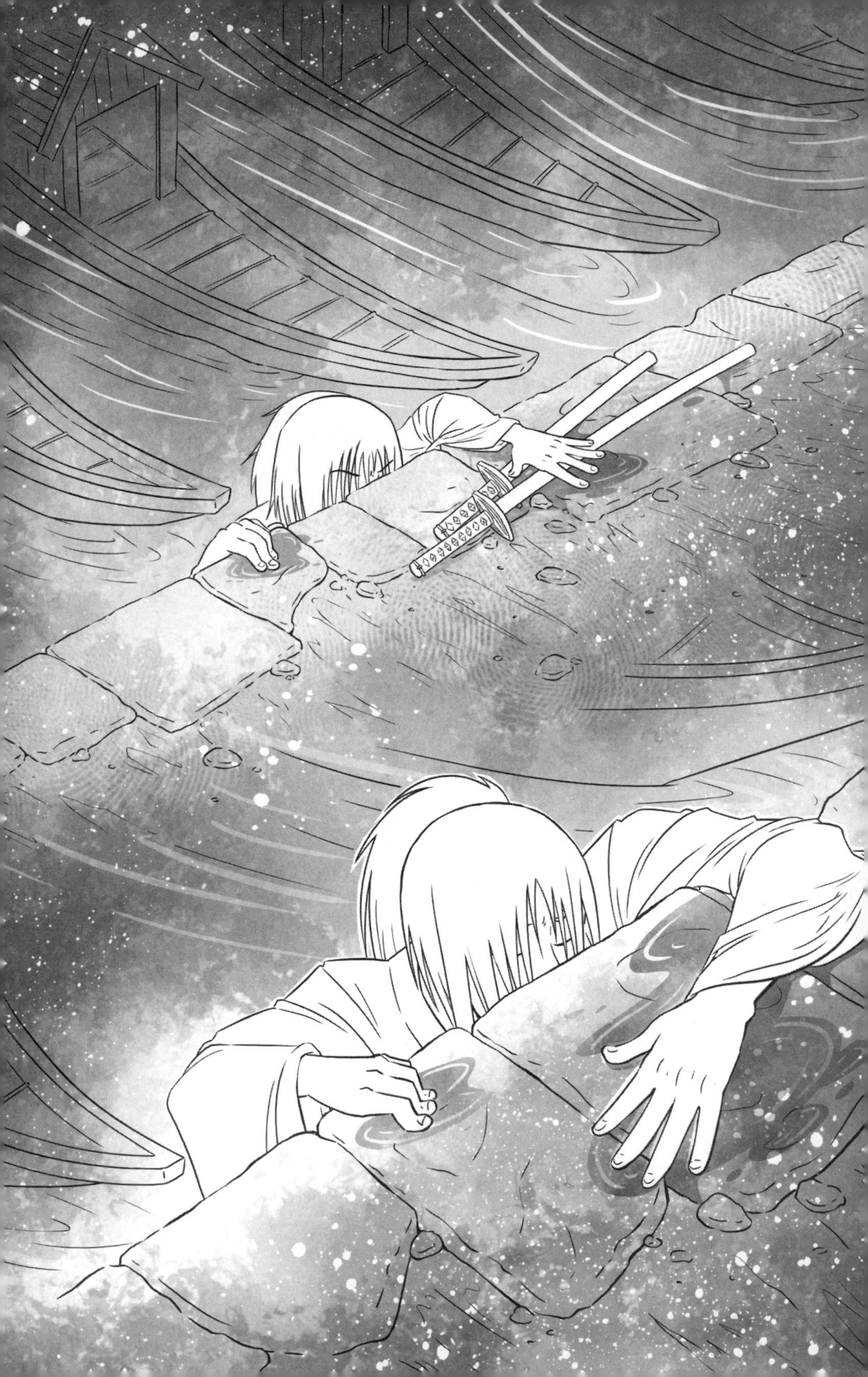

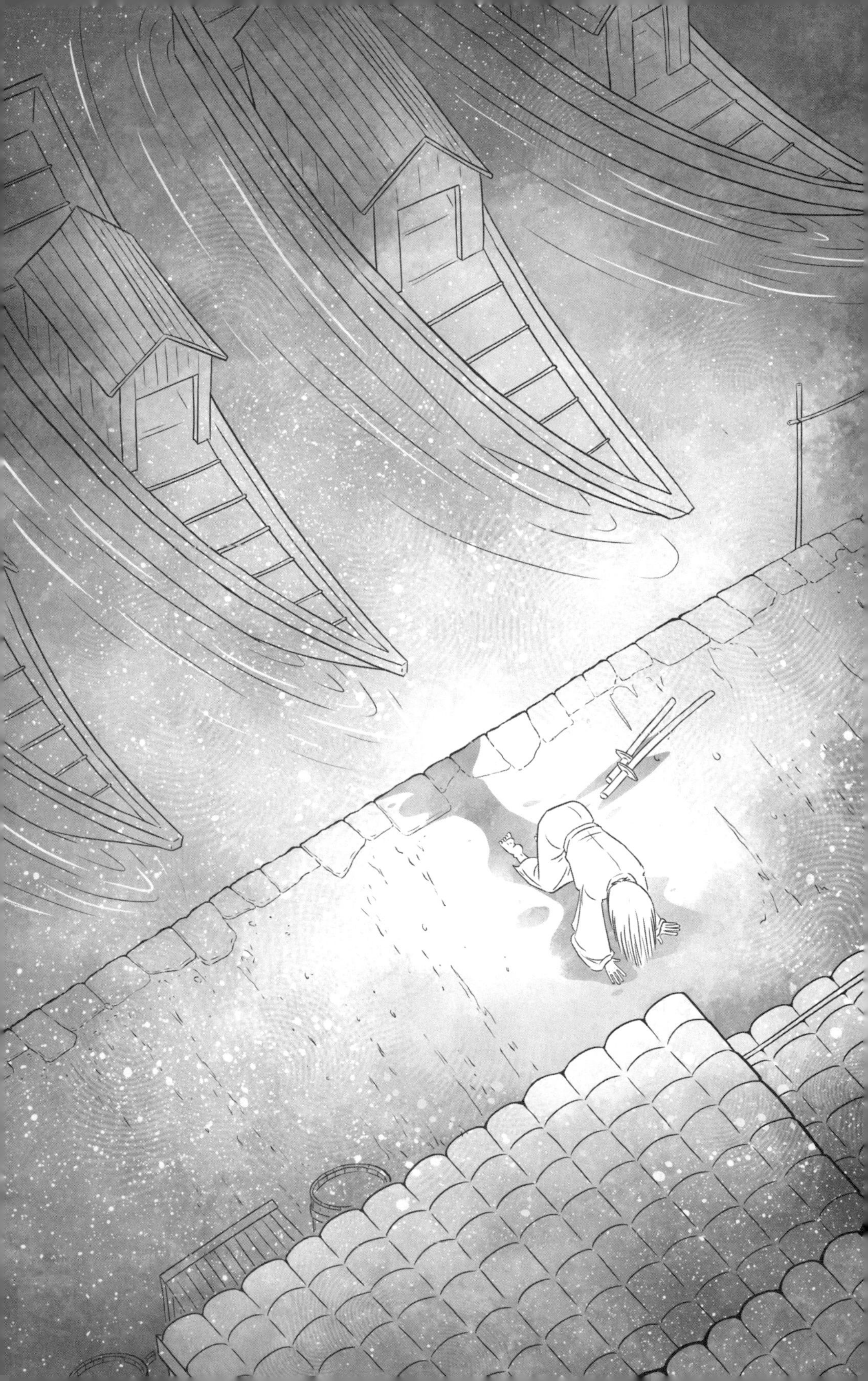

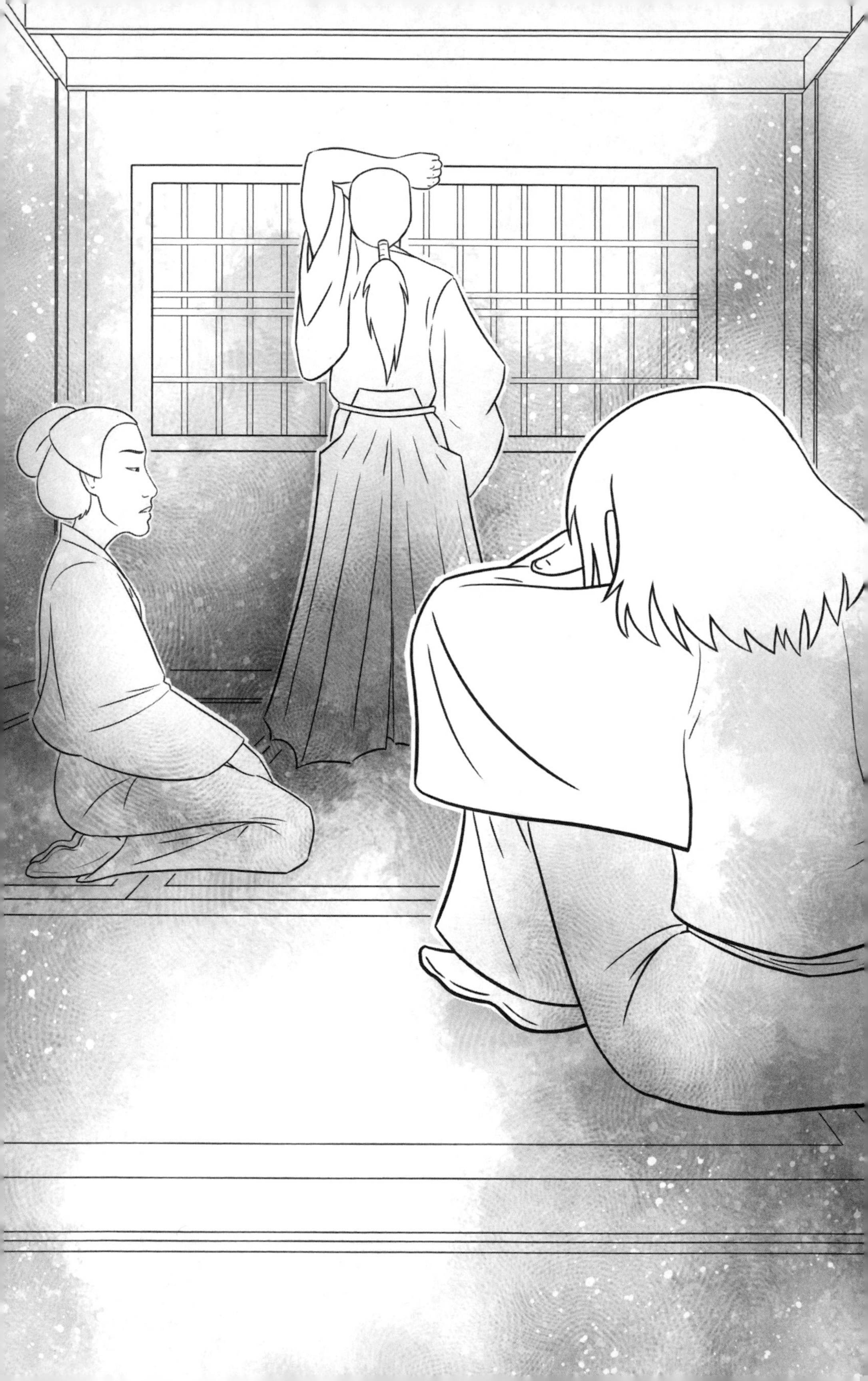

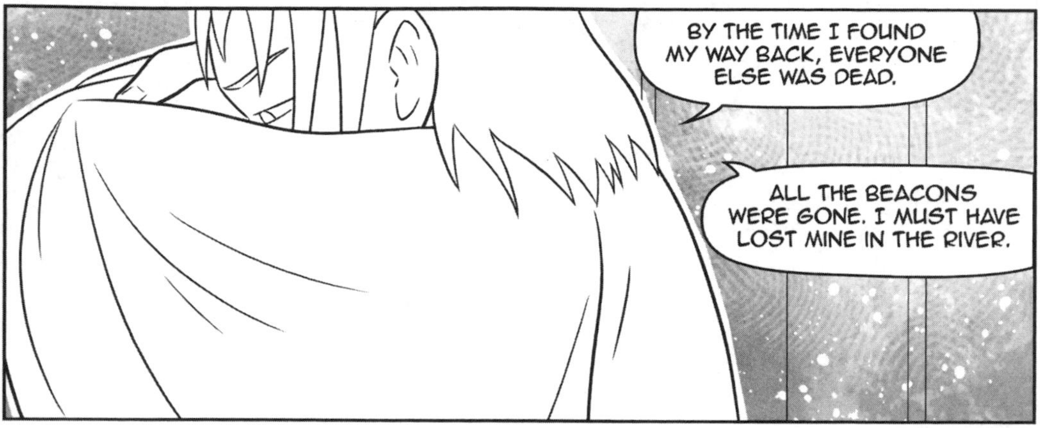
BY THE TIME I FOUND MY WAY BACK, EVERYONE ELSE WAS DEAD.
ALL THE BEACONS WERE GONE. I MUST HAVE LOST MINE IN THE RIVER.

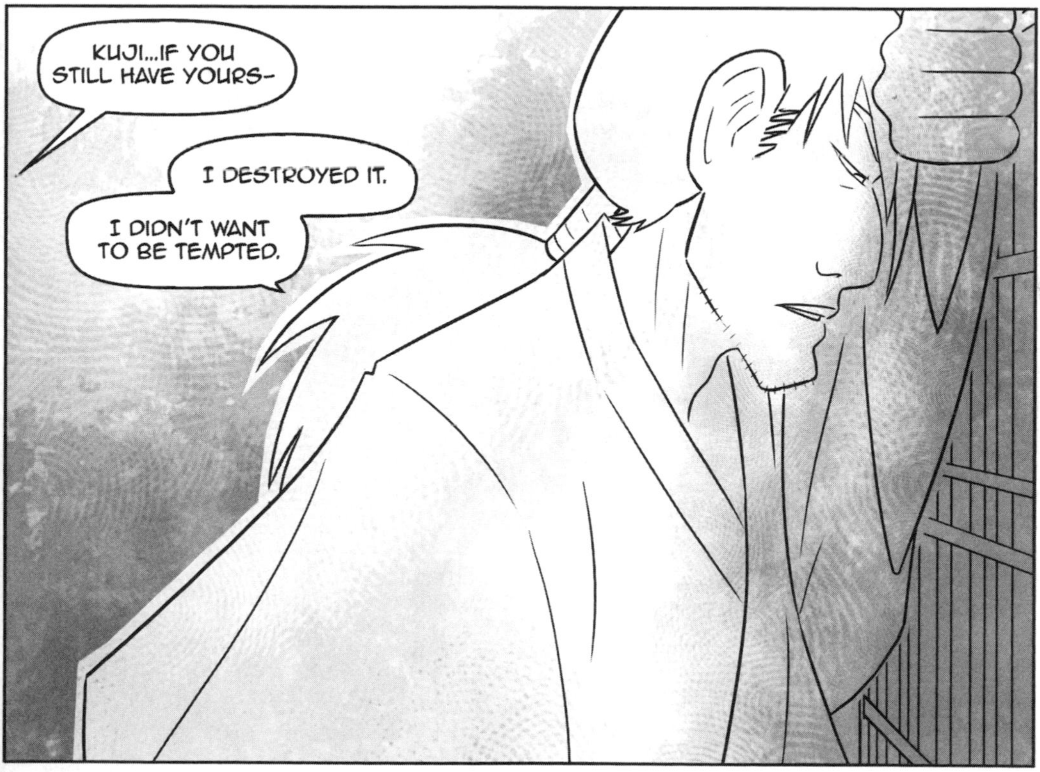
KUJI...IF YOU STILL HAVE YOURS-
I DESTROYED IT.
I DIDN'T WANT TO BE TEMPTED.

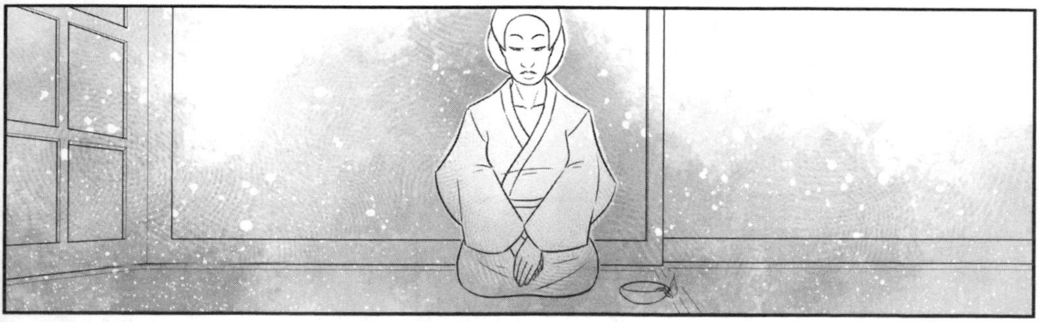

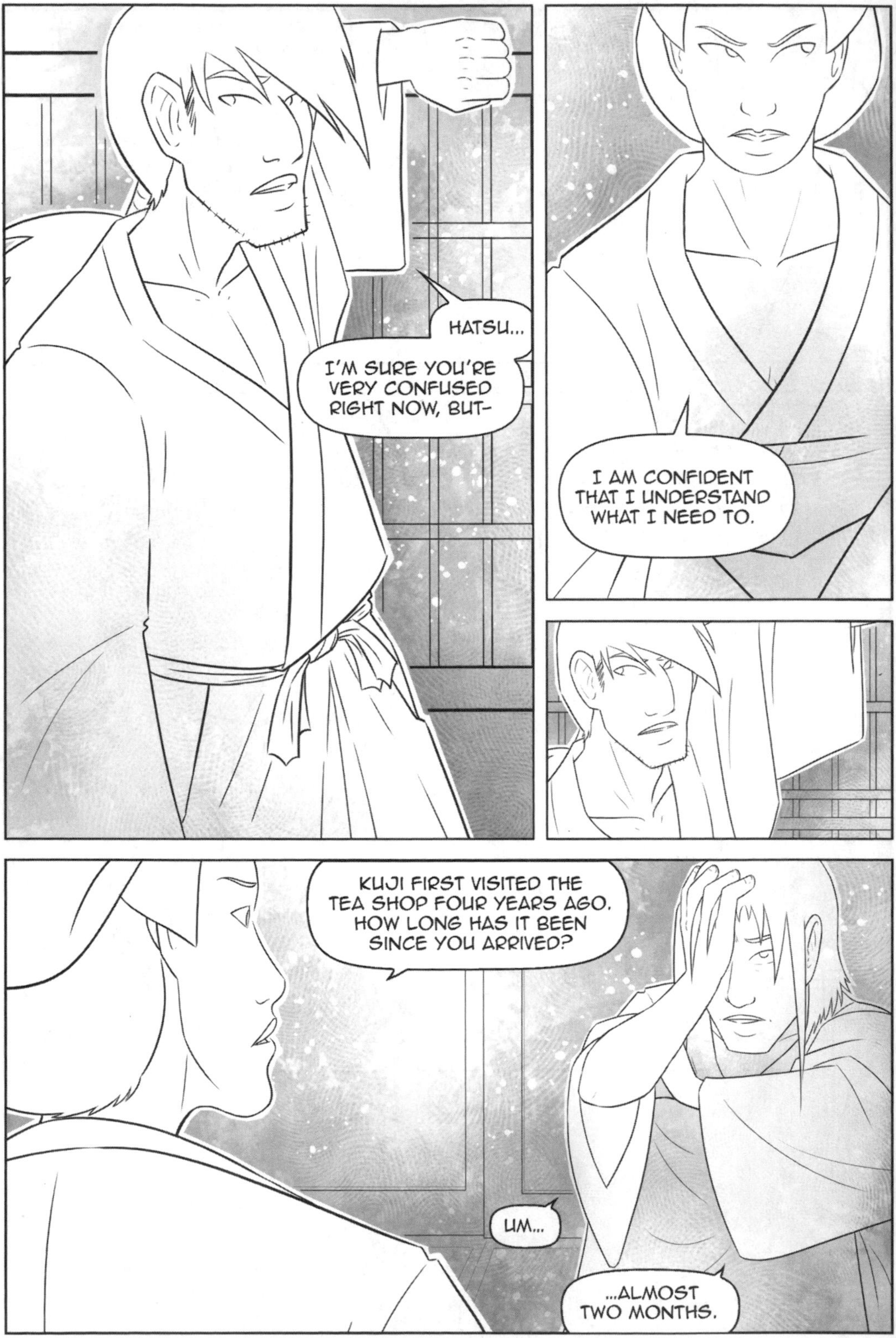
HATSU...
I'M SURE YOU'RE VERY CONFUSED RIGHT NOW, BUT-
I AM CONFIDENT THAT I UNDERSTAND WHAT I NEED TO.
KUJI FIRST VISITED THE TEA SHOP FOUR YEARS AGO. HOW LONG HAS IT BEEN SINCE YOU ARRIVED?
UM...
...ALMOST TWO MONTHS.

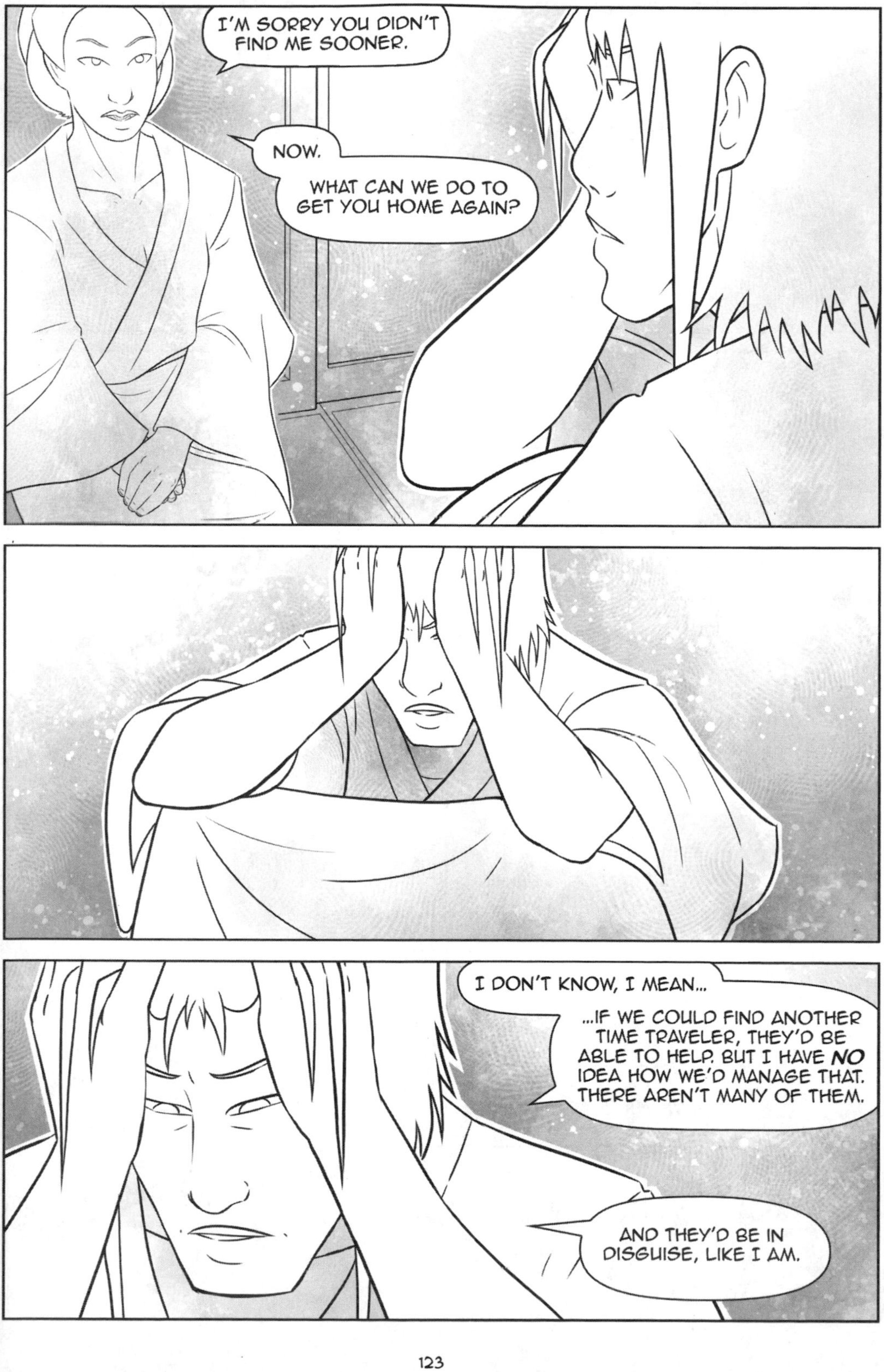
I'M SORRY YOU DIDN'T FIND ME SOONER.
NOW.
WHAT CAN WE DO TO GET YOU HOME AGAIN?
I DON'T KNOW, I MEAN...
...IF WE COULD FIND ANOTHER TIME TRAVELER, THEY'D BE ABLE TO HELP. BUT I HAVE ***NO*** IDEA HOW WE'D MANAGE THAT. THERE AREN'T MANY OF THEM.
AND THEY'D BE IN DISGUISE, LIKE I AM.

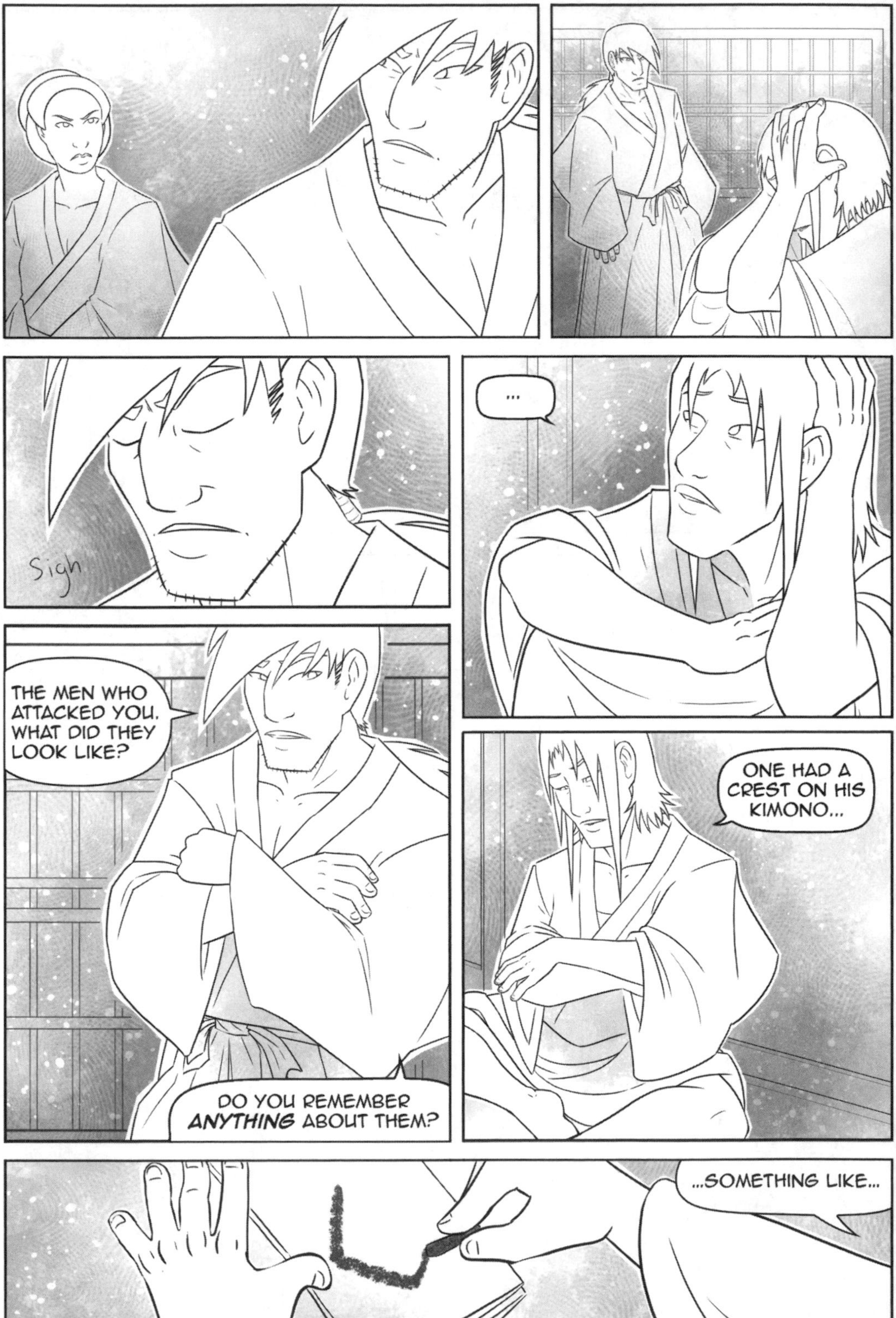
Sigh
...
THE MEN WHO ATTACKED YOU. WHAT DID THEY LOOK LIKE?
DO YOU REMEMBER ANYTHING ABOUT THEM?
ONE HAD A CREST ON HIS KIMONO...
...SOMETHING LIKE...

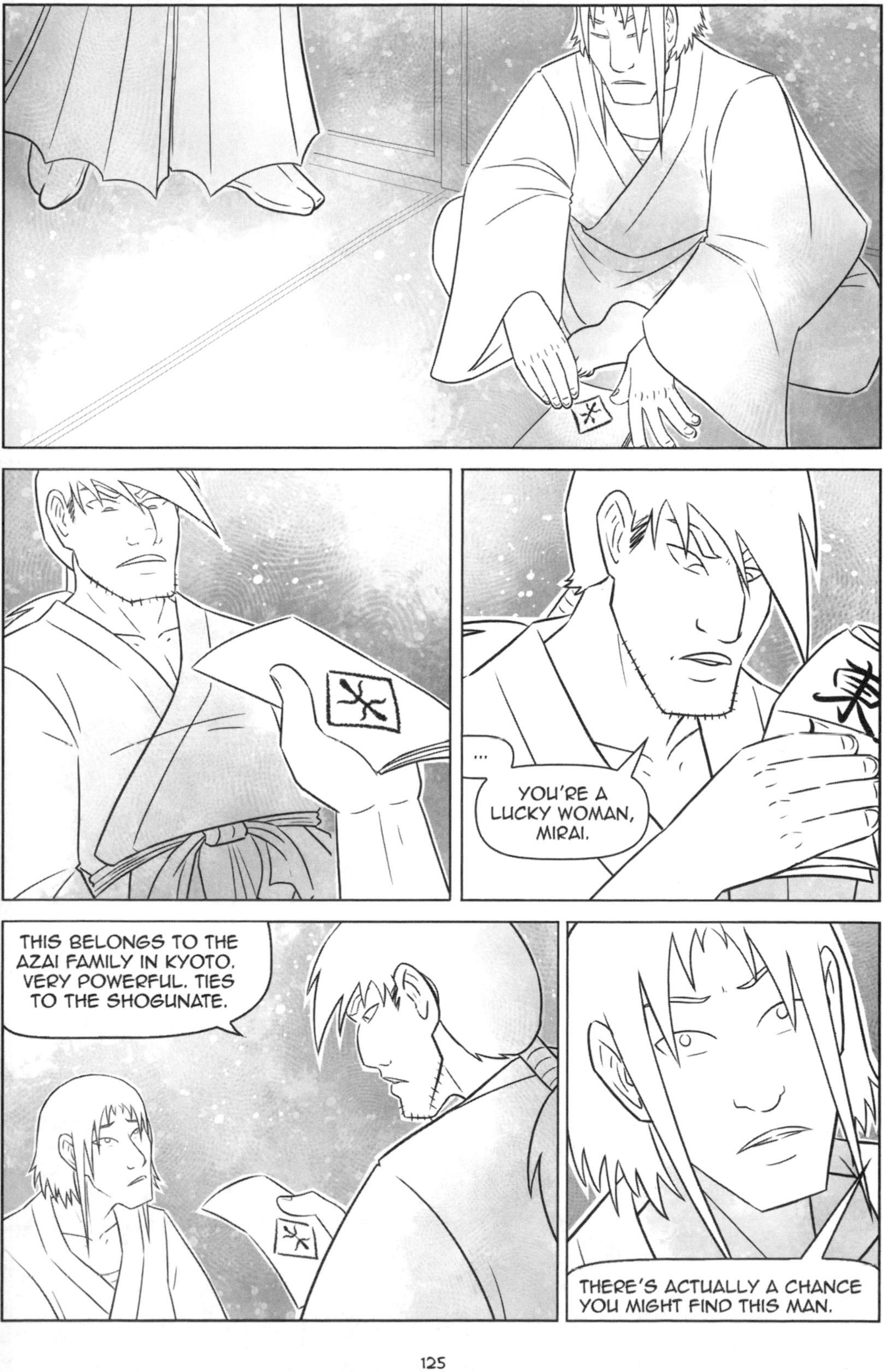
...
YOU'RE A LUCKY WOMAN, MIRAI.
THIS BELONGS TO THE AZAI FAMILY IN KYOTO. VERY POWERFUL. TIES TO THE SHOGUNATE.
THERE'S ACTUALLY A CHANCE YOU MIGHT FIND THIS MAN.

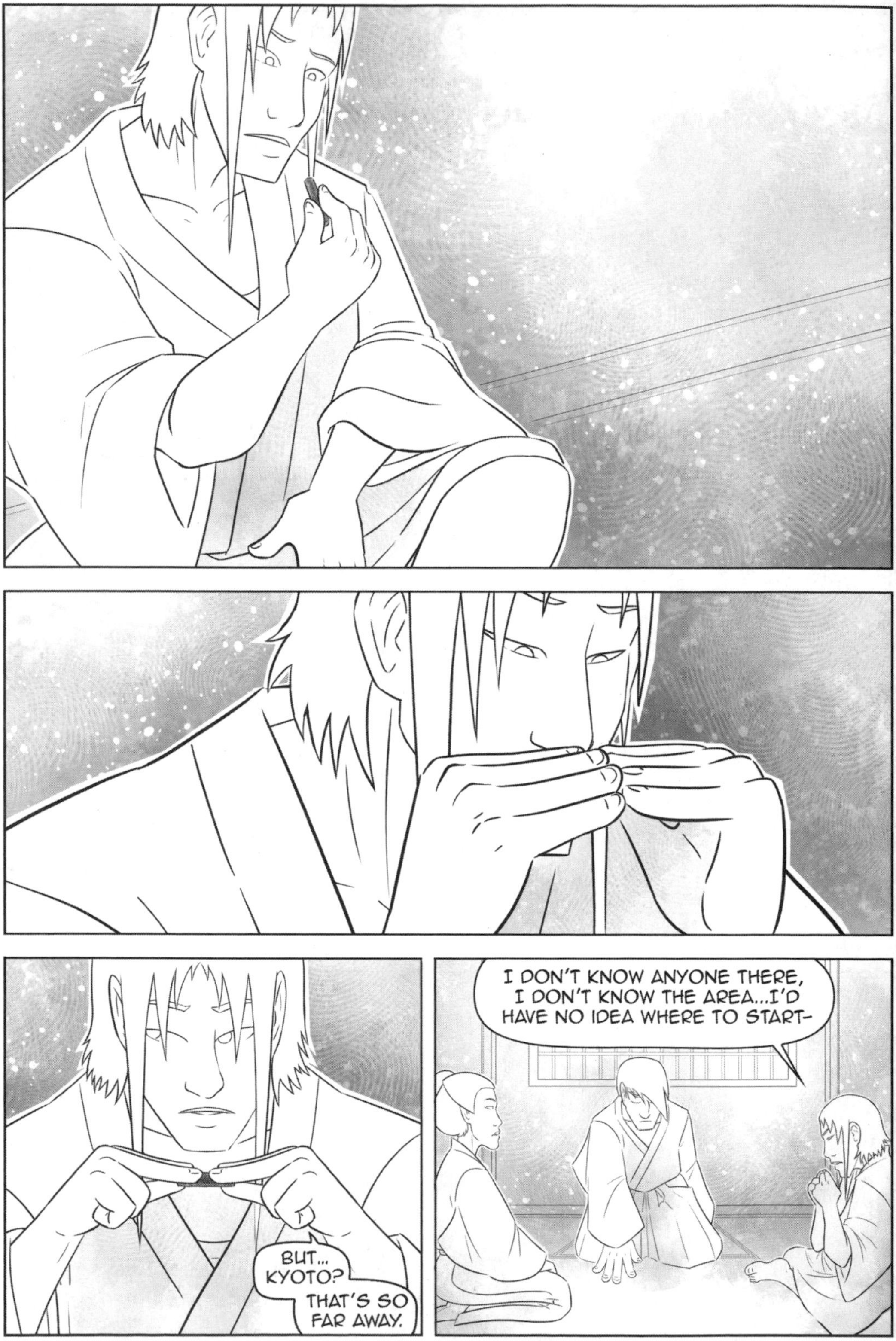
BUT... KYOTO?
THAT'S SO FAR AWAY.
I DON'T KNOW ANYONE THERE, I DON'T KNOW THE AREA...I'D HAVE NO IDEA WHERE TO START-

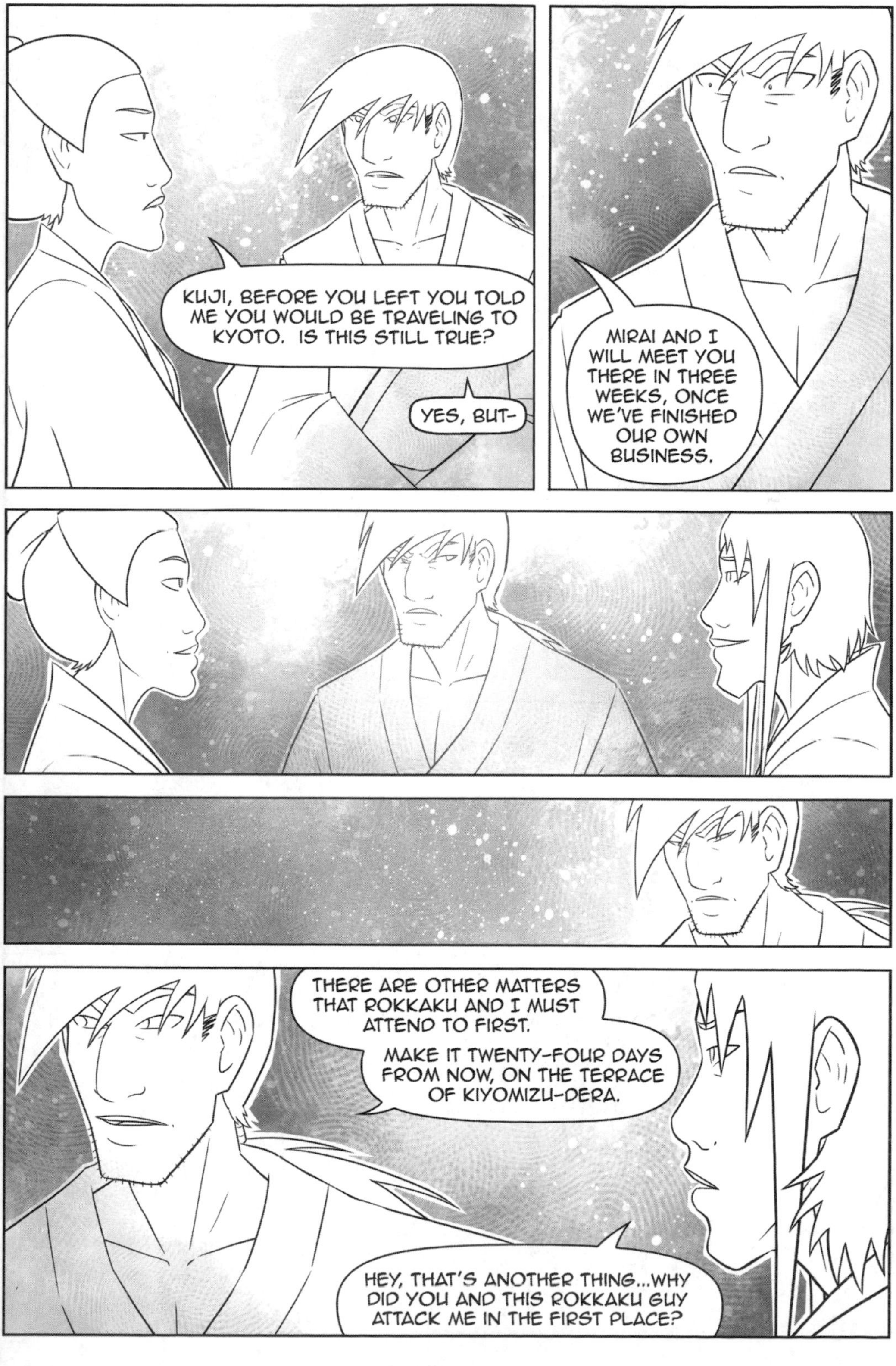
KUJI, BEFORE YOU LEFT YOU TOLD ME YOU WOULD BE TRAVELING TO KYOTO. IS THIS STILL TRUE?
YES, BUT-
MIRAI AND I WILL MEET YOU THERE IN THREE WEEKS, ONCE WE'VE FINISHED OUR OWN BUSINESS.
THERE ARE OTHER MATTERS THAT ROKKAKU AND I MUST ATTEND TO FIRST.
MAKE IT TWENTY-FOUR DAYS FROM NOW, ON THE TERRACE OF KIYOMIZU-DERA.
HEY, THAT'S ANOTHER THING...WHY DID YOU AND THIS ROKKAKU GUY ATTACK ME IN THE FIRST PLACE?

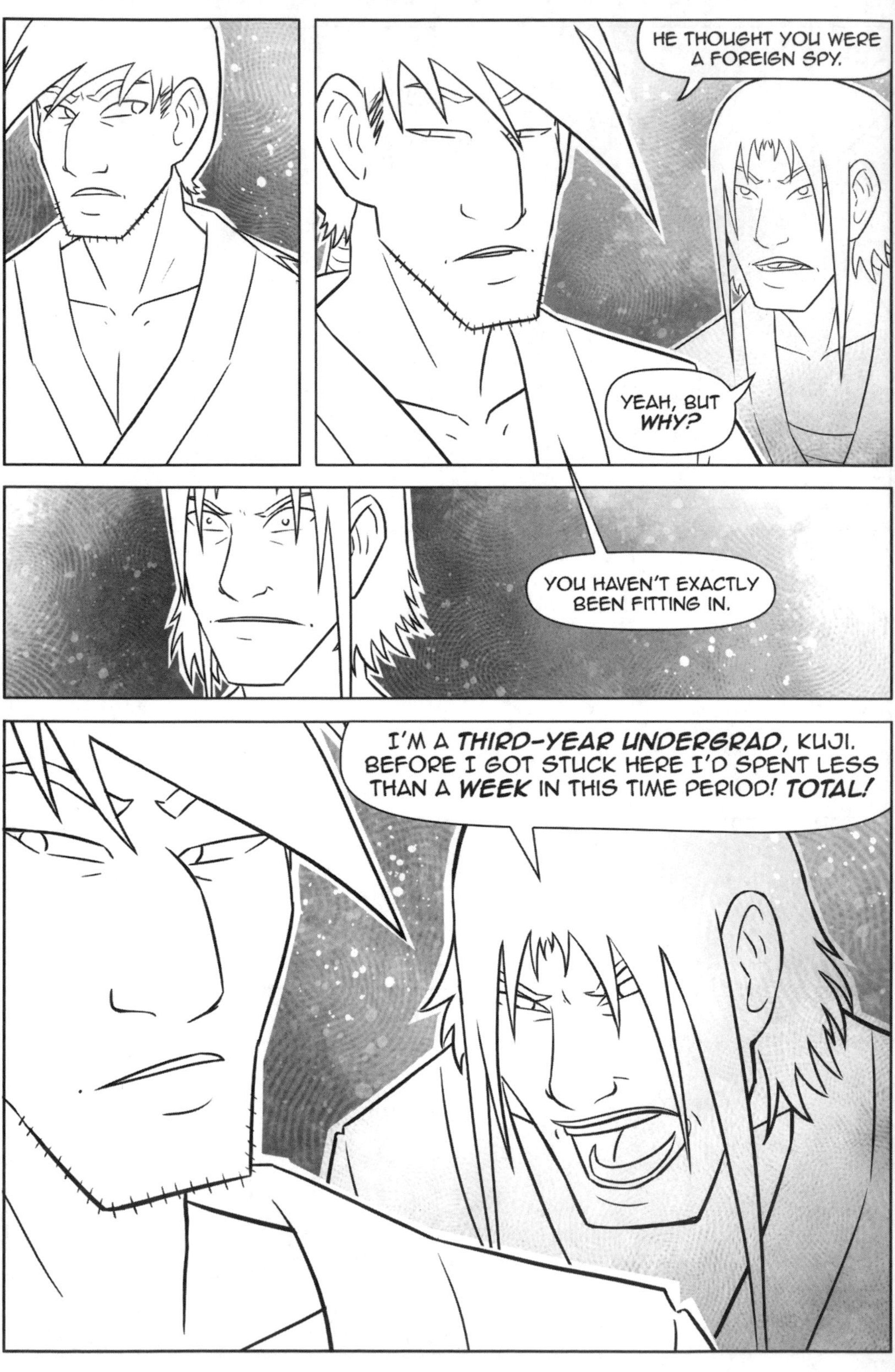
HE THOUGHT YOU WERE A FOREIGN SPY.
YEAH, BUT *WHY?*
YOU HAVEN'T EXACTLY BEEN FITTING IN.
I'M A ***THIRD-YEAR UNDERGRAD***, KUJI. BEFORE I GOT STUCK HERE I'D SPENT LESS THAN A ***WEEK*** IN THIS TIME PERIOD! ***TOTAL!***

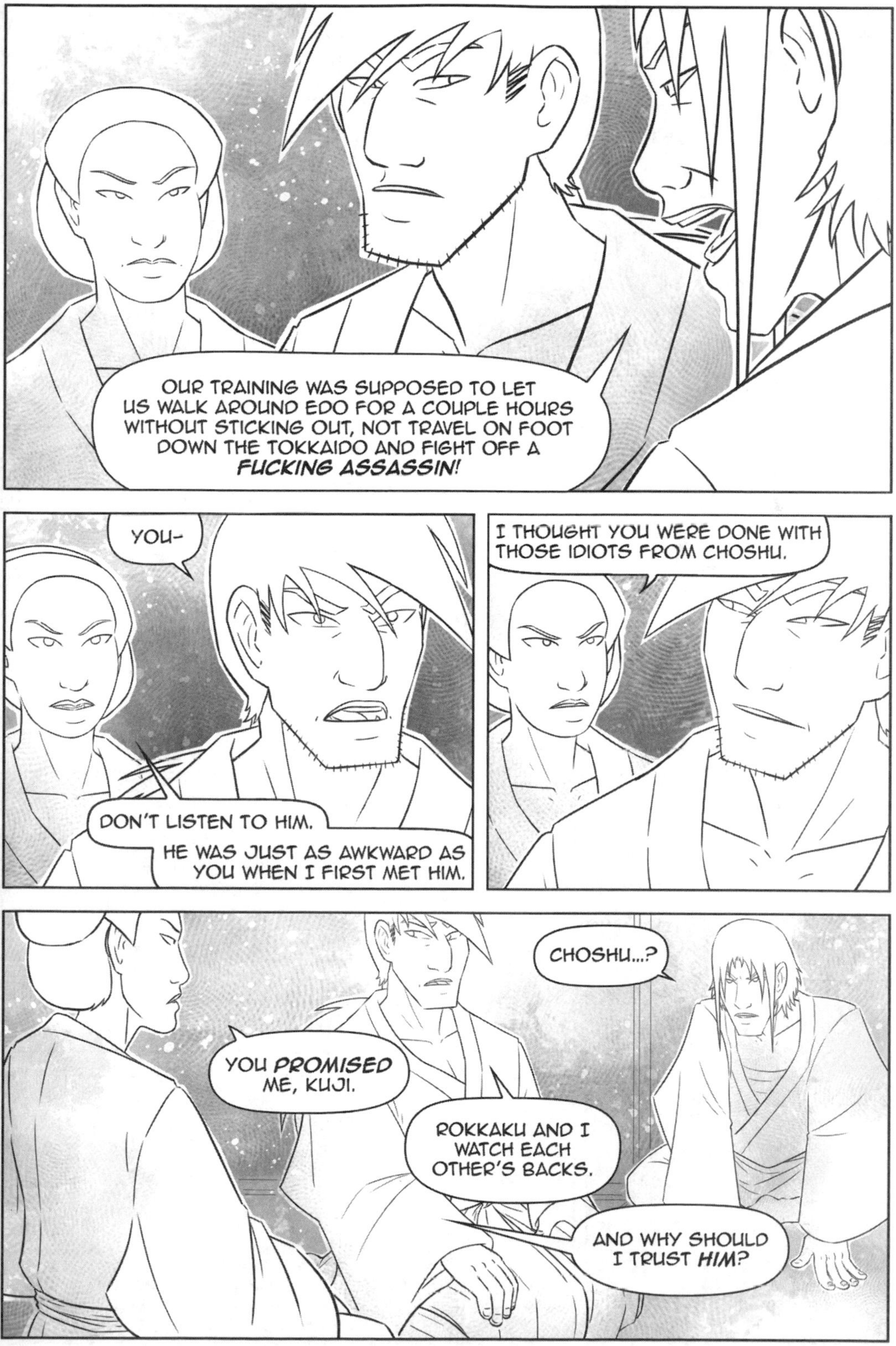
OUR TRAINING WAS SUPPOSED TO LET US WALK AROUND EDO FOR A COUPLE HOURS WITHOUT STICKING OUT, NOT TRAVEL ON FOOT DOWN THE TOKKAIDO AND FIGHT OFF A ***FUCKING ASSASSIN***!
YOU-
DON'T LISTEN TO HIM.
HE WAS JUST AS AWKWARD AS YOU WHEN I FIRST MET HIM.
I THOUGHT YOU WERE DONE WITH THOSE IDIOTS FROM CHOSHU.
CHOSHU...?
YOU ***PROMISED*** ME, KUJI.
ROKKAKU AND I WATCH EACH OTHER'S BACKS.
AND WHY SHOULD I TRUST ***HIM***?

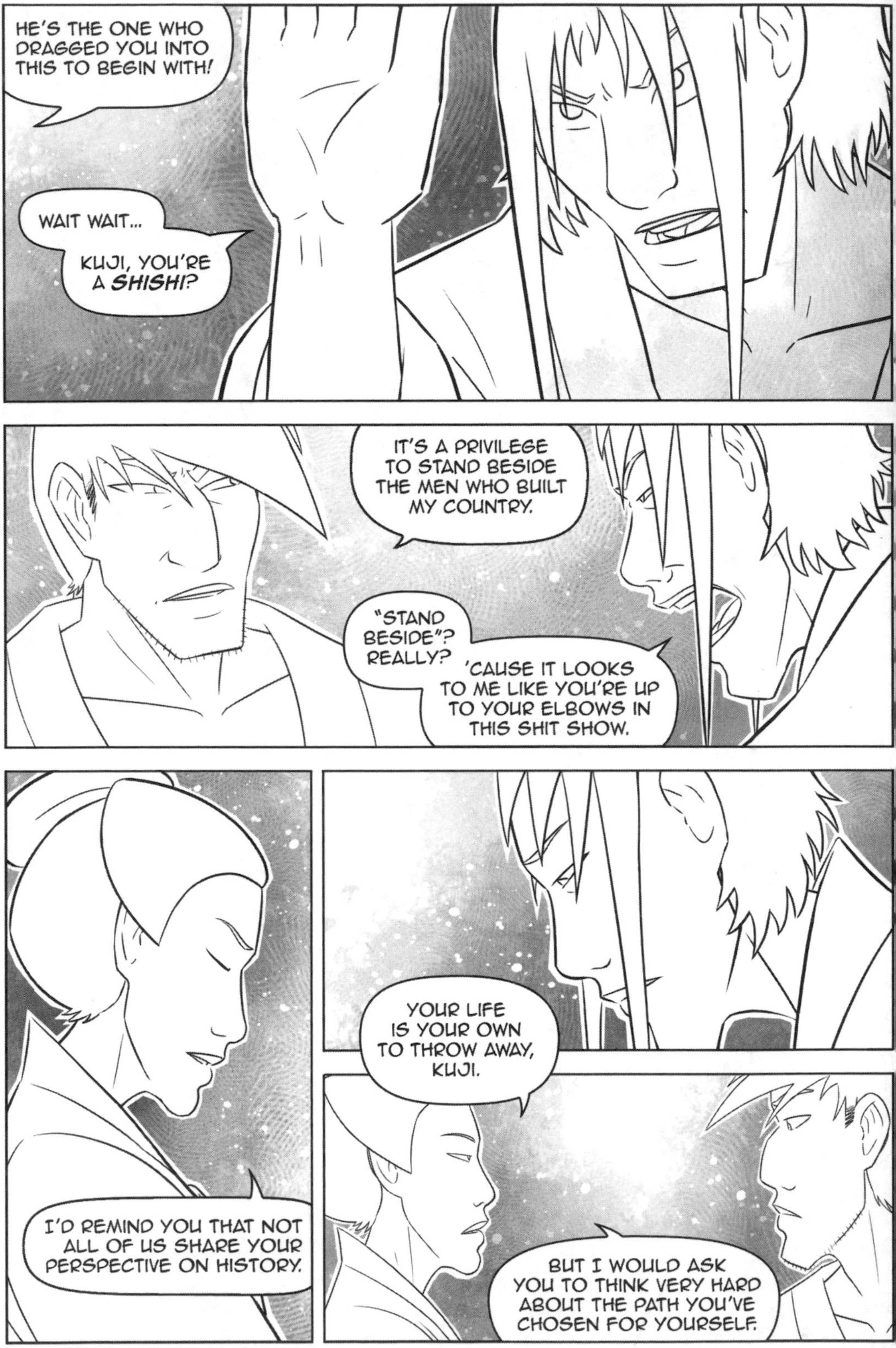
HE'S THE ONE WHO DRAGGED YOU INTO THIS TO BEGIN WITH!
WAIT WAIT...
KUJI, YOU'RE A *SHISHI*?
IT'S A PRIVILEGE TO STAND BESIDE THE MEN WHO BUILT MY COUNTRY.
"STAND BESIDE"? REALLY?
'CAUSE IT LOOKS TO ME LIKE YOU'RE UP TO YOUR ELBOWS IN THIS SHIT SHOW.
I'D REMIND YOU THAT NOT ALL OF US SHARE YOUR PERSPECTIVE ON HISTORY.
YOUR LIFE IS YOUR OWN TO THROW AWAY, KUJI.
BUT I WOULD ASK YOU TO THINK VERY HARD ABOUT THE PATH YOU'VE CHOSEN FOR YOURSELF.

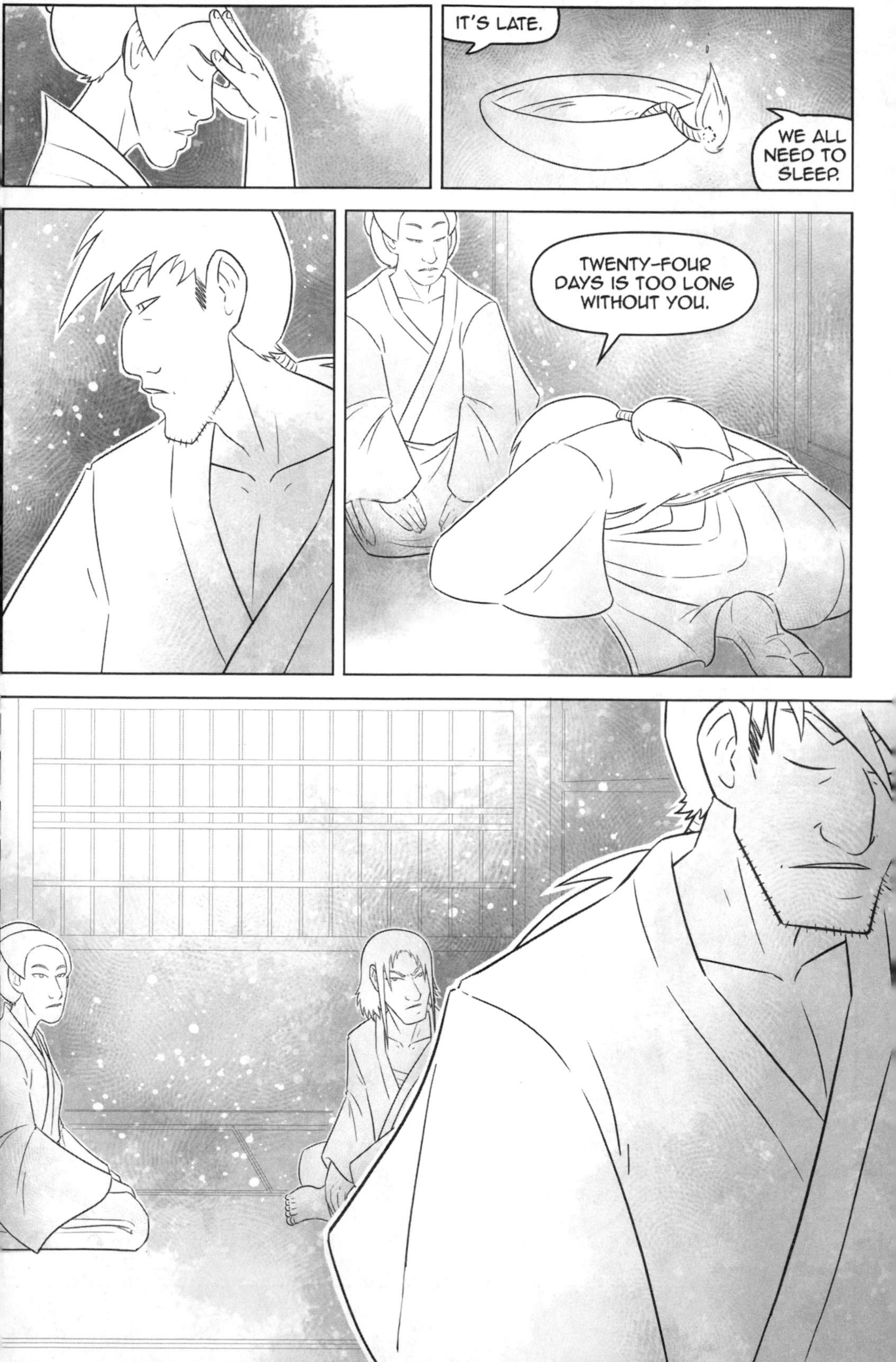
IT'S LATE.
WE ALL NEED TO SLEEP.
TWENTY-FOUR DAYS IS TOO LONG WITHOUT YOU.

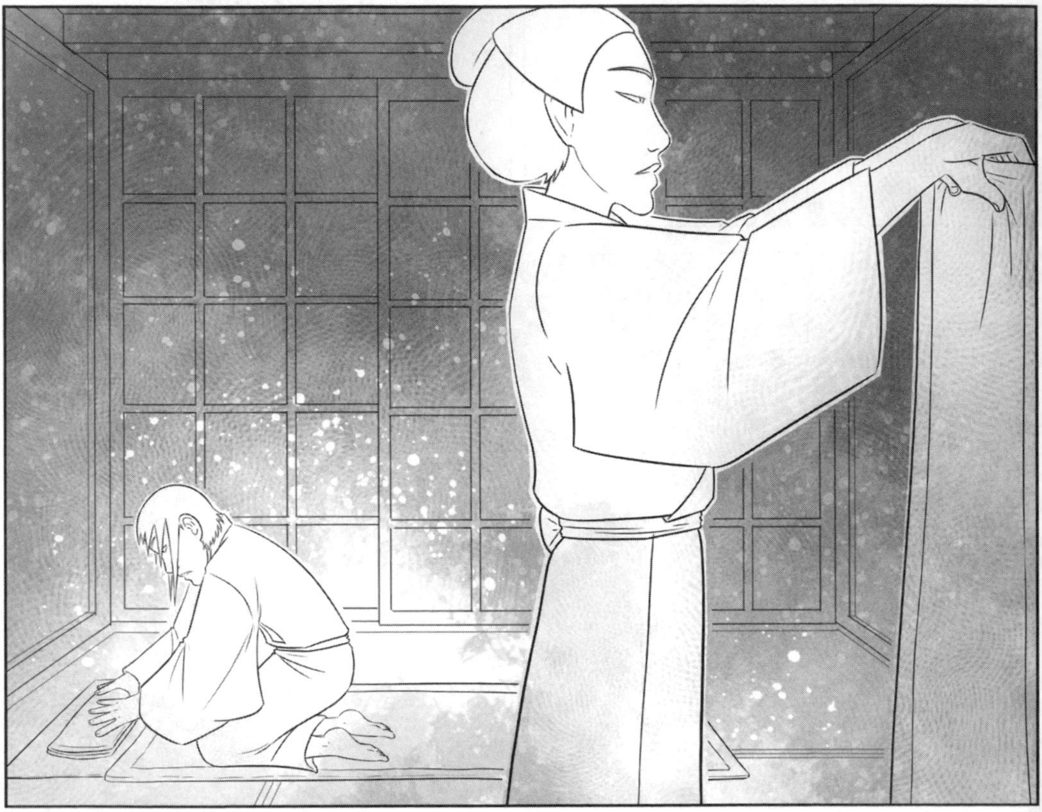

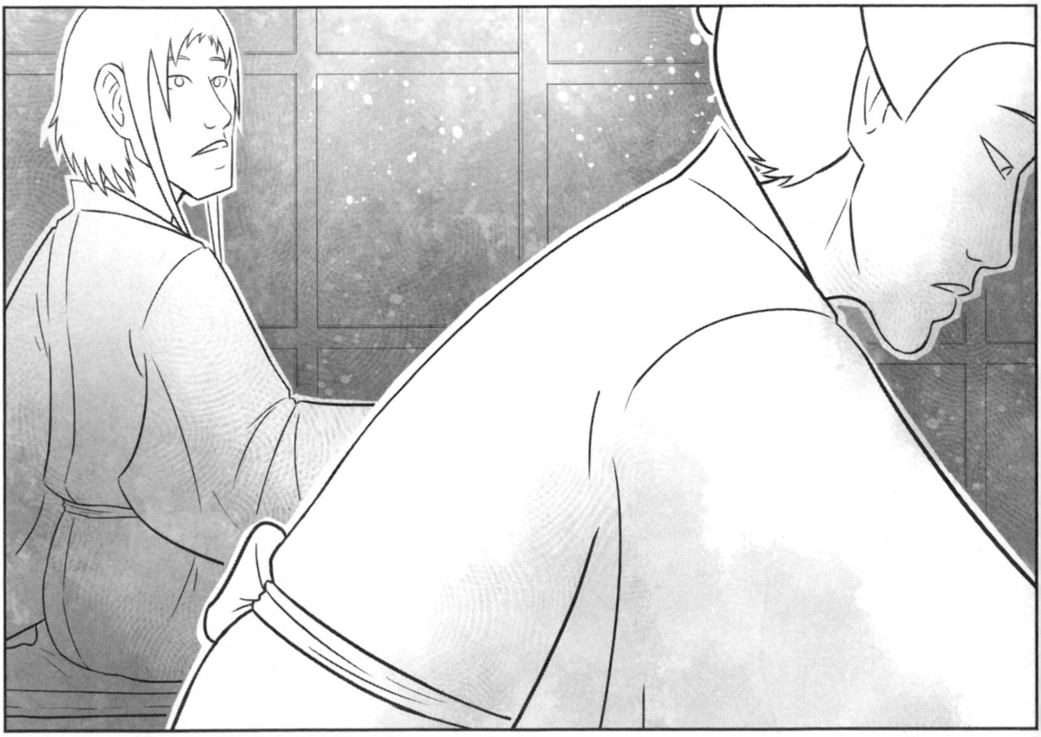

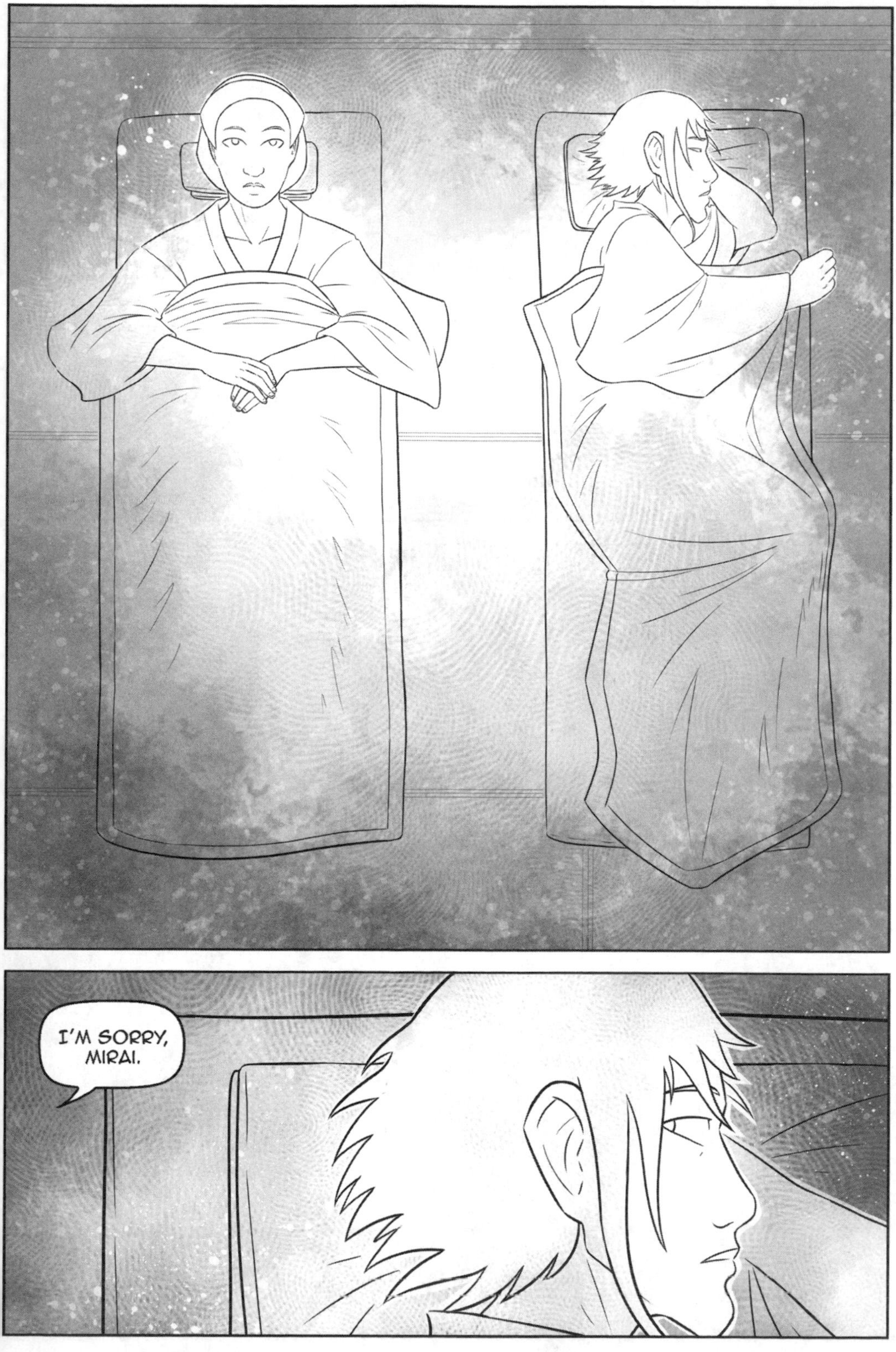
I'M SORRY, MIRAI.

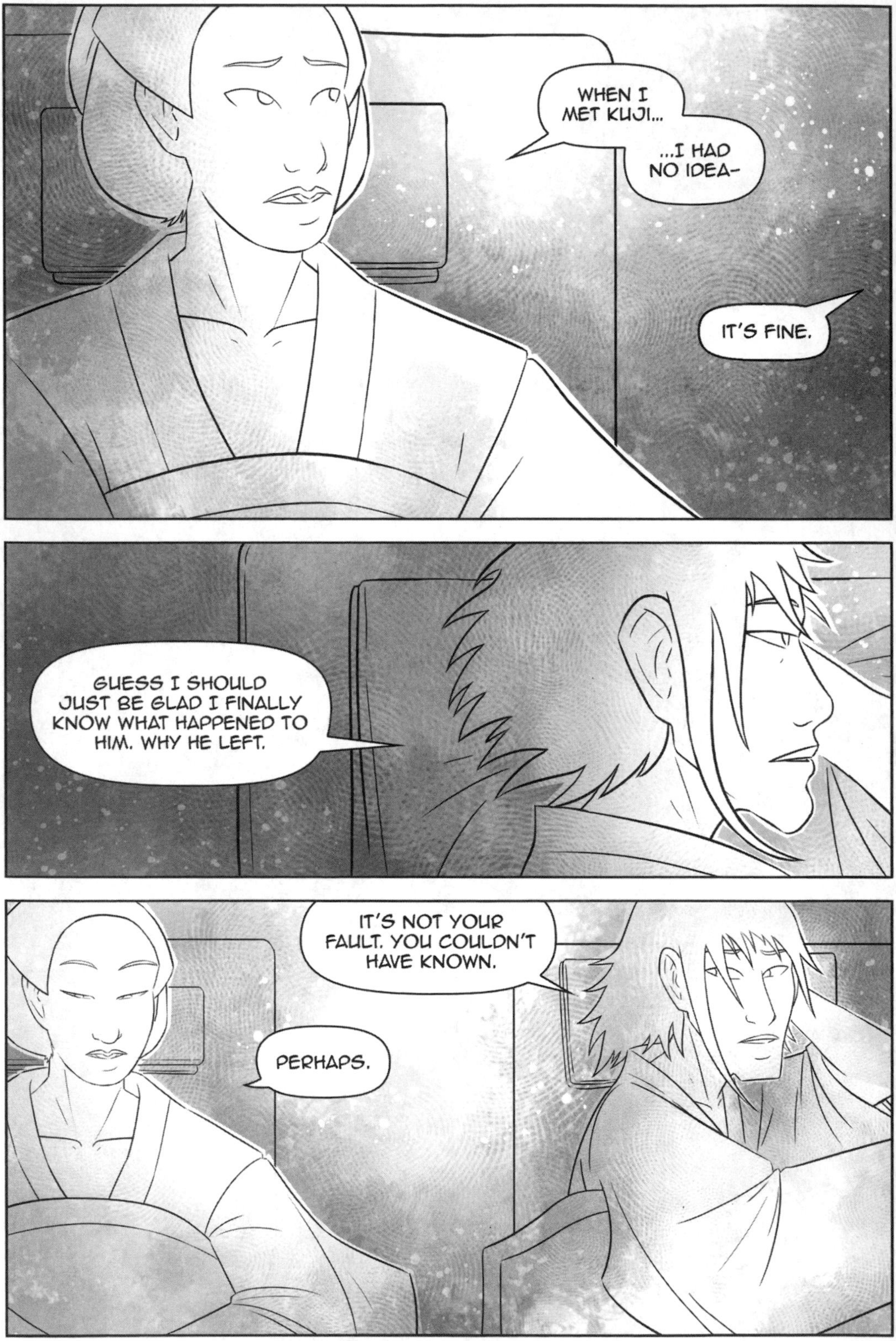
WHEN I MET KUJI...
...I HAD NO IDEA-
IT'S FINE.
GUESS I SHOULD JUST BE GLAD I FINALLY KNOW WHAT HAPPENED TO HIM. WHY HE LEFT.
IT'S NOT YOUR FAULT. YOU COULDN'T HAVE KNOWN.
PERHAPS.

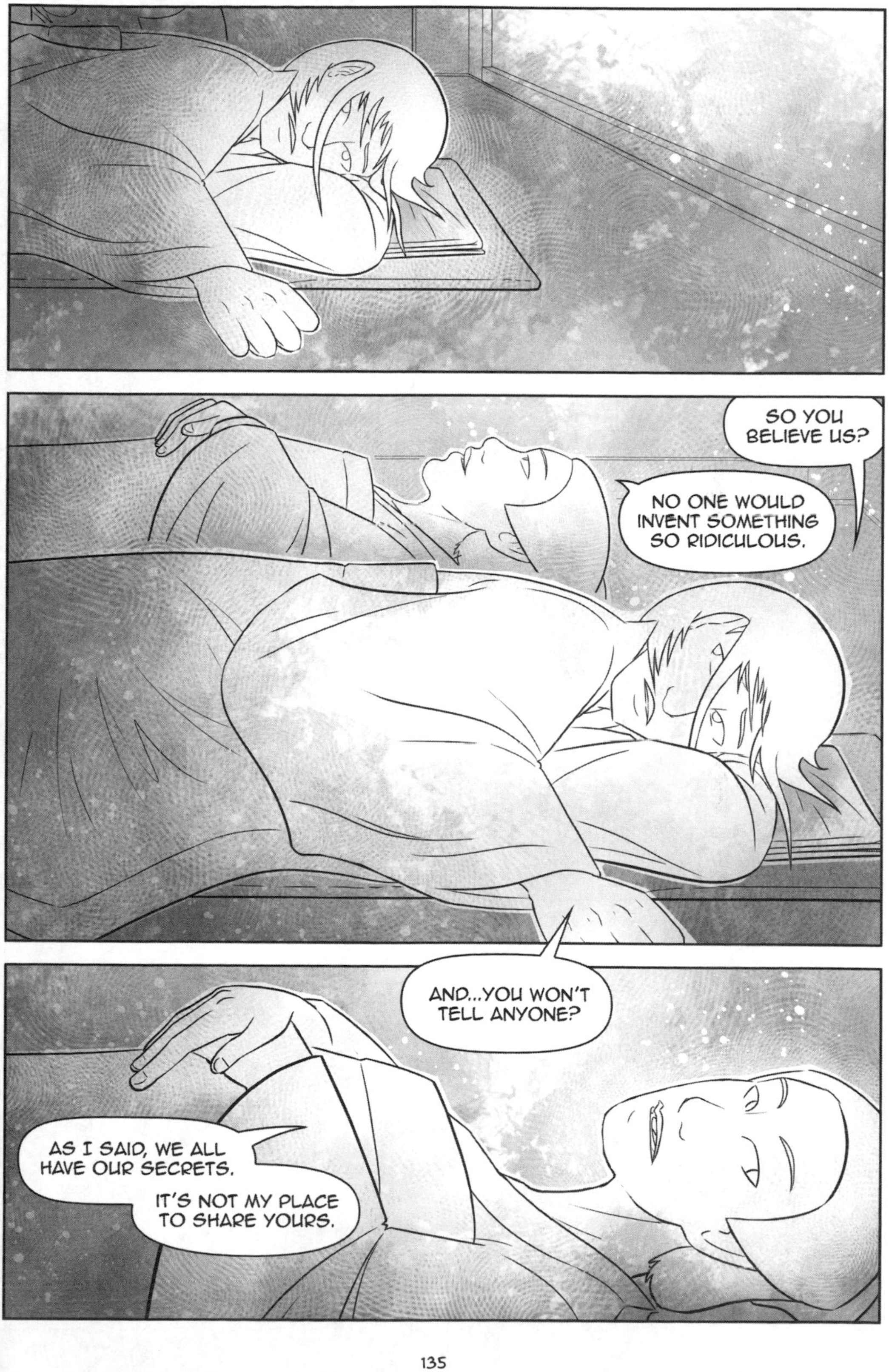
SO YOU BELIEVE US?
NO ONE WOULD INVENT SOMETHING SO RIDICULOUS.
AND...YOU WON'T TELL ANYONE?
AS I SAID, WE ALL HAVE OUR SECRETS.
IT'S NOT MY PLACE TO SHARE YOURS.

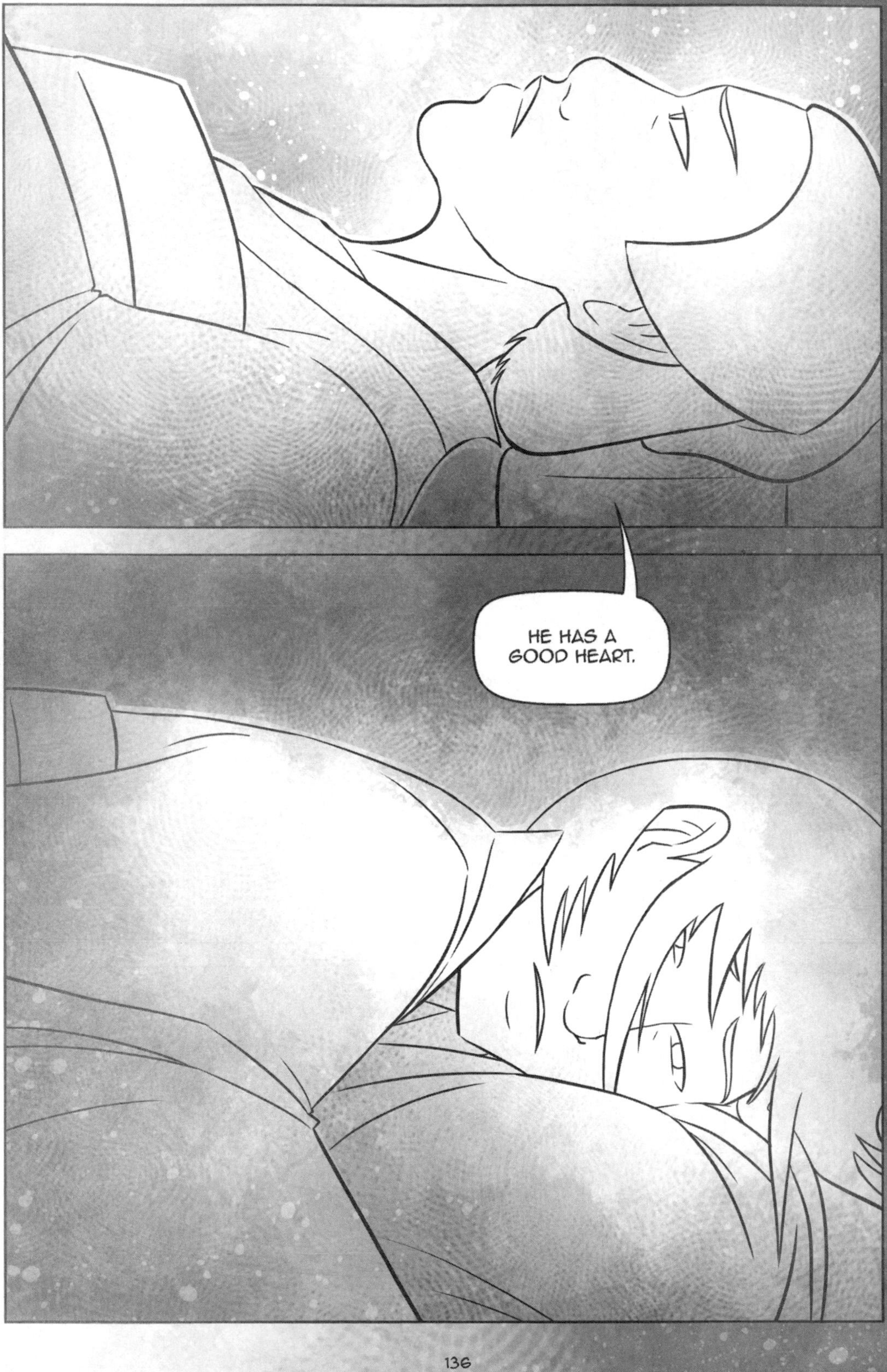
HE HAS A GOOD HEART.

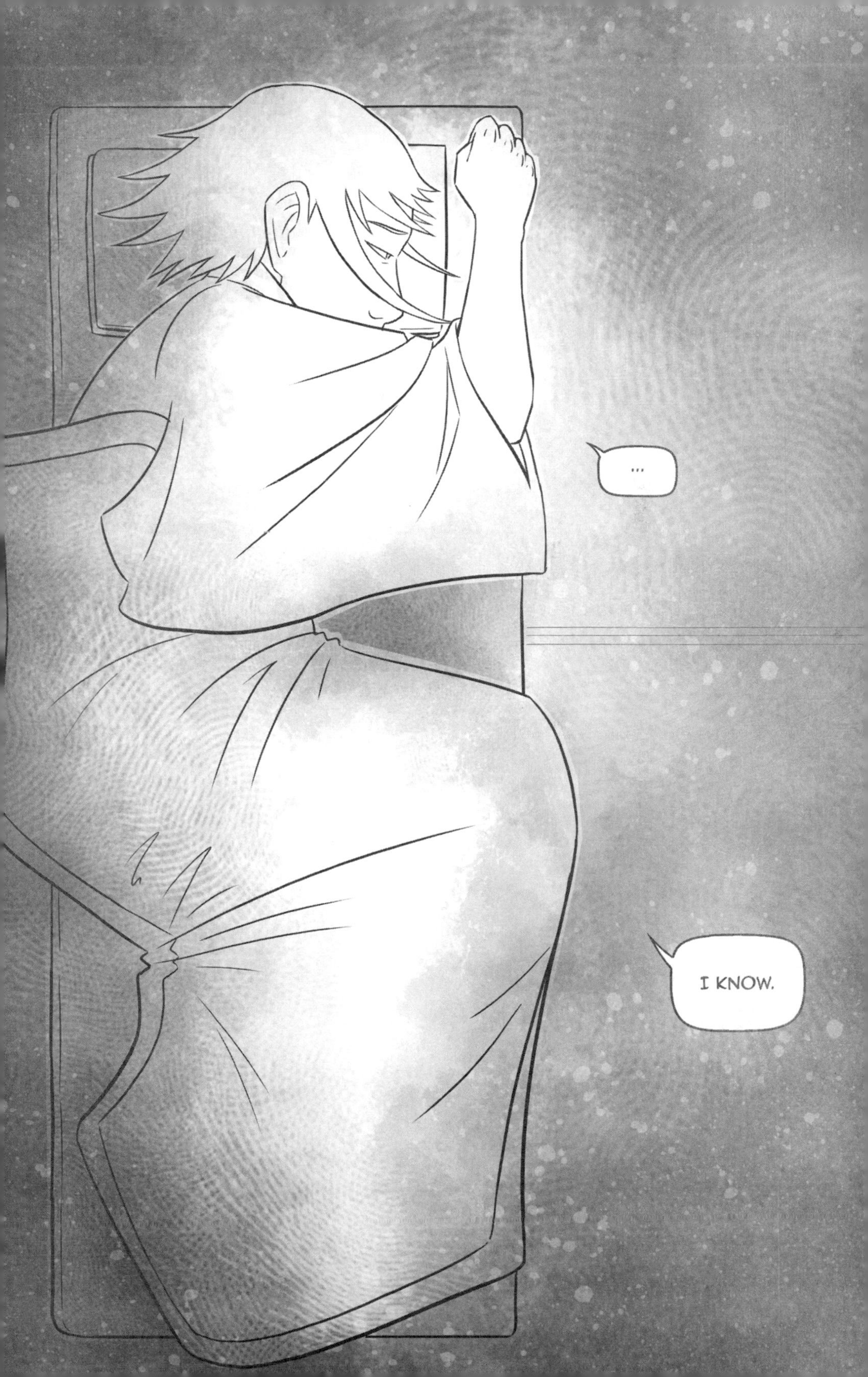
...
I KNOW.

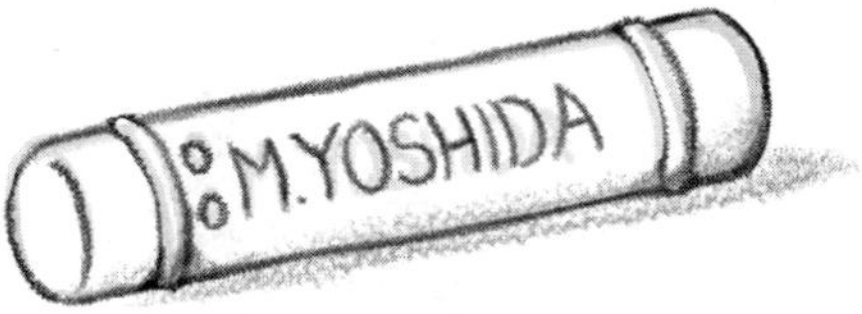

M.YOSHIDA

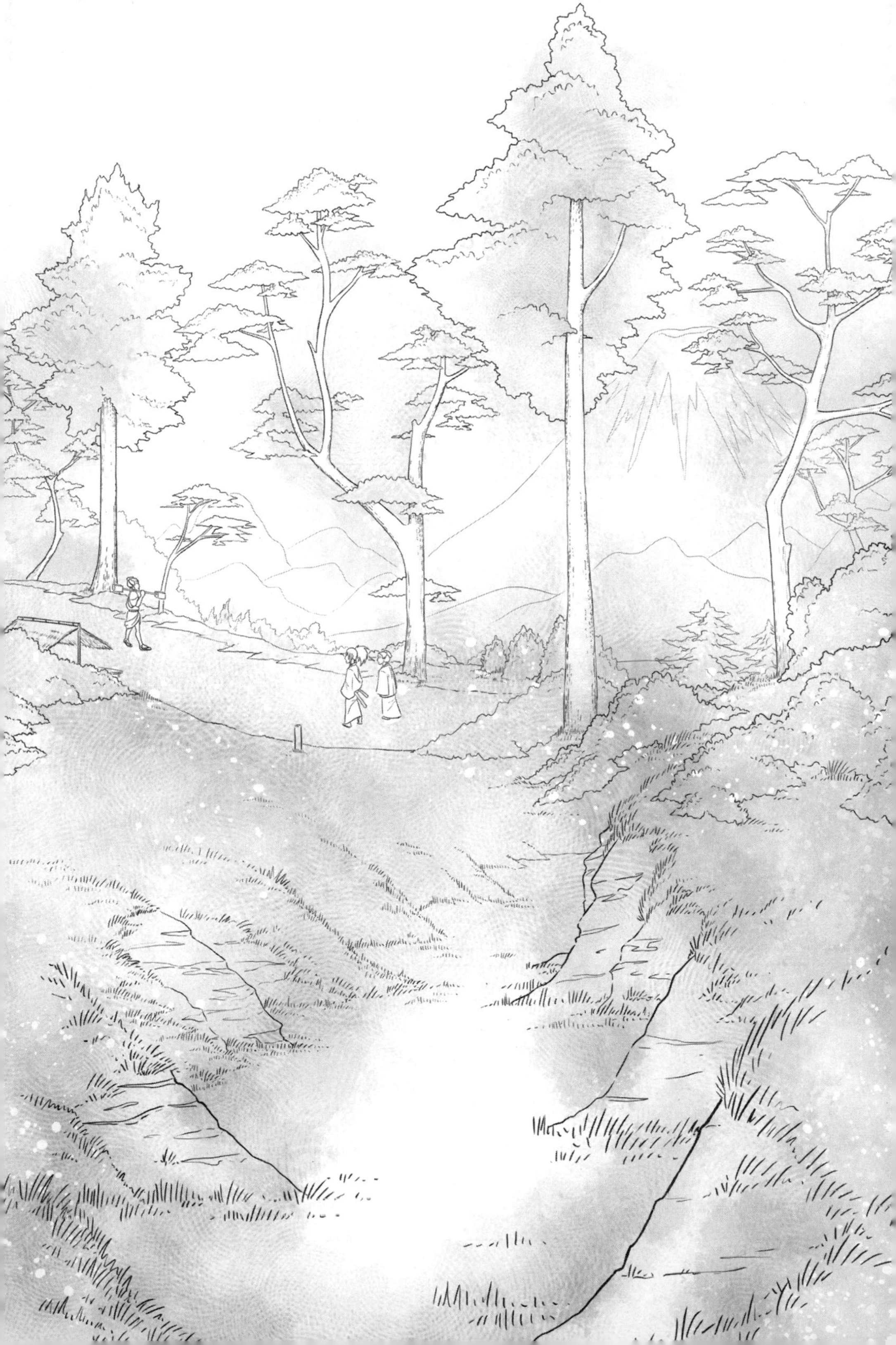

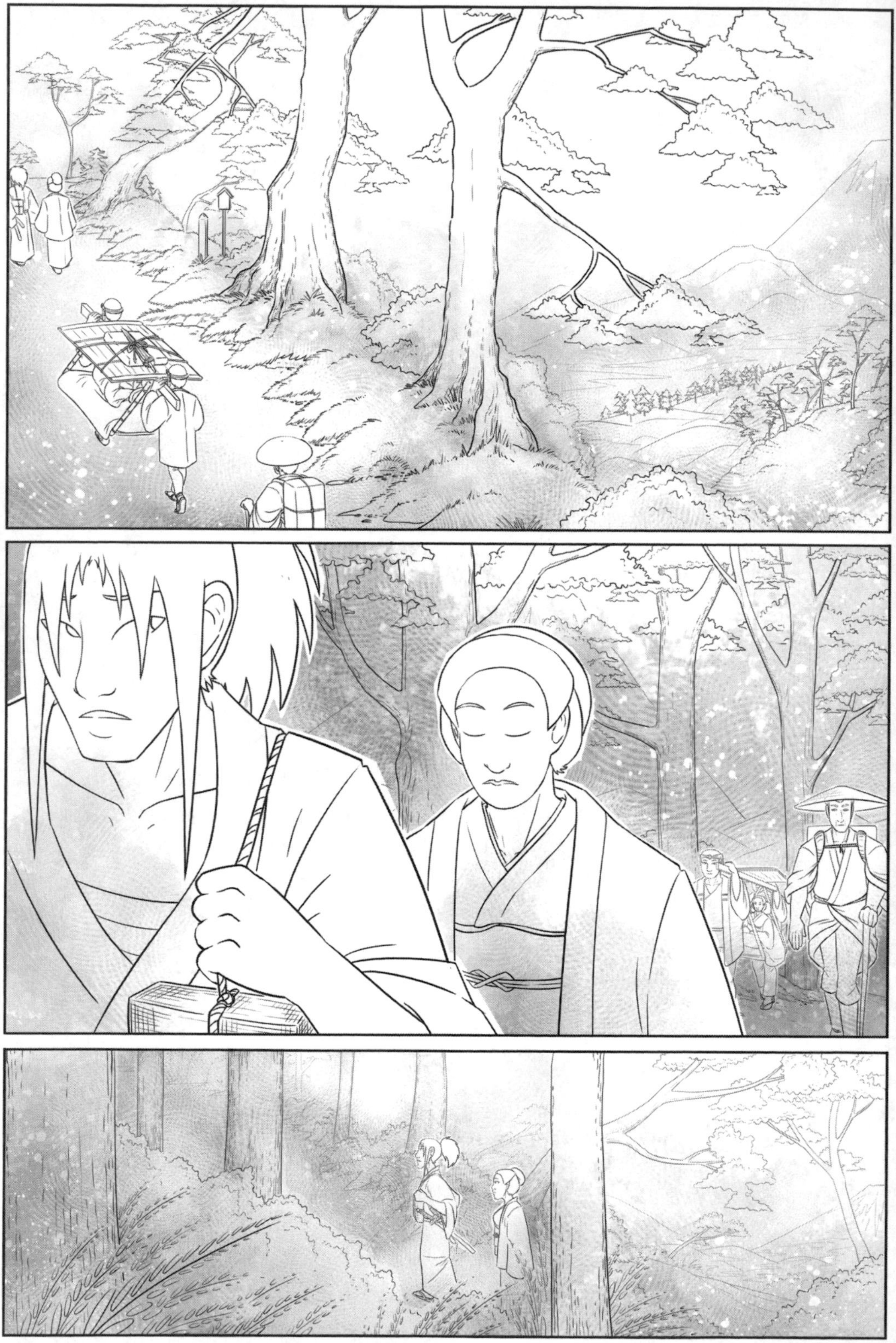

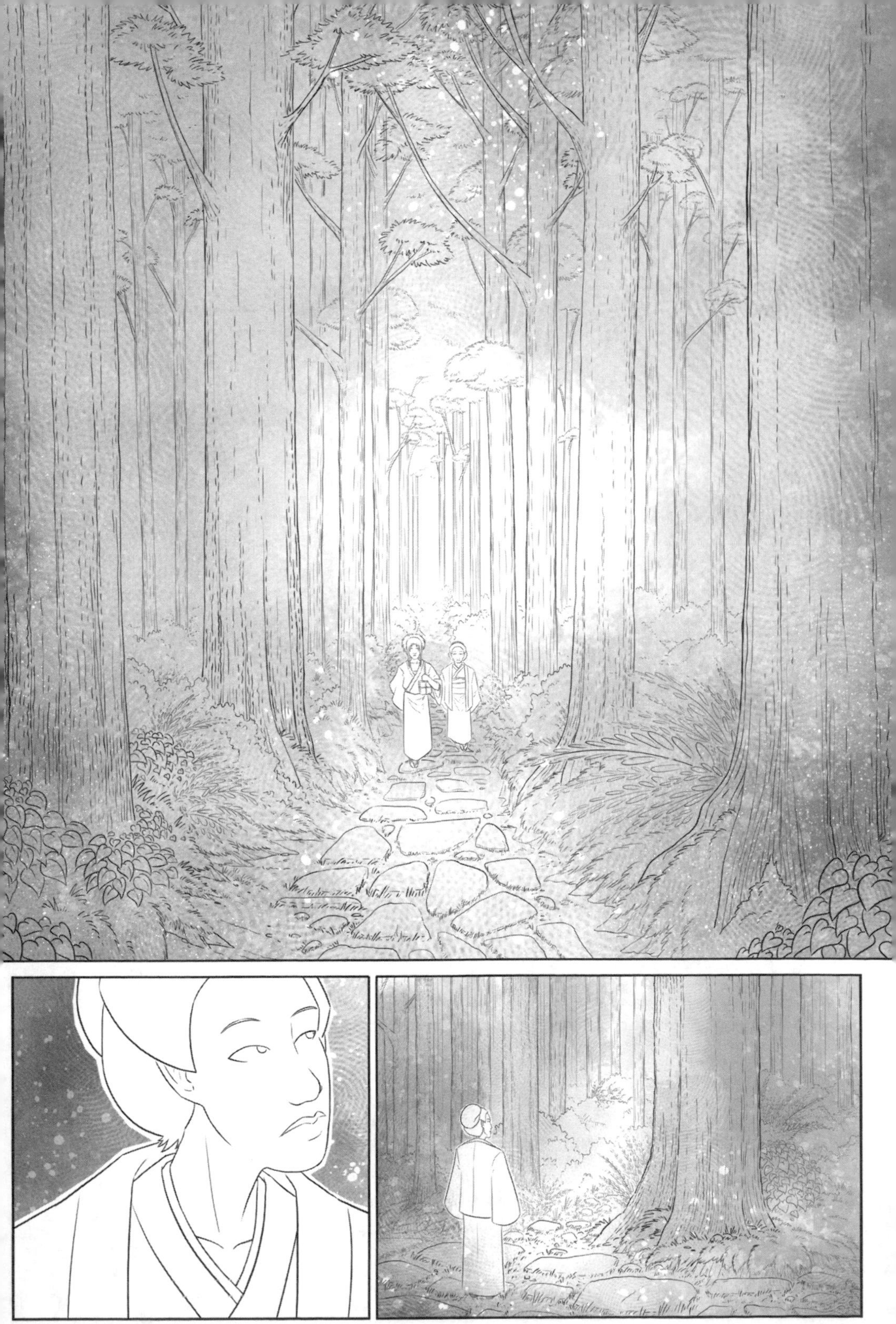

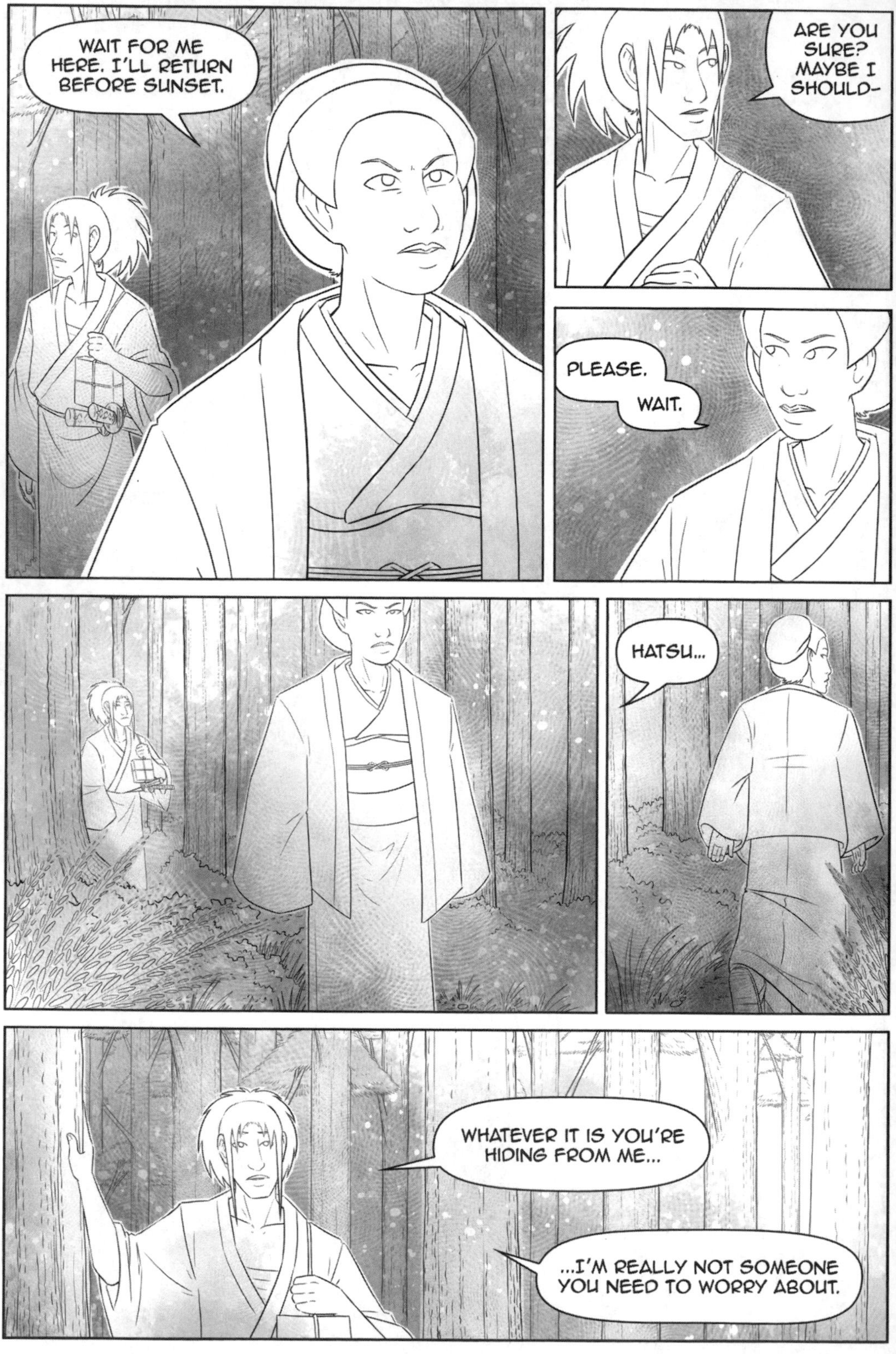
WAIT FOR ME HERE. I'LL RETURN BEFORE SUNSET.
ARE YOU SURE? MAYBE I SHOULD-
PLEASE.
WAIT.
HATSU...
WHATEVER IT IS YOU'RE HIDING FROM ME...
...I'M REALLY NOT SOMEONE YOU NEED TO WORRY ABOUT.

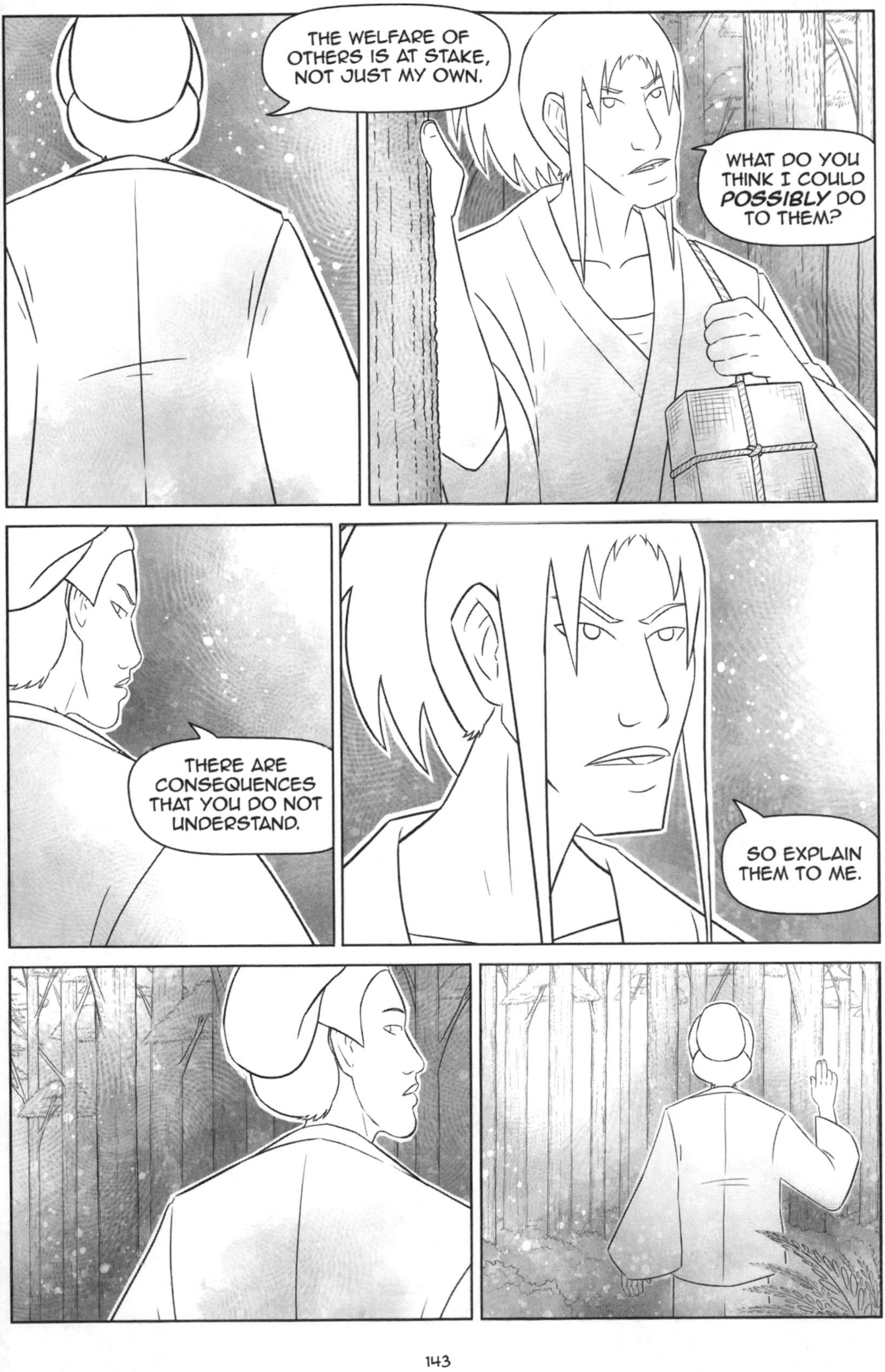
THE WELFARE OF OTHERS IS AT STAKE, NOT JUST MY OWN.
WHAT DO YOU THINK I COULD *POSSIBLY* DO TO THEM?
THERE ARE CONSEQUENCES THAT YOU DO NOT UNDERSTAND.
SO EXPLAIN THEM TO ME.

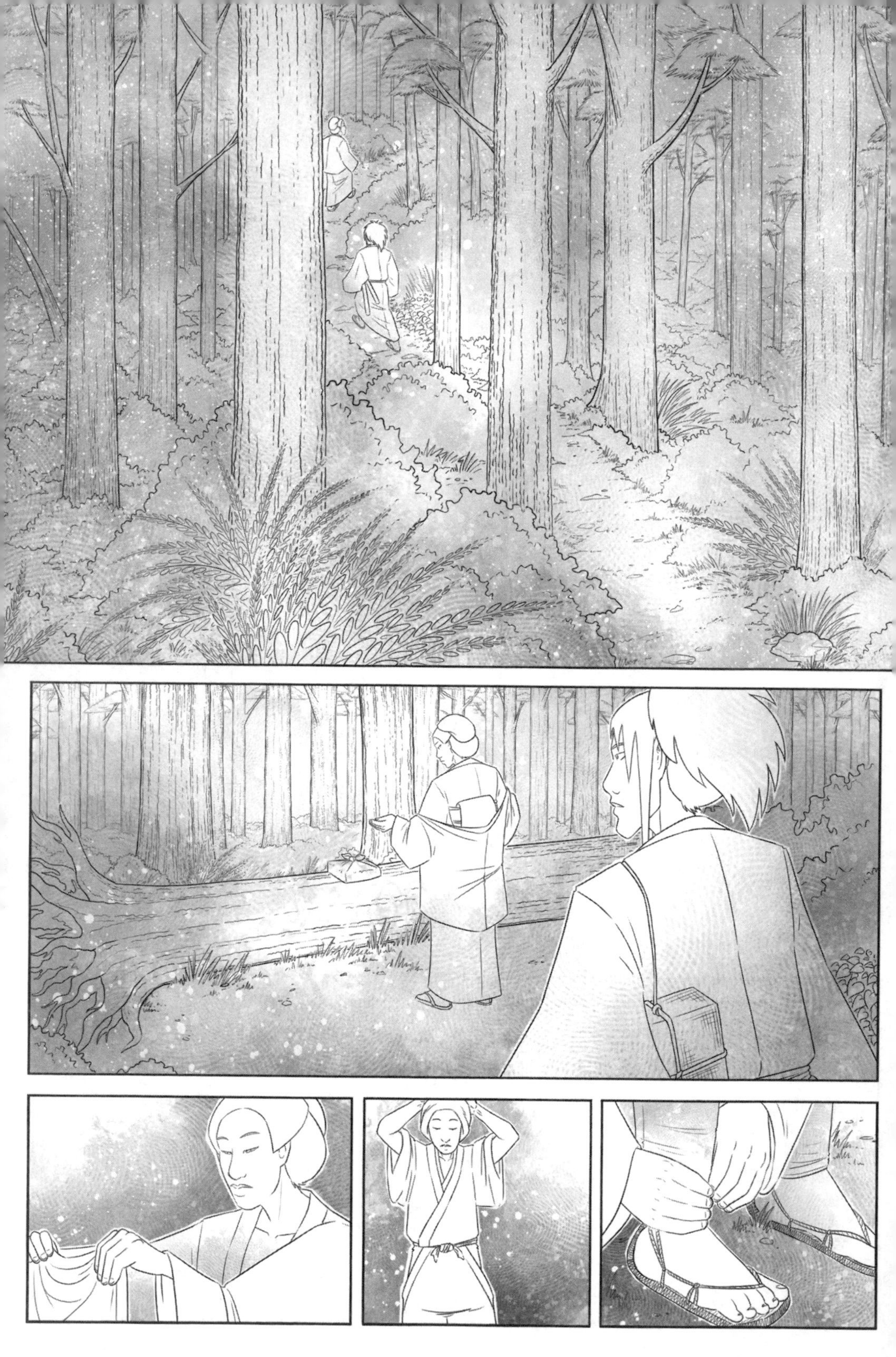

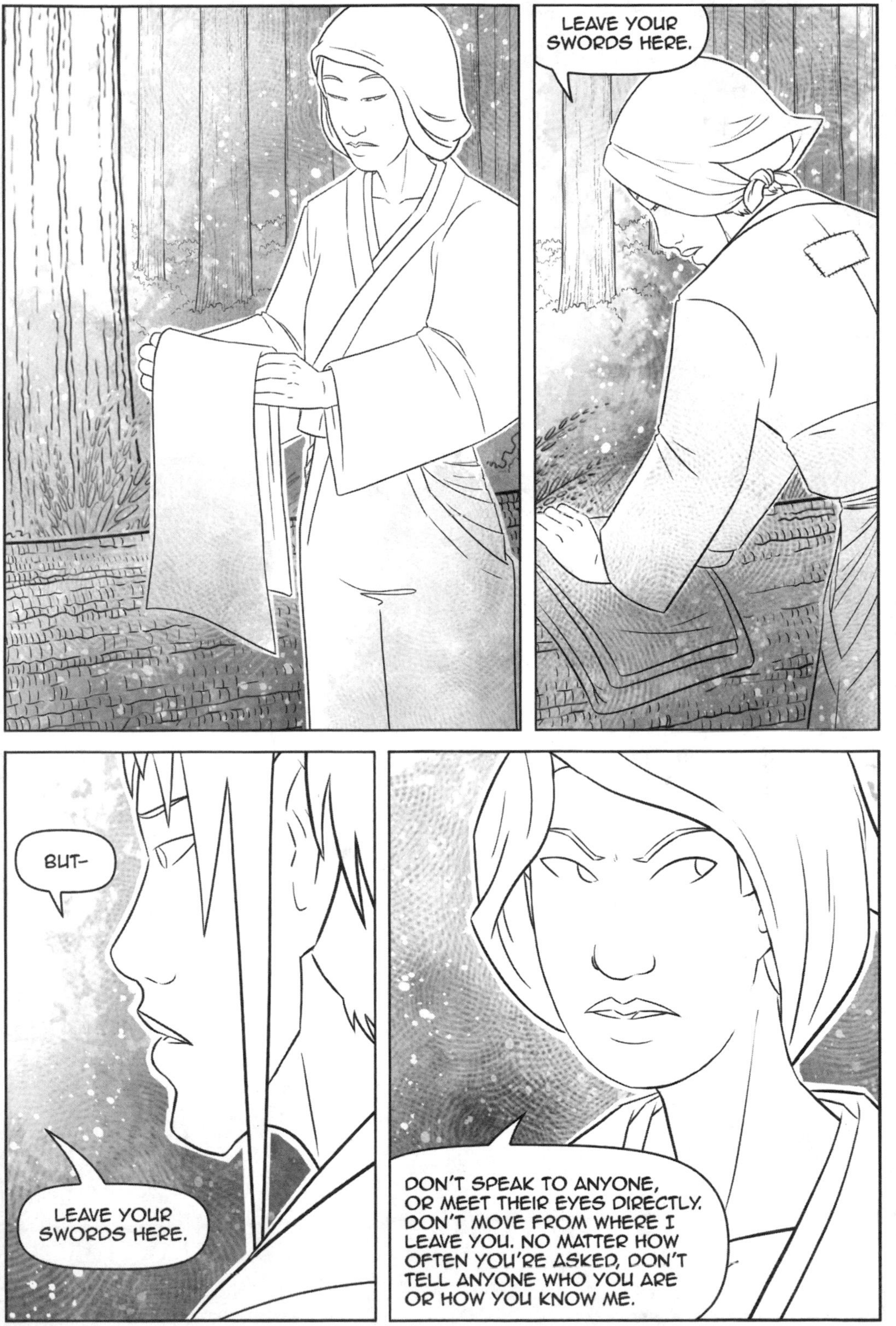
LEAVE YOUR SWORDS HERE.
BUT-
LEAVE YOUR SWORDS HERE.
DON'T SPEAK TO ANYONE, OR MEET THEIR EYES DIRECTLY. DON'T MOVE FROM WHERE I LEAVE YOU. NO MATTER HOW OFTEN YOU'RE ASKED, DON'T TELL ANYONE WHO YOU ARE OR HOW YOU KNOW ME.

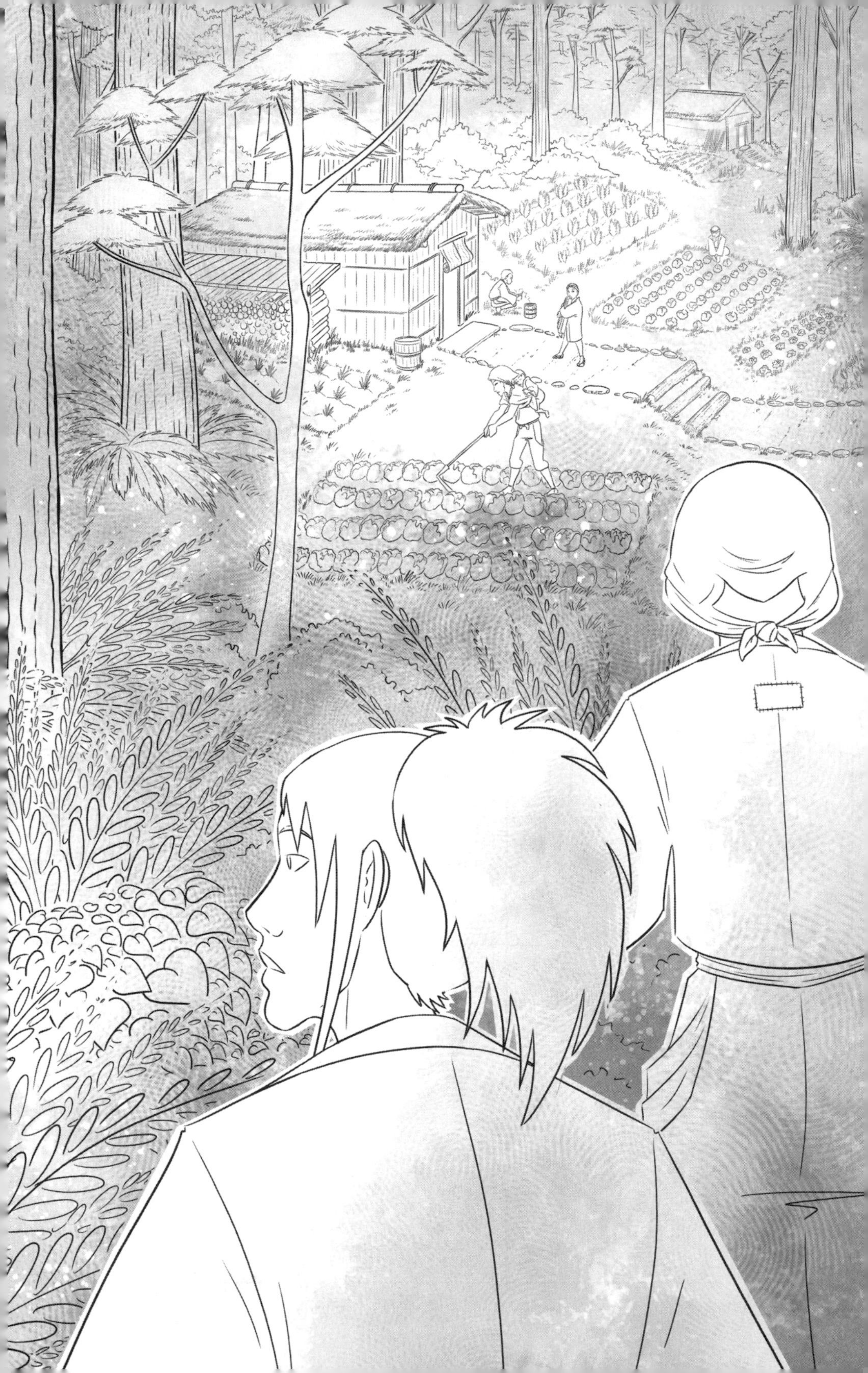

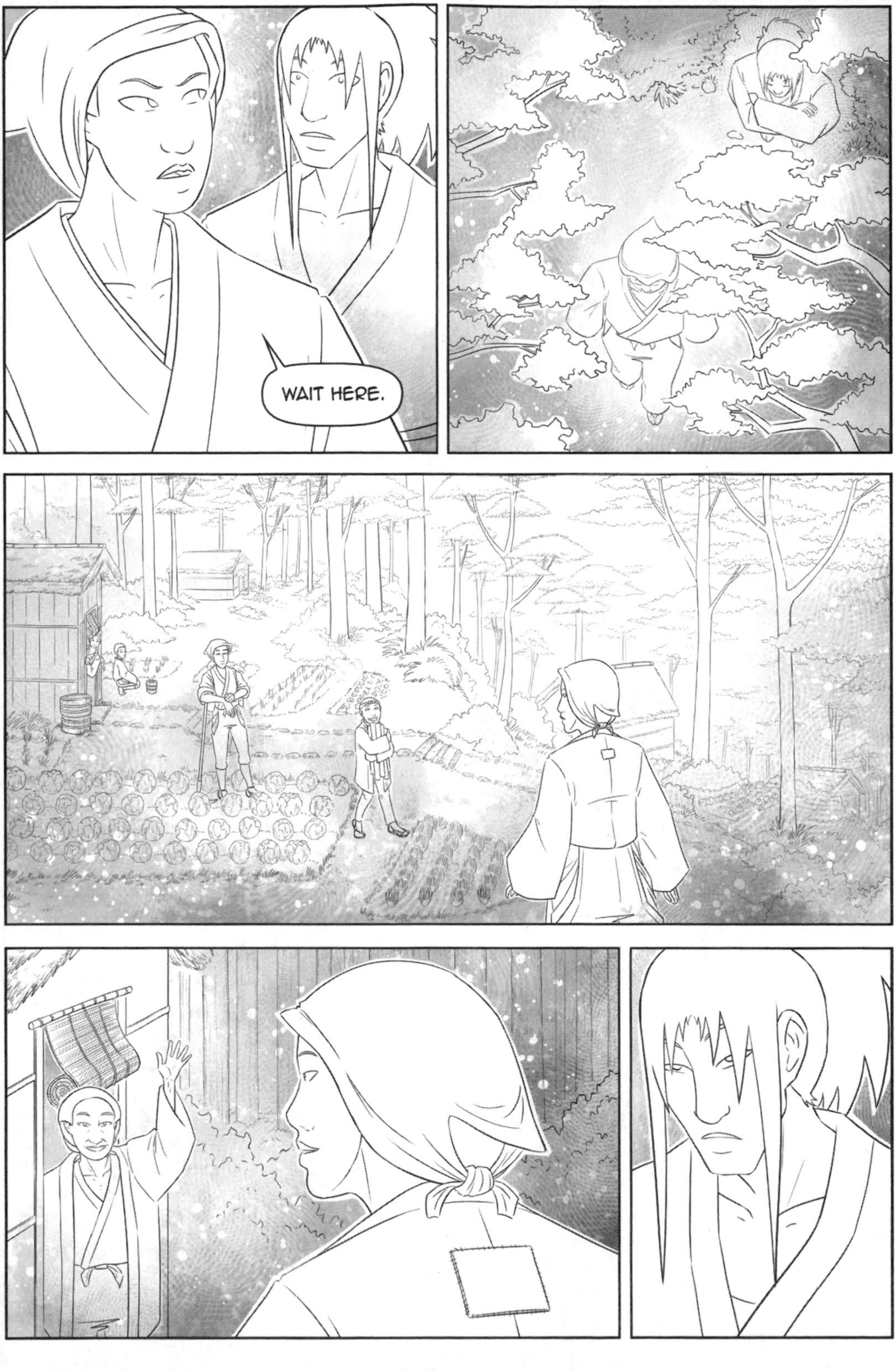
WAIT HERE.

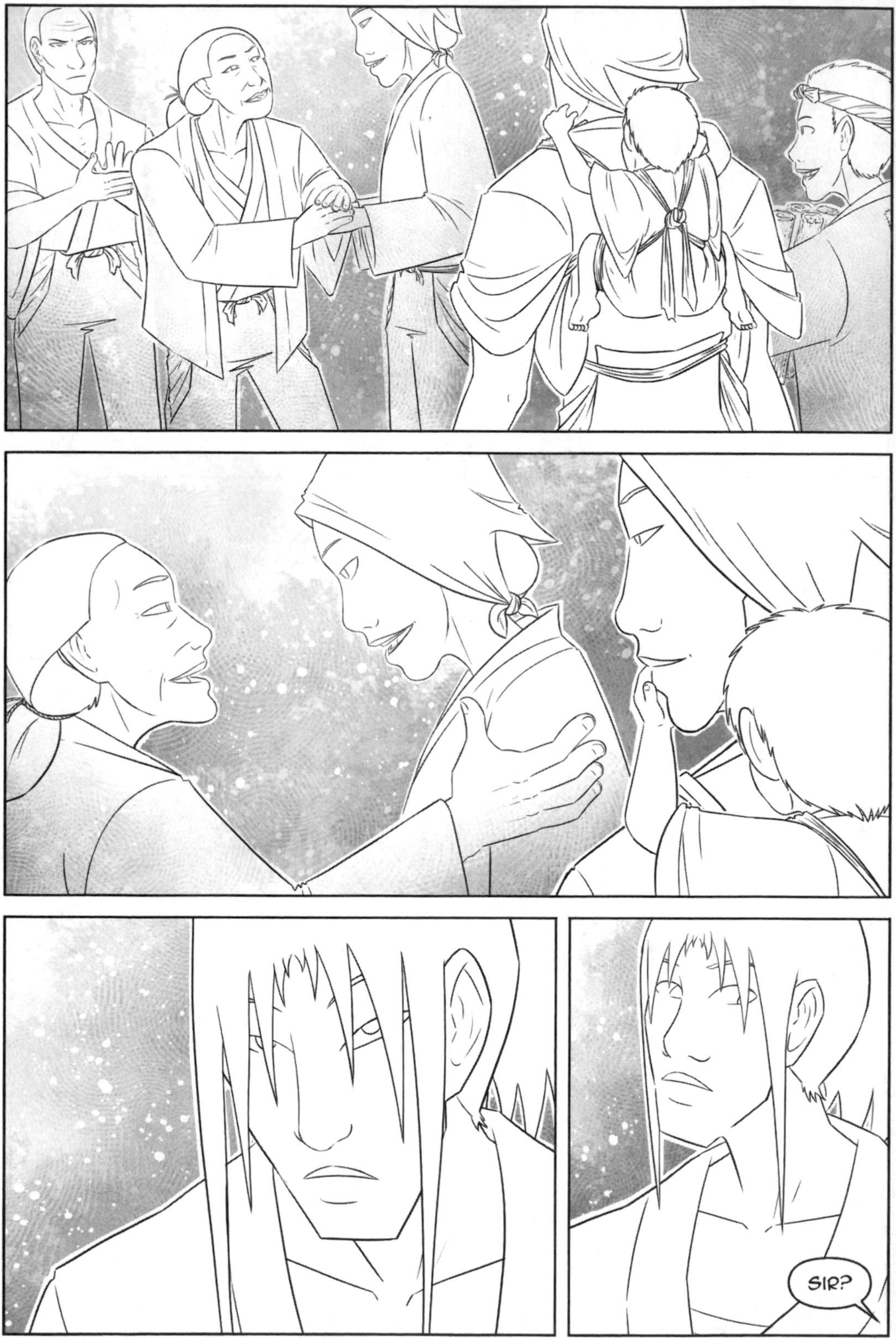
SIR?

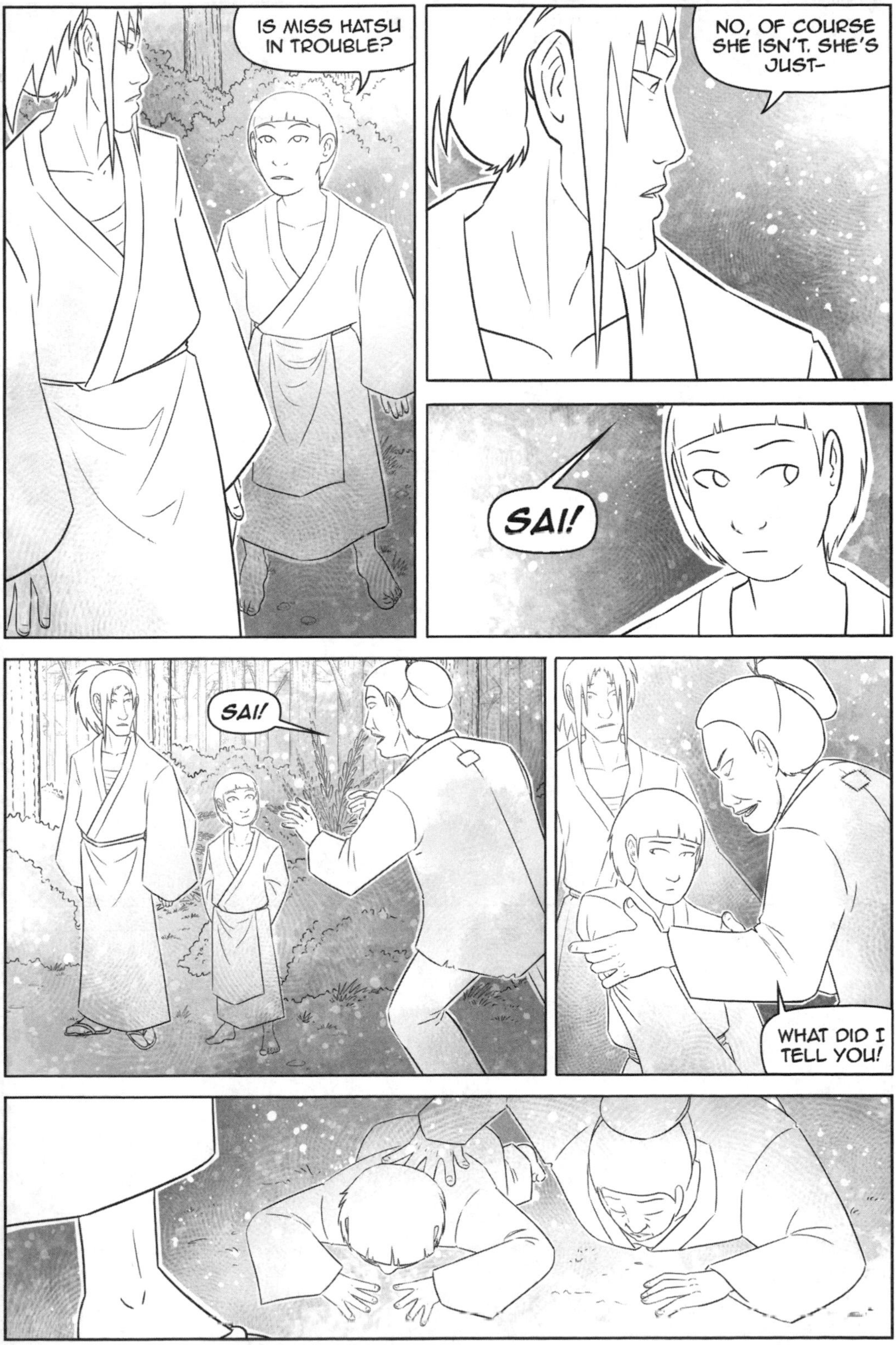
IS MISS HATSU IN TROUBLE?
NO, OF COURSE SHE ISN'T. SHE'S JUST-
SAI!
SAI!
WHAT DID I TELL YOU!

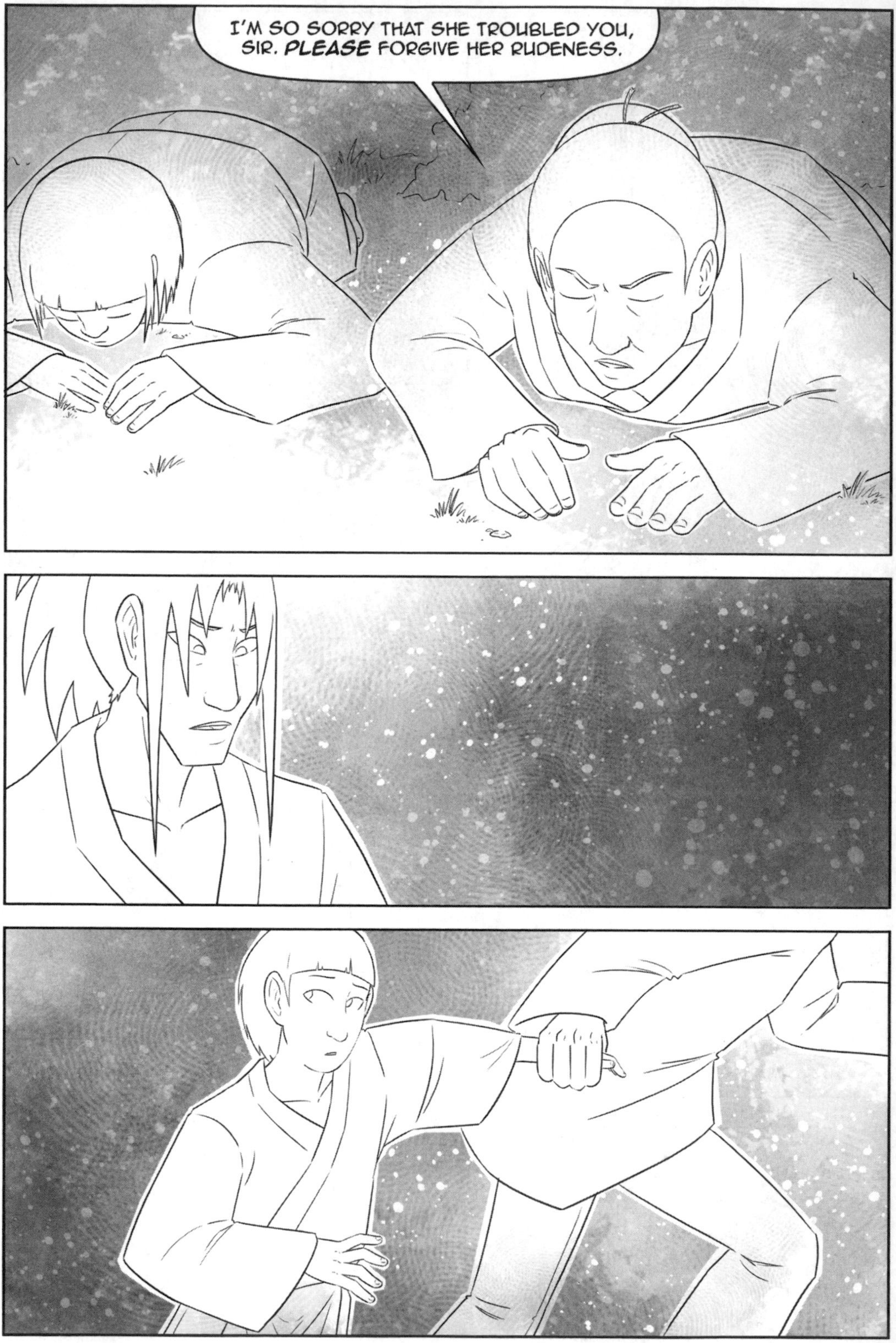
I'M SO SORRY THAT SHE TROUBLED YOU, SIR. PLEASE FORGIVE HER RUDENESS.

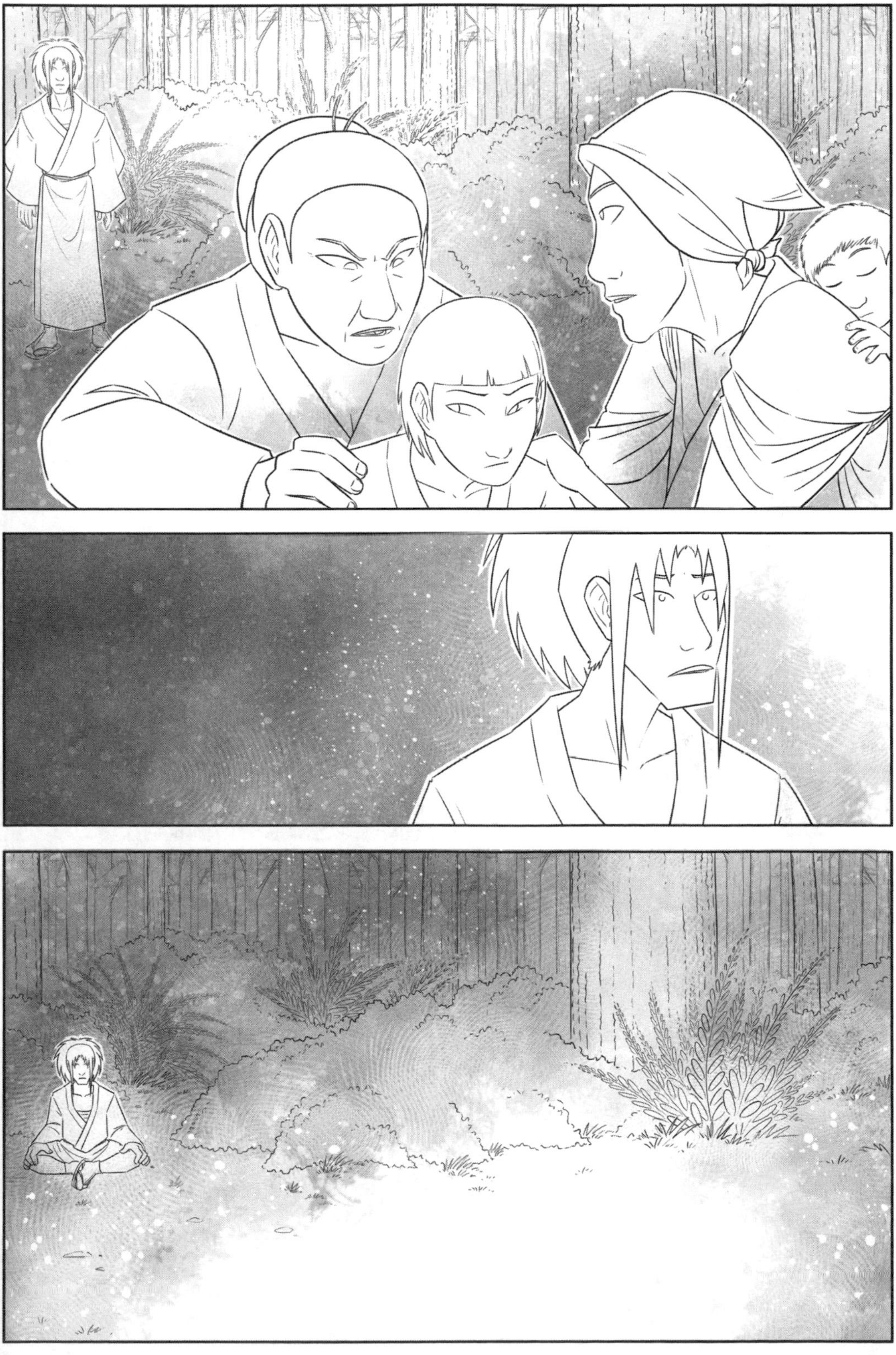

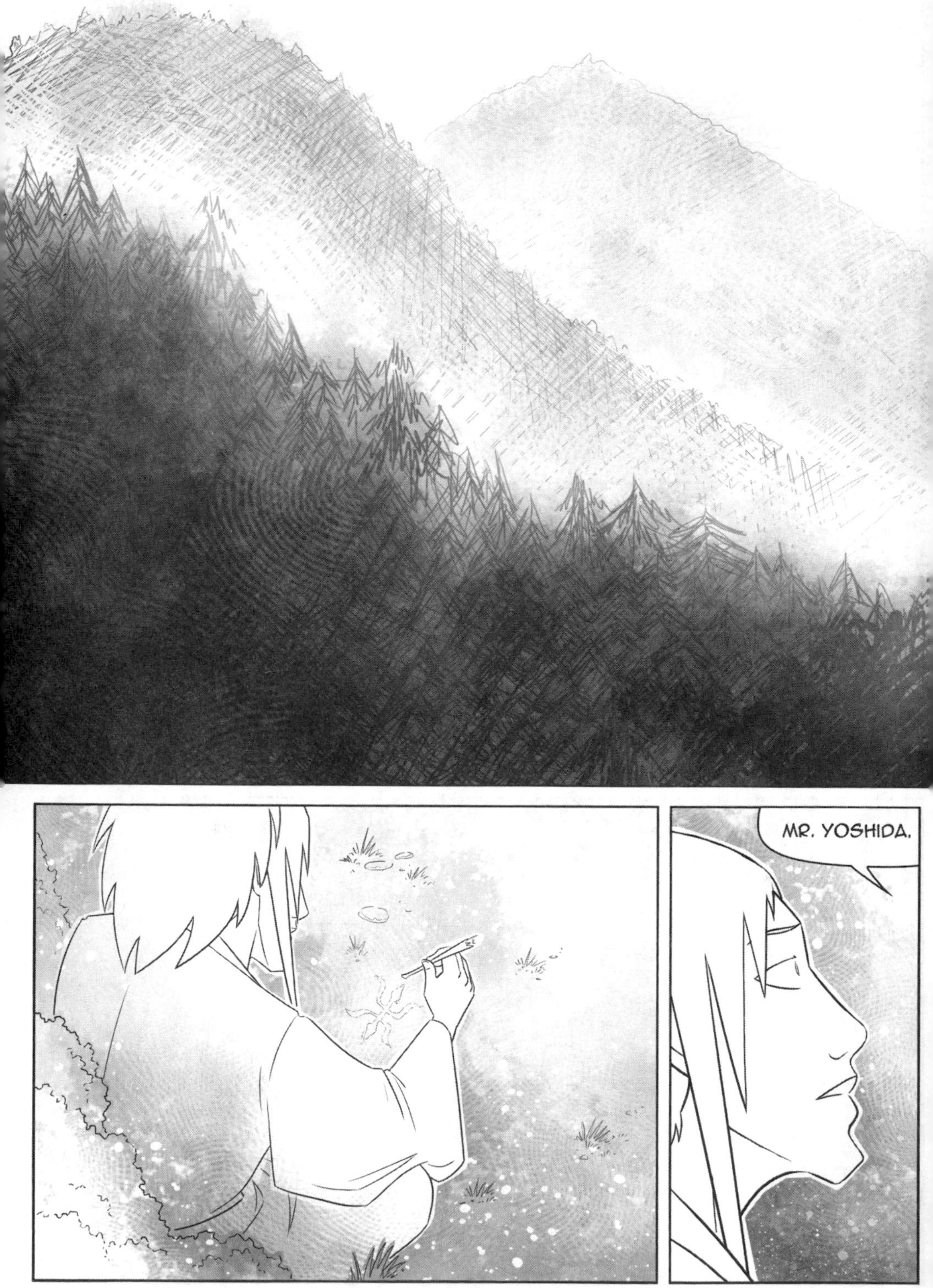
MR. YOSHIDA.

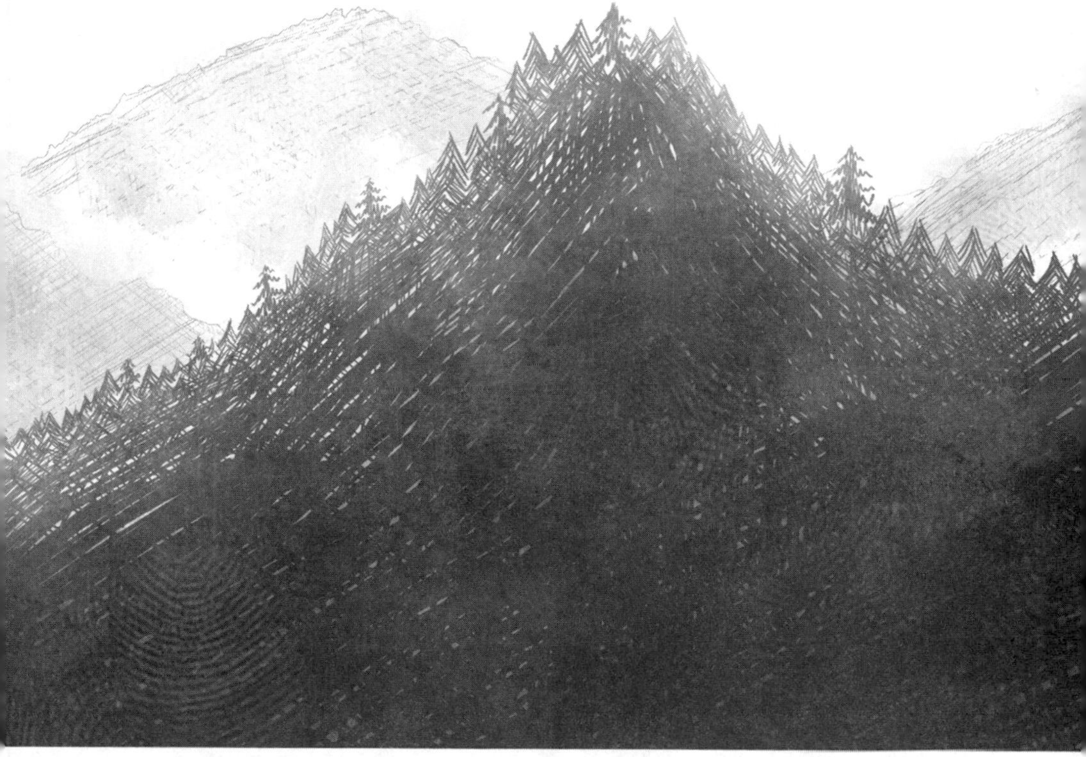

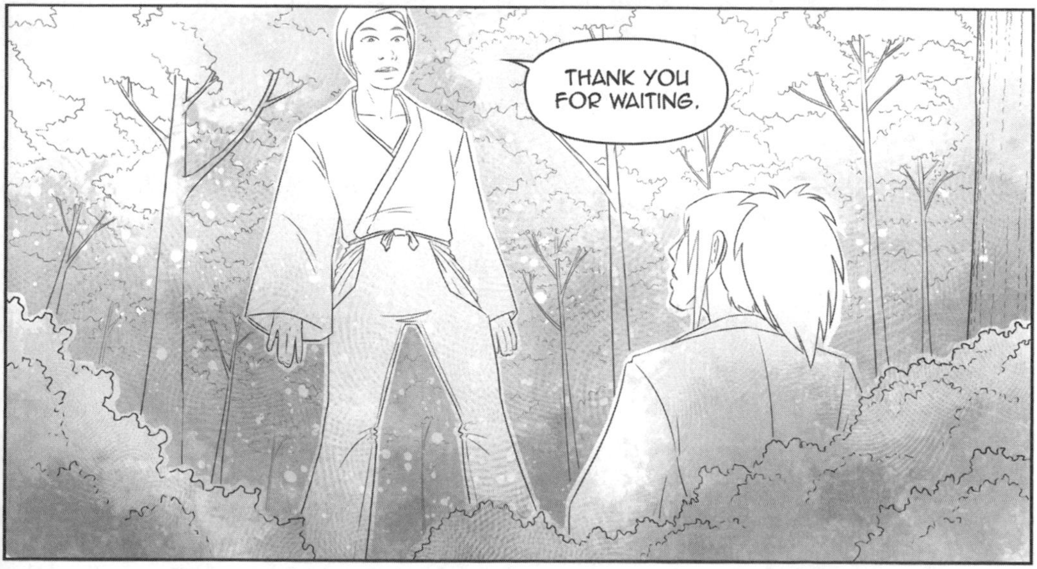
THANK YOU FOR WAITING.

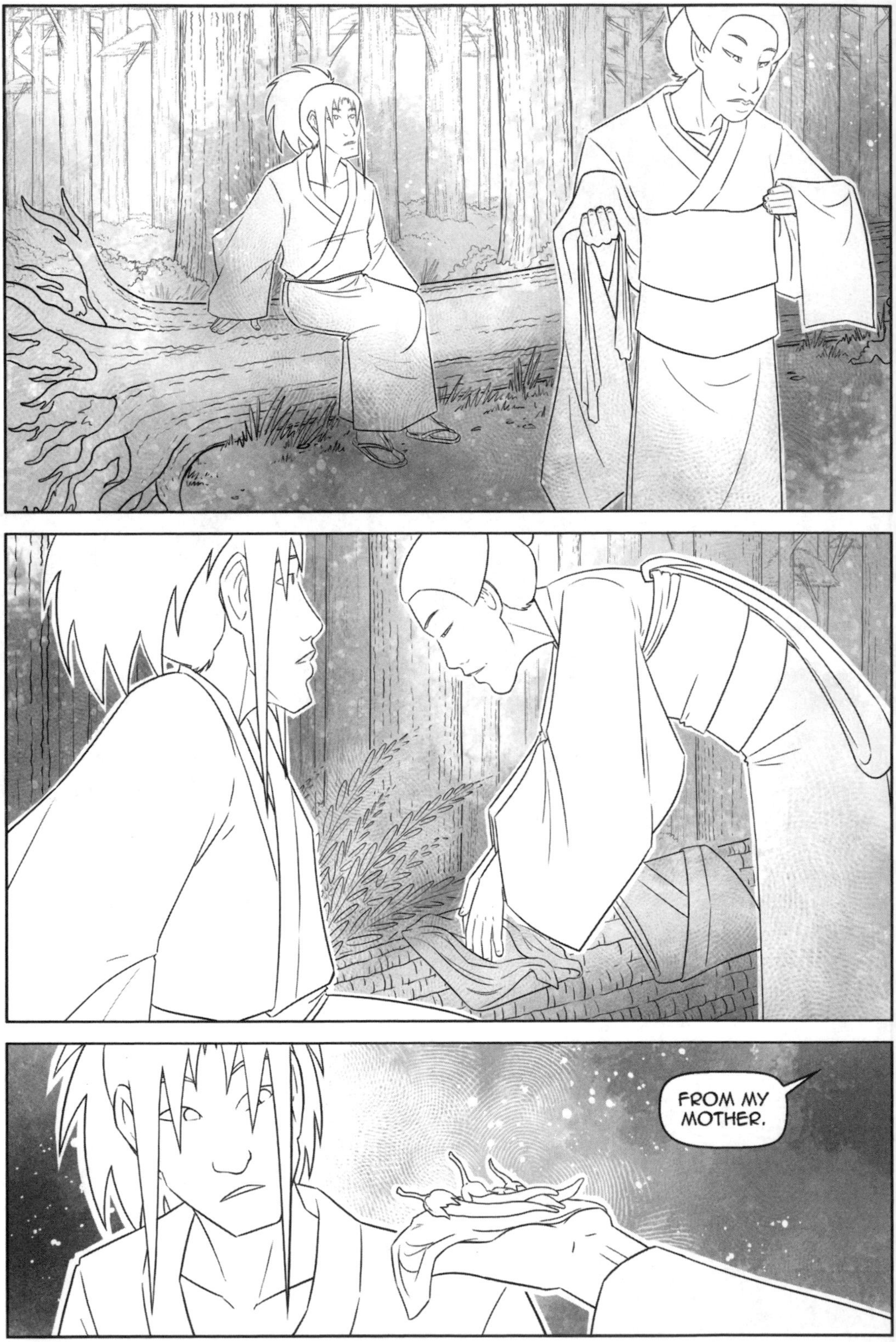
FROM MY MOTHER.

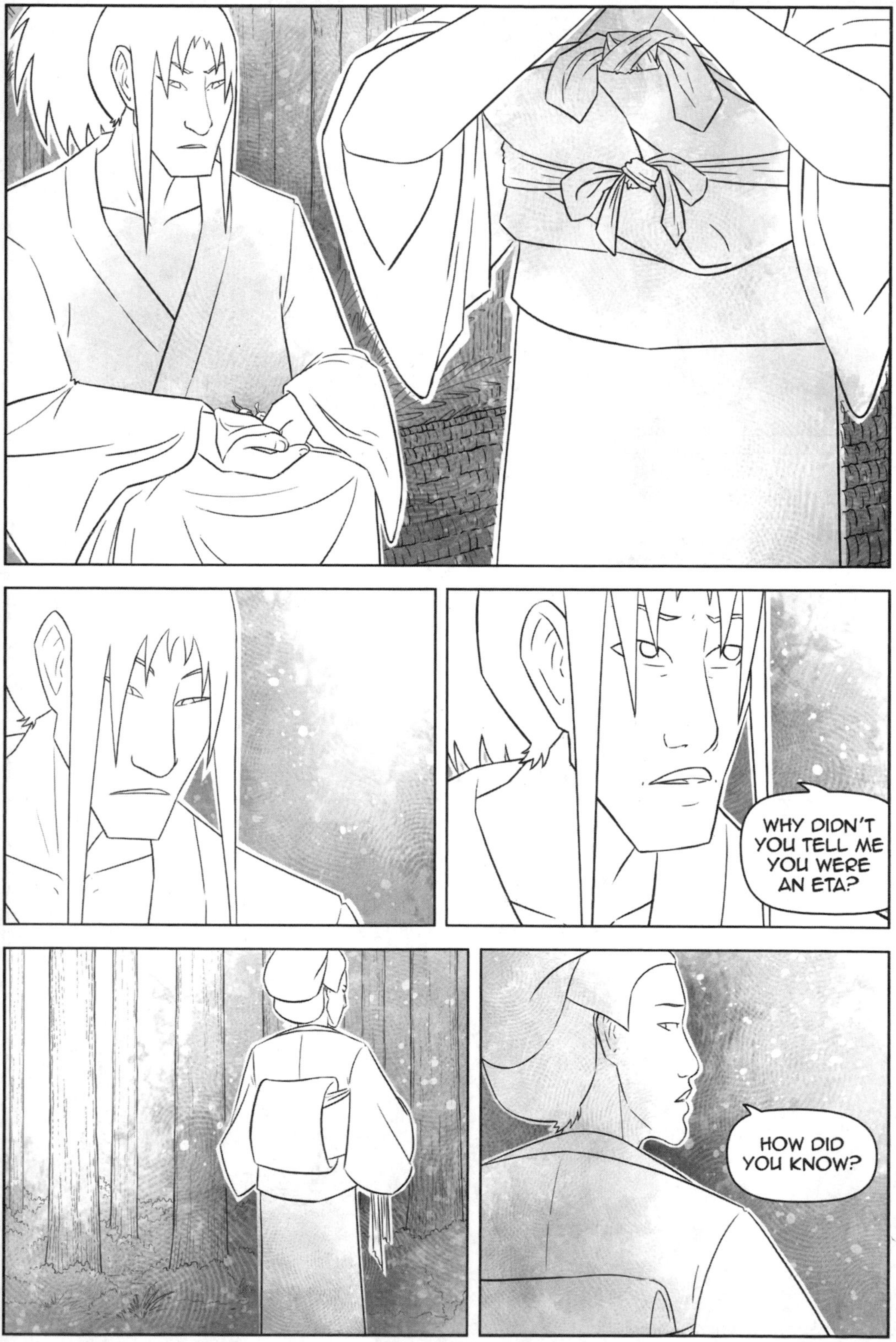
WHY DIDN'T YOU TELL ME YOU WERE AN ETA?
HOW DID YOU KNOW?

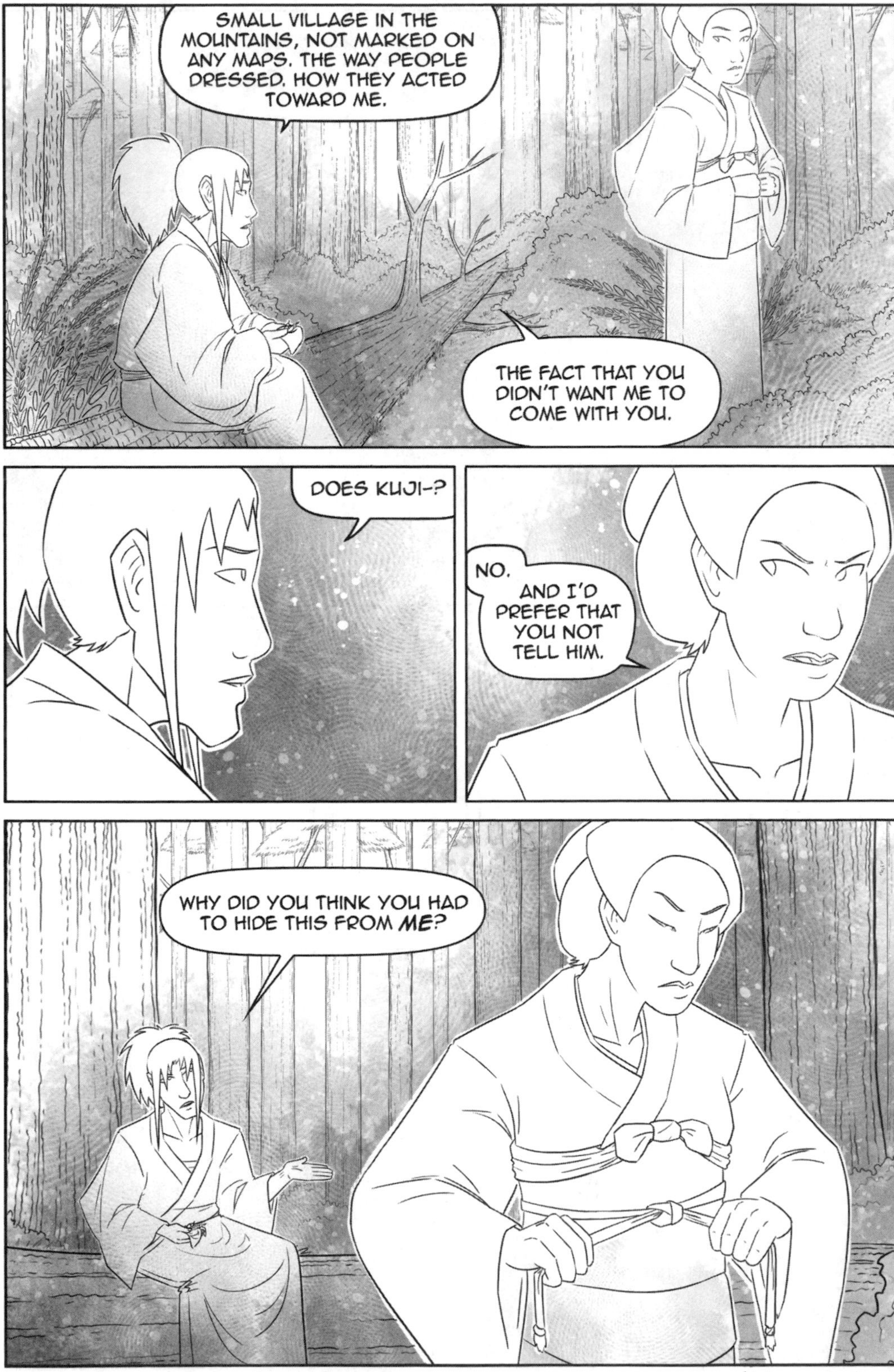
SMALL VILLAGE IN THE MOUNTAINS, NOT MARKED ON ANY MAPS. THE WAY PEOPLE DRESSED. HOW THEY ACTED TOWARD ME.
THE FACT THAT YOU DIDN'T WANT ME TO COME WITH YOU.
DOES KUJI-?
NO.
AND I'D PREFER THAT YOU NOT TELL HIM.
WHY DID YOU THINK YOU HAD TO HIDE THIS FROM *ME*?

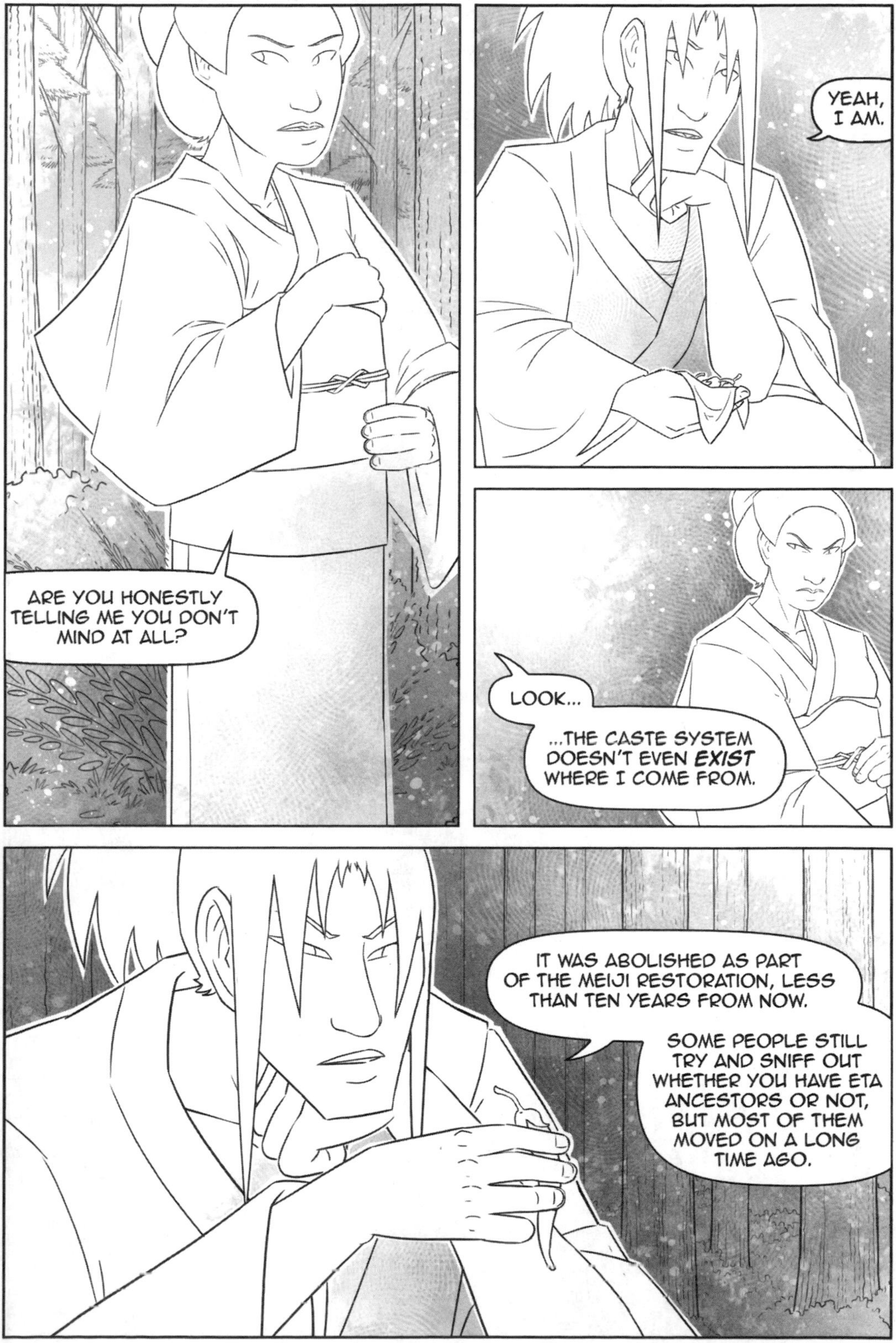
ARE YOU HONESTLY TELLING ME YOU DON'T MIND AT ALL?
YEAH, I AM.
LOOK...
...THE CASTE SYSTEM DOESN'T EVEN *EXIST* WHERE I COME FROM.
IT WAS ABOLISHED AS PART OF THE MEIJI RESTORATION, LESS THAN TEN YEARS FROM NOW.
SOME PEOPLE STILL TRY AND SNIFF OUT WHETHER YOU HAVE ETA ANCESTORS OR NOT, BUT MOST OF THEM MOVED ON A LONG TIME AGO.

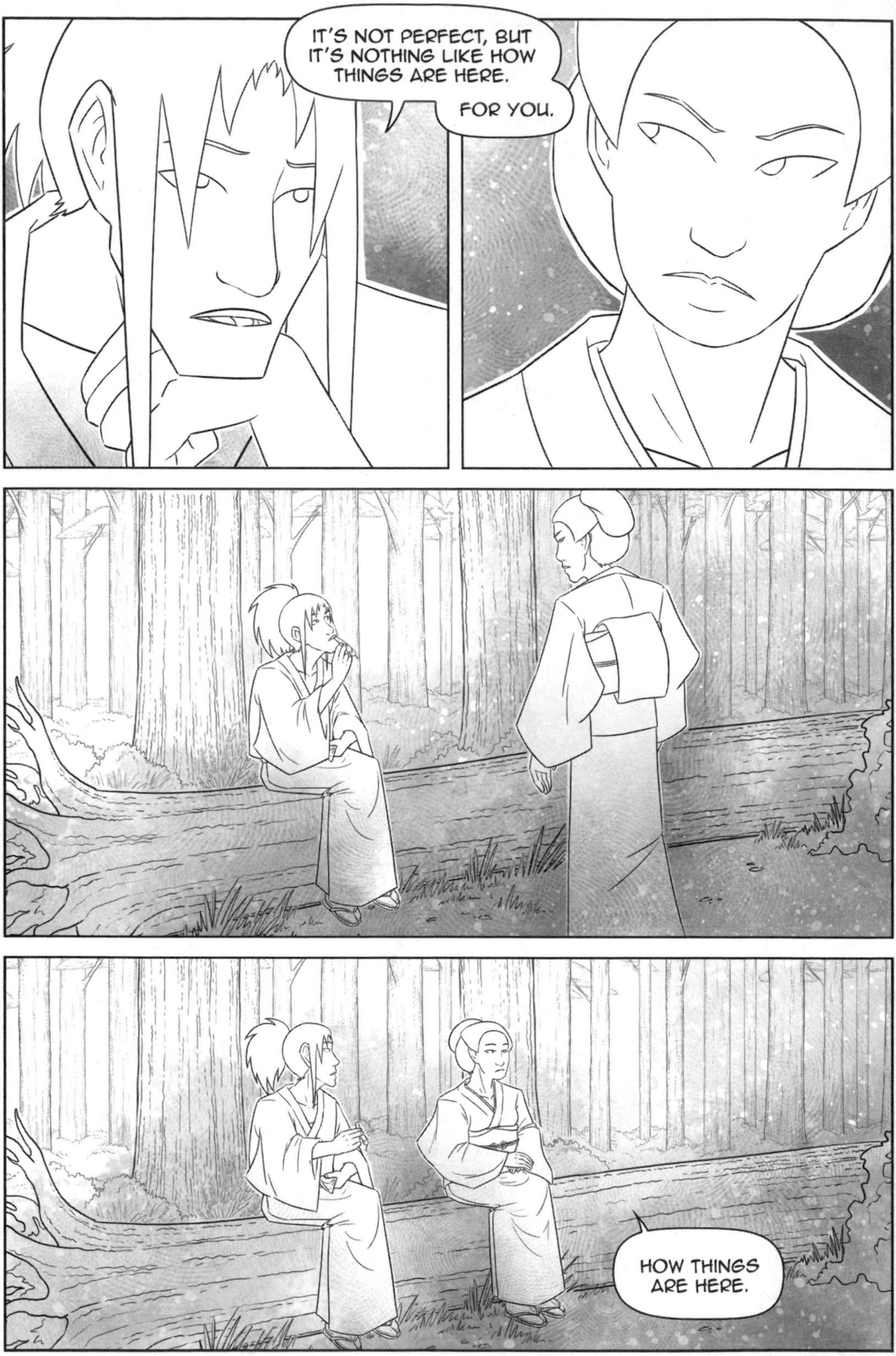
IT'S NOT PERFECT, BUT IT'S NOTHING LIKE HOW THINGS ARE HERE.
FOR YOU.
HOW THINGS ARE HERE.

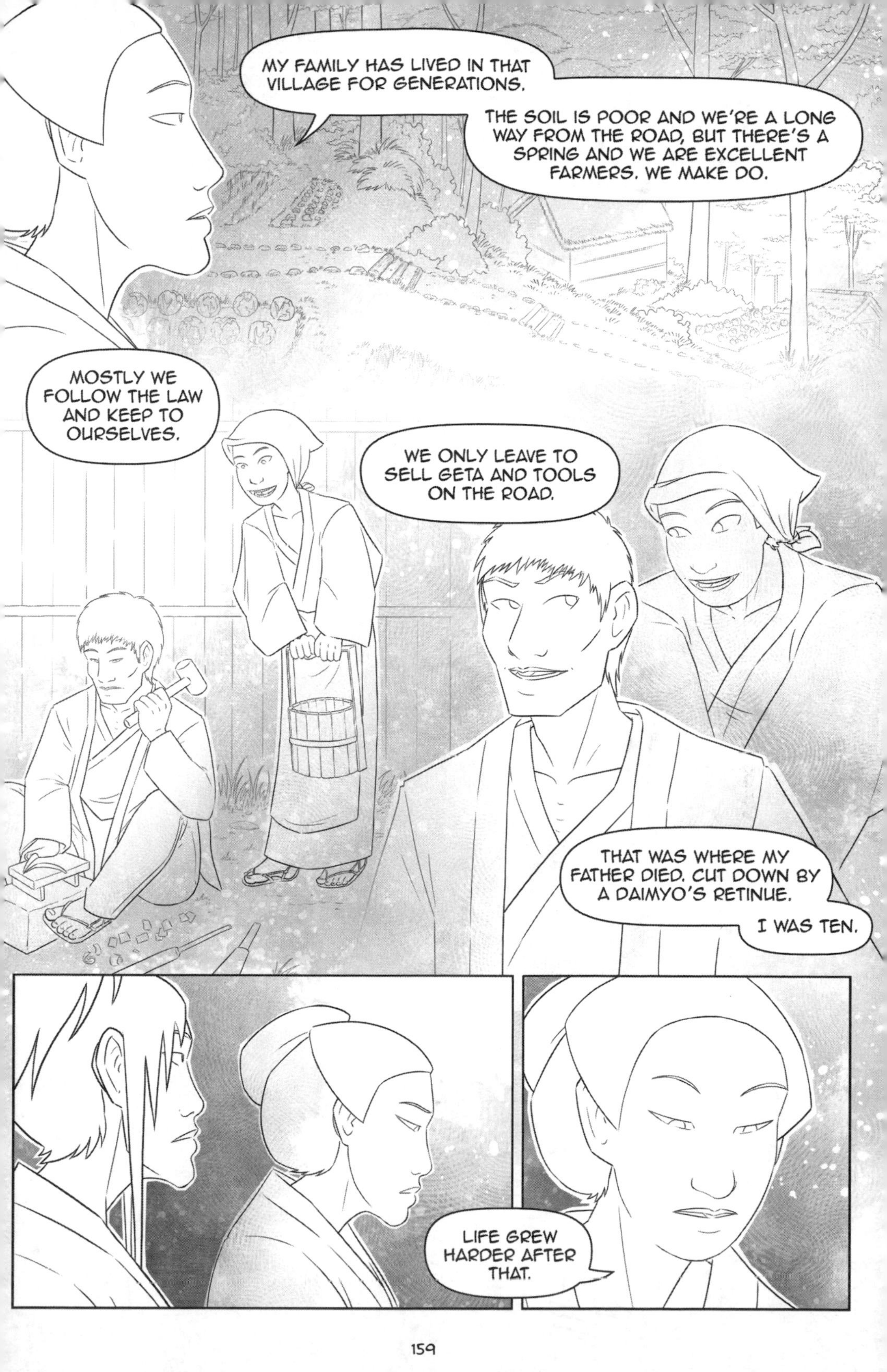
MY FAMILY HAS LIVED IN THAT VILLAGE FOR GENERATIONS.
THE SOIL IS POOR AND WE'RE A LONG WAY FROM THE ROAD, BUT THERE'S A SPRING AND WE ARE EXCELLENT FARMERS. WE MAKE DO.
MOSTLY WE FOLLOW THE LAW AND KEEP TO OURSELVES.
WE ONLY LEAVE TO SELL GETA AND TOOLS ON THE ROAD.
THAT WAS WHERE MY FATHER DIED. CUT DOWN BY A DAIMYO'S RETINUE.
I WAS TEN.
LIFE GREW HARDER AFTER THAT.

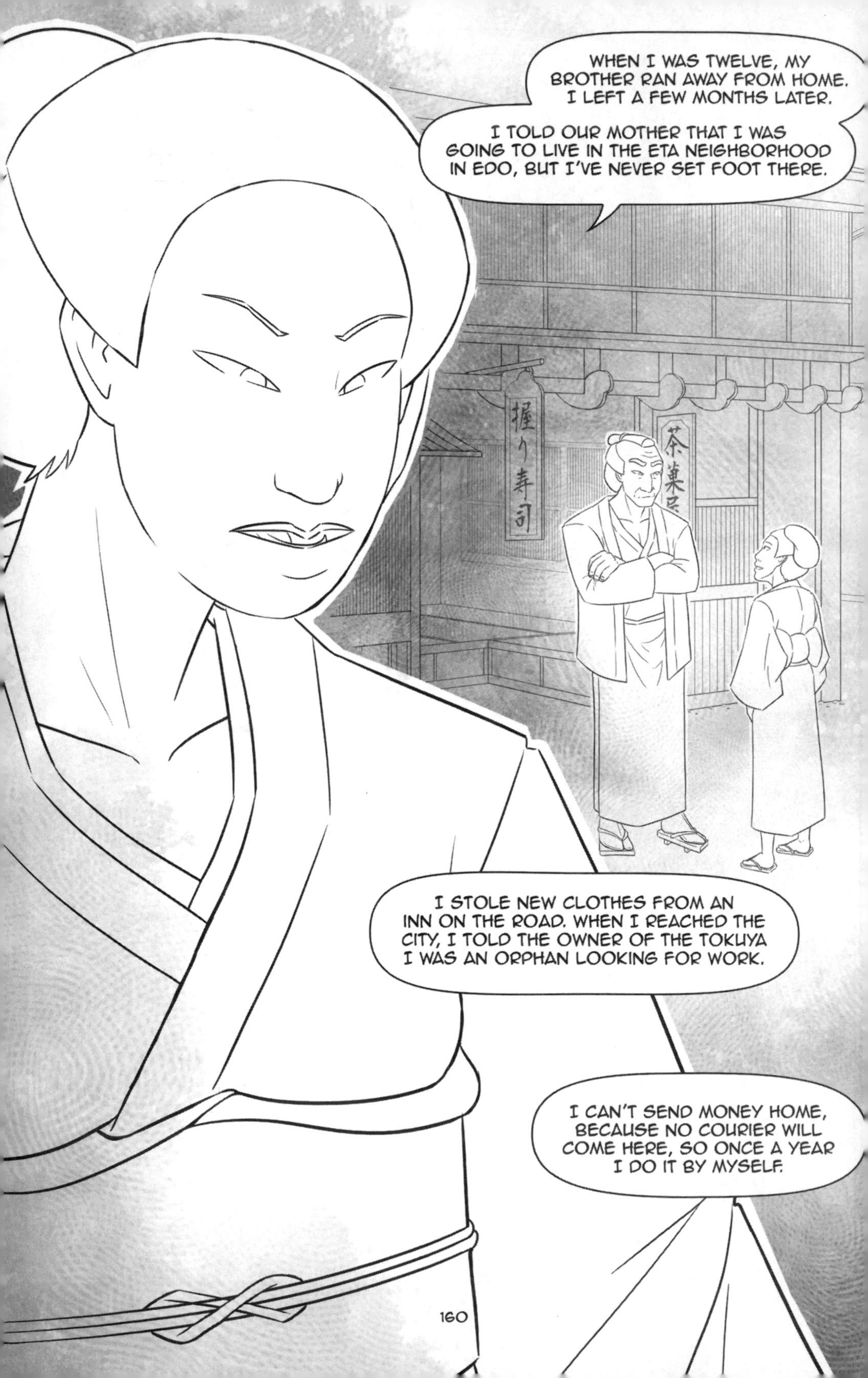
WHEN I WAS TWELVE, MY BROTHER RAN AWAY FROM HOME. I LEFT A FEW MONTHS LATER.
I TOLD OUR MOTHER THAT I WAS GOING TO LIVE IN THE ETA NEIGHBORHOOD IN EDO, BUT I'VE NEVER SET FOOT THERE.
握り寿司
I STOLE NEW CLOTHES FROM AN INN ON THE ROAD. WHEN I REACHED THE CITY, I TOLD THE OWNER OF THE TOKUYA I WAS AN ORPHAN LOOKING FOR WORK.
I CAN'T SEND MONEY HOME, BECAUSE NO COURIER WILL COME HERE, SO ONCE A YEAR I DO IT BY MYSELF.

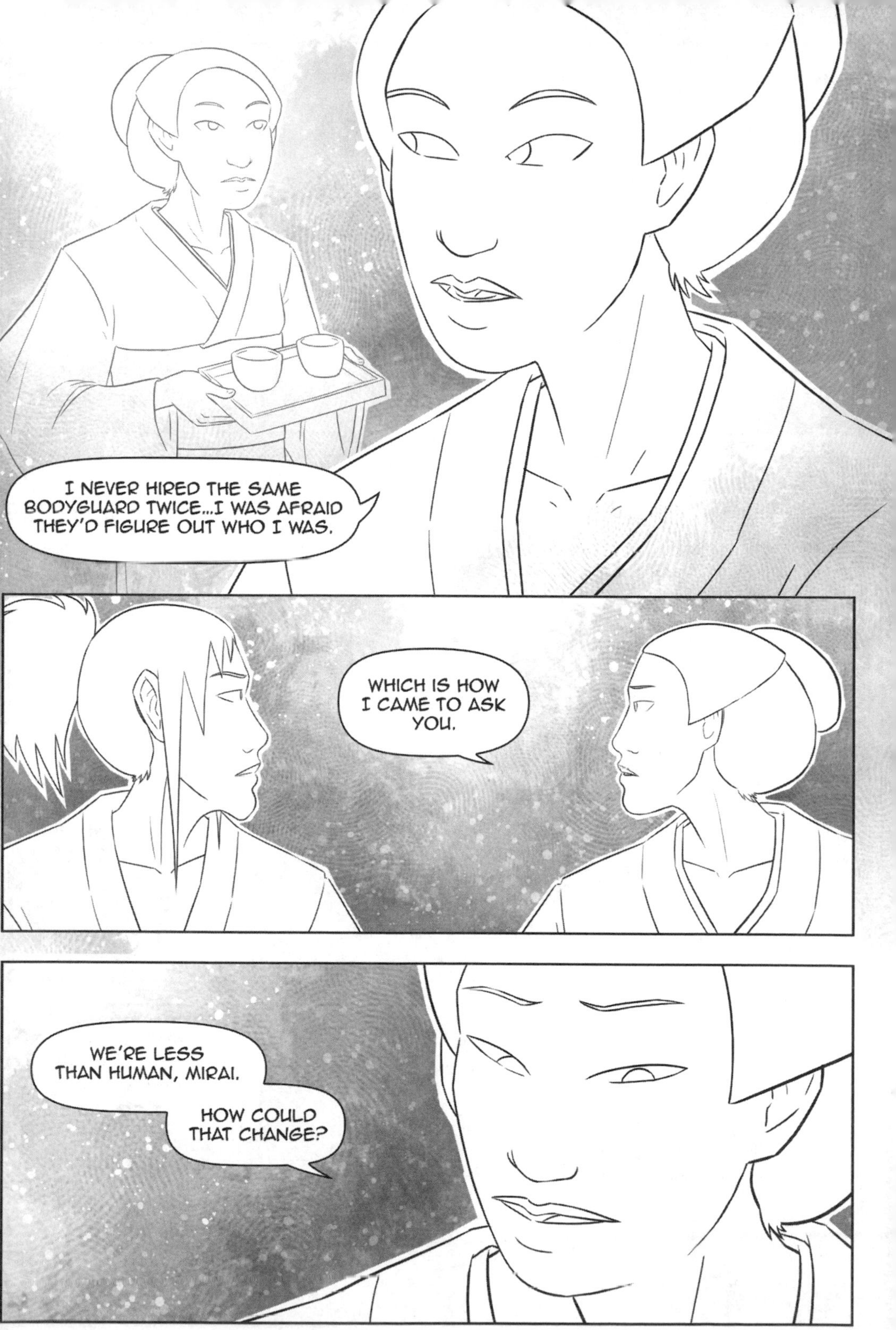
I NEVER HIRED THE SAME BODYGUARD TWICE...I WAS AFRAID THEY'D FIGURE OUT WHO I WAS.
WHICH IS HOW I CAME TO ASK YOU.
WE'RE LESS THAN HUMAN, MIRAI.
HOW COULD THAT CHANGE?

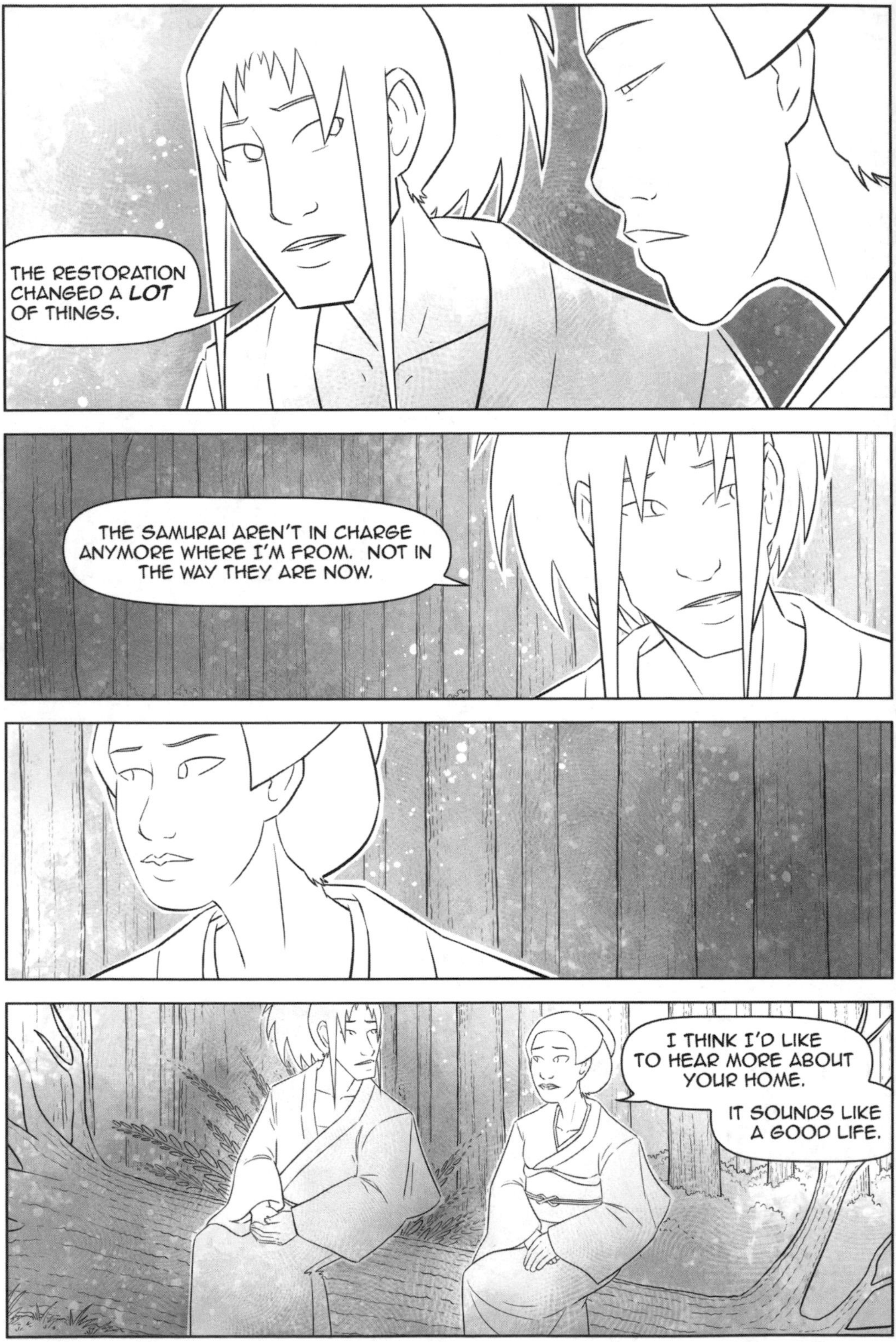
THE RESTORATION CHANGED A ***LOT*** OF THINGS.
THE SAMURAI AREN'T IN CHARGE ANYMORE WHERE I'M FROM. NOT IN THE WAY THEY ARE NOW.
I THINK I'D LIKE TO HEAR MORE ABOUT YOUR HOME.
IT SOUNDS LIKE A GOOD LIFE.

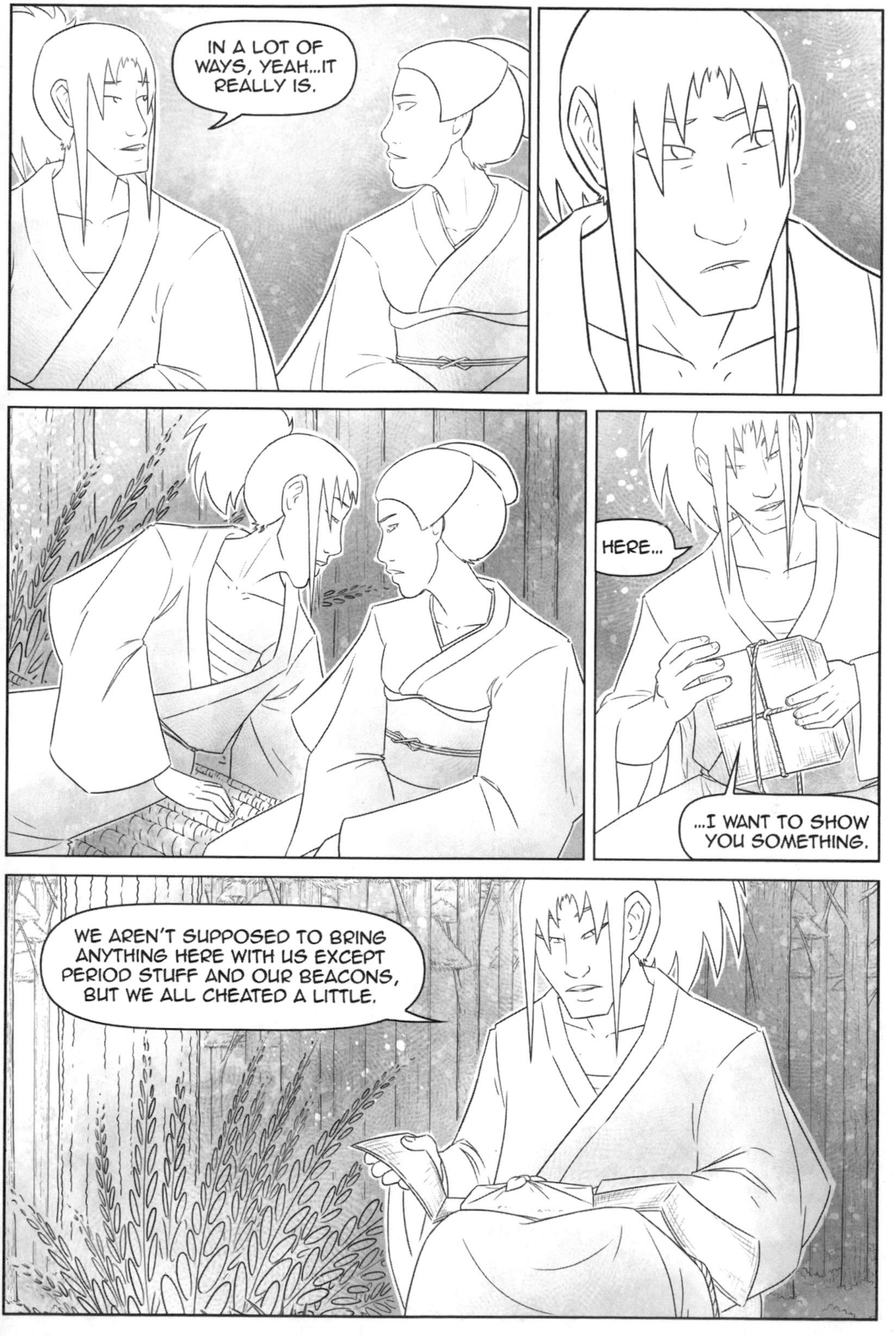
IN A LOT OF WAYS, YEAH...IT REALLY IS.
HERE...
...I WANT TO SHOW YOU SOMETHING.
WE AREN'T SUPPOSED TO BRING ANYTHING HERE WITH US EXCEPT PERIOD STUFF AND OUR BEACONS, BUT WE ALL CHEATED A LITTLE.

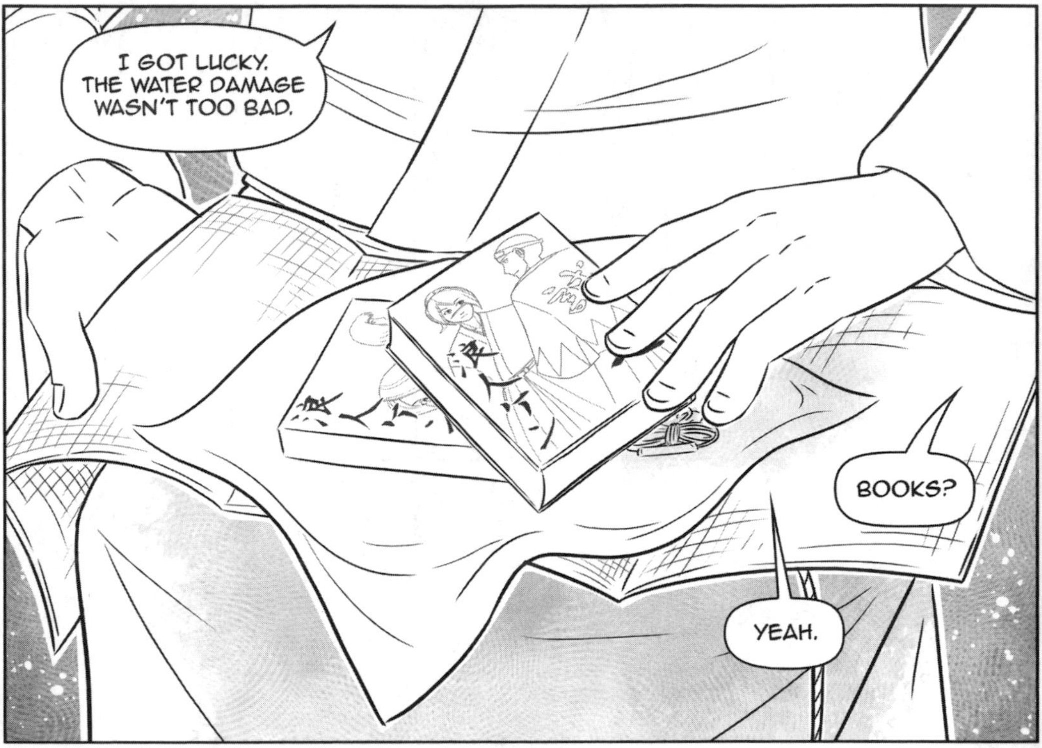
I GOT LUCKY. THE WATER DAMAGE WASN'T TOO BAD.
BOOKS?
YEAH.

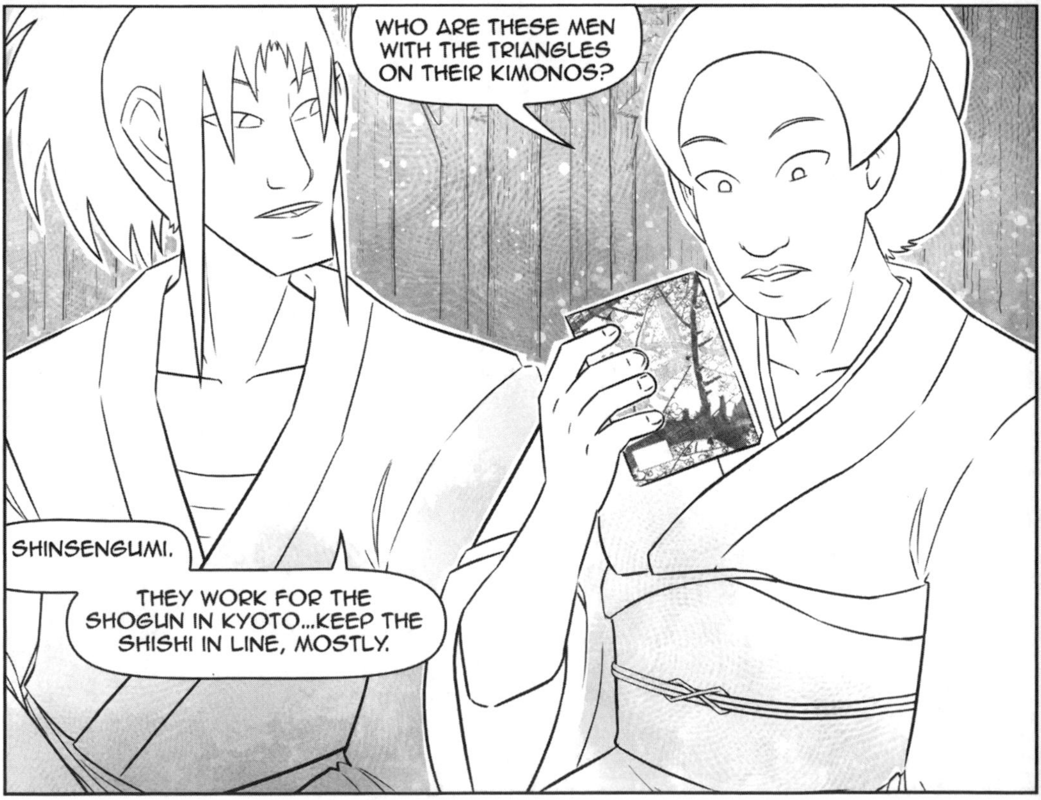
WHO ARE THESE MEN WITH THE TRIANGLES ON THEIR KIMONOS?
SHINSENGUMI.
THEY WORK FOR THE SHOGUN IN KYOTO...KEEP THE SHISHI IN LINE, MOSTLY.

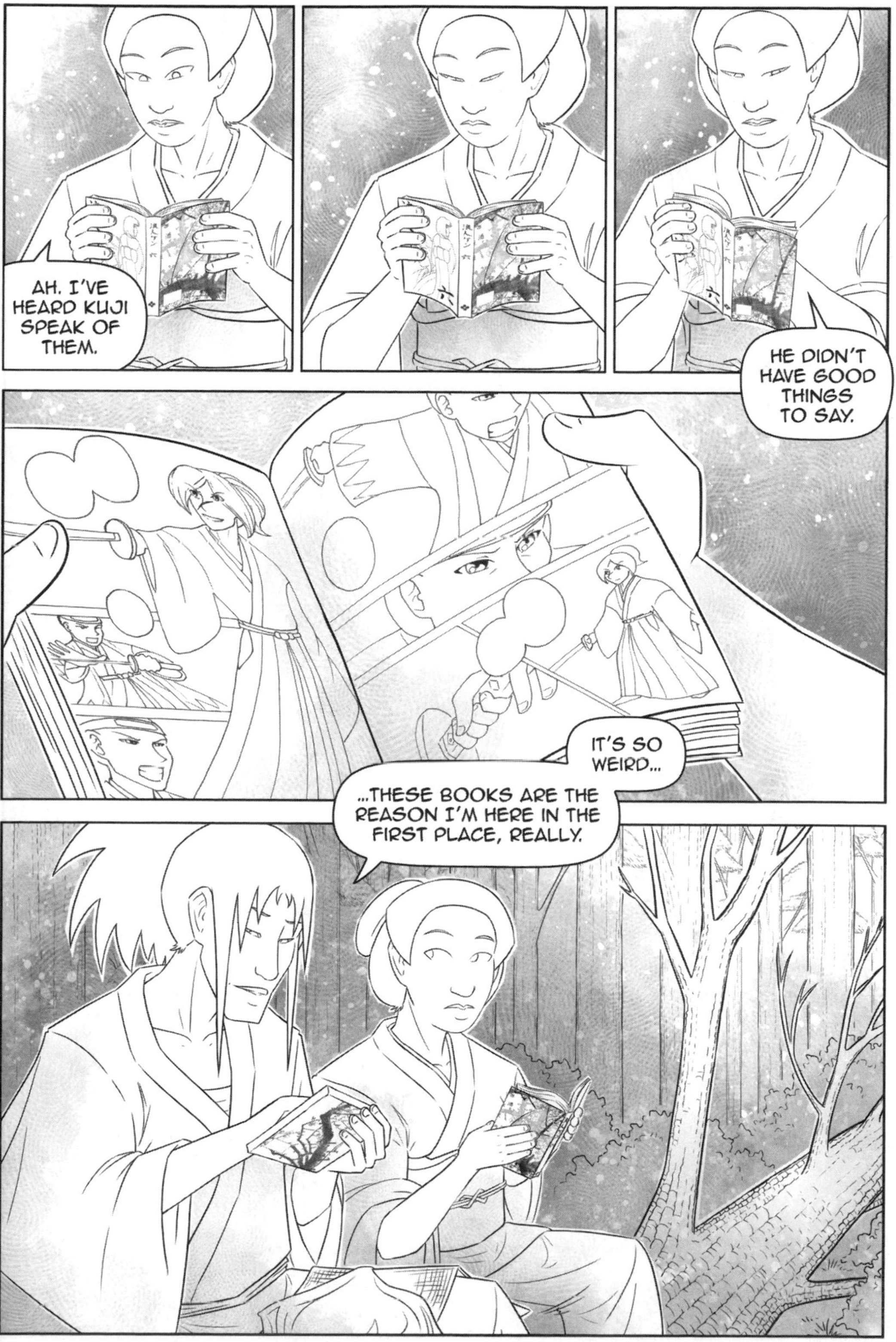
AH. I'VE HEARD KUJI SPEAK OF THEM.
HE DIDN'T HAVE GOOD THINGS TO SAY.
IT'S SO WEIRD...
...THESE BOOKS ARE THE REASON I'M HERE IN THE FIRST PLACE, REALLY.

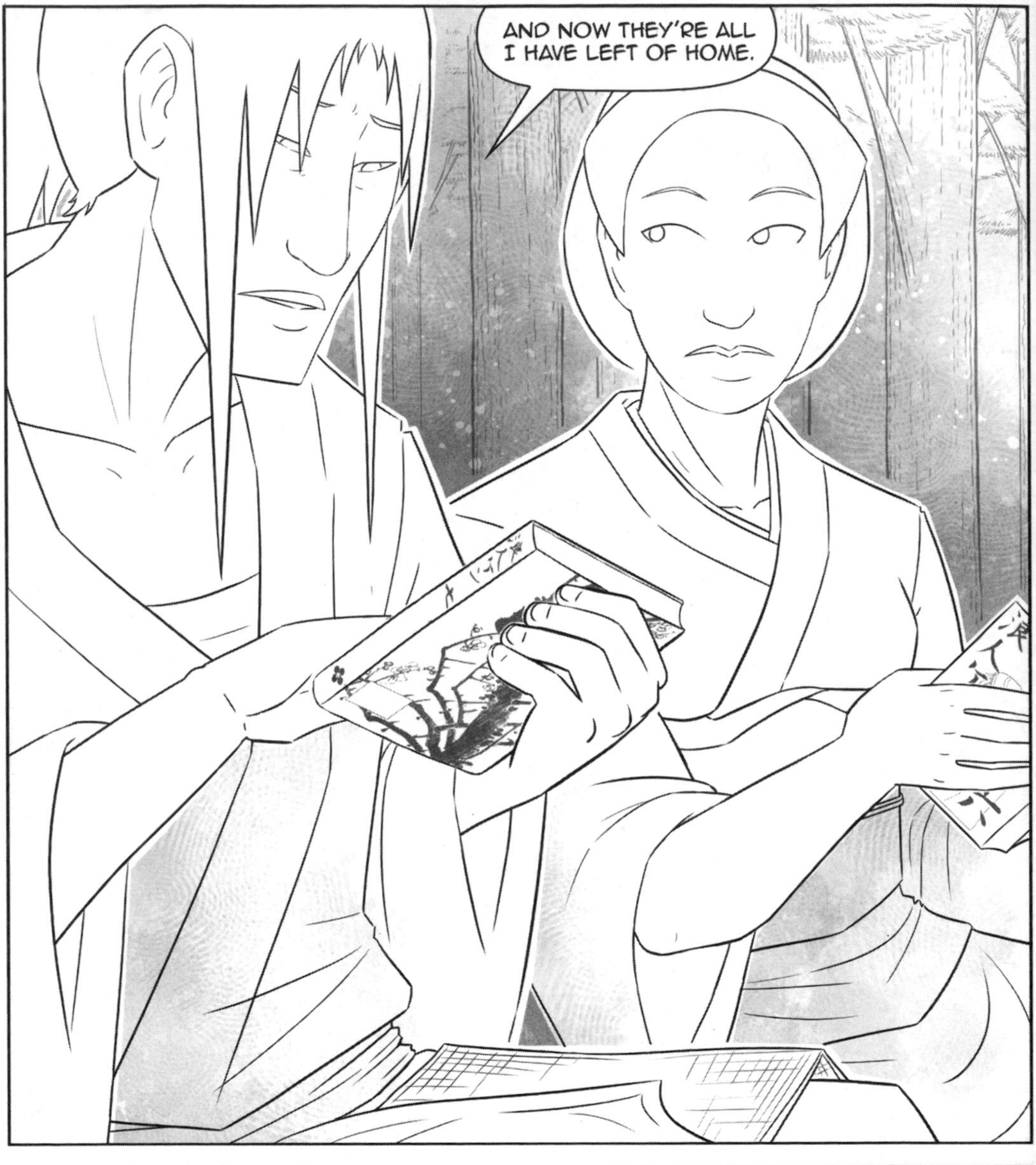
AND NOW THEY'RE ALL I HAVE LEFT OF HOME.

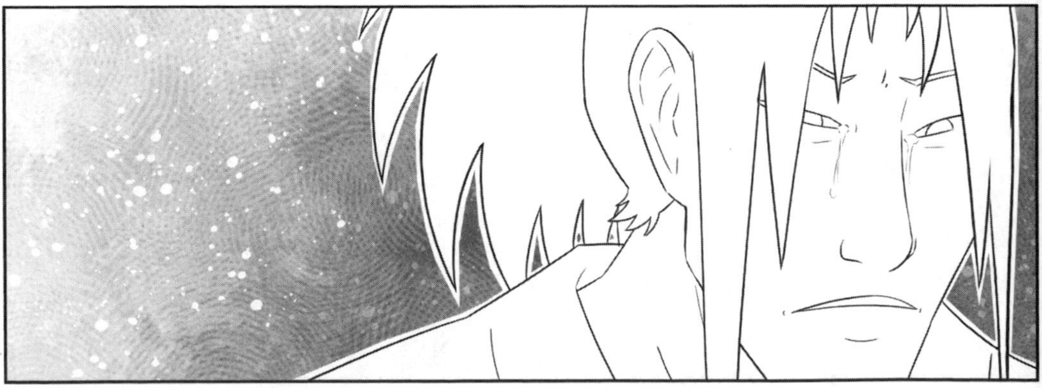

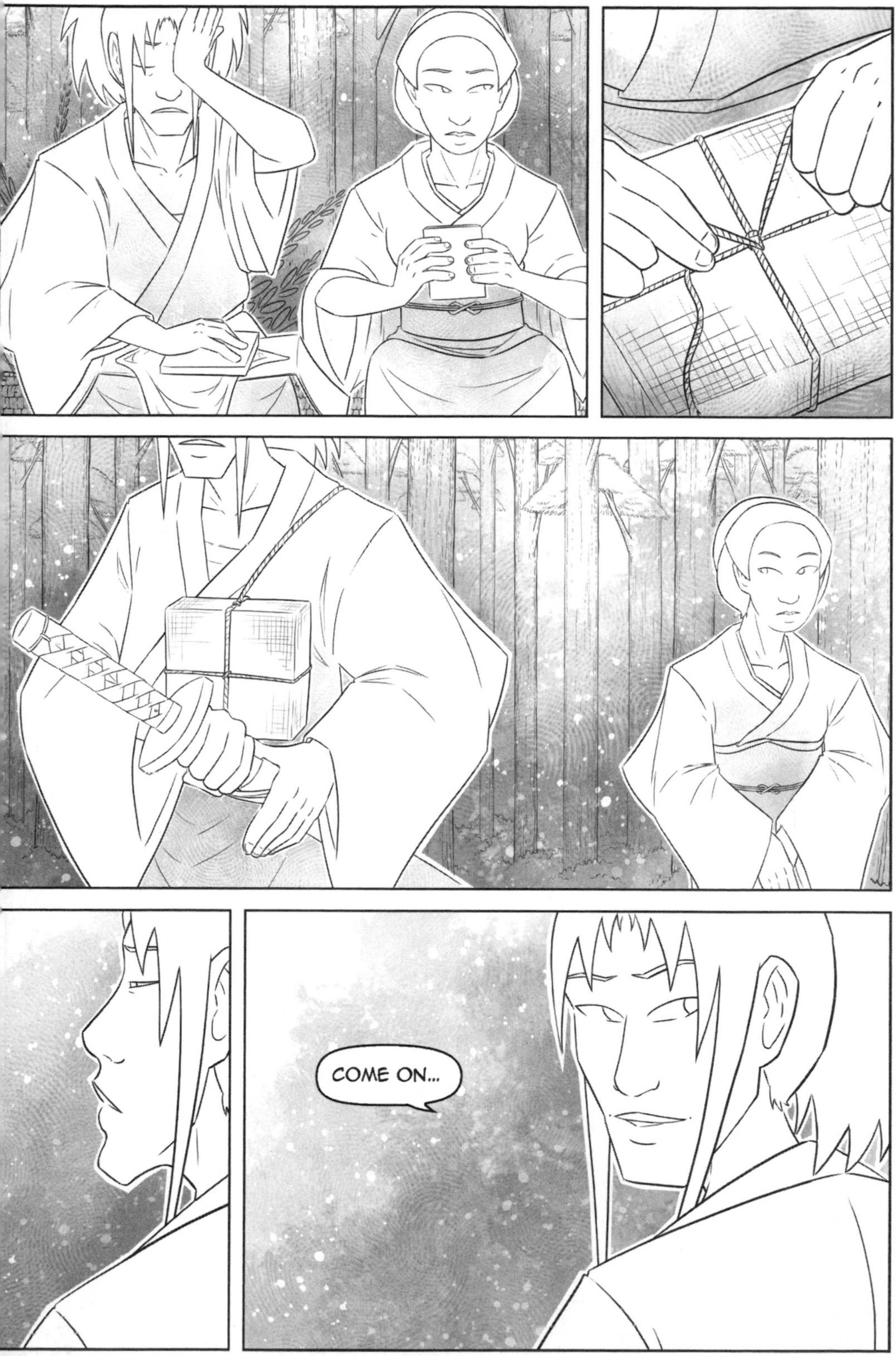
COME ON...

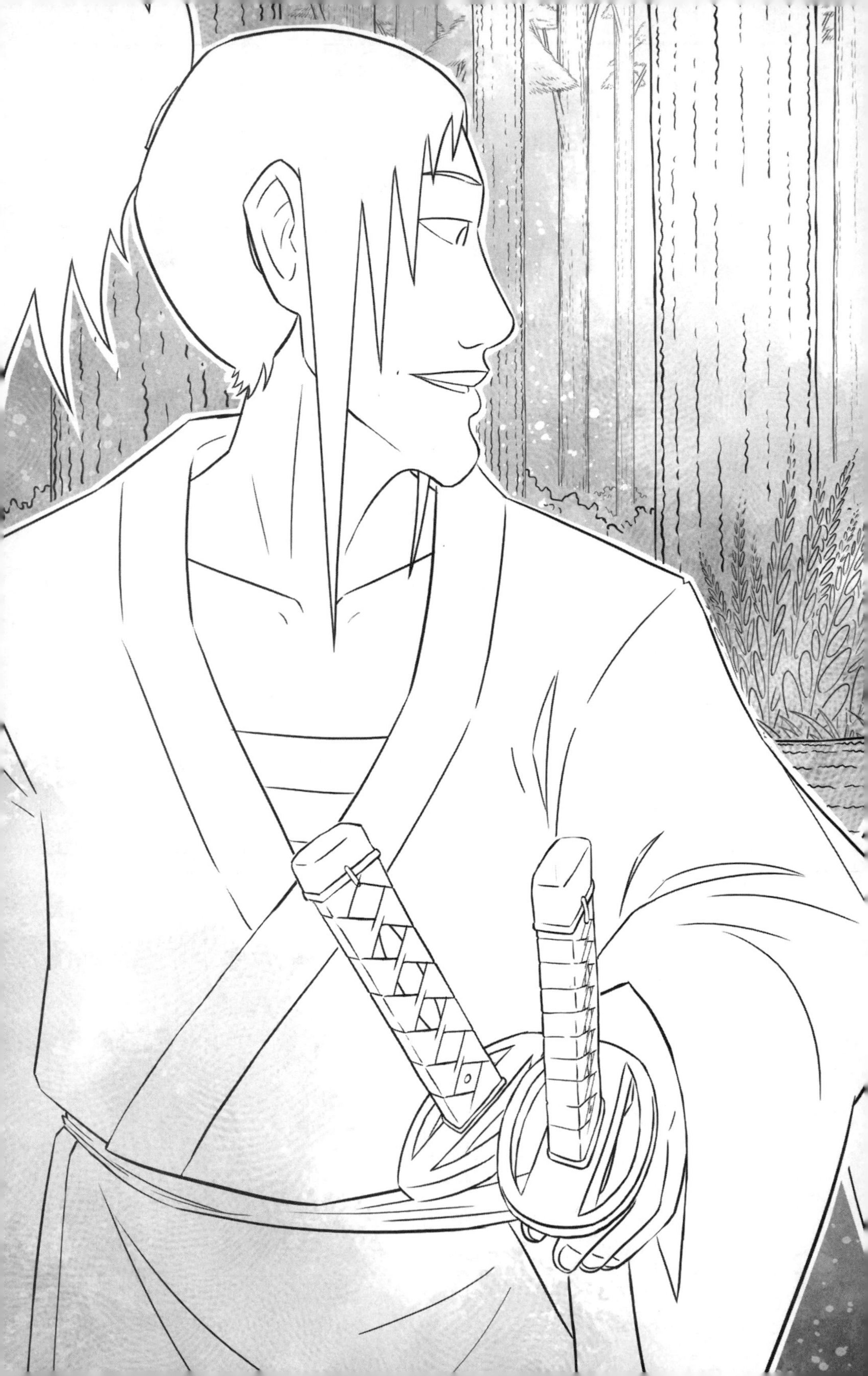

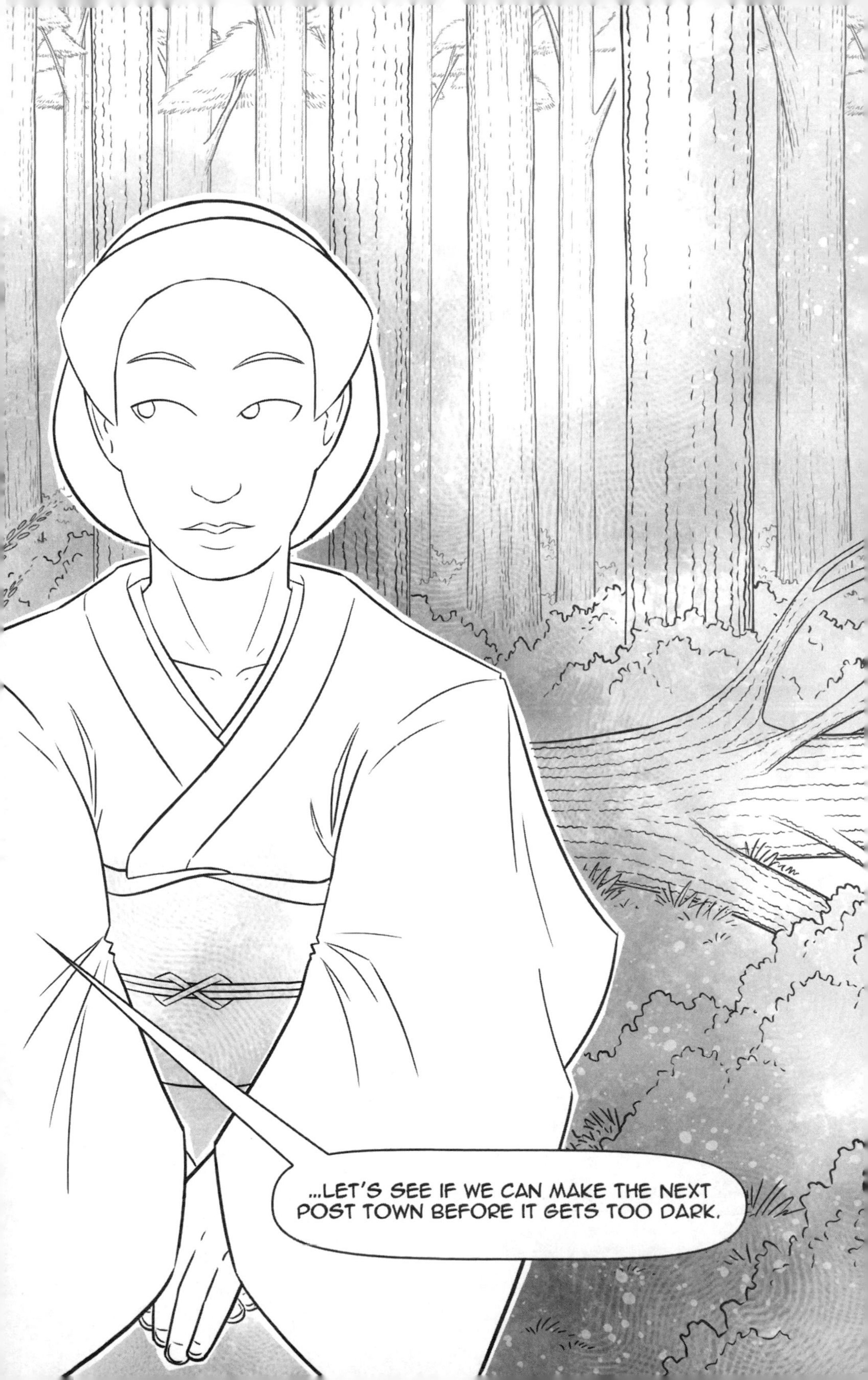
...LET'S SEE IF WE CAN MAKE THE NEXT POST TOWN BEFORE IT GETS TOO DARK.

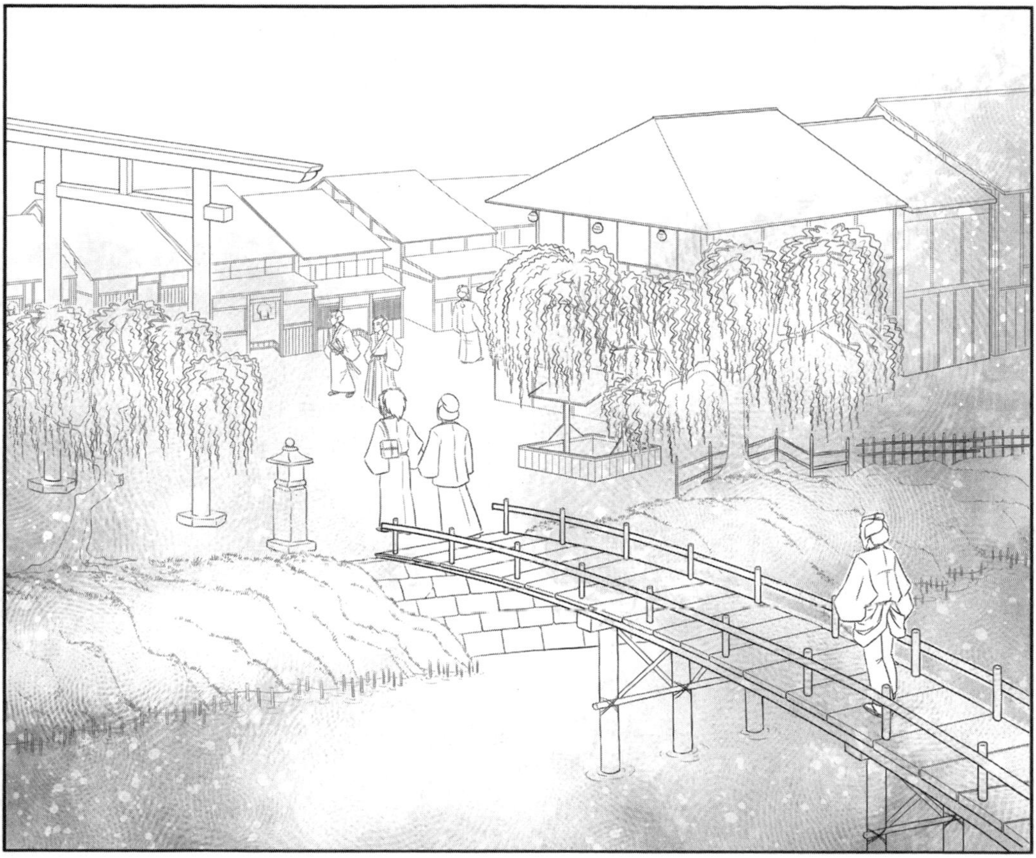

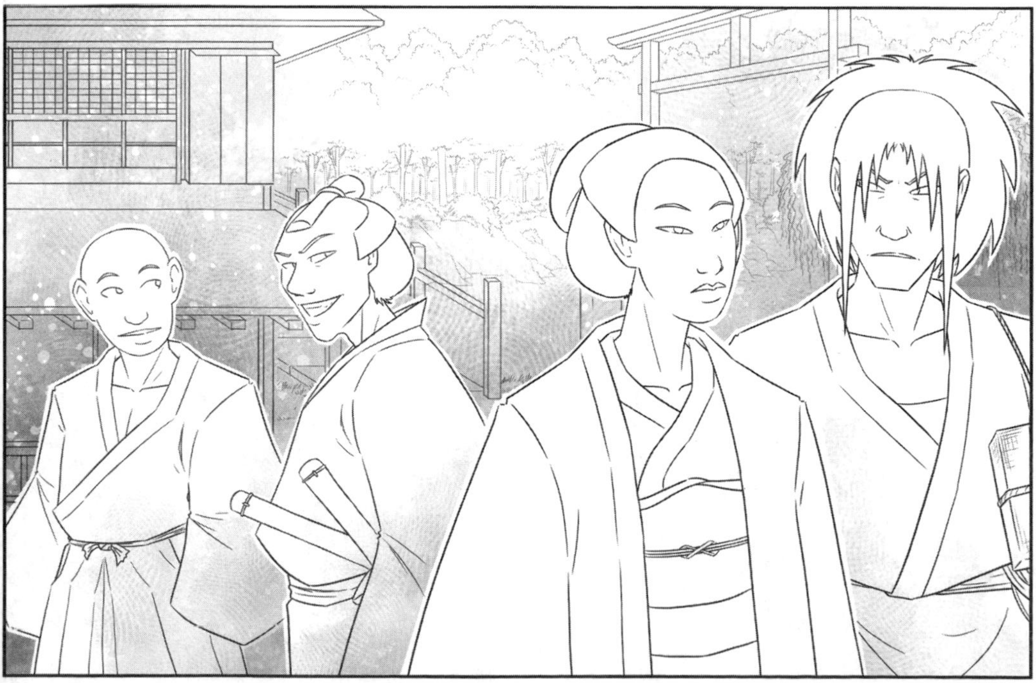

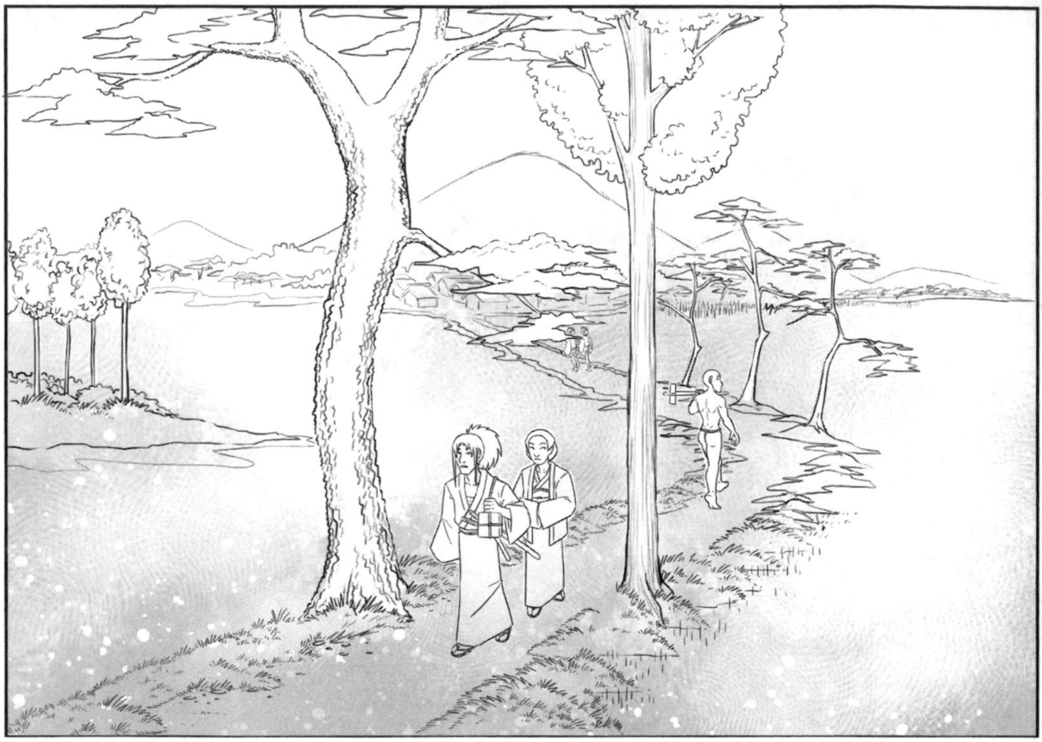

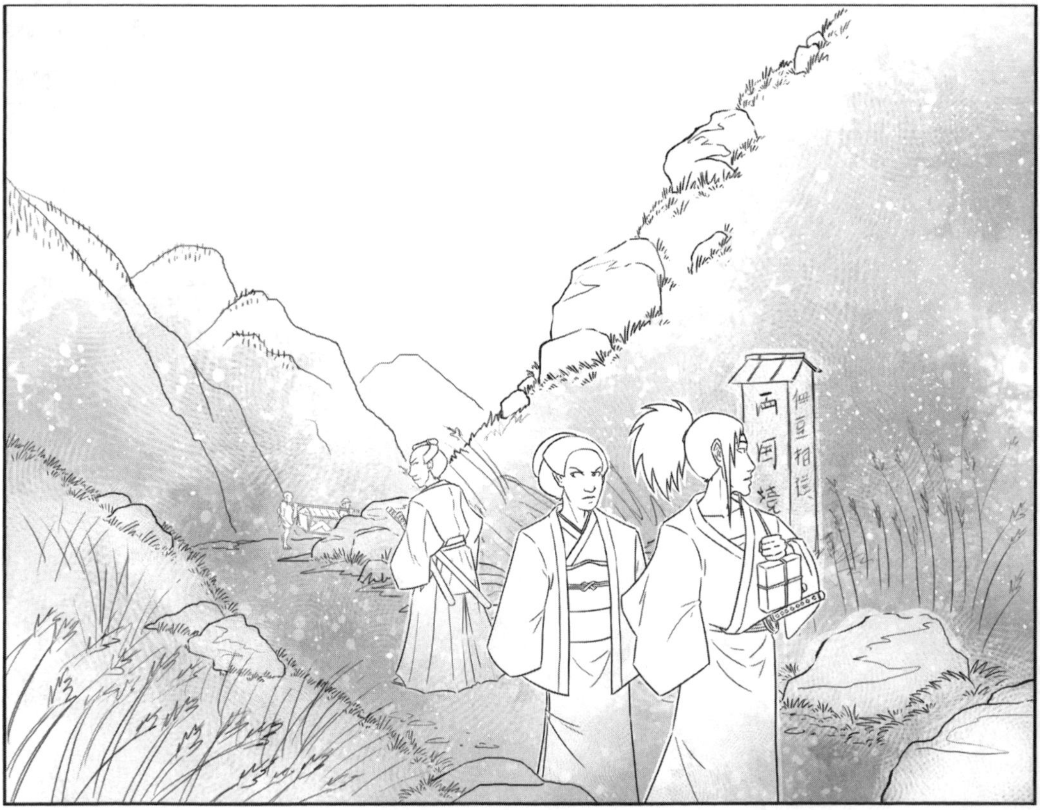
伊豆相模
両国境

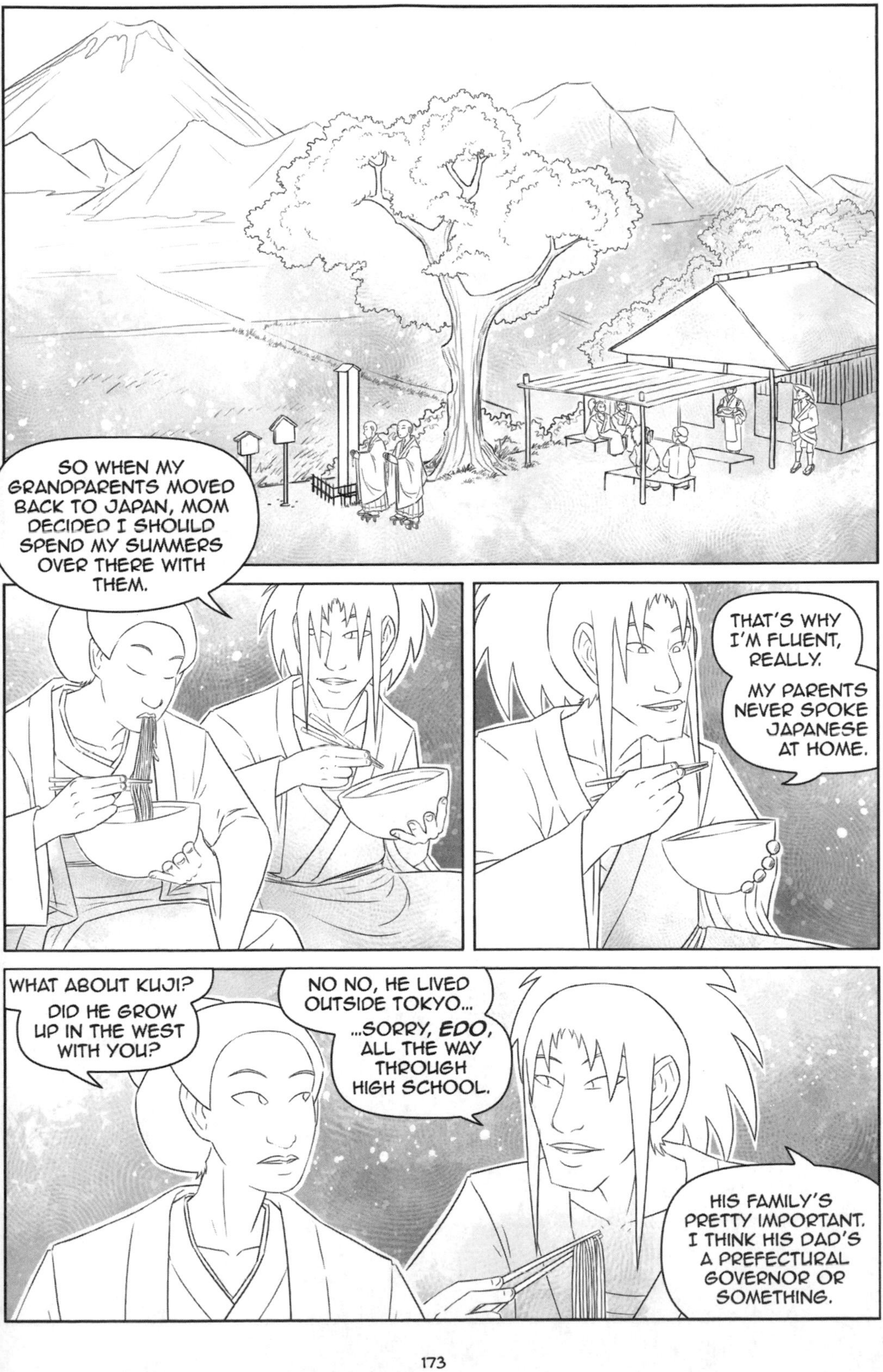
SO WHEN MY GRANDPARENTS MOVED BACK TO JAPAN, MOM DECIDED I SHOULD SPEND MY SUMMERS OVER THERE WITH THEM.
THAT'S WHY I'M FLUENT, REALLY.
MY PARENTS NEVER SPOKE JAPANESE AT HOME.
WHAT ABOUT KUJI?
DID HE GROW UP IN THE WEST WITH YOU?
NO NO, HE LIVED OUTSIDE TOKYO...
...SORRY, *EDO*, ALL THE WAY THROUGH HIGH SCHOOL.
HIS FAMILY'S PRETTY IMPORTANT. I THINK HIS DAD'S A PREFECTURAL GOVERNOR OR SOMETHING.

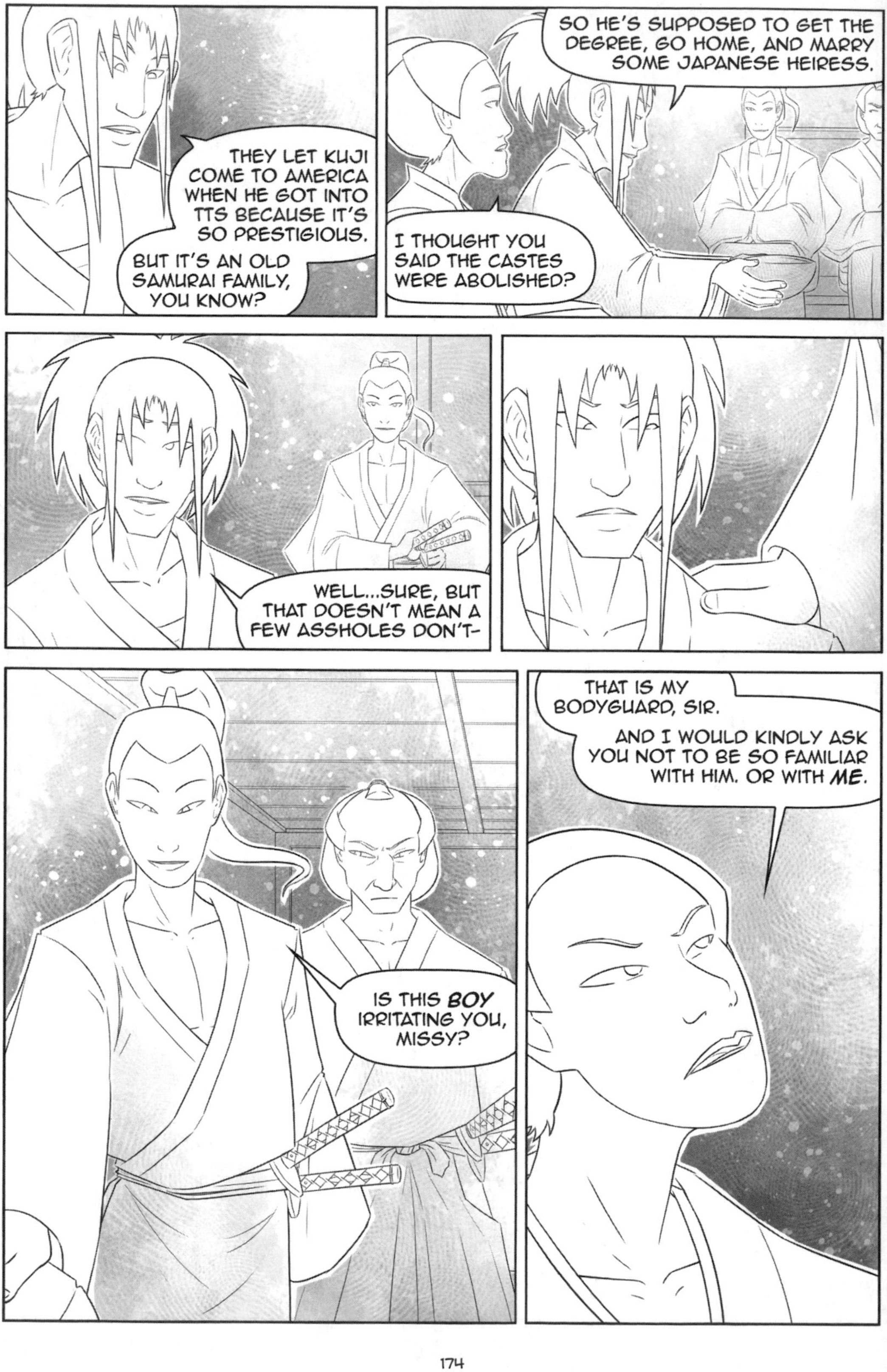
THEY LET KUJI COME TO AMERICA WHEN HE GOT INTO TTS BECAUSE IT'S SO PRESTIGIOUS.
BUT IT'S AN OLD SAMURAI FAMILY, YOU KNOW?
SO HE'S SUPPOSED TO GET THE DEGREE, GO HOME, AND MARRY SOME JAPANESE HEIRESS.
I THOUGHT YOU SAID THE CASTES WERE ABOLISHED?
WELL...SURE, BUT THAT DOESN'T MEAN A FEW ASSHOLES DON'T-
IS THIS *BOY* IRRITATING YOU, MISSY?
THAT IS MY BODYGUARD, SIR.
AND I WOULD KINDLY ASK YOU NOT TO BE SO FAMILIAR WITH HIM. OR WITH *ME*.

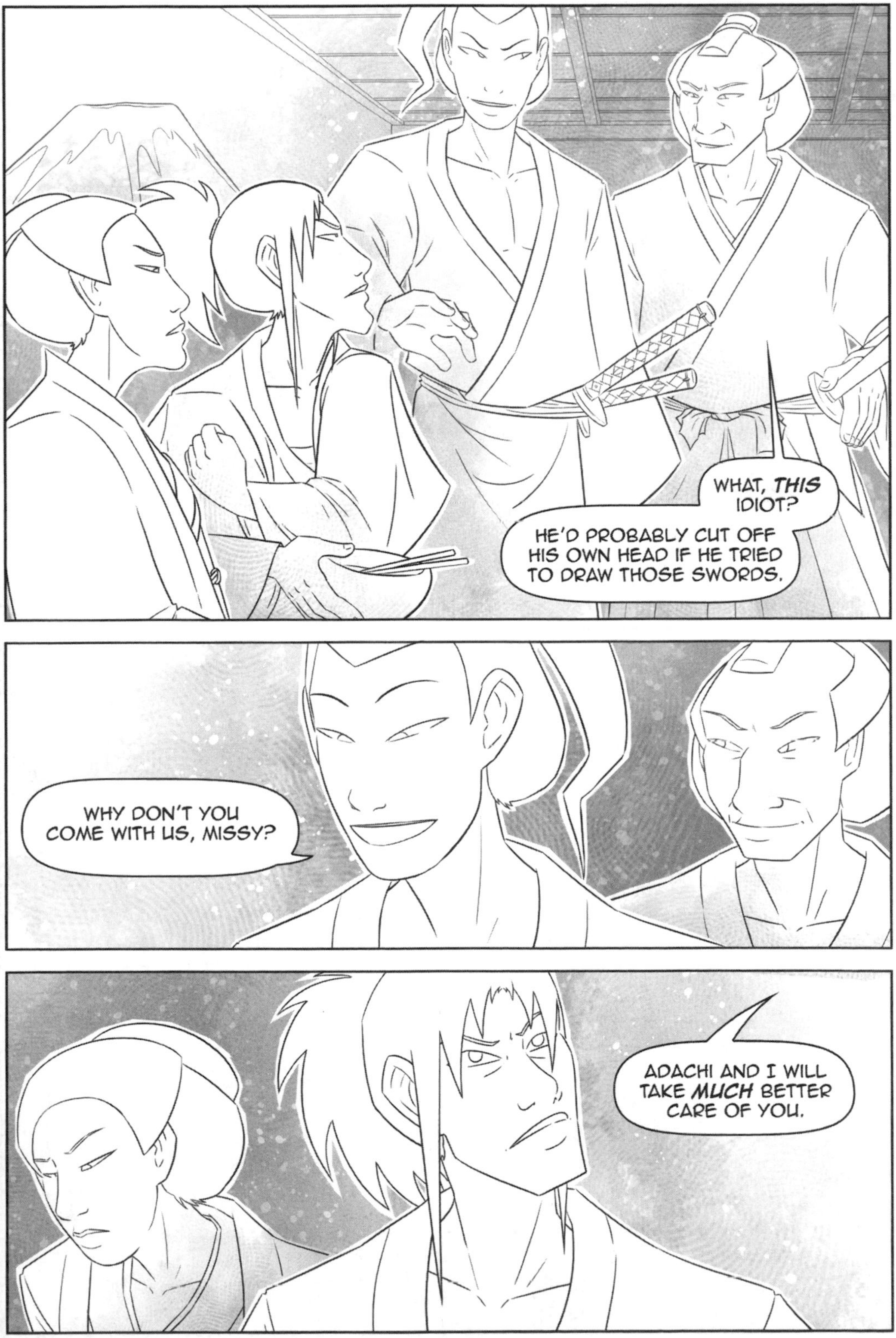
WHAT, THIS IDIOT?
HE'D PROBABLY CUT OFF HIS OWN HEAD IF HE TRIED TO DRAW THOSE SWORDS.
WHY DON'T YOU COME WITH US, MISSY?
ADACHI AND I WILL TAKE MUCH BETTER CARE OF YOU.

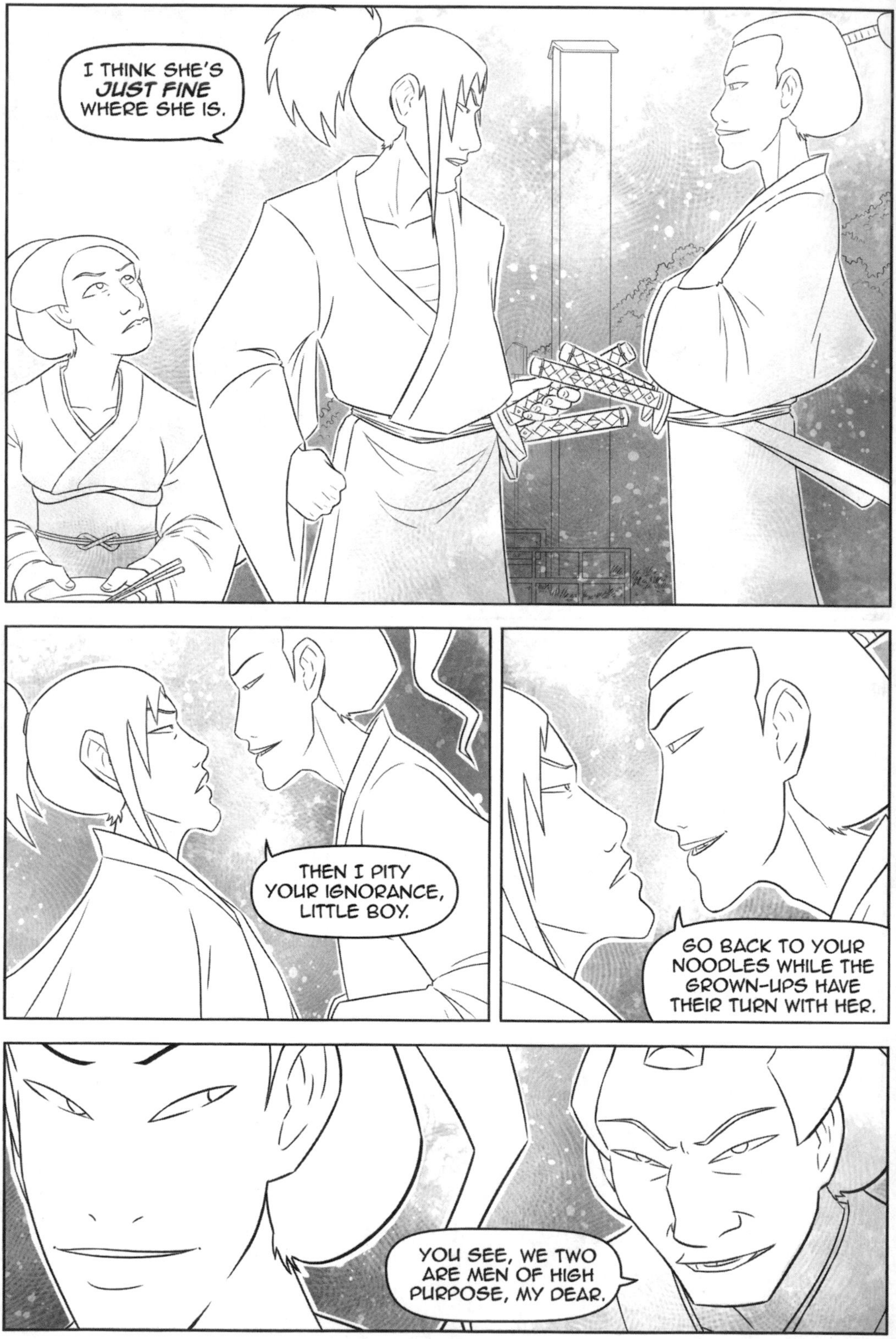
I THINK SHE'S *JUST FINE* WHERE SHE IS.
THEN I PITY YOUR IGNORANCE, LITTLE BOY.
GO BACK TO YOUR NOODLES WHILE THE GROWN-UPS HAVE THEIR TURN WITH HER.
YOU SEE, WE TWO ARE MEN OF HIGH PURPOSE, MY DEAR.

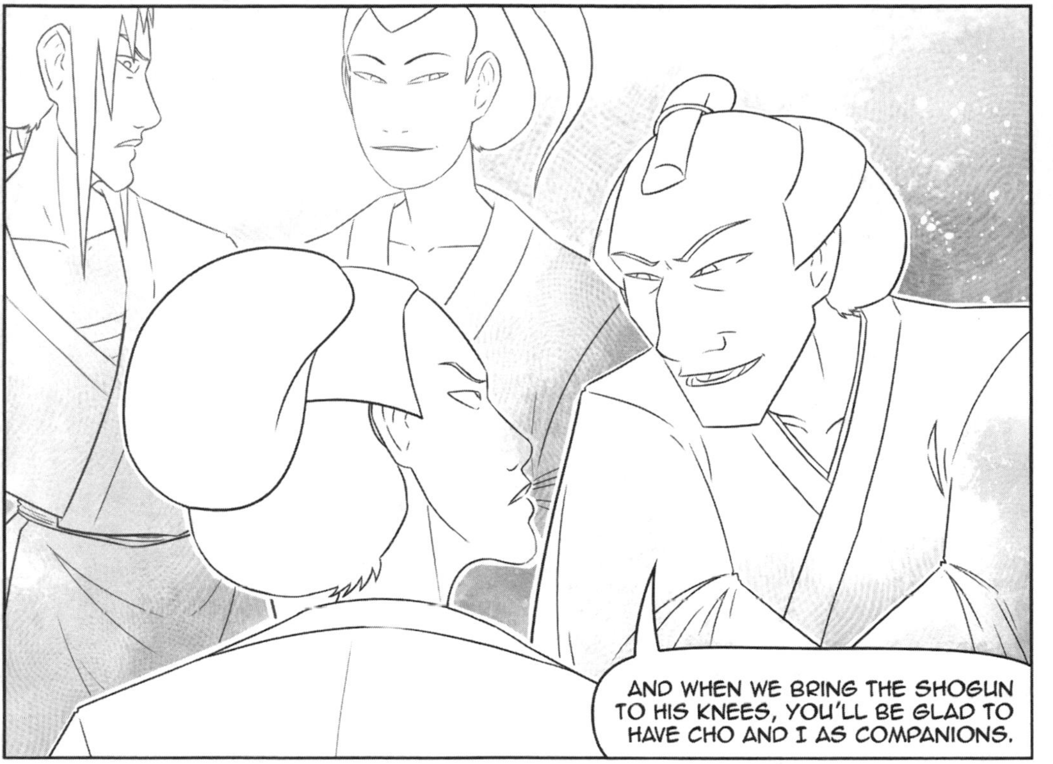
AND WHEN WE BRING THE SHOGUN TO HIS KNEES, YOU'LL BE GLAD TO HAVE CHO AND I AS COMPANIONS.

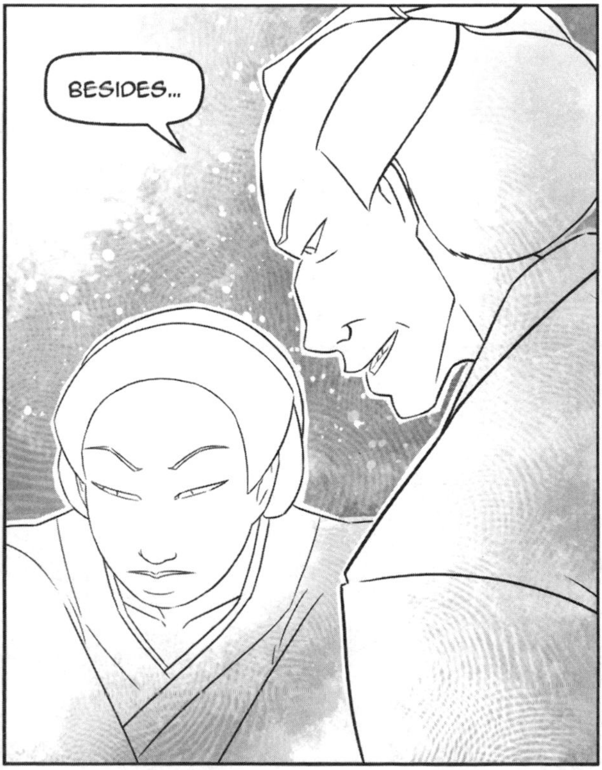
BESIDES...

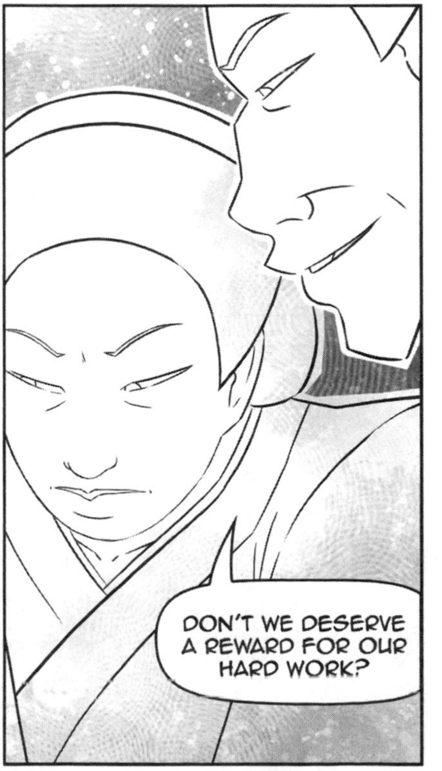
DON'T WE DESERVE A REWARD FOR OUR HARD WORK?

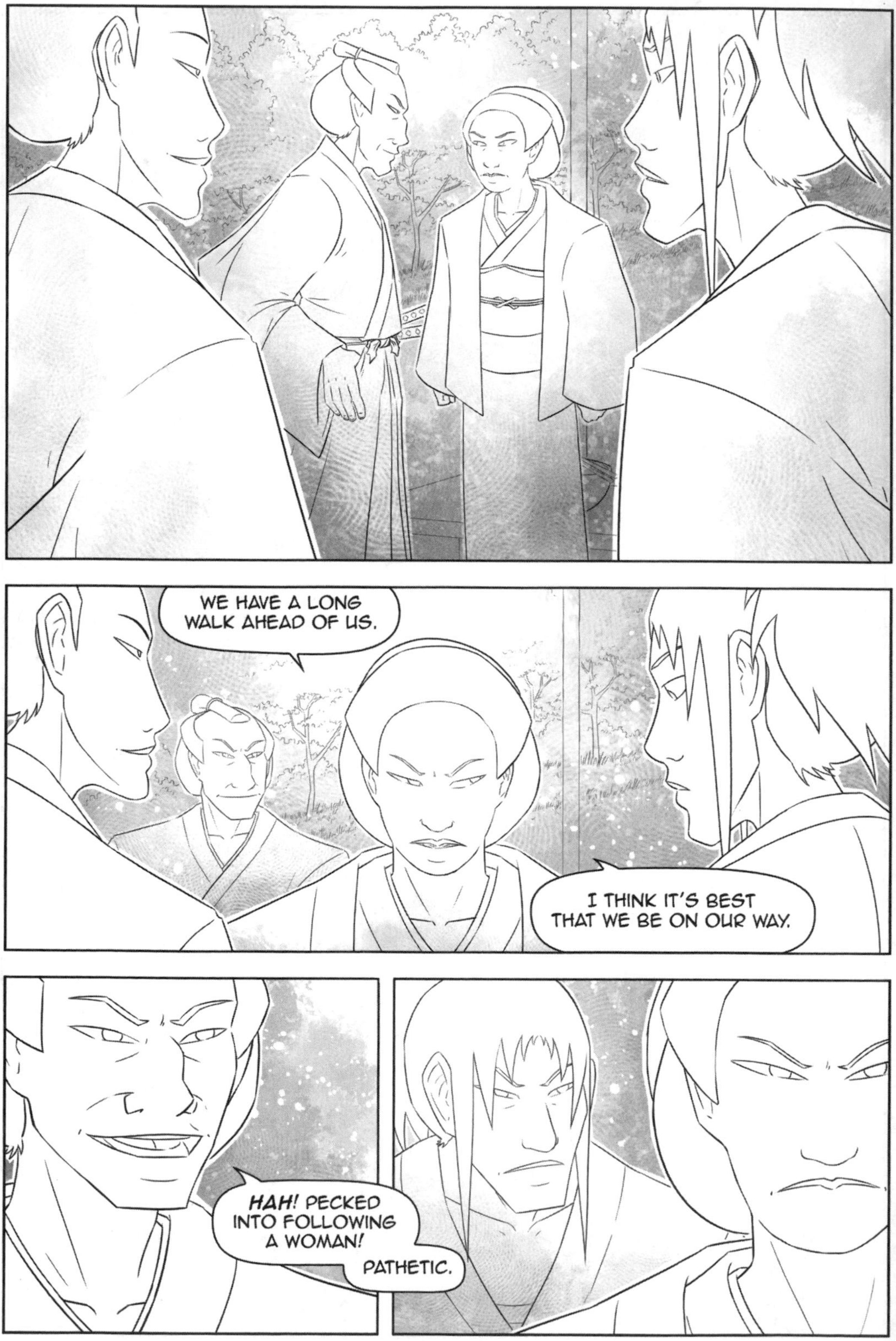
WE HAVE A LONG WALK AHEAD OF US.
I THINK IT'S BEST THAT WE BE ON OUR WAY.
HAH! PECKED INTO FOLLOWING A WOMAN!
PATHETIC.

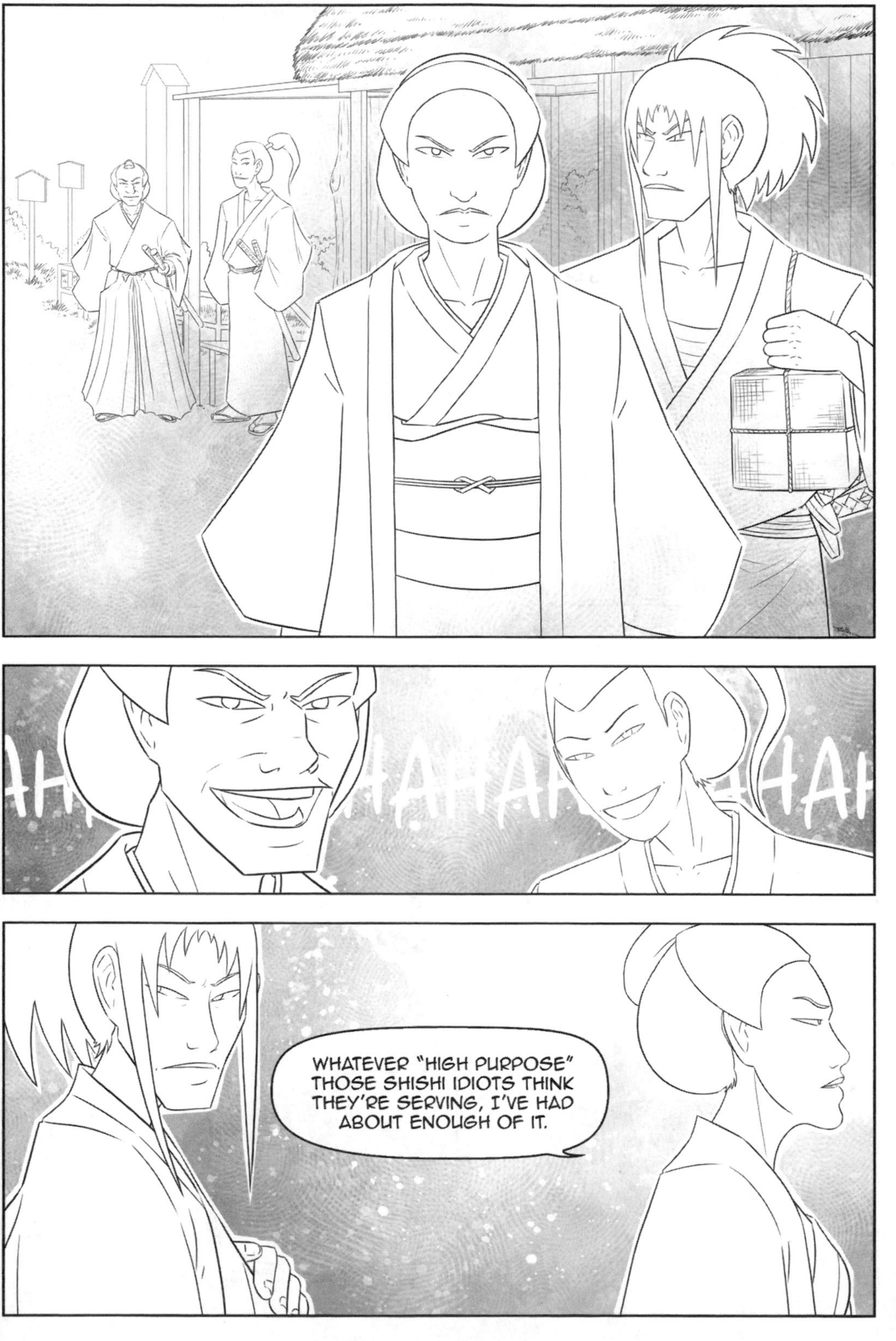
WHATEVER "HIGH PURPOSE" THOSE SHISHI IDIOTS THINK THEY'RE SERVING, I'VE HAD ABOUT ENOUGH OF IT.

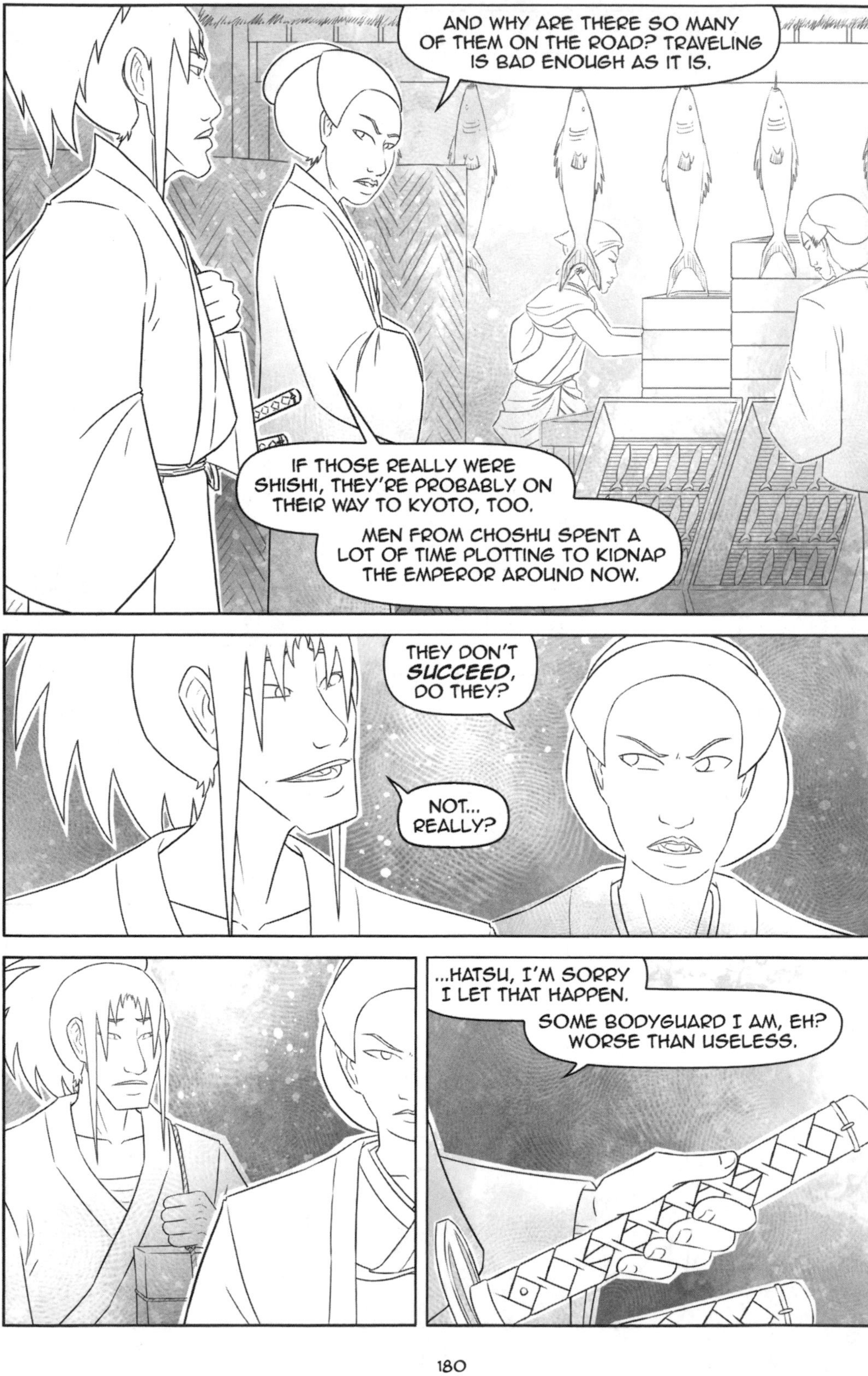
AND WHY ARE THERE SO MANY OF THEM ON THE ROAD? TRAVELING IS BAD ENOUGH AS IT IS.
IF THOSE REALLY WERE SHISHI, THEY'RE PROBABLY ON THEIR WAY TO KYOTO, TOO.
MEN FROM CHOSHU SPENT A LOT OF TIME PLOTTING TO KIDNAP THE EMPEROR AROUND NOW.
THEY DON'T *SUCCEED*, DO THEY?
NOT... REALLY?
...HATSU, I'M SORRY I LET THAT HAPPEN.
SOME BODYGUARD I AM, EH? WORSE THAN USELESS.

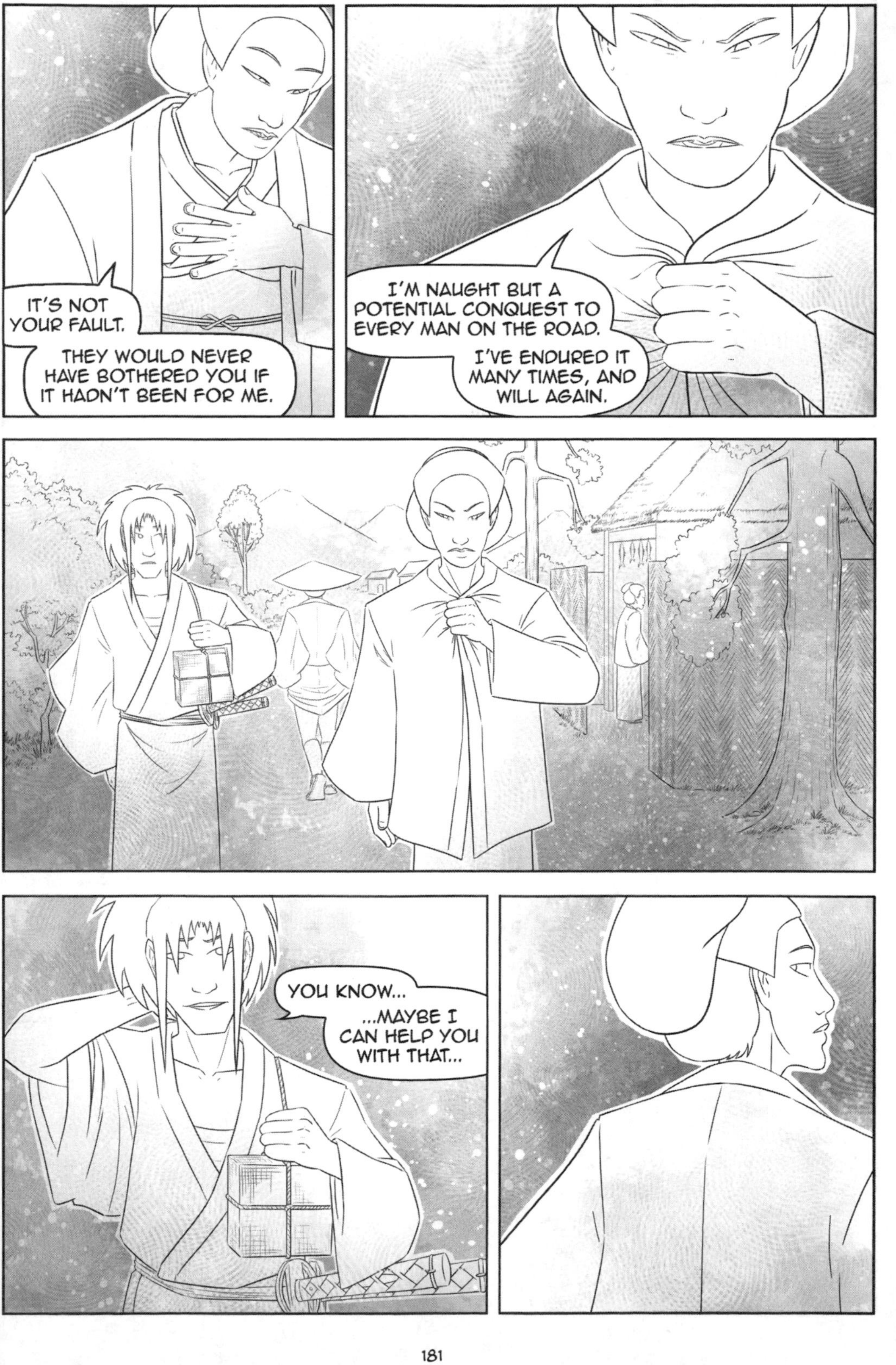
IT'S NOT YOUR FAULT.
THEY WOULD NEVER HAVE BOTHERED YOU IF IT HADN'T BEEN FOR ME.
I'M NAUGHT BUT A POTENTIAL CONQUEST TO EVERY MAN ON THE ROAD.
I'VE ENDURED IT MANY TIMES, AND WILL AGAIN.
YOU KNOW...
...MAYBE I CAN HELP YOU WITH THAT...

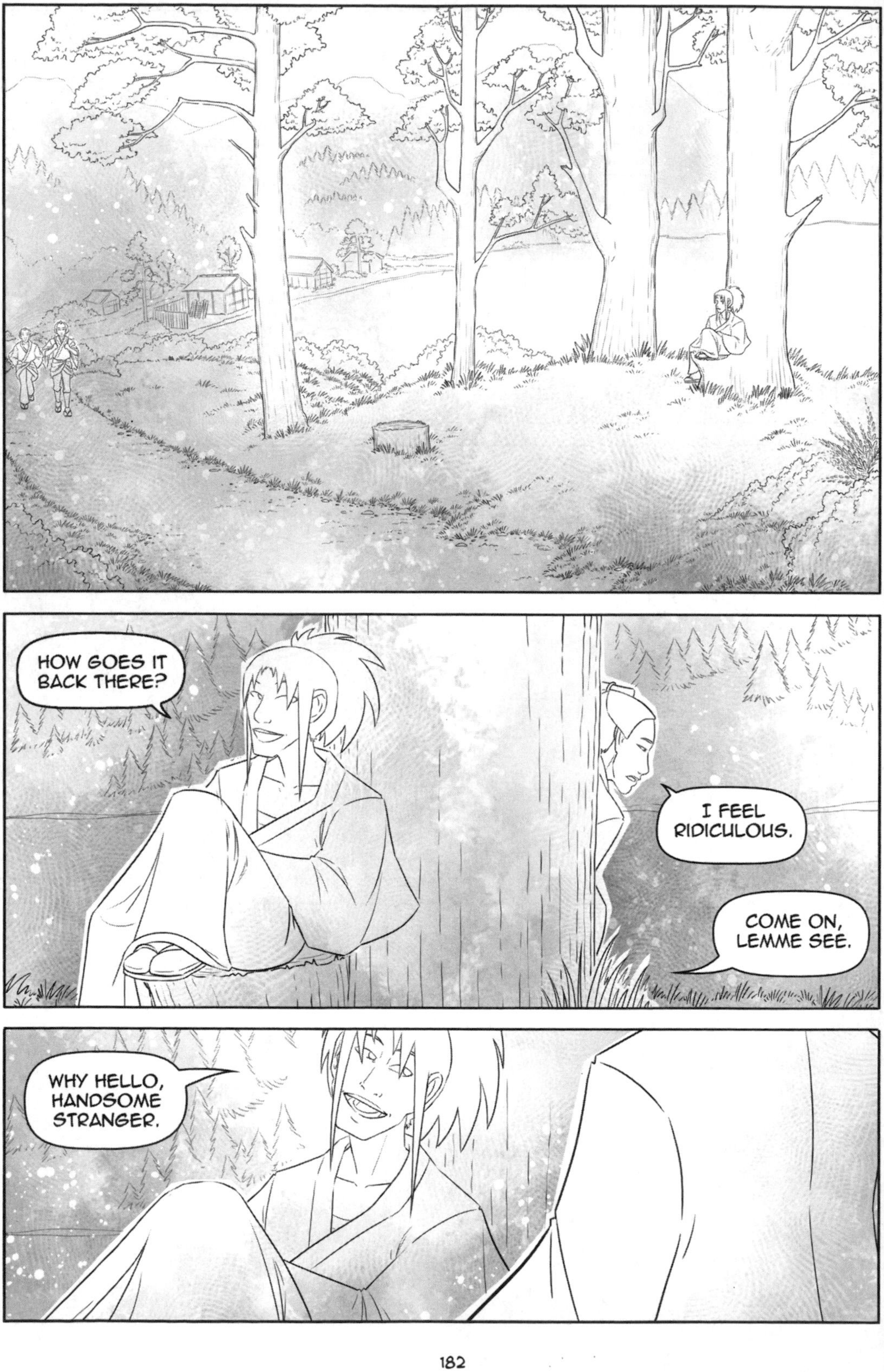
HOW GOES IT BACK THERE?
I FEEL RIDICULOUS.
COME ON, LEMME SEE.
WHY HELLO, HANDSOME STRANGER.

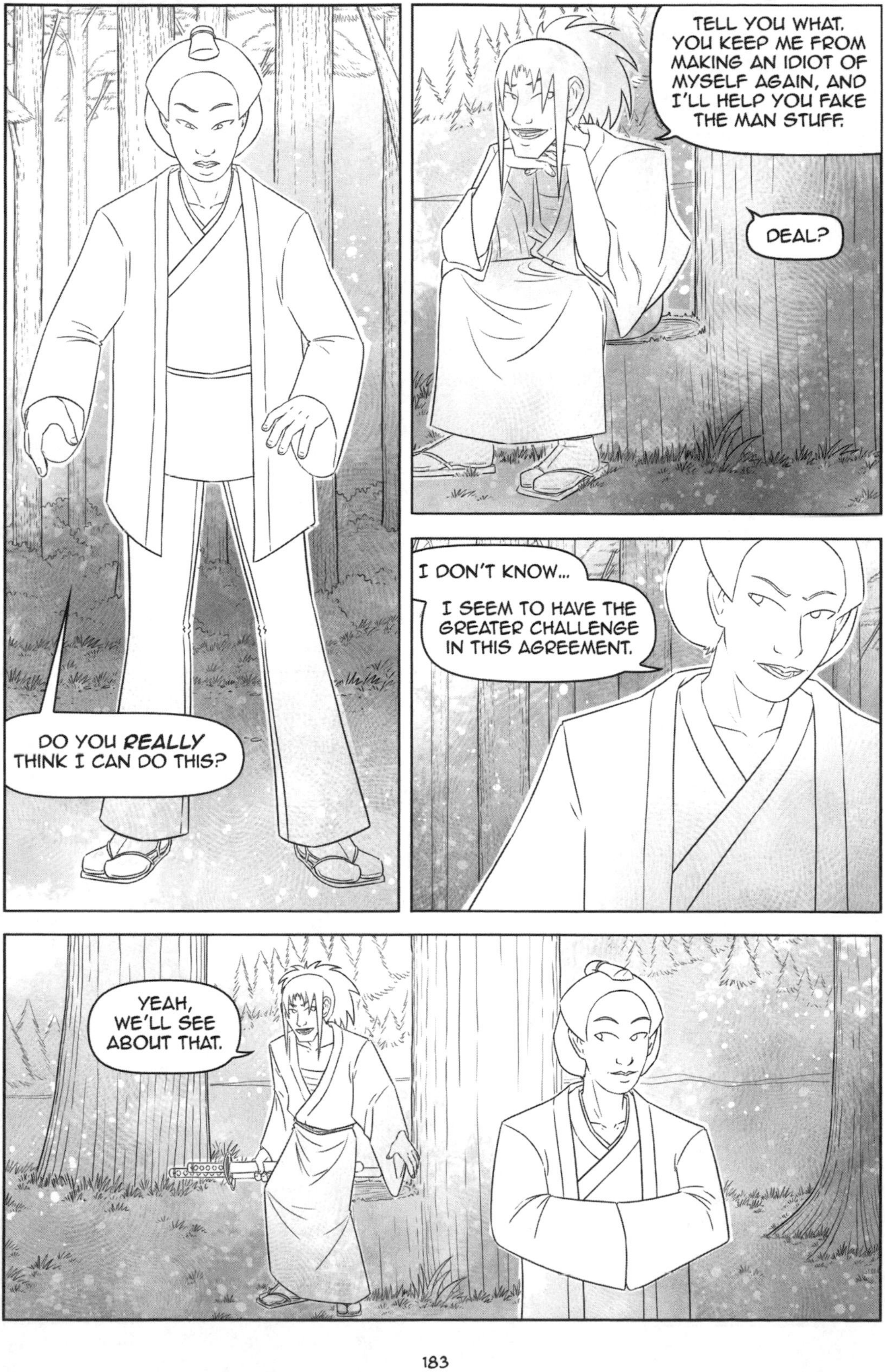
DO YOU *REALLY* THINK I CAN DO THIS?
TELL YOU WHAT. YOU KEEP ME FROM MAKING AN IDIOT OF MYSELF AGAIN, AND I'LL HELP YOU FAKE THE MAN STUFF.
DEAL?
I DON'T KNOW...
I SEEM TO HAVE THE GREATER CHALLENGE IN THIS AGREEMENT.
YEAH, WE'LL SEE ABOUT THAT.

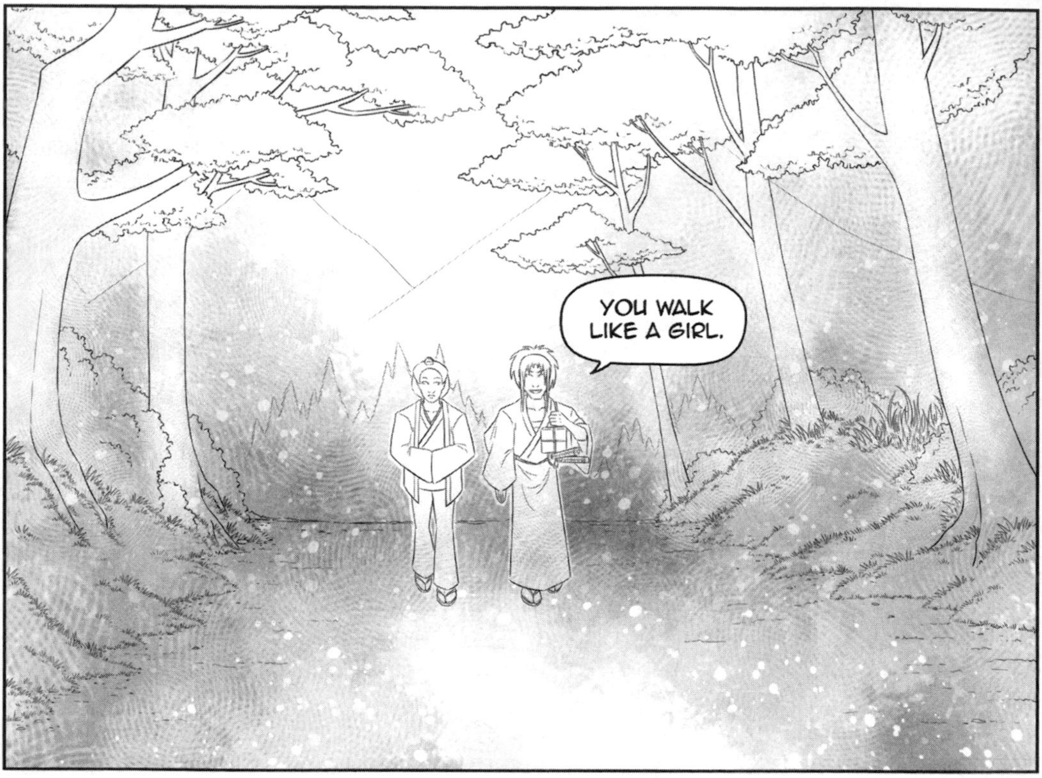
YOU WALK LIKE A GIRL.

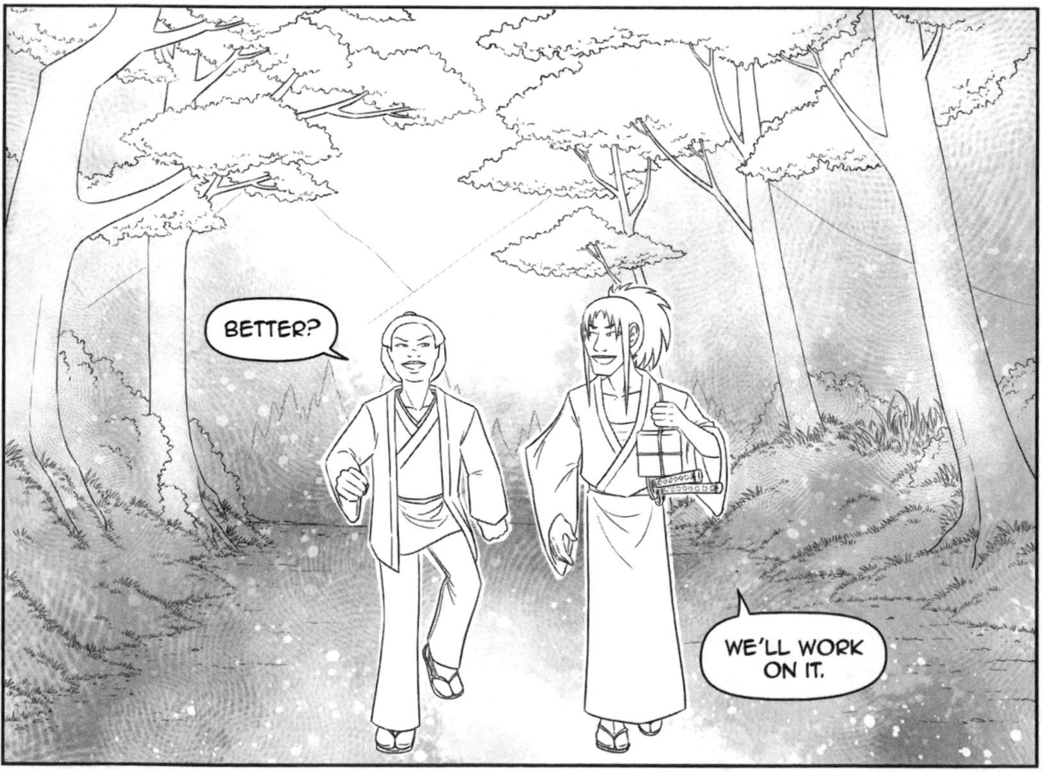
BETTER?
WE'LL WORK ON IT.

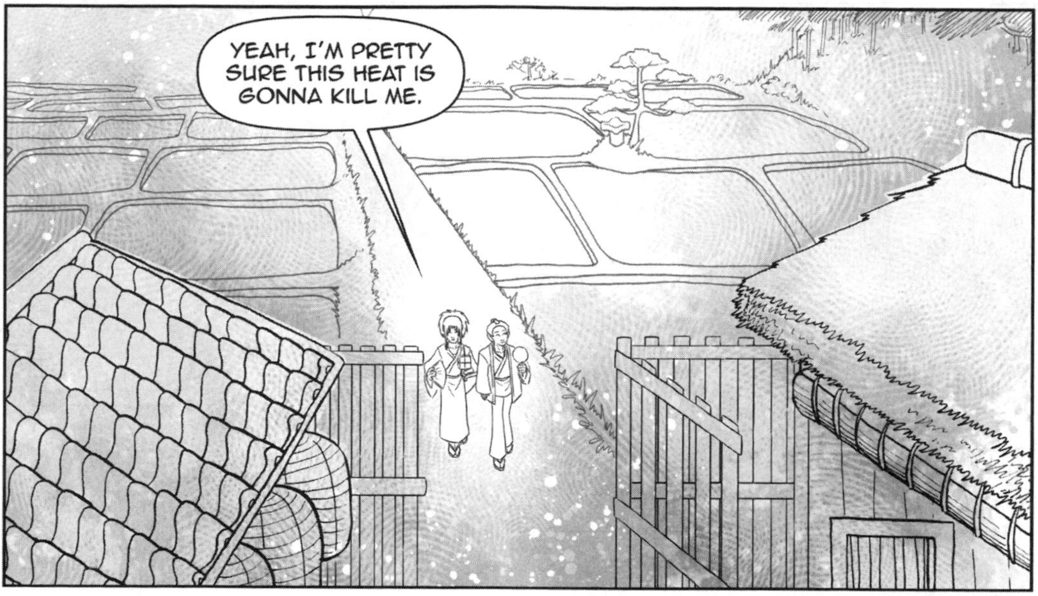
YEAH, I'M PRETTY SURE THIS HEAT IS GONNA KILL ME.

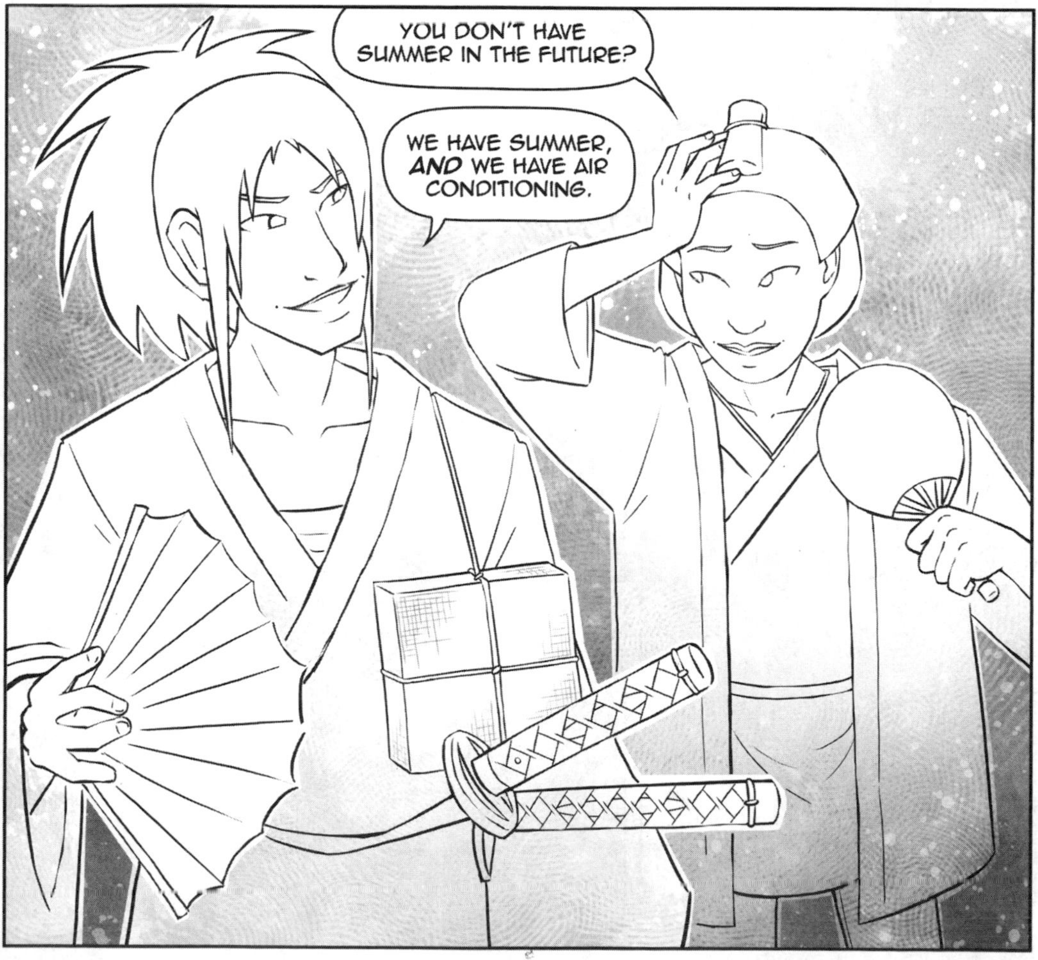
YOU DON'T HAVE SUMMER IN THE FUTURE?
WE HAVE SUMMER, ***AND*** WE HAVE AIR CONDITIONING.

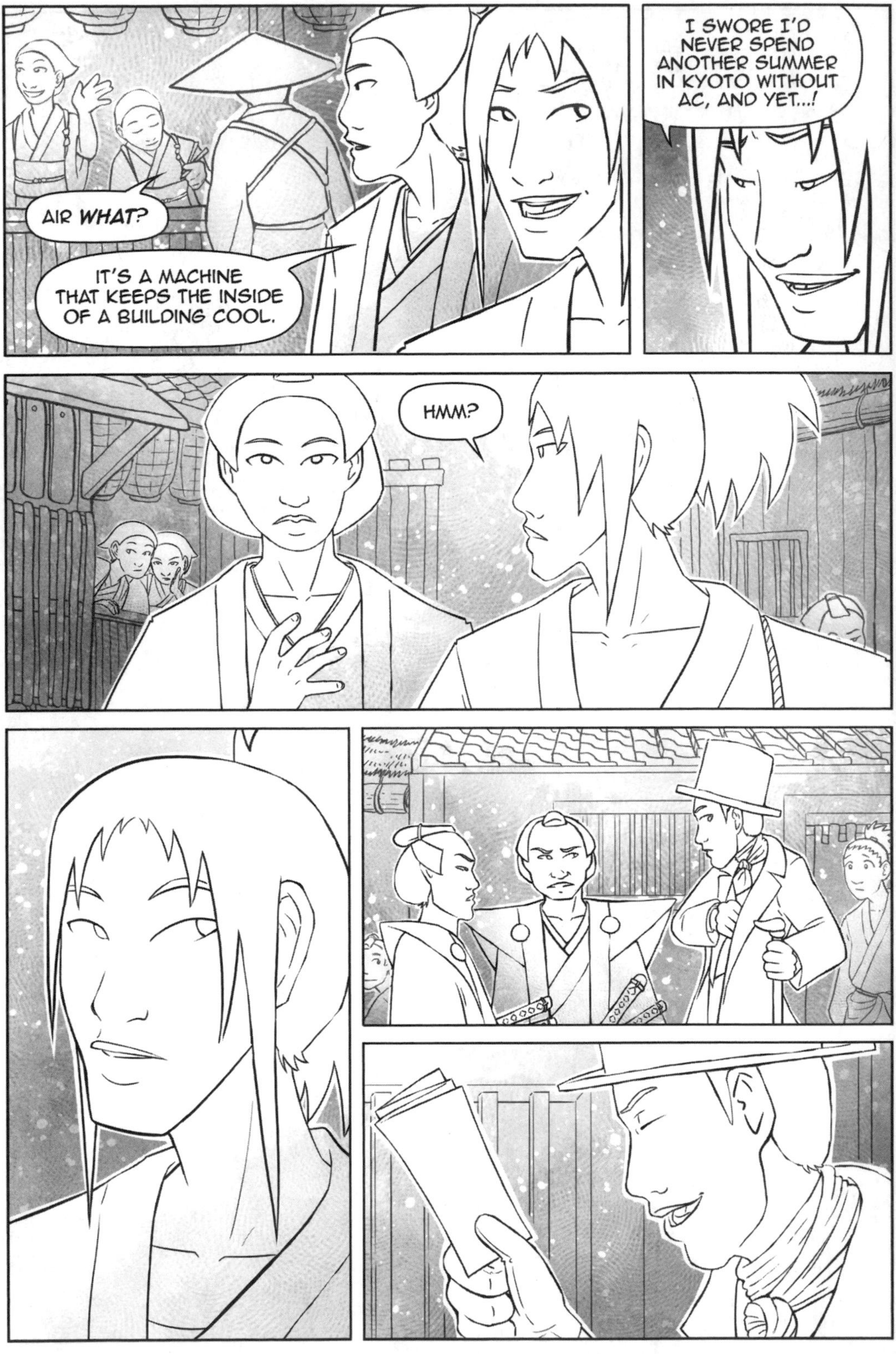
AIR *WHAT*?
IT'S A MACHINE THAT KEEPS THE INSIDE OF A BUILDING COOL.
I SWORE I'D NEVER SPEND ANOTHER SUMMER IN KYOTO WITHOUT AC, AND YET...!
HMM?

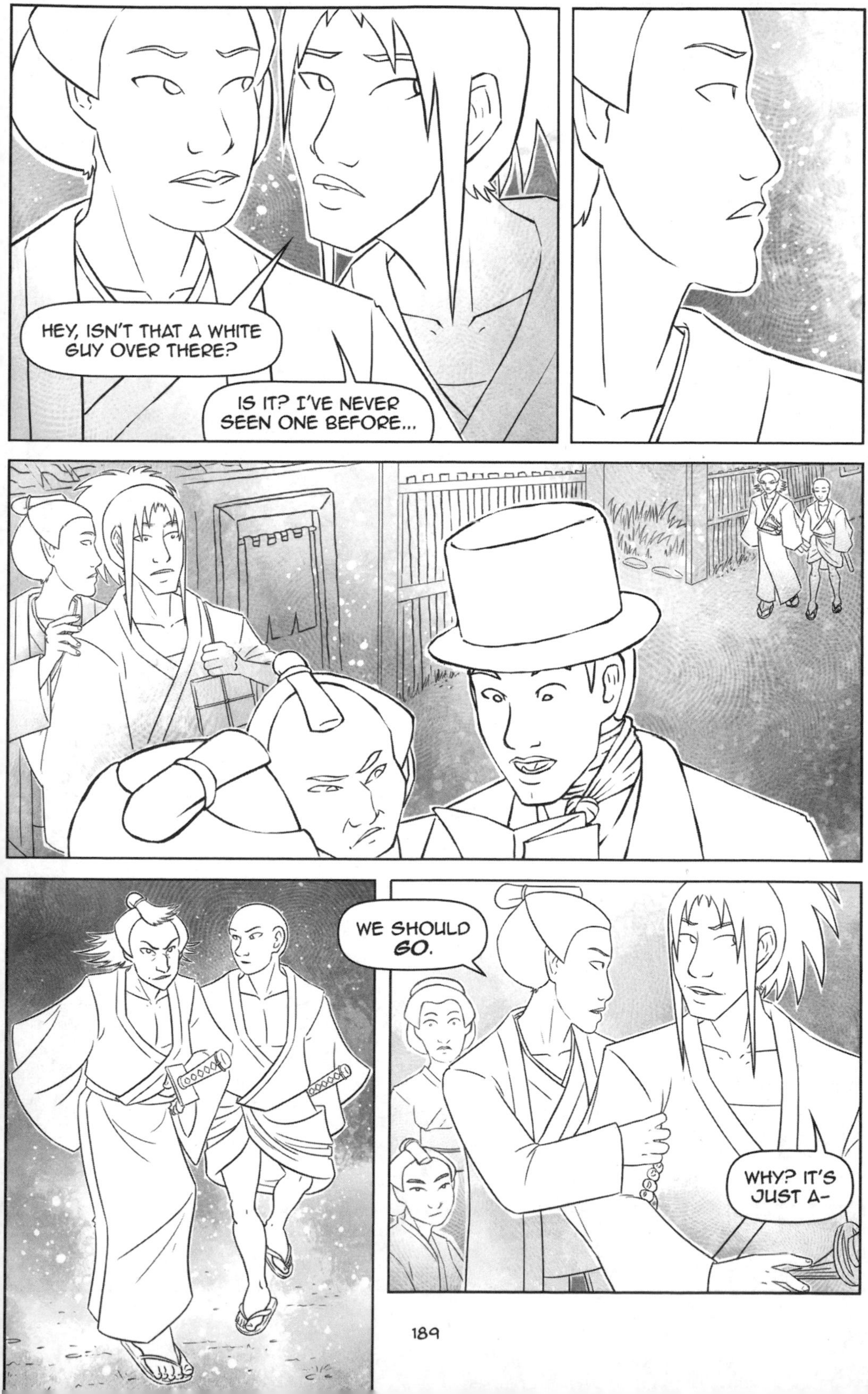
HEY, ISN'T THAT A WHITE GUY OVER THERE?
IS IT? I'VE NEVER SEEN ONE BEFORE...
WE SHOULD GO.
WHY? IT'S JUST A-

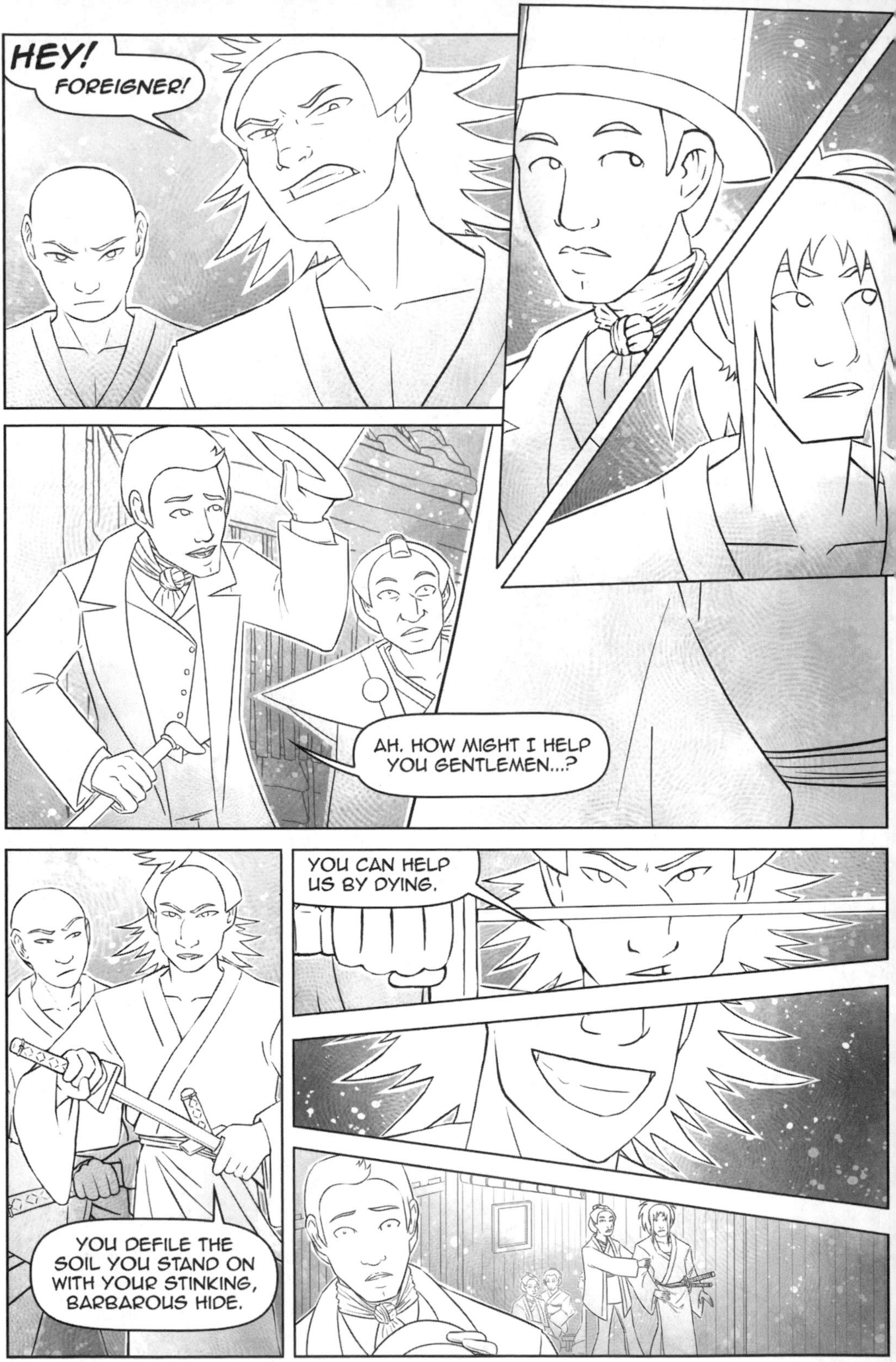
HEY! FOREIGNER!
AH. HOW MIGHT I HELP YOU GENTLEMEN...?
YOU DEFILE THE SOIL YOU STAND ON WITH YOUR STINKING, BARBAROUS HIDE.
YOU CAN HELP US BY DYING.

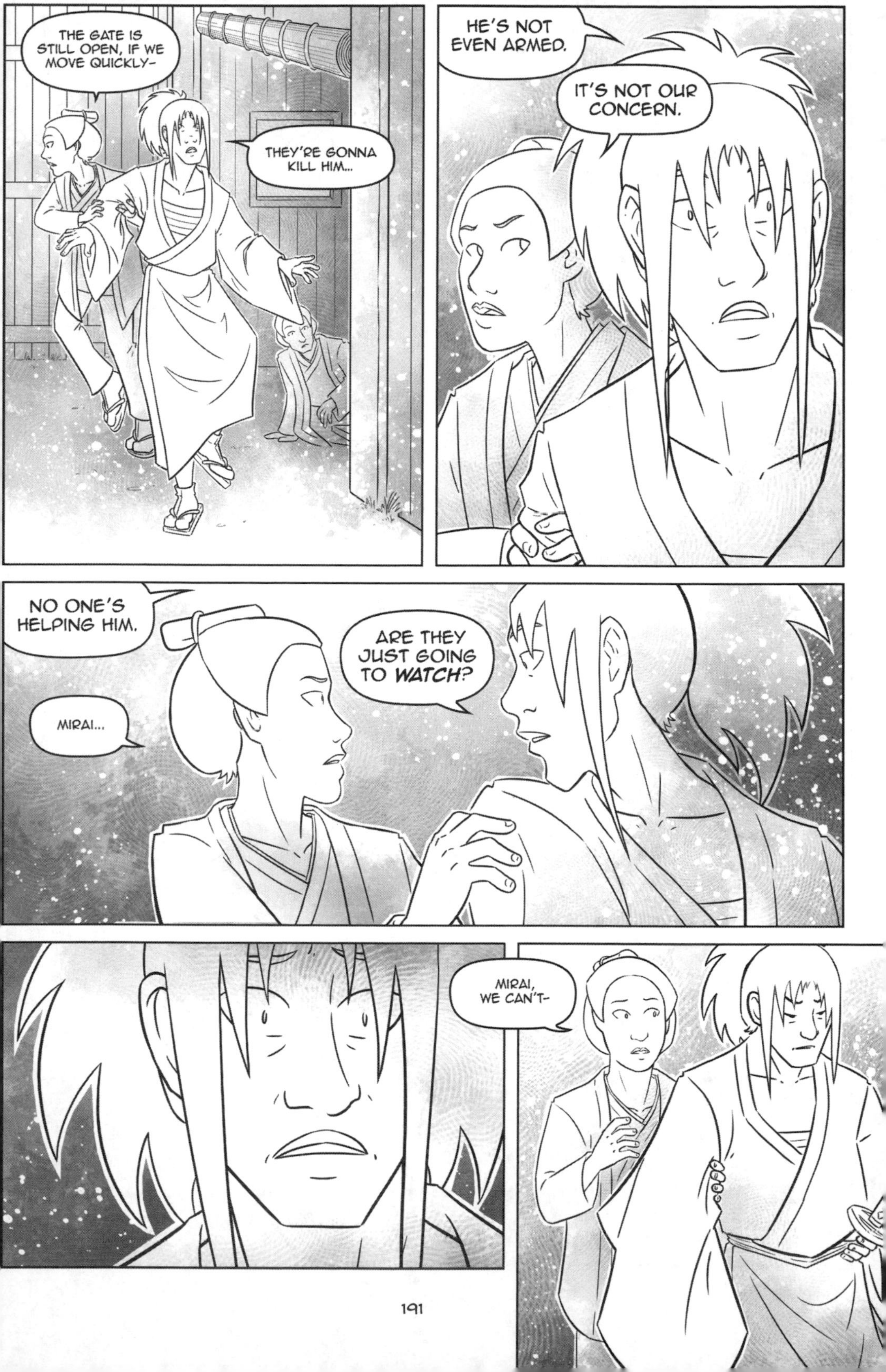
THE GATE IS STILL OPEN, IF WE MOVE QUICKLY-
THEY'RE GONNA KILL HIM...
HE'S NOT EVEN ARMED.
IT'S NOT OUR CONCERN.
NO ONE'S HELPING HIM.
ARE THEY JUST GOING TO *WATCH*?
MIRAI...
MIRAI, WE CAN'T-

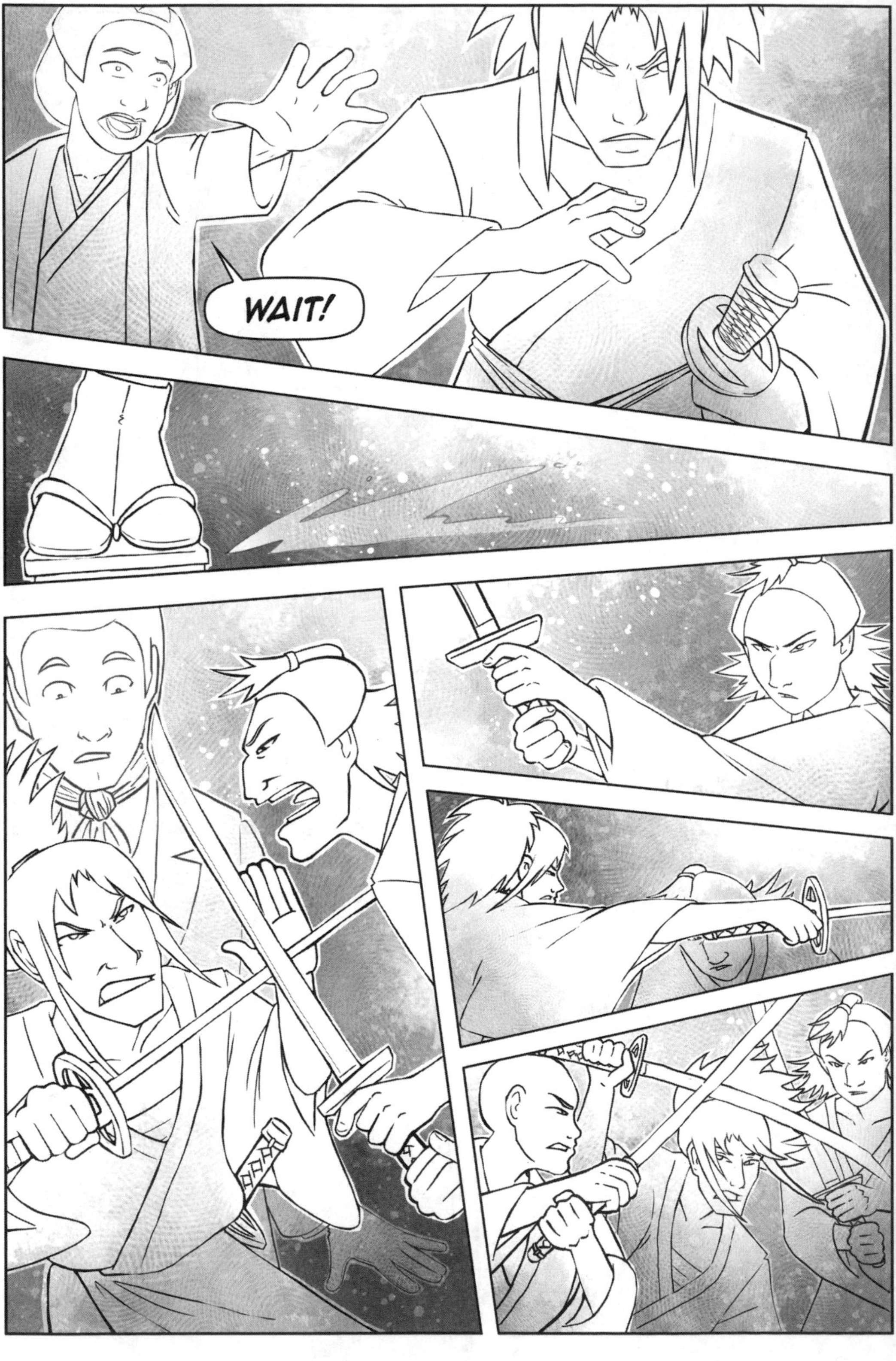
WAIT!

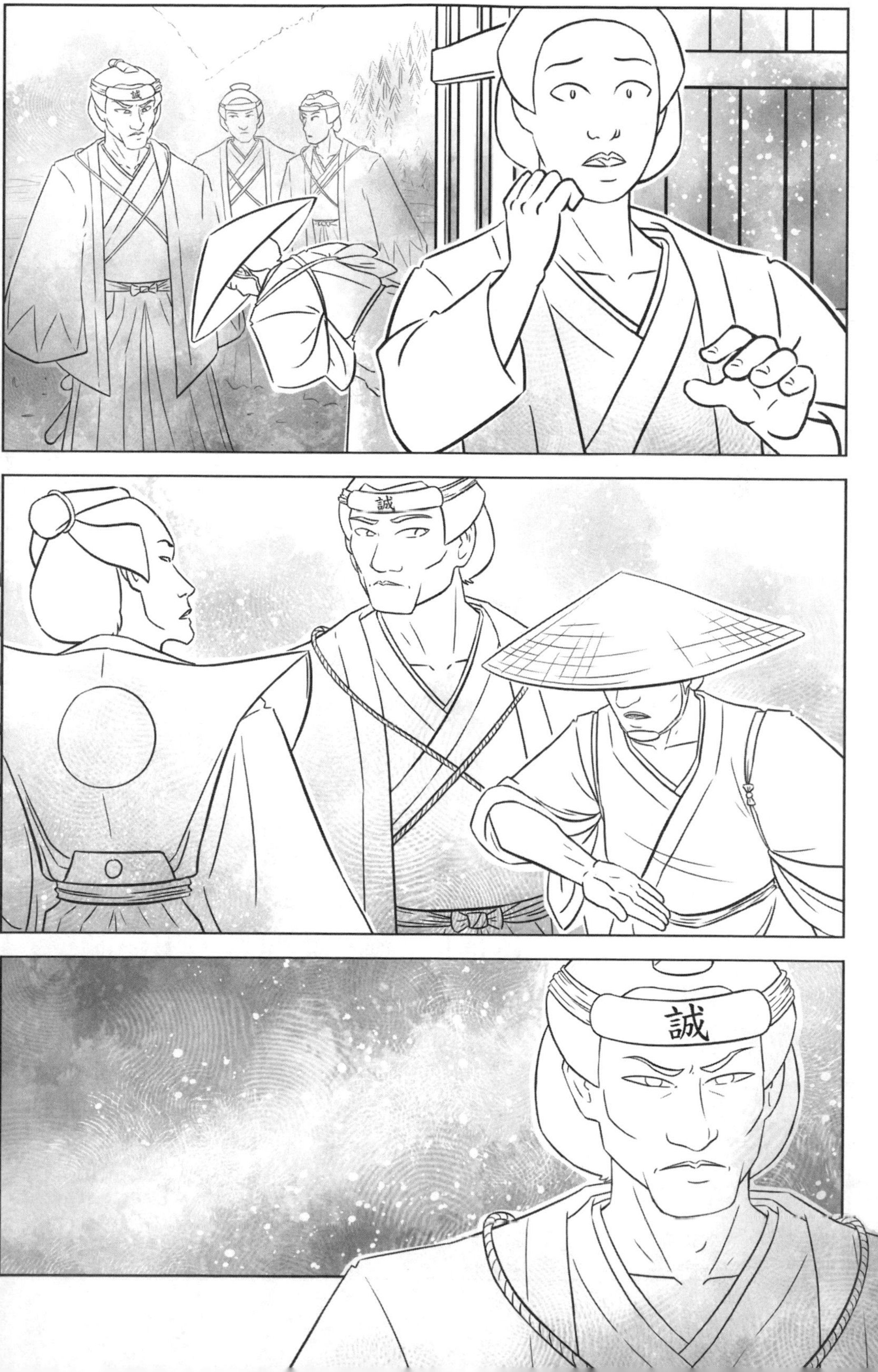
誠

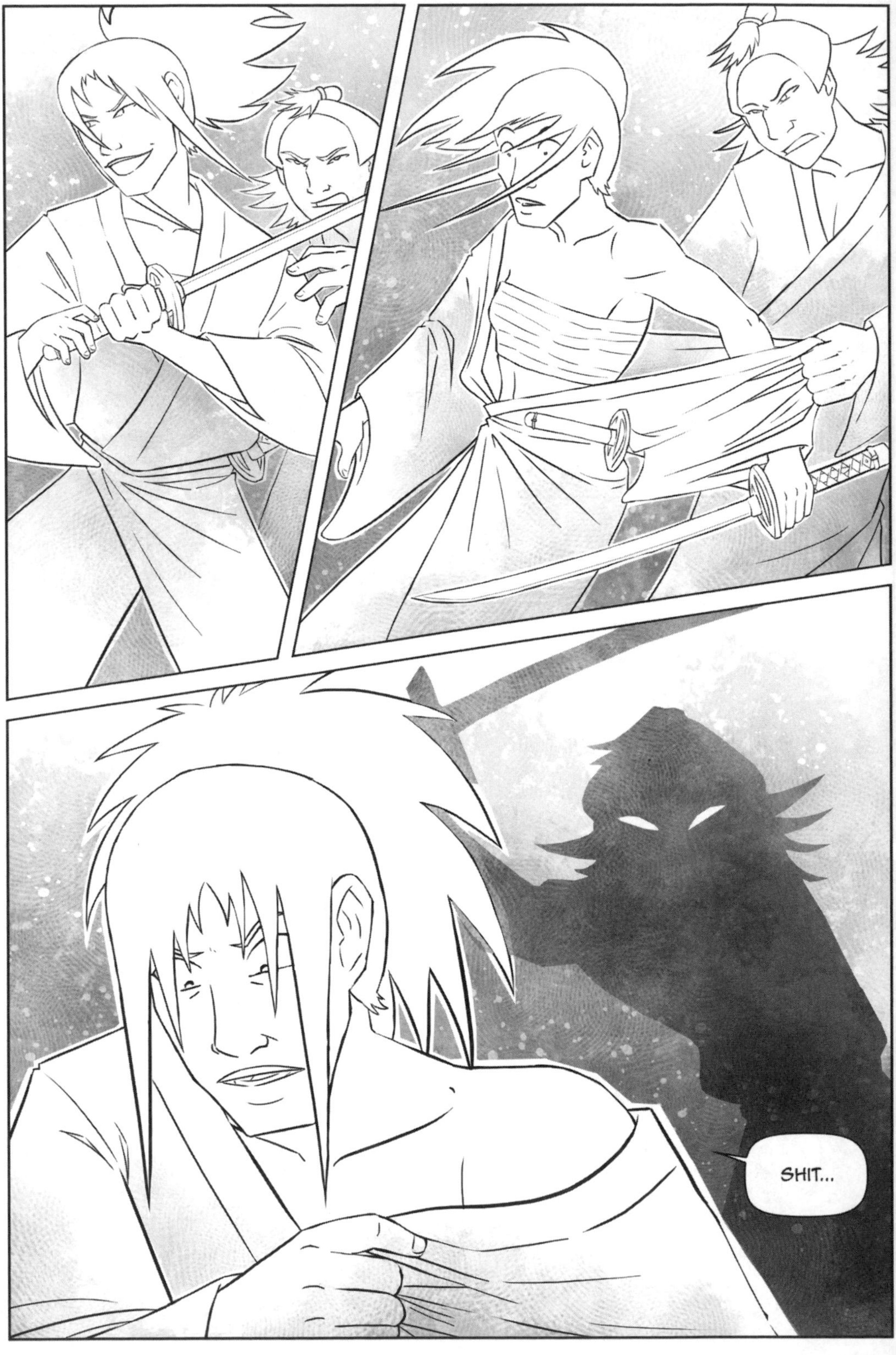
SHIT...

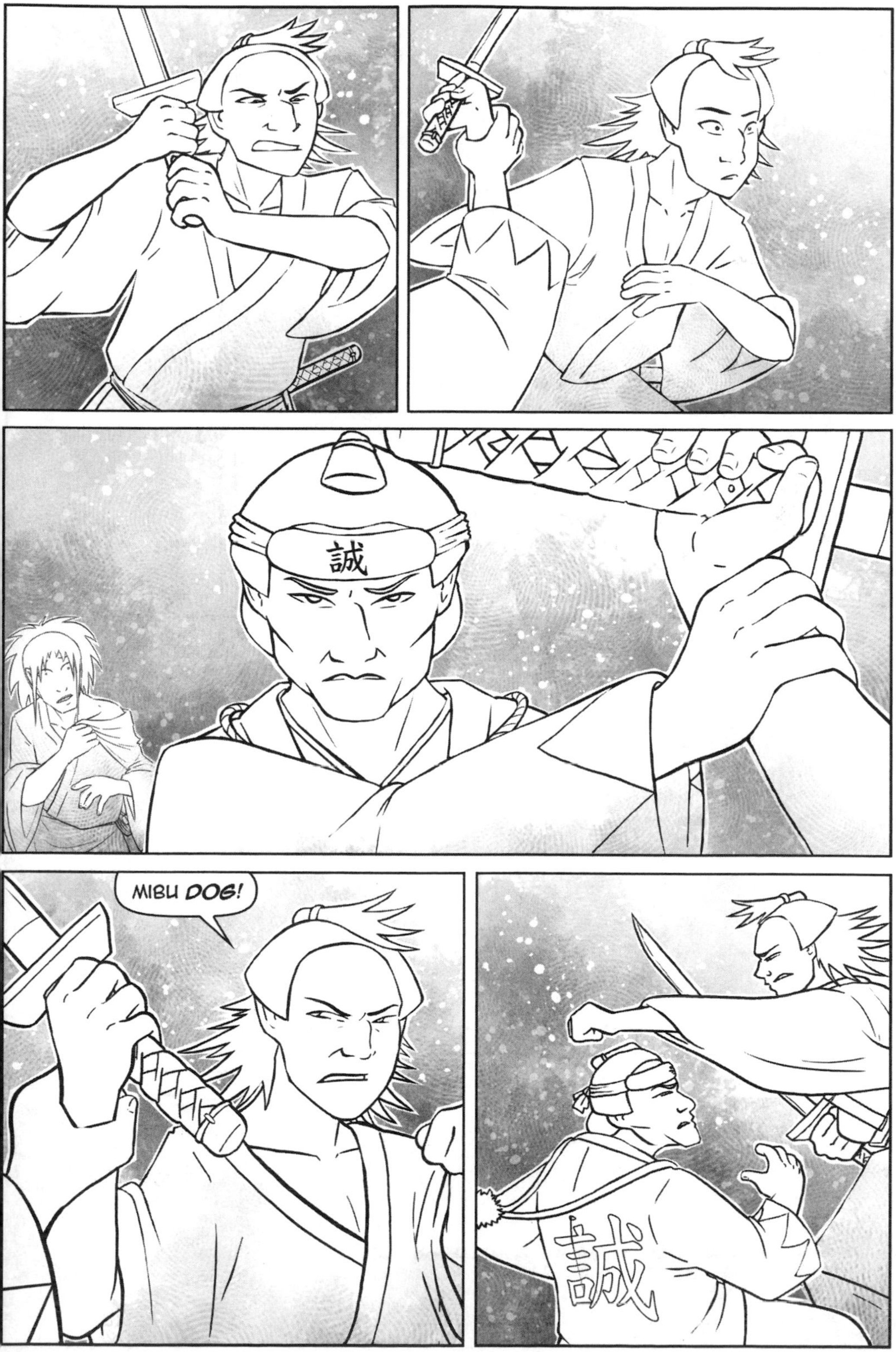
誠
MIBU DOG!
誠

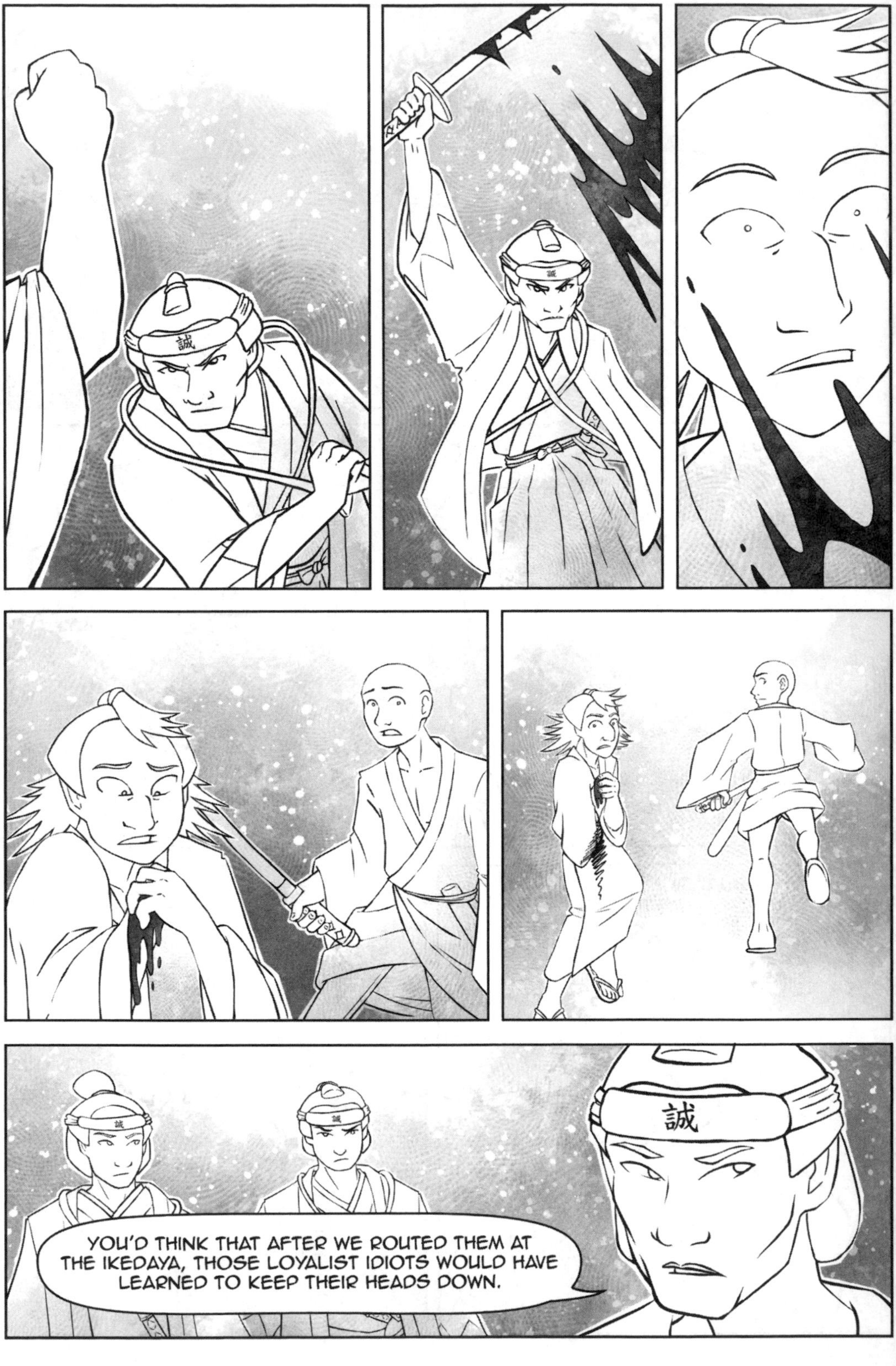
誠
誠
誠
誠
誠
YOU'D THINK THAT AFTER WE ROUTED THEM AT THE IKEDAYA, THOSE LOYALIST IDIOTS WOULD HAVE LEARNED TO KEEP THEIR HEADS DOWN.

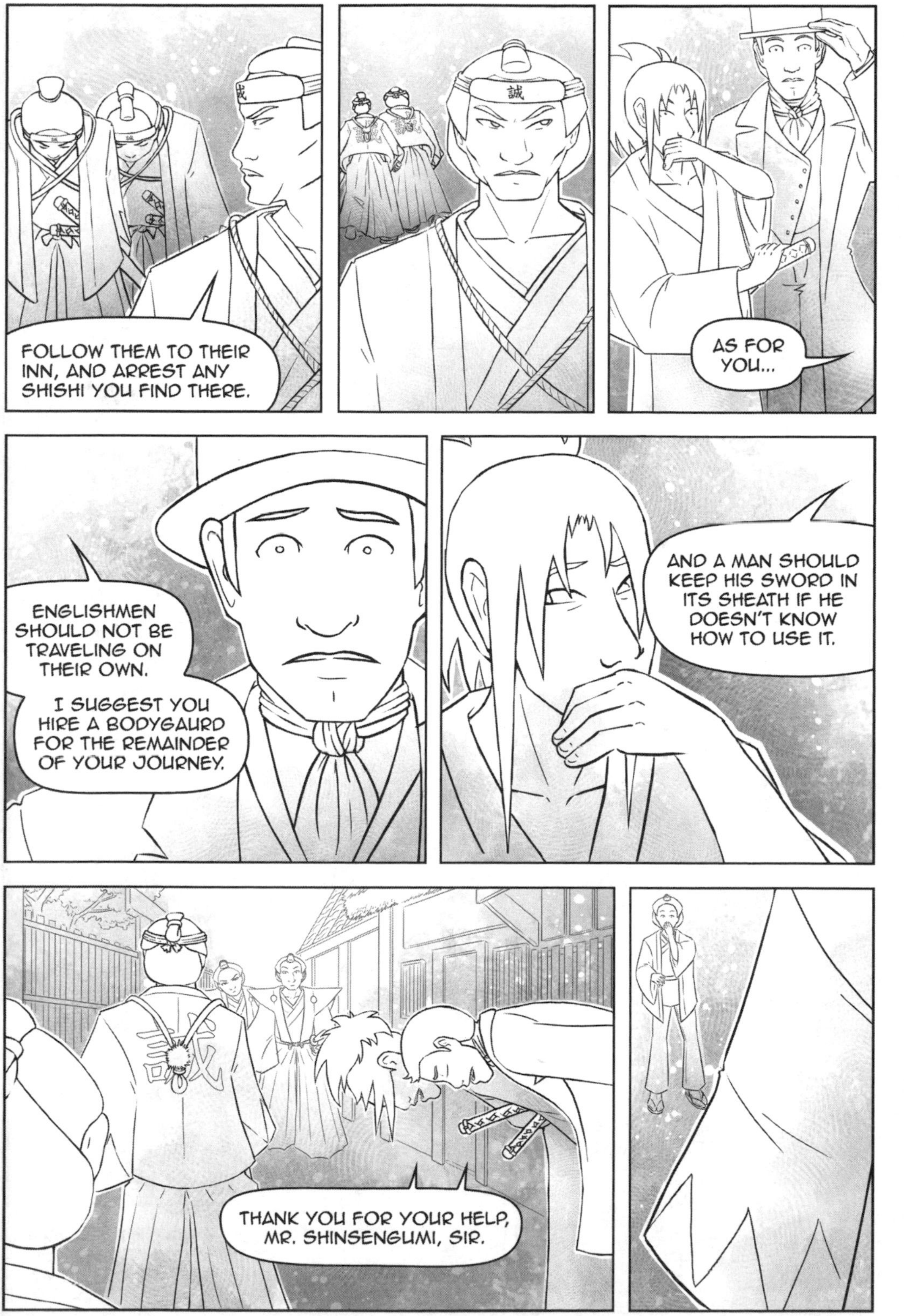
FOLLOW THEM TO THEIR INN, AND ARREST ANY SHISHI YOU FIND THERE.
AS FOR YOU...
ENGLISHMEN SHOULD NOT BE TRAVELING ON THEIR OWN.
I SUGGEST YOU HIRE A BODYGAURD FOR THE REMAINDER OF YOUR JOURNEY.
AND A MAN SHOULD KEEP HIS SWORD IN ITS SHEATH IF HE DOESN'T KNOW HOW TO USE IT.
THANK YOU FOR YOUR HELP, MR. SHINSENGUMI, SIR.

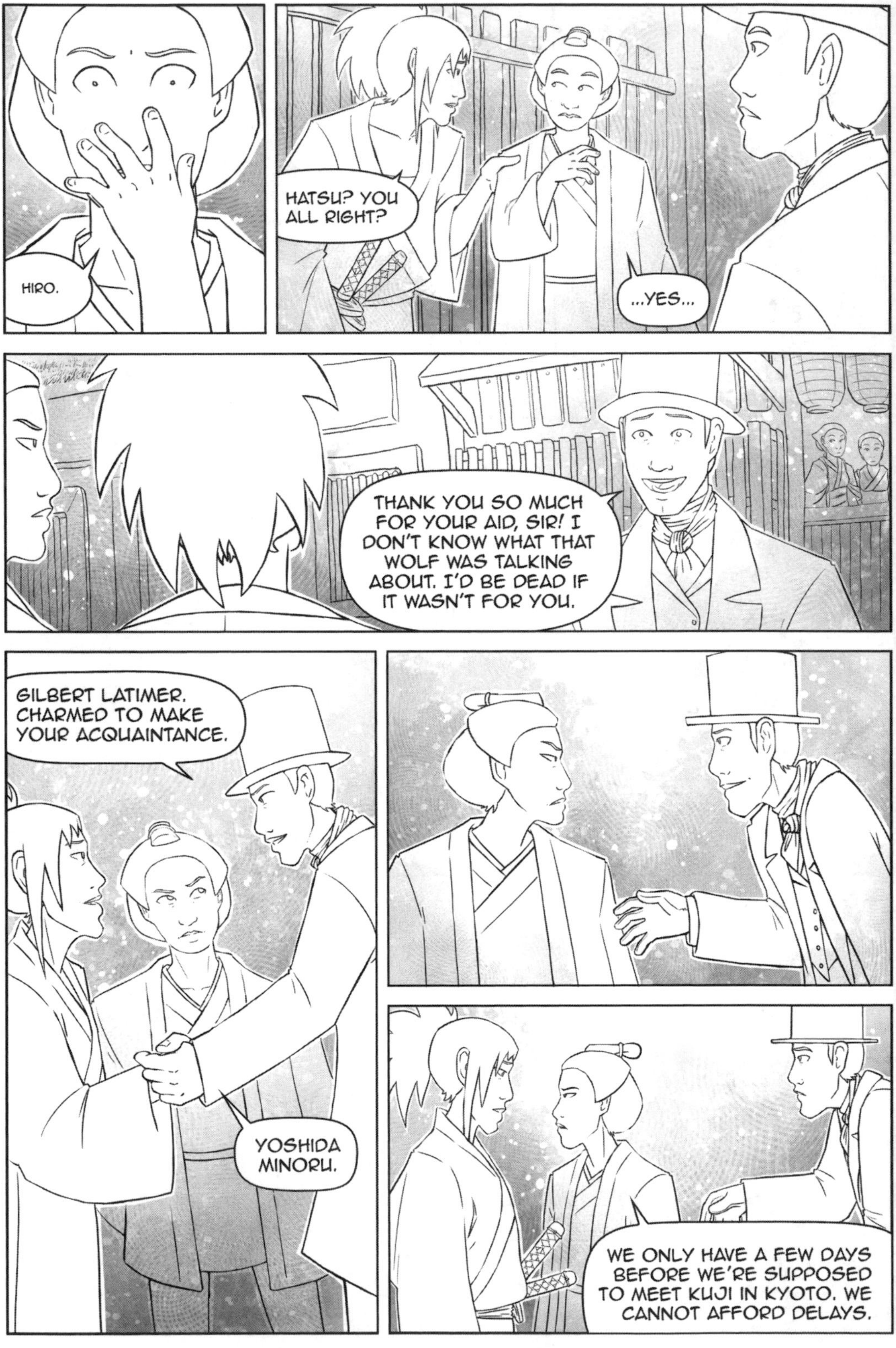
HIRO.
HATSU? YOU ALL RIGHT?
...YES...
THANK YOU SO MUCH FOR YOUR AID, SIR! I DON'T KNOW WHAT THAT WOLF WAS TALKING ABOUT. I'D BE DEAD IF IT WASN'T FOR YOU.
GILBERT LATIMER. CHARMED TO MAKE YOUR ACQUAINTANCE.
YOSHIDA MINORU.
WE ONLY HAVE A FEW DAYS BEFORE WE'RE SUPPOSED TO MEET KUJI IN KYOTO. WE CANNOT AFFORD DELAYS.

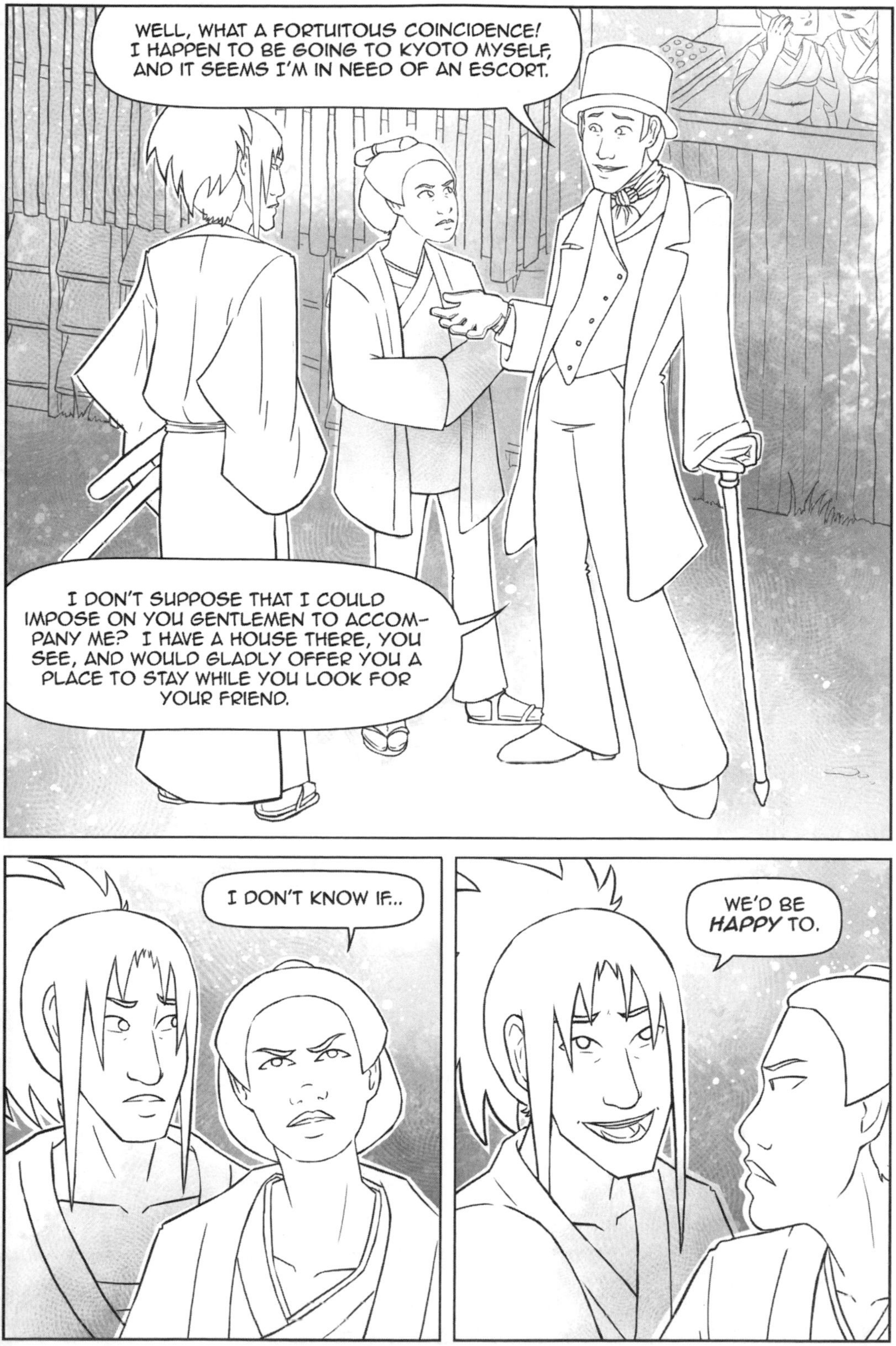
WELL, WHAT A FORTUITOUS COINCIDENCE! I HAPPEN TO BE GOING TO KYOTO MYSELF, AND IT SEEMS I'M IN NEED OF AN ESCORT.
I DON'T SUPPOSE THAT I COULD IMPOSE ON YOU GENTLEMEN TO ACCOMPANY ME? I HAVE A HOUSE THERE, YOU SEE, AND WOULD GLADLY OFFER YOU A PLACE TO STAY WHILE YOU LOOK FOR YOUR FRIEND.
I DON'T KNOW IF...
WE'D BE *HAPPY* TO.

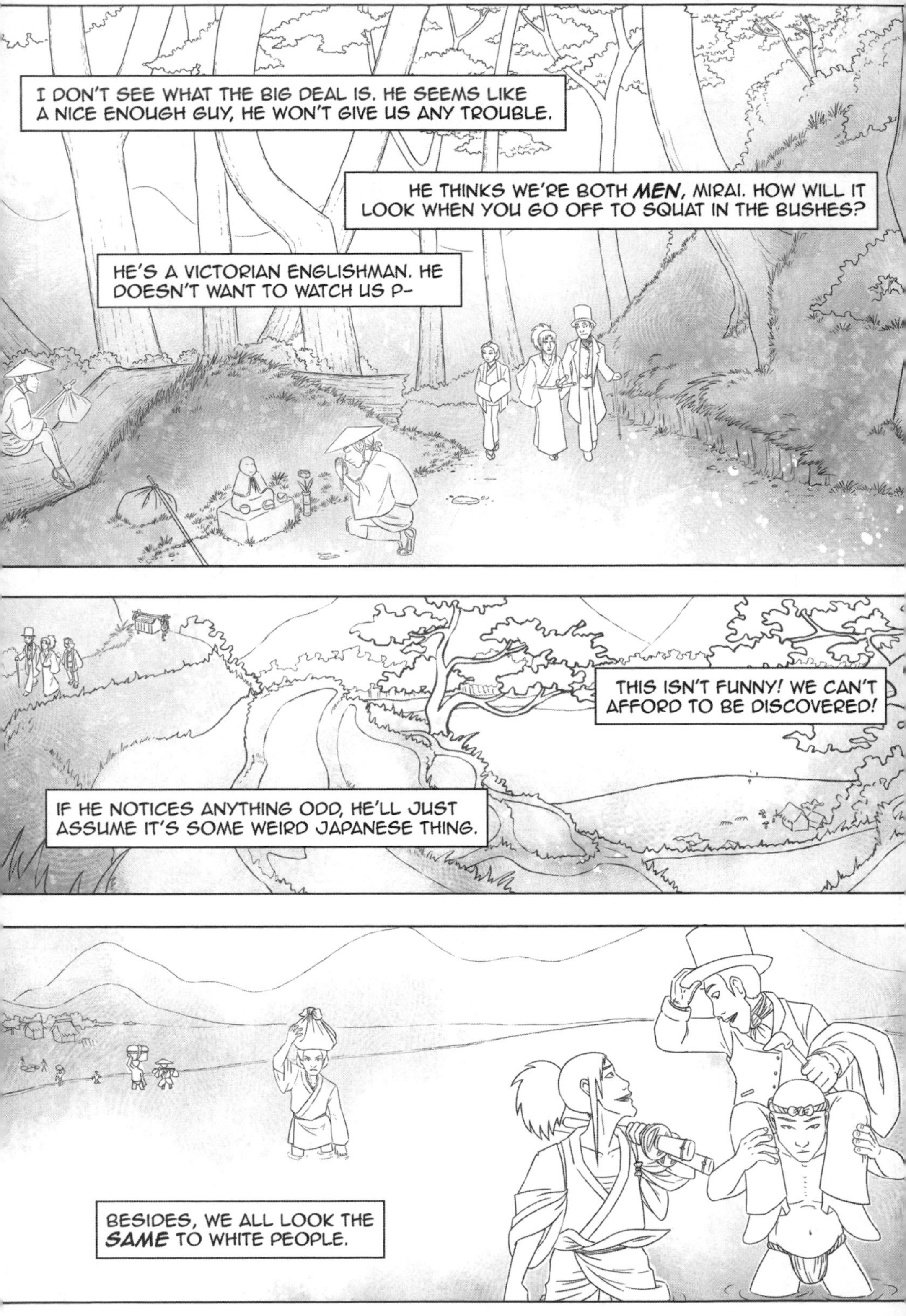

I DON'T SEE WHAT THE BIG DEAL IS. HE SEEMS LIKE A NICE ENOUGH GUY, HE WON'T GIVE US ANY TROUBLE.
HE THINKS WE'RE BOTH **MEN**, MIRAI. HOW WILL IT LOOK WHEN YOU GO OFF TO SQUAT IN THE BUSHES?
HE'S A VICTORIAN ENGLISHMAN. HE DOESN'T WANT TO WATCH US P-
THIS ISN'T FUNNY! WE CAN'T AFFORD TO BE DISCOVERED!
IF HE NOTICES ANYTHING ODD, HE'LL JUST ASSUME IT'S SOME WEIRD JAPANESE THING.
BESIDES, WE ALL LOOK THE **SAME** TO WHITE PEOPLE.

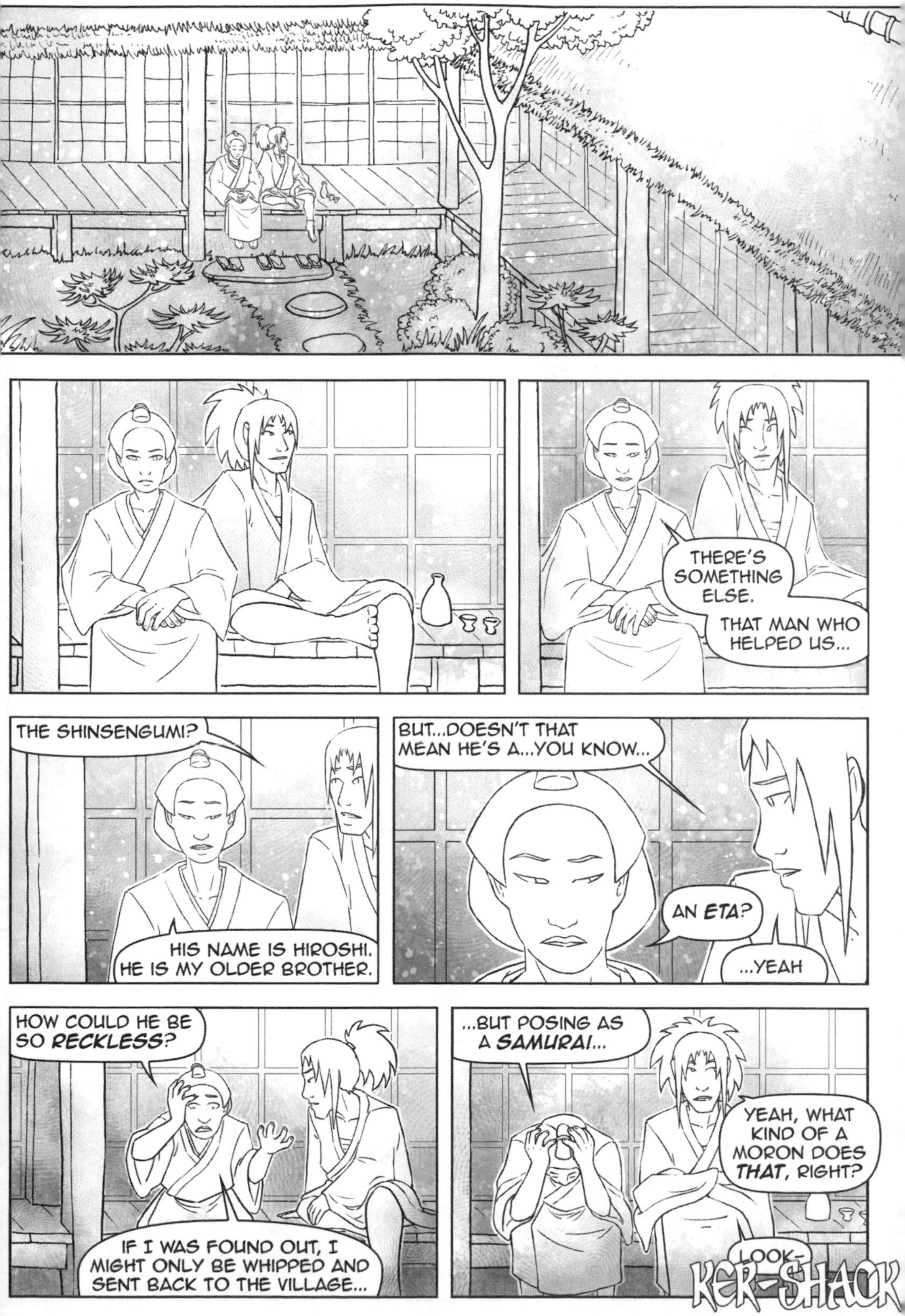

THERE'S SOMETHING ELSE.
THAT MAN WHO HELPED US...
THE SHINSENGUMI?
HIS NAME IS HIROSHI. HE IS MY OLDER BROTHER.
BUT...DOESN'T THAT MEAN HE'S A...YOU KNOW...
AN *ETA*?
...YEAH
HOW COULD HE BE SO ***RECKLESS***?
IF I WAS FOUND OUT, I MIGHT ONLY BE WHIPPED AND SENT BACK TO THE VILLAGE...
...BUT POSING AS A ***SAMURAI***...
YEAH, WHAT KIND OF A MORON DOES ***THAT***, RIGHT?
LOOK-
KER-SHACK

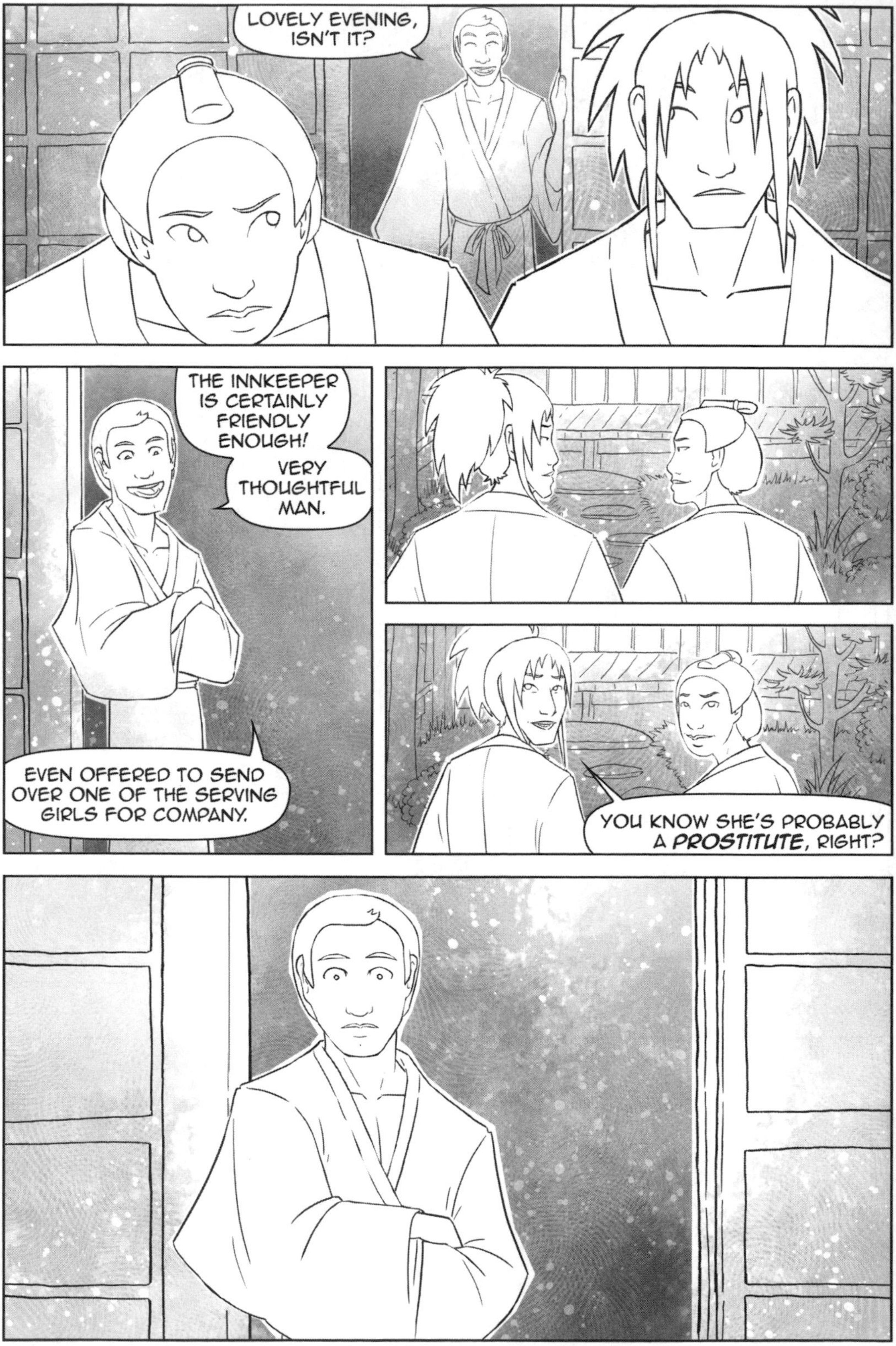
LOVELY EVENING, ISN'T IT?
THE INNKEEPER IS CERTAINLY FRIENDLY ENOUGH!
VERY THOUGHTFUL MAN.
EVEN OFFERED TO SEND OVER ONE OF THE SERVING GIRLS FOR COMPANY.
YOU KNOW SHE'S PROBABLY A *PROSTITUTE*, RIGHT?

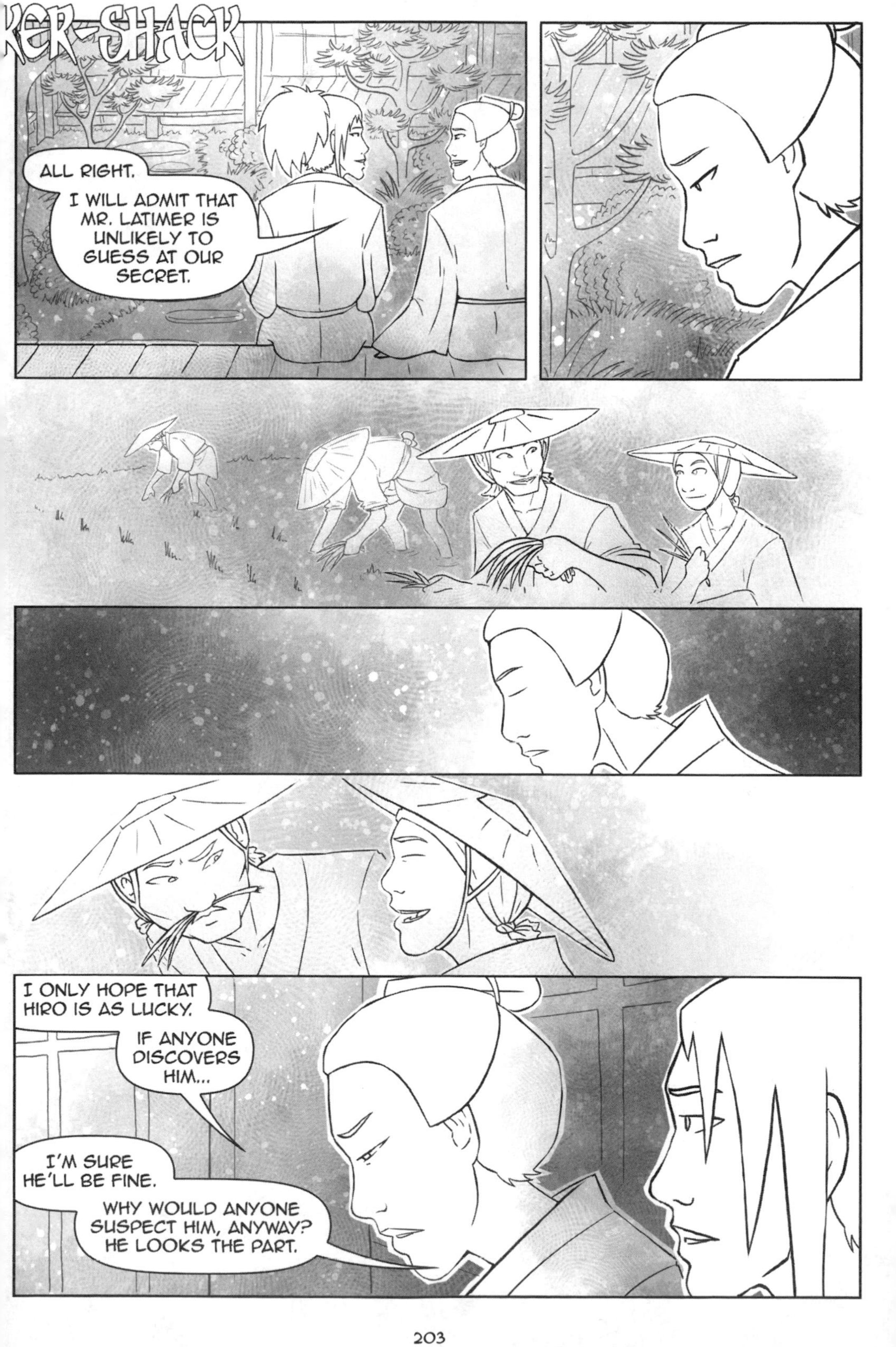
KER-SHACK
ALL RIGHT.
I WILL ADMIT THAT MR. LATIMER IS UNLIKELY TO GUESS AT OUR SECRET.
I ONLY HOPE THAT HIRO IS AS LUCKY.
IF ANYONE DISCOVERS HIM...
I'M SURE HE'LL BE FINE.
WHY WOULD ANYONE SUSPECT HIM, ANYWAY? HE LOOKS THE PART.

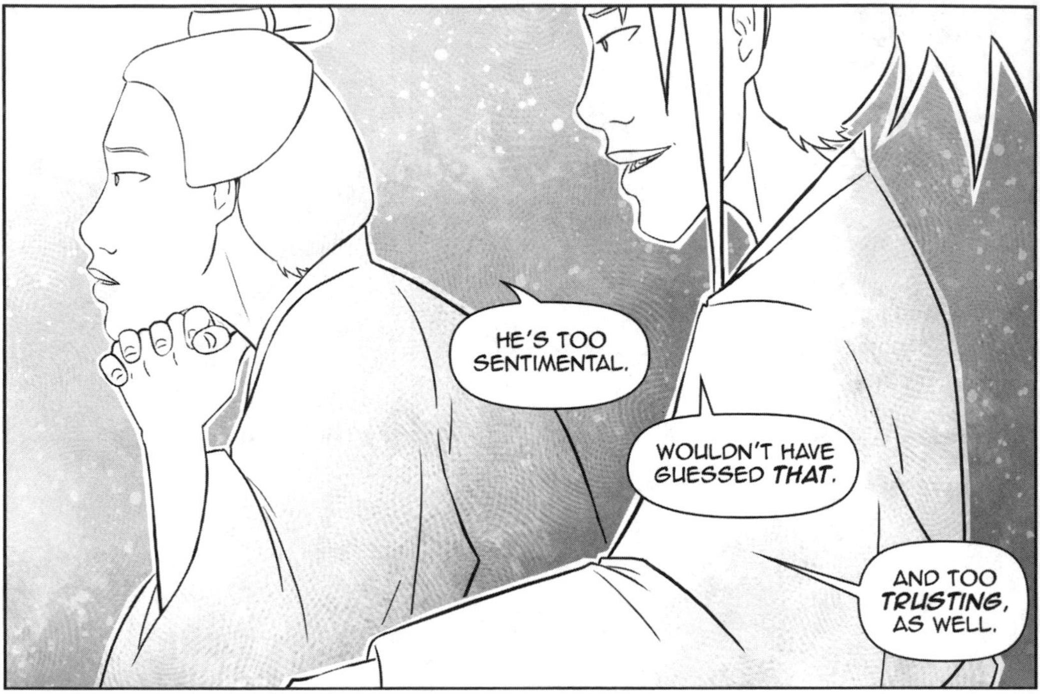
HE'S TOO SENTIMENTAL.
WOULDN'T HAVE GUESSED *THAT*.
AND TOO *TRUSTING*, AS WELL.

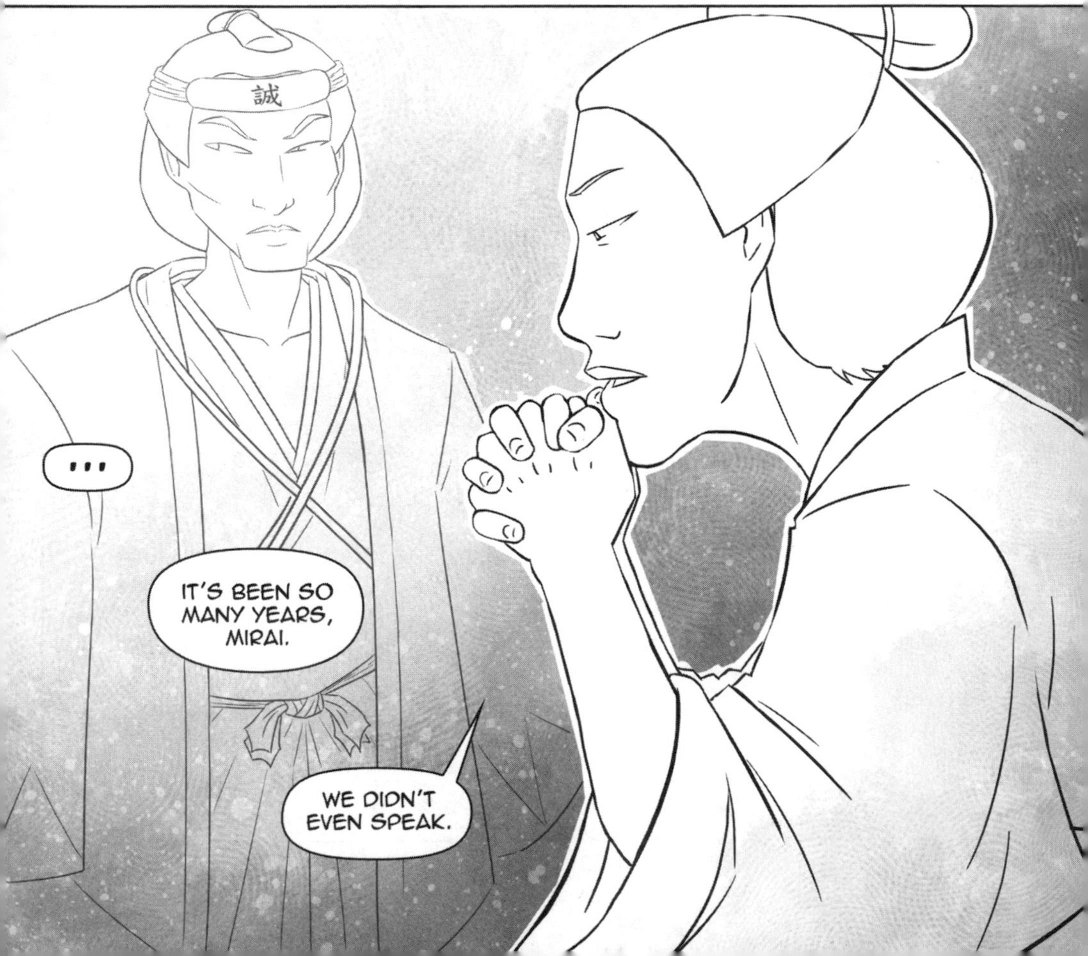
誠
...
IT'S BEEN SO MANY YEARS, MIRAI.
WE DIDN'T EVEN SPEAK.

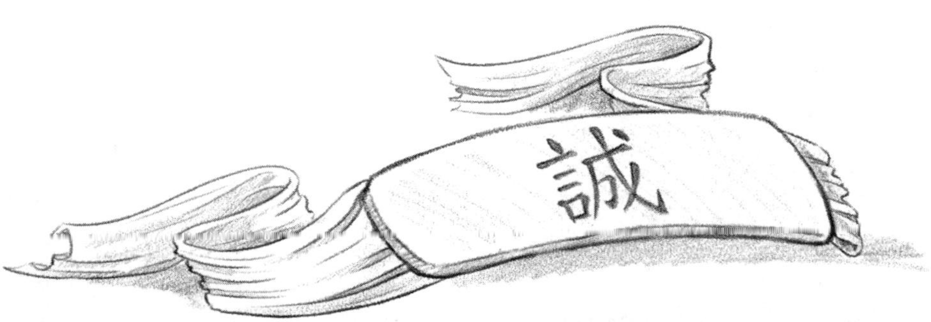
誠

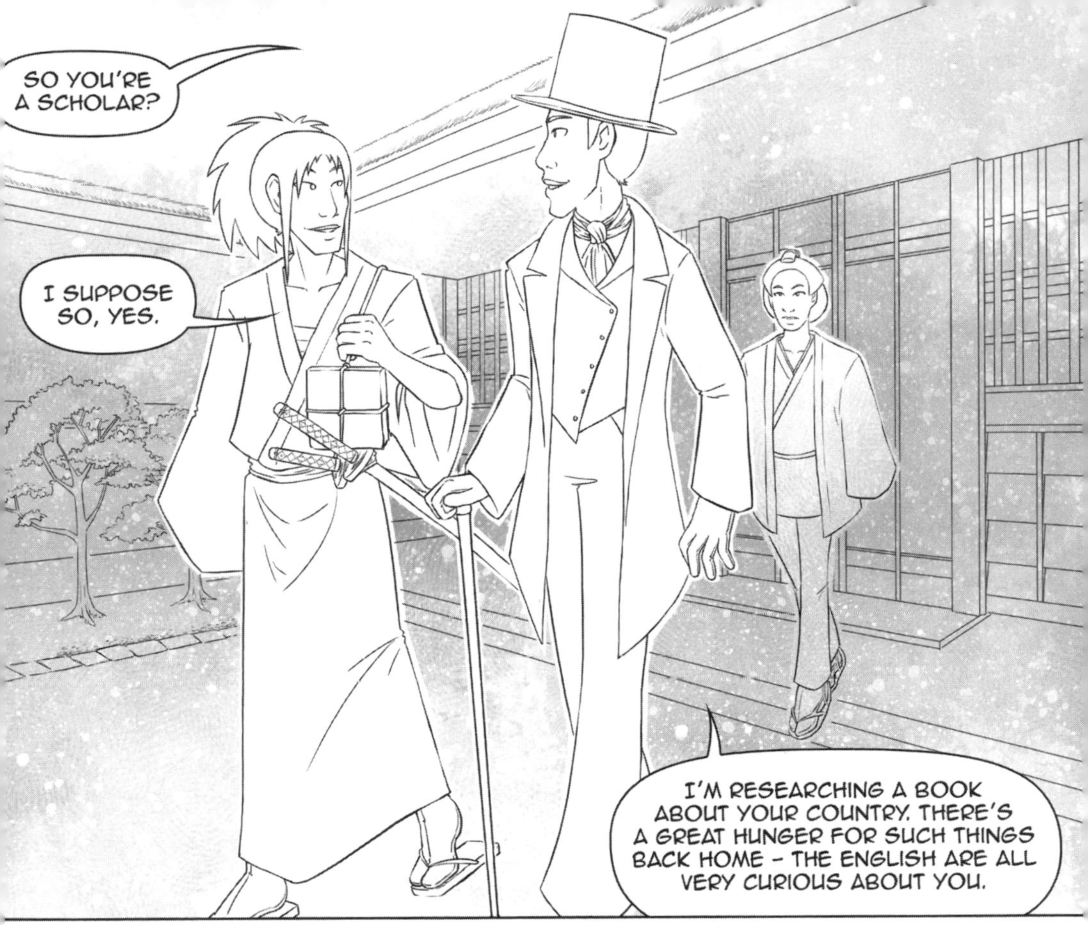
SO YOU'RE A SCHOLAR?
I SUPPOSE SO, YES.
I'M RESEARCHING A BOOK ABOUT YOUR COUNTRY. THERE'S A GREAT HUNGER FOR SUCH THINGS BACK HOME - THE ENGLISH ARE ALL VERY CURIOUS ABOUT YOU.

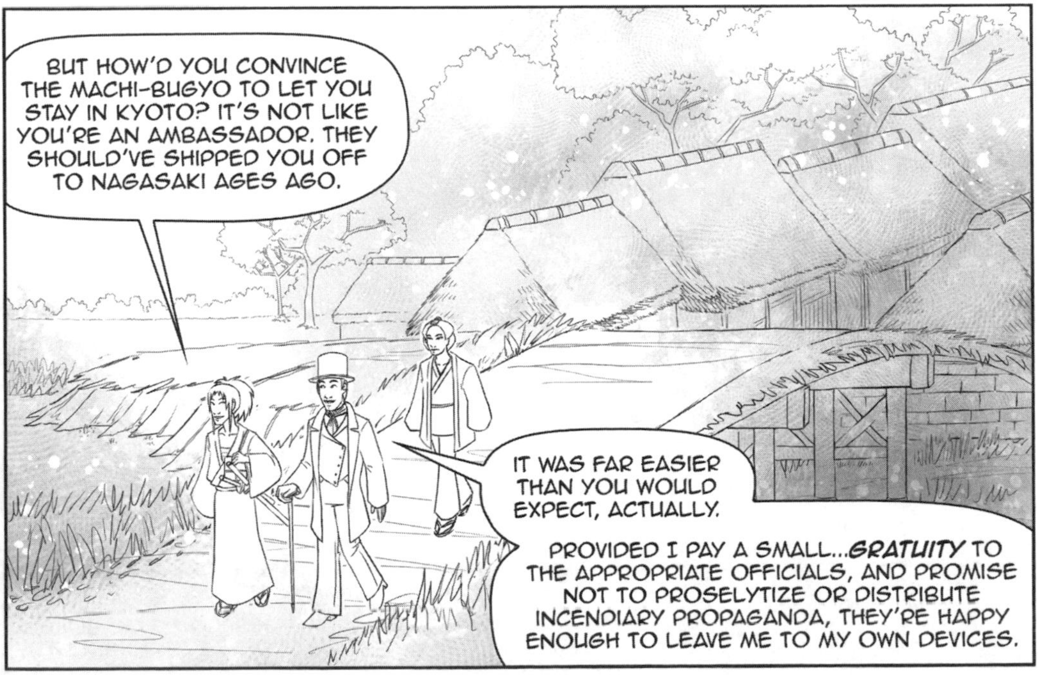
BUT HOW'D YOU CONVINCE THE MACHI-BUGYO TO LET YOU STAY IN KYOTO? IT'S NOT LIKE YOU'RE AN AMBASSADOR. THEY SHOULD'VE SHIPPED YOU OFF TO NAGASAKI AGES AGO.
IT WAS FAR EASIER THAN YOU WOULD EXPECT, ACTUALLY.
PROVIDED I PAY A SMALL...**GRATUITY** TO THE APPROPRIATE OFFICIALS, AND PROMISE NOT TO PROSELYTIZE OR DISTRIBUTE INCENDIARY PROPAGANDA, THEY'RE HAPPY ENOUGH TO LEAVE ME TO MY OWN DEVICES.

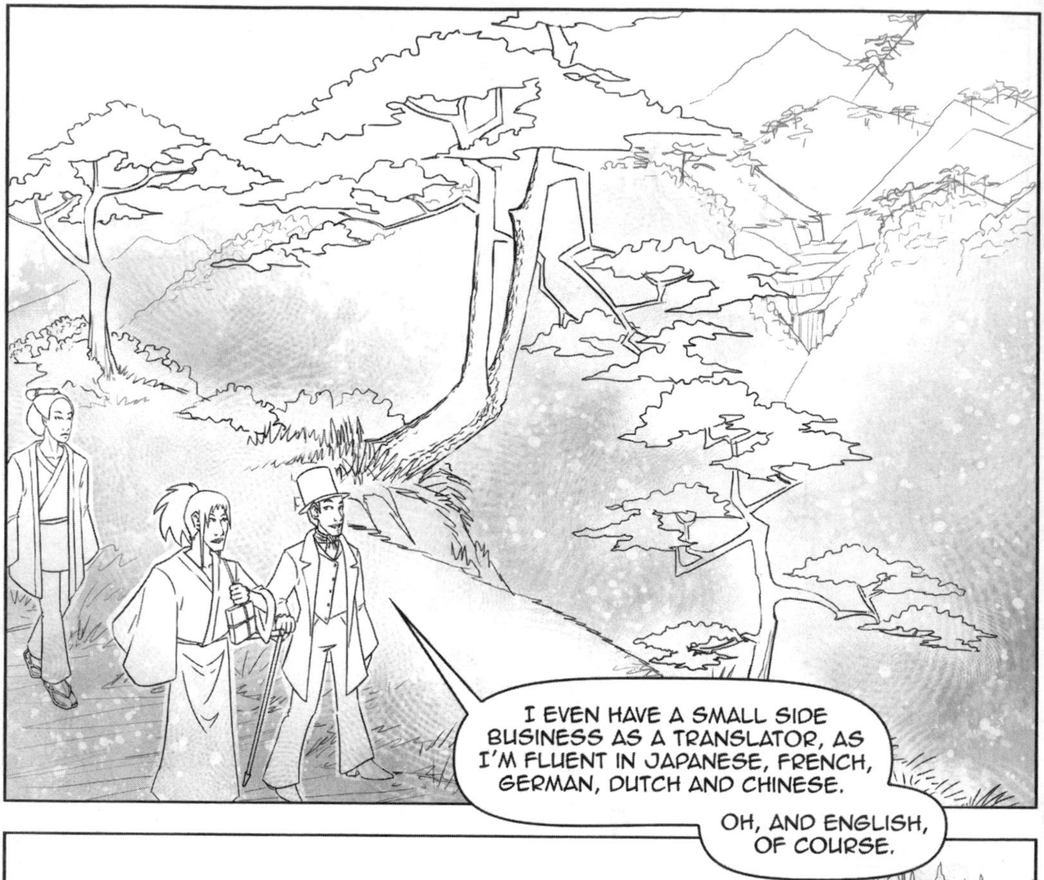
I EVEN HAVE A SMALL SIDE BUSINESS AS A TRANSLATOR, AS I'M FLUENT IN JAPANESE, FRENCH, GERMAN, DUTCH AND CHINESE.
OH, AND ENGLISH, OF COURSE.

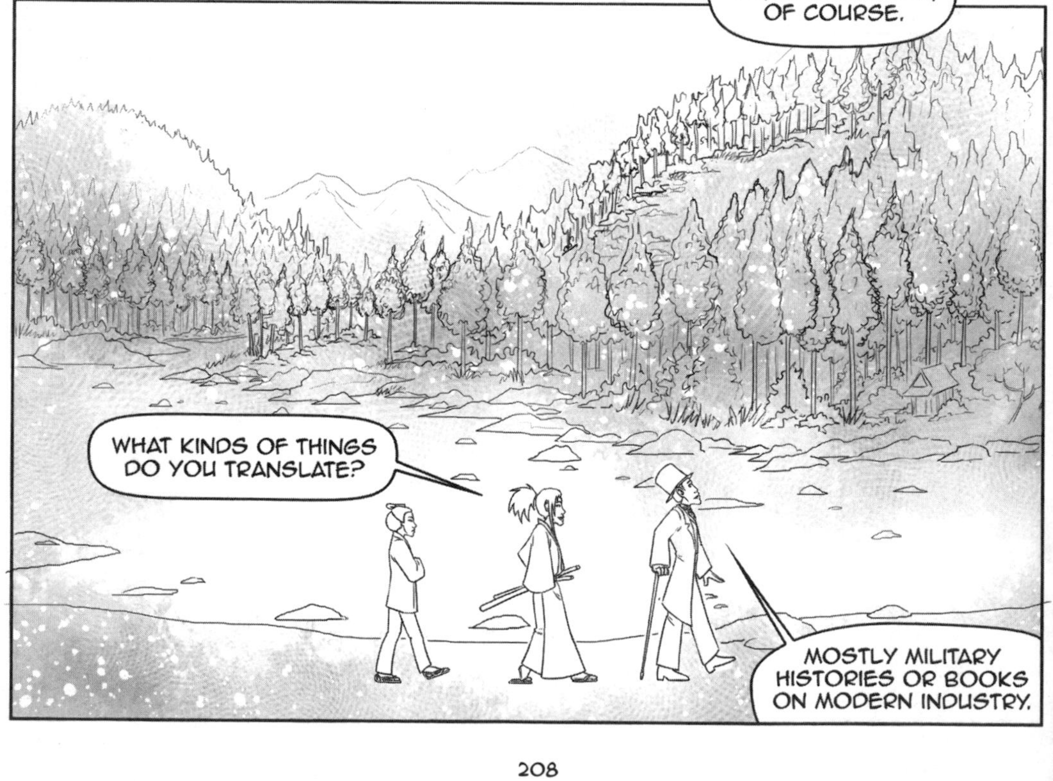
WHAT KINDS OF THINGS DO YOU TRANSLATE?
MOSTLY MILITARY HISTORIES OR BOOKS ON MODERN INDUSTRY.

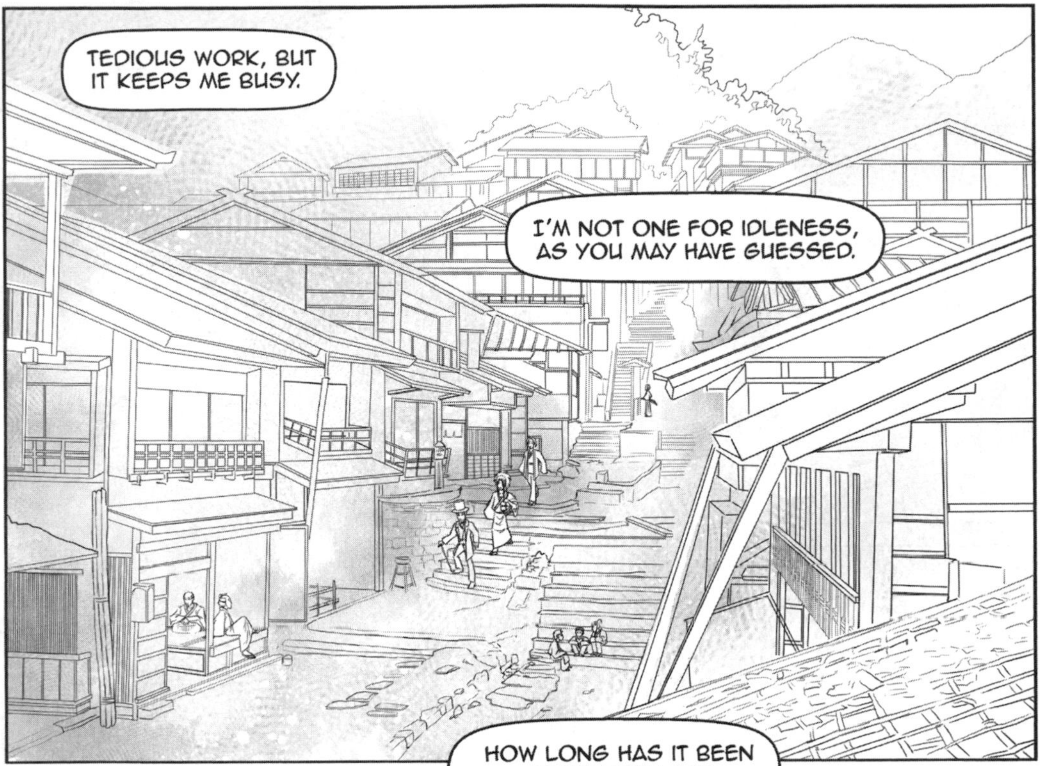
TEDIOUS WORK, BUT IT KEEPS ME BUSY.
I'M NOT ONE FOR IDLENESS, AS YOU MAY HAVE GUESSED.

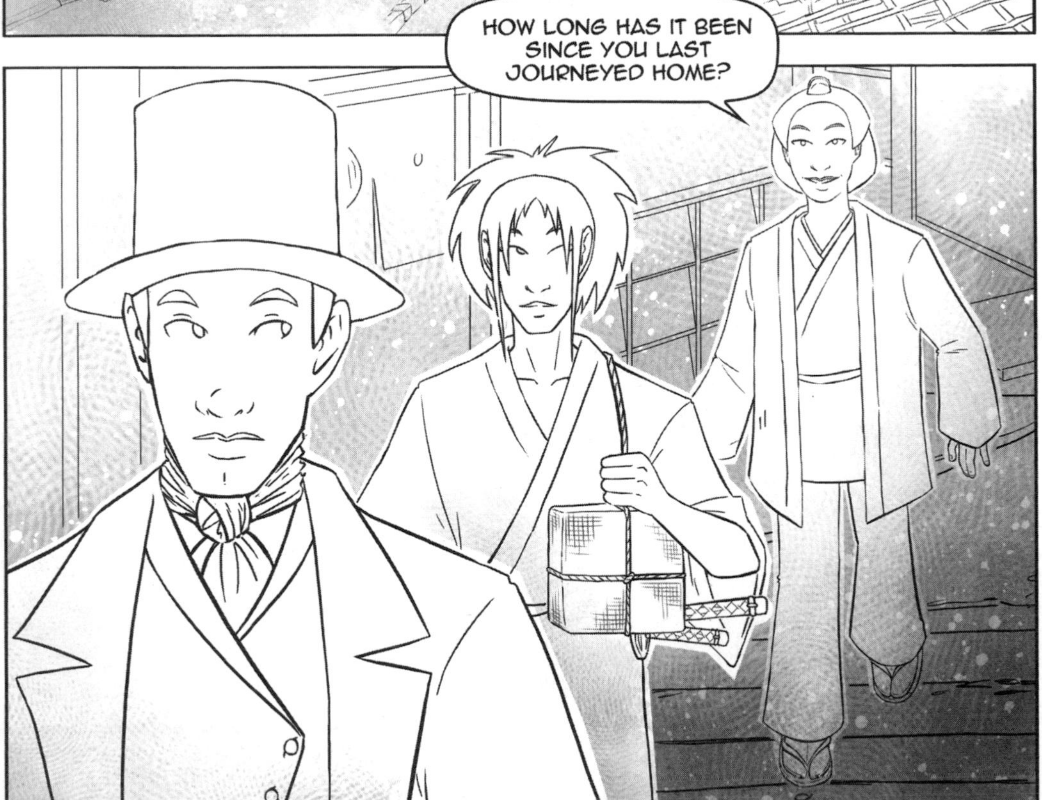
HOW LONG HAS IT BEEN SINCE YOU LAST JOURNEYED HOME?

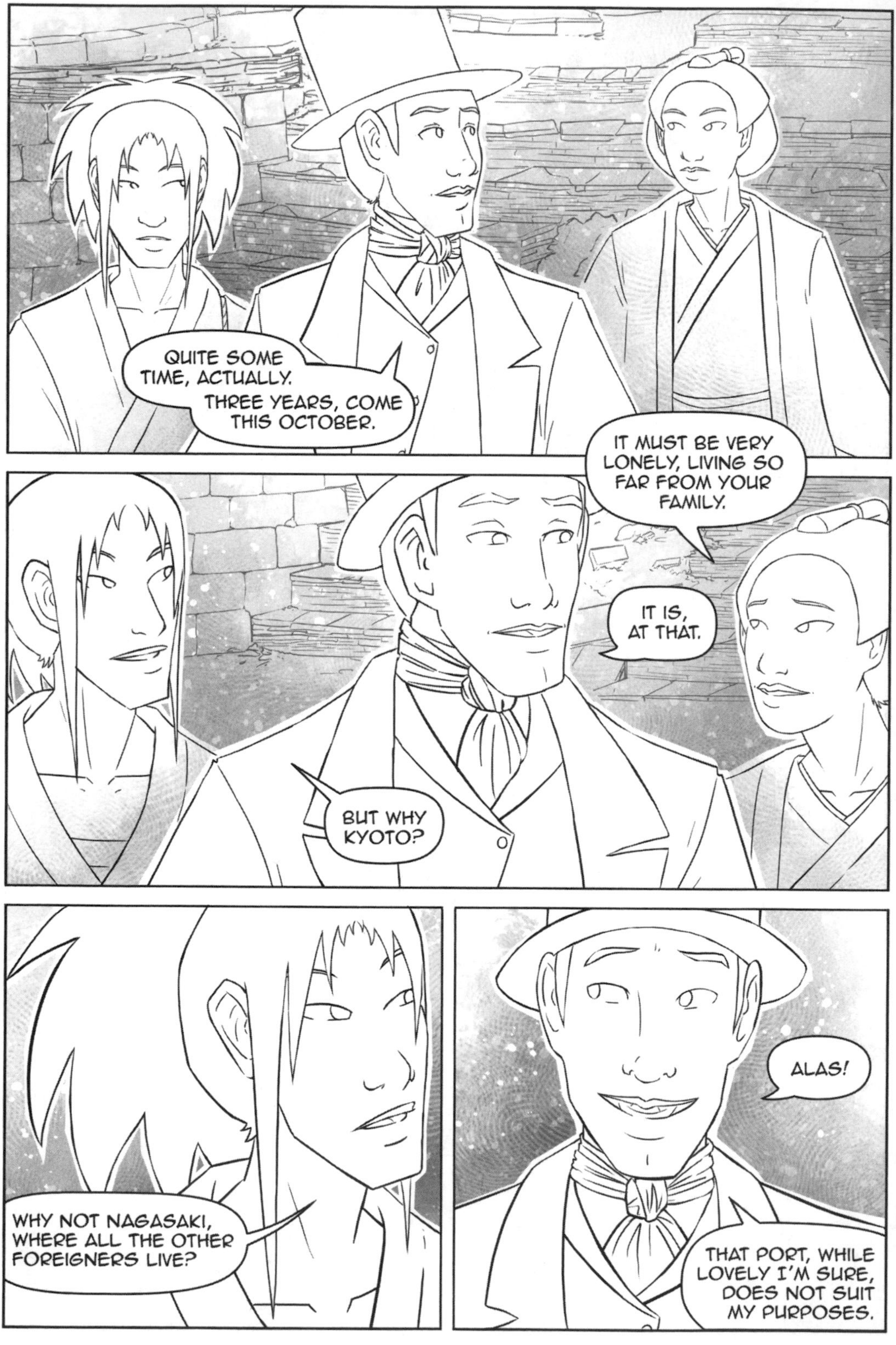
QUITE SOME TIME, ACTUALLY.
THREE YEARS, COME THIS OCTOBER.
IT MUST BE VERY LONELY, LIVING SO FAR FROM YOUR FAMILY.
IT IS, AT THAT.
BUT WHY KYOTO?
WHY NOT NAGASAKI, WHERE ALL THE OTHER FOREIGNERS LIVE?
ALAS!
THAT PORT, WHILE LOVELY I'M SURE, DOES NOT SUIT MY PURPOSES.

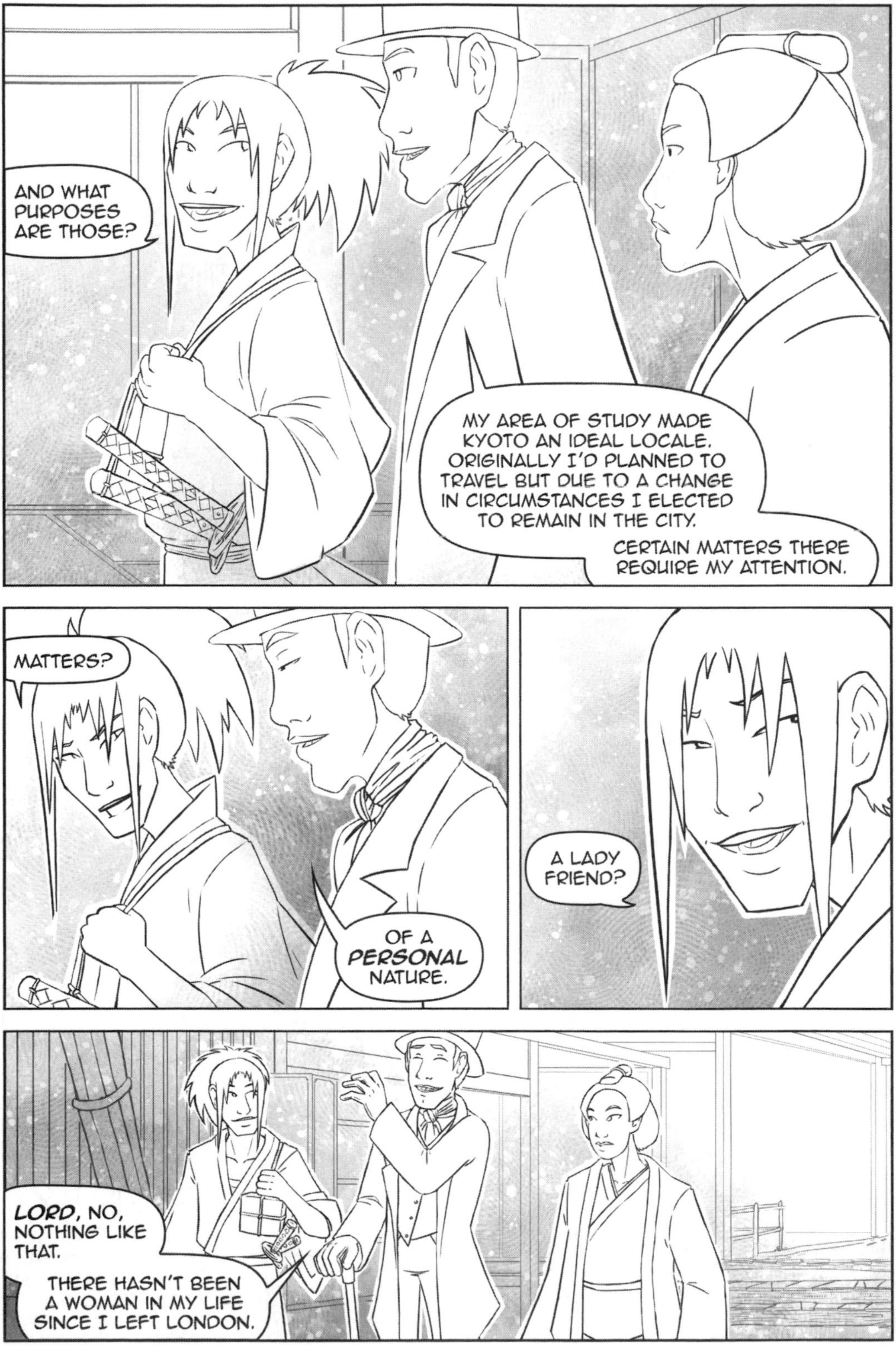
AND WHAT PURPOSES ARE THOSE?
MY AREA OF STUDY MADE KYOTO AN IDEAL LOCALE. ORIGINALLY I'D PLANNED TO TRAVEL BUT DUE TO A CHANGE IN CIRCUMSTANCES I ELECTED TO REMAIN IN THE CITY.
CERTAIN MATTERS THERE REQUIRE MY ATTENTION.
MATTERS?
OF A *PERSONAL* NATURE.
A LADY FRIEND?
LORD, NO, NOTHING LIKE THAT.
THERE HASN'T BEEN A WOMAN IN MY LIFE SINCE I LEFT LONDON.

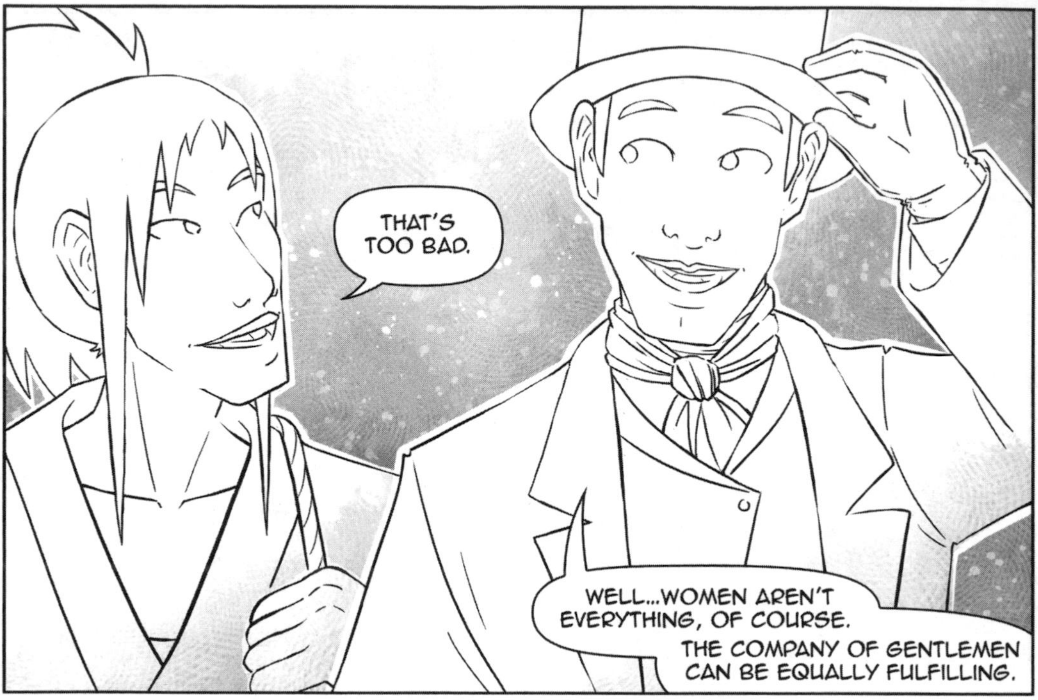
THAT'S TOO BAD.
WELL...WOMEN AREN'T EVERYTHING, OF COURSE.
THE COMPANY OF GENTLEMEN CAN BE EQUALLY FULFILLING.

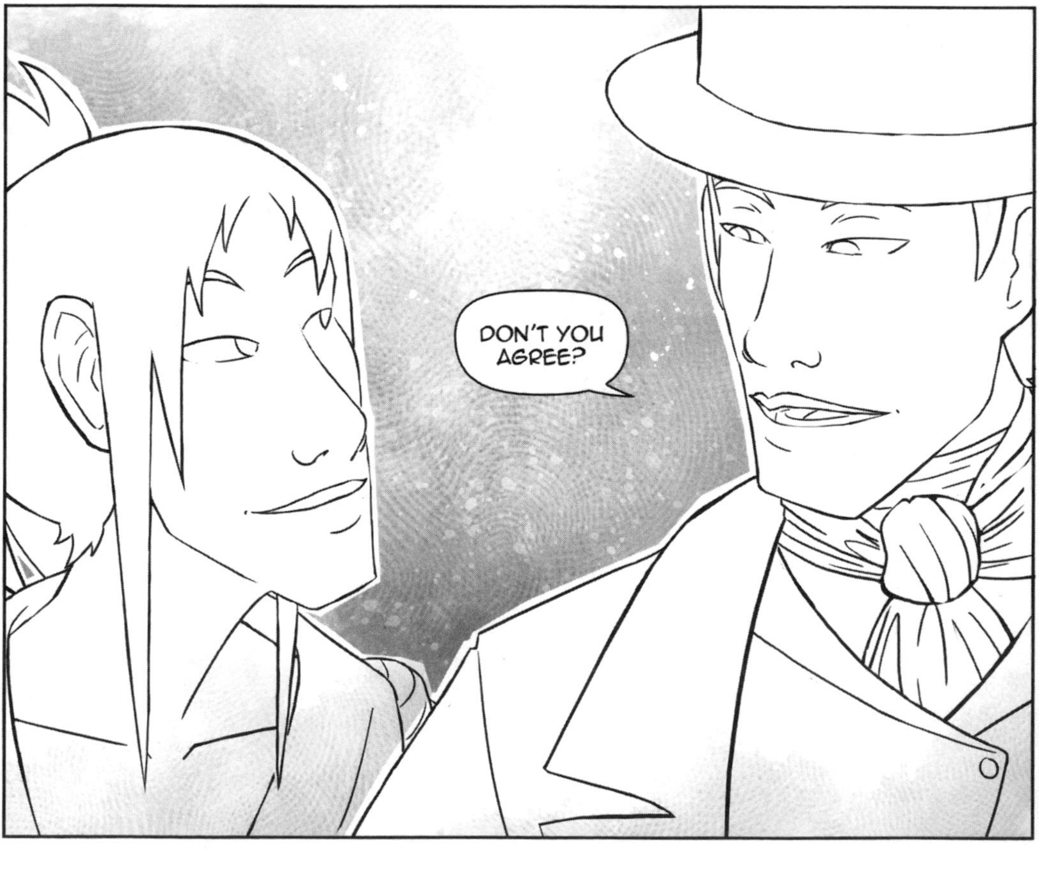
DON'T YOU AGREE?

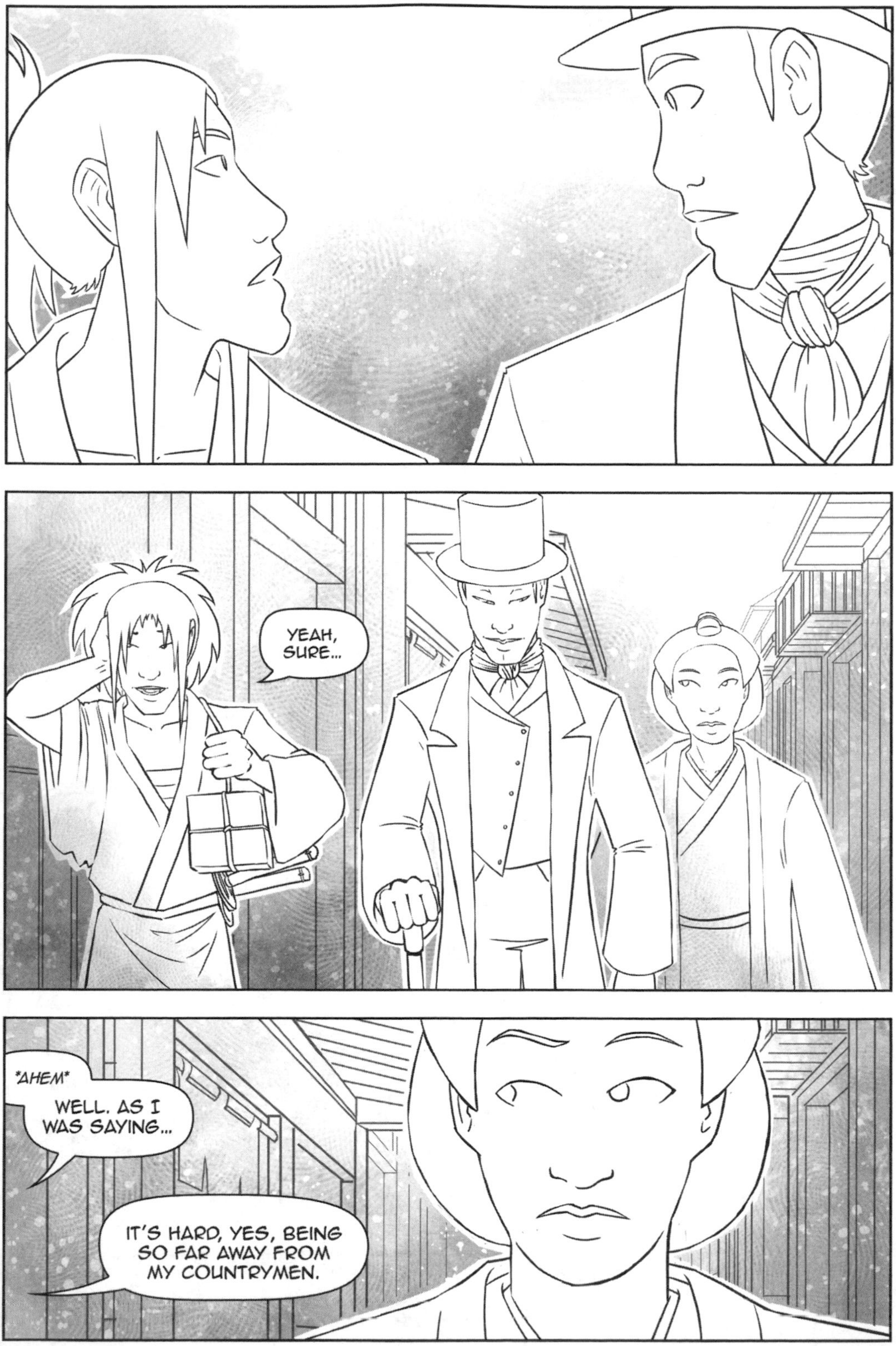
YEAH, SURE...
AHEM
WELL. AS I WAS SAYING...
IT'S HARD, YES, BEING SO FAR AWAY FROM MY COUNTRYMEN.

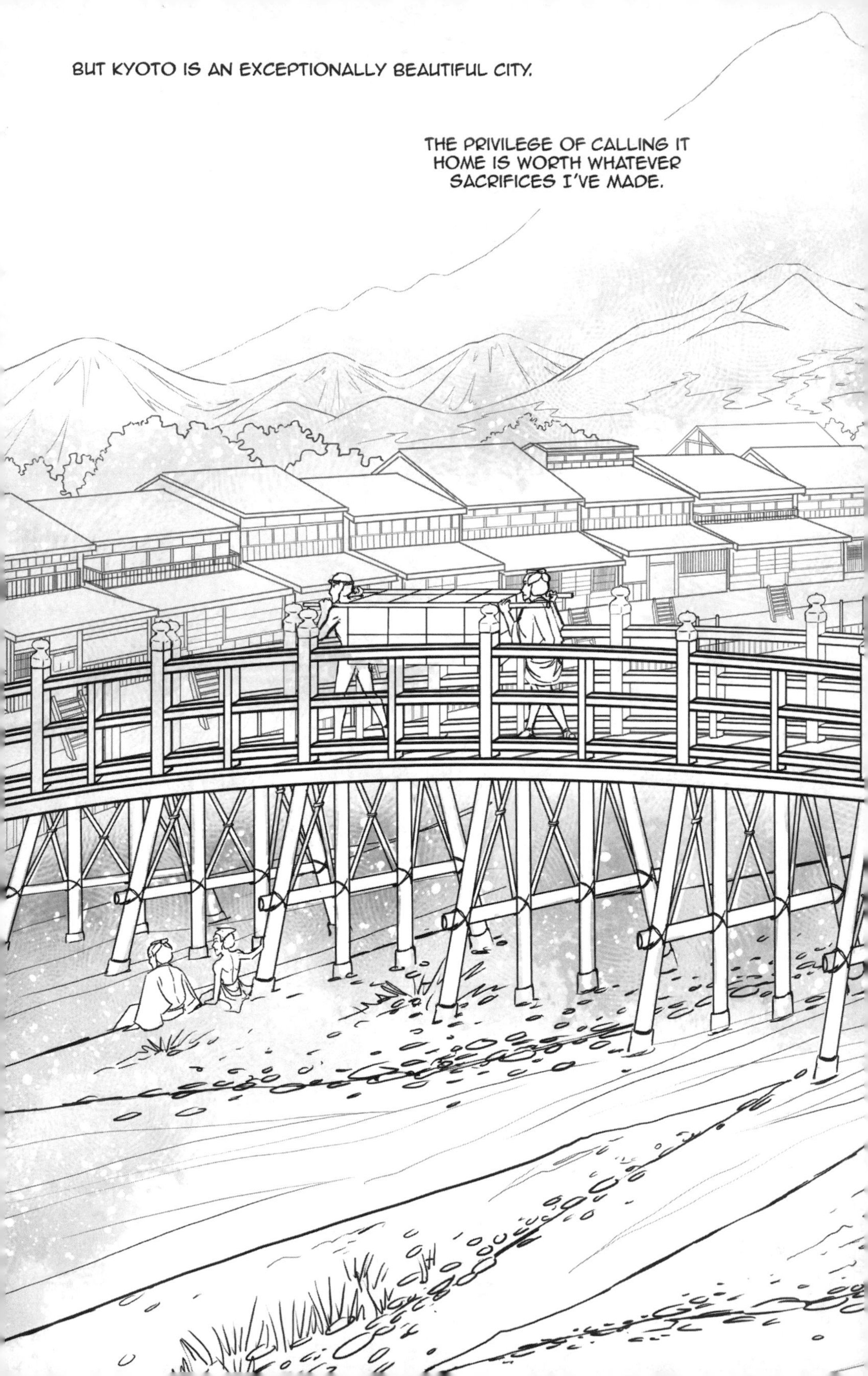
BUT KYOTO IS AN EXCEPTIONALLY BEAUTIFUL CITY.
THE PRIVILEGE OF CALLING IT HOME IS WORTH WHATEVER SACRIFICES I'VE MADE.

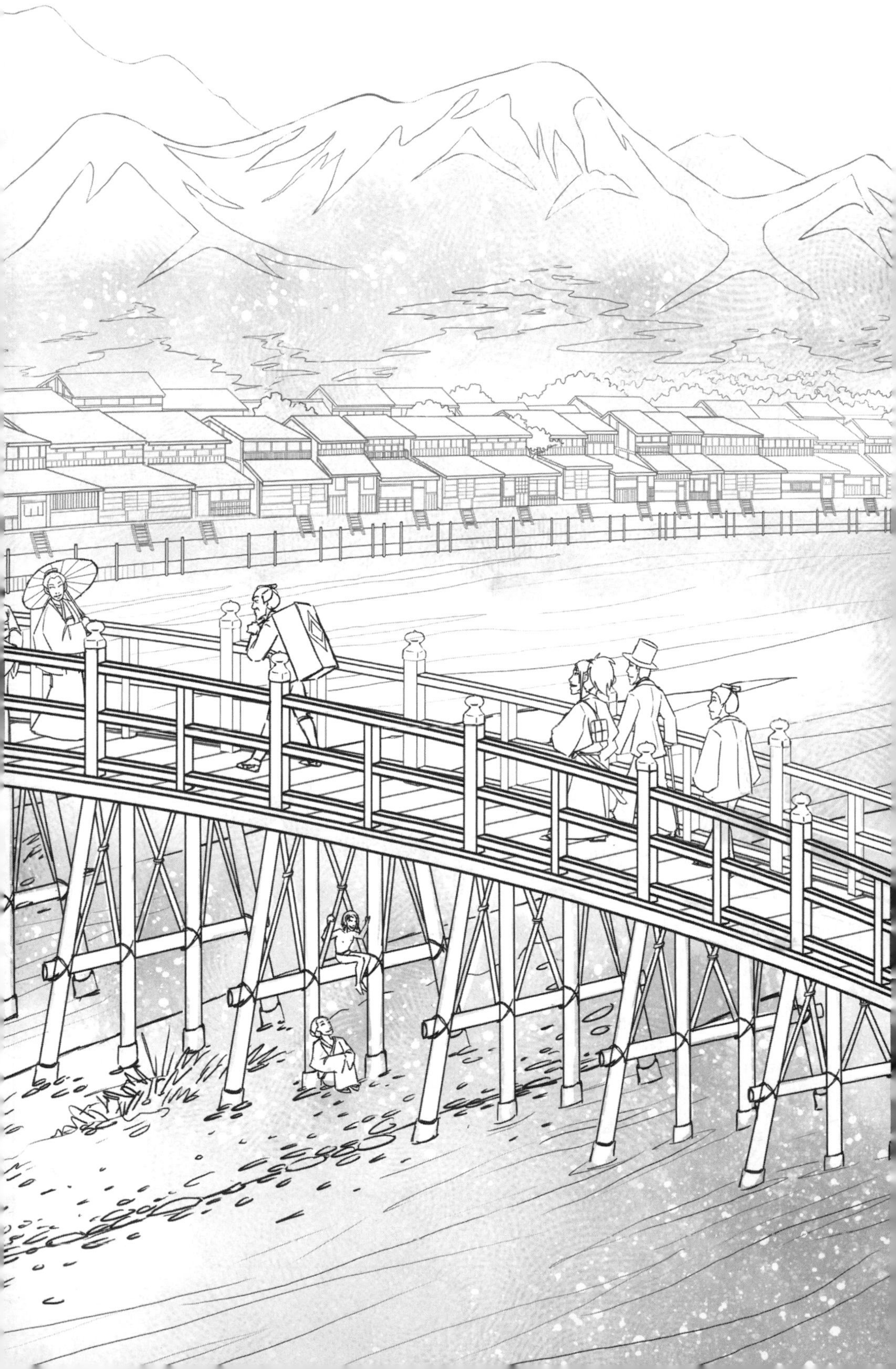

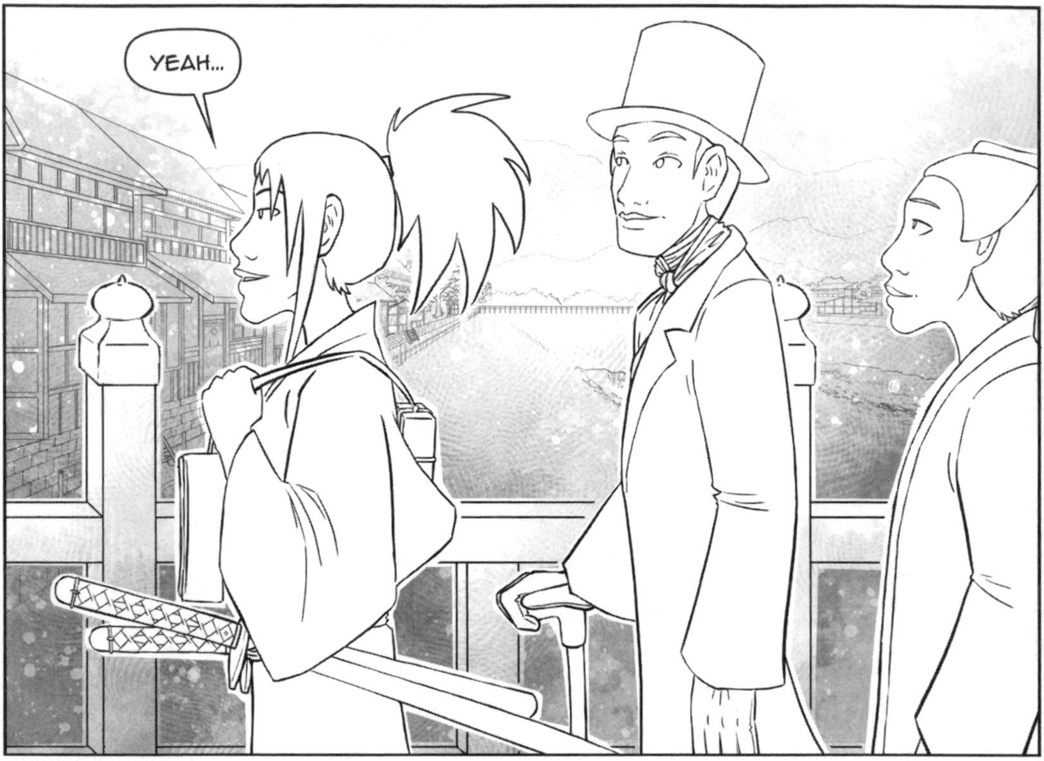
YEAH...

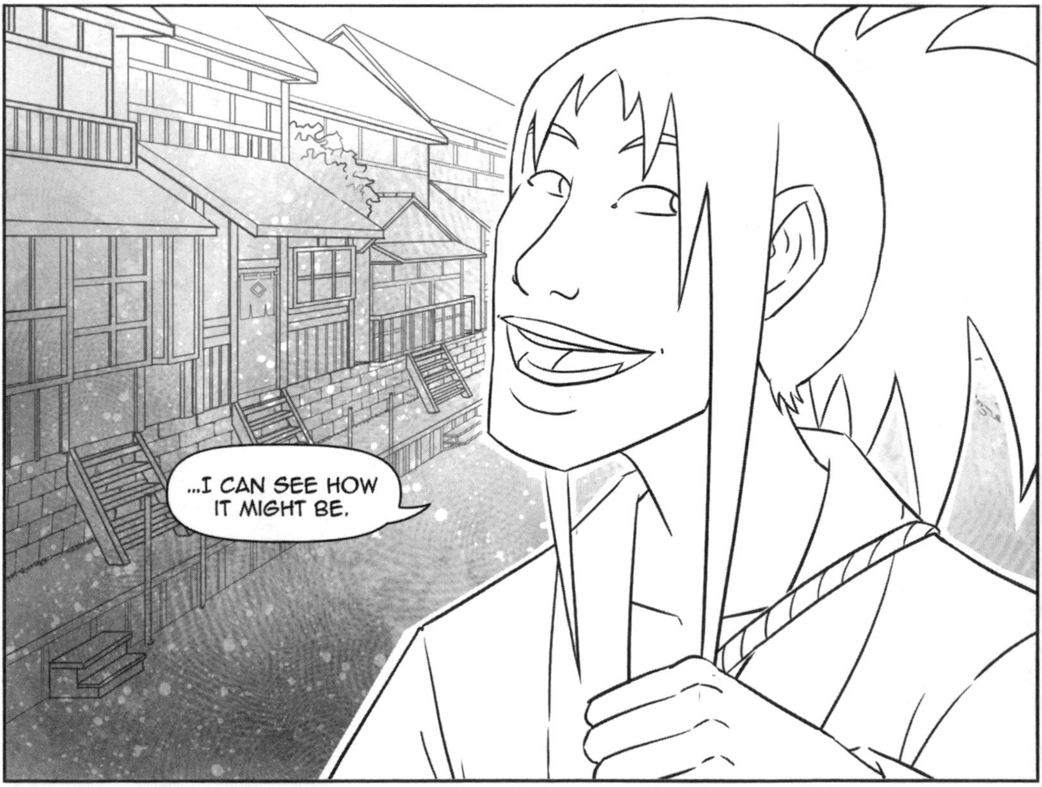
...I CAN SEE HOW
IT MIGHT BE.

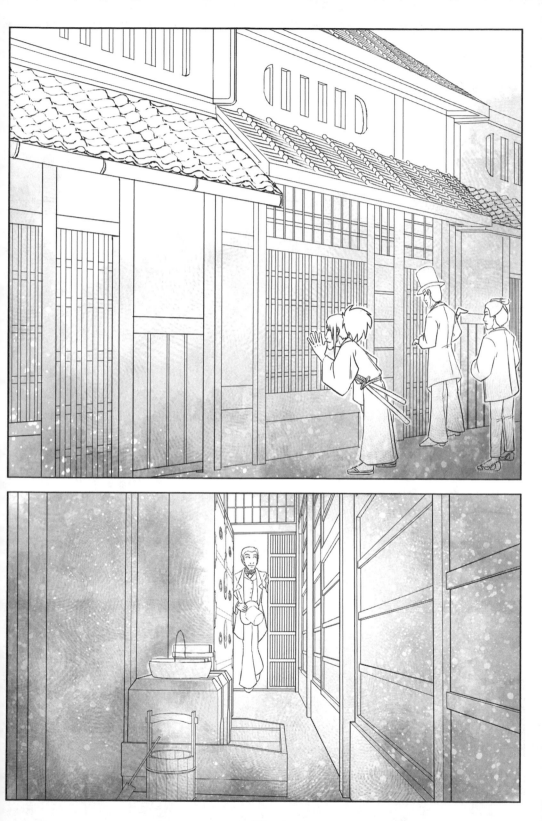

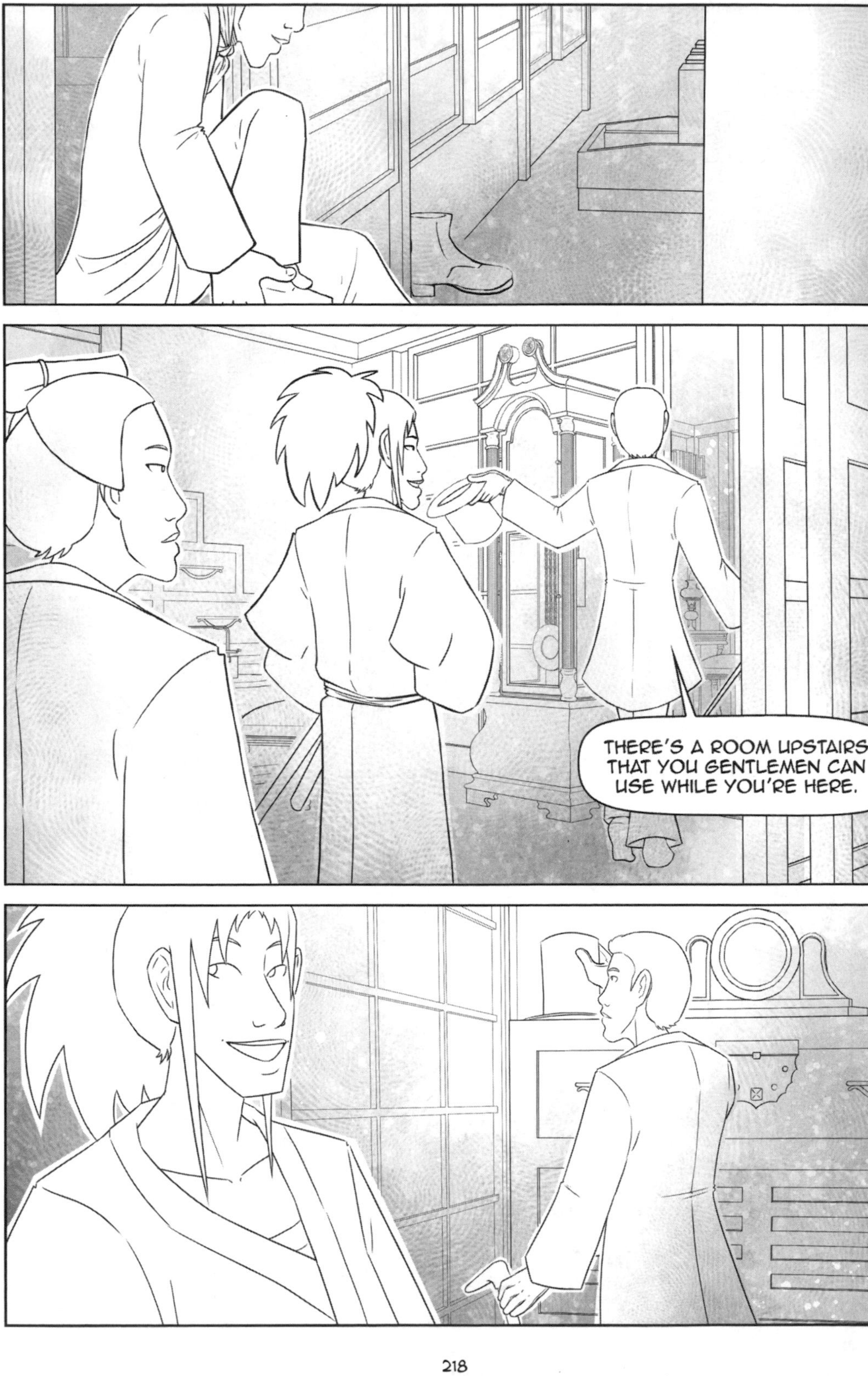
THERE'S A ROOM UPSTAIRS THAT YOU GENTLEMEN CAN USE WHILE YOU'RE HERE.

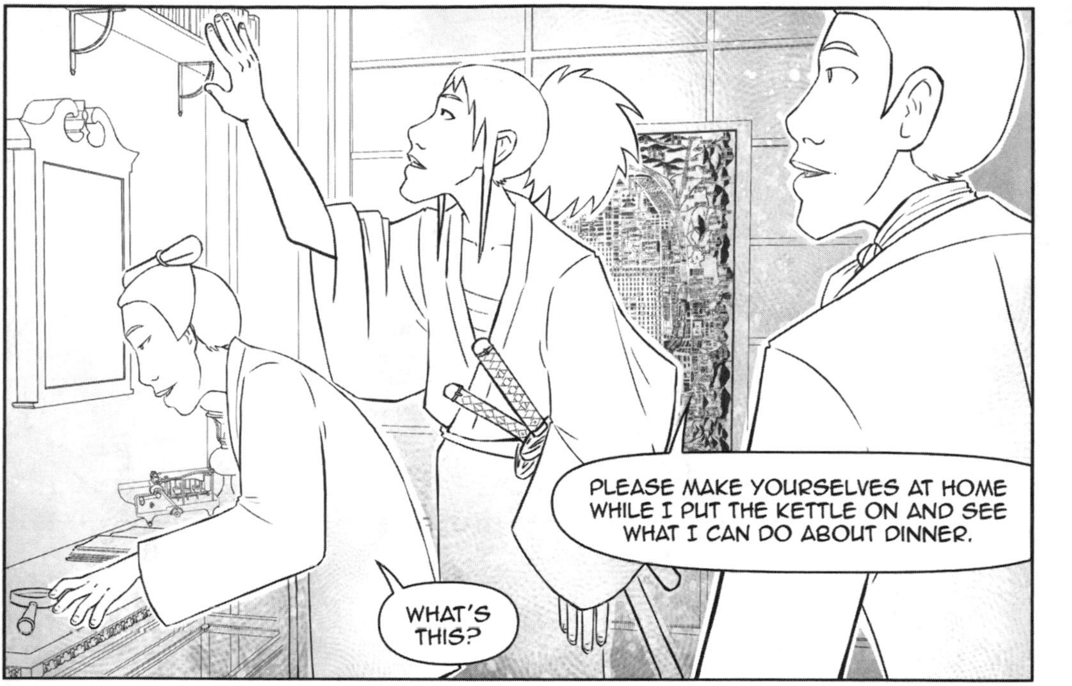
PLEASE MAKE YOURSELVES AT HOME WHILE I PUT THE KETTLE ON AND SEE WHAT I CAN DO ABOUT DINNER.
WHAT'S THIS?

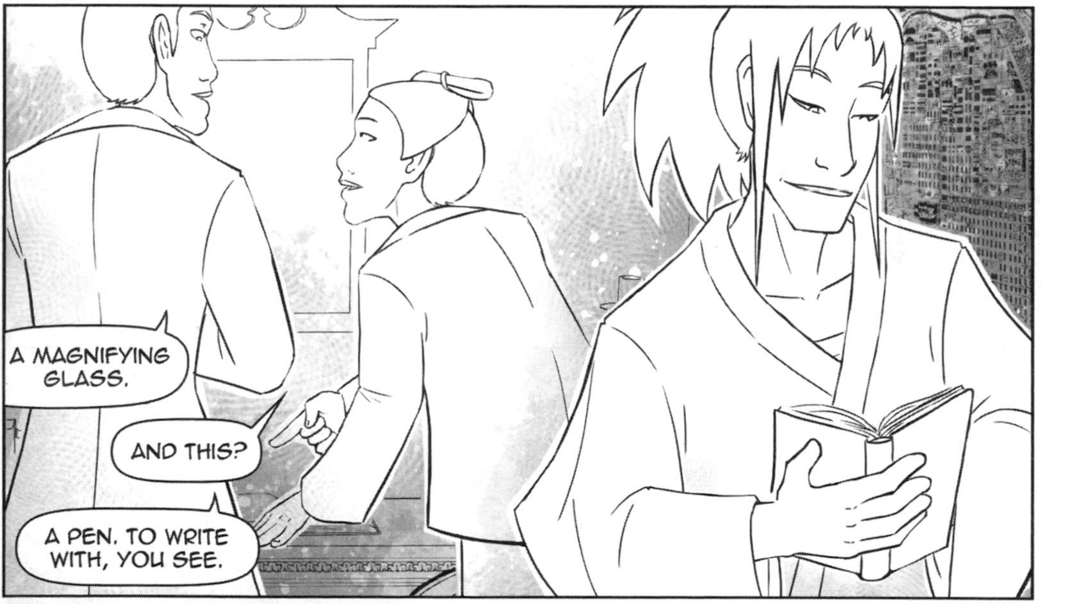
A MAGNIFYING GLASS.
AND THIS?
A PEN. TO WRITE WITH, YOU SEE.

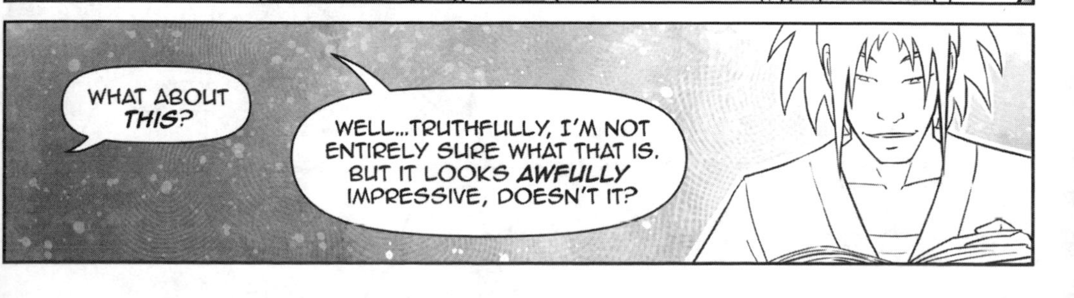
WHAT ABOUT *THIS*?
WELL...TRUTHFULLY, I'M NOT ENTIRELY SURE WHAT THAT IS. BUT IT LOOKS ***AWFULLY*** IMPRESSIVE, DOESN'T IT?

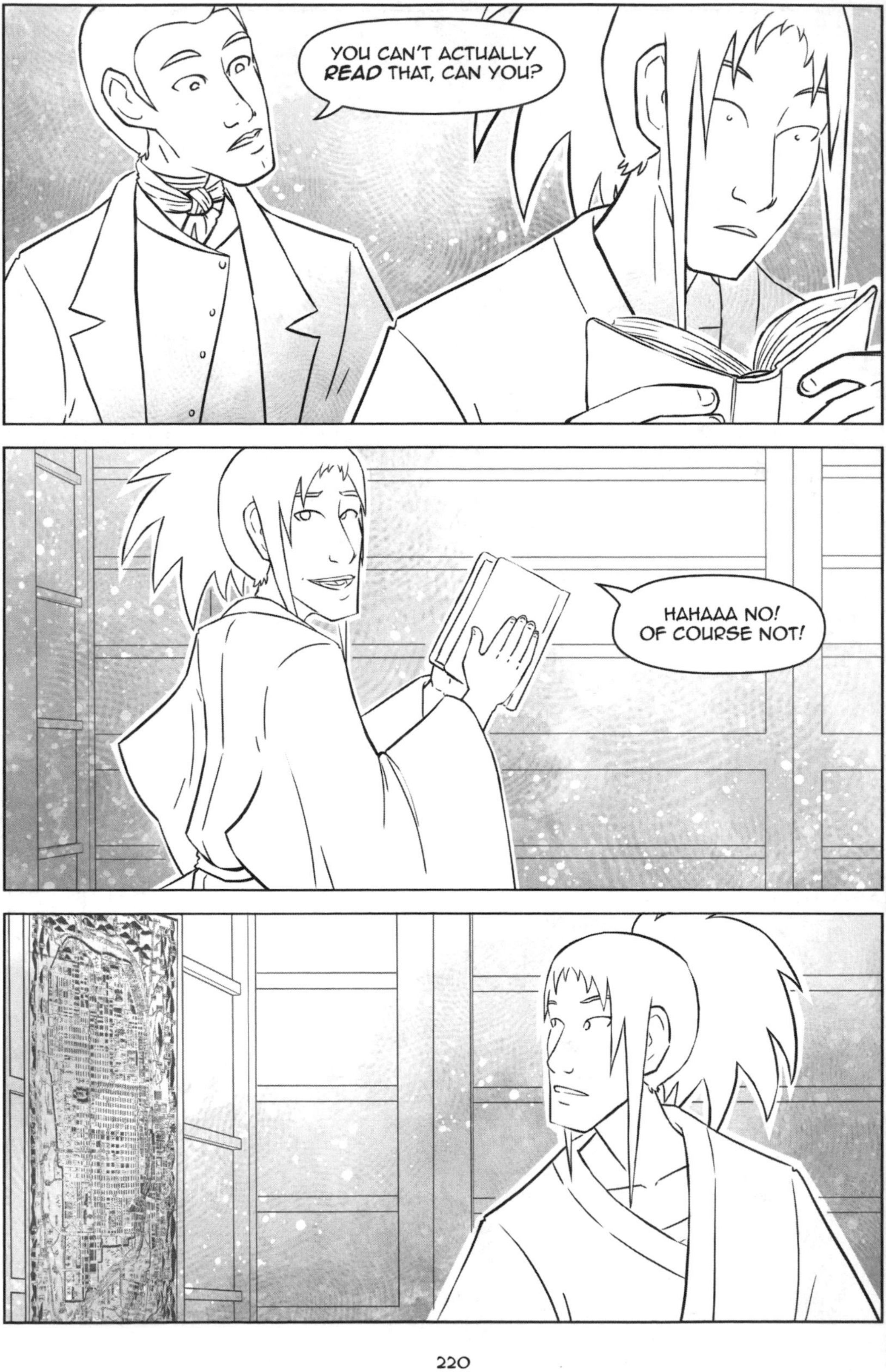
YOU CAN'T ACTUALLY READ THAT, CAN YOU?
HAHAAA NO! OF COURSE NOT!

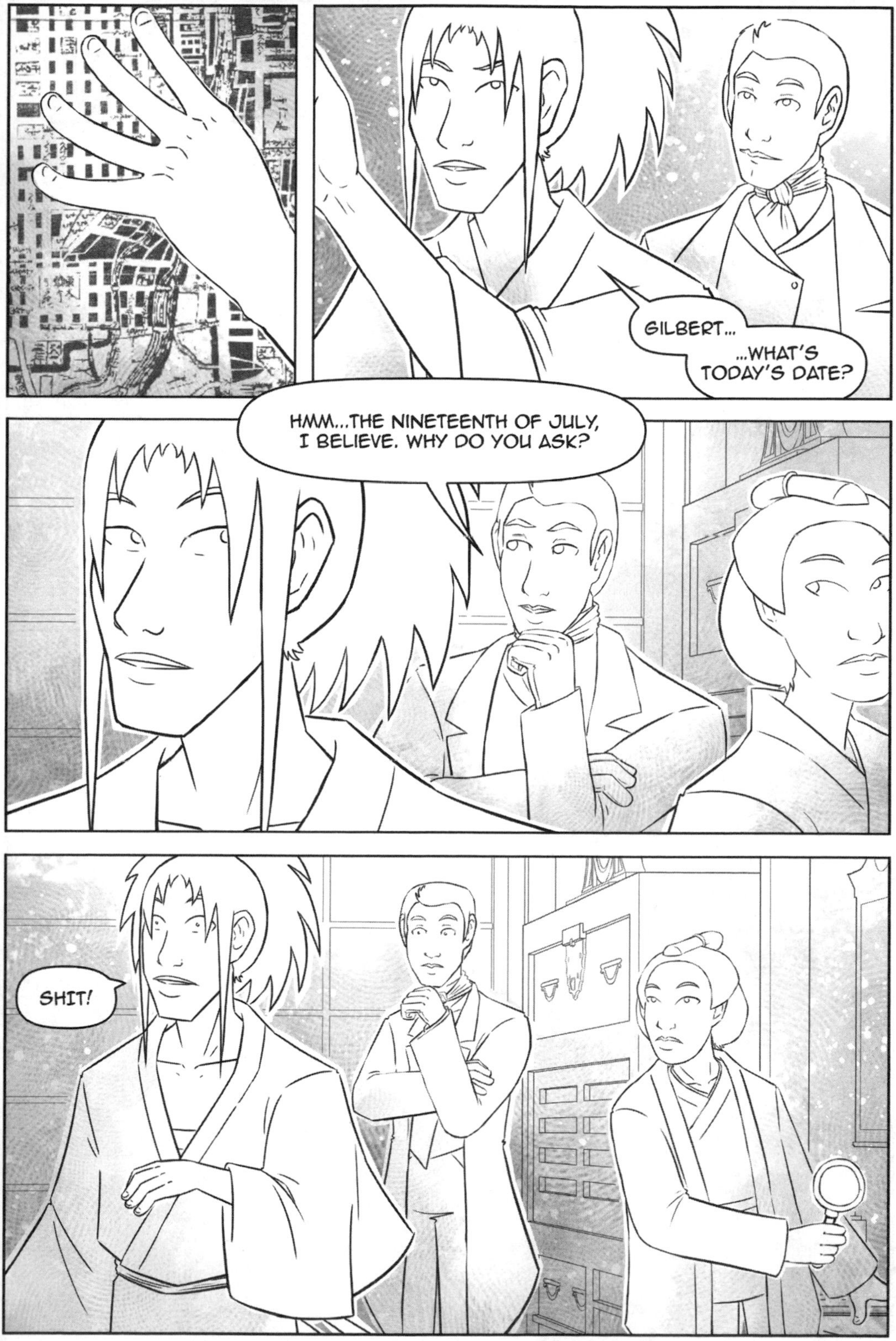
GILBERT...
...WHAT'S TODAY'S DATE?
HMM...THE NINETEENTH OF JULY, I BELIEVE. WHY DO YOU ASK?
SHIT!

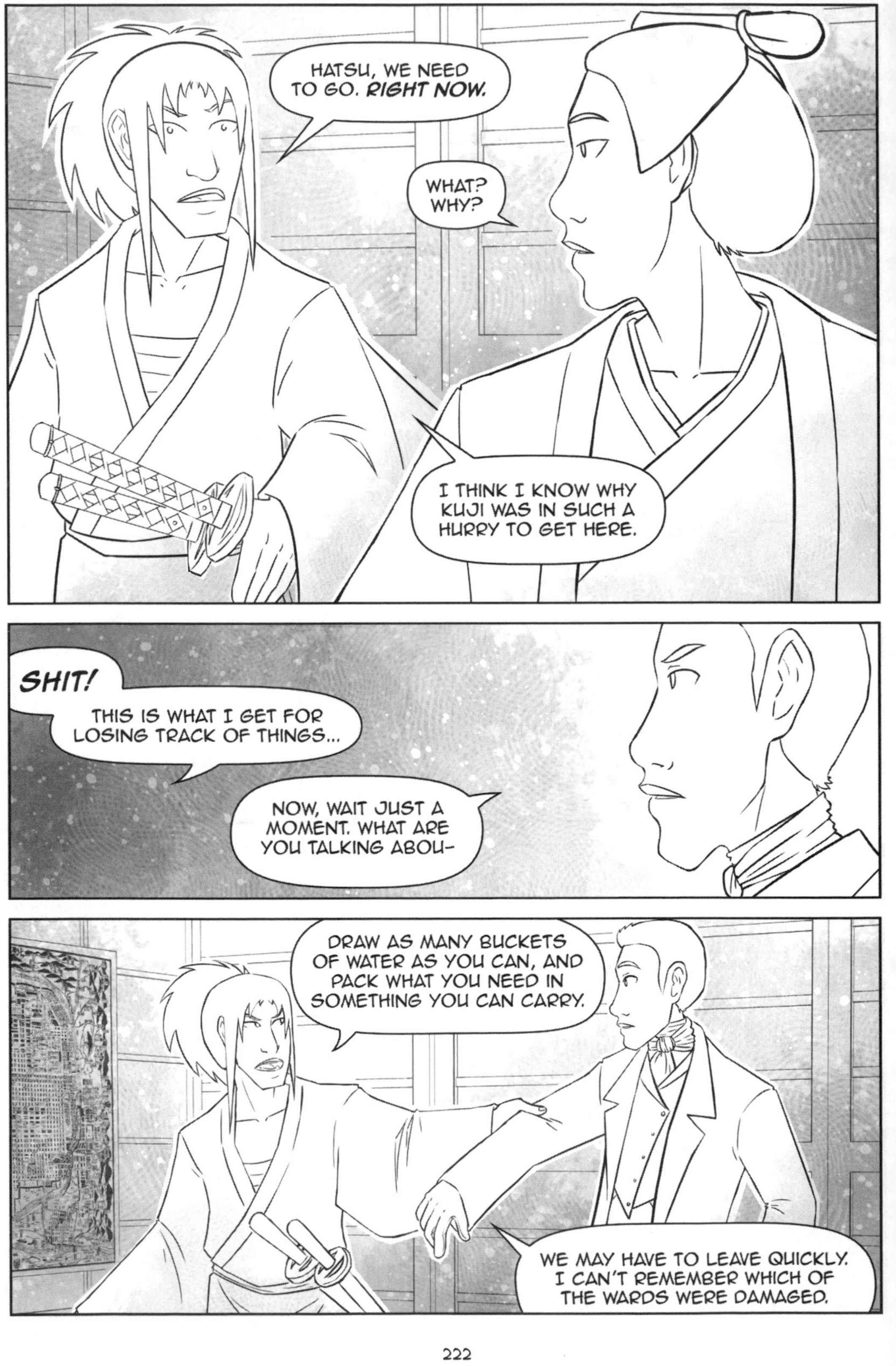
HATSU, WE NEED TO GO. RIGHT NOW.
WHAT? WHY?
I THINK I KNOW WHY KUJI WAS IN SUCH A HURRY TO GET HERE.
SHIT!
THIS IS WHAT I GET FOR LOSING TRACK OF THINGS...
NOW, WAIT JUST A MOMENT. WHAT ARE YOU TALKING ABOU-
DRAW AS MANY BUCKETS OF WATER AS YOU CAN, AND PACK WHAT YOU NEED IN SOMETHING YOU CAN CARRY.
WE MAY HAVE TO LEAVE QUICKLY. I CAN'T REMEMBER WHICH OF THE WARDS WERE DAMAGED.

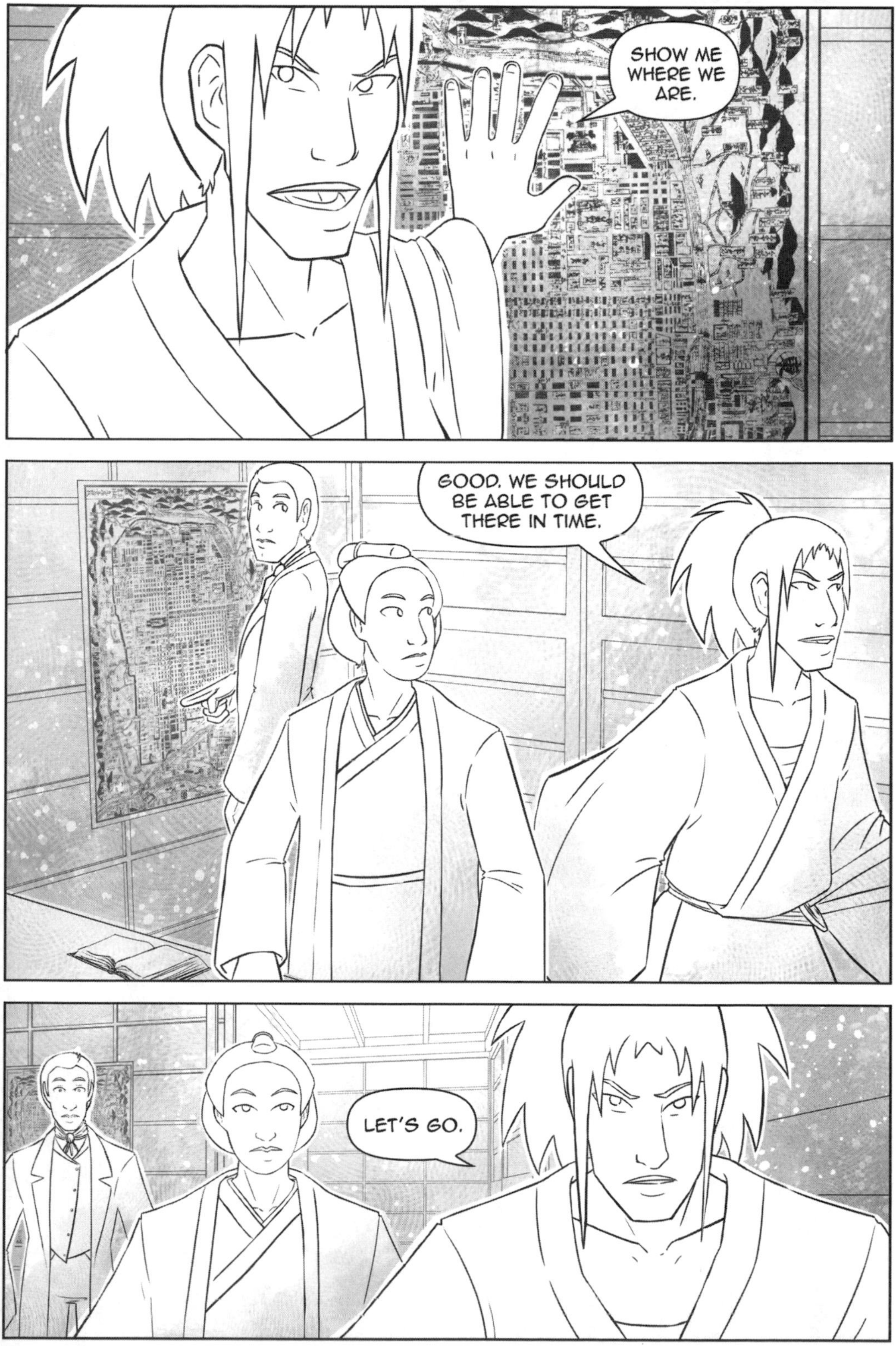
SHOW ME WHERE WE ARE.
GOOD. WE SHOULD BE ABLE TO GET THERE IN TIME.
LET'S GO.

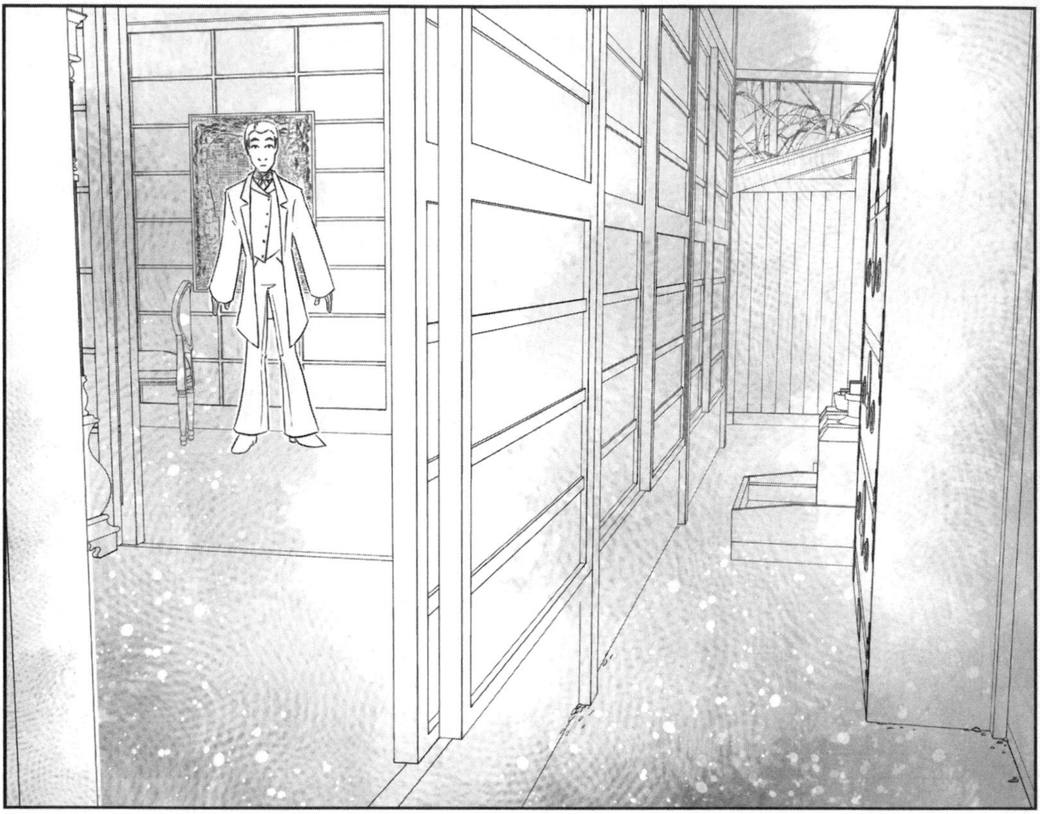

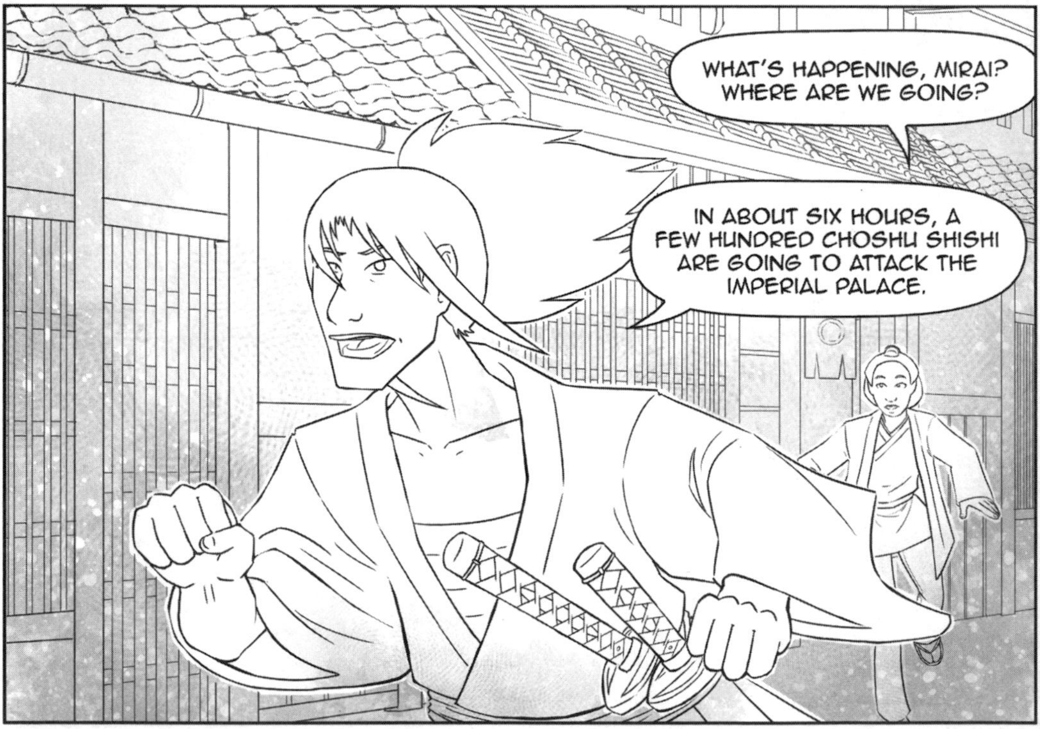
WHAT'S HAPPENING, MIRAI? WHERE ARE WE GOING?
IN ABOUT SIX HOURS, A FEW HUNDRED CHOSHU SHISHI ARE GOING TO ATTACK THE IMPERIAL PALACE.

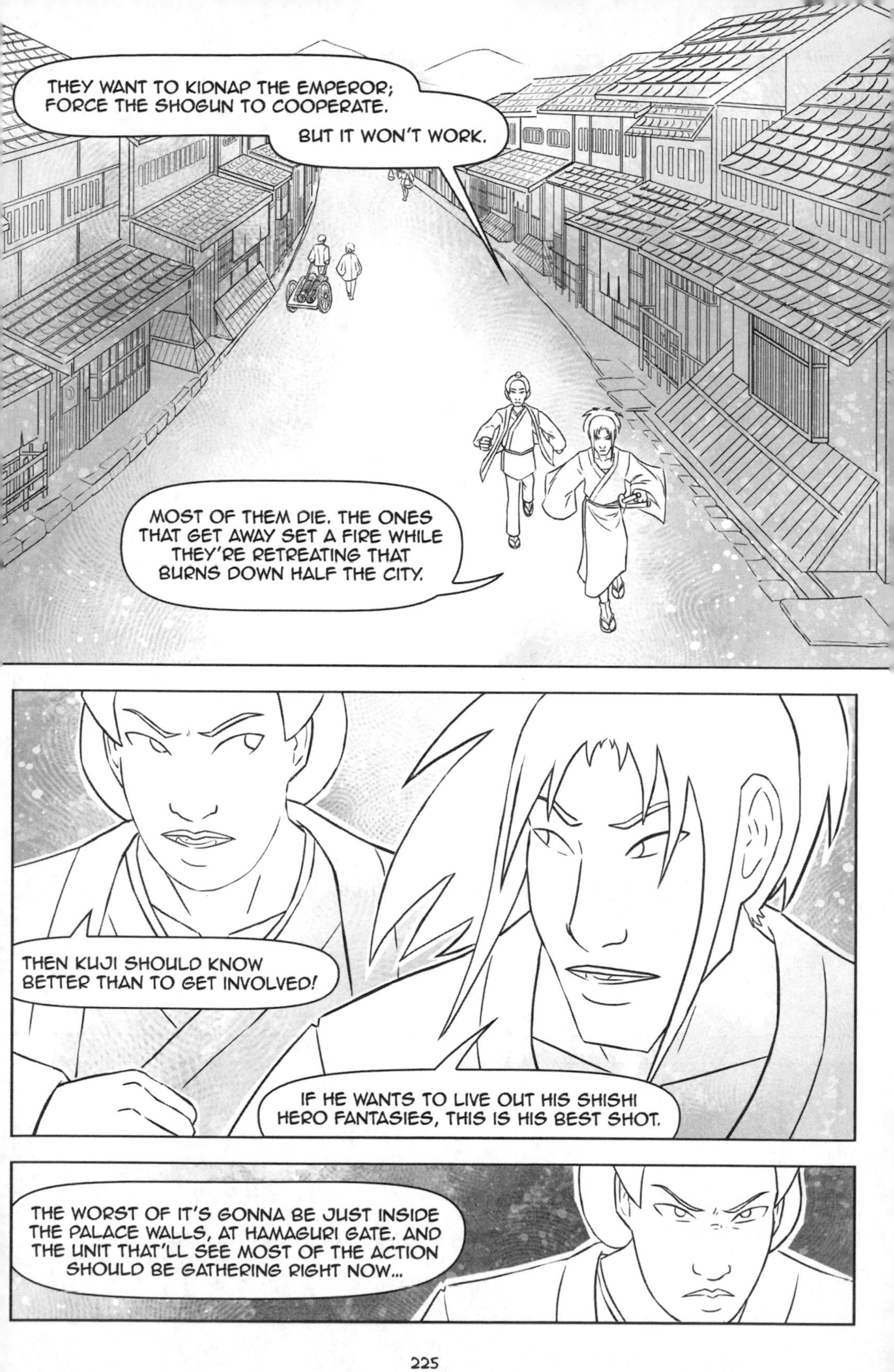
THEY WANT TO KIDNAP THE EMPEROR; FORCE THE SHOGUN TO COOPERATE.
BUT IT WON'T WORK.
MOST OF THEM DIE. THE ONES THAT GET AWAY SET A FIRE WHILE THEY'RE RETREATING THAT BURNS DOWN HALF THE CITY.
THEN KUJI SHOULD KNOW BETTER THAN TO GET INVOLVED!
IF HE WANTS TO LIVE OUT HIS SHISHI HERO FANTASIES, THIS IS HIS BEST SHOT.
THE WORST OF IT'S GONNA BE JUST INSIDE THE PALACE WALLS, AT HAMAGURI GATE. AND THE UNIT THAT'LL SEE MOST OF THE ACTION SHOULD BE GATHERING RIGHT NOW...

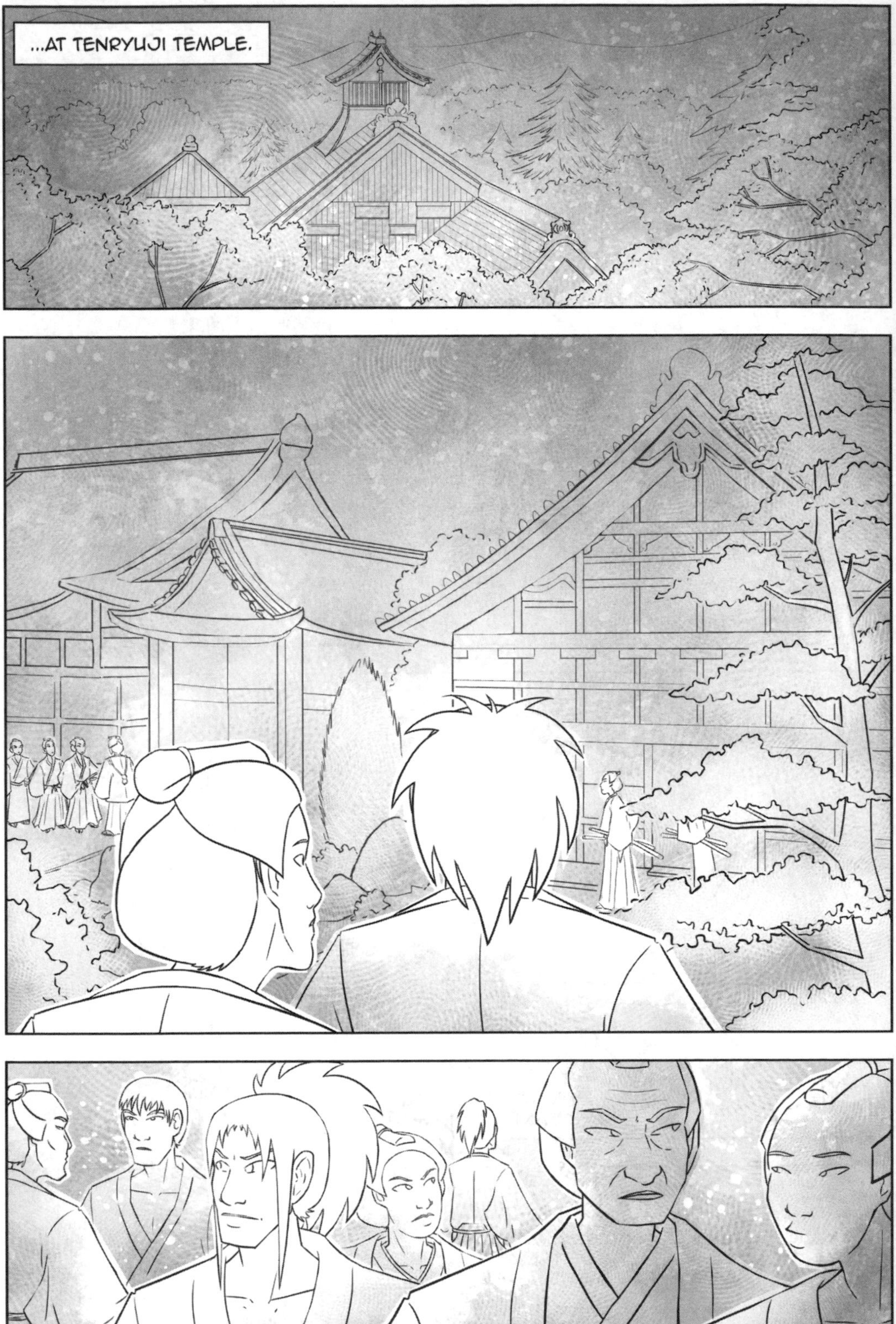
...AT TENRYUJI TEMPLE.

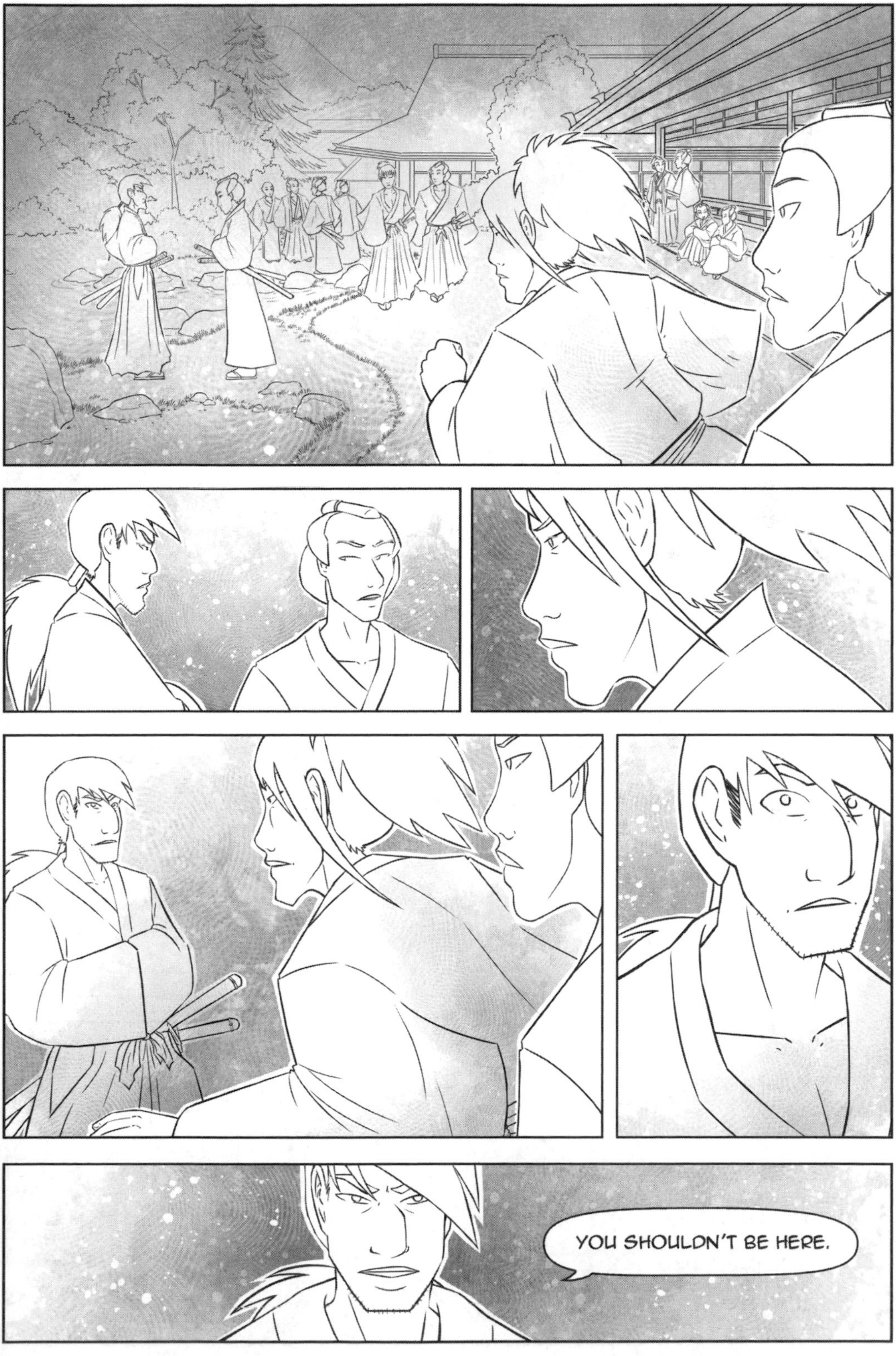
YOU SHOULDN'T BE HERE.

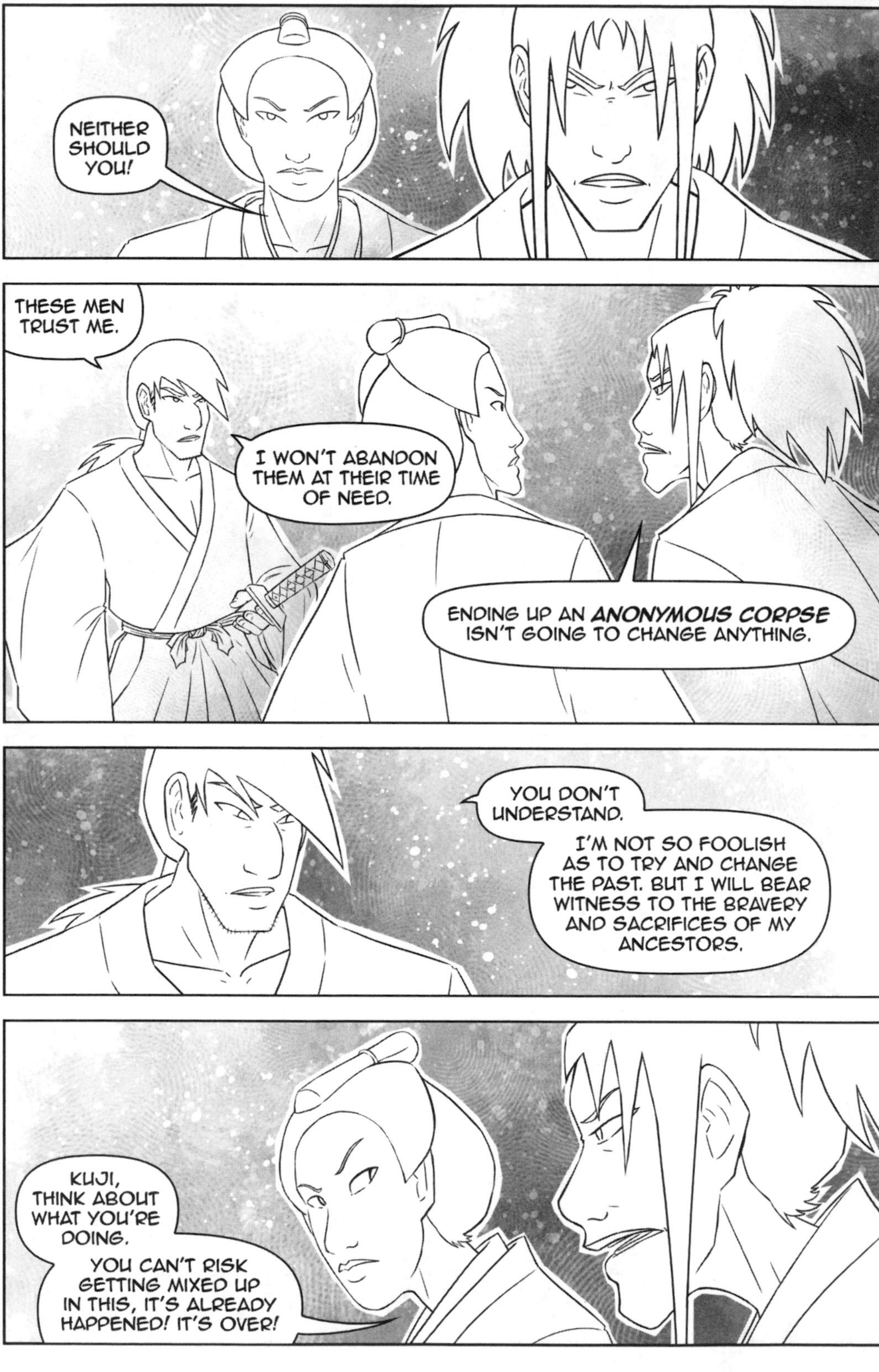
NEITHER SHOULD YOU!
THESE MEN TRUST ME.
I WON'T ABANDON THEM AT THEIR TIME OF NEED.
ENDING UP AN ***ANONYMOUS CORPSE*** ISN'T GOING TO CHANGE ANYTHING.
YOU DON'T UNDERSTAND.
I'M NOT SO FOOLISH AS TO TRY AND CHANGE THE PAST. BUT I WILL BEAR WITNESS TO THE BRAVERY AND SACRIFICES OF MY ANCESTORS.
KUJI, THINK ABOUT WHAT YOU'RE DOING.
YOU CAN'T RISK GETTING MIXED UP IN THIS, IT'S ALREADY HAPPENED! IT'S OVER!

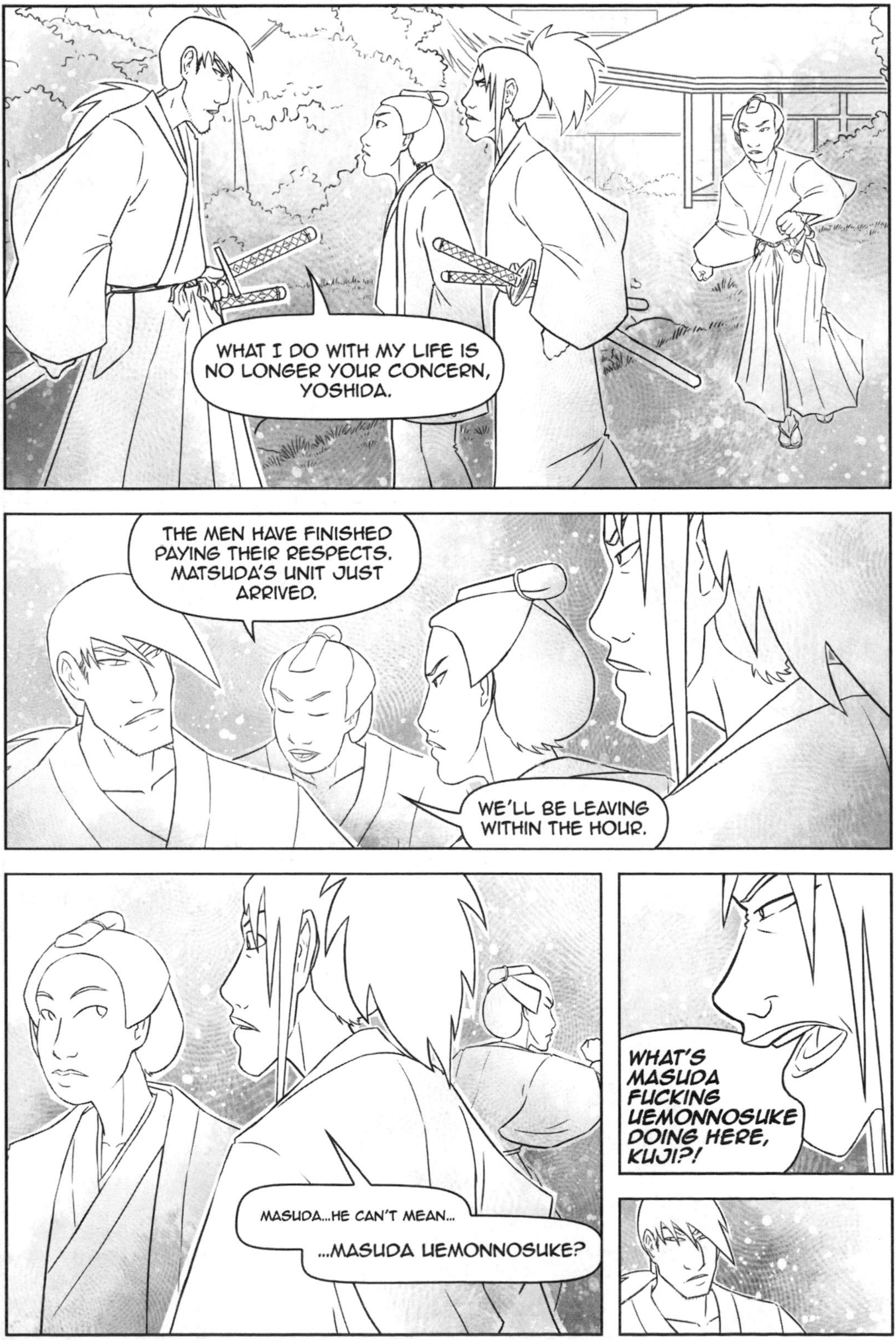
WHAT I DO WITH MY LIFE IS NO LONGER YOUR CONCERN, YOSHIDA.
THE MEN HAVE FINISHED PAYING THEIR RESPECTS. MATSUDA'S UNIT JUST ARRIVED.
WE'LL BE LEAVING WITHIN THE HOUR.
MASUDA...HE CAN'T MEAN...
...MASUDA UEMONNOSUKE?
WHAT'S MASUDA FUCKING UEMONNOSUKE DOING HERE, KUJI?!

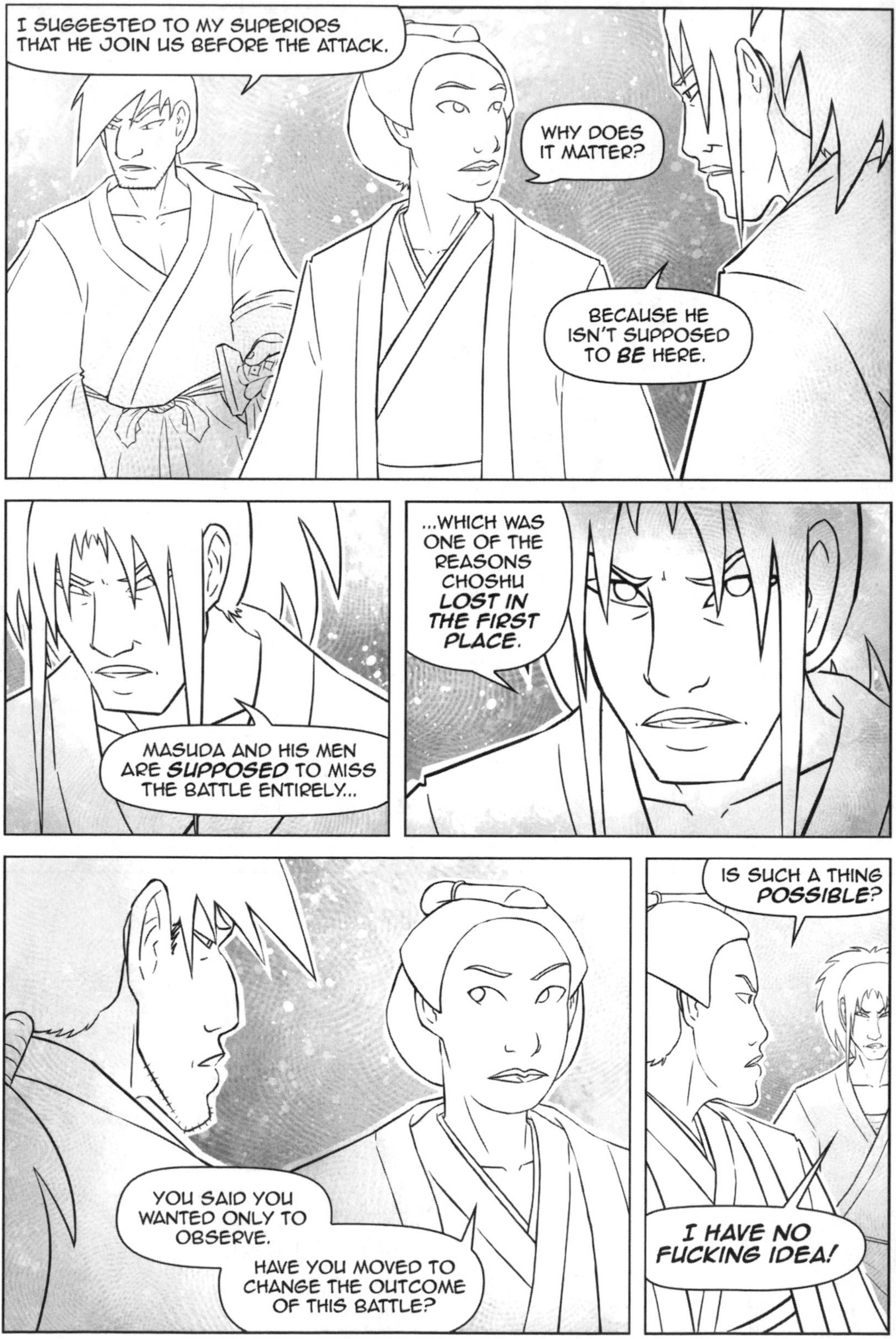
I SUGGESTED TO MY SUPERIORS THAT HE JOIN US BEFORE THE ATTACK.
WHY DOES IT MATTER?
BECAUSE HE ISN'T SUPPOSED TO *BE* HERE.
MASUDA AND HIS MEN ARE *SUPPOSED* TO MISS THE BATTLE ENTIRELY...
...WHICH WAS ONE OF THE REASONS CHOSHU *LOST IN THE FIRST PLACE*.
YOU SAID YOU WANTED ONLY TO OBSERVE.
HAVE YOU MOVED TO CHANGE THE OUTCOME OF THIS BATTLE?
IS SUCH A THING *POSSIBLE*?
I HAVE NO FUCKING IDEA!

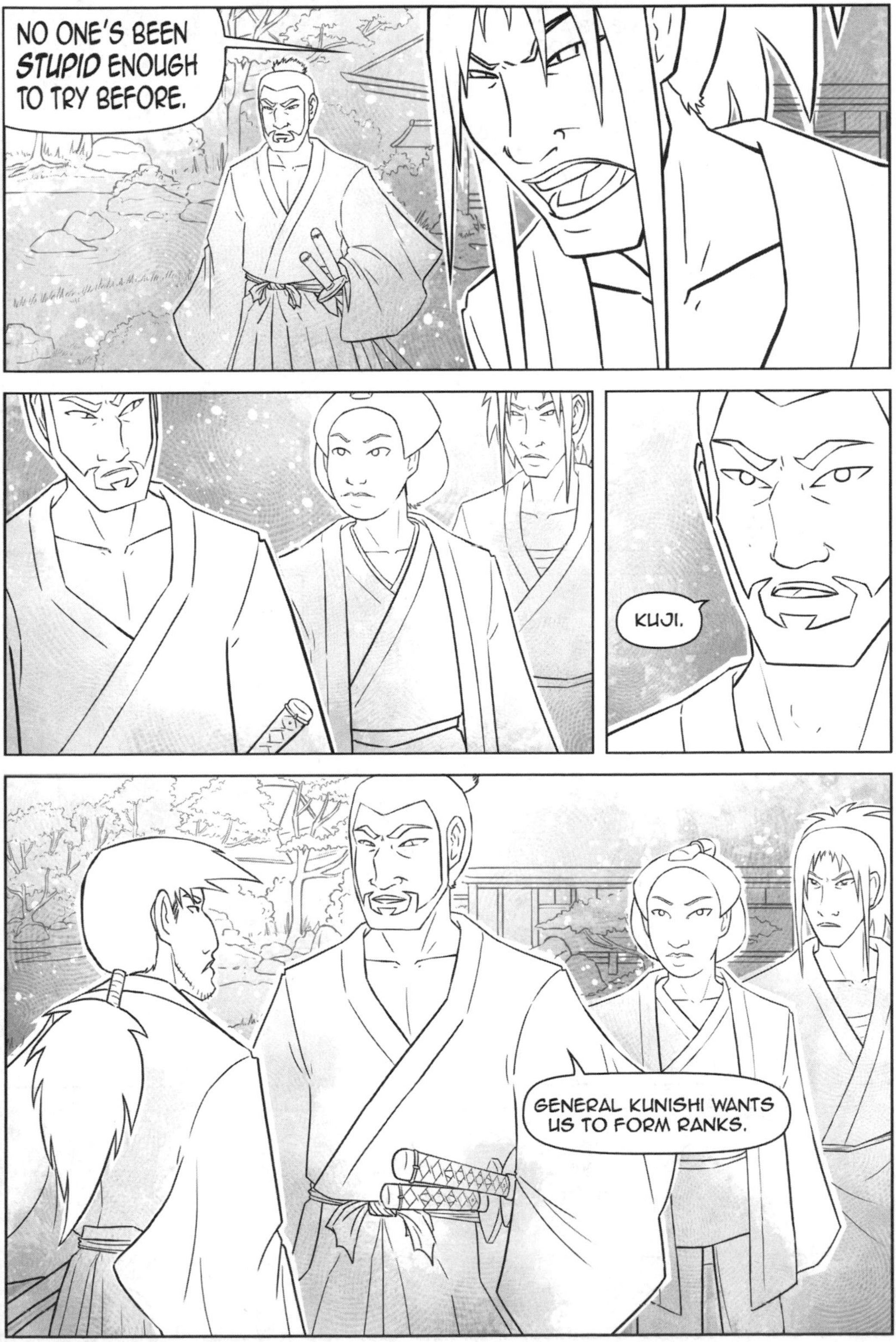
NO ONE'S BEEN STUPID ENOUGH TO TRY BEFORE.
KUJI.
GENERAL KUNISHI WANTS US TO FORM RANKS.

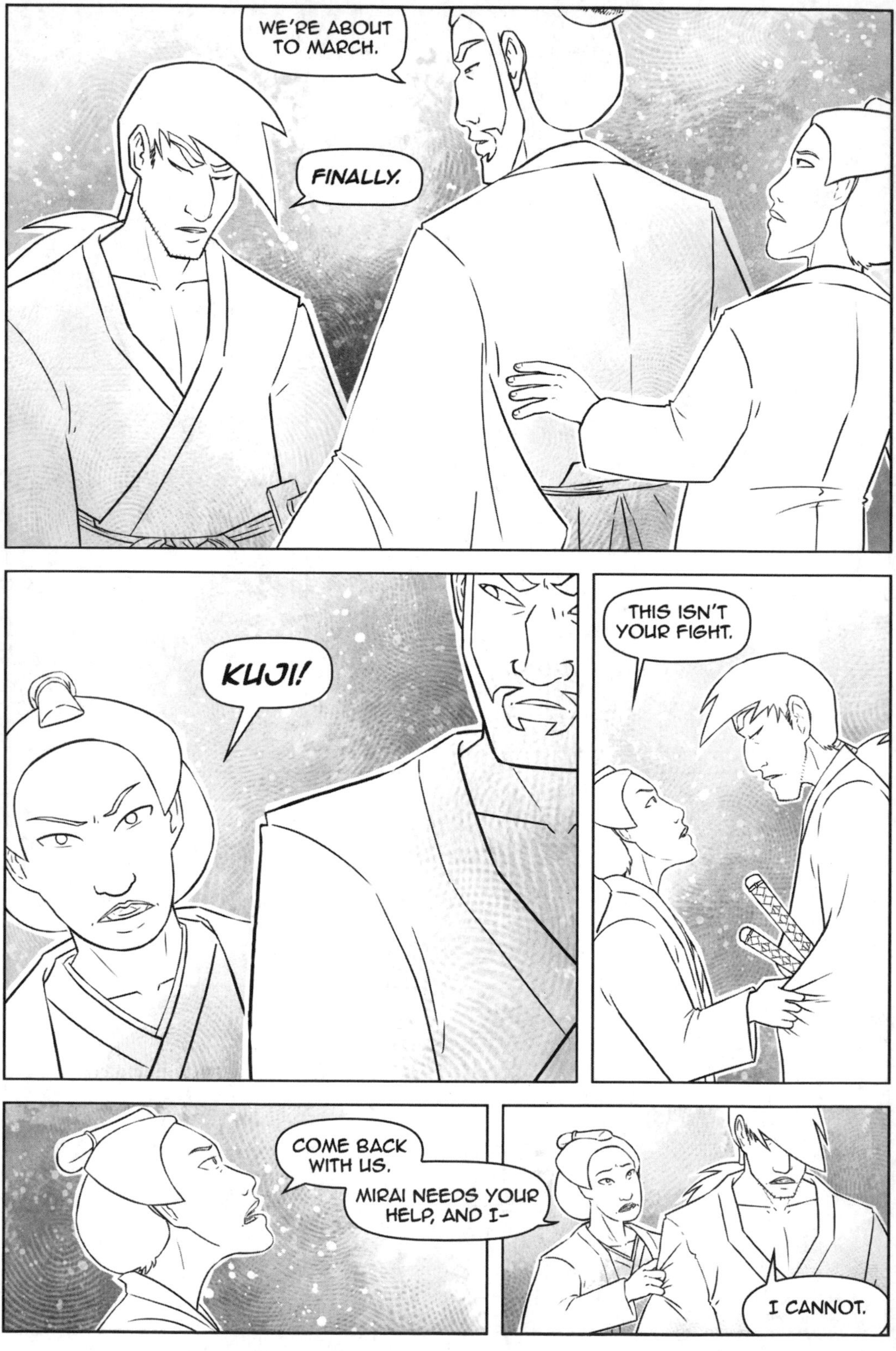
WE'RE ABOUT TO MARCH.
FINALLY.
KUJI!
THIS ISN'T YOUR FIGHT.
COME BACK WITH US.
MIRAI NEEDS YOUR HELP, AND I-
I CANNOT.

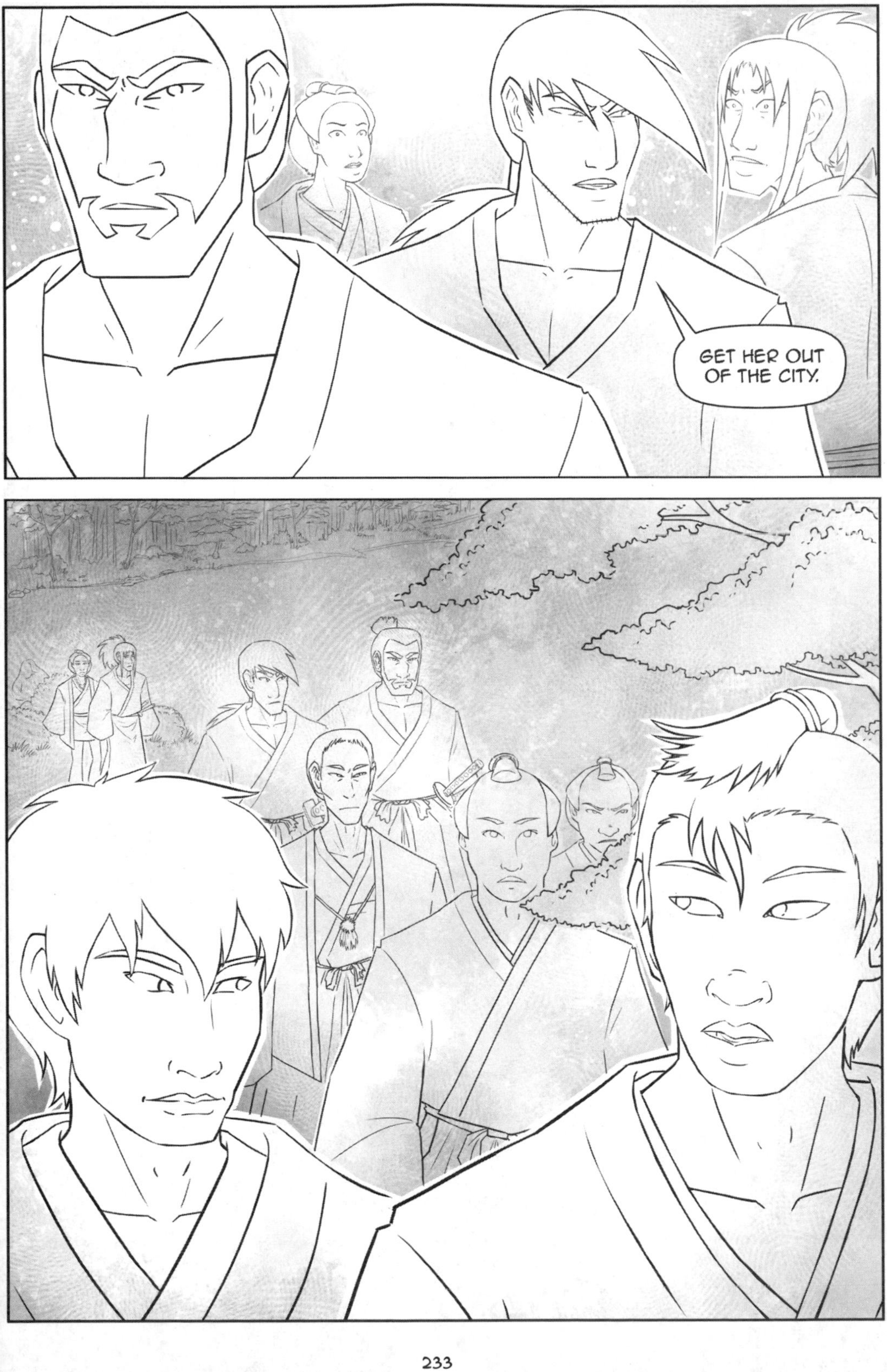
GET HER OUT OF THE CITY.

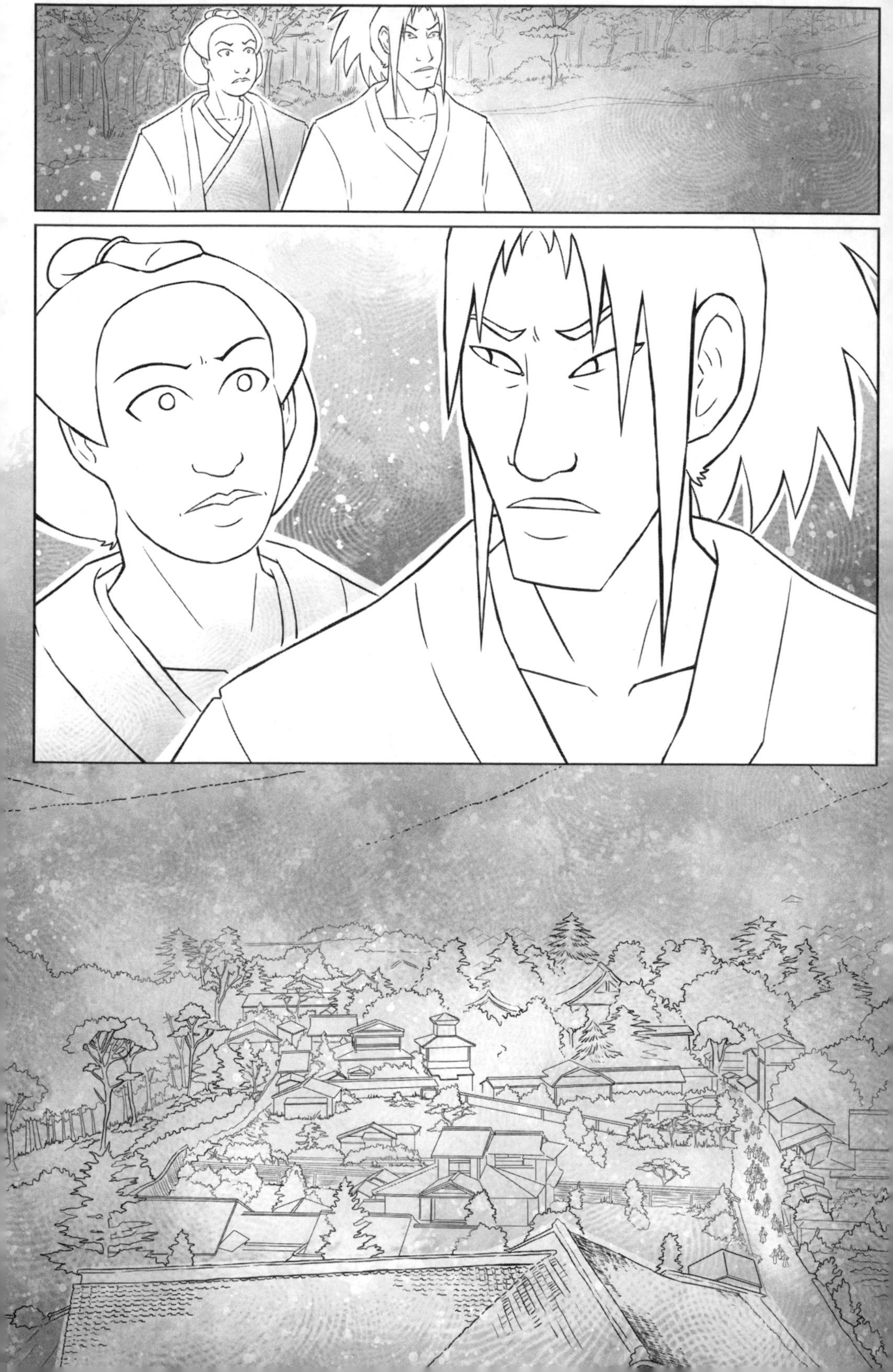

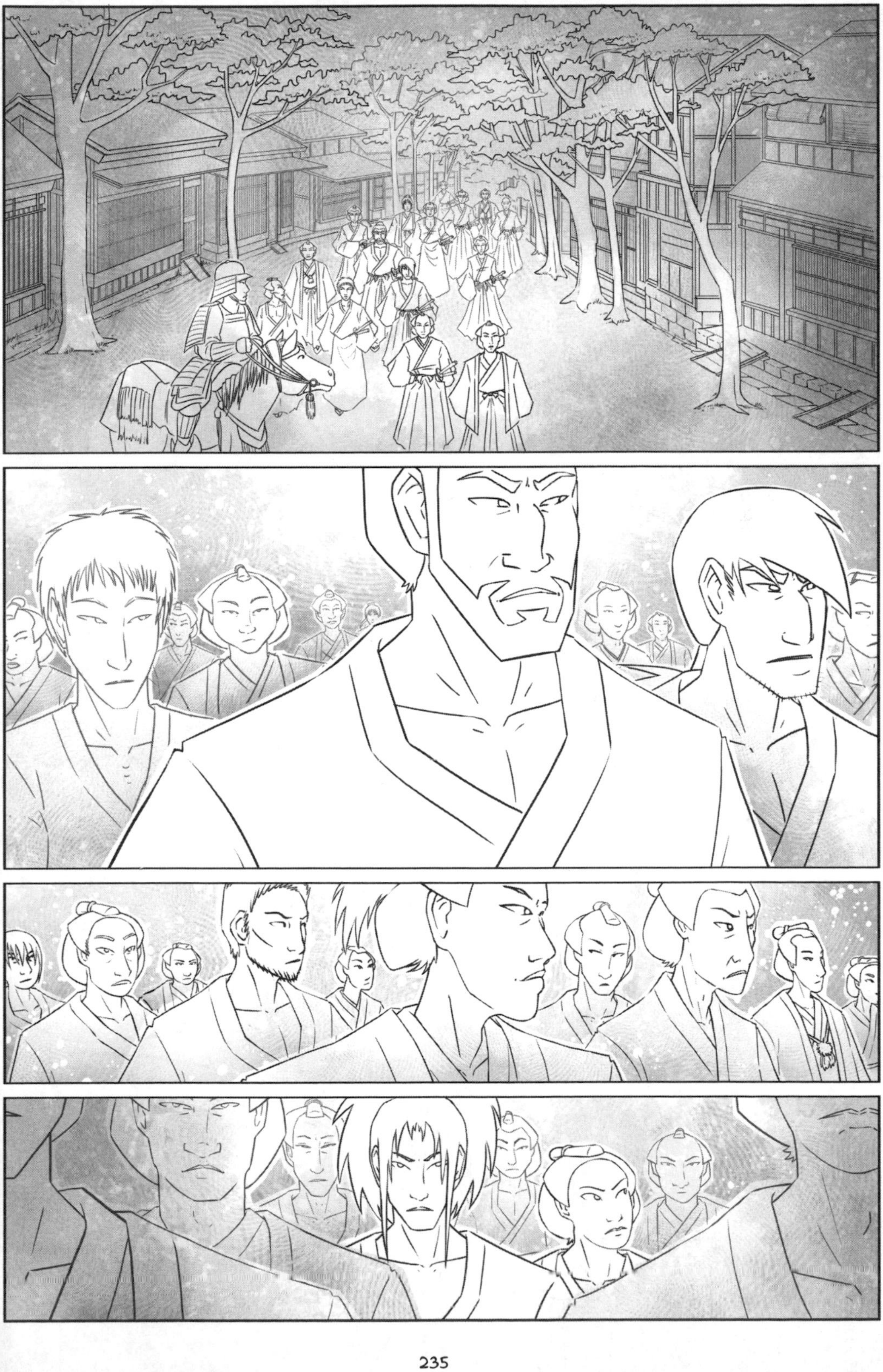

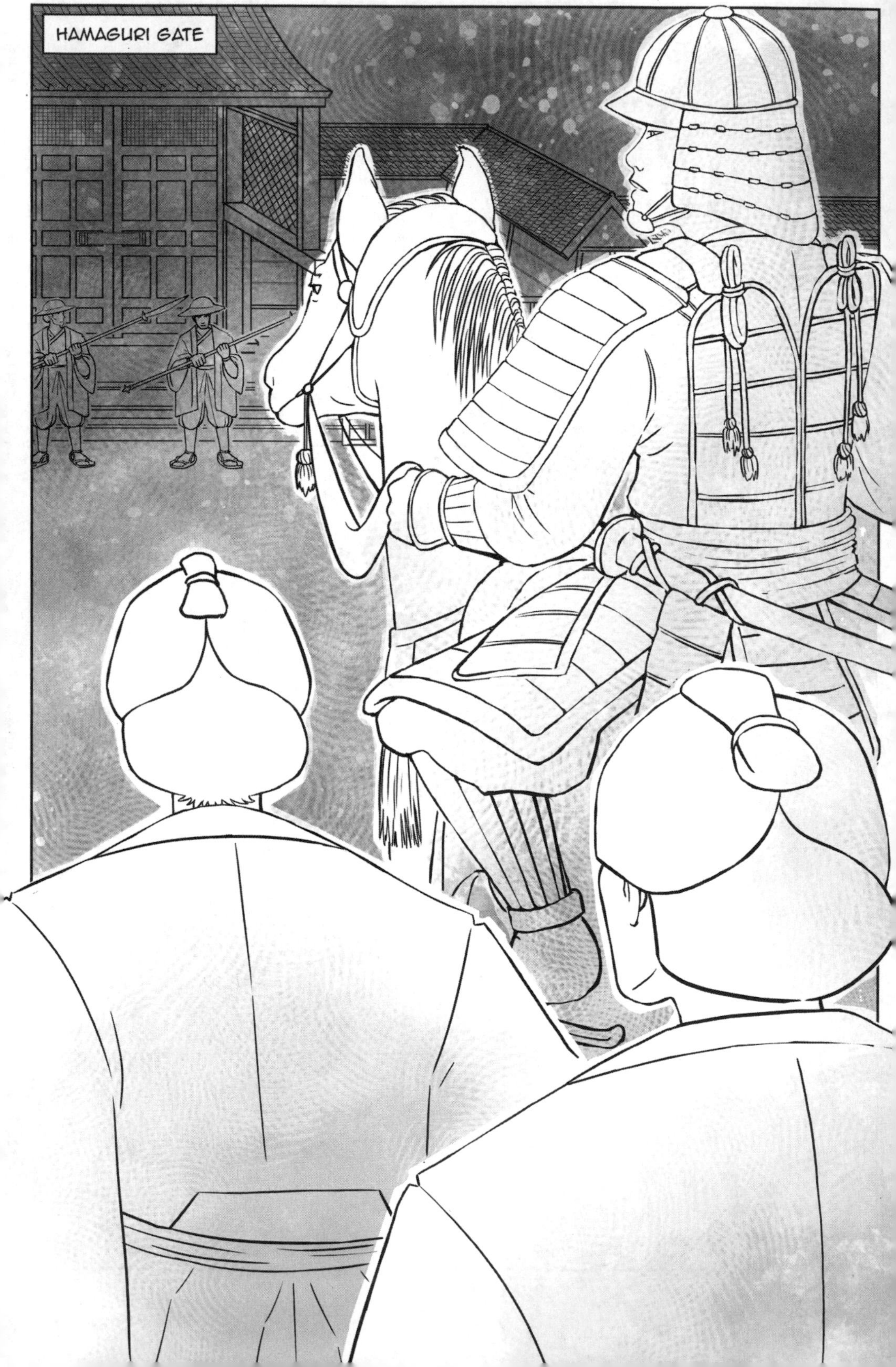
HAMAGURI GATE

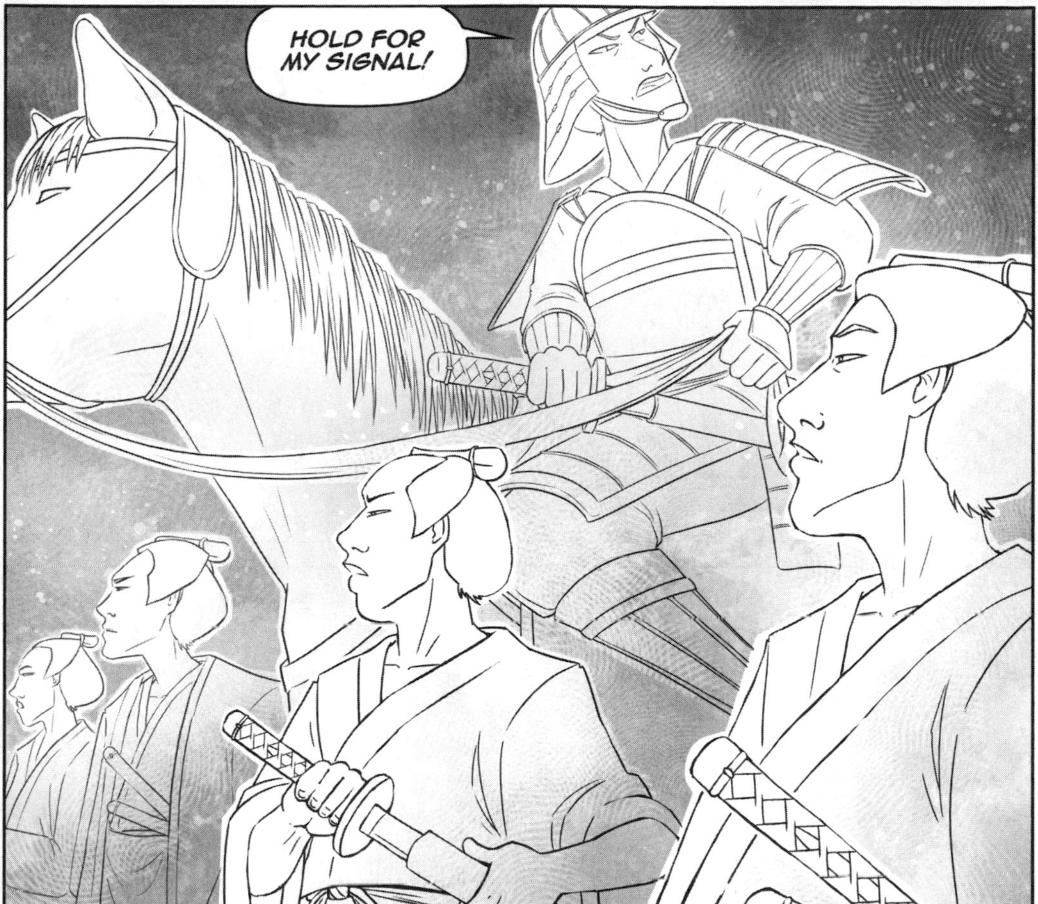
HOLD FOR MY SIGNAL!

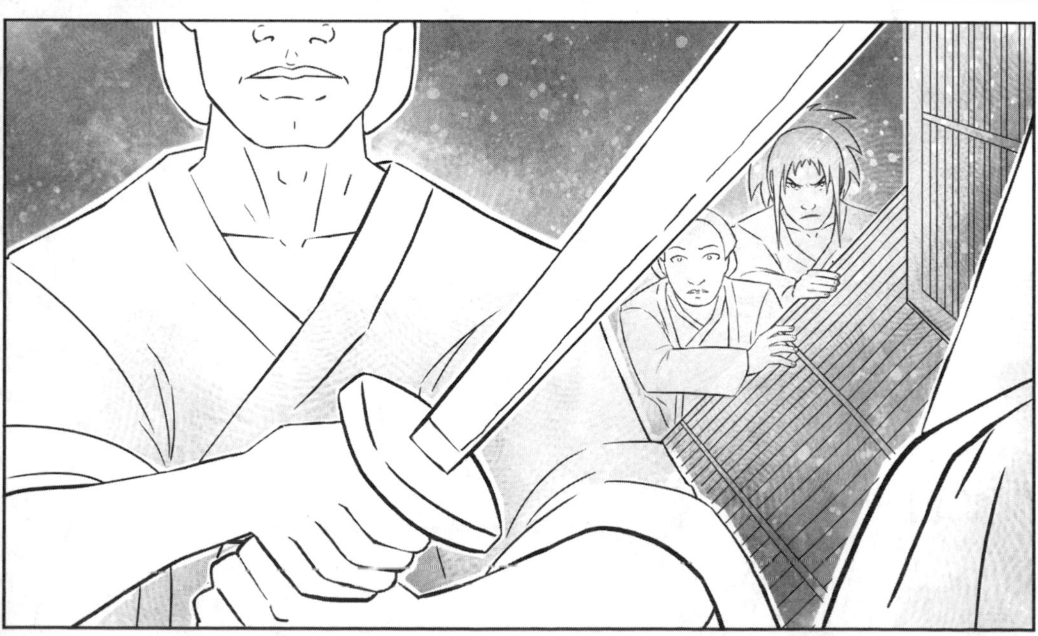

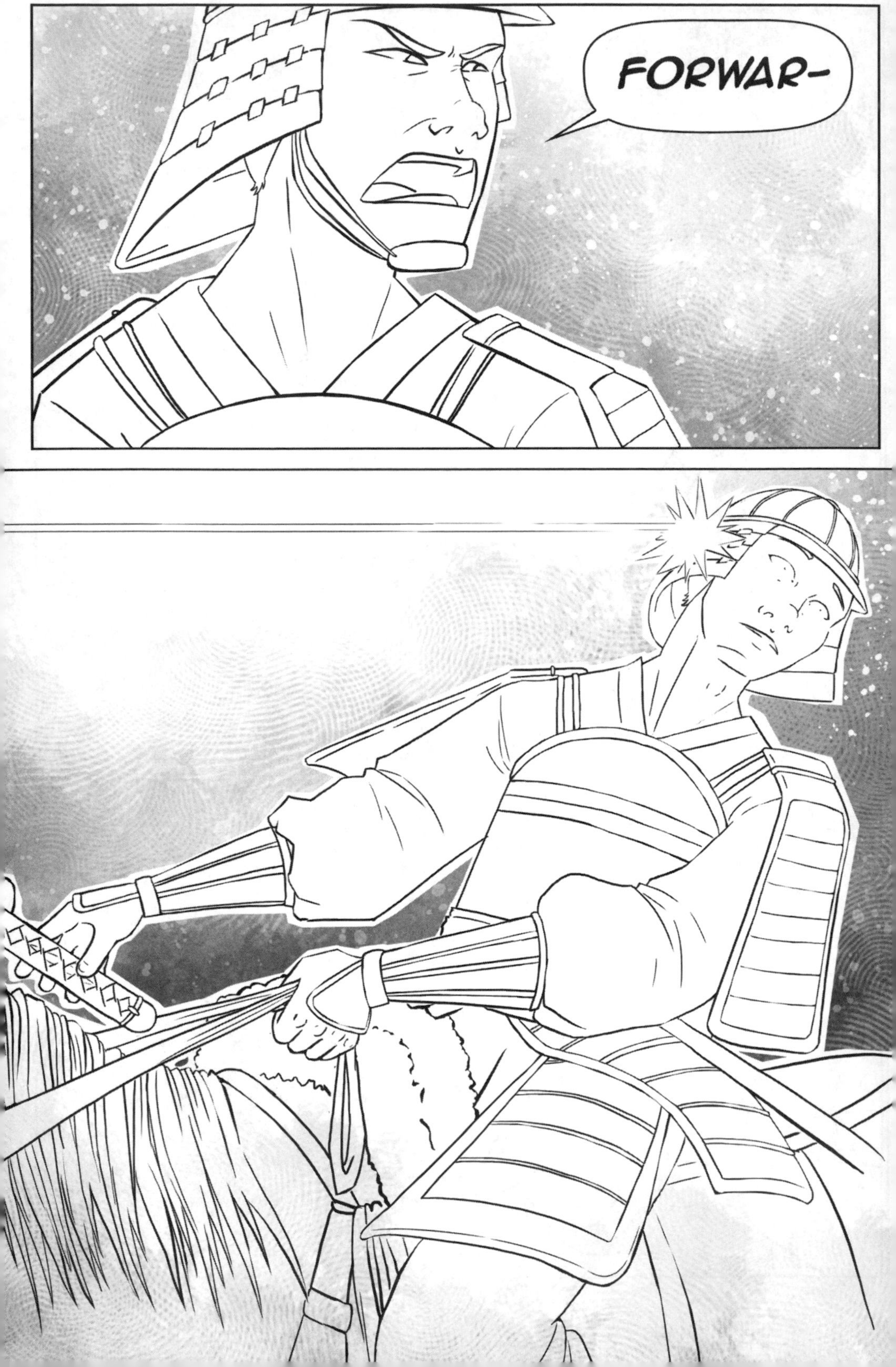
FORWAR-

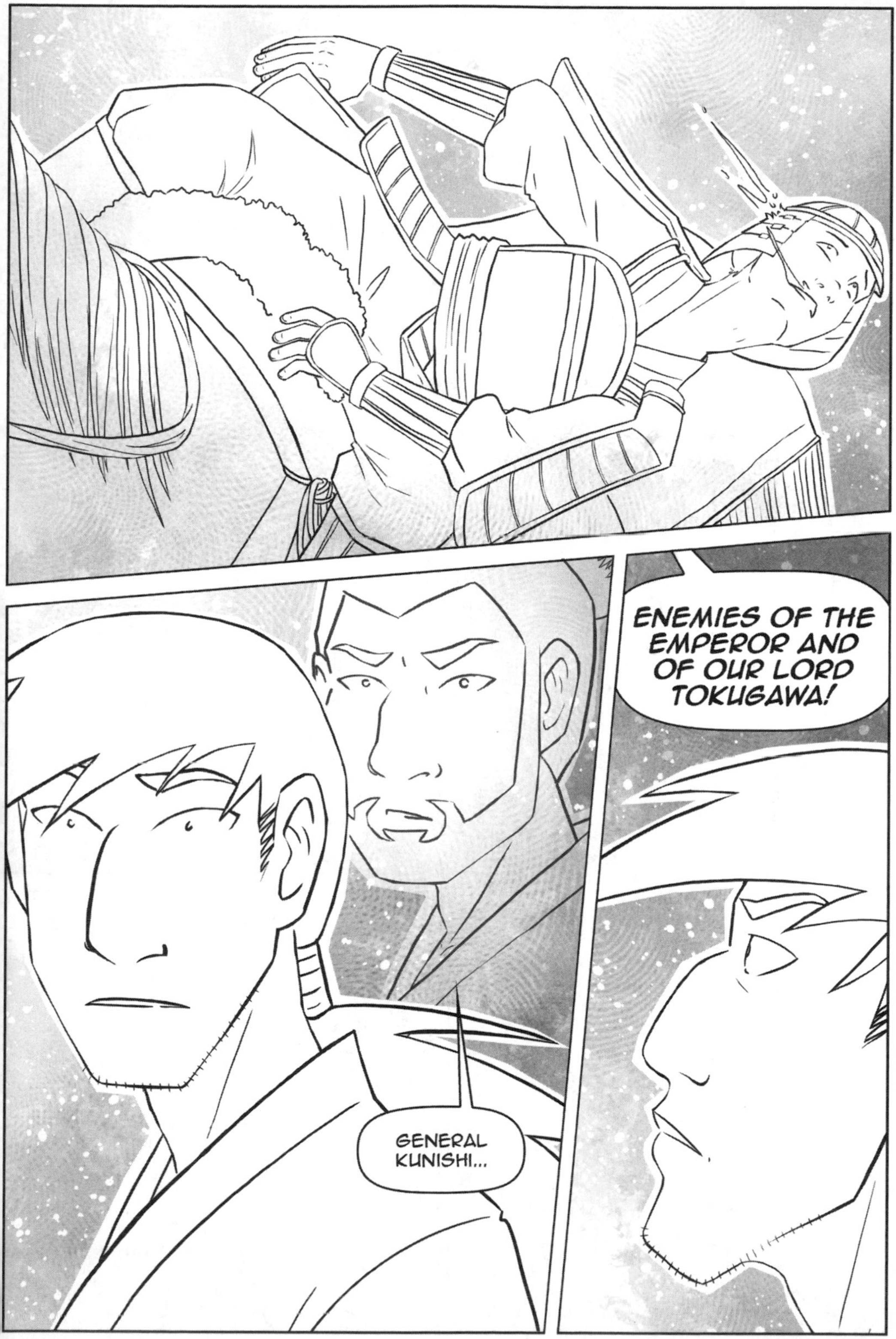
ENEMIES OF THE EMPEROR AND OF OUR LORD TOKUGAWA!
GENERAL KUNISHI...

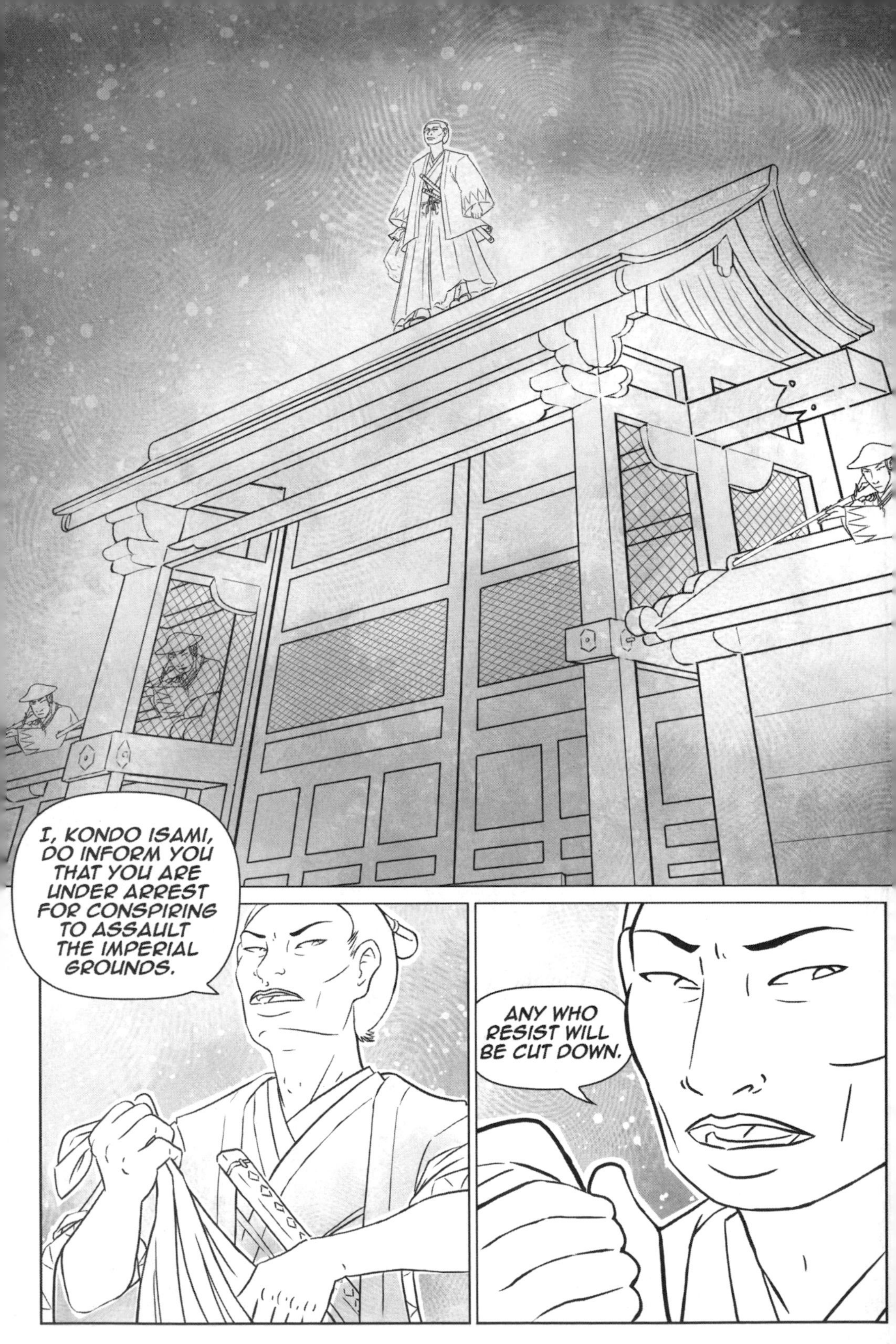
I, KONDO ISAMI, DO INFORM YOU THAT YOU ARE UNDER ARREST FOR CONSPIRING TO ASSAULT THE IMPERIAL GROUNDS.
ANY WHO RESIST WILL BE CUT DOWN.

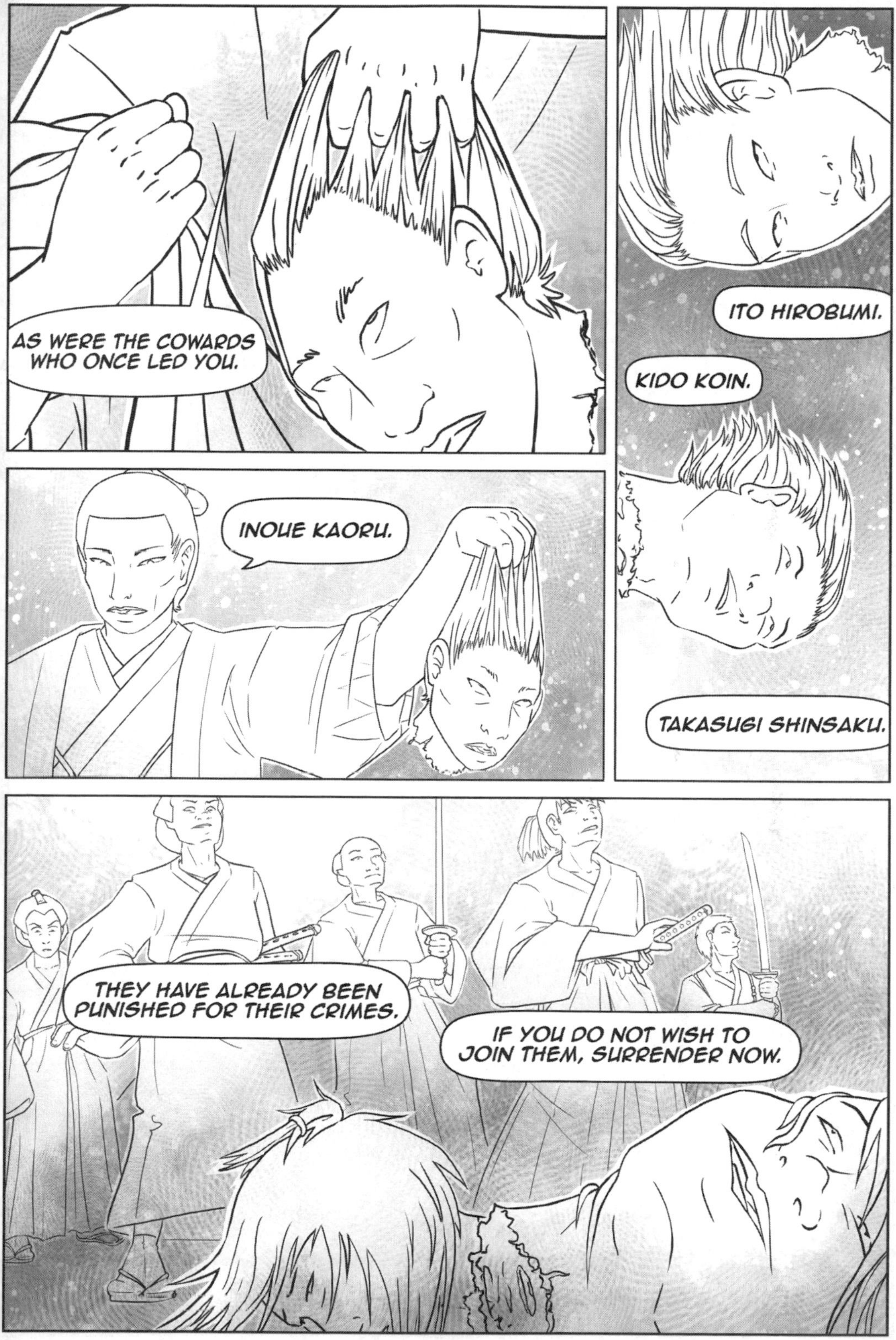
AS WERE THE COWARDS WHO ONCE LED YOU.
ITO HIROBUMI.
KIDO KOIN.
TAKASUGI SHINSAKU.
INOUE KAORU.
THEY HAVE ALREADY BEEN PUNISHED FOR THEIR CRIMES.
IF YOU DO NOT WISH TO JOIN THEM, SURRENDER NOW.

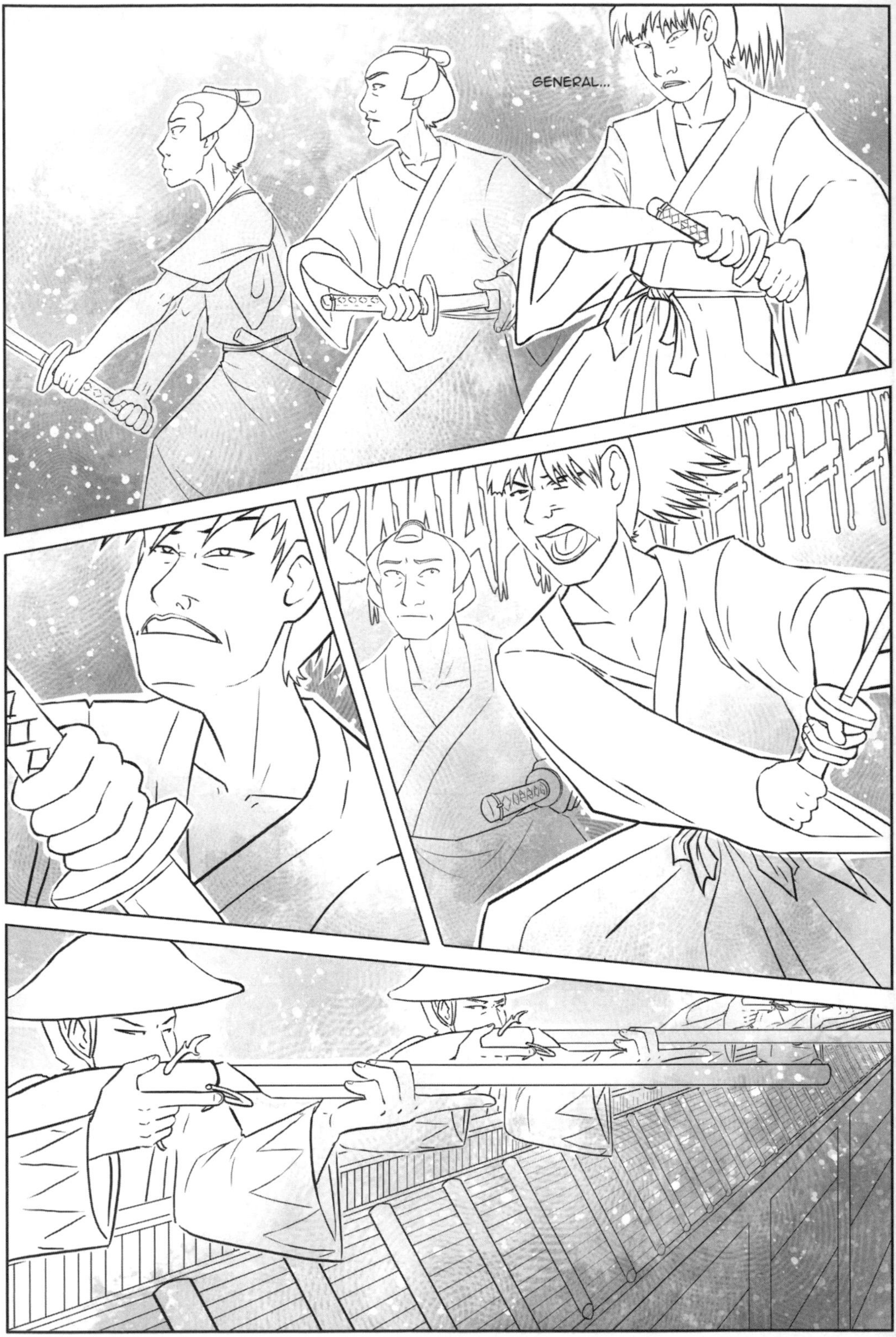
GENERAL...

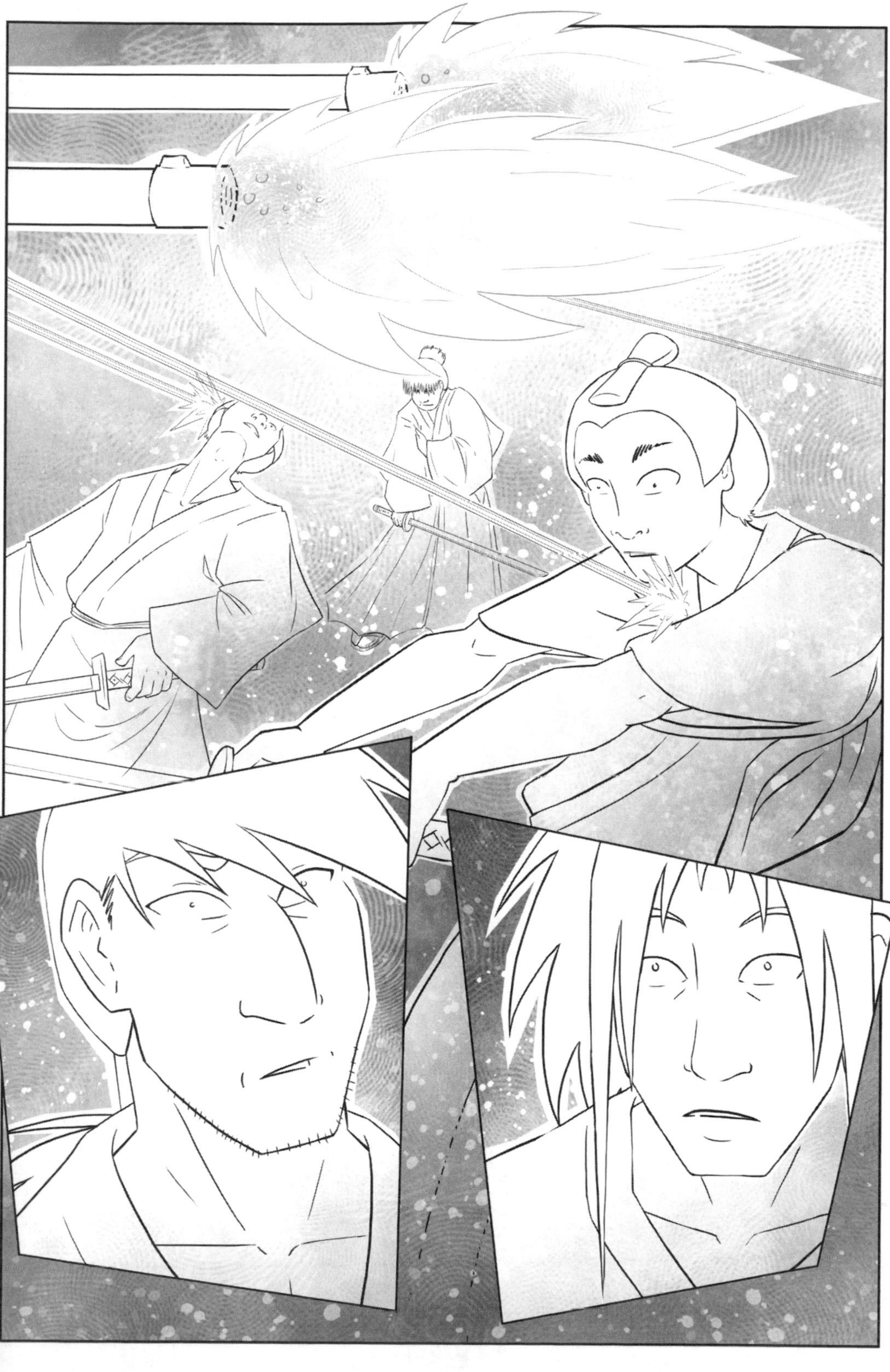

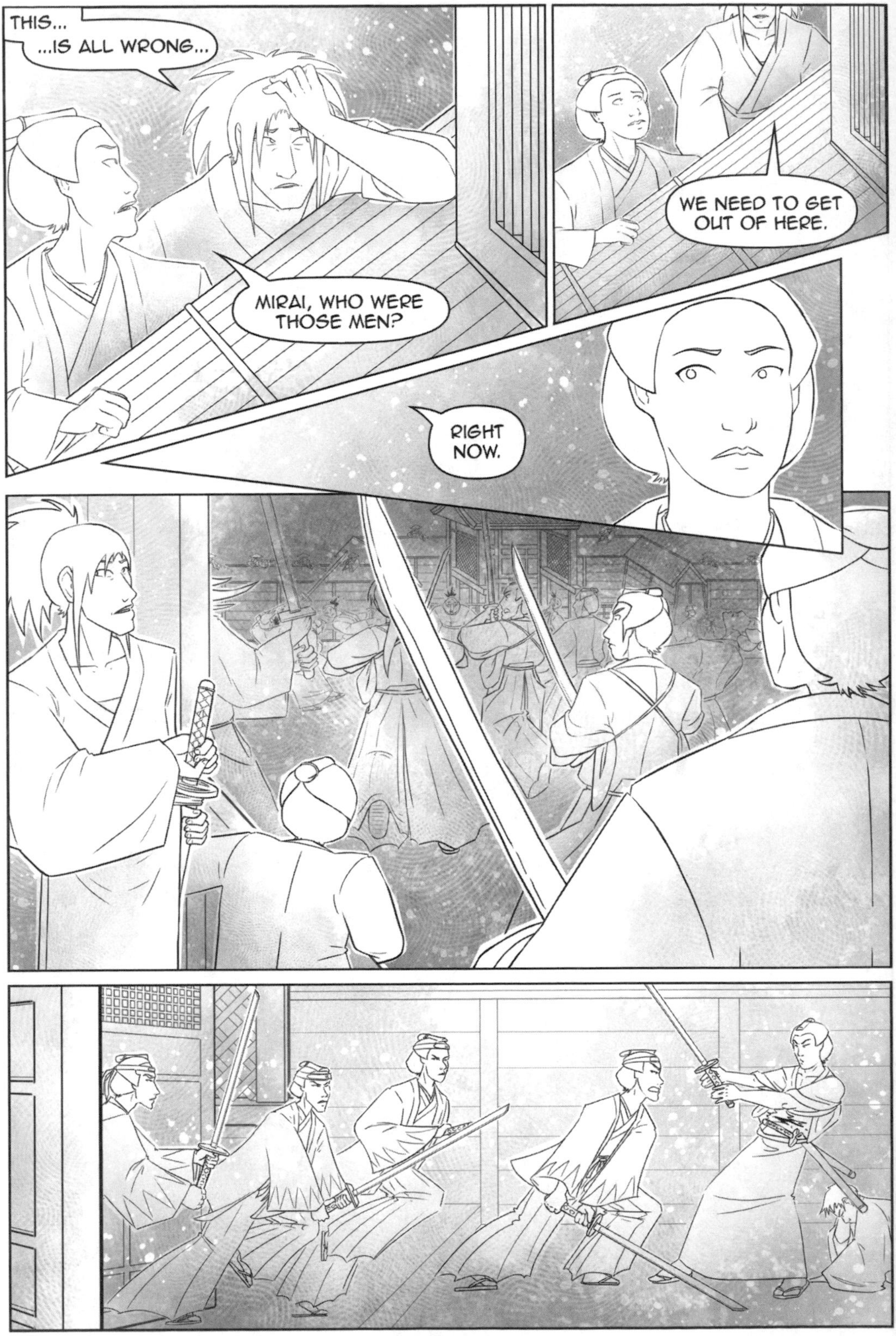
THIS...
...IS ALL WRONG...
WE NEED TO GET OUT OF HERE.
MIRAI, WHO WERE THOSE MEN?
RIGHT NOW.

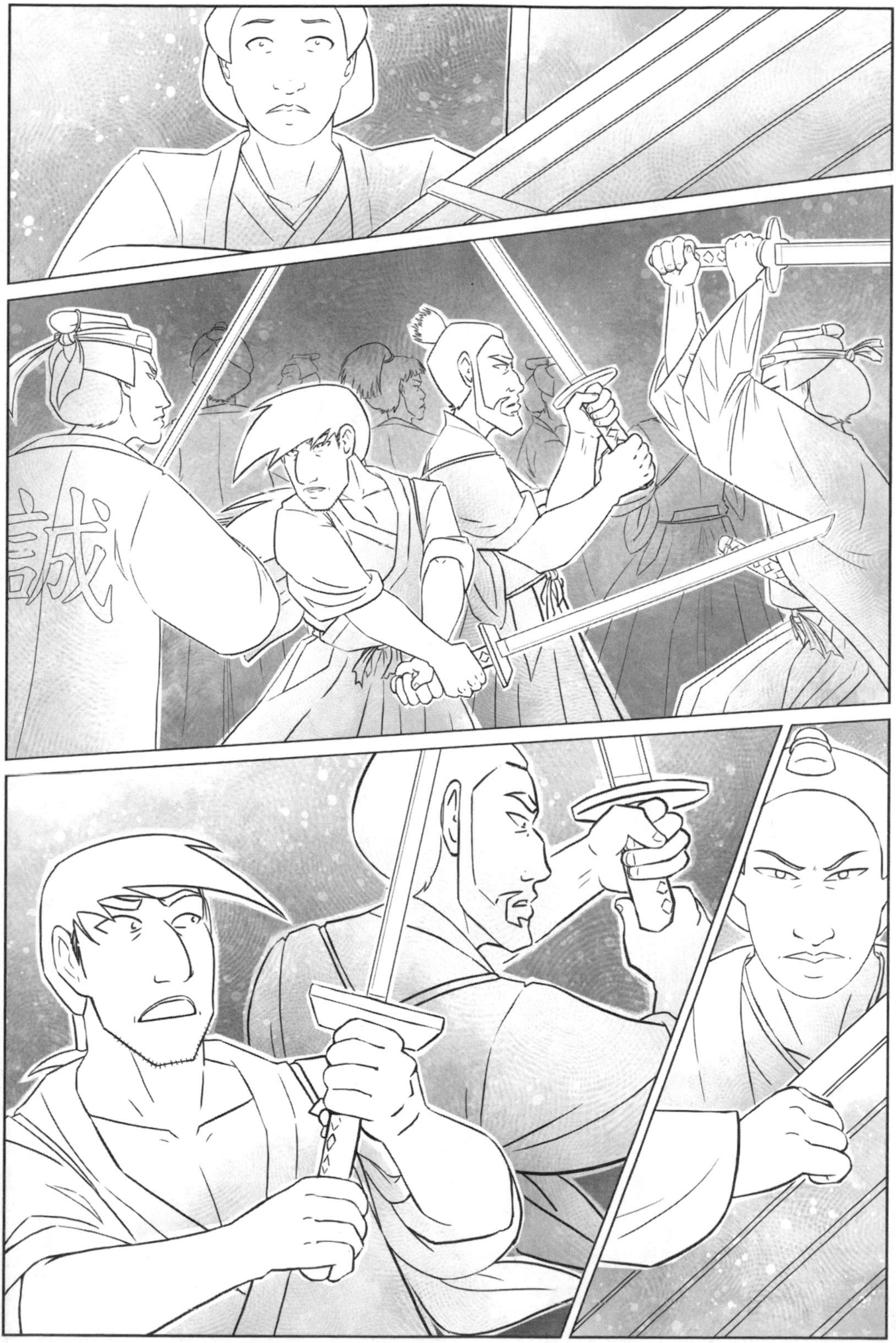
誠

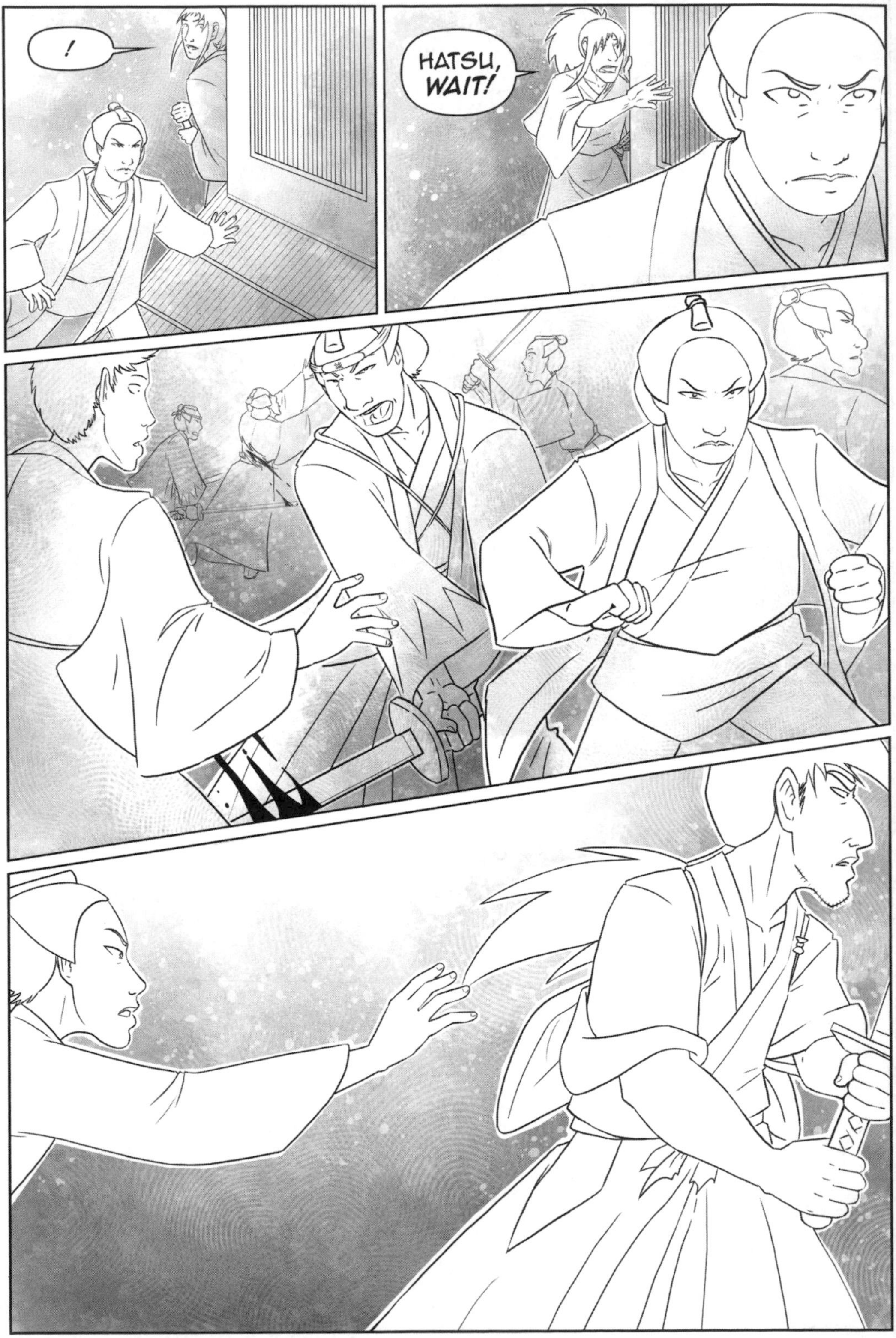
!
HATSU, WAIT!

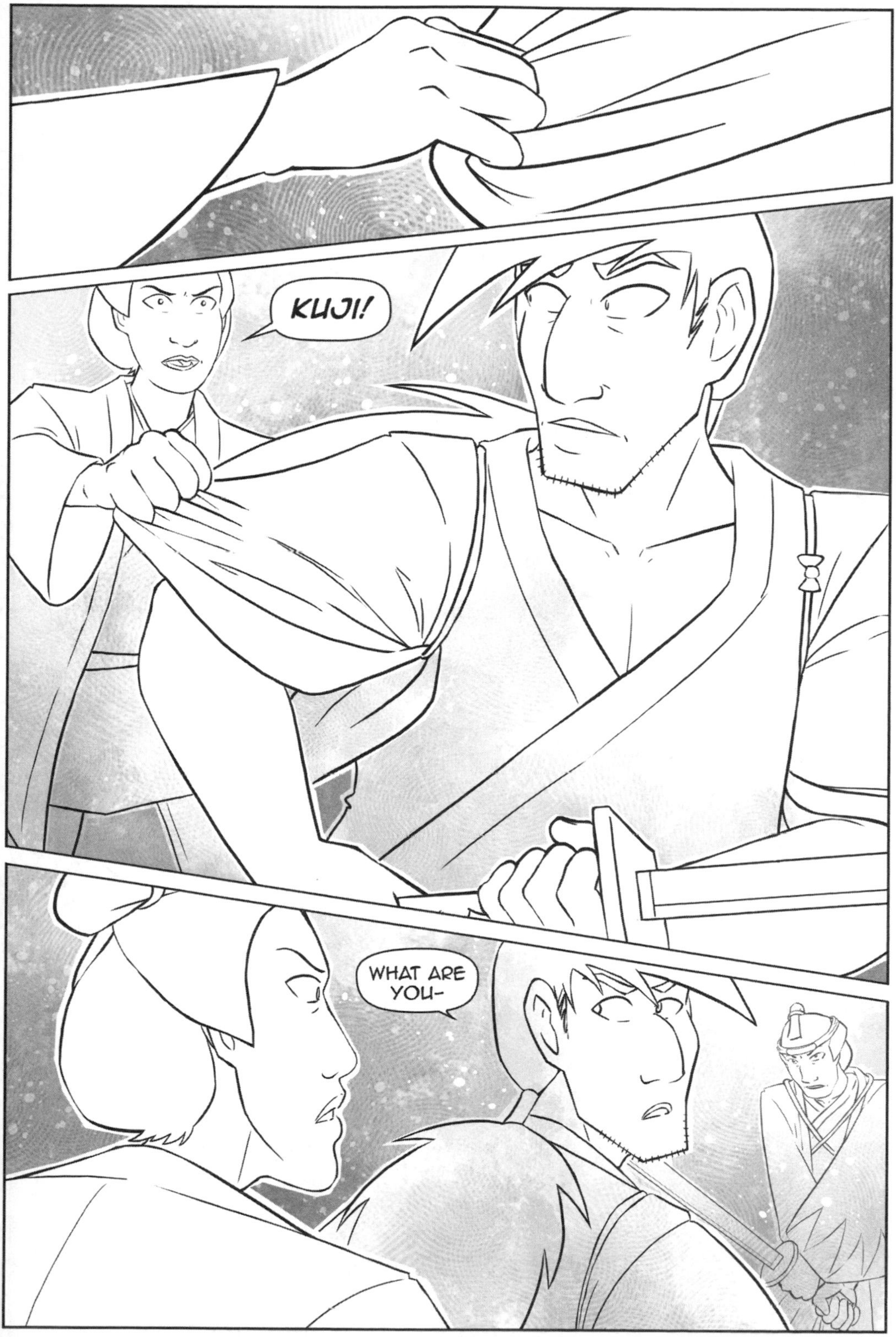
KUJI!
WHAT ARE YOU-

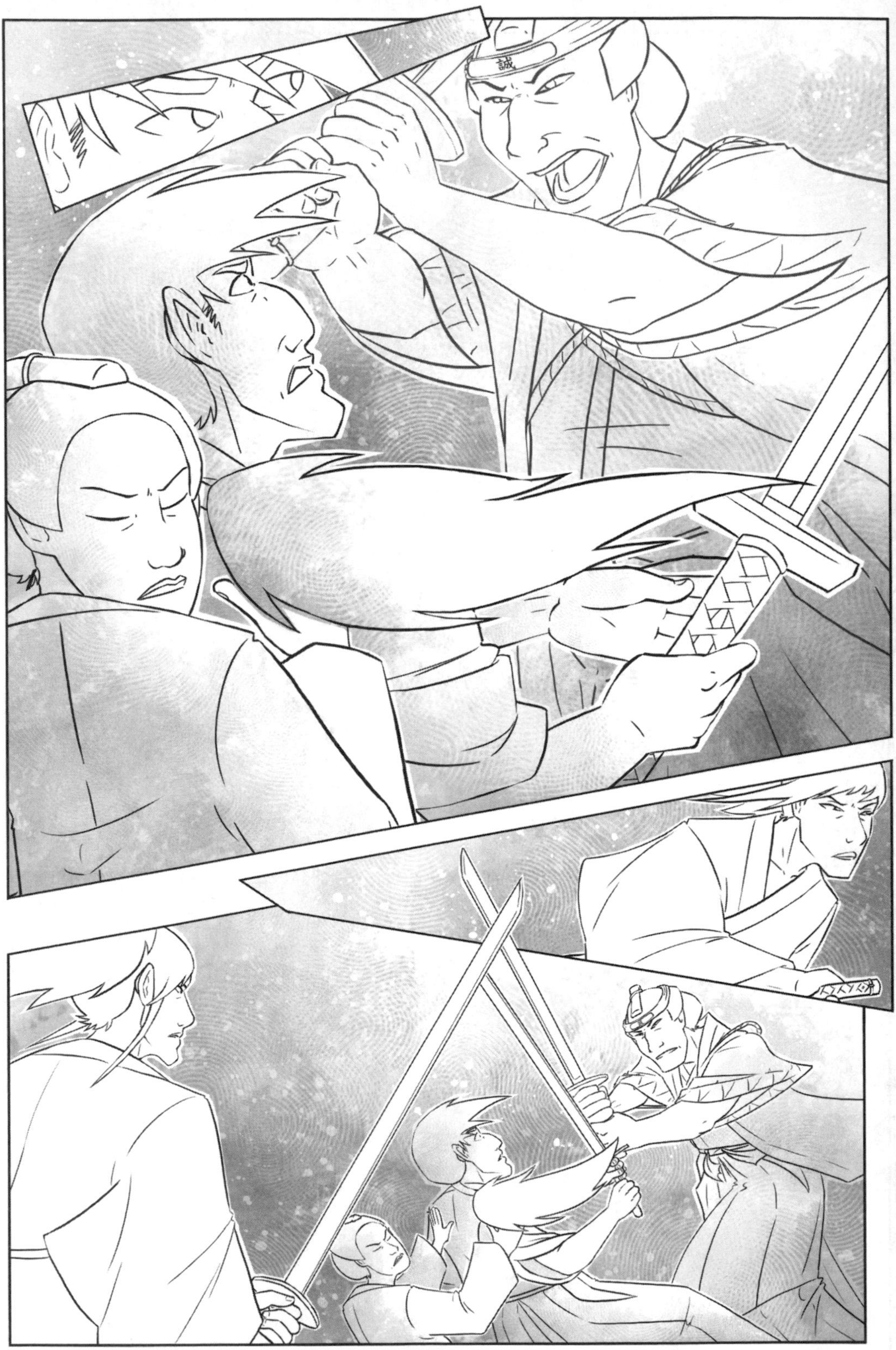
誠

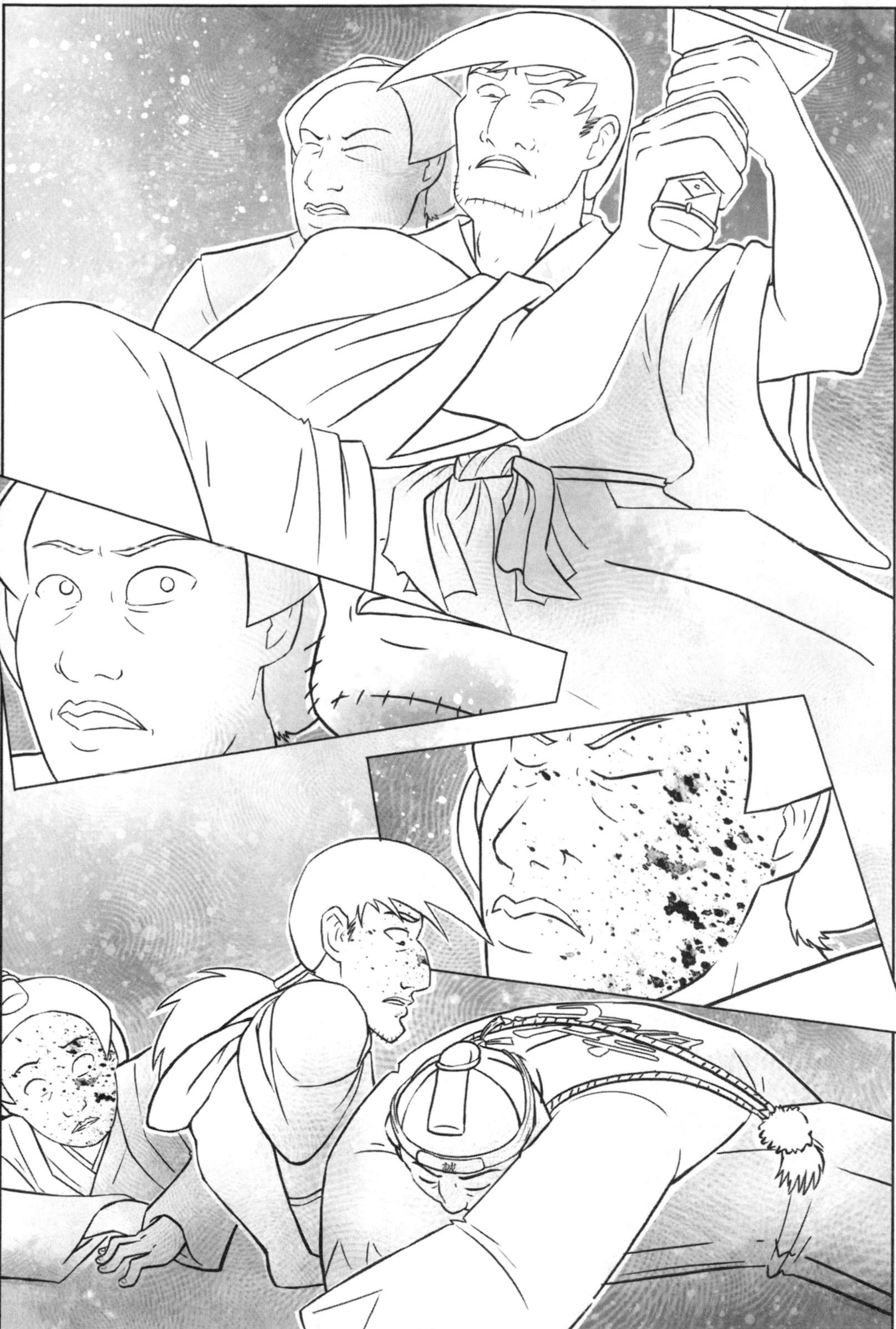

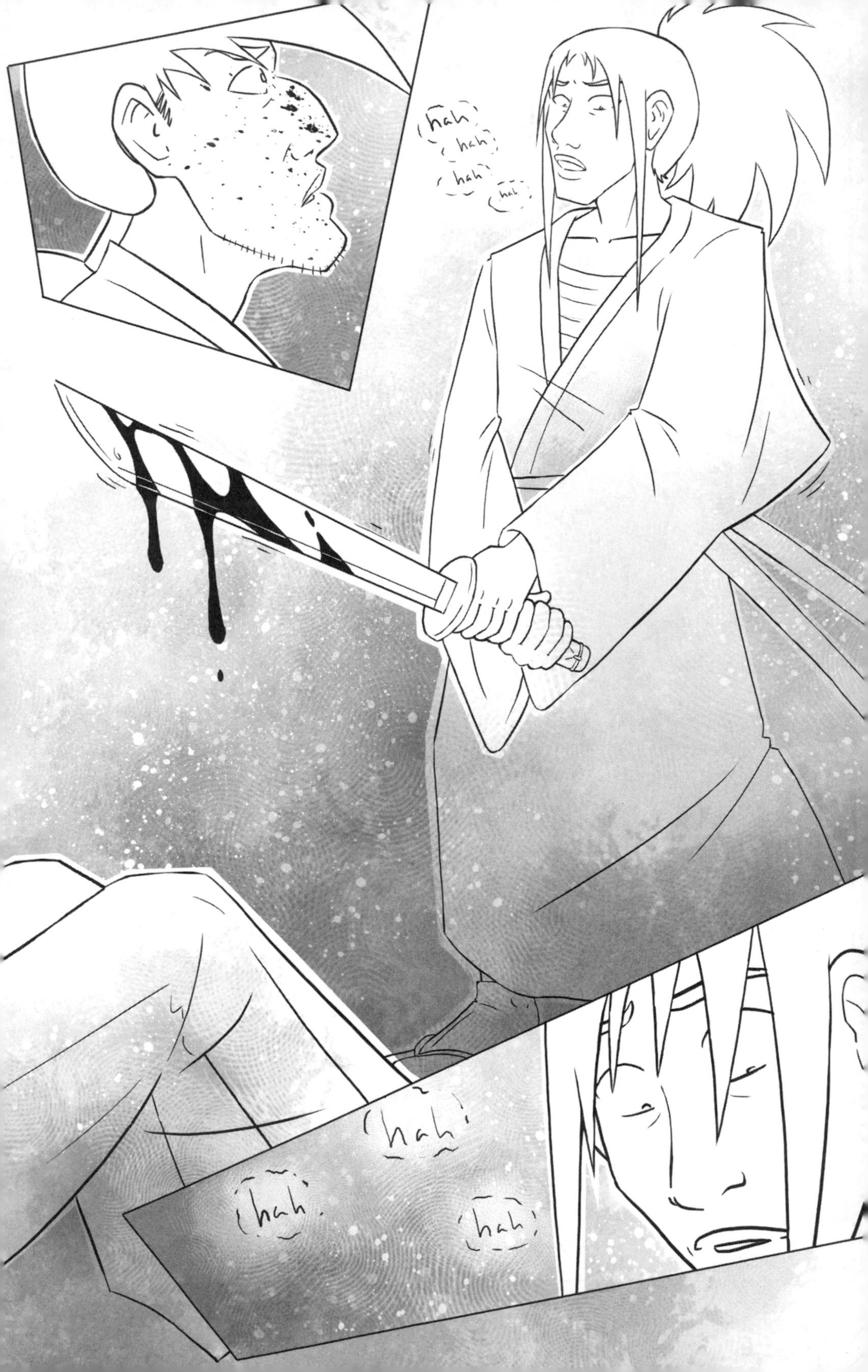
hah
hah
hah
hah
hah
hah
hah

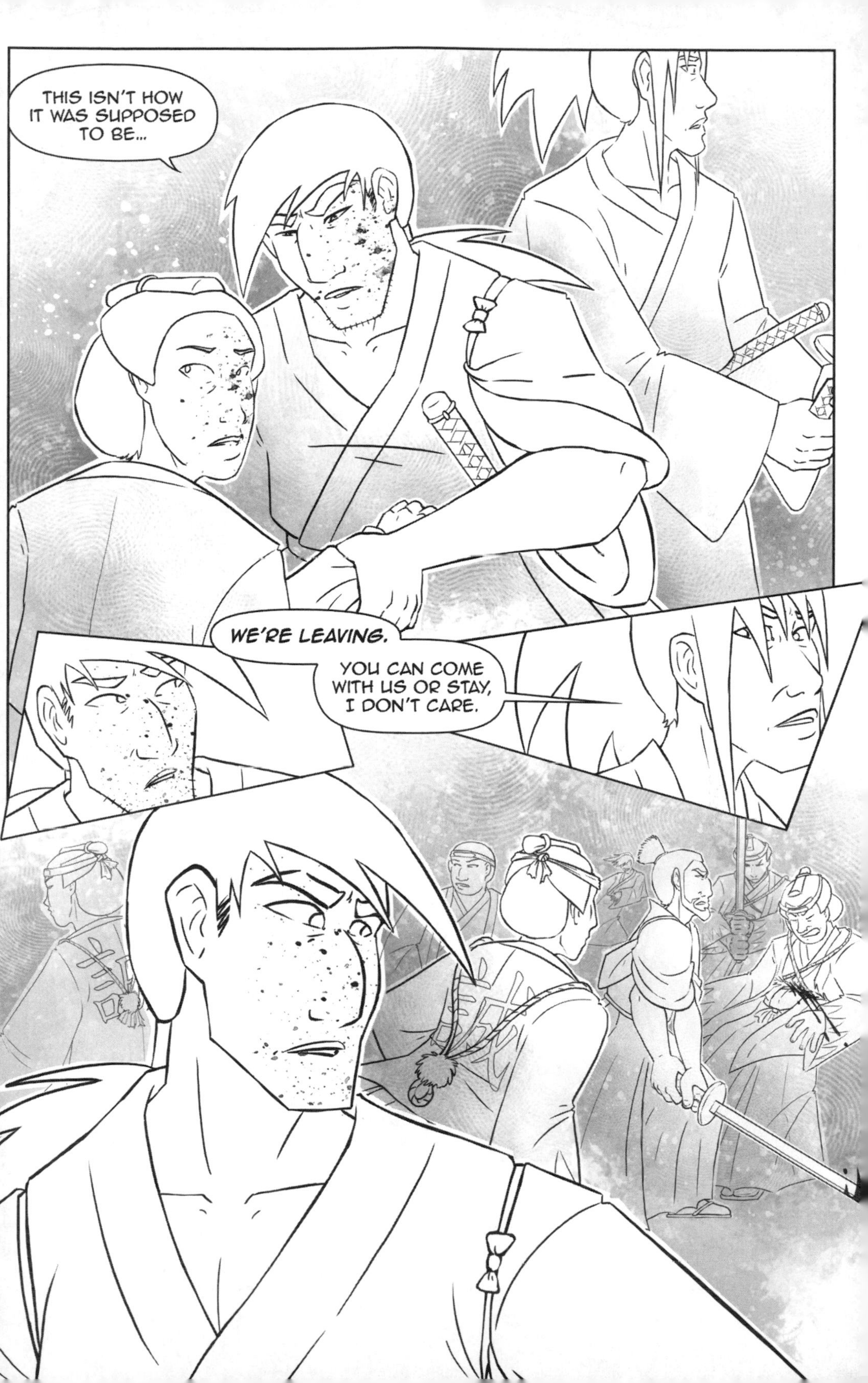
THIS ISN'T HOW IT WAS SUPPOSED TO BE...
WE'RE LEAVING.
YOU CAN COME WITH US OR STAY, I DON'T CARE.

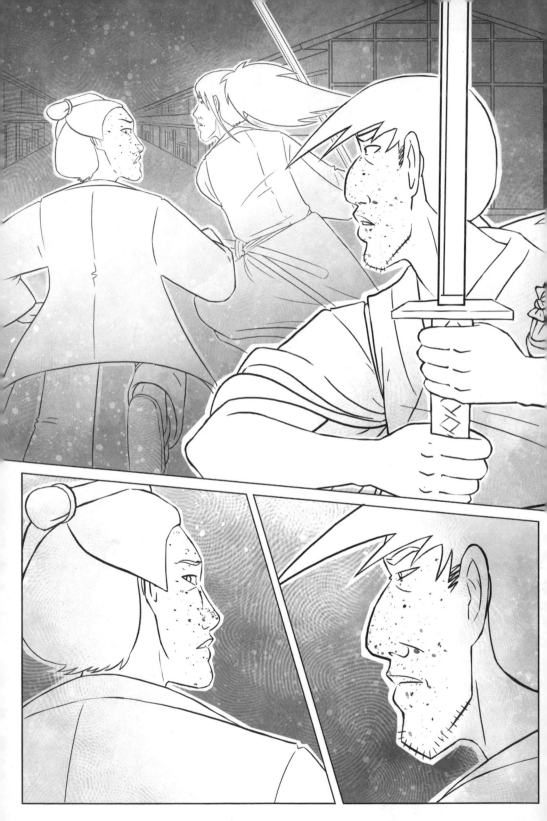

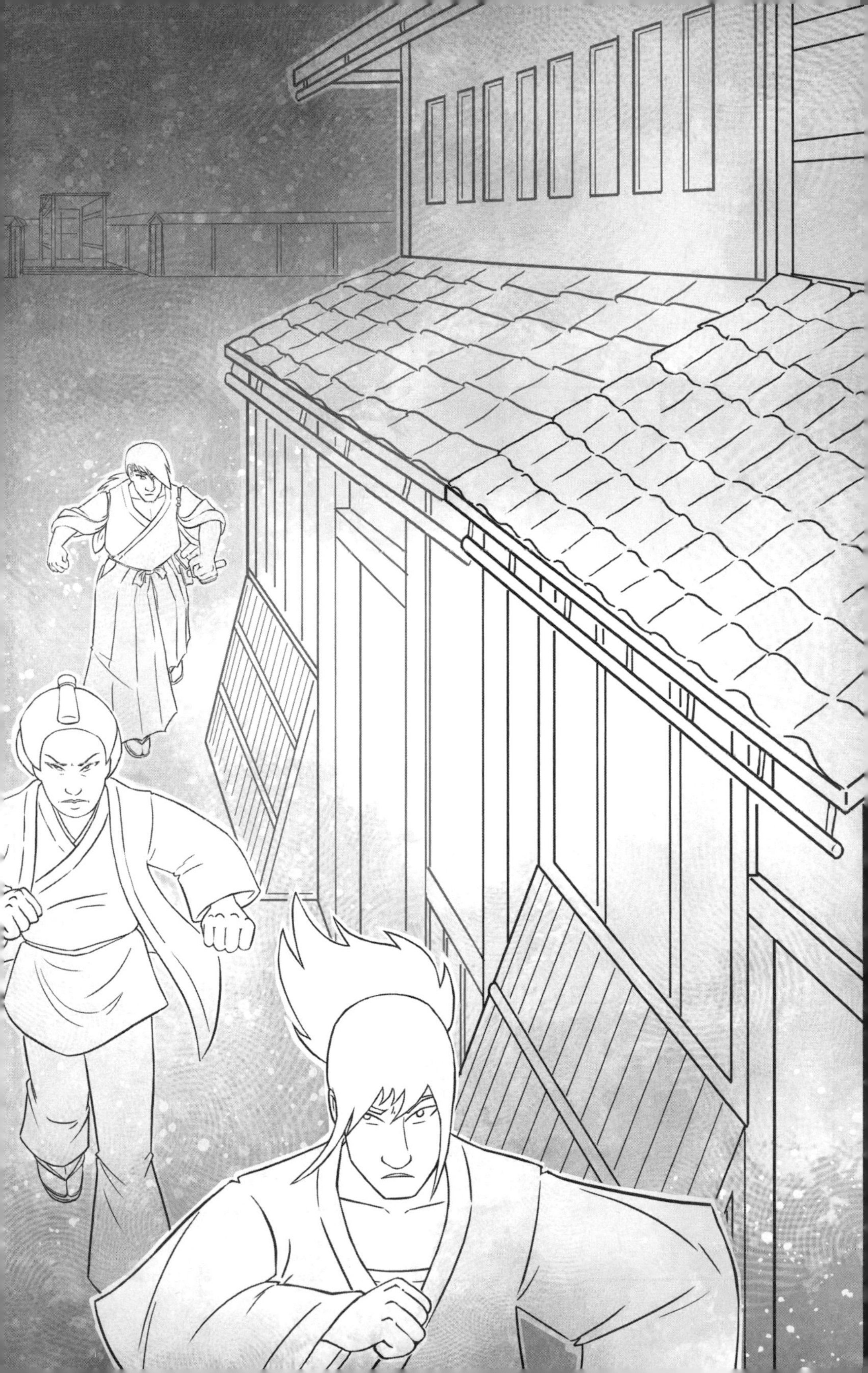

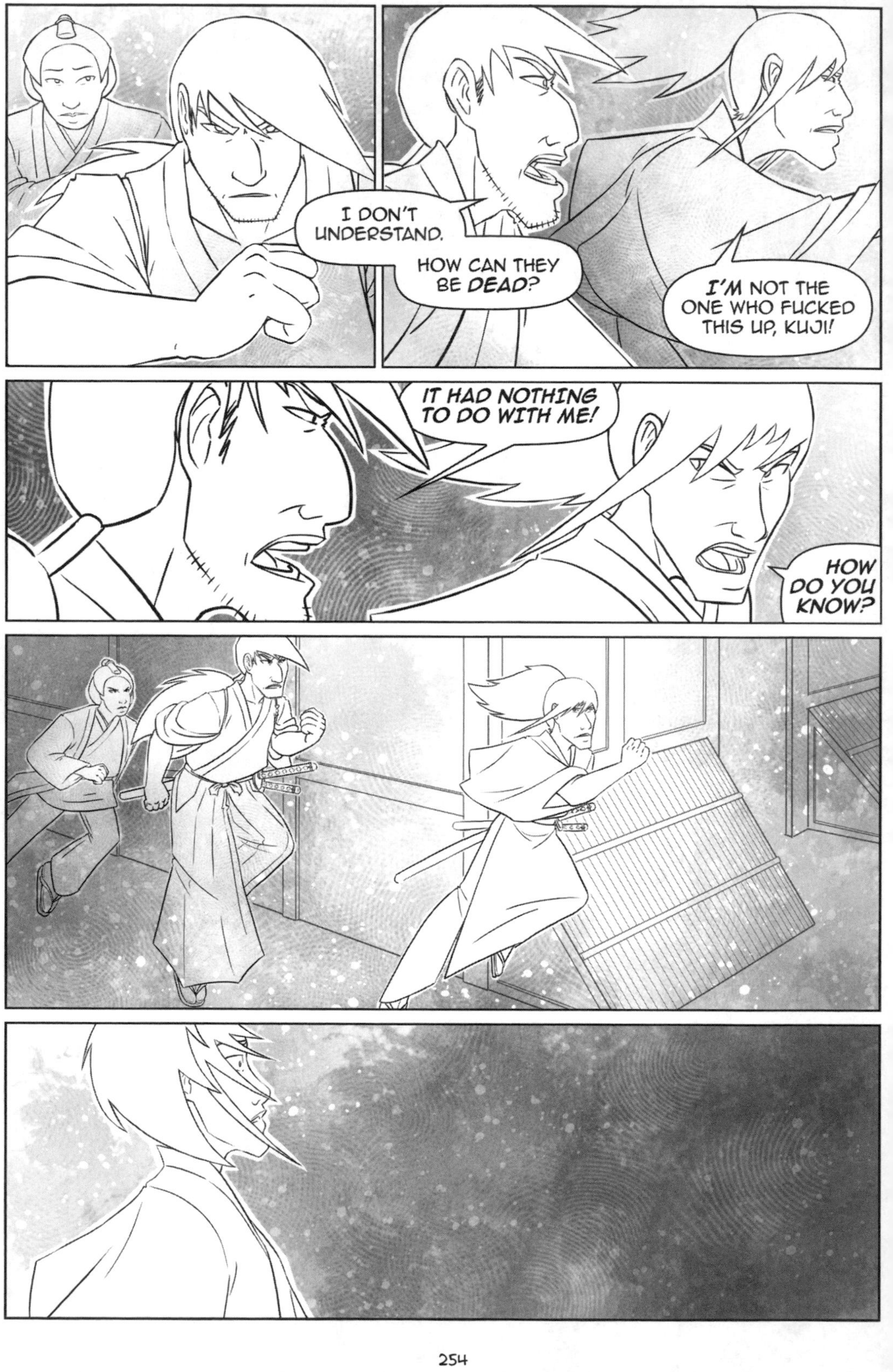
I DON'T UNDERSTAND.
HOW CAN THEY BE *DEAD*?
I'M NOT THE ONE WHO FUCKED THIS UP, KUJI!
IT HAD NOTHING TO DO WITH ME!
HOW DO YOU KNOW?

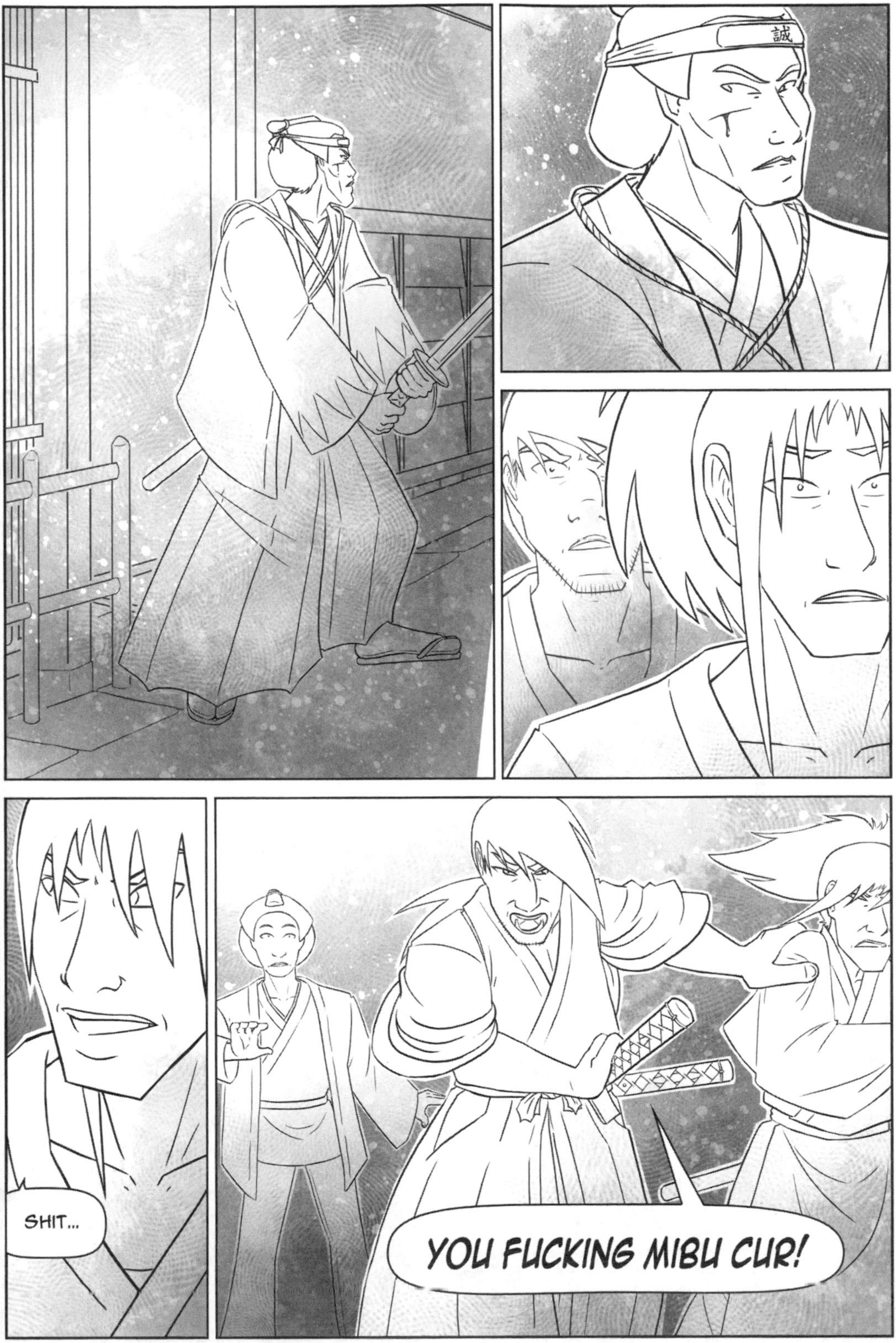

誠
SHIT...
YOU FUCKING MIBU CUR!

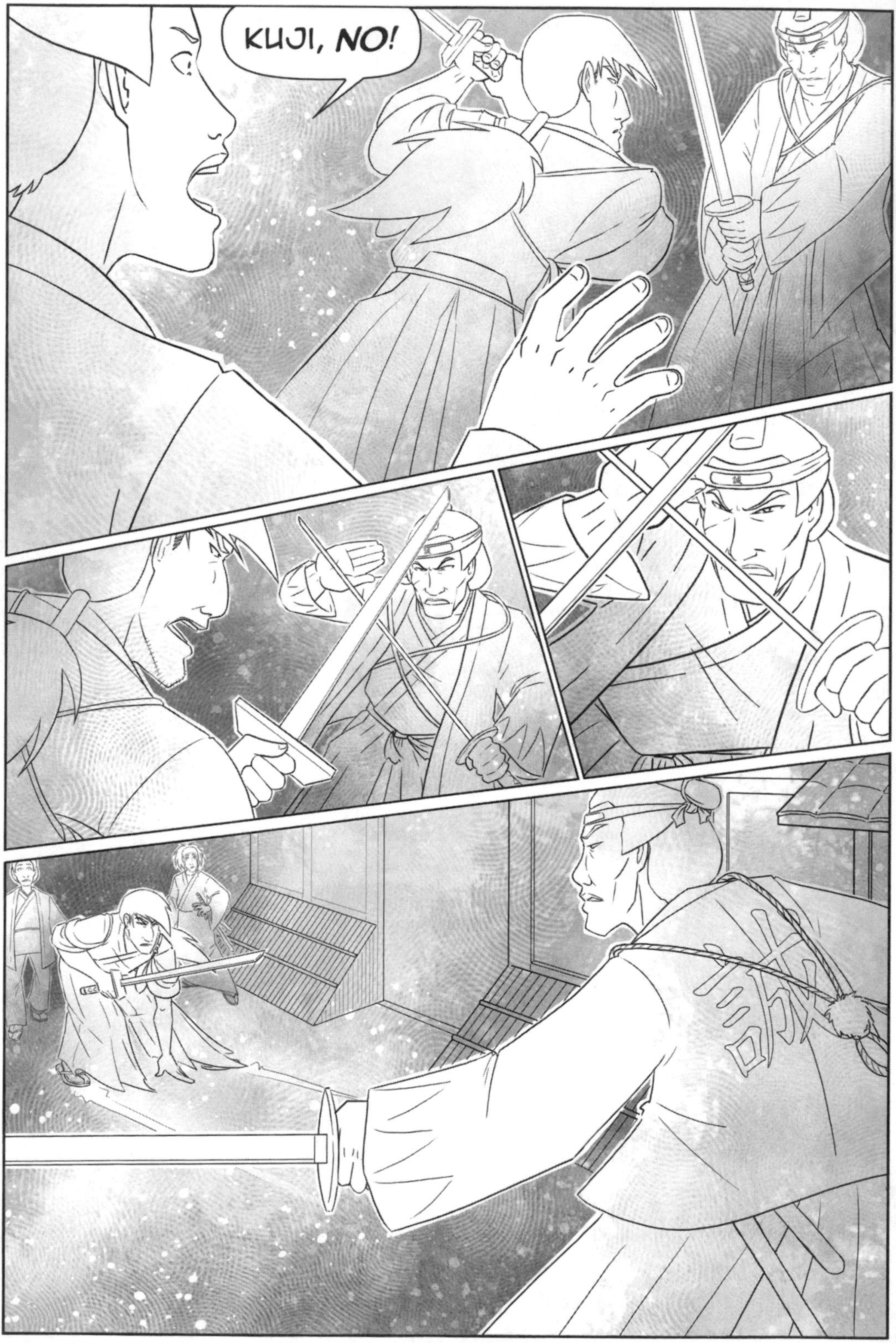
KUJI, NO!

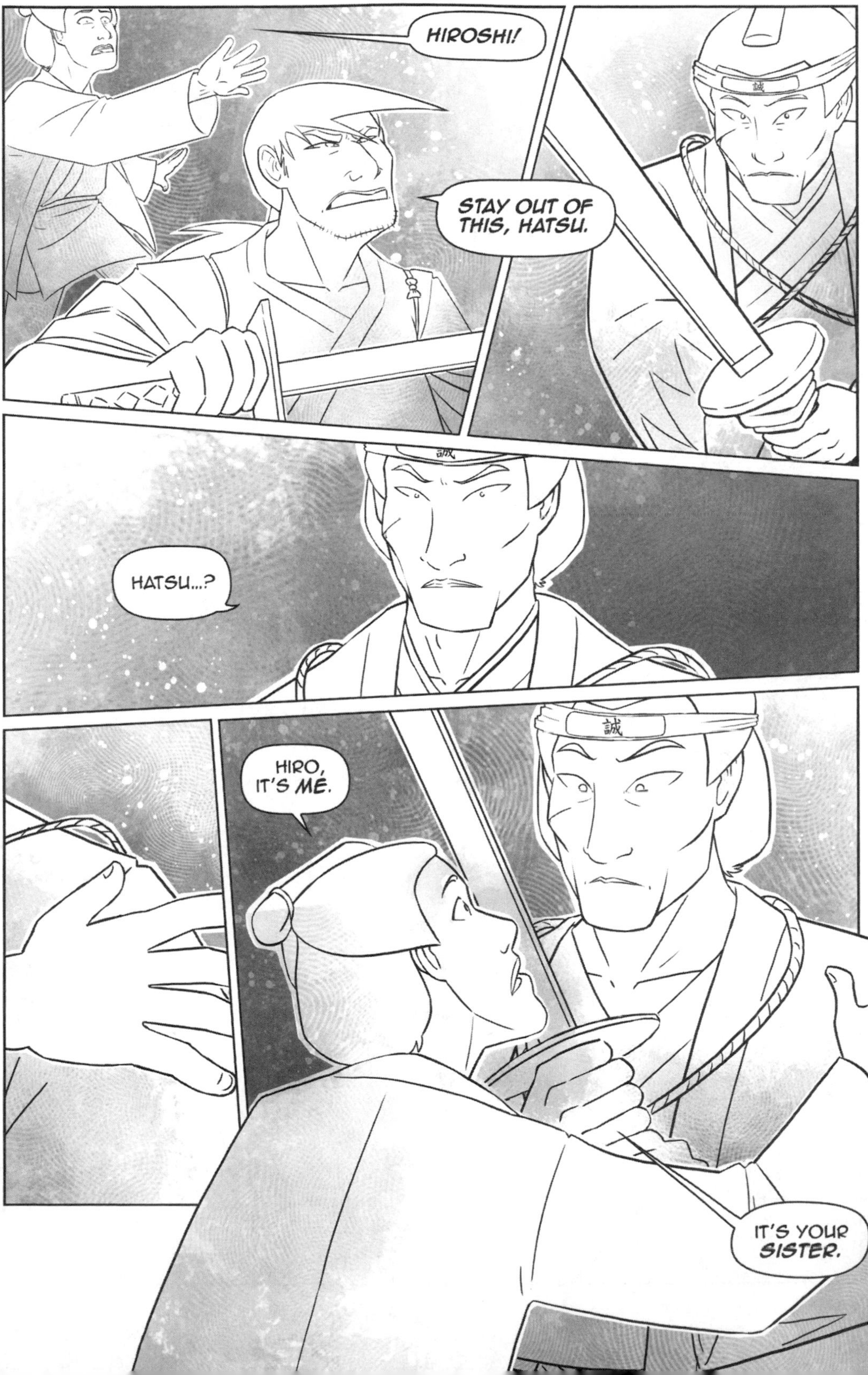
HIROSHI!
STAY OUT OF THIS, HATSU.
HATSU...?
HIRO, IT'S ME.
IT'S YOUR SISTER.

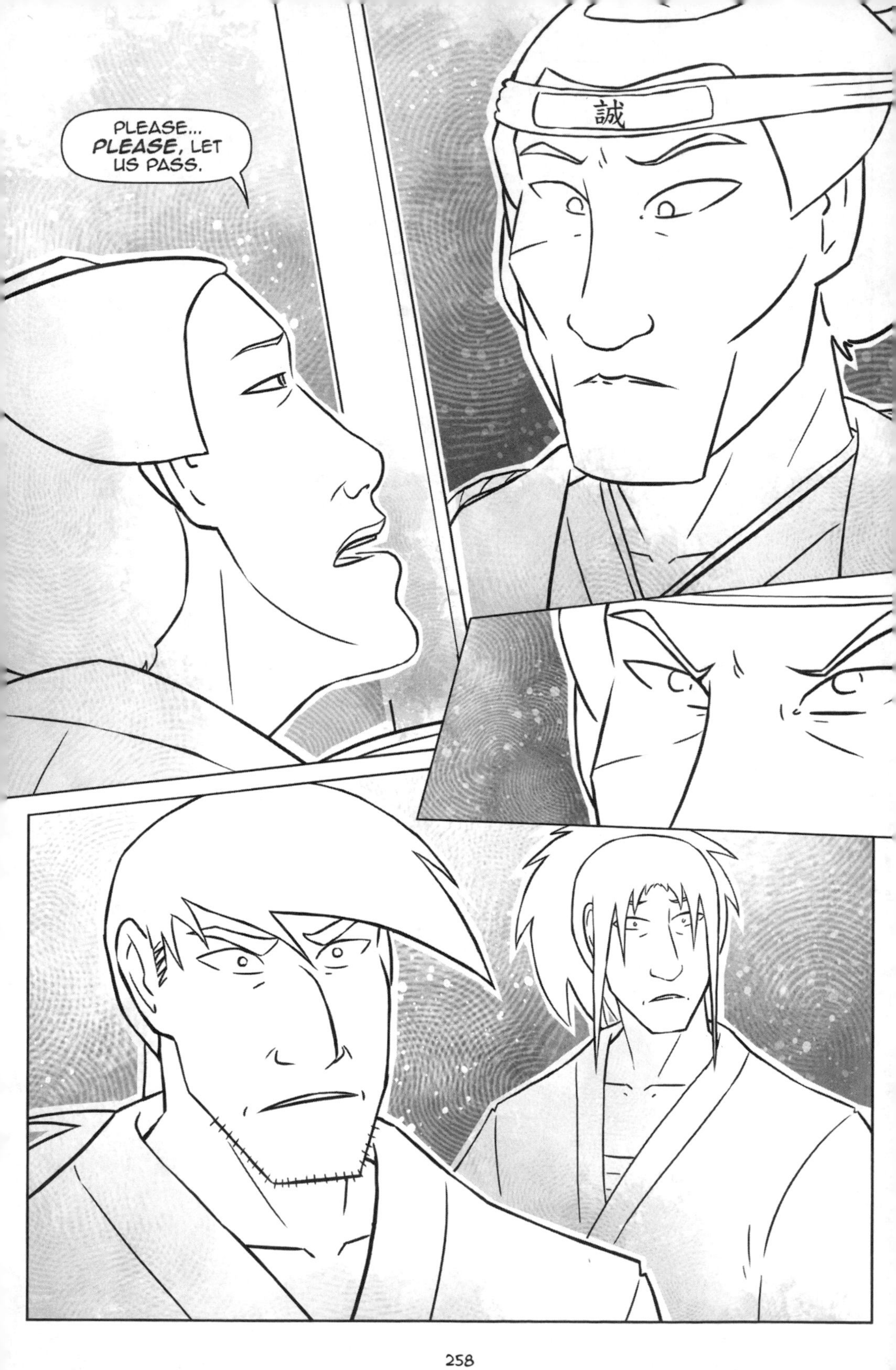
PLEASE... *PLEASE*, LET US PASS.
誠

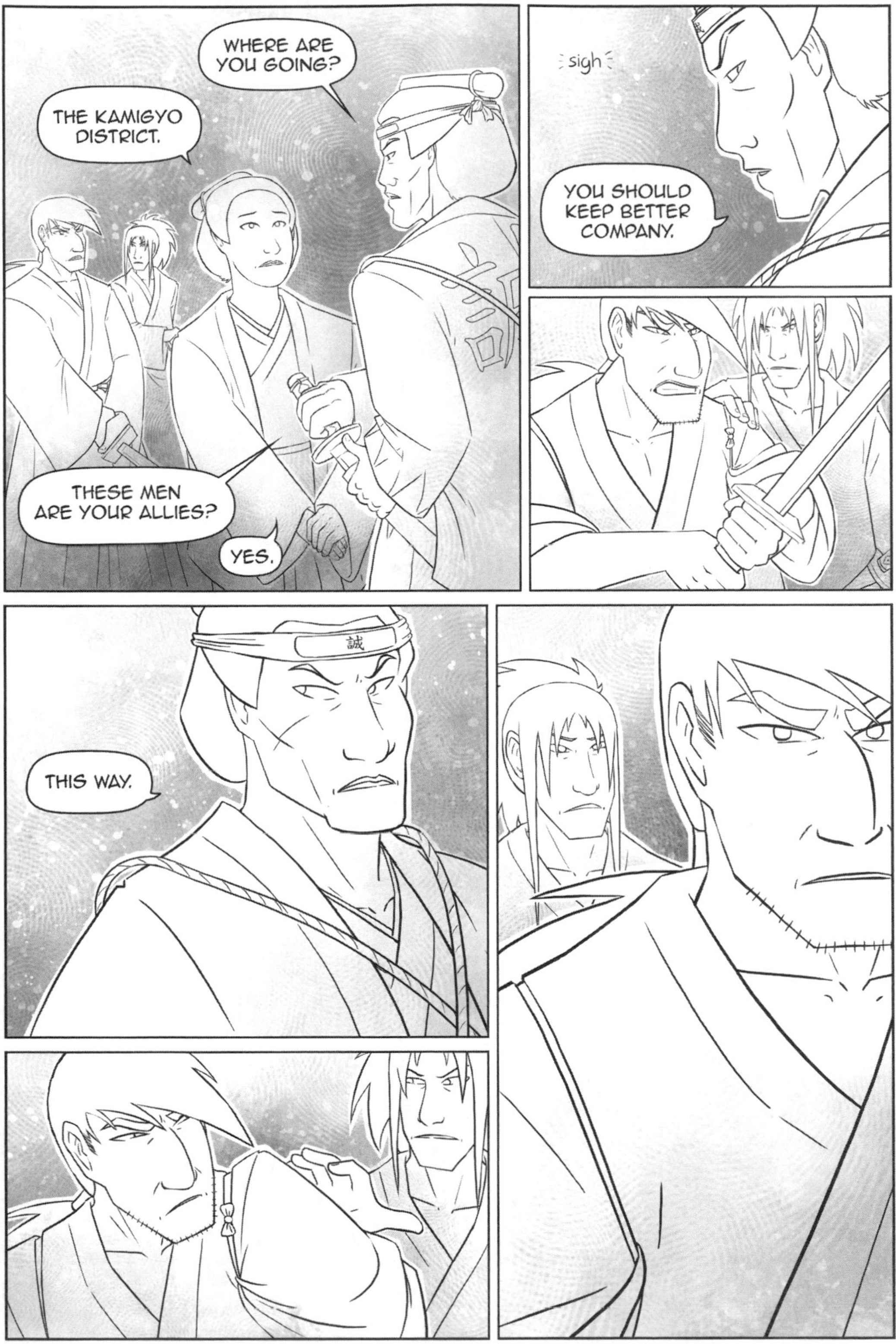
WHERE ARE YOU GOING?
THE KAMIGYO DISTRICT.
THESE MEN ARE YOUR ALLIES?
YES.
sigh
YOU SHOULD KEEP BETTER COMPANY.
THIS WAY.

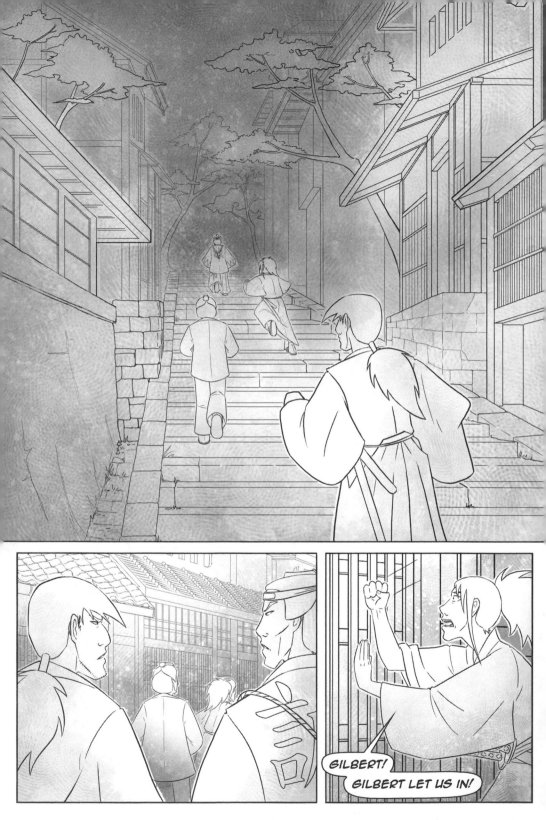

GILBERT!
GILBERT LET US IN!

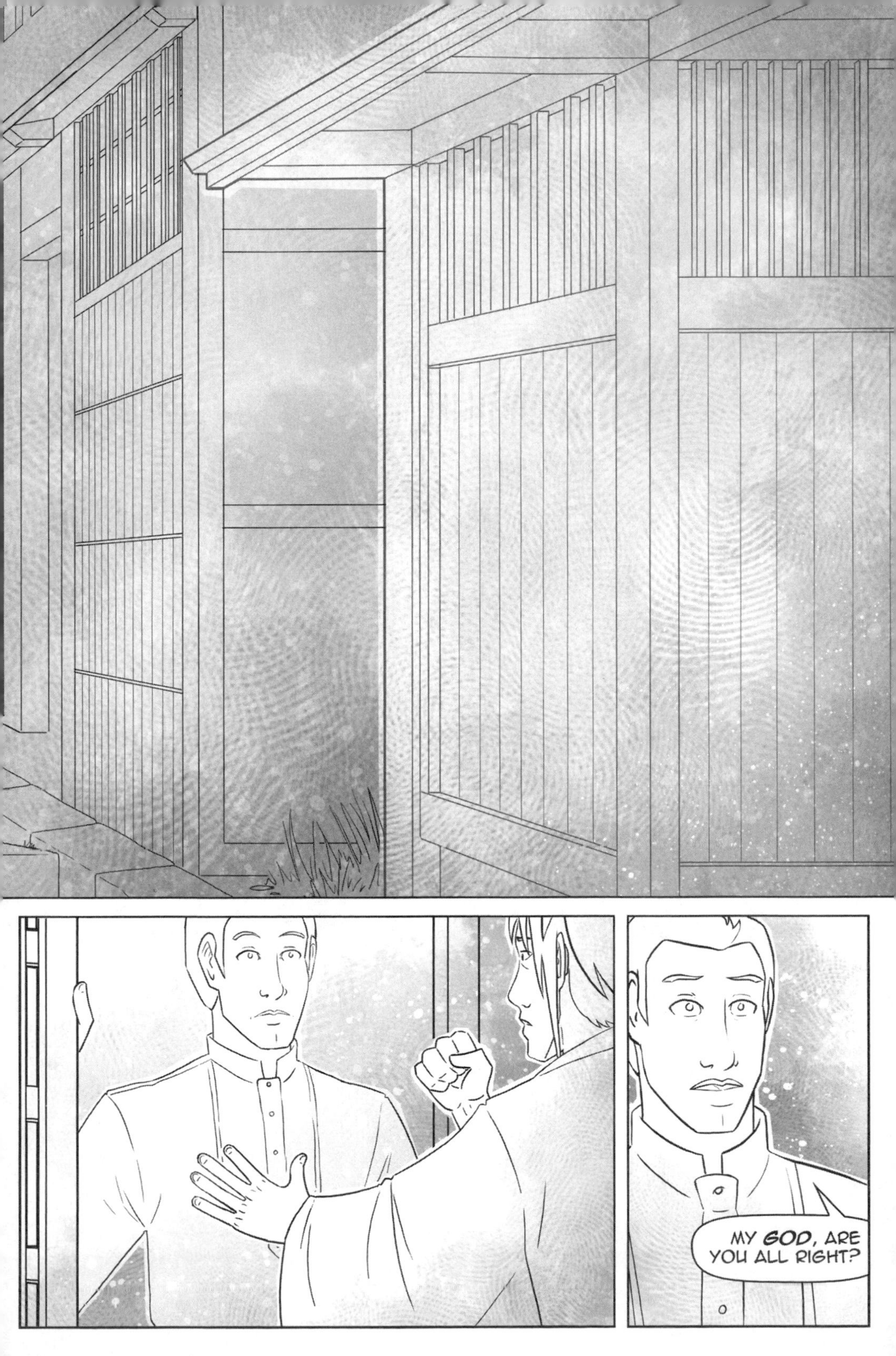
MY GOD, ARE YOU ALL RIGHT?

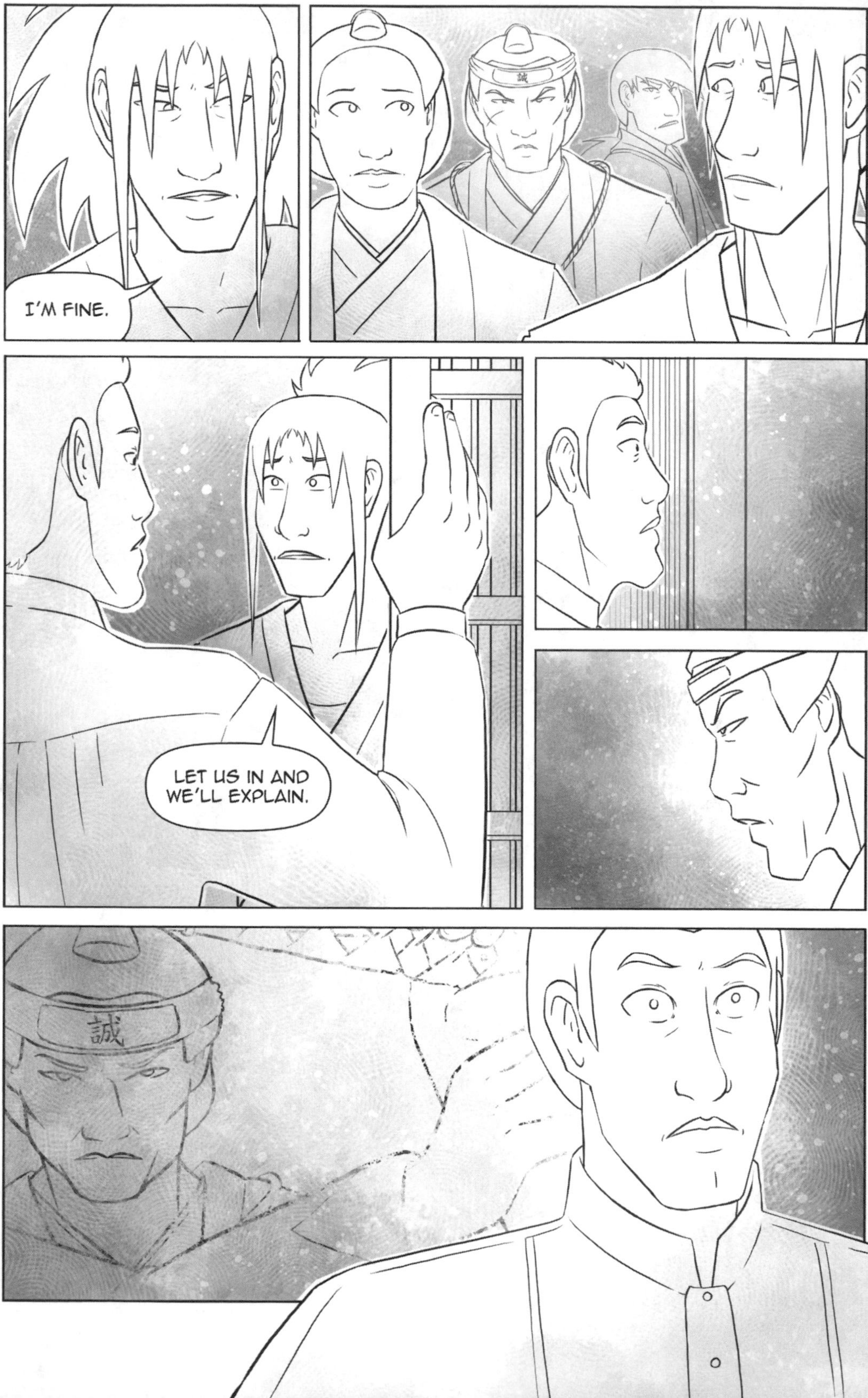
I'M FINE.
LET US IN AND WE'LL EXPLAIN.
誠

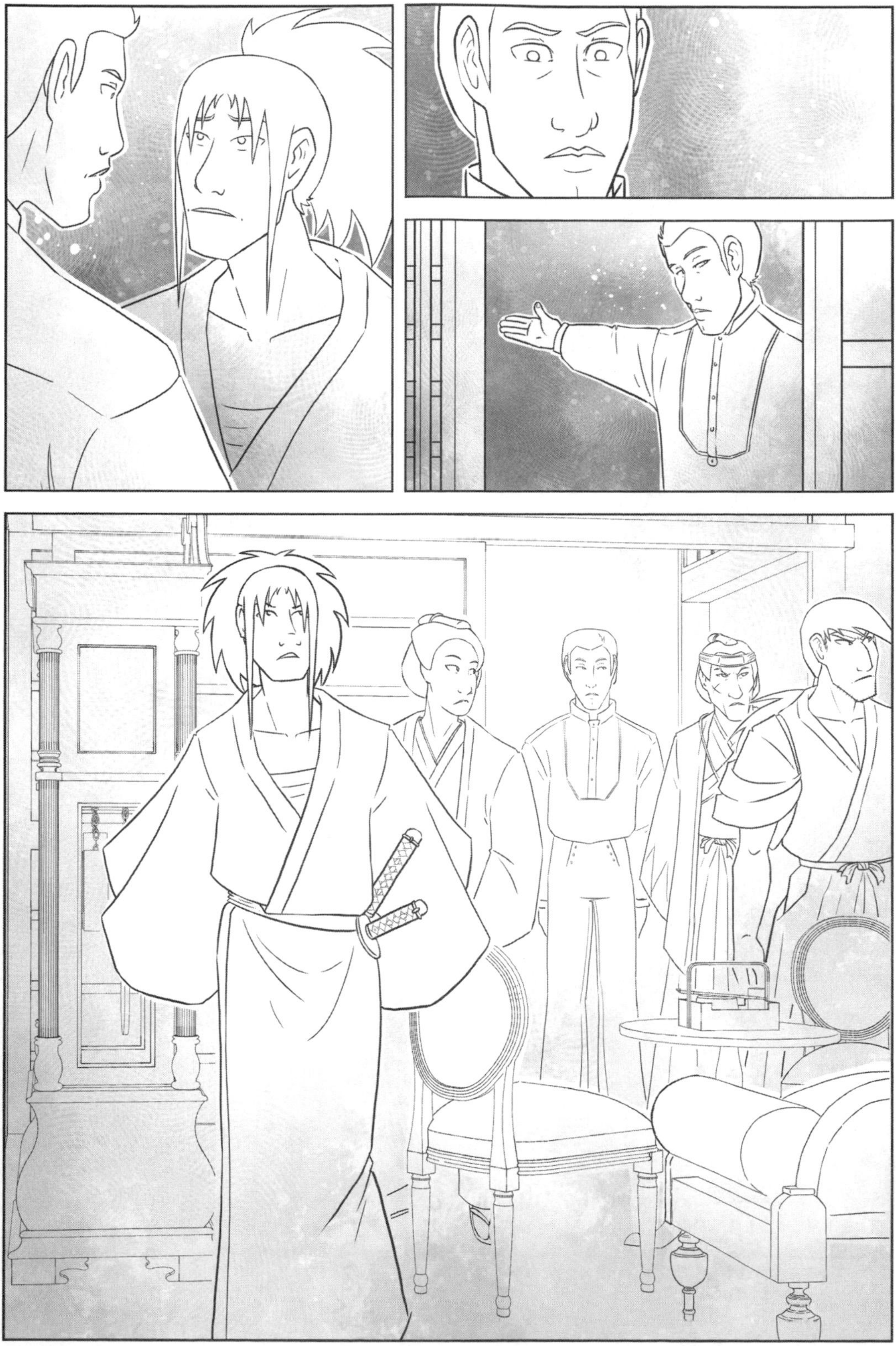

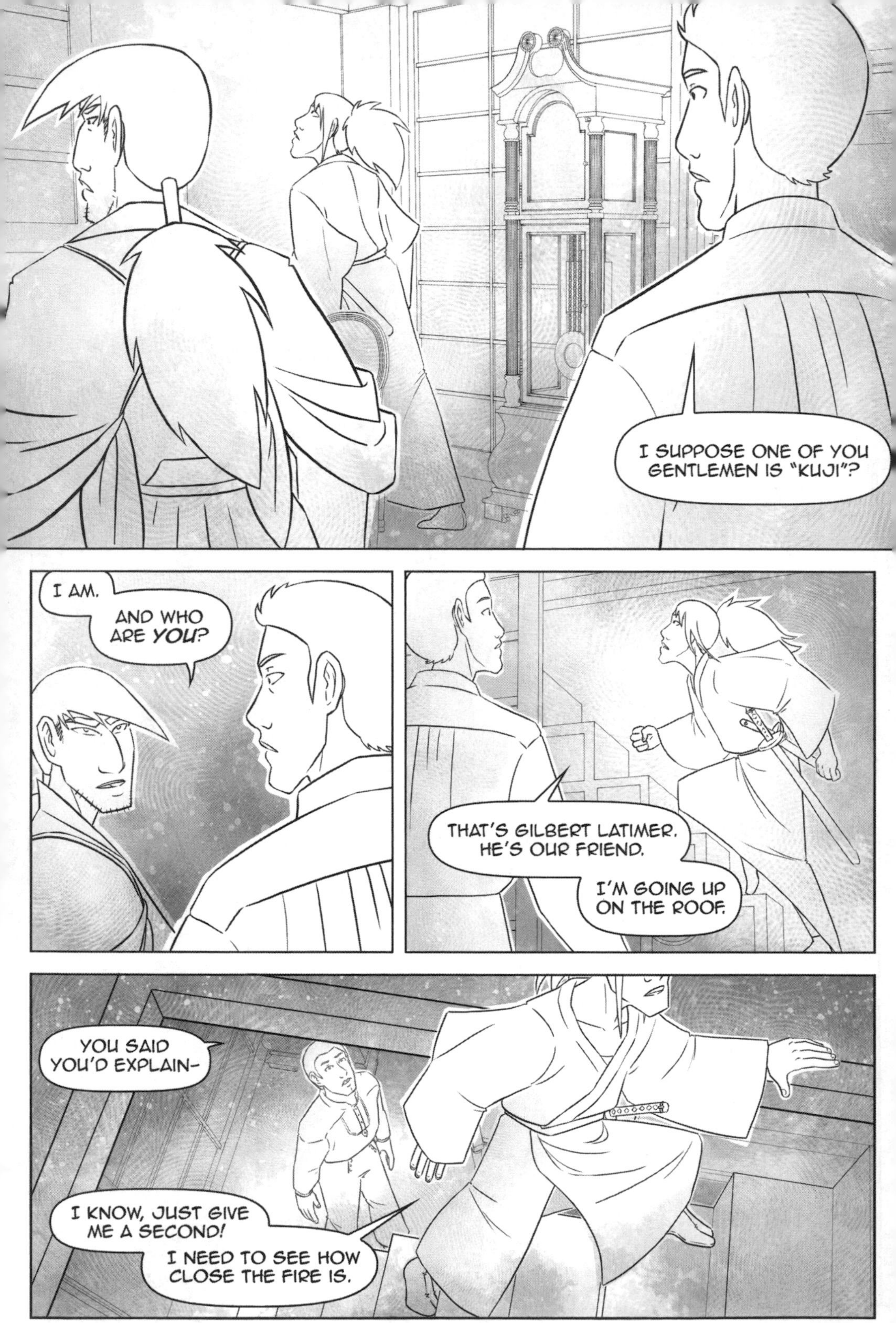
I SUPPOSE ONE OF YOU GENTLEMEN IS "KUJI"?
I AM.
AND WHO ARE *YOU*?
THAT'S GILBERT LATIMER. HE'S OUR FRIEND.
I'M GOING UP ON THE ROOF.
YOU SAID YOU'D EXPLAIN-
I KNOW, JUST GIVE ME A SECOND!
I NEED TO SEE HOW CLOSE THE FIRE IS.

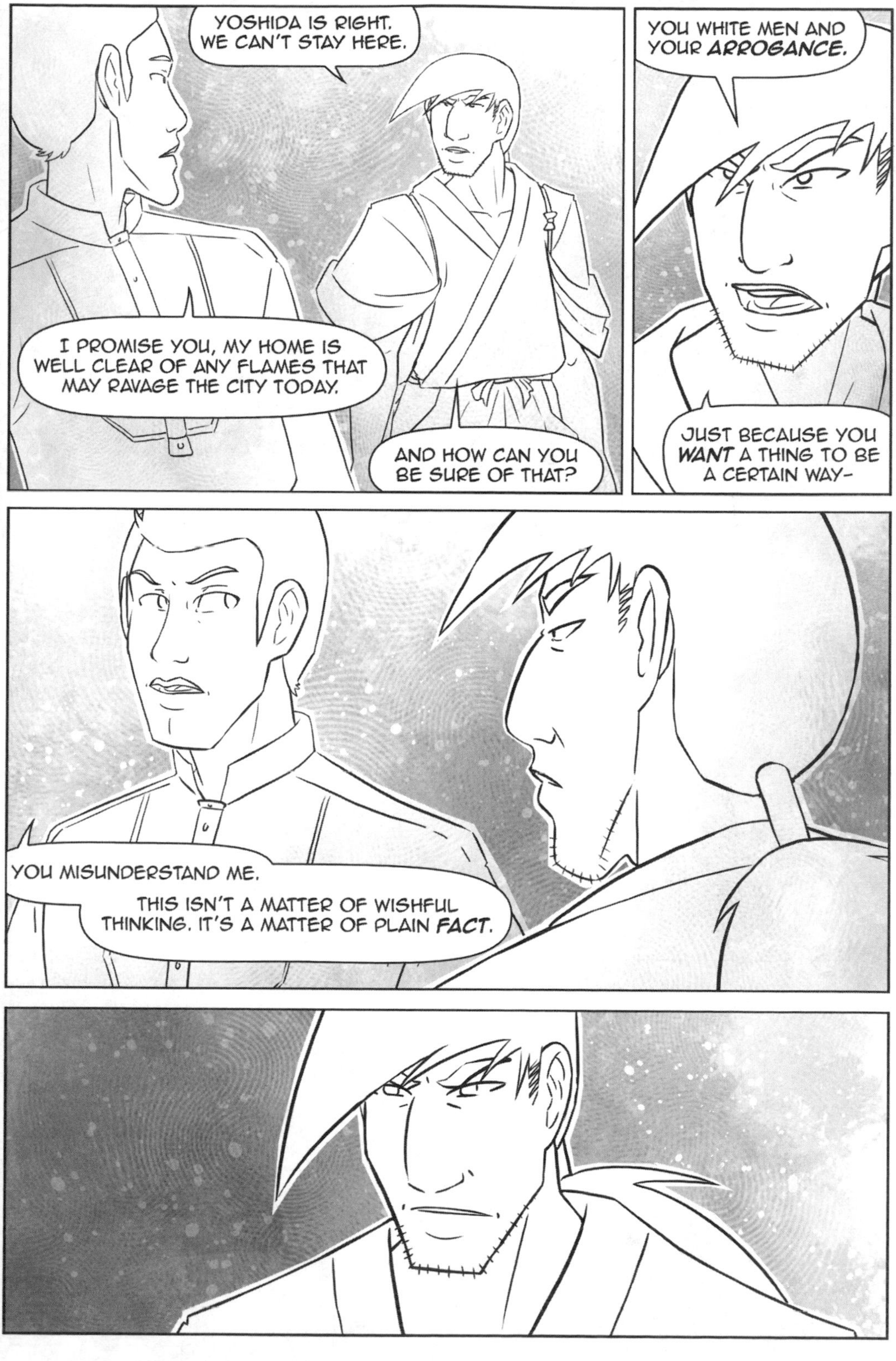
YOSHIDA IS RIGHT. WE CAN'T STAY HERE.
I PROMISE YOU, MY HOME IS WELL CLEAR OF ANY FLAMES THAT MAY RAVAGE THE CITY TODAY.
AND HOW CAN YOU BE SURE OF THAT?
YOU WHITE MEN AND YOUR ARROGANCE.
JUST BECAUSE YOU WANT A THING TO BE A CERTAIN WAY-
YOU MISUNDERSTAND ME.
THIS ISN'T A MATTER OF WISHFUL THINKING. IT'S A MATTER OF PLAIN FACT.

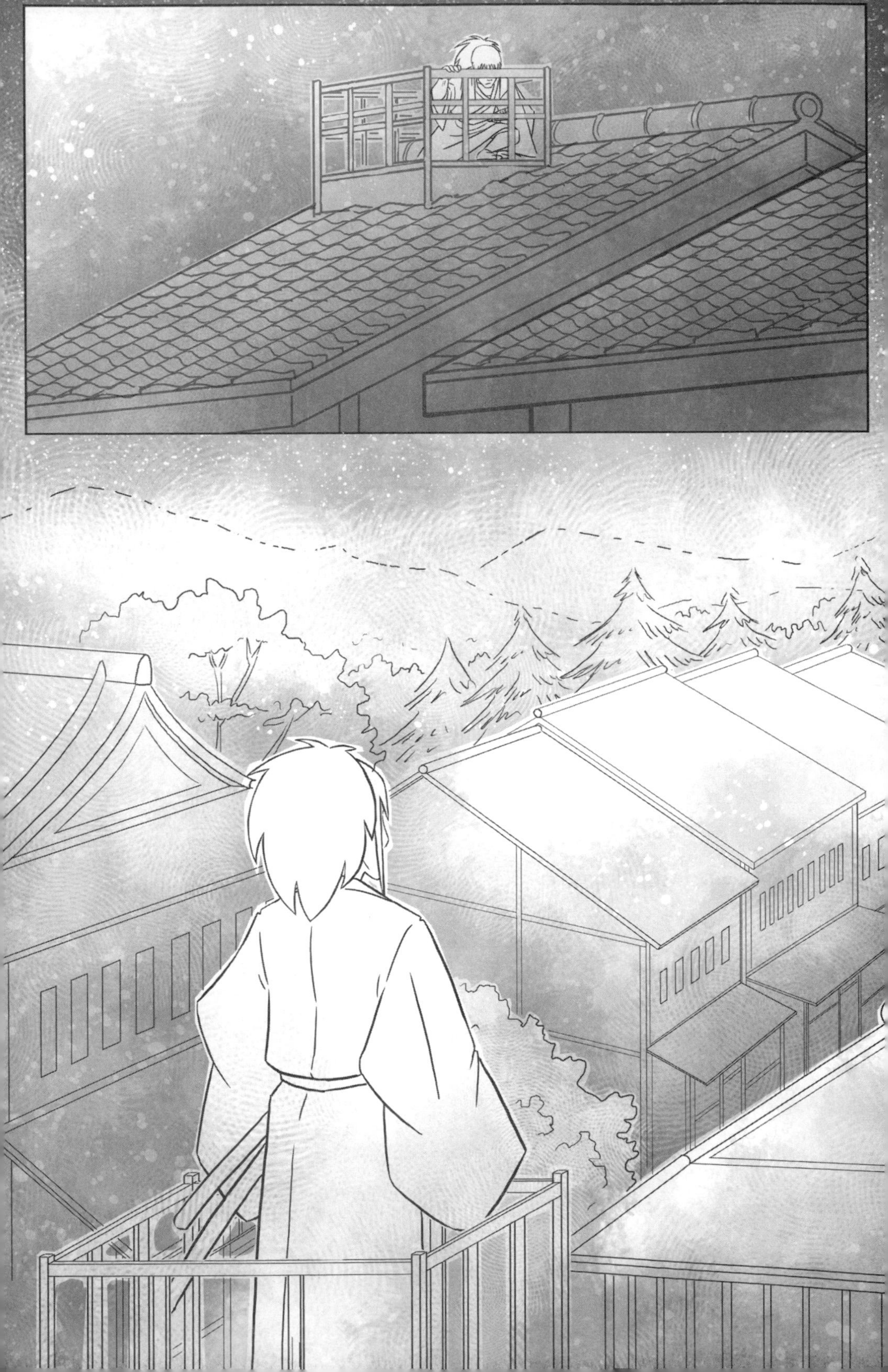

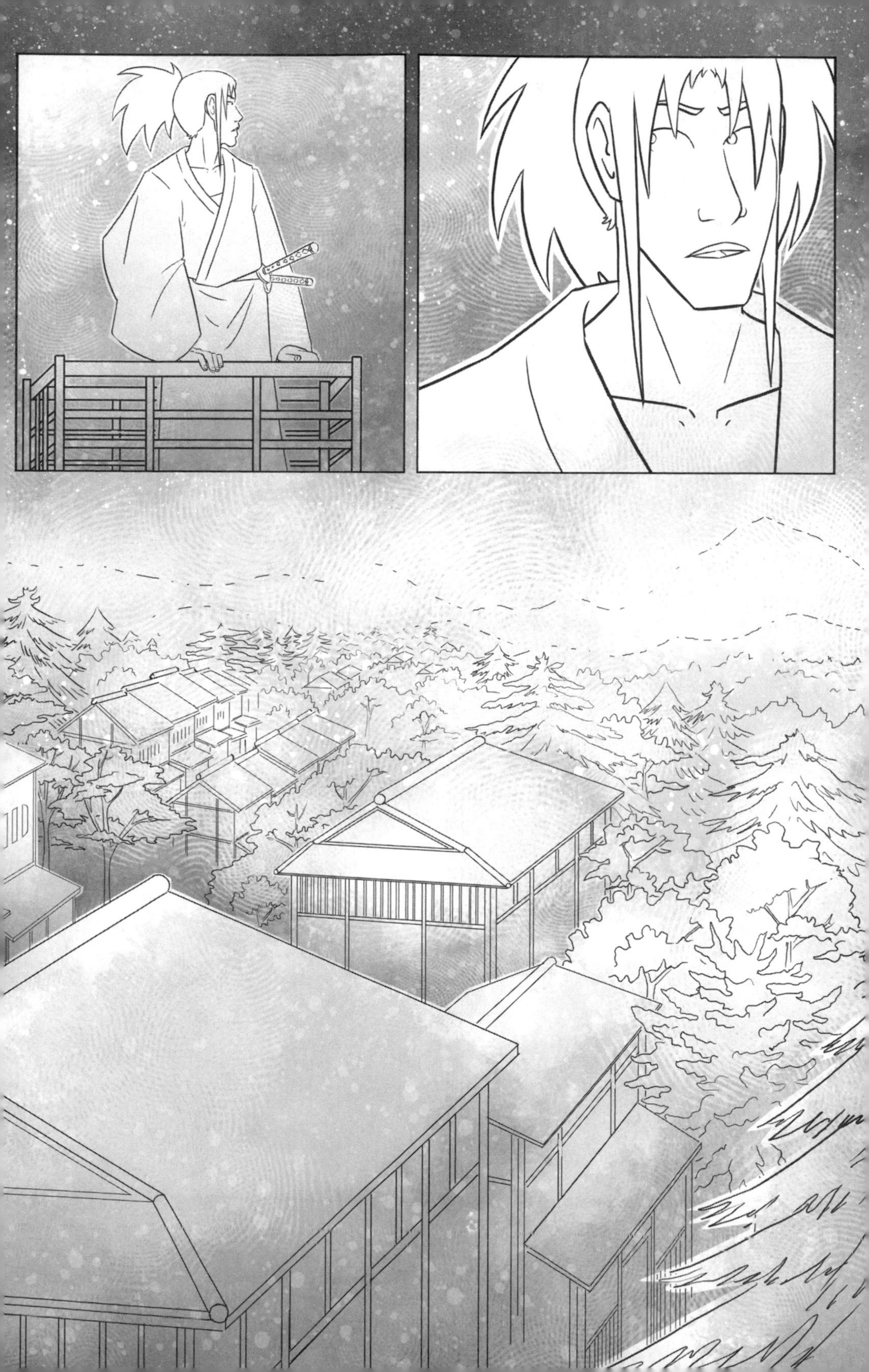

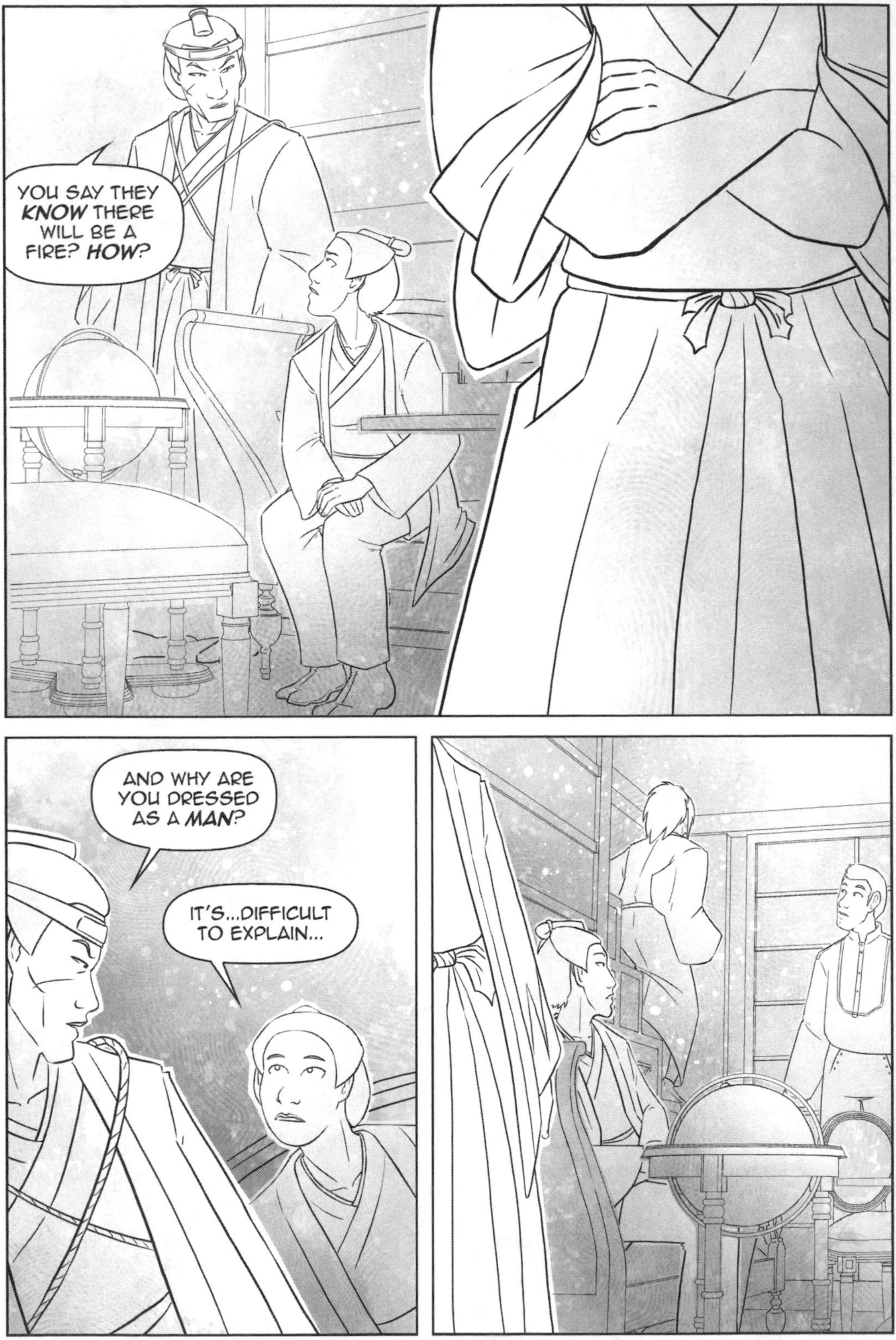
YOU SAY THEY *KNOW* THERE WILL BE A FIRE? *HOW*?
AND WHY ARE YOU DRESSED AS A *MAN*?
IT'S...DIFFICULT TO EXPLAIN...

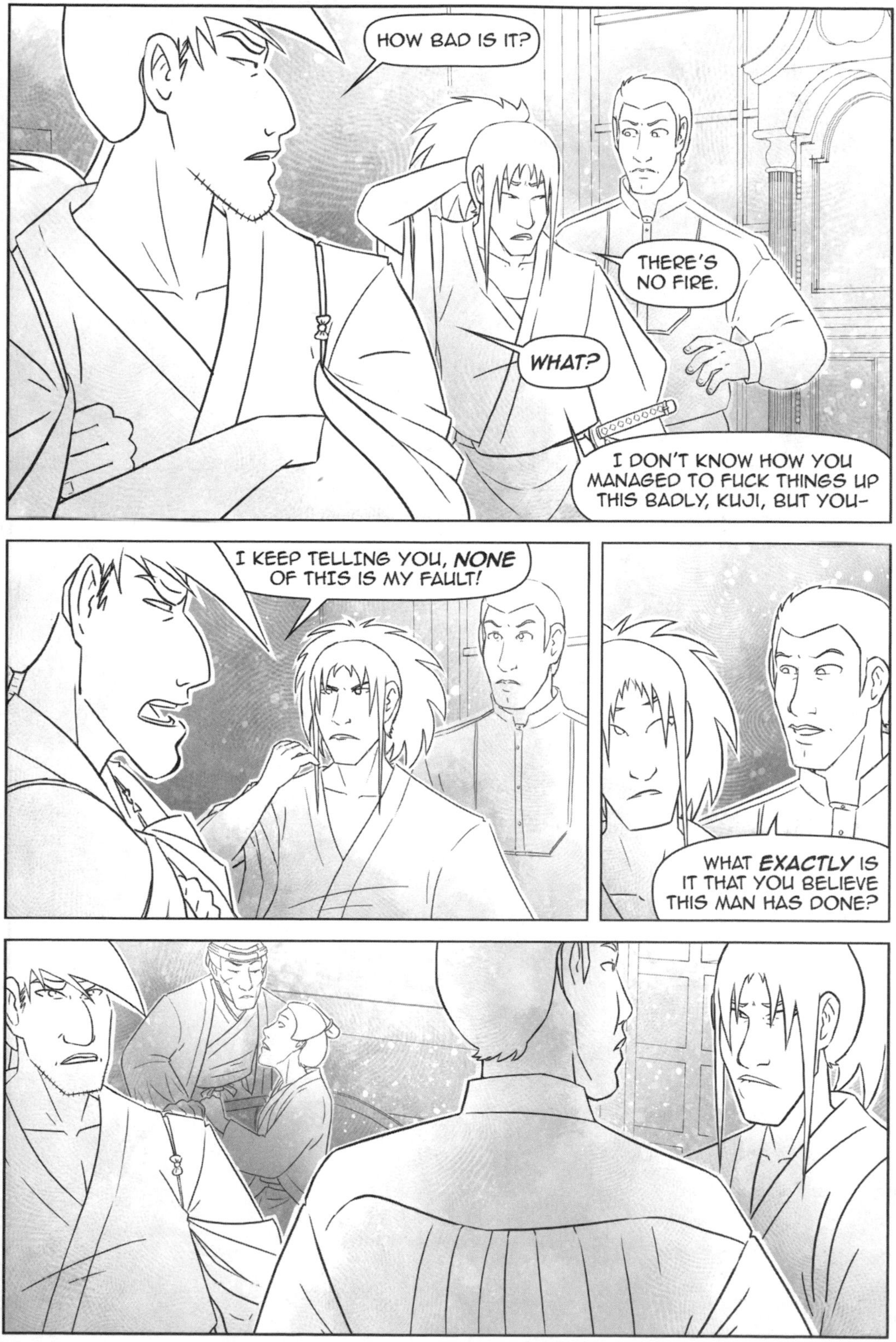
HOW BAD IS IT?
THERE'S NO FIRE.
WHAT?
I DON'T KNOW HOW YOU MANAGED TO FUCK THINGS UP THIS BADLY, KUJI, BUT YOU-
I KEEP TELLING YOU, NONE OF THIS IS MY FAULT!
WHAT EXACTLY IS IT THAT YOU BELIEVE THIS MAN HAS DONE?

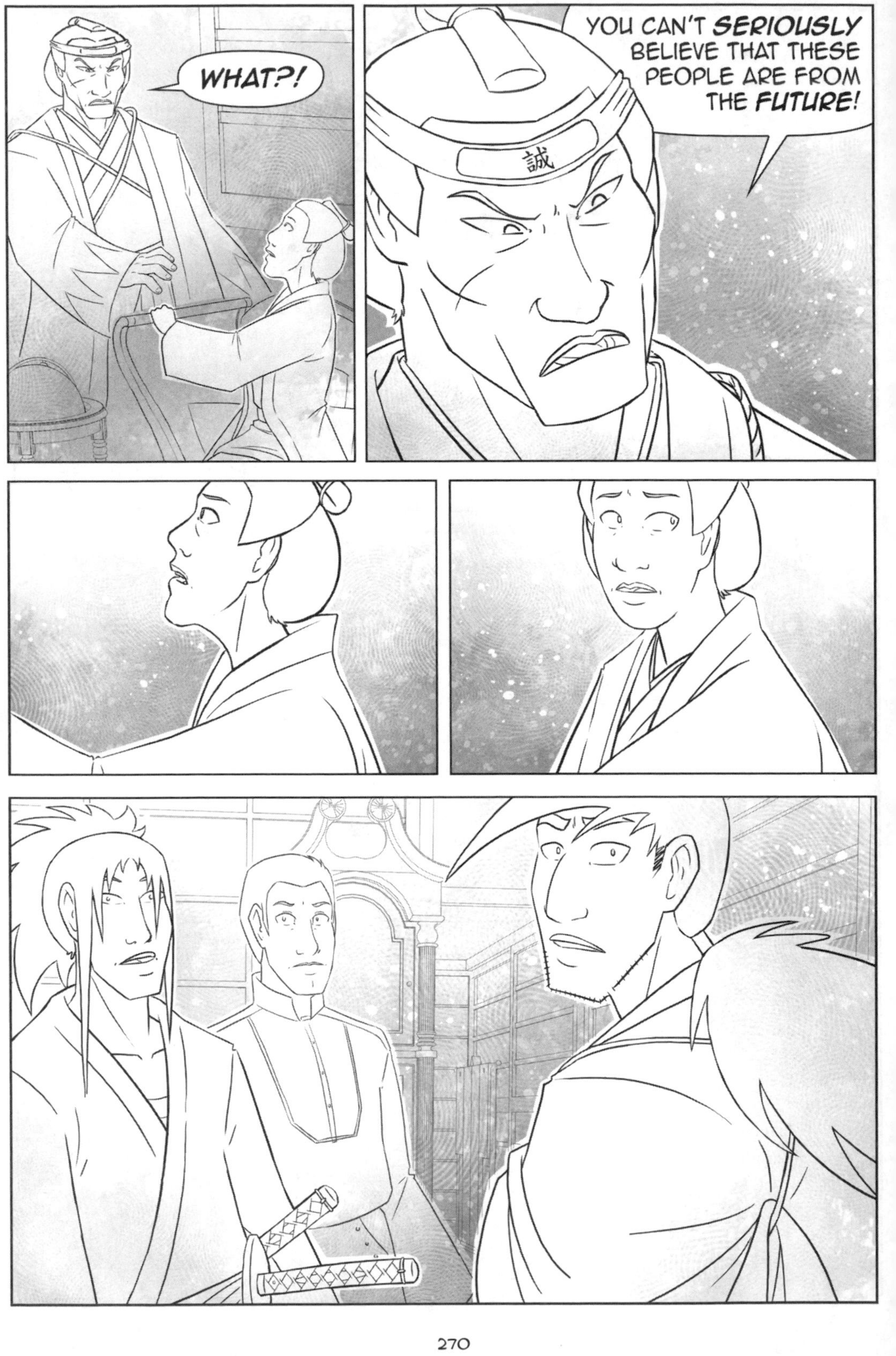
WHAT?!
YOU CAN'T SERIOUSLY BELIEVE THAT THESE PEOPLE ARE FROM THE FUTURE!
誠

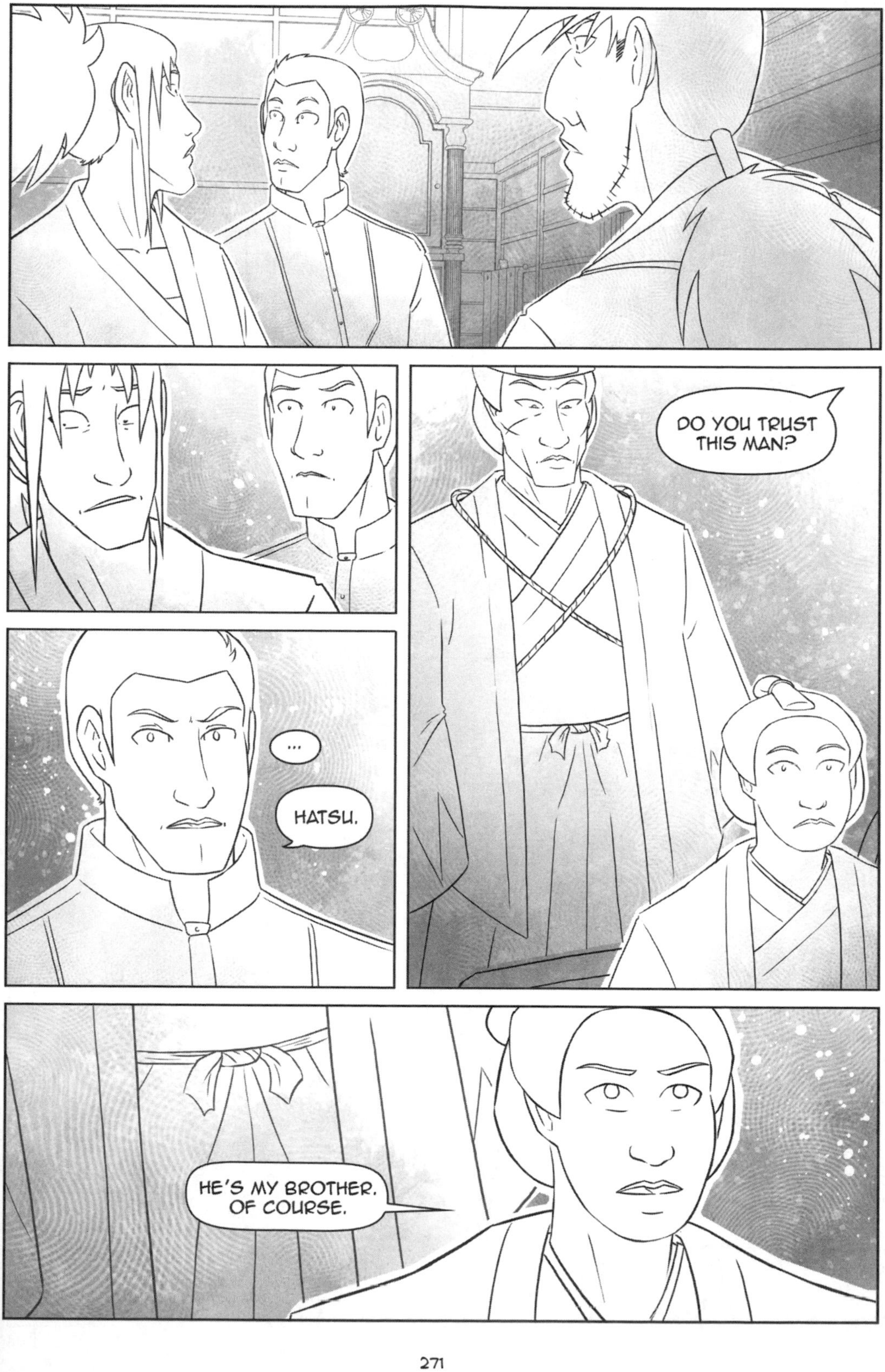
DO YOU TRUST THIS MAN?
...
HATSU.
HE'S MY BROTHER. OF COURSE.

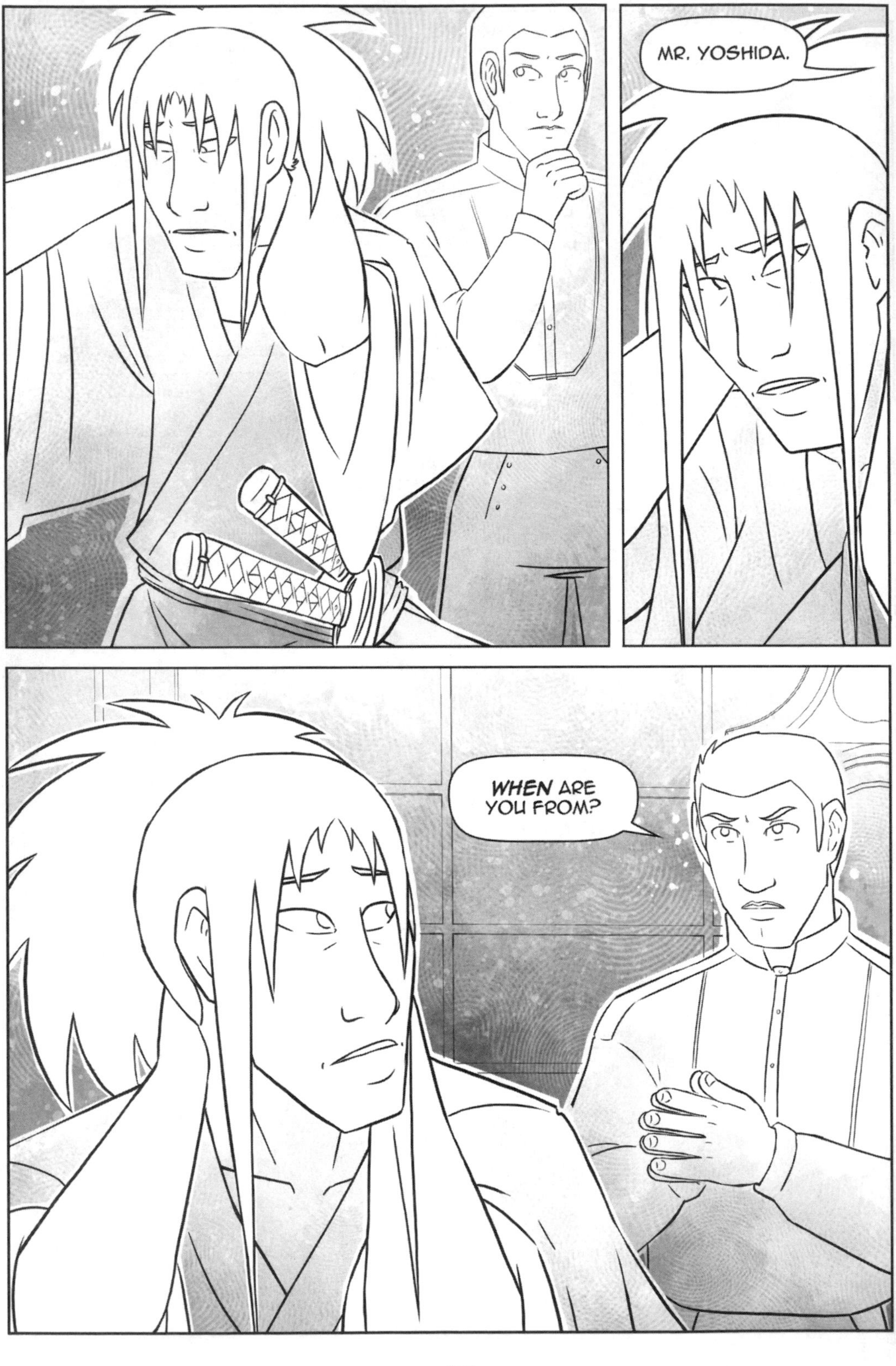
MR. YOSHIDA.
WHEN ARE YOU FROM?

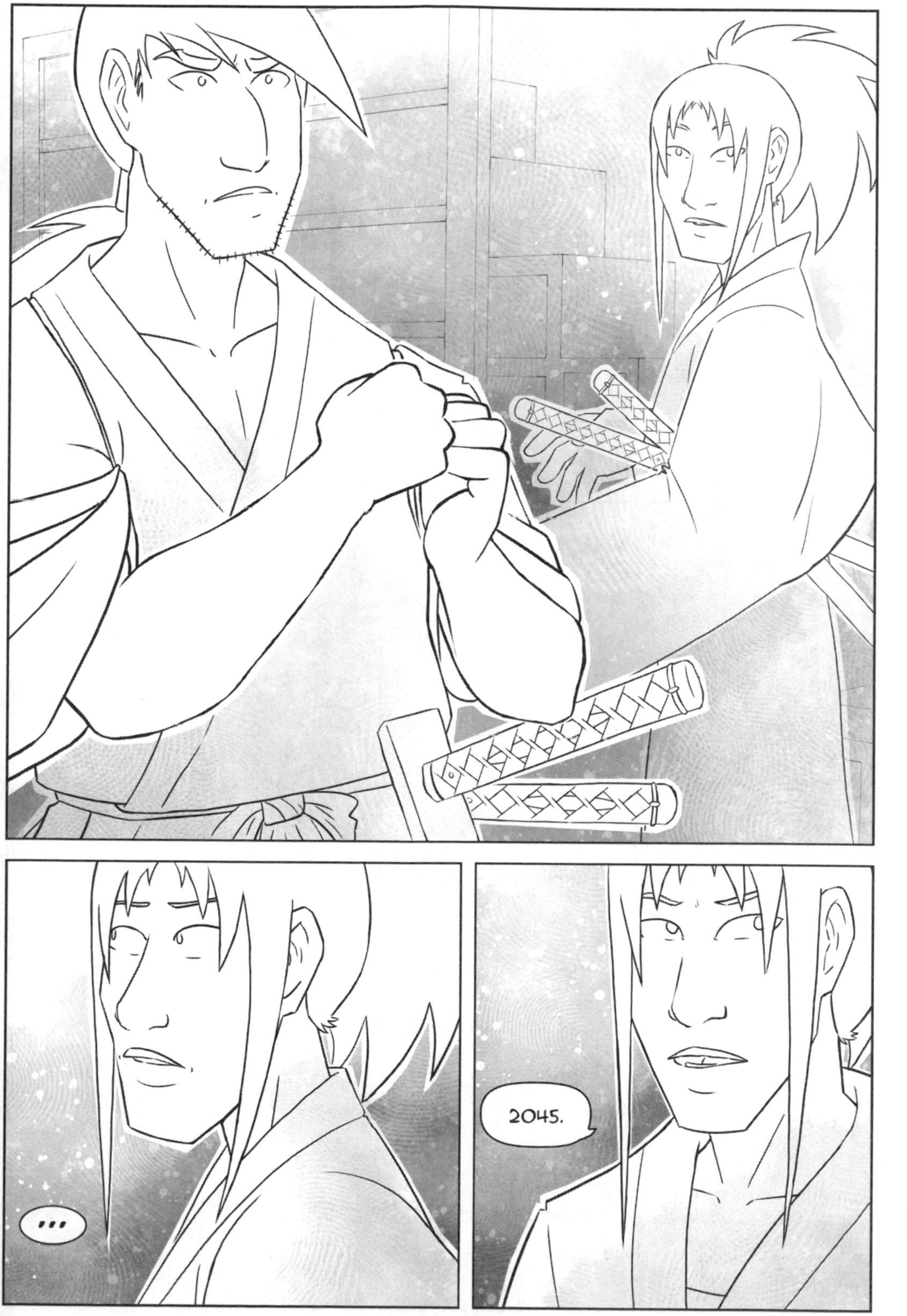
...
2045.

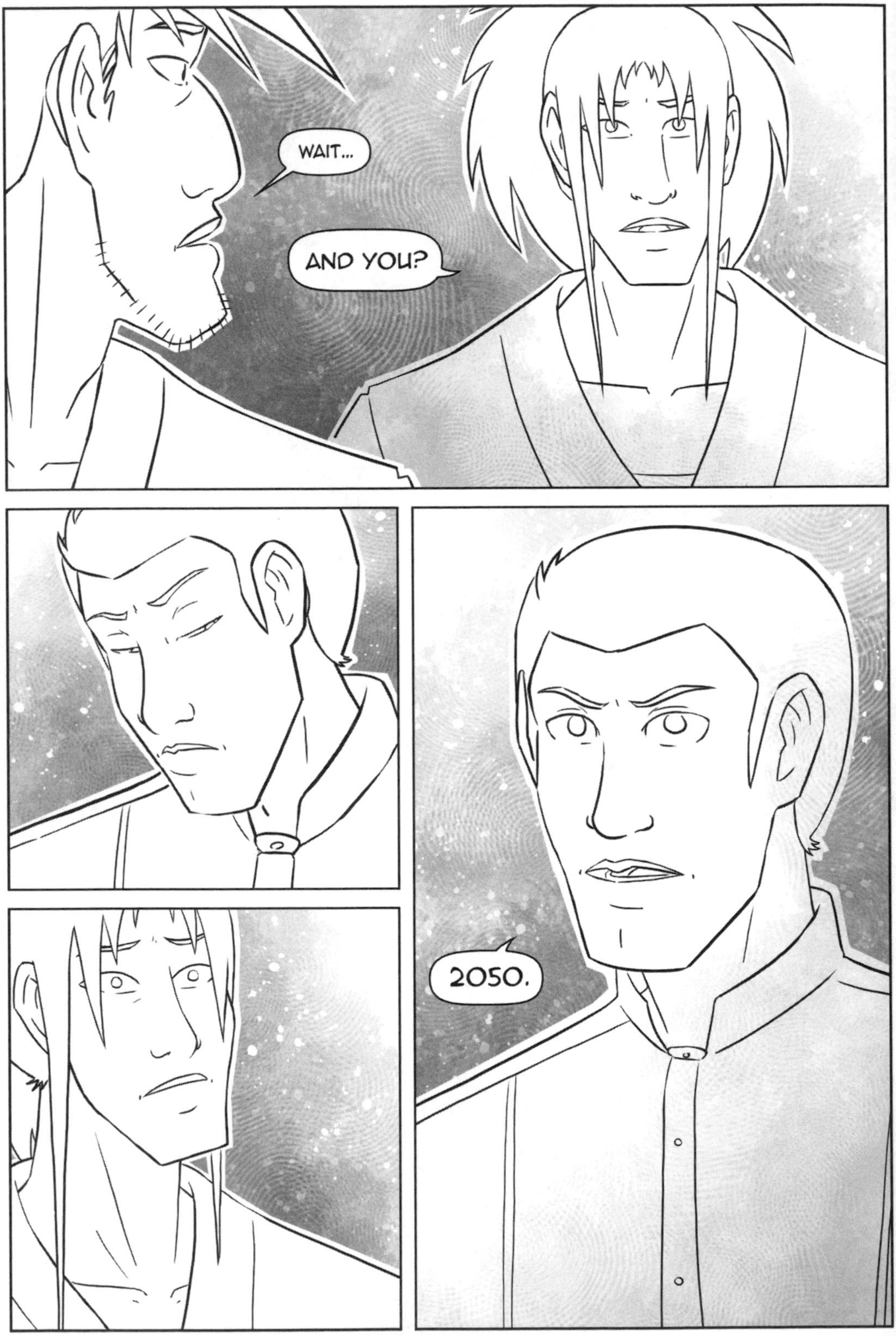
WAIT...
AND YOU?
2050.

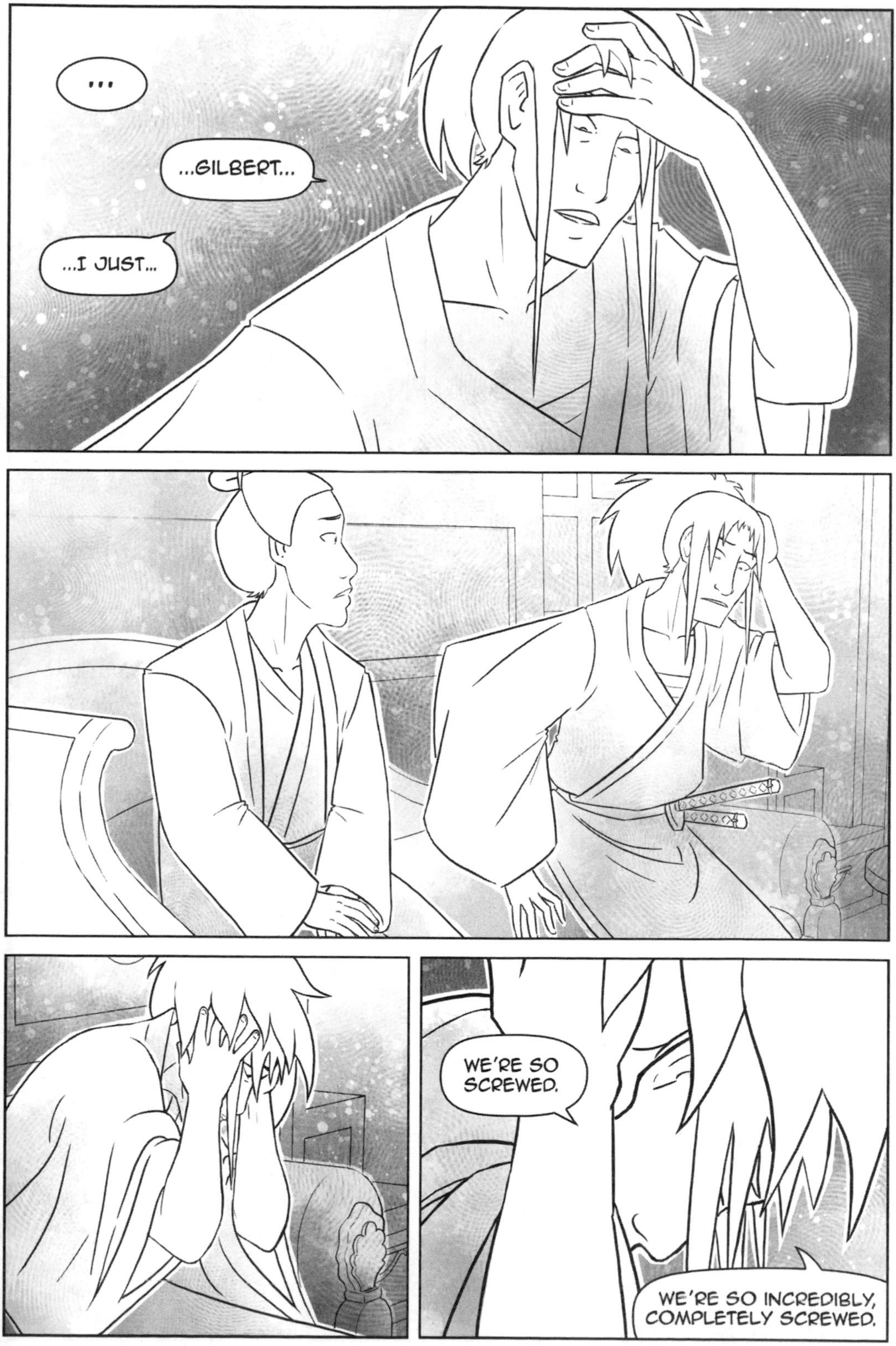
...
...GILBERT...
...I JUST...
WE'RE SO SCREWED.
WE'RE SO INCREDIBLY, COMPLETELY SCREWED.

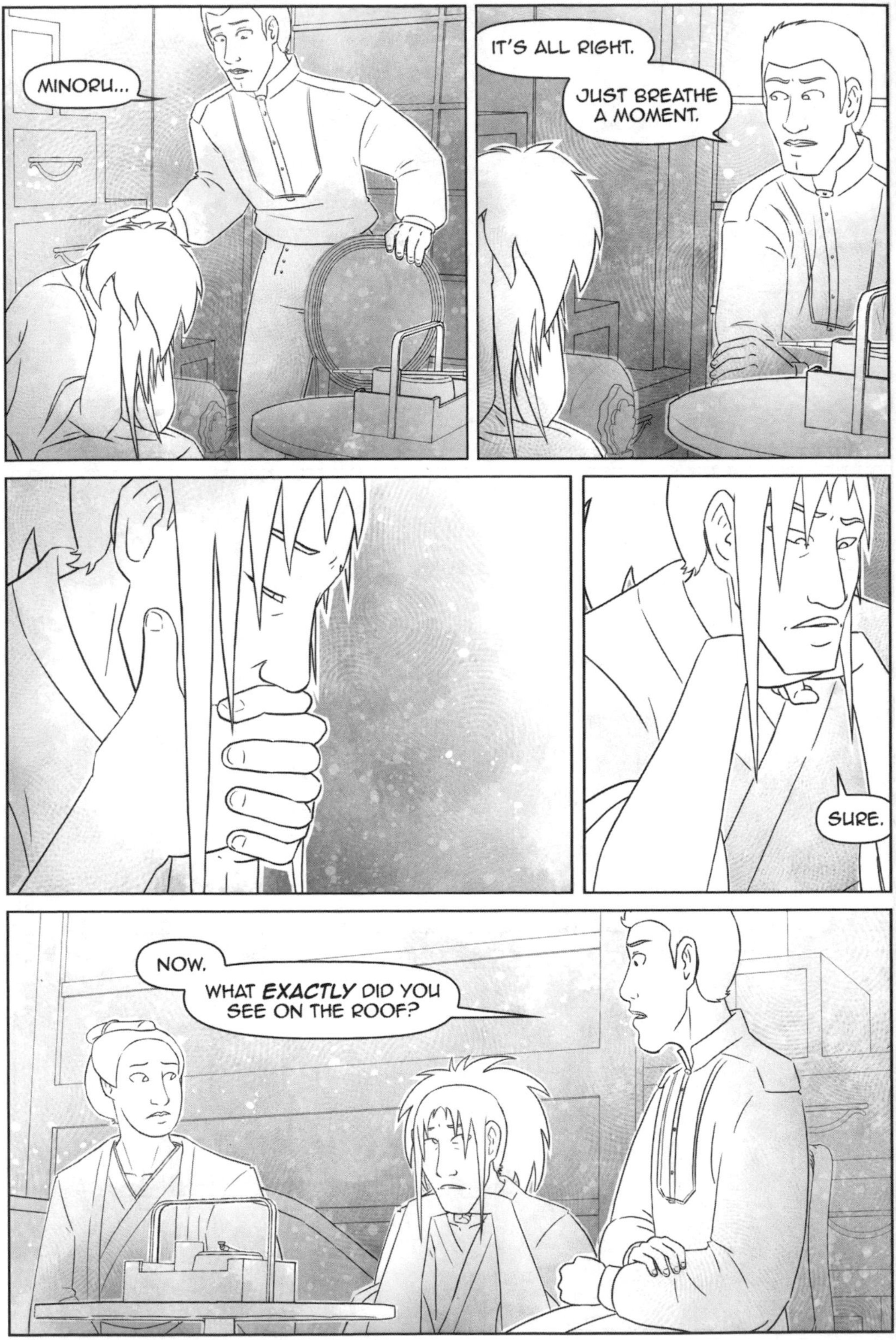
MINORU...
IT'S ALL RIGHT.
JUST BREATHE A MOMENT.
SURE.
NOW.
WHAT *EXACTLY* DID YOU SEE ON THE ROOF?

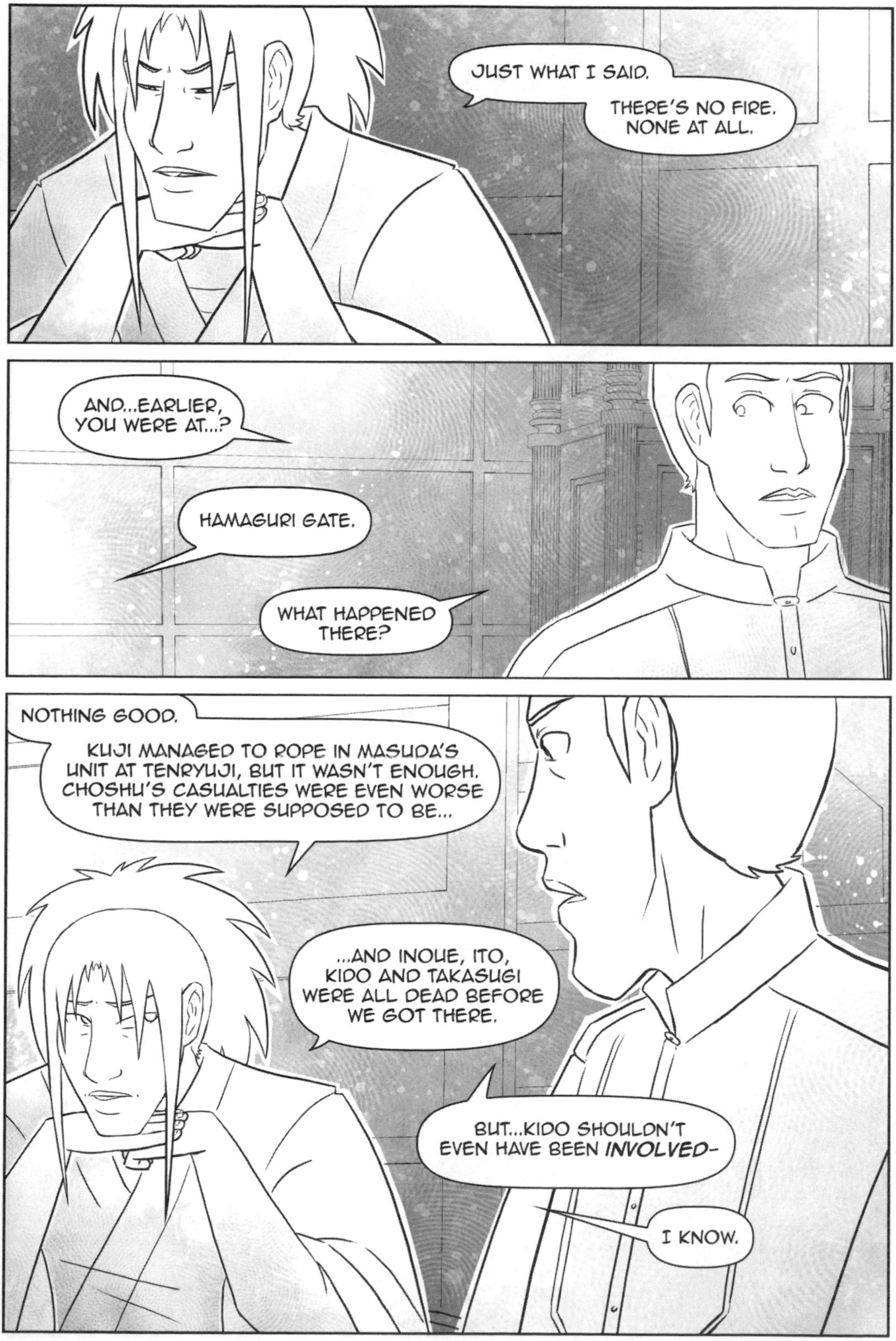
JUST WHAT I SAID.
THERE'S NO FIRE. NONE AT ALL.
AND...EARLIER, YOU WERE AT...?
HAMAGURI GATE.
WHAT HAPPENED THERE?
NOTHING GOOD.
KUJI MANAGED TO ROPE IN MASUDA'S UNIT AT TENRYUJI, BUT IT WASN'T ENOUGH. CHOSHU'S CASUALTIES WERE EVEN WORSE THAN THEY WERE SUPPOSED TO BE...
...AND INOUE, ITO, KIDO AND TAKASUGI WERE ALL DEAD BEFORE WE GOT THERE.
BUT...KIDO SHOULDN'T EVEN HAVE BEEN *INVOLVED*-
I KNOW.

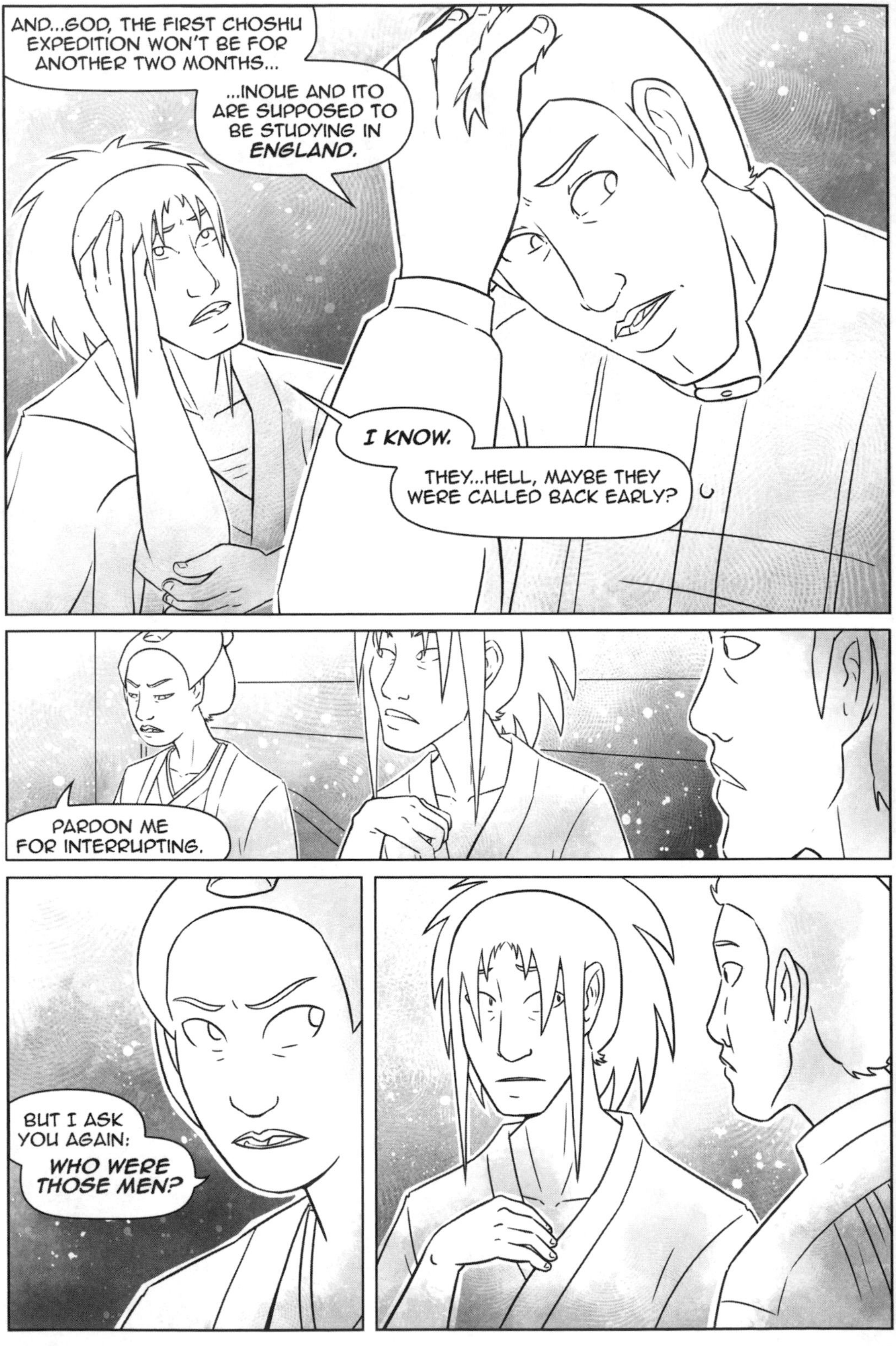
AND...GOD, THE FIRST CHOSHU EXPEDITION WON'T BE FOR ANOTHER TWO MONTHS...
...INOUE AND ITO ARE SUPPOSED TO BE STUDYING IN *ENGLAND.*
I KNOW.
THEY...HELL, MAYBE THEY WERE CALLED BACK EARLY?
PARDON ME FOR INTERRUPTING.
BUT I ASK YOU AGAIN: *WHO WERE THOSE MEN?*

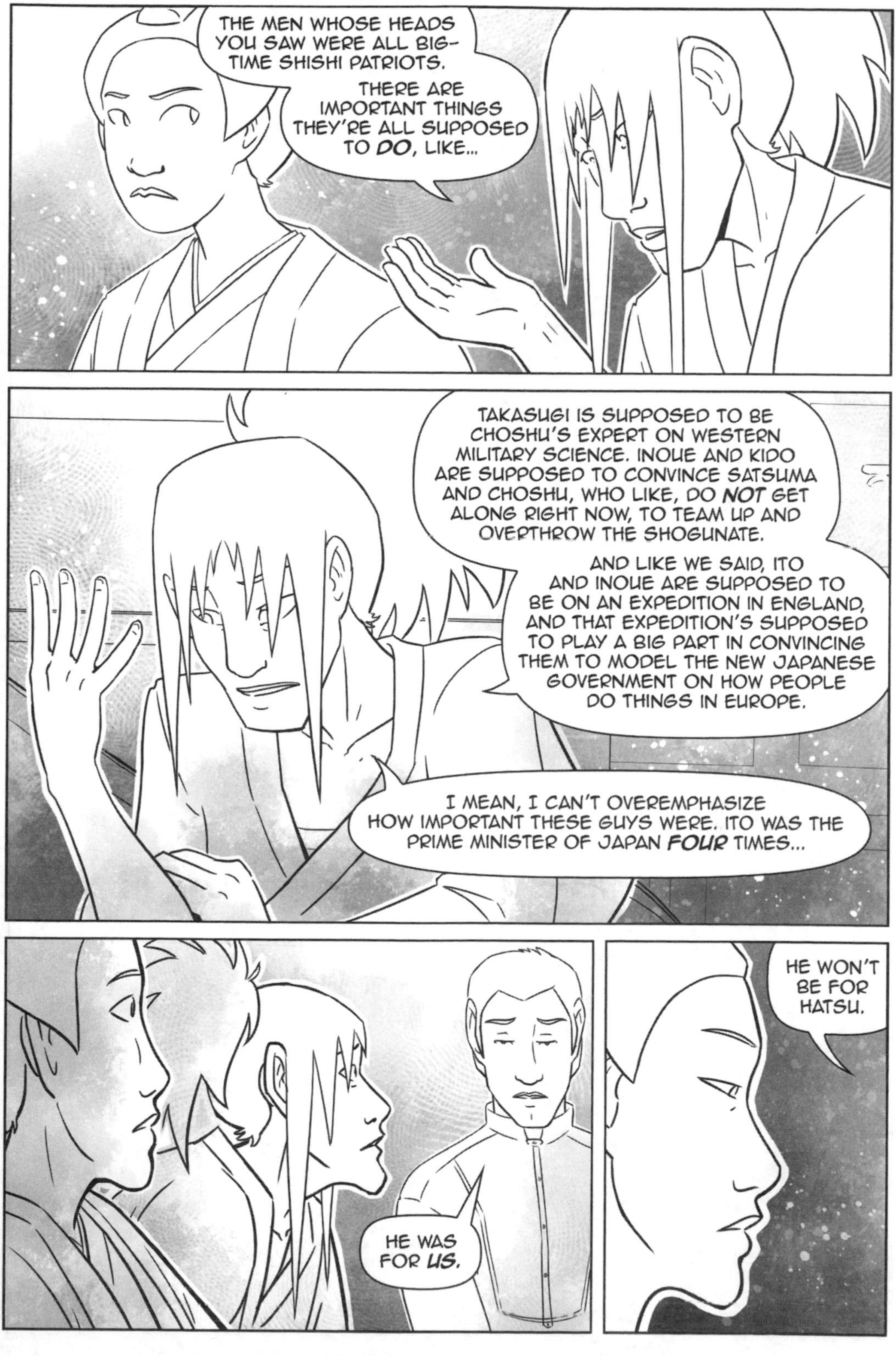
THE MEN WHOSE HEADS YOU SAW WERE ALL BIG-TIME SHISHI PATRIOTS.
THERE ARE IMPORTANT THINGS THEY'RE ALL SUPPOSED TO DO, LIKE...
TAKASUGI IS SUPPOSED TO BE CHOSHU'S EXPERT ON WESTERN MILITARY SCIENCE. INOUE AND KIDO ARE SUPPOSED TO CONVINCE SATSUMA AND CHOSHU, WHO LIKE, DO NOT GET ALONG RIGHT NOW, TO TEAM UP AND OVERTHROW THE SHOGUNATE.
AND LIKE WE SAID, ITO AND INOUE ARE SUPPOSED TO BE ON AN EXPEDITION IN ENGLAND, AND THAT EXPEDITION'S SUPPOSED TO PLAY A BIG PART IN CONVINCING THEM TO MODEL THE NEW JAPANESE GOVERNMENT ON HOW PEOPLE DO THINGS IN EUROPE.
I MEAN, I CAN'T OVEREMPHASIZE HOW IMPORTANT THESE GUYS WERE. ITO WAS THE PRIME MINISTER OF JAPAN FOUR TIMES...
HE WAS FOR US.
HE WON'T BE FOR HATSU.

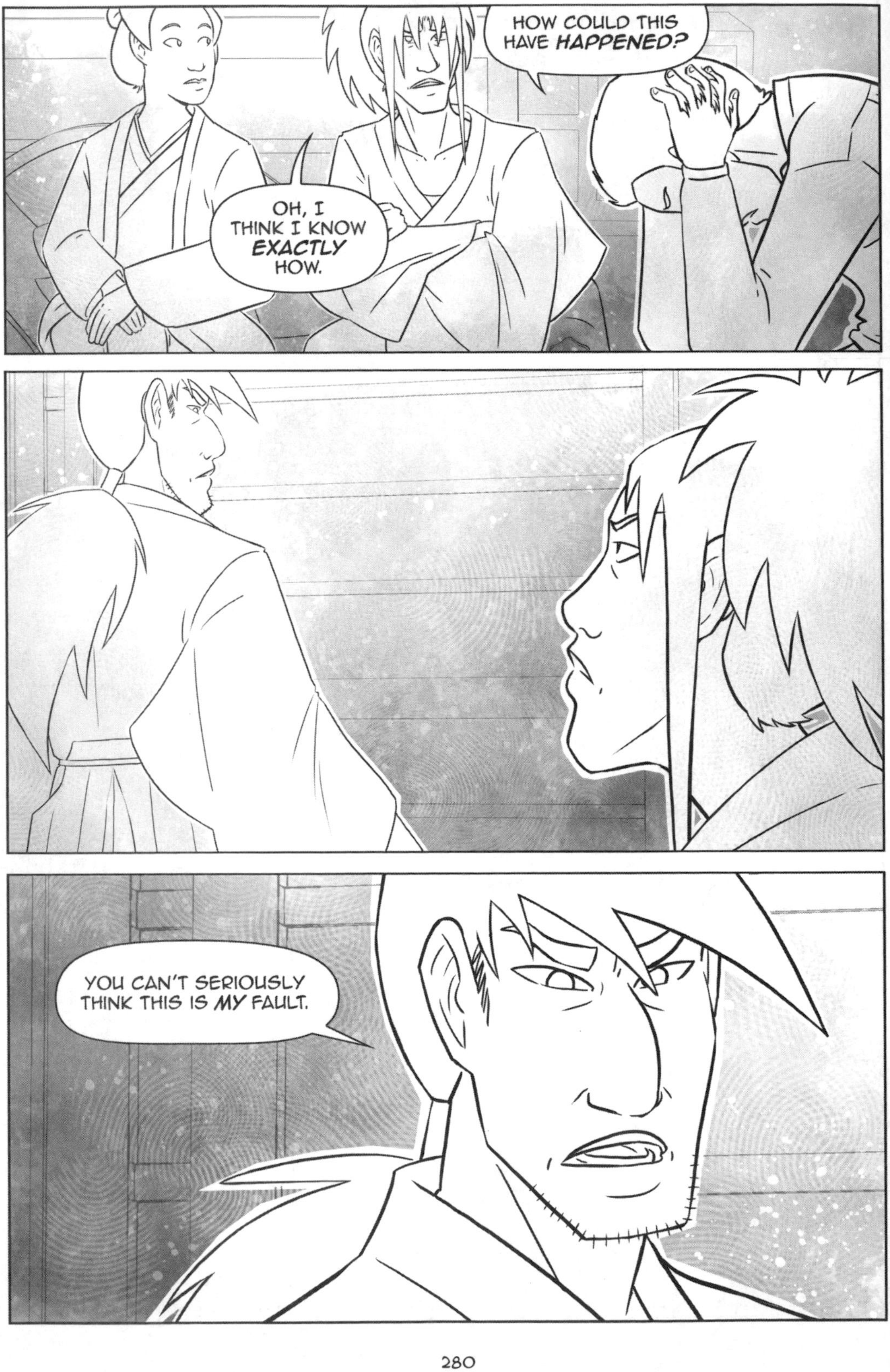
HOW COULD THIS HAVE HAPPENED?
OH, I THINK I KNOW EXACTLY HOW.
YOU CAN'T SERIOUSLY THINK THIS IS MY FAULT.

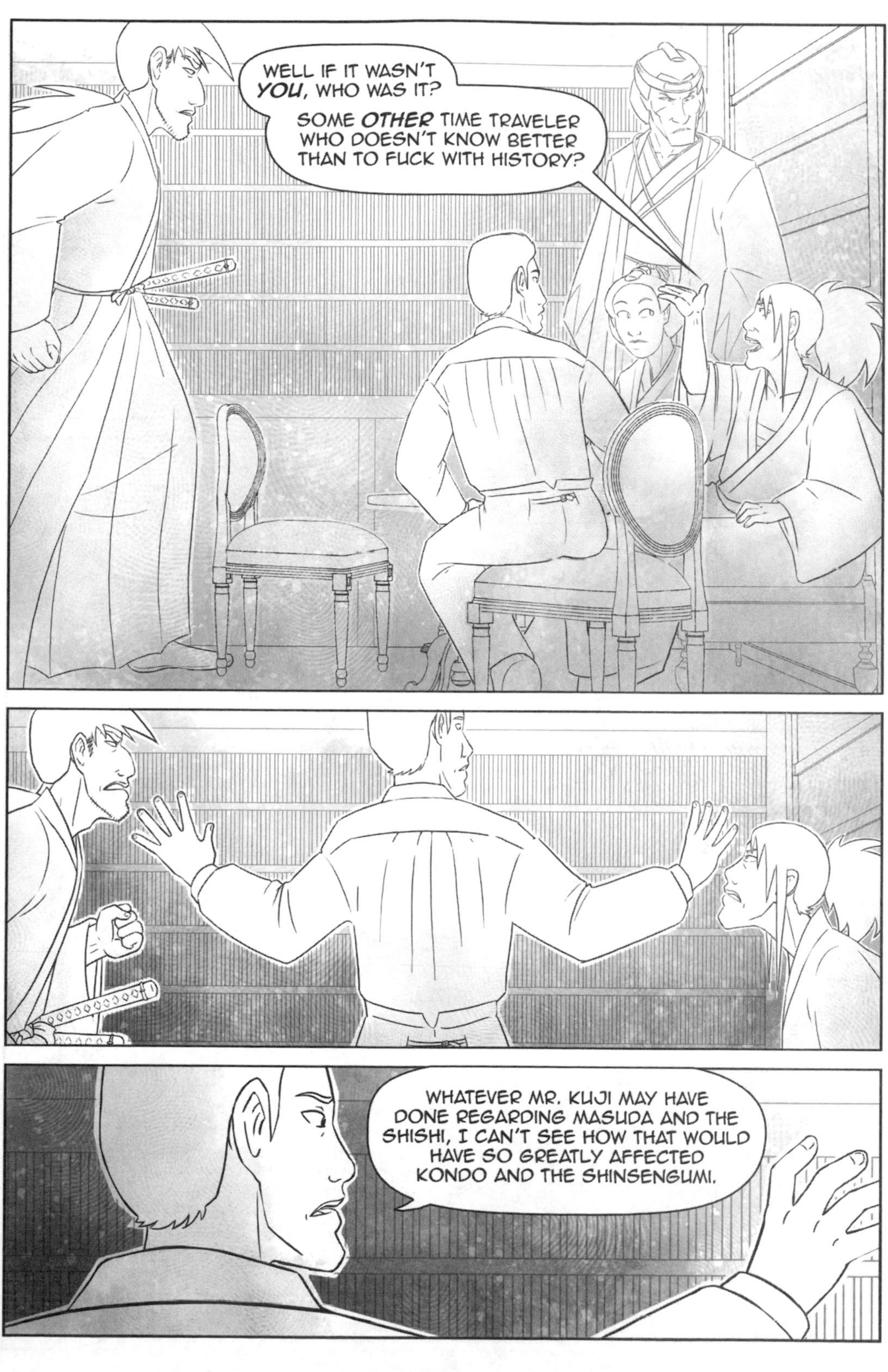
WELL IF IT WASN'T *YOU*, WHO WAS IT?
SOME *OTHER* TIME TRAVELER WHO DOESN'T KNOW BETTER THAN TO FUCK WITH HISTORY?
WHATEVER MR. KUJI MAY HAVE DONE REGARDING MASUDA AND THE SHISHI, I CAN'T SEE HOW THAT WOULD HAVE SO GREATLY AFFECTED KONDO AND THE SHINSENGUMI.

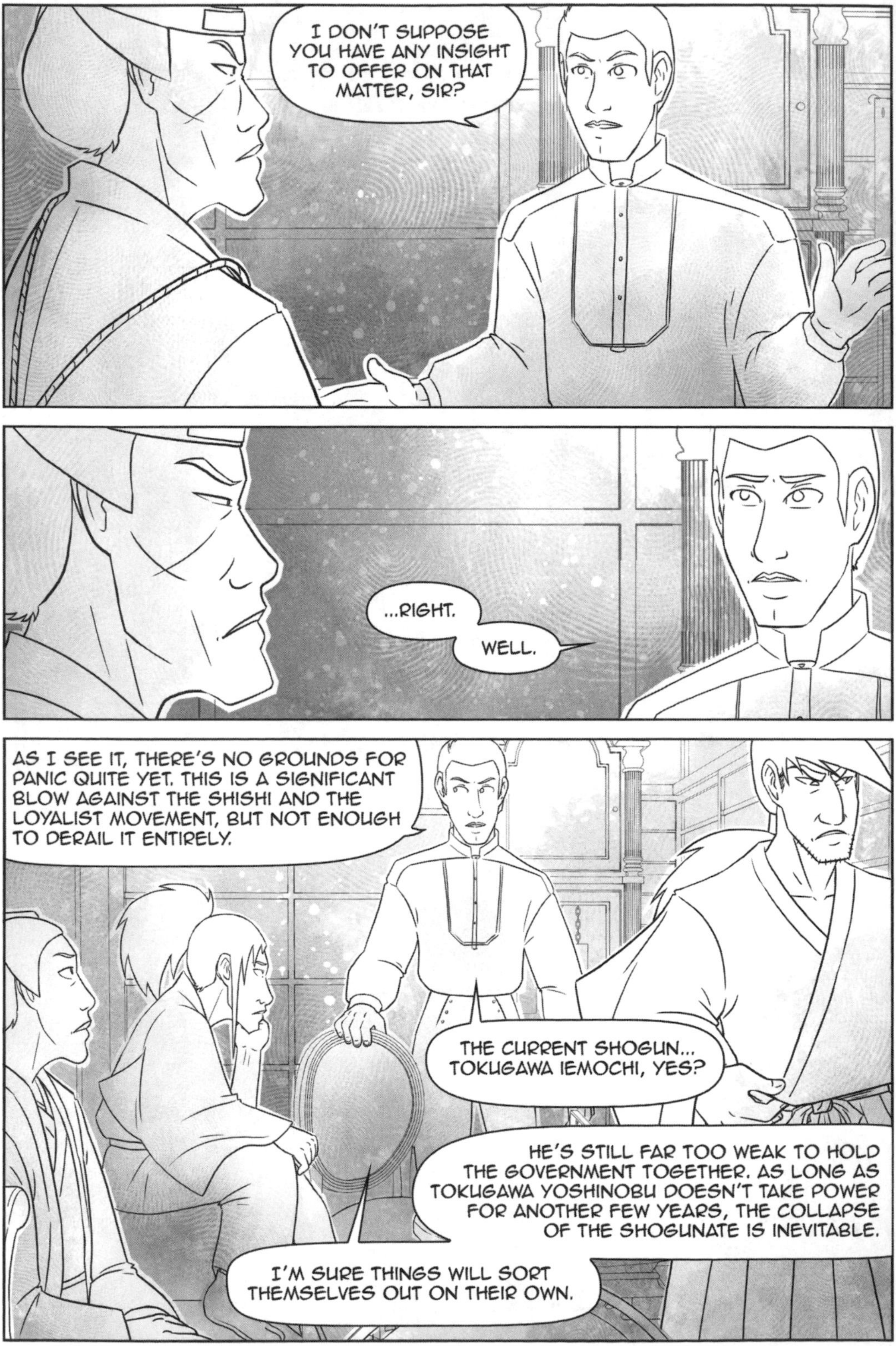
I DON'T SUPPOSE YOU HAVE ANY INSIGHT TO OFFER ON THAT MATTER, SIR?
...RIGHT.
WELL.
AS I SEE IT, THERE'S NO GROUNDS FOR PANIC QUITE YET. THIS IS A SIGNIFICANT BLOW AGAINST THE SHISHI AND THE LOYALIST MOVEMENT, BUT NOT ENOUGH TO DERAIL IT ENTIRELY.
THE CURRENT SHOGUN... TOKUGAWA IEMOCHI, YES?
HE'S STILL FAR TOO WEAK TO HOLD THE GOVERNMENT TOGETHER. AS LONG AS TOKUGAWA YOSHINOBU DOESN'T TAKE POWER FOR ANOTHER FEW YEARS, THE COLLAPSE OF THE SHOGUNATE IS INEVITABLE.
I'M SURE THINGS WILL SORT THEMSELVES OUT ON THEIR OWN.

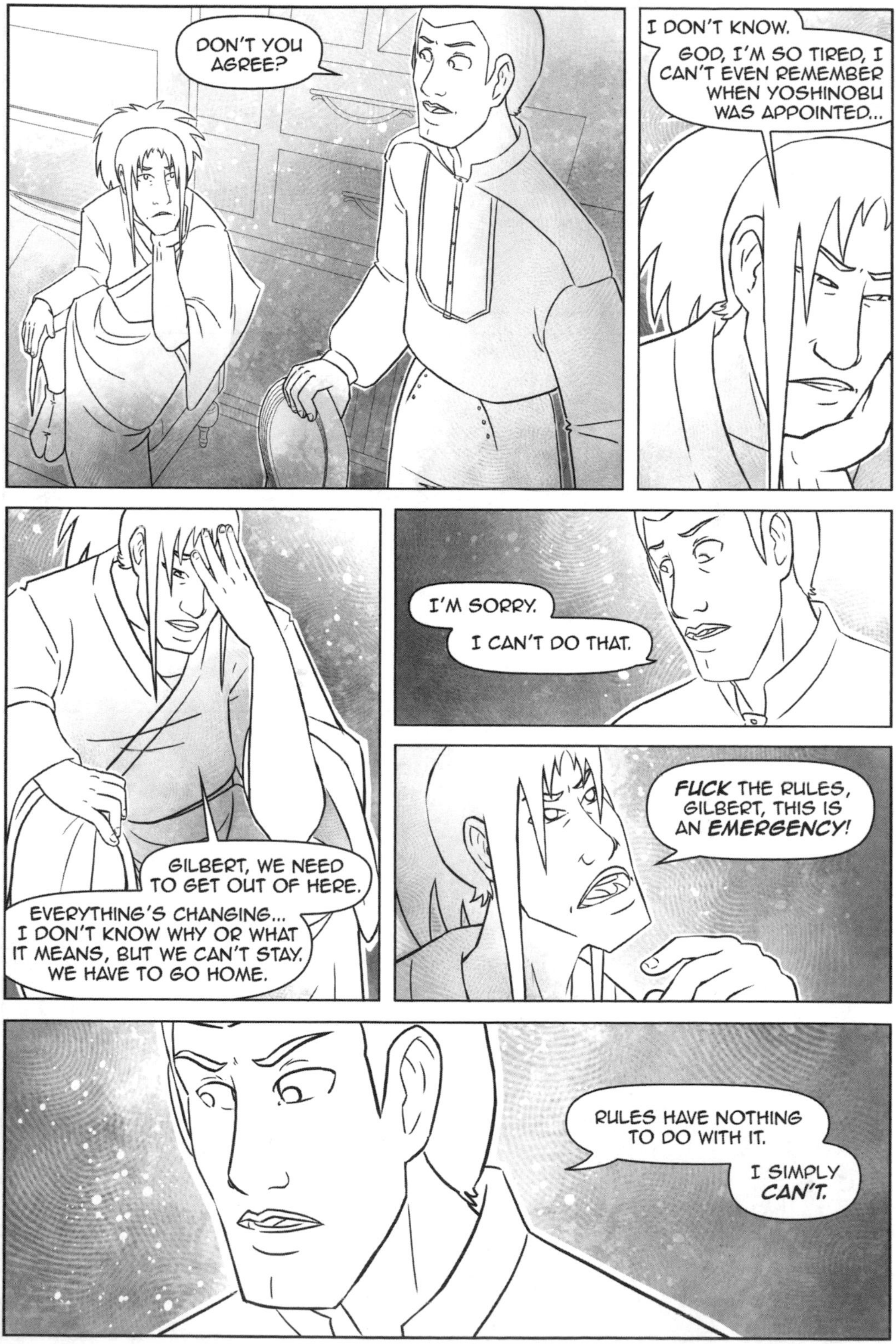
DON'T YOU AGREE?
I DON'T KNOW.
GOD, I'M SO TIRED, I CAN'T EVEN REMEMBER WHEN YOSHINOBU WAS APPOINTED...
GILBERT, WE NEED TO GET OUT OF HERE.
EVERYTHING'S CHANGING... I DON'T KNOW WHY OR WHAT IT MEANS, BUT WE CAN'T STAY. WE HAVE TO GO HOME.
I'M SORRY.
I CAN'T DO THAT.
FUCK THE RULES, GILBERT, THIS IS AN EMERGENCY!
RULES HAVE NOTHING TO DO WITH IT.
I SIMPLY CAN'T.

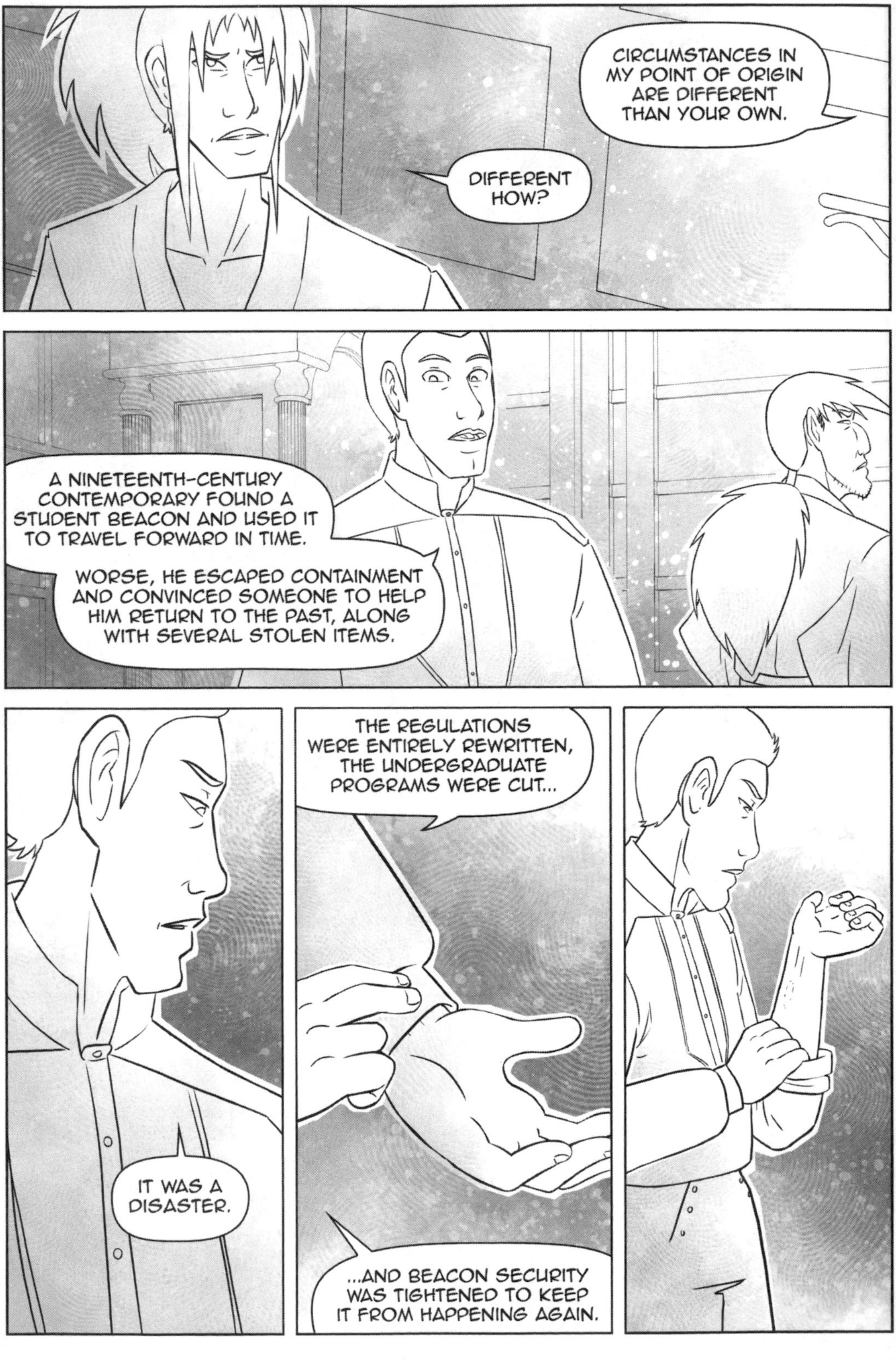
CIRCUMSTANCES IN MY POINT OF ORIGIN ARE DIFFERENT THAN YOUR OWN.
DIFFERENT HOW?
A NINETEENTH-CENTURY CONTEMPORARY FOUND A STUDENT BEACON AND USED IT TO TRAVEL FORWARD IN TIME.
WORSE, HE ESCAPED CONTAINMENT AND CONVINCED SOMEONE TO HELP HIM RETURN TO THE PAST, ALONG WITH SEVERAL STOLEN ITEMS.
IT WAS A DISASTER.
THE REGULATIONS WERE ENTIRELY REWRITTEN, THE UNDERGRADUATE PROGRAMS WERE CUT...
...AND BEACON SECURITY WAS TIGHTENED TO KEEP IT FROM HAPPENING AGAIN.

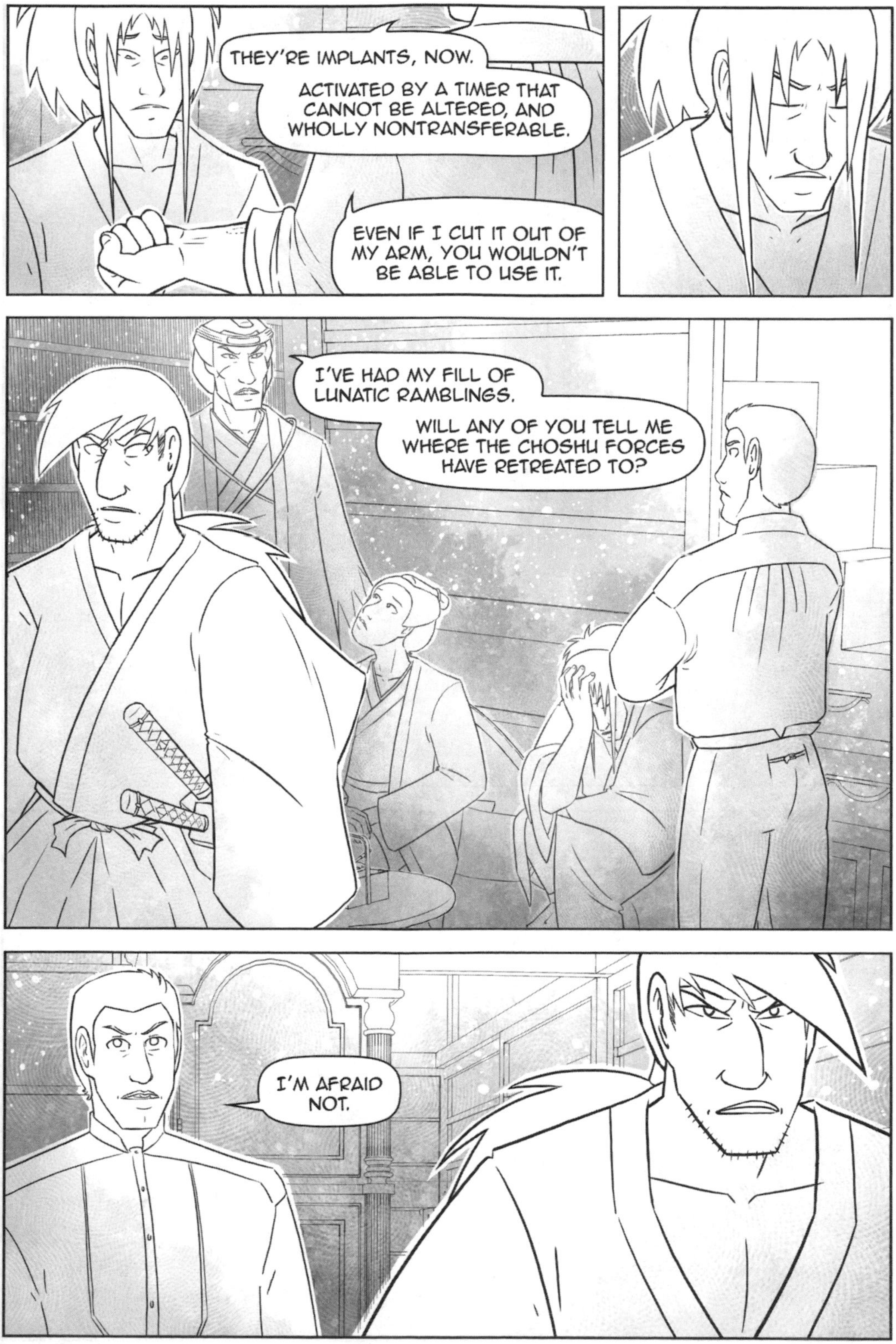
THEY'RE IMPLANTS, NOW.
ACTIVATED BY A TIMER THAT CANNOT BE ALTERED, AND WHOLLY NONTRANSFERABLE.
EVEN IF I CUT IT OUT OF MY ARM, YOU WOULDN'T BE ABLE TO USE IT.
I'VE HAD MY FILL OF LUNATIC RAMBLINGS.
WILL ANY OF YOU TELL ME WHERE THE CHOSHU FORCES HAVE RETREATED TO?
I'M AFRAID NOT.

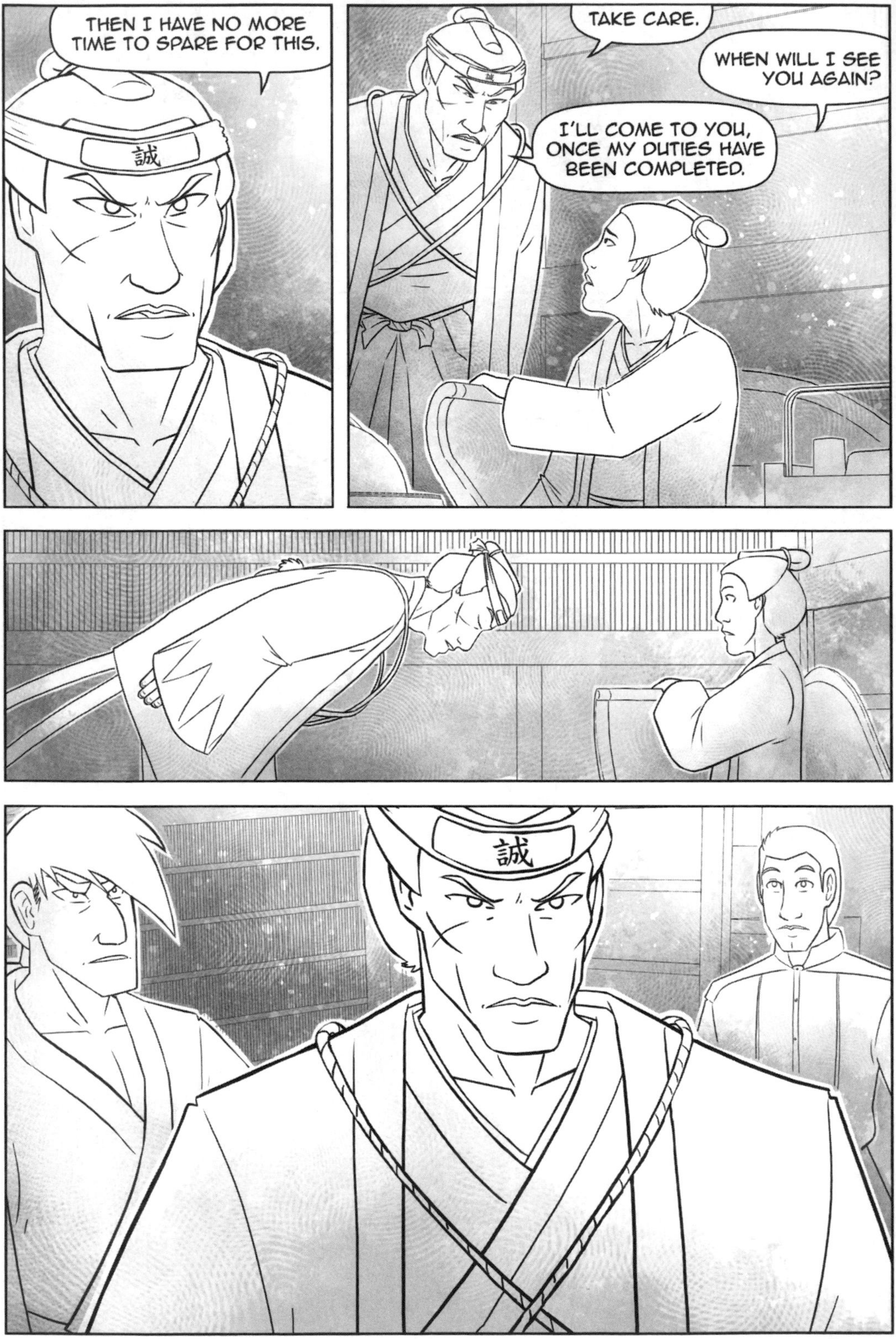
THEN I HAVE NO MORE TIME TO SPARE FOR THIS.
TAKE CARE.
WHEN WILL I SEE YOU AGAIN?
I'LL COME TO YOU, ONCE MY DUTIES HAVE BEEN COMPLETED.
誠

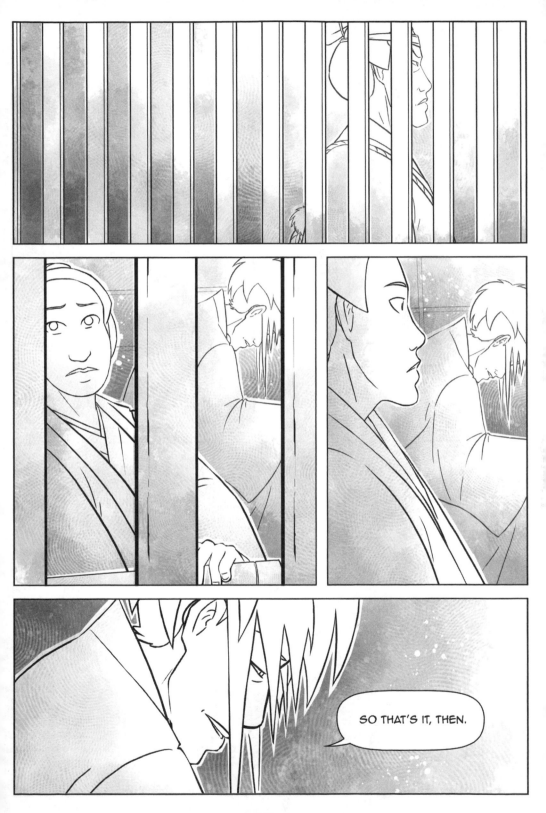

SO THAT'S IT, THEN.

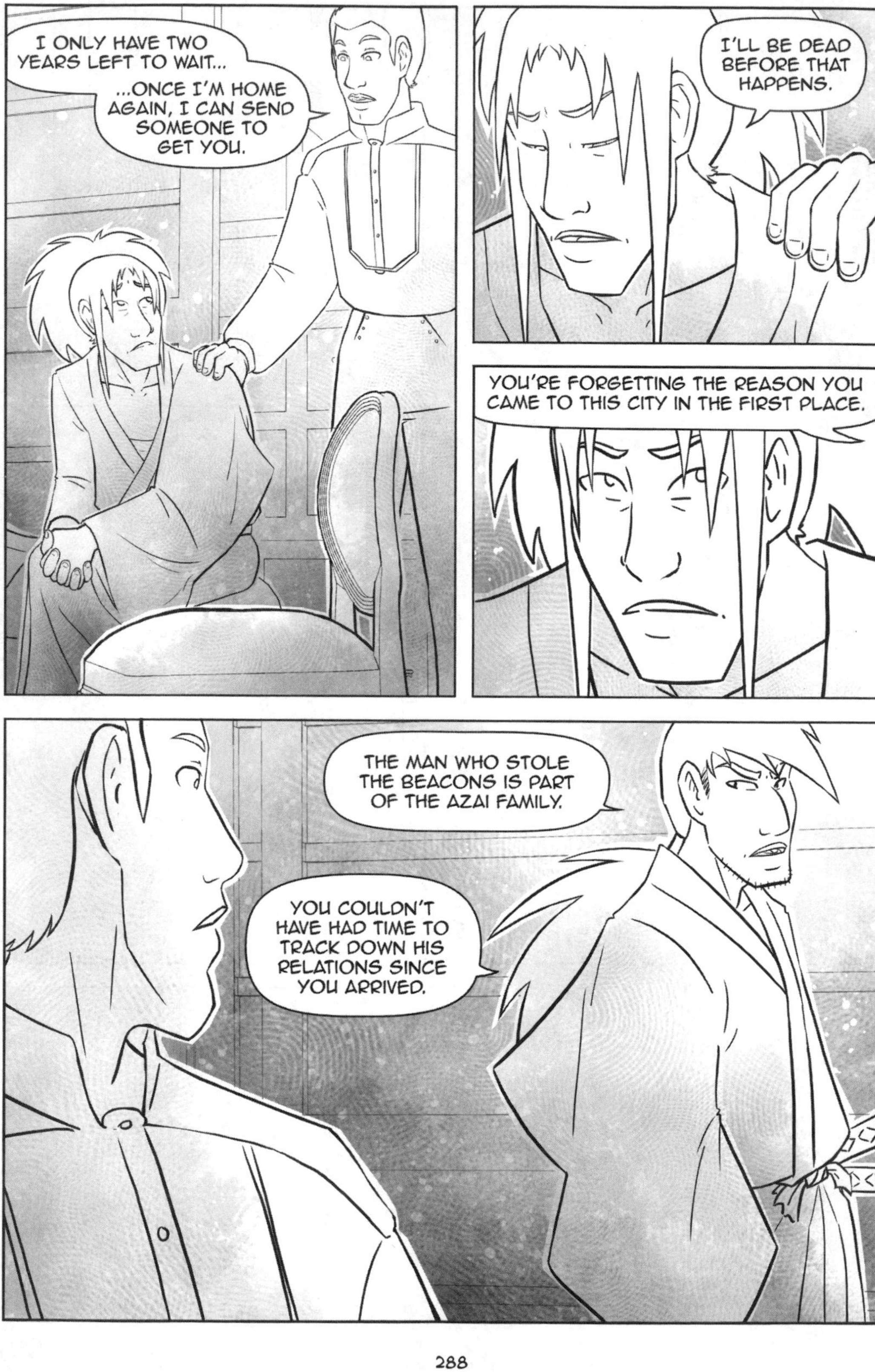

I ONLY HAVE TWO YEARS LEFT TO WAIT...
...ONCE I'M HOME AGAIN, I CAN SEND SOMEONE TO GET YOU.
I'LL BE DEAD BEFORE THAT HAPPENS.
YOU'RE FORGETTING THE REASON YOU CAME TO THIS CITY IN THE FIRST PLACE.
THE MAN WHO STOLE THE BEACONS IS PART OF THE AZAI FAMILY.
YOU COULDN'T HAVE HAD TIME TO TRACK DOWN HIS RELATIONS SINCE YOU ARRIVED.

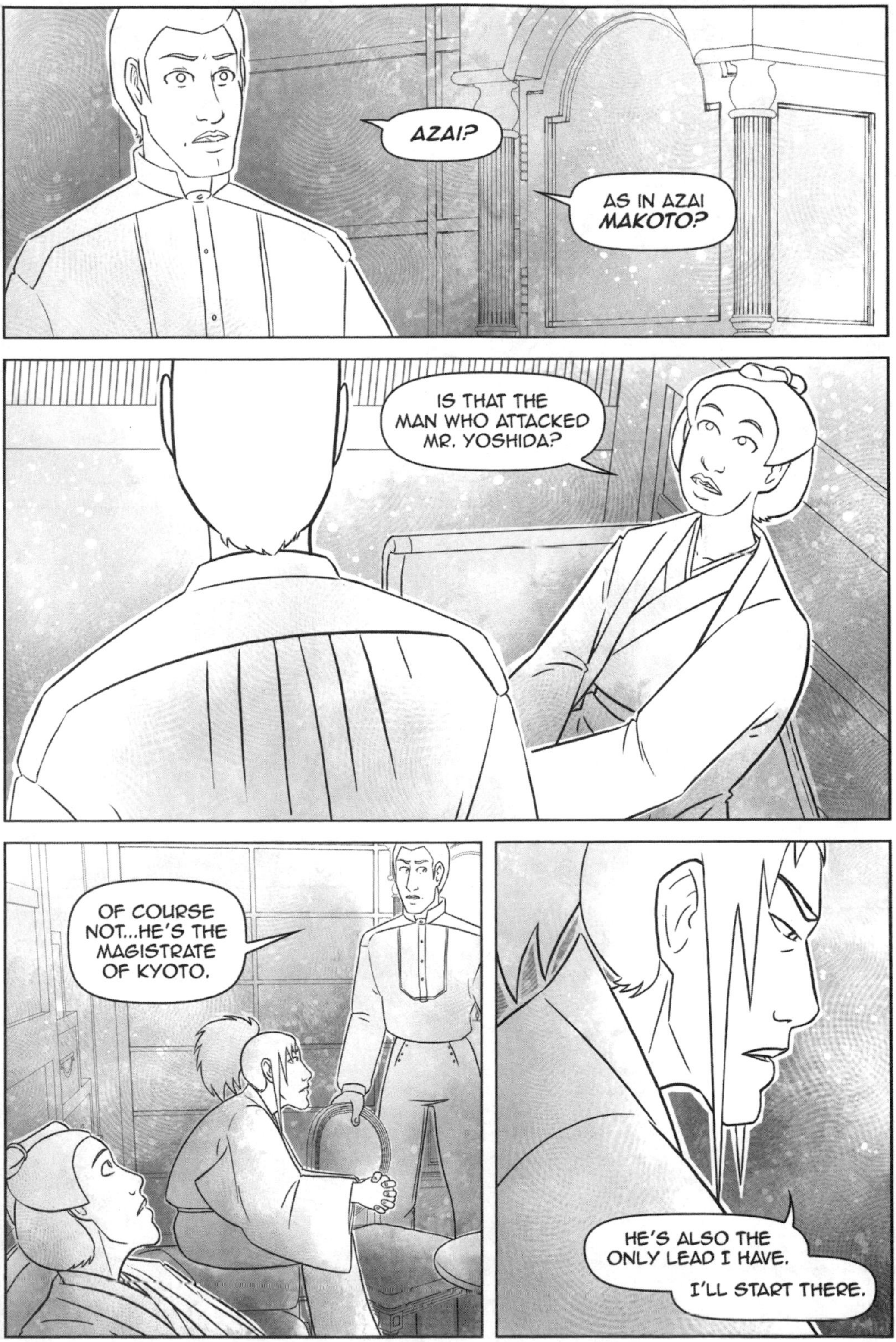
AZAI?
AS IN AZAI MAKOTO?
IS THAT THE MAN WHO ATTACKED MR. YOSHIDA?
OF COURSE NOT...HE'S THE MAGISTRATE OF KYOTO.
HE'S ALSO THE ONLY LEAD I HAVE.
I'LL START THERE.

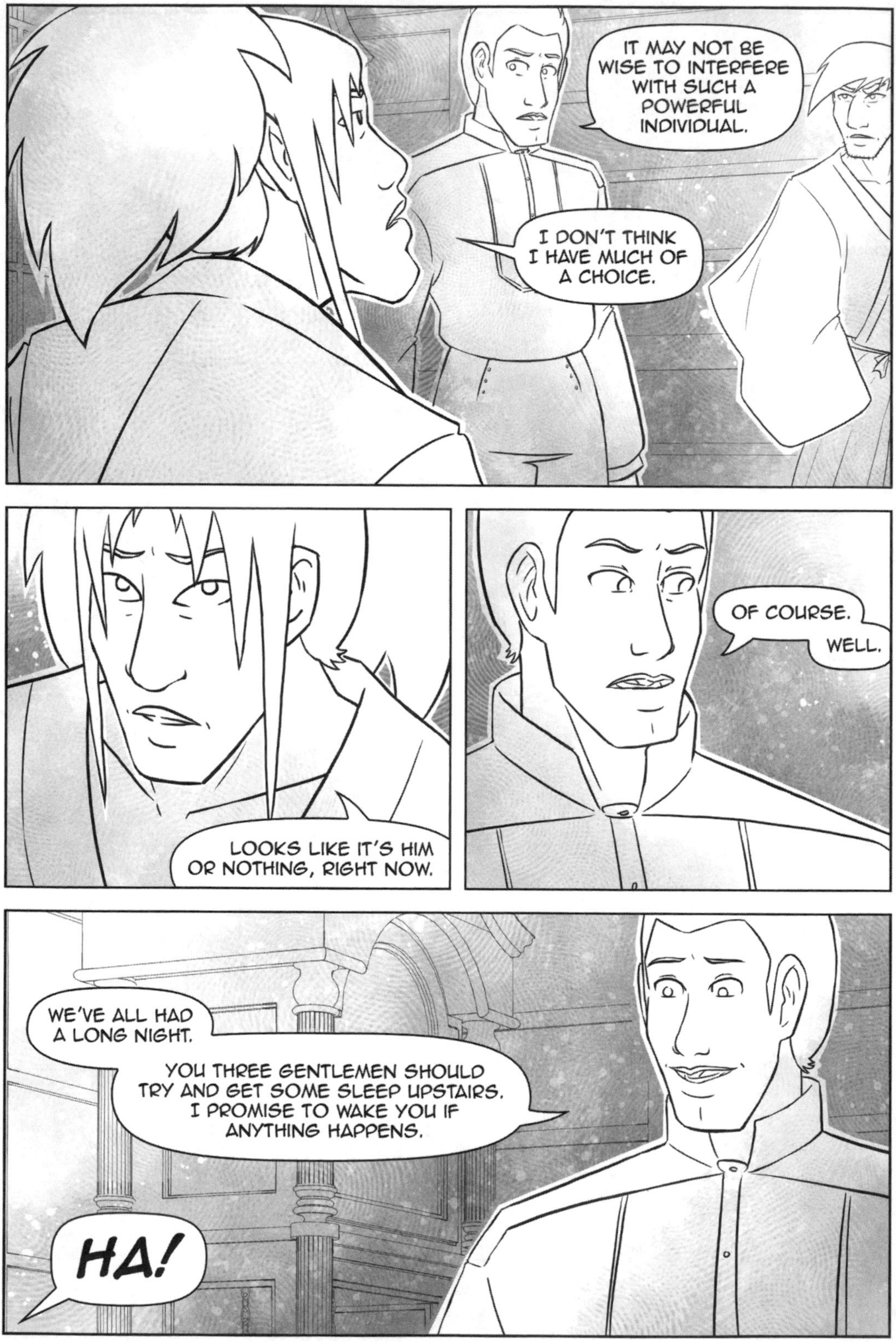
IT MAY NOT BE WISE TO INTERFERE WITH SUCH A POWERFUL INDIVIDUAL.
I DON'T THINK I HAVE MUCH OF A CHOICE.
LOOKS LIKE IT'S HIM OR NOTHING, RIGHT NOW.
OF COURSE.
WELL.
WE'VE ALL HAD A LONG NIGHT.
YOU THREE GENTLEMEN SHOULD TRY AND GET SOME SLEEP UPSTAIRS. I PROMISE TO WAKE YOU IF ANYTHING HAPPENS.
HA!

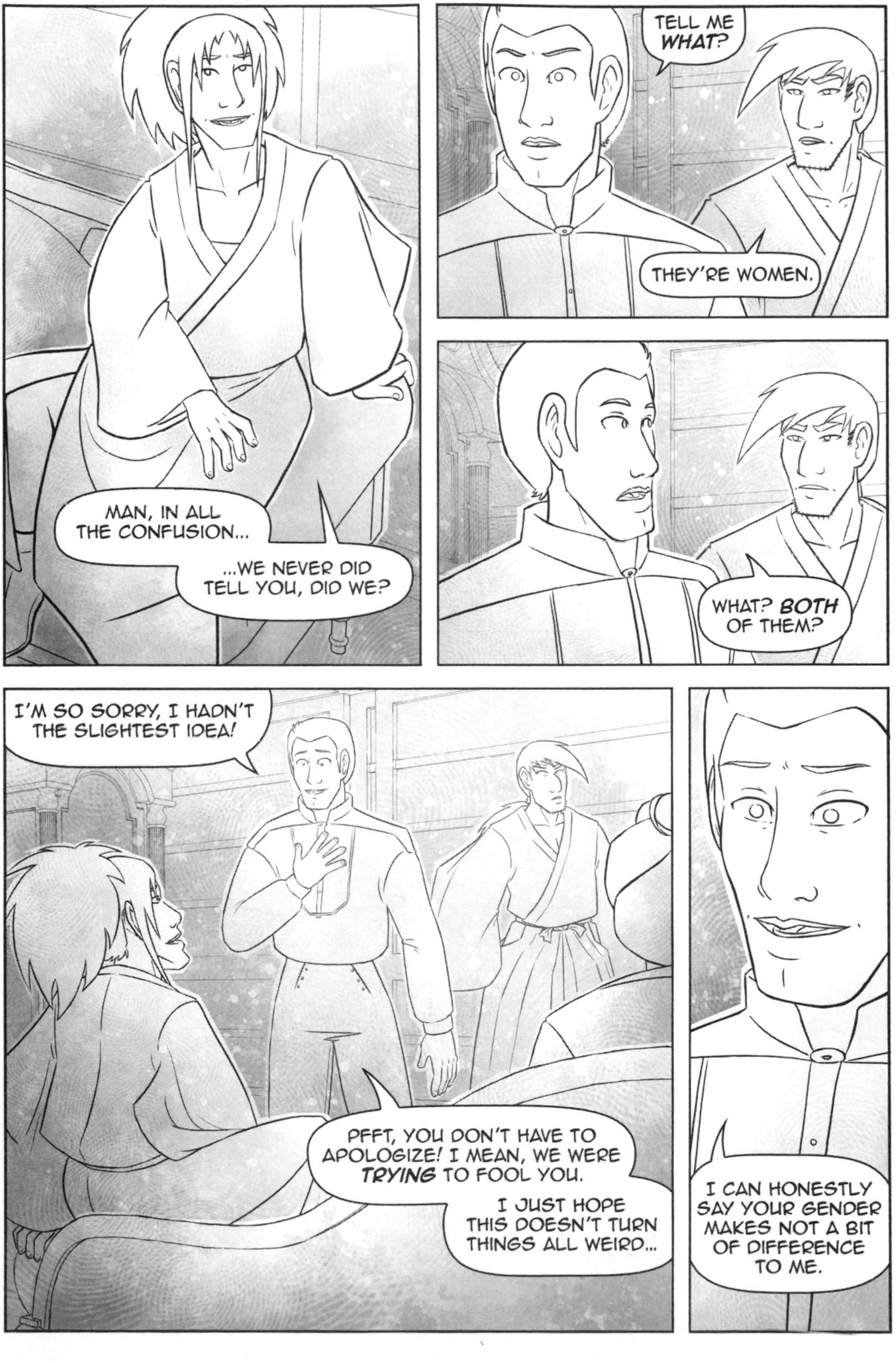
MAN, IN ALL THE CONFUSION...
...WE NEVER DID TELL YOU, DID WE?
TELL ME *WHAT?*
THEY'RE WOMEN.
WHAT? *BOTH* OF THEM?
I'M SO SORRY, I HADN'T THE SLIGHTEST IDEA!
PFFT, YOU DON'T HAVE TO APOLOGIZE! I MEAN, WE WERE *TRYING* TO FOOL YOU.
I JUST HOPE THIS DOESN'T TURN THINGS ALL WEIRD...
I CAN HONESTLY SAY YOUR GENDER MAKES NOT A BIT OF DIFFERENCE TO ME.

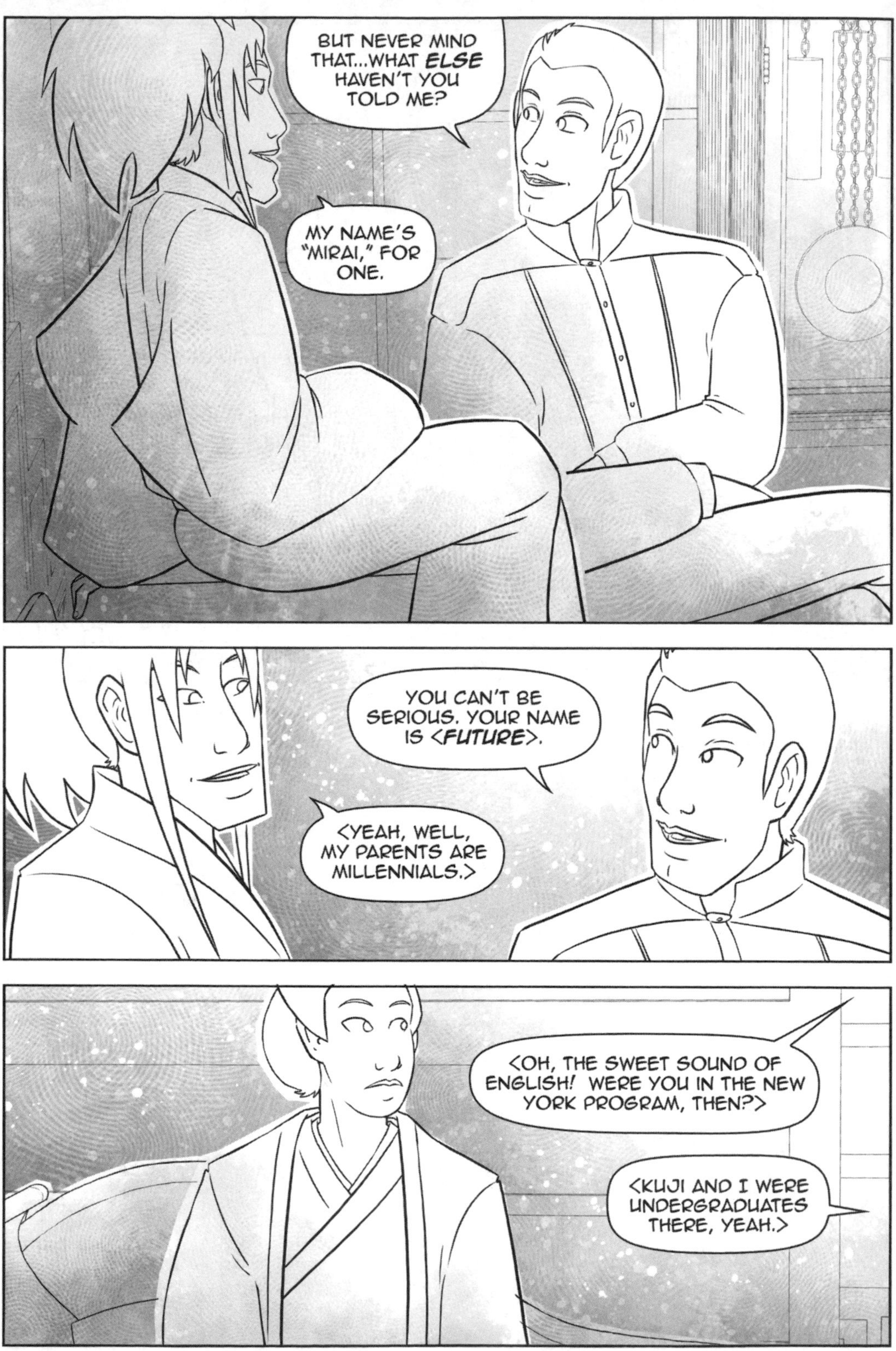
BUT NEVER MIND THAT...WHAT ELSE HAVEN'T YOU TOLD ME?
MY NAME'S "MIRAI," FOR ONE.
YOU CAN'T BE SERIOUS. YOUR NAME IS <FUTURE>.
<YEAH, WELL, MY PARENTS ARE MILLENNIALS.>
<OH, THE SWEET SOUND OF ENGLISH! WERE YOU IN THE NEW YORK PROGRAM, THEN?>
<KUJI AND I WERE UNDERGRADUATES THERE, YEAH.>

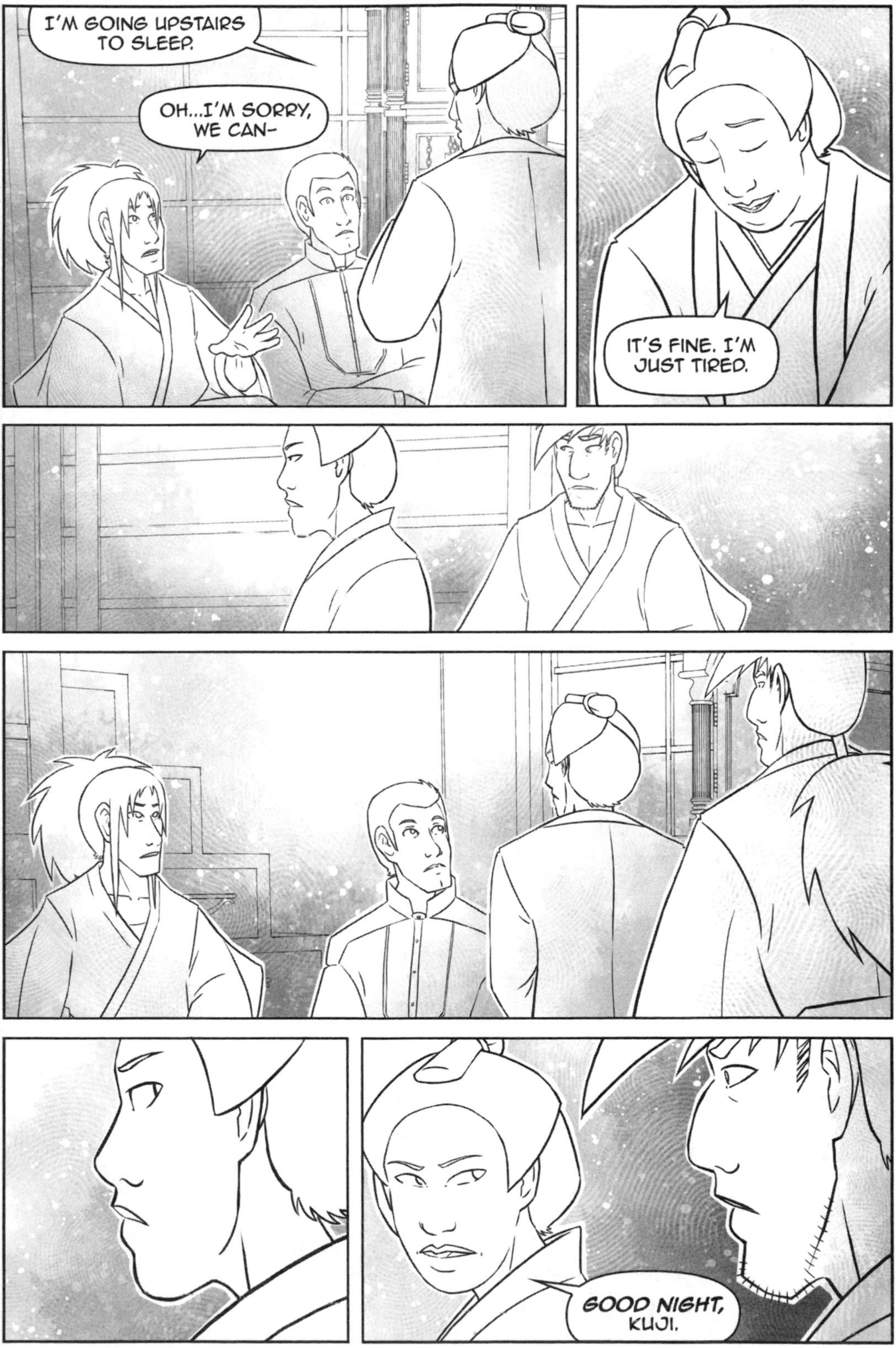
I'M GOING UPSTAIRS TO SLEEP.
OH...I'M SORRY, WE CAN-
IT'S FINE. I'M JUST TIRED.
GOOD NIGHT, KUJI.

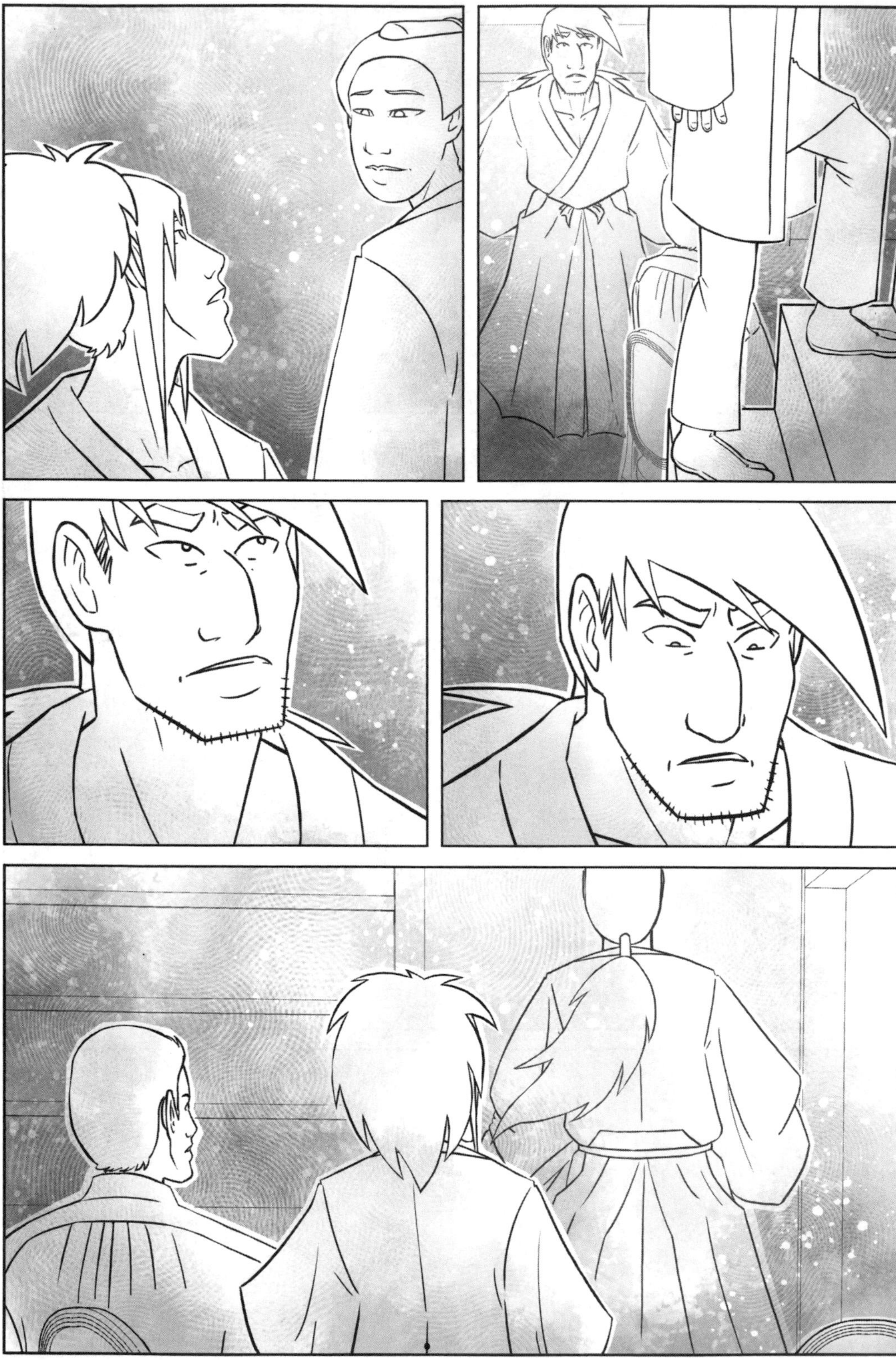

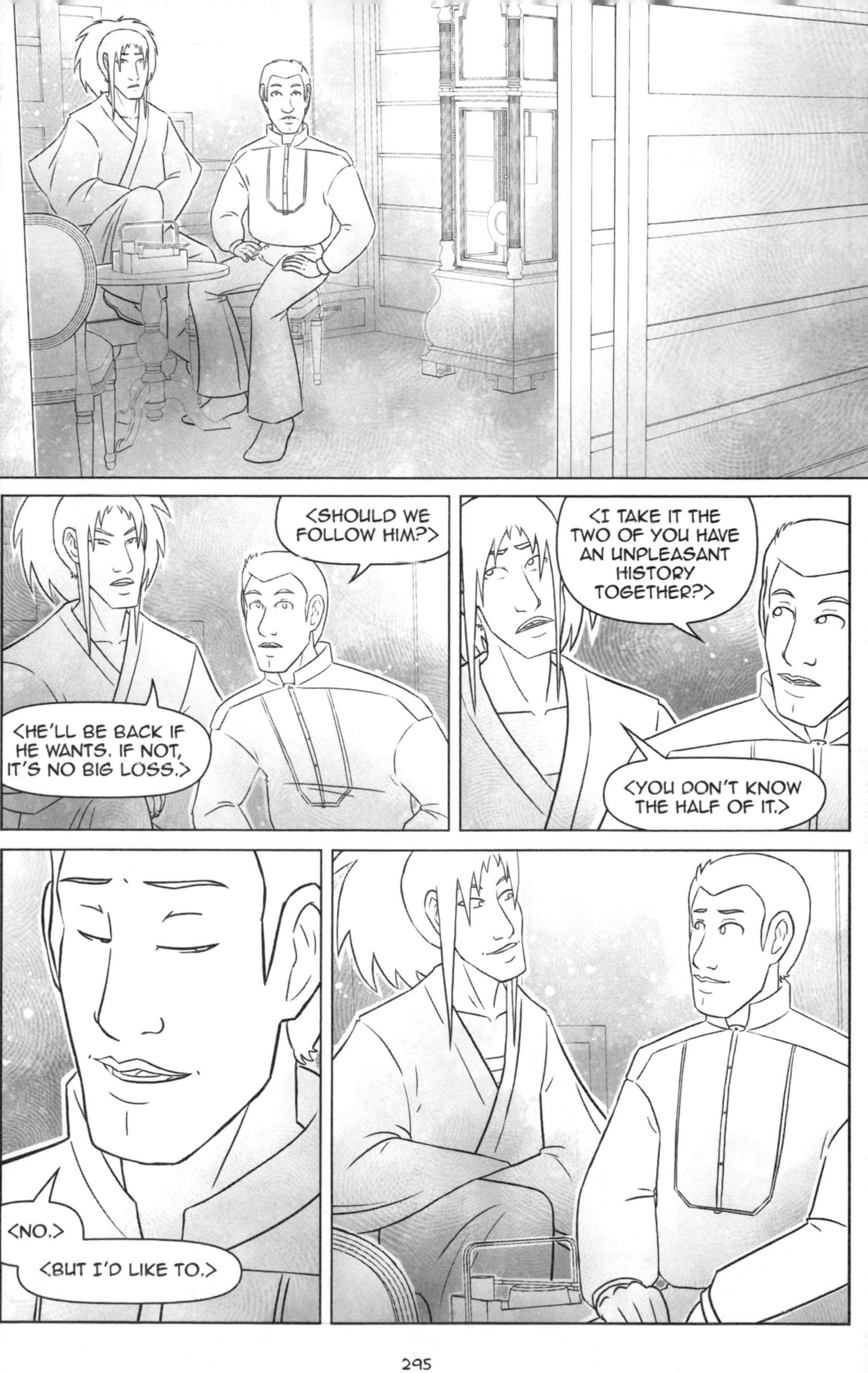
<SHOULD WE FOLLOW HIM?>
<HE'LL BE BACK IF HE WANTS. IF NOT, IT'S NO BIG LOSS.>
<I TAKE IT THE TWO OF YOU HAVE AN UNPLEASANT HISTORY TOGETHER?>
<YOU DON'T KNOW THE HALF OF IT.>
<NO.>
<BUT I'D LIKE TO.>

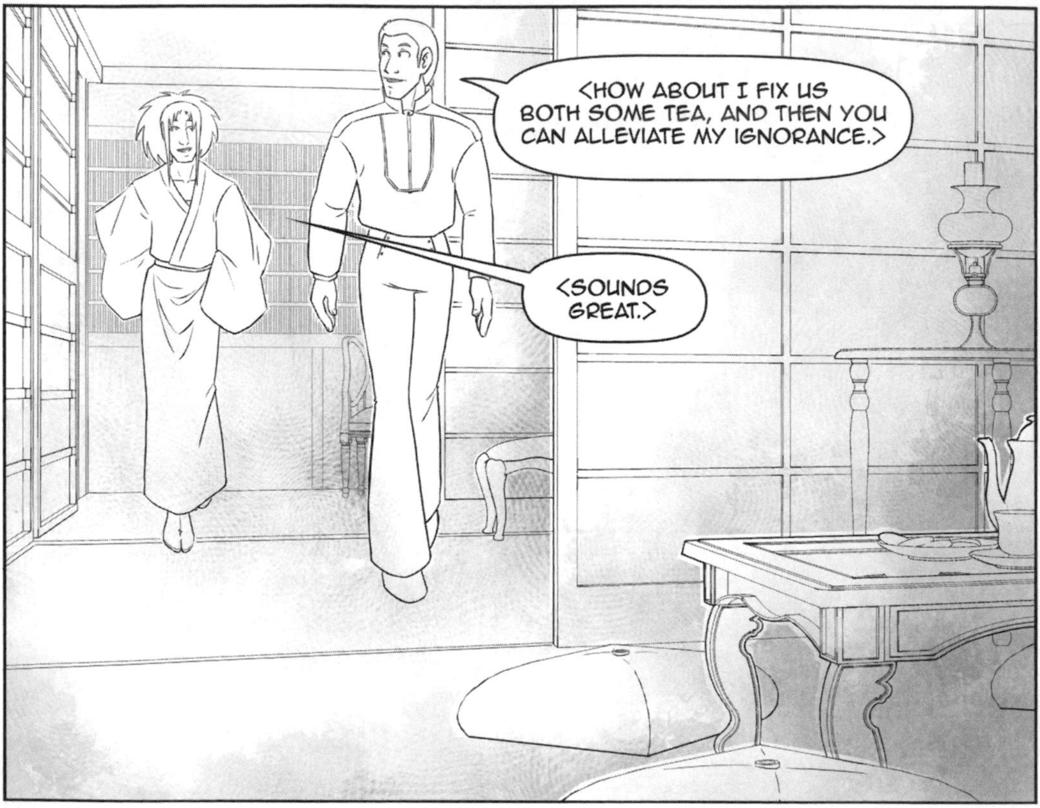
<HOW ABOUT I FIX US BOTH SOME TEA, AND THEN YOU CAN ALLEVIATE MY IGNORANCE.>
<SOUNDS GREAT.>

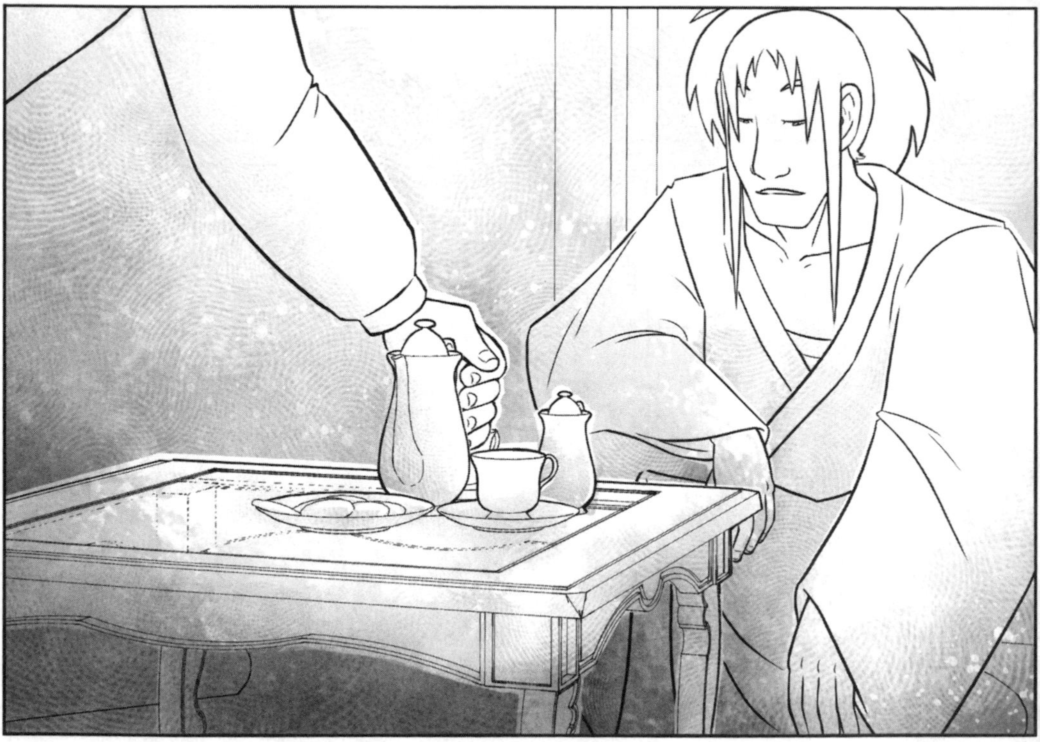

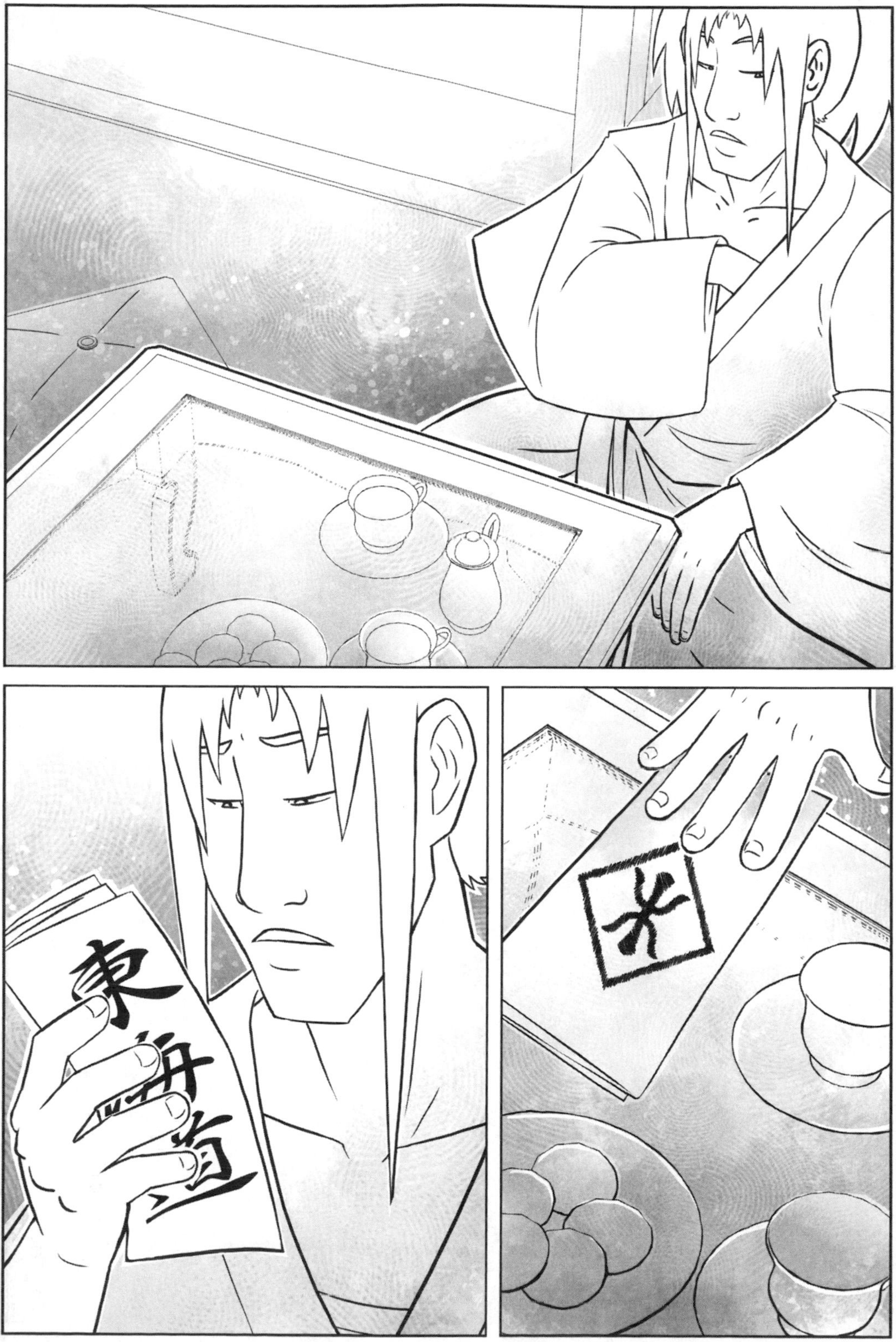

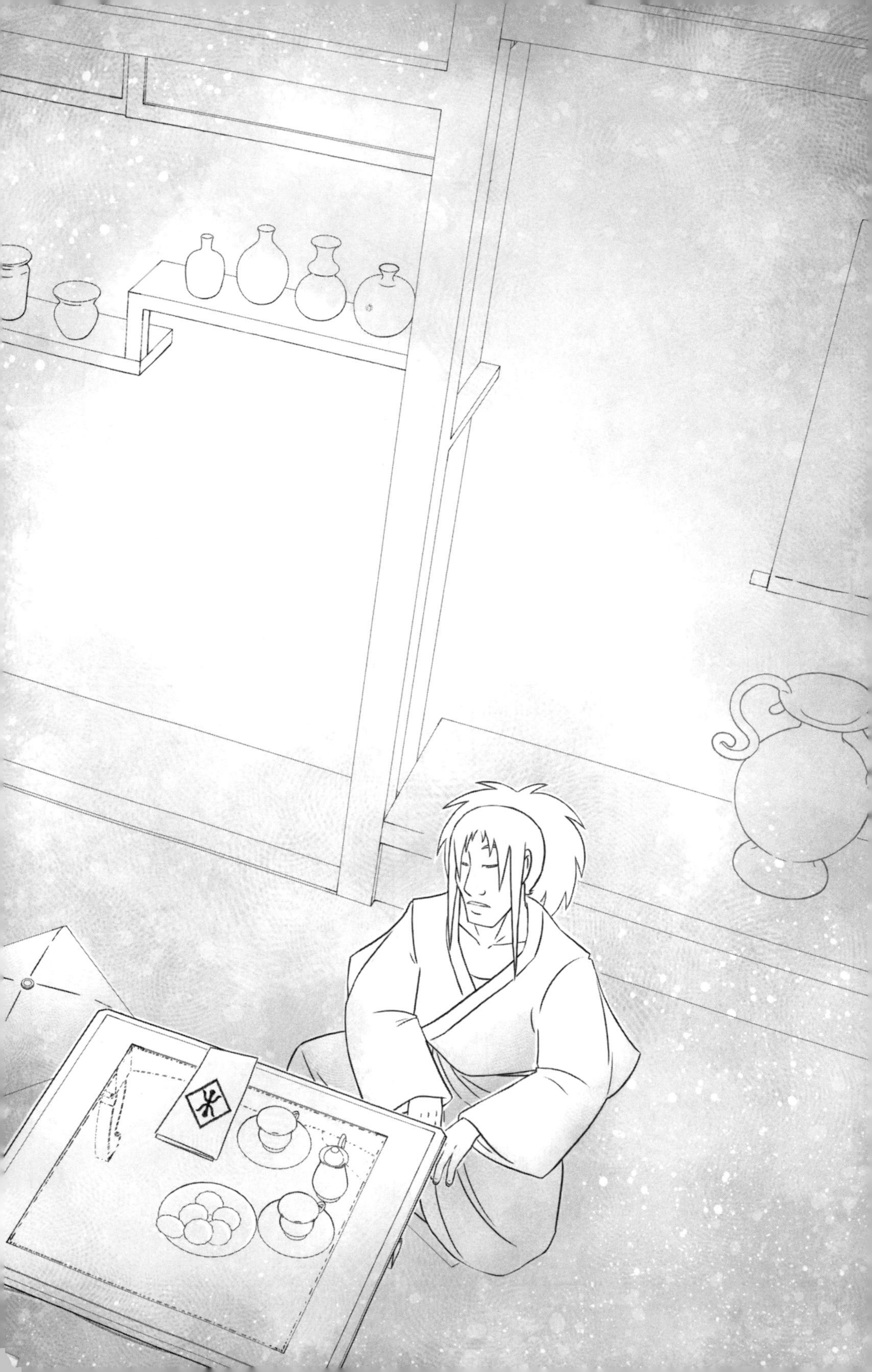

continued and concluded in

Chronin Volume 2: The Sword in Your Hand

ACKNOWLEDGMENTS

Thank you to Erin Finnegan, who helped me draw the earliest version of this story as a submission to Rising Stars of Manga approximately a million years ago, and who has thus been a part of this particular project for longer than anyone other than myself. Thank you to the whole team at Codename: Kids Next Door, but most especially to Tom for his advice on character design, to Mo for teaching me to approach every page turn as a barrier you need to bring your reader through, and to Grace for allowing me to skive off work early from time to time so I could go home and draw comics. Thank you to Hal for listening to me describe the basic plot and then replying, immediately, "You should call it 'Chronin.'" Thank you to everyone who read drafts of the script and offered invaluable feedback, including Clio, Erin F, Erin C, Gina, Evonne, and Scott. Thank you to the many friends—including Clio, Der-shing, Erin F, Erin C, Evonne, Gabbie, Gene, Julieta, Kari, Karlyl, Kitty, Paul, Meg, Marion, Matt, Meredith, Raina, Rawles, Rosemary, Scott, Tammy and Valvi—who followed along while I posted my lettered pencils in locked LiveJournal entries, helped me whip them into shape, and leant me the strength to keep going when things were hard. Thank you to everyone —particularly Anissa, EK and Nina—who drew fanart of a comic that technically didn't exist yet, reminding me that maybe folks would actually care about these nerds someday. Thank you to Jennifer for her early interest in this book and her encouragement to pursue it, which sustained me through some dark moments of the soul. Thank you to EK, Carey, Arthur, JoXn Costello and Tro Rex for their last-minute help with the cover for this first volume. Thank you to my crew of comics lady battle-axes—particularly Raina, Alisa, Marion and MK—who offered professional advice and personal support and excellent goddamn company. Thank you to Clio for keeping me grounded, and for sitting with me for many hours in my office while I cranked out pages, and for being the very best of friends.

Thank you to Indiana Scarlet Brown and Iori Kusano for their generous, exhaustive, thoughtful and invaluable feedback.

Thank you to my agent, Eddie Schneider, for his feedback and for his passionate advocacy on my behalf. Thank you to the entire team at the JABberwocky Literary Agency, particularly Lisa Rodgers, for all of their personal and practical support over the years.

Thank you to my editor, Diana Pho, for taking a chance on this book, for her enthusiasm and her insight and her professionalism, and for being an overall fantastic human being whom I feel very lucky to know in any context.

Thank you to my entire created family here in New York City, without whom I would never have survived the process of drawing this book. Thank you to my birth family, for never once suggesting I was crazy to dedicate a literal decade of my life to putting a comic together. Thank you to my husband, Scott Price, for his unflagging support of the person I was when I started this and the person I've become since.

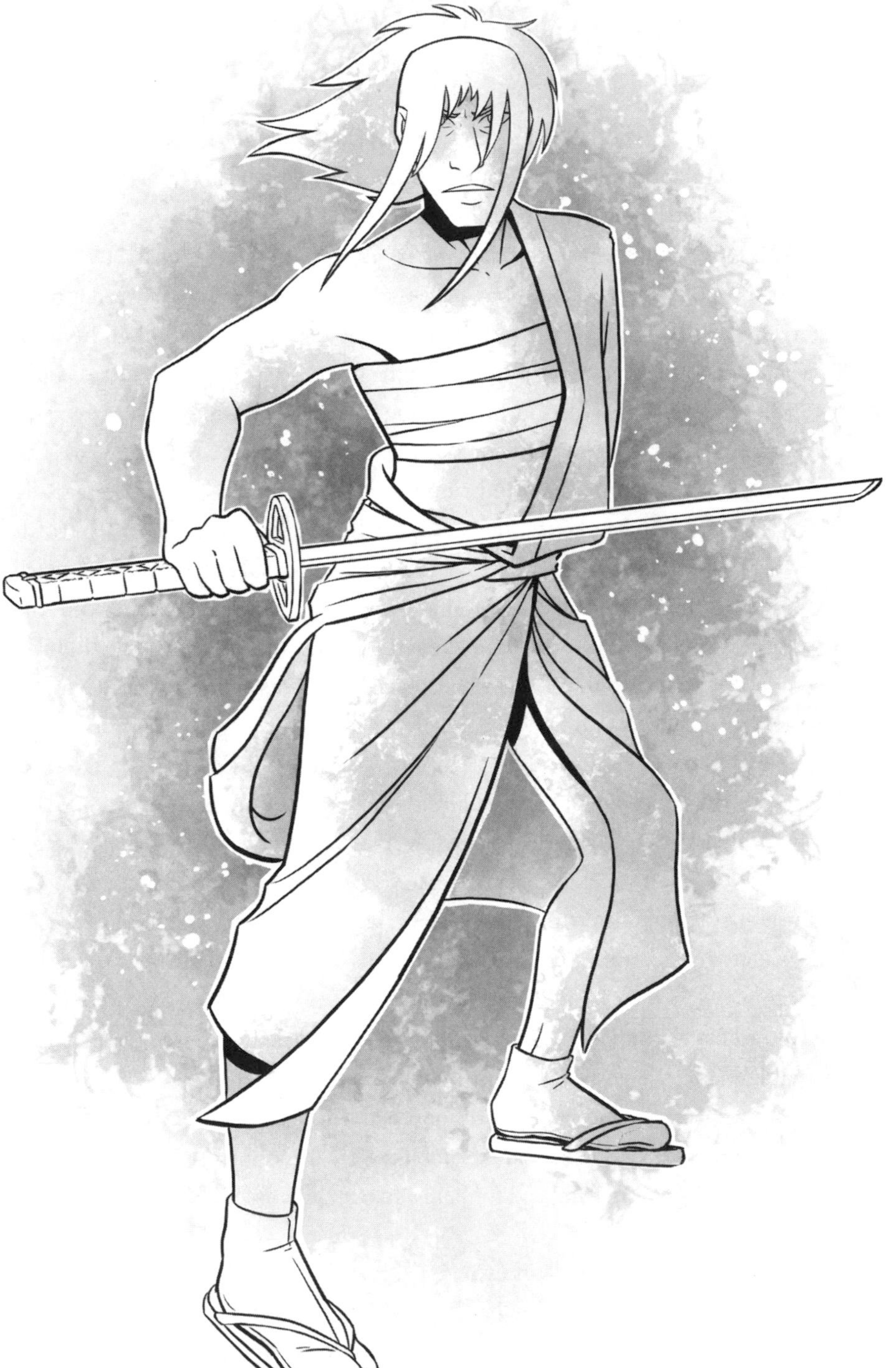

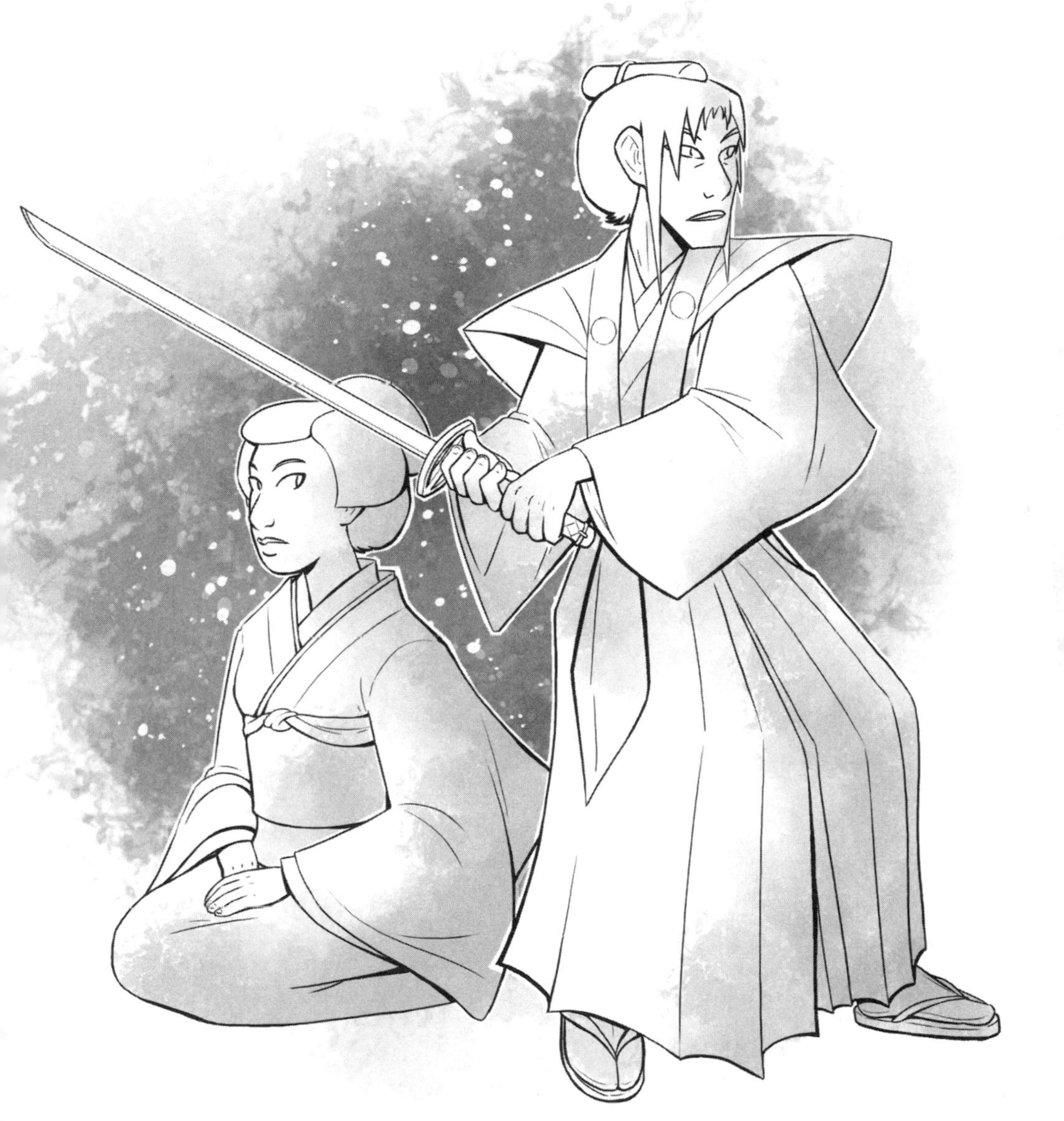

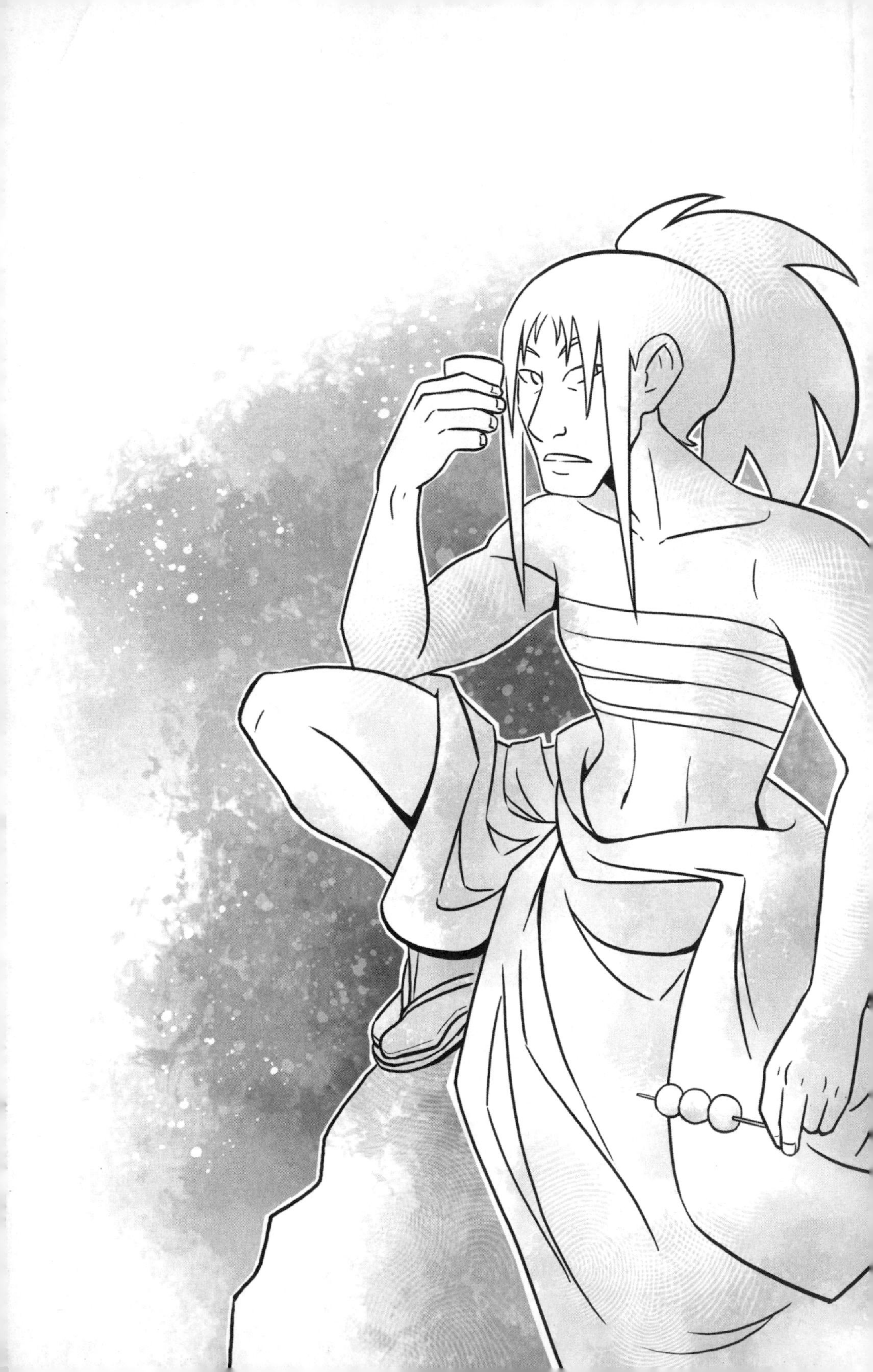